ROUTLEDGE HANDBOOK OF DISABILITY STUDIES

The *Routledge Handbook of Disability Studies* takes a multidisciplinary approach to disability and provides an authoritative and up-to-date overview of the main issues in the field around the world today. Adopting an international perspective and consisting entirely of newly commissioned chapters arranged thematically, it surveys the state of the discipline, examining emerging and cutting-edge areas as well as core areas of contention.

Divided in five parts, this comprehensive handbook covers:

- Different models and approaches to disability
- How key impairment groups have engaged with disability studies and the writings within the discipline
- Policy and legislation responses to disability studies and to disability activism
- Disability studies and its interaction with other disciplines, such as history, philosophy, and science and technology studies
- Disability studies and different life experiences, examining how disability and disability studies intersects with ethnicity, sexuality, gender, childhood and ageing.

Containing chapters from an international selection of leading scholars, this authoritative handbook is an invaluable reference for all academics, researchers and more advanced students in disability studies and associated disciplines such as sociology, health studies and social work.

Nick Watson is Professor of Disability Studies and Director of the Strathclyde Centre for Disability Research at the University of Glasgow, UK.

Alan Roulstone is Research Professor at Northumbria University, UK.

Carol Thomas is Professor of Sociology at the University of Lancaster, UK.

ROUTLEDGE HANDBOOK OF DISABILITY STUDIES

Edited by Nick Watson,
Alan Roulstone and Carol Thomas

Routledge
Taylor & Francis Group

LONDON AND NEW YORK

First published 2012
by Routledge
2 Park Square, Milton Park, Abingdon, Oxon OX14 4RN

Simultaneously published in the USA and Canada
by Routledge
711 Third Avenue, New York, NY 10017

Routledge is an imprint of the Taylor & Francis Group, an informa business

British Library Cataloguing in Publication Data
A catalogue record for this book is available from the British Library

Library of Congress Cataloging-in-Publication Data
Routledge handbook of disability studies / edited by Nick Watson,
Alan Roulstone and Carol Thomas.
p. cm.
Handbook of disability studies
Includes bibliographical references and index.
1. Disability studies. 2. People with disabilities. I. Watson, Nick, 1960-
II. Roulstone, Alan, 1962- III. Thomas, Carol, 1958- IV. Title: Handbook of disability studies.
[DNLM: 1. Disabled Persons. 2. Social Values. HV 1568.2]
HV1568.2.R68 2012
362.4--dc23
2011026773

ISBN13: 978-0-415-57400-6 (hbk)
ISBN13: 978-0-203-14411-4 (ebk)

Typeset in Bembo
by Integra Software Services Pvt. Ltd, Pondicherry, India

MIX
Paper from
responsible sources
FSC® C004839
www.fsc.org

Printed and bound in Great Britain by
CPI Antony Rowe, Chippenham, Wiltshire

CONTENTS

Contents

ILLUSTRATIONS

Figures

Tables

CONTRIBUTORS

Colin Barnes is Professor of Disability Studies at the Centre for Disability Studies, University of Leeds, UK and Visiting Professor of Disability Studies, University of Halmstad, Sweden.

Ana Bê is concluding her doctoral research at Lancaster University, UK. Her research interests are disability studies, feminist theory, the intersections of gender and disability, and health and illness.

Karen Beauchamp-Pryor is an honorary research fellow at Swansea University, UK. Following the completion of her PhD she was awarded an Economic and Social Research Council post-doctoral fellowship which supported the dissemination of her research findings through the publication and presentation of papers. She is writing a monograph about the participation of disabled students in Welsh higher education and co-editing a volume based on the experiences of an international network of 'new' researchers who question the purpose, process and future directions of researching disability.

Peter Beresford OBE is Professor of Social Policy and Director of the Centre for Citizen Participation at Brunel University, UK. He is also a long-term user of mental health services and Chair of Shaping Our Lives, the national independent service user-controlled organization and network. He has a long-standing involvement in issues of participation and empowerment as writer, researcher, educator, service user and campaigner. He is a member of many government bodies and co-author of *Supporting People* (Policy Press, 2011).

Jerome E. Bickenbach is a full professor in the Department of Philosophy and the Faculties of Law and Medicine at Queen's University, Canada. He is the author of *Physical Disability and Social Policy* (University of Toronto Press, 1993) and the co-editor of *Introduction to Disability* (W. B. Saunders, 1998), *Disability and Culture: Universalism and Diversity* (Hogrefe and Huber, 2000), *A Seat at the Table: Persons with Disabilities and Policy Making* (McGill-Queen's University Press, 2001), *Quality of Life and Human Difference* (Cambridge University Press, 2005) and numerous articles and chapters in disability studies focusing on the nature of disability and disability law and policy. He was a content editor of Sage Publications' five-volume *Encyclopaedia of Disability*. Since 1995 he has been a consultant with the World Health Organization (WHO), working on drafting, testing and the implementation of the International Classification of Functioning, Disability and

Health, and continues to consult with WHO on international disability social policy. As a lawyer, he was a human rights litigator, specializing in anti-discrimination for persons with intellectual impairments and mental illness. Since 2007 he has headed the Disability Policy Unit at Swiss Paraplegic Research in Nottwil, Switzerland, and is Professor at the Faculty of Humanities and Social Science at the University of Lucerne.

Christine Bigby is Professor of Social Work and Social Policy, Director of Postgraduate Programmes and leads a disability research group in the School of Social Work and Social Policy at Latrobe University, Melbourne, Australia. She has a long history of researching policy, programme and practice issues about adults with intellectual disability. She led research about ageing with an intellectual disability in Australia and is Chair of the International Association for the Scientific Study of Intellectual Disabilities' (IASSID) Special Interest Research Group on Ageing and Intellectual Disability. She is editor of *Australian Social Work* and has published widely in the peer-reviewed academic literature.

Stuart Blume has worked at the University of Sussex, the London School of Economics, the Organisation for Economic Co-operation and Development, and in various administrative positions including in the Cabinet Office and as Secretary of the Committee on Social Inequalities in Health (the Black Committee). From 1982 to 2007 he was Professor of Science and Technology Studies at the University of Amsterdam, and is now Emeritus Professor.

David Bolt is Lecturer, Recognized Researcher and Director of the Centre for Culture and Disability Studies, Faculty of Education, Liverpool Hope University, UK. He is editor of the *Journal of Literary & Cultural Disability Studies* and an editorial advisor for *Disability & Society* and *the Journal of Visual Impairment and Blindness*. He has more than three dozen publications to his name. He is currently working on a monograph entitled *The Metanarrative of Blindness*.

Anne Borsay is Professor of Healthcare and Medical Humanities at Swansea University, UK. Her recent publications include *Disability and Social Policy in Britain Since 1750: A History of Exclusion* (Palgrave Macmillan, 2004) and she is currently writing a cultural history of disability in Britain between 1500 and 2000. She sits on the editorial board of *Disability & Society* and is a member of the Wellcome Trust's Medical History and Humanities Expert Review Group.

John Davis is a senior lecturer in Childhood Studies at the University of Edinburgh and Chair of the Scottish Social Service Council Childhood Practice Development Group. He has produced research reports, seminars, conferences, training materials and publications on a range of topics including: inclusion and interagency working; participation in hospitals, mental health services, out-of-school clubs and respite care centres; skills, training and blended learning in early years, children and family services; equality issues in health, education, community, leisure and social services; and participatory research methods for working with children and adults.

Eric Emerson is Co-Director of the Improving Health and Lives Learning Disabilities Observatory and Professor of Disability and Health Research at Lancaster University, UK. He is also Visiting Professor at the Australian Family and Disabilities Studies Research Collaboration, University of Sydney. His research focuses on understanding the health and social inequalities faced by disabled children and people with intellectual disabilities.

Dan Goodley is Professor of Psychology and Disability Studies at Manchester Metropolitan University, UK. His research and teaching aims to shake up dominant myths in psychology and contribute in some small way to the development of critical disability studies theories that understand and eradicate disablism. His recent publications include *Disability Studies: An Interdisciplinary Introduction* (Sage, 2011).

Hilary Graham is Professor of Health Sciences at the University of York, UK. Her research focuses on how social inequalities influence health across people's lives. Her books include *Unequal Lives: Health and Socioeconomic Inequalities* (Open University Press, 2007) and *Understanding Health Inequalities* (Open University Press, 2009).

Chris Hatton is Professor of Psychology, Health and Social Care at the Centre for Disability Research, Lancaster University, UK. His research interests involve policy-relevant research designed to document, understand and reduce the inequalities experienced by disabled people and their families, principally people with intellectual disabilities.

Bill Hughes is Professor and the Dean of the School of Law and Social Sciences at Glasgow Caledonian University and is a sociologist 'to trade'. His research interests include disability and impairment, social theory and the body. He is co-author of *The Body, Culture and Society: An Introduction* (Open University Press, 2000). He is co-editor of a book entitled *Disability and Social Theory* (Palgrave, 2011), has published in the journals *Sociology* and *Body and Society*, and is a regular contributor to and a member of the editorial board of *Disability & Society*.

Gwynnyth Llewellyn is Dean of the Faculty of Health Sciences, University of Sydney and Director of the Australian Family and Disability Studies Research Collaboration. She is an international authority on family and disability studies. Her work on parents and parenting with intellectual disability has led national strategies in Australia, Sweden and the Netherlands.

Janice McLaughlin is Executive Director of the Policy, Ethics and Life Sciences Research Centre at Newcastle University, UK. She undertakes a range of sociological research on childhood, family and disability, looking at issues such as the influence of medical intervention and professionals, new diagnostic tools for framing childhood disability, experience of social integration and exclusion, and children's development of their own sense of self and identity. Her most recent book, with Dan Goodley, Emma Clavering and Pamela Fisher, is *Families Raising Disabled Children: Values of Enabling Care and Social Justice* (Palgrave, 2008).

Ros Madden leads the Australian International Classification of Functioning, Disability and Health (ICF) Disability and Rehabilitation Research Program in the Faculty of Health Sciences at the University of Sydney. She has played a major role in the development of national disability definition, measurement and statistics in Australia since 1992, and internationally in the development and implementation of the World Health Organization's ICF.

Claudia Malacrida is Professor in Sociology at the University of Lethbridge, Canada. Along with numerous articles on disability history, motherhood and the social control of difference, she has authored three books: *Mourning the Dreams: How Parents Create Meaning from Miscarriage, Stillbirth and Early Infant Death* (Left Coast Press, 2008); *Cold Comfort: Mothers, Professional Discourse and Attention Deficit Disorder* (University of Toronto Press, 2003); and *Sociology of the Body: A Reader*

(Oxford University Press, 2008). She is currently writing a book on eugenics and institutionalization in western Canada.

Helen Meekosha is Associate Professor in the School of Social Sciences and International Relations, University of New South Wales, Sydney, Australia. Her research interests cross boundaries of race, ethnicity, disability and gender and she has recently begun a research project on the experience of disability from the perspective of those who live in the Global South, including rural indigenous communities in Australia. She has been active in the disability movement since 1981.

David Mitchell and **Sharon Snyder** began collaborative work in disability studies in 1993. Their first edited collection, *The Body and Physical Difference: Discourses of Disability* (University of Michigan Press, 1997), offers work that analyses the unique terms by which disabled people inhabit the world, as depicted in memoir, film, literature, material cultures, and, broadly, across cultural and artistic traditions. As an adjunct to this effort, they have also overseen a book series, *Corporealities: Discourses of Disability* (University of Michigan Press). They both served as faculty for the United States' first PhD programme in disability studies (2000–8) and were founding members of the Committee on the Status of People with Disabilities in the Profession and the Disability Studies Discussion Group in the Modern Languages Association. They are currently writing a book on comparative contexts of disability developing globally at events such as disability film festivals, resistance movements led by persons with disabilities, and the labour of populations historically considered 'non-productive'.

Michele Moore is editor of the leading journal *Disability & Society*. She is Professor of Inclusive Education at Northumbria University, where she is working to advance the global agenda for inclusive education. Her current work also involves facilitation of the Iraq Research Fellowship Programme through the Council for Assisting Refugee Academics (http://academic-refugees. org).

Kevin Paterson is a research associate at Strathclyde Centre for Disability Research, University of Glasgow. His research interests include sociology of impairment, norms of communication and exclusion, and ageing with a lifelong impairment. He has worked on a variety of research projects and is currently researching the experience of ageing with cerebral palsy in Scotland.

Charlotte Pearson is a lecturer in Public Policy at the School of Social and Political Sciences, University of Glasgow. Over the past decade she has undertaken research that has focused on changes in policies promoting independent living for disabled people and issues surrounding disability equality legislation. She also teaches disability options at undergraduate and postgraduate levels.

Boika Rechel is a lecturer in Public Health at the University of East Anglia, UK and Consultant Physician in Public Health Medicine in the English National Health Service. Her research interests are in health inequalities and access to health care, with a special focus on the transitional societies of Central and Eastern Europe.

Donna Reeve is an honorary research fellow with the Centre for Disability Studies/Applied Social Science at Lancaster University, UK. Her research interests are psycho-emotional disablism and the complex relationships between disablism, impairment and identity. In addition to contributing to disability theory, she is also working to extend an awareness of psycho-emotional disablism into professional practice.

Janet Robertson is a lecturer in Health Research at the Centre for Disability Research, School of Health and Medicine, Lancaster University, UK.

Alan Roulstone is Research Professor at Northumbria University. He has produced over 60 publications in the field of disability, social inclusion, care, equality and employment policy. His books include *Understanding Disability Policy* (Policy Press, 2011, with Prideaux), *Disability Policy and Practice* (Sage, 2009, with Harris), *Enabling Technology* (Open University Press, 1998) and *Working Futures* (Policy Press, 2005, with Barnes). He is currently completing an edited collection on disablist hate crime (Routledge, 2012, with Mason-Bish). He is an executive editor of the journal *Disability & Society*.

Sasha Scambler is Lecturer in Sociology at King's College London Dental Institute. She has carried out extensive work on the experiences of families with Batten disease and researched and published on the application of disability and social theory to chronic disabling conditions and loneliness in later life. Sasha is co-editor of the journal *Social Science and Dentistry* and has published two books including a co-edited collection, *New Directions in the Sociology of Chronic and Disabling Conditions* (Palgrave Macmillan, 2004), which brings together leading international researchers in medical sociology and disability theory to critically review the sociological approach to chronic and disabling conditions.

Jackie Leach Scully is Reader in Social Ethics and Bioethics, and Co-Director of the Policy, Ethics and Life Sciences Research Centre, Newcastle University, UK. She is also Honorary Senior Lecturer at the University of Sydney Medical School. After a first degree in biochemistry and a doctorate in molecular biology she worked for some years in neuroscience research before becoming involved in bioethics. Her research interests include disability and identity, embodiment and disembodiment, feminist bioethics, reproductive and genetic bioethics, the formation of moral opinion, and psychoanalytic theory. She is the author of *Disability Bioethics: Moral Bodies, Moral Difference* (Rowman & Littlefield, 2008), *Quaker Approaches to Moral Issues in Genetics* (Mellen, 2002) and co-editor of *Feminist Bioethics: At the Center on the Margins* (Johns Hopkins University Press, 2010). She has been a disability activist since before she knew what the term meant.

Tom Shakespeare has researched and taught at the Universities of Cambridge, Sunderland, Leeds and Newcastle. His books include *The Sexual Politics of Disability* (Continuum, 1996) and *Disability Rights and Wrongs* (Routledge, 2006). He is currently a technical officer in the Department of Violence and Injury Prevention and Disability at the World Health Organization, where he is one of the editors and authors of the *World Report on Disability*.

Margrit Shildrick is Professor of Gender and Knowledge Production at Linkoping University and Adjunct Professor of Critical Disability Studies at York University, Toronto. Her research covers postmodern feminist and cultural theory, bioethics, critical disability studies and body theory. She is the author of *Dangerous Discourses of Disability, Subjectivity and Sexuality* (Palgrave Macmillan, 2009), *Embodying the Monster* (Sage, 2002) and *Leaky Bodies and Boundaries* (Routledge, 1997); and joint editor of *Ethics of the Body* (MIT Press, 2005) with Roxanne Mykitiuk, and *Feminist Theory and the Body* (Edinburgh University Press, 1999) and *Vital Signs* (Edinburgh University Press, 1998) both with Janet Price.

Roger Slee holds the Chair of Inclusive Education at the Institute of Education, University of London. He is the founding editor of the *International Journal of Inclusive Education*. He has been the Deputy Director General of the Queensland Department of Education and his most recent book, *The Irregular School*, is published by Routledge (2010). Roger has been appointed as Director of the Institute for Diversity, Education Access and Success at Victoria University in Melbourne, Australia.

Brett Smith is a senior lecturer in the School of Sport, Exercise and Health Sciences, a member of the Peter Harrison Centre for Disability Sport and co-director of the Qualitative Digital Research Lab (LiQuiD) at Loughborough University. His theoretical and empirical research interests concern spinal cord injury, health and well-being; the development of qualitative research methods and methodologies; and narrative inquiry. He is editor of the journal *Qualitative Research in Sport, Exercise and Health*.

Karen Soldatic is the Postgraduate Research Coordinator at the Centre for Human Rights Education, Curtin University, Perth, Australia. She recently completed her PhD on the neoliberal restructuring of disability within Australia and her main research interests include critical sociologies and geographies of disability, gender, race and class.

Andrew C. Sparkes is Professor of Sport and Body Pedagogy in the Faculty of Education, Community and Leisure at Liverpool John Moores University. His research interests revolve around the ways that people experience different forms of embodiment over time in a variety of contexts. Recent work has focused on performing bodies and identity formation; catastrophic spinal cord injury in sport and the narrative reconstruction of self; and ageing bodies.

Kirsten Stalker is Professor of Disability Studies in the School of Applied Social Science at the University of Strathclyde. From 1991 to 2006 she worked in the Social Work Research Centre, University of Stirling and, prior to that, in the Norah Fry Research Centre at Bristol University. Much of her research has focused on disabled children and people with learning disabilities. She is a member of the editorial boards of *Disability & Society* and the *British Journal of Learning Disabilities*.

Deborah Stienstra is Professor in Disability Studies at the University of Manitoba. She held the Royal Bank Research Chair in Disability Studies from 2000 to 2003 at the Canadian Centre on Disability Studies. Her publications and research interests are related to intersectionality, vulnerability and public services, women's experiences of economic restructuring, the experiences of people with disabilities in end-of-life and cancer care, and access and inclusion in telecommunications policy.

Carol Thomas is Professor of Sociology, specializing in disability studies and the sociology of health and illness. She has published widely in the field and in addition to her work on disability she has also written on the sociology of cancer, care and domestic labour. She is the author of *Female Forms: Experiencing and Understanding Disability* (Open University Press, 1999) and *Sociologies of Disability and Illness. Contested Ideas in Disability Studies and Medical Sociology* (Palgrave Macmillan, 2007).

Simo Vehmas is Professor of Special Education at the University of Jyväskylä, Finland and the President of the Nordic Network on Disability Research. His training is in both special education and philosophy, and his research interests mainly focus on philosophical issues related to disability.

Brandon Vick is a PhD student in Economics at Fordham University, USA. He has worked on a number of projects investigating the relationships between poverty, mental health and disability.

Nick Watson is Professor of Disability Studies and Director of the Strathclyde Centre for Disability Research at the University of Glasgow. He has written on a range of disability issues, including disability and technology, disability and identity, and disability theory. He is a member of the executive editorial board of the journal *Disability & Society*.

PART 1

Theorizing disability

1

THE CHANGING TERRAIN
OF DISABILITY STUDIES

Alan Roulstone, Carol Thomas and Nick Watson

Disability studies is at a crossroads. From its political foundations and early theoretical formulations in the late 1960s and early 1970s it has now become recognized as an academic discipline in its own right. It is available as a core subject of study at undergraduate and postgraduate levels and has firmly established national and international organizations that hold their own academic conferences, including the Society for Disability Studies (SDS) in the United States (US), the Disability Studies Association (DSA) in the United Kingdom (UK), the Nordic Network of Disability Research (NNDR) and the Academic Network of European Disability Experts (ANED). There also exist a range of international, peer reviewed academic journals rooted in disability studies, including *Disability & Society,* the *Scandinavian Journal of Disability Research, Disability Studies Quarterly, ALTER – the European Journal of Disability Research* and the *Journal of Literary and Cultural Disability Studies.*

Disability studies can trace its origins to the organizations of disabled people whose voices emerged in the late 1960s and who shared ideas drawn from those of other previously excluded groups such as African Americans in the US, black and other minority ethnic groupings elsewhere, women, and lesbians and gay men. Disability activists in the US, the UK, Scandinavia and other Western European countries campaigned for a change in the way that disability was understood, demanding the redefinition of disability from a personal, medical problem to a political one (Driedger 1991). No longer, they argued, should disability be seen as a problem of the individual's 'body' and thus something to be treated by health and social care professionals, but instead it should be seen as a political and socially constructed problem with a focus on the disabling barriers faced by people with an impairment (De Jong 1981; Finkelstein 1980).

It can be argued that there have been three key elements to the development of the disability studies agenda (Shakespeare and Watson 2001). First was the idea that disabled people are a marginalized and disadvantaged constituency; second was the idea that disabled people constitute a minority group; and third, and perhaps key, was the idea that disability be reconstructed as a social rather than a medical problem – what Mike Oliver in 1983, drawing on the ideas of the Union of the Physically Impaired against Segregation (UPIAS 1976), termed the social model of disability. The former two points have combined and been used to reinforce the latter, and the three elements together are broadly constitutive of what has become known as disability studies. Disability is thus described in terms of social discrimination and prejudice rather than individual medical conditions. Discrimination, according to disability studies writers, can be rooted in institutional, personal and interpersonal processes of exclusion and oppression and are viewed as endemic to most societies irrespective of levels of economic and cultural development.

The acknowledgement and conceptualization of disabled people as a disadvantaged group was the main focus of early disability scholars, supporting the claim for the politicization of disability by disabled people and their allies throughout the world. Writers such as Kleinfield (1979), Hahn (1985) and Barnes (1991) all presented evidence for this claim, in different cultural contexts. Economic considerations and materialist analyses were central to first-wave disability studies perspectives. Very soon afterwards, feminist disability activists and scholars were keen to name this disadvantage as social oppression: the concept 'disablism' sat comfortably alongside sexism and racism (Morris 1991).

Through its close ties with disabled people and their political movements and organizations, and by stretching beyond and across disciplinary boundaries, disability studies has become fully international, multidisciplinary and has transformed the intellectual scene. Disability studies has produced not just an intellectual challenge to the way that disability is understood and theorized but has resulted in the establishment of a new paradigm around disability. Large-scale international organizations such as the United Nations and the World Health Organization (WHO), national governments and voluntary and third sector organizations everywhere have engaged with – and been influenced by – the ideas that have emerged as a direct result of the way that disability studies scholars and activists have engaged with disability.

As disability studies has grown, its central ideas and concepts have increasingly attracted critical academic scrutiny and with this has come increasing demands for academic validity (Shakespeare 2006). New ideas and concepts have emerged that have sought to challenge the key tenets of the discipline. These challenges have emerged both from within the discipline and from outside it. Disabled feminists such as Jenny Morris, Carol Thomas, Simi Linton and Rosemary Garland-Thomson have argued that disability studies has failed to adequately theorize the experience of disability from a gendered perspective and needs to engage more with feminist perspectives. Similar points have been made in relation to ethnicity (Stuart 1993), sexuality (Shakespeare *et al.* 1996) and social class (Gallagher and Skidmore 2006).

Since the 1990s, disability scholars have also begun a critique from outside of first-wave disability studies by pointing to the need to go beyond largely economistic arguments and their correctives by critically unpacking structures of 'ableism', normalcy and the construction of disabled people as categorically 'other' (Chouinard 2009; Davis 1995; Kasnitz 2001; Goodley 2010). Instead of simply navigating around the results of disablism, these writers attempt to get to the core of ableist thinking as structures of categorical exclusion. Such writers argue for root and branch and educational reappraisals of how we view difference in contemporary society.

Of significance, both first-wave and subsequent disability writings share a concern for the results of exclusionary societies and the impact this has on disabled people. Not surprisingly, the theoretical and thus policy responses to disablism/ableism differ in their emphasis, whilst ideas can be increasingly characterized as pluralized in pursuit of understanding disabled people's lives. Some see such plurality as a risk to disability studies; others view these developments as evidence of the growing maturity and openness of debate within disability studies. We see these developments as contributing to the enrichment of the discipline as it grows and diversifies. This book seeks to capture a sense of the discipline in transition.

Structure of the book

In putting this book together we have sought to cover the key debates in disability studies and it is our hope that this collection will act as a major reference text for the future development of disability studies. The invited contributions are designed to help further define and develop the social scientific approach to the study of disability. The chapters in this volume bring together established and leading scholars in the field of disability studies and some of the discipline's rising stars. We deliberately sought to include authors from around the world and arrive at an international 'take' on disability. We wanted a mix of both distinguished scholars as well as those at an earlier stage in their career trajectory. All of the contributors were asked to address the key challenging questions in their area of expertise, to give pointers as to the way ahead and to reflect on how they see future developments within their particular areas of expertise.

As disability studies has matured it has moved beyond its original disciplinary bases and we wanted to produce a collection that reflects that development. We therefore sought to include authors from as wide a range of specialties as possible – combining the more traditional sociological and social policy approaches with new perspectives. This, we feel, is a major success of this collection. At its heart is a desire to bring together disciplines from across the arts, humanities and social sciences and to create a truly interdisciplinary approach to the study of disability. We have therefore included contributions from sociologists, social and public policy analysts, anthropologists, demographers, political scientists, philosophers, cultural theorists, psychologists, historians and statisticians.

The volume has five overarching themes: theorizing disability; disablement, impairment and impairment effects; health matters, social policy and disability; disability studies across the disciplines; and finally, experiences of disablement.

Part 1: Theorizing disability

The collection opens with a section on theoretical approaches to disability within disability studies, and what it is that makes disability studies both unique and dynamic. This defines the discipline and illustrates how new theories of disability are impacting on our understanding. The first chapters explore how various approaches to disability have sought to define the nature of disability. Colin Barnes, one of the key thinkers behind the development of the discipline in the UK, lays out the basic tenets of the quintessential social model of disability. In his chapter, Barnes restates his commitment to the social model and to what he sees as its lasting value at the core of disability studies. In this chapter, he lays out the origins of the social model and how it has influenced insights into disability both within and beyond the academy. He also addresses many of its critics and concludes that without the social model of disability, disability studies would not exist.

Margrit Shildrick, in the next chapter, presents a very different perspective as she argues the case for *critical disability studies*, developing what she terms a postconventional approach to disability. Bringing together ideas from feminism, postcolonial studies and queer theory, she challenges the categories 'disabled' and 'non-disabled', arguing for a rejection of conventional binary thinking. She argues that the way forward for disability studies is to deconstruct the very categories that define disabled people as 'different' from their non-disabled peers. She suggests that such differences are not viable and neither are they sustainable; only by such a deconstruction can we further the position of disabled people and promote their inclusion and full social participation.

In the next chapter, David Mitchell and Sharon Snyder take a similar line, developing the arguments employed by Henri-Jacques Stiker (1999) in his *A History of Disability*. In this chapter they argue against the conventional categorization of disability, suggesting that such an approach will not further the rights of disabled people and must be transcended. Many of the key themes in these opening three chapters are taken up and engaged with in the rest of the book.

Jerome Bickenbach takes the debate on definitions in an altogether different direction. He argues that the WHO's International Classification of Functioning, Disability and Health (ICF) provides a useful epidemiological tool that allows for the generation of data that can help make the case for equality and human rights for disabled people. He takes on and addresses – and in some cases accepts – many of the critiques of the ICF made by those within disability studies. His contribution finishes with a plea for further engagement with the ICF by disability theorists, arguing that it is only through such engagement that the ICF can be further refined to accommodate more sensitive and relevant indicators.

Bill Hughes, employing ideas emerging from the sociology of emotions and what Carol Thomas termed psycho-emotional disablism, explores how emotions are used to construct disability and our responses to disabled people. He examines how the emotions of fear, pity and disgust contribute to the social distance between disabled and non-disabled people and how they construct the discrimination and exclusion experienced.

Donna Reeve's contribution continues the theme of emotions as she explores the experience of psycho-emotional disablism per se. This offers a phenomenologically informed theoretical analysis of this inner dimension of disablism. Using the accounts of disabled people, she highlights both direct and indirect forms of this type of disablism and shows the different ways in which 'the body' is also present when looking at their experiences.

The final chapter in Part 1 – by Nick Watson – looks at the way that disability studies has approached research on disability. He argues that whilst it has been very successful in pointing out the disadvantage experienced by disabled people, and providing evidence for their exclusion, disability studies has failed to provide us with an understanding of what it is like to live as a disabled person. This, he argues, is largely a result of its reliance on emancipatory research. Watson argues that the way forward is to adopt a more critical realist approach, and to explore both the experience of disablement and the experience of impairment.

Part 2: Disablement, disablism and impairment effects

This part explores how different groups of people with particular impairment types ('real' or 'constructed') have engaged with disability studies and the writings within the discipline, especially published ideas about the relationship between impairment and disablement. It opens with a chapter by Jackie Leach Scully on deafness, which examines how the experiences of deafness are contained – or not – within disability theory. In doing this, she looks both at how disability studies has approached the idea of *disability* identity and why deafness might need to be considered differently, especially in view of the existence of the Deaf community and the concept Deaf culture. She argues that deafness and disability should be understood as instances of embodied human diversity and that how they are experienced is contextual rather than biological, arguing that the most decisive factor is the degree to which the normality of deafness is endorsed by family and community. This mirrors some of the arguments of Shildrick, and Mitchell and Snyder in chapters three and four.

In the next chapter, Kirsten Stalker examines how learning disabilities have been theorized, or rather *not* theorized, in disability studies. Not only were people with a learning disability absent from the original formulation of disability as defined by UPIAS (1976), they have also, she argues, been largely absent from much that is published in the discipline. She presents an overview of the dominant theoretical frameworks within the academic study of learning disability and considers how these have impacted on policy-making and service delivery. She is highly critical of some of the more recent post-structuralist approaches to learning disability, and finishes her chapter with an exploration of how critical realism might be the way forward for further development in this area.

Sasha Scambler, closely associated with medical sociology, examines the intersection between critical illness and other long-term disabling conditions, which are the main causes of impairment in the developed world. As in the previous chapter, Scambler makes the case for a realist approach to the study of disability. Using the examples of diabetes and Batten disease, she argues that the study of long-term disabling conditions, and the people who live with them on a daily basis, can offer fresh insights into existing debates within the field of disability studies. She also makes the case for much greater collaboration between medical sociologists and disability theorists.

The relationship between mental health and disability studies is the focus of the next chapter. Peter Beresford explores what has, at times, been an uncomfortable relationship between the two areas; he does this through the lens of the psychiatric system survivors' movement. The chapter documents how this movement has emerged and explores its impact on both people labelled with a mental health problem and its intersection with disability studies. He argues that whilst there are differences there are also shared values and beliefs that underpin both disability studies and the survivors' movement. Thus, both can learn – and need to learn – from each other.

Speech impairment is another area that disability studies has not yet fully engaged with, and in the next chapter Kevin Paterson seeks to develop an understanding of 'communication disablement' from the standpoint of a person with speech impairment. He draws on phenomenology to argue that norms of communication are oppressive to people with speech impairment but that disability studies has not been able to theorize this oppression. He argues that whilst it is possible to augment or facilitate people with a speech impairment, the temporal dimension of conversation cannot be accommodated and it is difficult for people with speech impairment to acquire and sustain the physical and cultural capital necessary to participate in everyday social encounters.

The final chapter in this part explores the relationship between social and individual approaches to the study of blindness through an exploration of how equal opportunity is experienced by blind and visually impaired students in the context of higher education in the UK. Karen Beauchamp-Pryor makes the case for a perspective that includes both approaches, arguing that that if blind students are to be included changes are required at the level of the institution but that these must take account of, and be sensitive to, individual experiences – and that the latter have to be included in policy and practice to ensure equality and inclusion.

Part 3: Social policy and disability: health, personal assistance, employment and education

In Part 3 we present a series of chapters that examine the policy response to the disability 'problem'. It starts with a chapter from scholars in Australia, Karen Soldatic and Helen Meekosha, which explores how social policy both creates and sustains hegemonic constructions of disability. They argue that the widespread ideology of neoliberalism has generated a political economy and state formation that has resulted in regulatory state practices of great significance for disabled people. Most notable is a restructuring of social rights, a remapping of disability labour market programming, and the rise of the informal 'care economy' and ideologies of 'care'. The state therefore plays a central role in creating social, moral and political understandings of disability. Thus, the state must form a central part of our understanding and analysis of disability. Indeed, the relationship between the state and disabled people is the main focus of this section and is picked up in the next three chapters on employment, education and independent living.

In the first of these, Alan Roulstone presents an analysis of the barriers faced by disabled people globally in accessing paid work. He suggests that, largely as a result of the turn to neoliberalism, 'work' in many countries has come to be seen as an antithesis of welfare, and that this has the consequence of positioning people in receipt of welfare as either unable or unwilling to move to work-based social activities – with the latter deemed to be less worthy than their non-disabled peers. This approach, he suggests, ignores all of the many barriers disabled people face as they attempt to access the employment marketplace.

Similar points are made by Michele Moore and Roger Slee as they explore the foundations of educational exclusion and consider emerging patterns of exclusion. They argue that as educational systems have embraced a neo-liberal ethic of competitive individualism so the exclusion of disabled children has increased. The solution to this, they argue, is for disability studies to be included in education as a strategy pursuant to inclusive education. This would critically engage with, and challenge, dominant and oppressive practices and promote the voices of disabled students and school children.

Charlotte Pearson presents an overview of the independent living movement and shows how the ideas behind this movement have led to the increased marketization of social care. Independent living, and the move to individual budgets in the UK, marks an important shift in the relationship between the state and the individual in that, whilst the provision of support for disabled people is moved away from the patchwork of benefits towards a more coherent policy framework, it also marks the end of the role of the state in the direct delivery of social care and the end of socialized care.

The final two chapters in Part 3 are broadly concerned with health and disability. In the first, Eric Emerson and his colleagues explore: the nature and determinants of the health inequalities faced by disabled people; the association between health and disability; the reasons why disabled people experience poorer health than their non-disabled peers; and the processes that may link disability and health. They also identify the implications of this knowledge for policy and future research, arguing that policies must be developed to improve and protect the living standards of disabled people and their families.

In the final chapter in this part, Tom Shakespeare explores disability in the global South, drawing on work for the WHO/The World Bank *World Report on Disability* (2011). He argues that we currently know little about disability and how it is experienced in many low and middle income countries. Moreover, in many of these countries disability is not well understood and developed as an equality issue. Disabled people in the global South live in very disadvantaged conditions – far removed from what pertains in North America, Europe or Australasia. The chapter gives some examples of good practice in developing countries, but points out that many of these policies need to be evaluated and the results disseminated to share best practice. Shakespeare argues that there is a need for policies that can promote equality in a way that is sensitive to local customs and traditions.

Part 4: Disability studies and interdisciplinarity

As disability studies has developed, so too has its links to other disciplines, and it has moved beyond its original disciplinary basis in sociology and social policy. In this part we present six chapters that explore how other disciplines have engaged with disability studies and how that relationship has developed. The aim of this part is to show not only what other disciplines can contribute to disability studies but also what disability studies can contribute to them.

In the first chapter, David Bolt explores how cultural studies and disability studies intersect, examining both how a cultural studies approach can deepen our understanding of disability and how the study of disability can enrich our understanding of culture. He points out that there has been a general reluctance within cultural studies to critically engage with disability studies – and to a certain extent vice-versa – and that both need each other. He makes a plea to those who work in literary studies, cultural studies, film studies and media studies for disability studies to be taken more seriously.

In the next chapter, Simo Vehmas presents an overview of what philosophy has to offer disability studies. He shows how philosophy and disability studies can be combined to question and examine carefully the essential concepts and conceptions of disability studies and their rational credibility, logical tenability and normative soundness. The chapter discusses the ontology of disability, ethics and the moral significance of disability. He finishes with a discussion on political philosophy, drawing on the ideas of Amartya Sen and how the concept of capabilities can be used in relation to disabled people's social status.

Dan Goodley explores the relationship between disability studies and psychology, an area where there has been considerable conceptual conflict. Psychology, with its focus on rehabilitation, treatment, therapy and cure, coupled with its tendency to individualize the disability experience, is often seen as incompatible with disability studies. Goodley argues, however, that combining the two approaches would allow the exploration of a number of important and neglected issues, including: the psychological impact of living with impairment in a disabling society; exploring the ways in which disabled people deal psychologically with demanding publics; and exposing non-disabled people's unresolved, unconscious conflicts around difference. He makes the case for the development of a critical psychology of disability in which psychology is recast and becomes a discipline of and for disabled people, one that seeks to challenge the disabling conditions of everyday life.

The relationship between disability studies and history forms the basis of Anne Borsay's contribution. She argues that history has, to a large extent, ignored disability mainly because disabled people were seen as being too marginal and of little historical interest. She also points out that disability studies has largely ignored disability history, especially in the UK where the materialist focus is strongest. She contrasts the approach in the UK with that found in the US, where there has been a much greater engagement with individual biographies of disabled people. The chapter maps the changing relationship between disability, history and disability studies.

Brett Smith and Andy Sparks examine the intersection between disability and sport and leisure studies, and explore disabled people's participation in both elite sports and in more leisurely activities. They argue that this newly burgeoning area of research in which disability studies and the social study of sports science are combined allows for an exploration of a range of issues including how participation can be promoted, the barriers to participation, the impact of sport and leisure on an individual's health and well-being, and how it affects non-disabled people's views of disability and disabled people. Also, from a more theoretical perspective, they point to the way that sport and leisure studies can be used to further our understanding of the embodied experience of living with an impairment – and the nature of impairment and impairment effects.

In the final chapter in Part 4, Stuart Blume presents an overview of science and technology studies and explores how studying technologies – and how they are used and not used – can provide insights into the meaning of disability. Using examples of specific technologies such as cochlear implants, he describes how science and technology studies can help in uncovering and exploring the gap that exists between the social model and the embodied experiences of disability and impairment.

Part 5: Contextualizing the disability experience

In this final part, we present a series of chapters that examine disability and its intersection with a range of different social and political factors. It opens with two chapters that focus on the concept of intersectionality in relation to disability and gender and disability and ethnicity. In the first chapter, Ana Bê presents an overview of how feminist scholars from within disability studies have used feminism to develop and enrich our understandings of disability. She argues that feminism has made a substantial contribution to theorizations of disability and that this has often gone unacknowledged. Her chapter finishes with an exploration of intersectionality and points to the possibilities this approach offers in relation to the heterogeneity of the disability experience, both in terms of impairment and in terms of social identity and location.

The concept of intersectionality is used again in the next chapter. Here, Deborah Stienstra explores the intersectionality between race/ethnicity and disability studies. Stienstra calls for greater reflexivity around issues to do with race/ethnicity and, in particular, on the 'whiteness' of disability studies. This involves the recognition that disability studies has largely ignored issues to do with ethnicity and cultural identity. She suggests that 'White privilege' and the ability to use English has shaped the culture and practices of many services in North America and that we need to unpack these experiences if we are to develop a truly inclusive approach to the study of disability.

The next three chapters all explore the intersection between disability and family. In the first, Claudia Malacrida explores the relationship between mothering and disability. She highlights the dearth of information on, and understanding of, the experiences and needs of mothers with disabilities. She argues that this is often at the root of the challenges faced by disabled women in giving birth to, raising and maintaining custody of their children. This, she argues, is the result of historical and enduring ideas about disability – impacting on the right of disabled women to reproduce and rear children. She explores the intersections between disabled women's multiple sources of oppression and their embodied relationships of interdependency. The chapter concludes with a call for more inclusive framings of disability which include gendered inequalities and a research approach that takes women's specifically situated perspectives into account.

Kinship forms the basis of the next chapter, in which Janice McLaughlin explores the intersection between disability and family. The chapter challenges dominant narratives around family and disability, which emphasize 'the burden' disability produces and the 'special' qualities of families who are able to 'cope'. It examines care and caring responsibilities, the notion of interdependency and the effects of therapy on family life. The chapter highlights aspects of family life that are often ignored because of the 'burden' focus, and argues that disabled family members are usually full and valued participants in family life.

John Davis takes up this last point in his analysis of disability and childhood. In this chapter, Davis brings together key themes from disability studies and childhood studies and offers a synthesis that presents a view of childhood disability that moves beyond the materialist focus within UK disability studies. By bringing these two disciplines together, a more complex and politically nuanced approach to childhood and disability emerges – one that recognizes the diverse identities of disabled children and balances notions of agency, fluidity and social oppression.

The last chapter in this collection, perhaps fittingly, looks at disability at the end of the life course, and examines the intersection between disability and ageing. Christine Bigby explores the issue of ageing for people with an intellectual disability – a relative new group of disabled people emerging largely as a result of improvements in health care. She employs a life course perspective and, in doing so, shows how important earlier experiences are in shaping the life course and the ageing experience. Her chapter points to the importance of good provision of services and the importance of the family, of relationships and the intersection between the lived experience and the provision of good social care and social support.

Concluding comments

Our hope in bringing this collection together is that disability studies can be enriched and boosted by the new ideas and perspectives presented here, and that readers will learn much for their own thinking, research, scholarship and activism. The inclusion of authors representing a broad mix of disciplines, perspectives and nationalities has brought together expertise and knowledge in an innovative fashion. This has allowed for the positive and constructive examination and questioning of the dominant discourses within disability studies. We believe that this collection will act as a starting point for new developments in disability studies, and can point the way to exciting initiatives in research and theorizing.

References

Barnes, C. (1991) *Disabled People in Britain and Discrimination: A Case for Anti-discrimination Legislation* (London: C. Hurst & Co.).

Chouinard, V. (2009) 'Impairment and Disability', in T. Brown, S. McLafferty and G. Moon, eds, *A Companion to Health and Medical Geography* (Oxford: Wiley-Blackwell).

Davis, L. (1995) *Enforcing Normalcy: Disability, Deafness and the Body* (London: Verso).

De Jong, G. (1981) *Environmental Accessibility and Independent Living Outcomes* (East Lansing, Michigan: University Centre for International Rehabilitation).

Driedger, D. (1991) *The Last Civil Rights Movement* (London: Hurst and Co).

Finkelstein, V. (1980) *Attitudes and Disabled People* (New York: World Rehabilitation Fund).

Gallagher, D. J. and Skidmore, D. (2006) 'On Social Class, Disability, and Discursive Spaces: Using Dialogical Pedagogy to Promote Inclusive Education', in *Disability Studies in Education*, 18–21 May (Michigan: Michigan State University).

Goodley, D. (2010) *Disability Studies: An Interdisciplinary Introduction* (London: Sage).

Hahn, H. (1985) 'Toward a Politics of Disability: Definitions, Disciplines, and Policies', *The Social Science Journal* 22(4) Oct: 87–105.

Kasnitz, D. (2001) 'Life Event Histories and the US Independent Living Movement', in M. Priestley, ed., *Disability and the Life Course: Global Perspectives* (Cambridge: Cambridge University Press): pp. 67–79.

Kleinfield, S. (1979) *The Hidden Minority: A Profile of Handicapped Americans* (Boston, Mass.: Atlantic Monthly Press).

Morris, J. (1991) *Pride Against Prejudice* (London: Women's Press).

Oliver, M. (1983) *Social Work with Disabled People* (Basingstoke: Macmillan).

Shakespeare, T. (2006) *Disability Rights: Disability Wrongs* (London: Routledge).

Shakespeare, T. and Watson, N. (2001) 'Making the Difference: Disability, Politics, Recognition', in G. Albrecht, K. D. Seelman and M. Bury, eds, *Handbook of Disability Studies* (Sage: London): pp. 546–64.

Shakespeare, T., Gillespie-Sells, K. and Davies, D. (1996) *The Sexual Politics of Disability: Untold Desires* (London: Cassell).

Stiker, H.-J. (1999) *A History of Disability*, translated by W. Sayers (Michigan: University of Michigan Press).

Stuart, O. (1993) 'Double Oppression: An Alternative Starting Point', in J. Swain, V. Finkelstein, S. French and M. Oliver, eds, *Disabling Barriers: Enabling Environments* (London: Sage): pp. 101–6

UPIAS (Union of the Physically Impaired Against Segregation) (1976) *Fundamental Principles of Disability* (London: UPIAS).

WHO and The World Bank (2011) *World Report on Disability* (New York: World Health Organization).

2

UNDERSTANDING THE SOCIAL MODEL OF DISABILITY

Past, present and future

Colin Barnes

Introduction

As someone with a congenital visual impairment with working class disabled parents, I grew up with impairment and disability. I found the social model of disability in the 1980s in a book by Mike Oliver (1983), *Social Work with Disabled People*, when I entered university to study disability. It summarized what I already knew about disability: that people with any form of accredited impairment are disabled by an unjust and uncaring society. It has influenced my work ever since. Subsequently, thinking inspired by the social model has had a major impact on policy circles and universities across the world. Yet in many respects there remains a general misunderstanding about what the social model actually is and what it is for.

This chapter will address this unfortunate state of affairs, in particular the debates surrounding the usefulness of the social model within the academy. It is divided into three main sections. The first section will examine the origins of the social model. This is followed by a review of the influence of social model insights within and beyond the academy. The final section will address the various debates that have emerged since the late 1990s and argue that, without the social model of disability, disability studies will be rendered meaningless. Therefore, the struggle for a fairer and more just society will be that bit harder.

The origins of the social model

To understand the significance of the implications of social model reasoning it is important to remember that until very recently 'disability' was viewed almost exclusively as an individual medical problem or 'personal tragedy' in western culture. Yet there is a wealth of anthropological and sociological evidence to suggest that societal responses to people with impairments or long-term health conditions vary considerably across time, culture and location. (See, for example, Hanks and Hanks 1948; Lemert 1951; Ingstad and Whyte 1995; Miles 1995, 2001; Ingstad 2001.)

The philosophical and cultural basis upon which the individualistic negative response to impairment rests is rooted firmly in the foundations of western culture. Whilst the vast majority of people with impairments were integrated into the community prior to the industrial revolution, there is substantial evidence that oppression and prejudice was widespread (Ryan and Thomas 1980; Garland 1995; Stiker 1999). There is also general agreement that the economic and social upheavals that accompanied the coming of industrial capitalism precipitated the institutionalization of discriminatory policies and practices. Industrialization, urbanization, changing work patterns and accompanying ideologies: liberal utilitarianism, medicalization, eugenics and social Darwinism – all contributed to and compounded ancient fears and prejudices. Taken together, these structural forces provided intellectual justification for more extreme discriminatory practices; notably the systematic removal of disabled people from mainstream economic and social life (Finkelstein 1980; Oliver 1990; Barnes 1990, 1991, 1997; Gleeson 1999; Borsay 2005).

Since the mass 'euthanasia' policy for disabled people, defined as 'useless eaters', introduced by Germany's then Nazi Government in the 1930s and 40s (Gallagher 1995; Burleigh 1994), there has been a general 'softening' of attitudes in policy circles in wealthy states such as the United Kingdom (UK), Europe and the United States of America (USA). This led to an expansion of community-based services provided by state and voluntary agencies and a proliferation of professional helpers underpinned by traditional deficit understandings of disability (Oliver 1981; Brisenden 1986; Barnes 1991; Morris 1993; Priestley 1999).

This policy change was the result of several factors. These included a moral obligation felt by politicians and the general population towards the large numbers of civilians and military personnel injured during the war. There was also an unprecedented growth in the numbers of disabled and elderly people due to increasing affluence and medical advances. All of this contributed to the politicization of disability by disabled people and their organizations in the latter half of the twentieth century in countries as diverse as Sweden (Hőjer 1951; Nordqvist 1972), the UK (Hunt 1966a; Campbell and Oliver 1996; Barton 2001), the USA (De Jong 1979; Scotch 1989; Shapiro 1993) and Japan (Tateiwa 2010).

In the UK, disability activism revolved around a rejection of 'residential care' and control by what Finkelstein (1999) termed 'professionals allied to medicine', poverty and the exclusion from mainstream economic and social activity. Until the late 1960s, support for 'severely' disabled people was generally unavailable outside institutions and there were no disability-related welfare payments. Consequently, 'severely' disabled people were either incarcerated in residential homes run by professionals or living in relative poverty and social isolation in the community. A crucial factor for all disabled people and their families at this time was a lack of money, which resulted in the formation of the Disabled Incomes Group (DIG) by two disabled women in 1965 (Campbell and Oliver 1996).

The DIG attracted the attention of disability activists across the country. These included future key figures in the UK's disabled people's movement: Paul Hunt, Vic Finkelstein, Maggie Hines and Ken Davis. They soon rejected the narrow incomes approach favoured by DIG and later the Disability Alliance (DA). The DA brought together several disability organizations to campaign for a comprehensive disability income. Disillusioned by this approach and its domination by non-disabled 'experts', Hunt, Finkelstein and Davis along with other like-minded disabled activists set up the Union of the Physically Impaired Against Segregation (UPIAS) in 1974 (UPIAS 1976).

Undoubtedly the most influential organization in the history of social model thinking, UPIAS functioned mainly through confidential correspondence and circulars distributed amongst its members. Drawing on personal experience and sociological insights, although none were trained sociologists, UPIAS members argued that disability was a complex form of social oppression similar to that encountered by women, ethnic minorities, lesbians and gay men. An early expression of this view is found in *Stigma: The Experience of Disability*: a book of 12 personal accounts of living with impairment by six disabled men and six disabled women, initiated and edited by Paul Hunt, then a resident of the Le Court residential home in Hampshire (Hunt 1966a).

Hunt selected the chapters from over 60 responses to a letter he had published in national newspapers and magazines requesting contributions. His aim was to avoid 'sentimental autobiography' or a 'preoccupation with the medical and practical details of a particular affliction'. In his chapter, Hunt argues that:

> the problem of disability lies not only in the impairment of function and its effects on us individually but more importantly in our *relationship* with 'normal' people (emphasis added).
>
> *(Hunt 1966b: 146)*

Disabled people 'are set apart from the ordinary' in ways which see them as posing a direct 'challenge' to commonly held social values by appearing 'unfortunate, useless, different, oppressed and sick' (p. 146).

Thus, for UPIAS, lack of income is a symptom rather than a cause of disabled people's individual and collective disadvantage:

> Disability is something imposed on top of our impairments by the way we are unnecessarily isolated and excluded from society. Disabled people are therefore an oppressed group. It follows from this analysis that having low incomes, for example, is only one aspect of our oppression. It is a consequence of our isolation and segregation in every area of social life, such as education, work, mobility, housing etc.
>
> *(UPIAS 1976: 4)*

In contrast to previous definitions that cited impairment as the cause of disability and 'handicap' (Harris *et al.* 1971), UPIAS produced a socio-political definition of disability that made the crucial distinction between the biological (impairment) and the social (disability). Hence, 'impairment' denotes 'lacking part or all of a limb, or having a defective limb or mechanism of the body' but 'disability' is:

> the disadvantage of restriction of activity caused by a contemporary social organisation which takes no or little account of people who have physical impairments and thus excludes them from participation in the mainstream of social activities.
>
> *(UPIAS 1976: 14)*

Subsequently, the restriction to 'physical impairments' was dropped to incorporate all impairments – physical, sensory and cognitive. This is because some conditions, both congenital and acquired, affect all bodily functions and in a disablist society all impairments – whatever their cause – have to a greater or lesser degree negative physical and psychological implications. Also, impairment-specific labels may have relevance when accessing appropriate medical and support needs, but they are usually imposed rather than chosen and therefore socially and politically divisive (Barnes 1996; Oliver and Barnes 1998).

Thereafter, the UPIAS definition was adopted and adapted by national and international organizations controlled and run by disabled people. These included the British Council of Organisations of Disabled People (BCODP), the national umbrella for organizations controlled and run by disabled people in the UK, and Disabled People's International (DPI), an international body for national organizations like BCODP (Campbell and Oliver 1996).

Other important developments during the 1970s included increased disability activism in the USA and the emergence of the Independent Living Movement (ILM). The ILM emerged partly from within the campus culture of American universities and partly from repeated efforts by American disability activists, swelled by the growing numbers of disabled Vietnam War veterans, to influence US disability legislation. During the 1960s, some American universities had introduced various self-help programmes to enable students with 'severe' physical impairments to attend mainstream courses. Such schemes were rarely available outside university campuses. This prompted some disabled students to develop their own services under the banner of Centres for Independent Living (CILs) (De Jong 1979).

Unlike conventional services *for* disabled people, CILs are self-help organizations run and controlled by disabled people. Traditional professionally dominated provision focused almost exclusively on medical treatments and therapies within institutional settings that effectively removed disabled people from everyday life. In contrast, CILs provided a new and innovative range of services designed to empower people with impairments for a lifestyle of their own choosing within, rather than apart from, the local community. The activities of the ILM had a significant impact on activists in the UK and led to the establishment of user-led organizations providing services and support for disabled people and their families. Early examples include the Spinal Injuries Association (SIA), established in 1973. The UK's first CILs, the Hampshire Centre for Independent Living (HCIL) and the Derbyshire Centre for Integrated Living (DCIL), opened in 1985 (Barnes and Mercer 2006).

The 1970s also witnessed the introduction of various legislative measures and policy initiatives to address disability issues. In the UK, the Chronically Sick and Disabled Person's Act entered the statute books following a Private Members' Bill by a Labour MP, Alf Morris, in 1970. The Act is widely regarded as the first piece of legislation in the world to introduce policies to improve equal opportunities for disabled people in community-based services, education, housing and public buildings (Topliss and Gould 1981). Three years later, the US Congress passed the 1973 Rehabilitation Act, which included Section 504 prohibiting discrimination against disabled people in any federally funded programme. The United Nations (UN) introduced its Declaration on the Rights of Mentally Retarded Persons in 1971 and the Declaration on the Rights of Disabled Persons in 1975. The latter states that:

> Disabled persons, whatever the origin, nature and seriousness of their handicaps and disabilities, have the same fundamental rights as their fellow-citizens of the same age, which implies first and foremost the right to enjoy a decent life, as normal and full as possible.
>
> *(UN 1975, article 3)*

Growing interest in disability at the international level led to in 1980 the World Health Organization's (WHO) first attempt to provide a universally acceptable definition of disability – the International Classification of Impairment Disability and Handicap (ICIDH) – and a year later the UN's International Year of Disabled People (IYDP).

The ICIDH was developed by a group of social scientists led by Philip Wood at the University of Manchester without the involvement of disabled people. Published in 1980, four years after the UPIAS definition, the stated aim of the ICIDH was to clarify concepts and terminology surrounding disability to facilitate accurate and comparable research and policy within and across nation states (Bury 1997). Designed to complement the WHO's International Classification of Disease (WHO 1976), the ICIDH separates the concepts *impairment, disability* and *handicap* as follows:

- Impairment: 'Any loss or abnormality of psychological, physiological or anatomical structure or function'
- Disability: 'Any restriction or lack (resulting from an impairment) of ability to perform an activity in the manner or within the range considered normal for a human being'

- Handicap: 'A disadvantage for a given individual, resulting from an impairment or disability, that limits or prevents the fulfilment of a role (depending on age, sex, social and cultural factors) for that individual.

(Adapted from WHO 1980: 29)

The ICIDH has been subject to several criticisms by disabled activists and allies. First, it relies exclusively on individualistic medical definitions and bio-physical assumptions of 'normality'. But 'normality' is a contentious concept influenced by various historical, cultural and situational forces (Abberley 1993; Davis 1995). Second, 'impairment' is identified as the cause of both 'disability' and 'handicap'. Although handicap, or social disadvantage, is presented as neutral and the inevitable consequence of either impairment or disability, this is difficult to sustain. Many impairments do not inhibit an individual's physical or intellectual capability. Examples include short stature, hair loss and skin blemishes. What is and what is not an impairment is historically, culturally and socially variable. For example, homosexuality is no longer considered an impairment in some cultures but in others it is (Weeks 1991). Handicap is therefore ideologically and culturally determined; neither ideology nor culture is politically neutral.

Finally, this approach places people with an actual or accredited impairment in a dependent position. Their condition is individualized and medicalized and therefore assumes that they are reliant upon professional experts and others to provide therapeutic and social support. As impairments are presented as the root cause of disability, logic dictates that they must be eradicated, minimized or 'cured'. But where 'cures' are ineffective, which is more often than not the case, people labelled 'disabled' are viewed as economically and socially inadequate and in need of 'care'. This has resulted in the generation of a thriving and costly 'disability' industry comprised of state institutions, private businesses, charities and voluntary agencies staffed by vast armies of professional helpers. The result is that disabled people's assumed inadequacy and dependence is reified and assured (Stone 1984; Wolfensberger 1989; Albrecht 1992; Oliver 1990).

The growing interest in disability issues at the international level led to the UN declaring 1981 the International Year of Disabled People. This signified a formal recognition that national governments are responsible for securing equal rights for disabled people. The following year the UN General Assembly adopted by consensus a World Programme of Action Concerning Disabled Persons and a global strategy on the prevention of disability. Other international initiatives quickly followed, including the African Decade of Persons with Disabilities (2000–9), the European Year of People with Disabilities 2003, the Asian and Pacific Decade of Disabled Persons (2003–12) and the Arab Decade of Disabled Persons (2003–12) (Albert 2006).

Also in 1981, disabled activists formed DPI. This was established because of Rehabilitation International (RI)'s refusal to accept the equal participation of disabled delegates on its controlling body. Formed in 1922 as the International Society for Crippled Children, RI is an international organization composed of rehabilitation professionals (Driedger 1989: 18). DPI's first world congress was held in Singapore in the following year and attracted 400 delegates representing national organizations run by disabled people from around the world, including representatives of BCODP. As well as adopting a socio-political definition of disability, DPI's stated policy revolves around the promotion of grass roots organizations and the development of public awareness of disability issues in the struggle for equality. Its slogan 'Nothing About Us Without Us' has been embraced by disabled people's organizations around the world (Charlton 1998). Taken together, these forces were instrumental in the thinking behind the use of the phrase 'the social model of disability'.

The arrival and impact of the social model

Prior to the 1970s, apart from one or two notable exceptions, academic interest in disability was limited almost exclusively to conventional, individualistic medical explanations. An important example is Talcott Parsons's (1951) functionalist analysis of the role of the medical profession. For Parsons, 'health' is 'normal' and 'sickness', and, by implication 'impairment', is not and is therefore socially deviant. The role of medicine is to regulate and control sickness by curing and returning 'sick' people back to health. Although this account is concerned with 'acute' rather than 'chronic' conditions, it has dominated sociological analyses of reactions to and the management of ascribed social deviance, including disablement, ever since (Barnes *et al.* 1999; Barnes and Mercer 2003, 2010).

A notable example is Erving Goffman's (1968) account of the interactions between 'normal' and 'abnormal' people. Also during the 1960s, particular attention was paid to the social construction of 'mental illness'. Examples include Scheff (1966), Szasz (1971) and Rosenhan (1973). The idea that mental illness and other forms of ascribed social deviance are little more than social constructs generated by an increasingly dominant and moralistic social order was given a further boost by the writings of the French philosopher Michel Foucault (1976, 1977).

Consequently, academic interest in the general area of 'disability' increased. Notable publications in the UK include *The Meaning of Disability* (Blaxter 1976) and *Poverty in the United Kingdom* (Townsend 1979); American examples include *The Making of Blind Men* (Scott 1969), *The Sociology of Physical Disability and Rehabilitation* (Albrecht 1976) and *Handicapping America* (Bowe 1978). But whilst each of these studies drew attention to the various economic and social consequences of the ascription of a conventional 'disabled' identity, none made any serious attempt to question its ideological and cultural underpinnings. The theoretical insights applied to the concept of cognitive impairments were never extended to address other conditions and, particularly, 'physical disability'. The groundwork for this endeavour was laid by writers such as Finkelstein (1980), *Attitudes and Disabled People*; Ryan and Thomas (1980), *The Politics of Mental Handicap*; Shearer (1981), *Disability: Whose Handicap*; and Sutherland (1981), *Disabled We Stand*; and the emergence of what is now referred to as disability studies.

The UK's first 'disability' studies course, 'The Handicapped Person in the Community', was conceived and produced by an interdisciplinary team at the Open University (OU) in 1975 as an optional module on the OU's Health and Social Studies degree. A key figure in the development of this course was Vic Finkelstein, a clinical psychologist and founder member of UPIAS. Initially aimed at professionals and voluntary workers, the course's primary objective was to help students improve their 'professional and social skills in order to assist handicapped people to achieve *maximum autonomy*' (emphasis added) (Finkelstein 1997: 41). From the outset the course was criticized for its 'sociological bias' (Finkelstein 1997: 46). It was updated twice before its abolition in 1994, and each time more and more disabled people were involved in the production of course materials. The final version of the programme was re-titled 'The Disabling Society' to reflect its wider content. Over the years, the OU team generated a wealth of material that provided the basis for the development of a whole host of disability studies-related courses and professional training schemes at both undergraduate and postgraduate levels in mainstream colleges and universities across the UK (Barnes *et al.* 2002a).

Disability studies was pioneered in American universities by disability advocates and academics. The first course, structured around 'living with a disability', was situated in the general area of medical sociology (Pfeiffer and Yoshida 1995: 476). In 1981, Irving Zola, a disabled sociologist and chairperson of the medical sociology section of the American Sociology Association, founded the *Disability Studies Quarterly* and co-founded America's Society for Disability Studies. At the turn of the 1980s, 12 disability studies courses at various levels were offered in American institutions. By 1986 the number had risen to 23 (Pfeiffer and Yoshida 1995).

Taken together, these developments led Mike Oliver, a disabled activist and lecturer, to coin the phrase 'social model of disability' in his contribution to a collection of five papers edited by a practising social worker, Jo Campling, in 1981, entitled *The Handicapped Person: A New Perspective for Social Workers*. Campling's previous work had included *Better Lives for Disabled Women* (1979) and *Images of Ourselves: Women with Disabilities Talking* (1981); both focused on women's experiences of living with impairment in the UK in the 1970s. Oliver's initial aim was to provide an accessible key to understanding the importance of the UPIAS's definition of disability and its implications for policy and practice for social work students. Hence:

> This new paradigm involves nothing more or less fundamental than a switch away from focusing on the physical limitations of particular individuals to the way the physical and social environment impose limitations upon certain categories of people.
>
> *(Oliver 1981: 28)*

It is therefore an 'heuristic device' or aid to understanding which entails the adoption of the following key principles.

First, a social model perspective is not a denial of the importance or value of appropriate individually based interventions, whether they be medically, re/habilitative, educational or employment-based. Instead, it draws attention to their limitations in terms of furthering disabled people's empowerment. Second, the social model is a deliberate attempt to shift attention away from the functional limitations of individuals with impairments onto the problems caused by disabling environments, barriers and cultures. In short, the social model of disability is a tool with which to provide insights into the disabling tendencies of modern society in order to generate policies and practices to facilitate their eradication. For advocates, impairment may be a human constant but 'disability' need not and should not be. Although the concept 'social model' has been linked to several sociological theories of disability (Priestley 1998), it is generally associated with materialist perspectives (adapted from Oliver 1996, 2004; Barnes 1996; Barnes *et al.* 1999; Barnes and Mercer 2003, 2010).

Even so, social model insights were ignored by many social scientists in the UK until the turn of the millennium. Sociologists in particular continued to favour a 'conventional' functionalist, deviance approach, albeit within a broader sociological framework. This has generated a growing literature on the mechanisms and processes by which people adapt to the onset of 'chronic illness' and impairment. See, for example, Anderson and Bury (1988). This burgeoning 'sociology of chronic illness and disability' has dampened down sociological interest in the wider social processes that create disability and as a result produced little in terms of theory and research (Thomas 2007: 40).

The bulk of this literature focuses almost exclusively on the 'failing body' and 'personal troubles', disregarding the significance of social barriers to inclusion. This has recently been acknowledged by some medical sociologists such as Gareth Williams (2001) and Graham Scambler (2004). The latter provides a reappraisal of his earlier work on stigma in which he identifies a 'hidden distress model' of epilepsy (Scambler 1989). He now maintains that this approach is at best *partial and at worst deficient* in its failure to address sociologically a series of theoretical questions' (original emphasis) (Scambler 2004: 29). Yet this critique does not reject or abandon the medically dominated perceptions of impairment as social deviance. Instead, the deviance perspective must be strengthened with the development of a 'new' research agenda based on the assertion that:

> Any appreciation of why and how epilepsy persists as a significant condition must be articulated against the background of the logics of capitalist accumulation (of the economy) and mode of regulation (of the state) and their respective relations of class and command.
>
> *(Scambler 2004: 42)*

It is perhaps testament to the inward-looking practices of many medical sociologists, and academia generally (Barnes *et al.* 2002b), that Scambler chose to ignore the wealth of material already produced by disabled people and their organizations and writers working from a social model perspective in the UK and elsewhere that deal with these very issues.

Indeed, the social model had become the 'big idea' (Hasler 1993) and a key factor in the mobilization of disability activism during the 1980s and 1990s. Notable examples include the struggle for anti-discrimination legislation to outlaw discrimination against disabled people and the campaign to legalize direct payments to enable disabled people to employ their own support workers (Campbell and Oliver 1996). At its inception in 1981, the BCODP had seven member organizations; its membership had increased to 80 by 1990 (Barnes 1991: 6). Disabled activists developed a range of innovative user-led initiatives, including a national network of telephone Disability Information and Advice Lines (DIAL) (Davis 1981), integrated accessible housing schemes for disabled and non-disabled residents (Davis and Woodward 1981) and direct payments for disabled people to employ personal assistants (HCIL 1981).

In a paper inspired by a 'social barriers model of disability', Ken Davis describes how DCIL implemented a comprehensive 'operational framework' for service support based on seven needs and priorities formulated by disabled people. These included information, peer counselling and support, accessible housing, technical aids and equipment, personal assistance, accessible transport and access to the built environment (Davis 1990: 7). By the turn of the decade there were at least 85 user-led CIL-type organizations offering or aspiring to offer these and other services for disabled people and their families (Barnes and Mercer 2006).

The politicization of disability also prompted the emergence of a burgeoning disability culture and arts movement. This includes disabled artists, musicians, poets and film-makers. The general aim is to give expression to the experience of living with impairment in a disabling society and help generate a celebration of difference and a positive disabled identity (Sutherland 1997, 2006; Peters 2000; Swain and French 2000). The social model was also central to the development of Disability Equality.

These activities generated an expanding literature produced mainly by disabled writers. A key factor was the establishment in 1986 of the first international journal devoted exclusively to disability issues, *Disability, Handicap and Society*, renamed *Disability & Society* in 1993. Disabled researchers inspired by social model thinking produced ethnographic accounts of coming to terms with impairment and disability. Examples include Oliver *et al.* (1988), Morris (1989) and Barnes (1990). Building on UPIAS's insights and Finkelstein's (1980) account of the link between capitalism and the emergence of the disability category, Oliver produced the first comprehensive materialist theory of disability in 1990: *The Politics of Disablement*. The following year the BCODP produced *Disabled People in Britain and Discrimination: A Case for Anti Discrimination Legislation* (Barnes 1991) to bolster their campaign for an anti-discrimination law.

Social model thinking was instrumental to the development of Disability Equality Training (DET) courses devised and presented by disabled people. Primarily aimed at professionals and practitioners, these courses focus on environmental and social barriers to generate possible solutions (Gillespie-Sells and Campbell 1991). This is in contrast to Disability Awareness Training, presented by non-disabled professionals, that tend to reaffirm disability as an individual problem with the use of simulation exercises (French 1996).

The year 1991 also heralded the emergence of a new approach to doing disability research founded on social model principles that placed disabled people and a social model approach at the centre of the research process: emancipator disability research (DHS 1992). Thereafter, a host of studies appeared focusing on a range of disability issues and conducted mainly by disabled researchers. Examples include disabling imagery and the media (Barnes 1992; Hevey 1992; Cumberbatch and Negrine 1992), ageing and disability (Zarb and Oliver 1993), direct payments and personal assistance (Oliver and Zarb 1992; Barnes 1993; Zarb and Nadash 1994), independent living (Morris 1993), ethnicity and 'race' (Begum 1992; Begum *et al.* 1994), sexuality (Shakespeare *et al.* 1996), parenting (Wates 1997) and employment (Roulstone 1998).

All of this has had a major influence on disability policy. In 1992, the British Government acknowledged for the first time that disability discrimination was a major problem and three years later the Disability Discrimination Act became law. In 1996, the Community Care (Disabled Persons) Act allowed local authorities to offer direct payments to disabled people. Hitherto, this was technically illegal under the 1948 National Assistance Act (Zarb and Nadash 1994). The Disability Rights Commission (DRC) was established in 2000 employing a social model definition of disability (DRC 2002). The Government formally adopted a social model definition in its report of 2005 *Improving the Life Chances of Disabled People* (PMSU 2005). Social model rhetoric – if not policy – is now clearly evident in the publications of a host of agencies dealing with disability and related issues in both the statutory and voluntary sectors across the UK (Oliver and Barnes 2006; Shakespeare 2006; Barnes and Mercer 2010).

Social model thinking is also evident in policy statements and documents at the international level. In 1993, the UN produced the *Standard Rules on the Equalisation of Opportunity for People with Disabilities*. This document outlines a radical programme for governments to follow in identifying and securing equality for disabled people (UN 2003/4). The UN's Convention on the Rights of Persons with Disabilities and its Optional Protocol were adopted in December 2006. Negotiated over eight sessions of an ad hoc committee of the General Assembly, including representatives of disability organizations, it marks the first human rights treaty of the twenty-first century. With 50 articles, the Convention is the most comprehensive document yet produced on the rights of disabled people (UN Enable 2009). The European Union sanctioned the social model of disability in its policy Action Plan of 2003 (Commission of the European Communities 2003: 4).

A social model perspective played a key role in 'Rethinking Care from Disabled People's Perspectives', sponsored by the WHO's Disability and Rehabilitation Team. This was a two-year project and conference supported by the Norwegian Government that involved professionals, disabled people and their families from all over the world (WHO 2001). Furthermore, the WHO's recent International Classification of Functioning and Health (ICF), which replaced the much maligned ICIDH, also claims to incorporate social model insights into its construction (WHO 2005). Whilst there is not the space here to provide an extensive critique of the ICF, it is sufficient to point out that it is a three-tier construct, albeit with different terms for disability and handicap – 'activity' and 'participation' respectively – and founded on western notions of 'scientific' medicine and normality. Furthermore, the ICF is presented as apolitical and acknowledges the role of the environment in shaping our understanding of disability. Yet the inference that impairment is the main cause of disablement is clearly retained in its title: the 'biopsychosocial' model of disability (Barnes and Mercer 2010).

In addition, due to the critique of its activities from disabled people and their organizations (Hurst and Albert 2006) and the appointment in 2004 of Judy Heumann, a key activist in America's disabled people's movement as principal advisor on disability and development (Coleridge 2006), The World Bank has since adopted a policy of 'mainstreaming disability' in all its programmes. In 2007 it published its *Social Analysis and Disability: A Guidance Note*, which 'offers a practical guide to integrating social analysis and disability inclusive development into sector and thematic projects and programs of the World Bank' (p. 1).

But, although this document focuses on the importance of disability rights and institutional change, the guidelines therein are not binding. Their impact depends on various factors including: the project or programme, local context and, most importantly, 'available resources' (p. 2). These must come from other sources such as international non-governmental organizations (INGOs), non-governmental organizations (NGOs) and charities. The Bank is neither a charity nor a human rights organization. Its policies are determined by a neo-liberal/capitalist philosophy that strongly upholds the interests of big business and transnational corporations. Its primary function is to provide loans for economic development, which have to be repaid (Yeo 2005).

Moreover, many governments, as diverse as the USA and China, have employed social model-type rhetoric to introduce policies to secure disabled people's rights (Doyle 2008). Yet these policies have had only a marginal impact on the growing numbers of people labelled disabled in both rich and poor countries alike (Charlton 1998; Albert 2006; Chen and Ravallion 2008; Inclusion Europe 2008; Sheldon 2010). All of which raises important issues for the growing numbers of academics and researchers engaged in disability studies.

The social model and its discontents

Since the 1980s, there has been an unprecedented upsurge of interest in the general area of disability amongst social scientists in universities and colleges across the world. This generated a growth in the number of journals dealing with disability issues and networks of researchers studying disablement from a variety of academic disciplines. Disability studies is now an internationally recognized academic discipline, with courses, research centres and professorial chairs (Barnes *et al.* 2002a). This is to be welcomed as it raises the profile of disability issues in colleges and universities: the seed-beds for tomorrow's politicians, policy makers and professionals. Perhaps inevitably with this heightened interest, a number of important challenges to social model thinking have emerged which raise concerns about the discipline's future direction and role in society.

As indicated earlier, theoretical analyses of disability in the UK and the USA are rooted in the political activities of disabled people in the 1960s and 1970s. The American approach, however, differed from that of the UK in that it was dominated by professional academics and adhered to a conventional functionalist/deviance analysis commensurate with American ideology and culture: 'radical consumerism' and 'independent living' (De Jong 1979). By way of contrast, the foundations for a more comprehensive and radical social model-inspired materialist analysis were laid by disabled activists outside the academy (Barnes *et al.* 2002a).

This perspective is still prominent within the disability studies agenda in the UK and elsewhere (Charlton 1998; Gleeson 1999; Hahn 2002). However, its significance has been seriously undermined over recent years by the emergence within the social sciences generally and disability studies in particular of postmodernist/structuralist perspectives. Since the coming to power of right-of-centre governments in America and in the UK in the 1980s and the collapse of Soviet-style communism, there has been a gradual but significant de-radicalization of the social sciences generally and a retreat from radical theories which pose a direct challenge to a capitalist neo-liberal world view (Harvey 2010).

This finds expression in disability studies in America and Canada in the work of Davis (1995), Mitchell and Snyder (1997), Thomson (1997, 2006) and Tremain (2002, 2005) and in the UK and Europe the writings of Corker and Shakespeare (2002), Shakespeare and Watson (2002), Shakespeare (2006), Kristiansen *et al.* (2009) and Goodley (2011).

In sum, these approaches shift attention away from the primacy of economic forces in the creation of disablement toward a politically benign focus on culture, language and discourse. Whilst some studies acknowledge that cultural responses to impairment were transformed with the onset of industrialization and non-disabled 'normalcy' (Davis 1995), the focus is on the role of discourse rather than the economy and associated ideologies. Constructions of the body rather than the economic and social relations of capitalism are prioritized. Standards of physical health, mental balance and moral soundness are closely linked, so that defective bodies and minds are associated with 'degeneracy' (Young 1990) and social anxieties (Thomson 1997, 2006). 'People with disabilities' are therefore recast as a disadvantaged minority in the tradition of American politics and writings (Hahn 2002).

The postmodernist rejection of a 'modernist' world view, 'grand theorising' and associate conceptual dualisms generated a critique of the social model and the impairment/disability distinction upon which it rests (Tremain 2002, 2005; Shakespeare and Watson 2002; Shakespeare 2006). These arguments are fuelled by disabled feminists' early assertions that impairment-related experiences must be included in disability theorizing (Morris 1991; Crow 1996), and that the removal of barriers would not solve the problems encountered by all disabled people because of the complexity and severity of particular conditions (French 1993; Thomas 1999). All of these writers have subsequently acknowledged the importance of a social model analysis. For example, Jenny Morris stated in 2002:

> The social model of disability gives us the words to describe our inequality. It separates out (disabling barriers) from impairment (not being able to walk or see or having difficulty learning). ... Because the social model separates out disabling barriers and impairments, it enables us to focus on exactly what it is which denies us our human and civil rights and what action needs to be taken.
>
> *(Morris 2002: 1–3)*

Even so, the social model as advocated by UPIAS and evident in the writings of Finkelstein (1980) and Oliver (1990), amongst others, is criticized for generating a totalizing grand theory that excludes important dimensions of disabled people's lived experience and knowledge. Critics and former advocates, such as Shakespeare and Watson (1997) for example, argue that the social model is an outdated ideology as the impairment/disability division upon which it rests is difficult to sustain and its emphasis on barrier removal is unrealistic.

However, to claim that the impairment/disability distinction is false is to suggest that the division between the biological and the social is false. Whilst such assertions may be of interest to philosophers and some social theorists, they have little, if any, meaningful or practical value in terms of research, policy and practice. Besides helping to fuel further criticism of social model-inspired writings by medical sociologists (Bury 1996, 2000; Williams 2003), they serve only to re-enforce within policy circles the traditional bias for 'changing the person rather than changing the world' (Bickenbach 2009: 110).

To reiterate the social model impairment, disability dichotomy is a pragmatic one that does not deny that some impairments limit people's ability to function independently. Nor does it deny that disabled people have illnesses at various points in their lives and that appropriate medical interventions are sometimes necessary. Most people experience illness at various stages of the life course (Priestley 2003). Impairment is a common occurrence often due to environmental and social causes (WHO 1999, 2002). How people deal with impairment – whatever its cause and severity – is determined in many ways by their access to a range of social and material resources. The fact that increasing numbers of people with impairments do not have access to these resources in both rich and poor nation states is due in large part to the globalization of a particular materialist world view that prioritizes the pursuit of profit over equality and social justice.

Whilst postmodernist accounts reaffirm the importance of the cultural in the process of disablement, they downplay the material reality of disabled people's lives. They provide no meaningful insight into how the problem of institutional disablism might be resolved in either policy or politics. Indeed, if the postmodernist denial of the impairment/disability distinction is accepted then disability activism and politics are rendered inconceivable and 'Impaired people might as well lie down to the discrimination and exclusion that disables their lives' (Hughes 2005: 90).

As the problems with postmodernism have become overt some disability theorists have turned to a critical realist perspective similar to that favoured by medical sociologists. Shakespeare, for instance, argues that this is 'the most helpful way of understanding the social world, because it allows for complexity' (2006: 55). This enables him to justify an allegiance to the ICF and a 'relational' understanding of disability promoted by researchers in Nordic countries (see also Watson 2010 and Goodley 2011).

However, such arguments fail to address Williams's (1999) assertion that a critical realist approach runs in marked contrast to recent developments in disability theory, and postmodernist thinking in particular, as a basis upon which to fashion 'health care "fit" for the 21st century' (Williams 1999: 815). It is notable too that in Nordic states welfare and educational policies continue to rely on medical and psychological interpretations and labels. Research is essentially top down, apolitical and often concerned with defining and measuring impairment with reference to impairment-specific groups such as those with 'learning disabilities', for example, rather than oppression or discrimination (Tøssebro and Kittelsaa 2004; Soder 2009). Consequently, discrimination and oppression remain largely unchecked (Gustavsson 2004; Kristiansen and Traustadottier 2005; Inclusion Europe 2008).

Moreover, the shift in emphasis away from a social model focus on structural forces has important implications for disabled people, their families and indeed the general population in both wealthy and poor countries alike. Since the coming of capitalism, inequality within and across nation states has escalated. This has been exacerbated over recent years by a succession of deepening global economic crises. These have fuelled long-standing concerns over environmental decay due to unregulated industrial development and its implications for a sustainable food supply in light of an unprecedented expanding global population (Harvey 2010). Consequently, as we move further into the new millennium economic and political stability in all countries is likely to be increasingly fragile and the struggle for a fairer and inclusive global society more difficult (Barnes and Sheldon 2010). Social model insights have provided a theoretical and practical framework with which to explore and address these concerns. To ignore these achievements is to usher in the demise of disability studies and its relevance to disabled people, their families and the population as a whole and the struggle for a fairer and just society.

Final word

This chapter has focused on the various forces that have shaped what is generally referred to as the social model of disability. The combination of political activism and scholarship has helped generate a shift in perceptions of disability both nationally and internationally. Disability is now regarded in policy circles as not simply a medical issue but also a human rights concern. A major catalyst for this development has been the social model emphasis on the material and structural causes of disabled people's disadvantage. This has led to the introduction of numerous legislative measures and policy initiatives to address the various economic and social deprivations encountered by disabled people across the world.

Yet these policies have had only a marginal impact on the everyday experience of disablement, and the majority of disabled people remain the poorest in all societies. And given the unprecedented economic, environmental and demographic challenges that lie ahead, this situation is likely to get worse before it gets better, if it does at all. Consequently, now more than ever we need to build on the insights of the social model and uncover the reasons why the policies to address disablism have been unsuccessful, and so contribute to the on-going struggle for change. To shy away from this task and focus instead on abstract and obscure theorizing that has little or no relevance beyond the sterile confines of university lecture theatres and seminar rooms will almost certainly usher in the demise of disability studies as a credible and meaningful academic discipline (Sheldon 2006).

References

Abberley, P. (1993) 'Disabled People and "Normality'", in J. Swain, V. Finkelstein, S. French and M. Oliver, eds, *Disabling Barriers – Enabling Environments* (London: Sage, in association with the Open University) pp. 107–15.★

Albert, B., ed. (2006) *In or Out of the Mainstream? Lessons from Research on Disability and Development Cooperation* (Leeds: The Disability Press).

Albrecht, G. L., ed. (1976) *The Sociology of Physical Disability and Rehabilitation* (Pittsburgh: The University of Pittsburgh Press).

Albrecht, G. L. (1992) *The Disability Business. Rehabilitation in America* (London: Sage).

Anderson, R. and Bury, M., eds (1988) *Living With Chronic Illness: The Experience of Patients and their Families* (London: Unwin Hyman).

Barnes, C. (1990) *Cabbage Syndrome: The Social Construction of Dependence* (Lewes: Falmer Press).★

Barnes, C. (1991) *Disabled People in Britain and Discrimination: A Case for Anti-discrimination Legislation* (London: Hurst and Co. in association with the British Council of Organisations of Disabled People).★

Barnes, C. (1992) *Disabling Imagery and the Media: An Exploration of Media Representations of Disabled People* (Belper: British Council of Organisations of Disabled People).★

Barnes, C., ed. (1993) *Making Our Own Choices: Independent Living, Personal Assistance and Disabled People* (Belper: British Council of Organisations of Disabled People).★

Barnes, C. (1996) 'The Social Model of Disability: Myths and Misrepresentations', *Coalition*, the magazine of the Greater Manchester Coalition of Disabled People, August: 25–30.

Barnes, C. (1997) 'A Legacy of Oppression: A History of Disability in Western Culture', in L. Barton and M. Oliver, eds, *Disability Studies: Past, Present and Future* (Leeds: The Disability Press) pp. 3–25.★

Barnes, C. and Mercer, G., eds (2003) *Disability* (Cambridge: Polity).

Barnes, C. and Mercer, G. (2006) *Independent Futures. Creating User-led Disability Services in a Disabling Society* (Bristol: The Policy Press).

Barnes C. and Mercer, G. (2010) *Exploring Disability*, 2nd edn (Cambridge: Palgrave).

Barnes, C. and Sheldon, A. (2010) 'Disability, Politics and Poverty in a Majority World Context', *Disability & Society* 25(7): 771–82.

Barnes, C., Mercer, G. and Shakespeare, T. (1999) *Exploring Disability: A Sociological Introduction* (Cambridge: Polity).

Barnes, C., Oliver, M. and Barton, L. (2002a) 'Introduction', in C. Barnes, M. Oliver and L. Barton, eds, *Disability Studies Today* (Cambridge: Polity) pp. 1–17.

Barnes, C., Oliver, M. and Barton, L. (2002b) 'Disability, the Academy and the Inclusive Society', in C. Barnes, M. Oliver and L. Barton, eds, *Disability Studies Today* (Cambridge: Polity) pp. 250–60.

Barton, L., ed. (2001) *Disability, Politics and the Struggle for Change* (London: David Fulton).

Begum, N. (1992) *Something to be Proud of: The Lives of Asian Disabled People and Carers in Waltham Forest* (London: Waltham Forest Race Relations Unit).

Begum, N., Hill, M. and Stevens, A., eds (1994) *Reflections: Views of Black Disabled People on Their Lives and Community Care* (London: Central Council for Education and Training of Social Workers).

Bickenbach, J. E. (2009) 'Disability, Non-talent, and Distributive Justice', in K. Kristiansen, S. Velmas and T. Shakespeare, eds, *Arguing About Disability: Philosophical Perspectives* (London: Routledge) pp. 105–23.

Blaxter, M (1976) *The Meaning of Disability* (London: Heinemann).

Borsay, A. (2005) *Disability and Social Policy in Britain Since 1750* (Basingstoke: Palgrave Macmillan).

Bowe, F. (1978) *Handicapping America* (New York: Harper and Rowe).

Brisenden, S. (1986) 'Independent Living and the Medical Model of Disability', *Disability, Handicap and Society* 1(2): 173–78.

Burleigh, M. (1994) *Death and Deliverance: Euthanasia in Germany 1900–1945* (Cambridge: Cambridge University Press).

Bury, M. (1996) 'Defining and Researching Disability: Challenges and Responses', in C. Barnes and G. Mercer, eds, *Exploring the Divide: Illness and Disability* (Leeds: The Disability Press) pp. 17–38.★

Bury, M. (1997) *Health and Illness in a Changing Society* (London: Routledge).

Bury, M. (2000) 'On Chronic Illness and Disability', in C. E. Bird, P. Conrad and A. M. Freemont, eds, *Handbook of Medical Sociology*, 5th edn (Upper Saddle River, NJ: Prentice Hall International) pp. 173–83.

Campbell, J. and Oliver, M. (1996) *Disability Politics: Understanding Our Past, Changing Our Future* (London: Routledge).

Campling, J. (1979) *Better Lives for Disabled Women* (London: Virgo).★

Campling, J. (1981) *Images of Ourselves: Women with Disabilities Talking* (London: Routledge and Kegan Paul).★

Campling, J. (1981a) *The Handicapped Person: A New Perspective for Social Workers* (London: RADAR).★

Charlton, J. I. (1998) *Nothing About Us Without Us: Disability Oppression and Empowerment* (Berkeley, CA: University of California Press).

Chen, S. and Ravallion, M. (2008) *The Developing World is Poorer Than We Thought But No Less Successful in the Fight Against Poverty*. Policy Research Working Paper 4703 (Washington, DC: The World Bank).

Coleridge, P. (2006) 'CBR as Part of Community Development and Poverty Reduction', in S. Hartley, ed., *CBR as Part of Community Development: A Poverty Reduction Strategy* (London: Centre for International Child Health, University College London) pp. 19–39.

Commission of the European Communities (2003) *Equal Opportunities for People with Disabilities: A European Action Plan* (Brussels: [COM (2003)0650]).

Corker, M. and Shakespeare, T., eds (2002) *Disability/Postmodernity: Embodying Disability Theory* (London: Continuum).

Crow, L. (1996) 'Including All of Our Lives: Renewing the Social Model of Disability', in C. Barnes and G. Mercer, eds, *Exploring the Divide: Illness and Disability* (Leeds: The Disability Press): pp. 55–73.★

Cumberbatch, G. and Negrine R. (1992) *Images of Disability on Television* (London: Routledge).

Davis, K. (1981) '28–38 Grove Road: Accommodation and Care in a Community Setting', in A. Brechin, P. Liddiard and J. Swain, eds, *Handicap in a Social World* (London: Hodder and Stoughton, in association with the Open University) pp. 322–7.

Davis, K. (1990) *A Social Barriers Model of Disability: Theory into Practice – The Emergence of the Seven Needs*. A paper prepared for the Derbyshire Coalition of Disabled People.★

Davis, K. and Woodward, J. (1981): 'DIAL UK: Development in the National Association of Disablement Information and Advice Services', in A. Brechin, P. Liddiard and J. Swain, eds, *Handicap in a Social World* (London: Hodder and Stoughton, in association with the Open University) pp. 328–34.

Davis, L. J. (1995) *Enforcing Normalcy: Disability, Deafness, and the Body* (London and New York: Verso).

De Jong, G. (1979) *The Movement for Independent Living: Origins, Ideology and Implications for Disability Research* (Michigan: University Centre for International Rehabilitation, Michigan State University).

DHS (1992) 'Special Issue: Researching Disability', *Disability, Handicap and Society* 7(2).

Doyle, B. (2008) *Disability Discrimination: Law and Practice*, 6th edn. (Bristol: Jordans).

DRC (2002) *Independent Living and the DRC Vision* (London: Disability Rights Commission).

Driedger, D. (1989) *The Last Civil Rights Movement: Disabled People's International* (London: Hurst and Co.).

Finkelstein, V. (1980) *Attitudes and Disabled People: Issues for Discussion* (New York: World Rehabilitation Fund).★

Finkelstein, V. (1997) 'Emacipating Disability Studies', in T. Shakespeare, ed., *The Disability Studies Reader* (London: Cassell) pp. 28–49.★

Finkelstein, V. (1999) 'A Profession Allied to the Community: The Disabled People's Trade Union', in E. Stone, ed., *Disability and Development: Learning from Action and Research in the Majority World* (Leeds: The Disability Press) pp. 21–4.★

Foucault, M. (1976) *The Birth of the Clinic* (London: Tavistock).

Foucault, M. (1977) *Discipline and Punish* (Harmondsworth, London: Peregrine).

French, S (1993) 'Disability, Impairment or Something In-between?', in J. Swain, V. Finkelstein, S. French and M. Oliver, eds, *Disabling Barriers – Enabling Environments* (London: Sage in association with the Open University): pp. 17–25.

French, S. (1996) 'Simulation Exercises in Disability Awareness Training: A Critique', in G. Hales, ed., *Beyond Disability: Towards an Enabling Society* (London: Sage in association with the Open University) pp. 114–23.

Gallagher, H. (1995) *By Trust Betrayed: Patients, Physicians and the Licence to Kill in the Third Reich* (Arlington, VA: Vandamere Press).

Garland, R. R. J. (1995) *The Eye of the Beholder: Deformity and Disability in the Graeco-Roman World* (London: Duckworth).

Gillespie-Sells, K. and Campbell, J. (1991) *Disability Equality Training: Trainers Guide* (London: Central Council for the Education and Training of Social Workers and the London Boroughs Disability Resource Team).★

Gleeson, B. J. (1999) *Geographies of Disability* (London: Routledge).

Goffman, E. (1968) *Stigma: Notes on the Management of a Spoiled Identity* (Harmondsworth, London: Penguin).

Goodley, D. (2011) *Disability Studies: An Interdisciplinary Introduction* (London: Sage).

Gustavsson, A. (2004) 'The Role of Theory in Disability Research – Springboard or Strait-jacket?', *Scandinavian Journal of Disability Research* 6(1): 55–70.

Hahn, H. (2002) 'Academic Debates and Political Advocacy: The US Disability Movement', in C. Barnes, M. Oliver and L. Barton, eds, *Disability Studies Today* (Cambridge: Polity) pp. 162–89.

Hanks, J. and Hanks, L. (1948) 'The Physically Handicapped in Certain Non-Occidental Societies', *Journal of Social Issues* 4(4): 11–20.

Harris, A., Cox, E. and Smith, C. (1971) *Handicapped and Impaired in Great Britain, Part 1* (London: HMSO).

Harvey, D. (2010) *The Enigma of Capital* (London: Profile Books).

Hasler, F. (1993) 'Developments in the Disabled People's Movement', in J. Swain, V. Finkelstein, S. French and M. Oliver, eds, *Disabling Barriers – Enabling Environments* (London: Sage, in association with The Open University) pp. 278–83.

HCIL (1981) *Project 81, One Step Up: Consumer Directed Housing and Care for Disabled People* (Petersfield, Hampshire: Hampshire Coalition of Disabled People).★

Hevey, D. (1992) *The Creatures that Time Forgot: Photography and Disability Imagery* (London: Routledge).

Höjer, S. (1951) 'Cripple Welfare in Sweden', *Svensk Vanföretidskrift* 28: 130–4.★

Hughes, B. (2005) 'What Can a Foucauldian Analysis Contribute to Disability Theory?', in S. Tremain, ed., *Foucault and the Government of Disability* (Ann Arbor: University of Michigan Press) pp. 78–92.

Hunt, P., ed. (1966a) *Stigma: The Experience of Disability* (London: Geoffrey Chapman).★

Hunt, P. (1966b) 'A Critical Condition', in P. Hunt, ed., *Stigma: The Experience of Disability* (London: Geoffrey Chapman) pp. 145–59.★

Hurst, R. and Albert, B. (2006) 'The Social Model of Disability: Human Rights and Development Cooperation', in B. Albert, ed., *In or Out of the Mainstream? Lessons from Research on Disability and Development Cooperation* (Leeds: The Disability Press) pp. 24–39.

Inclusion Europe (2008) *The Specific Risks of Discrimination Against Persons in Situations of Major Dependence or with Complex Needs* (Brussels: Inclusion Europe).★

Ingstad, B. (2001) 'Disability in the Developing World', in G. L. Albrecht, K. D. Seelman and M. Bury, eds, *Handbook of Disability Studies* (London: Sage) pp. 772–92.

Ingstad, B. and Whyte, S. R., eds, (1995) *Disability and Culture* (Berkeley: University of California Press).

Kristiansen, K. and Traustadottier K., eds (2005) *Gender and Disability: Research in the Nordic Countries* (Sweden: Studentlitteratur).

Kristiansen, K., Velmas, S. and Shakespeare, T., eds (2009) *Arguing About Disability: Philosophical Perspectives* (London: Routledge).

Lemert, E. (1951) *Social Pathology* (New York: McGraw Hill).

Miles, M. (1995) 'Disability in an Eastern Religious Context: Historical Perspectives', *Disability & Society* 10(1): 49–69.

Miles, M. (2001) 'ICIDH Meets Postmodernism, or "Incredulity Toward Meta-Terminology"', *Disability World* (March–April); available at http://www.disabilityworld.org/03–04_01/resources/icidh.shtml (accessed 25 July 2011).

Mitchell, D. T. and Snyder, S. L., eds (1997) *The Body and Physical Difference* (Ann Arbor: University of Michigan Press) pp. 89–110.

Morris, J. (1989) *Able Lives – Women's Experience of Paralysis* (London: The Women's Press).

Morris, J. (1991) Pride Against Prejudice. *Transforming Attitudes to Disability* (London: The Women's Press).

Morris, J. (1993) *Independent Lives, Community Care and Disabled People* (Basingstoke: Macmillan).

Morris, J. (2002) Untitled conference presentation, in *Reclaiming the Social Model of Disability Report* (London: Greater London Action on Disability) pp. 1–3.★

Nordqvist, I. (1972) *Life Together: The Situation of the Handicapped* (Stockholm: Swedish Central Committee for Rehabilitation).

Oliver, M. (1981) 'A New Model of the Social Work Role in Relation to Disability', in J. Campling, ed., *The Handicapped Person: A New Perspective for Social Workers* (London: RADAR) pp. 19–32.★

Oliver, M. (1983) *Social Work with Disabled People* (Basingstoke: Macmillan).

Oliver, M. (1990) *The Politics of Disablement* (Basingstoke: Macmillan).★

Oliver, M. (1996) *Understanding Disability: From Theory to Practice* (London: Macmillan).

Oliver, M. (2004) 'The Social Model in Action: If I had a Hammer?', in C. Barnes and G. Mercer, eds, *Implementing the Social Model of Disability: Theory and Research* (Leeds: The Disability Press) pp. 18–32.★

Oliver, M. and Barnes, C. (1998) *Social Policy and Disabled People: From Exclusion to Inclusion* (London: Longman).

Oliver, M. and Barnes C. (2006) 'Disability Politics: Where Did it All Go Wrong?' *Coalition*, the magazine of the Greater Manchester Coalition of Disabled People, August, 8–13.★

Oliver, M. and Zarb, G (1992) *Personal Assistance Schemes in Greenwich: An Evaluation* (London: University of Greenwich).★

Oliver, M., Zarb, G., Silver, J., Moore, M. and Sainsbury, V. (1988) *Walking Into Darkness: The Experience of Spinal Cord Injury* (Basingstoke: Macmillan).

Parsons, T. (1951) *The Social System* (New York: Free Press).

Pfeiffer, D. and Yoshida, K. (1995) 'Teaching Disability Studies in Canada and the USA', *Disability & Society* 10(4): 475–500.

Peters, S. (2000) 'Is There a Disability Culture? A Syncretisation of Three Possible World Views', *Disability & Society* 15(4): 583–601.

PMSU (Prime Minister's Strategy Unit) (2005) *Improving the Life Chances of Disabled People: Final Report* (London: Cabinet Office); available online at http://webarchive.nationalarchives.gov.uk/+/http://www.cabinetoffice.gov.uk/strategy/work_areas/disability.aspx (accessed 25 July 2011).

Priestley, M. (1998) 'Constructions and Creations: Idealism, Materialism and Disability Theory', *Disability & Society* 13(1): 75–95.

Priestley, M. (1999) *Community Care or Independent Living* (Cambridge: Polity).

Priestley, M. (2003) *Disability: A Life Course Approach* (Cambridge: Polity).

Rosenhan, D. (1973) 'On Being Sane in Insane Places', *Science* 179: 250–58.

Roulstone, A. (1998) *Enabling Technology: Disabled People, Work and New Technology* (Milton Keynes: Open University Press).

Ryan, J. and Thomas, F. (1980) *The Politics of Mental Handicap* (Harmondsworth, London: Penguin).

Scambler, G. (1989) *Epilepsy* (London: Tavistock and Routledge).

Scambler, G. (2004) 'Re-framing Stigma: Felt and Enacted Stigma and Challenges to the Sociology of Chronic and Disabling Conditions', *Social Theory and Health* 2(1): 29–46.

Scheff, T. J. (1966) *Being Mentally Ill* (New York: Aldine).

Scotch, R. (1989) 'Politics and Policy in the History of the Disability Rights Movement', *Milbank Quarterly*, 67 (Supplement 2, Part 2): 380–400.

Scott, R. A. (1969) *The Making of Blind Men* (London: Sage).

Shakespeare, T. W. (2006) *Disability Rights and Wrongs* (London: Routledge).

Shakespeare, T. and Watson, N. (1997) 'Defending the Social Model', *Disability & Society* 12(2): 293–300.

Shakespeare, T. and Watson, N. (2002) 'The Social Model of Disability: An Outdated Ideology?', *Research in Social Science and Disability* 2: 9–28.★

Shakespeare, T. W., Gillespie-Sells, K. and Davies, D. (1996) *The Sexual Politics of Disability* (London: Cassell).★

Shapiro, J. (1993) *No Pity: People with Disabilities Forging a New Civil Rights Movement* (New York: Times Books).

Shearer, A. (1981) *Disability: Whose Handicap?* (Oxford: Basil Blackwell).

Sheldon, A. (2006) 'Disabling the Disabled People's Movement: The Influence of Disability Studies on the Struggle for Liberation'. Keynote address at the third Disability Studies Association Conference, Lancaster University, 18 September.★

Sheldon, A. (2010) 'Locating Disability in the Majority World: Geography or Poverty?'. *Paper delivered at the Disability and the Majority World: Challenging Dominant Epistemologies conference*, Manchester Metropolitan University, 9 July.★

Soder, M. (2009) 'Tensions, Perspectives and Themes in Disability Studies', *Scandinavian, Journal of Disability Research* 11(2): 67–81.

Stiker, H.-J. (1999) *A History of Disability* (Ann Arbor: University of Michigan Press).

Stone, D. A. (1984) *The Disabled State* (London: Macmillan).

Sutherland, A. (1981) *Disabled We Stand* (London: Suvenier Press).★

Sutherland, A. (2006) 'The Other Tradition: From Personal Politics to Disability Arts'. Presentation at the Disability Association Conference, Lancaster University, 19 September.★

Sutherland, D. (1997) 'Disability Arts and Disability Politics', in A. Pointon and C. Davies, eds, *Framed: Interrogating Disability in the Media* (London: British Film Institute) p. 159.

Swain, J. and French, S. (2000) 'Towards an Affirmative Model of Disability', *Disability & Society* 15(4): 569–82.

Szasz, T. S. (1971) *The Manufacture of Madness* (London: Routledge and Kegan Paul).

Tateiwa, T. (2010) 'The Disability Movement', *Studies in Japan, 1: Beginning, and 2: The People.*★

The World Bank (2007) *Social Analysis and Disability: A Guidance Note. 39385* (Washington, DC: Social Development Department, The World Bank).

Thomas, C. (1999) *Female Forms: Experiencing and Understanding Disability* (Buckingham: Open University Press).

Thomas, C. (2007) *Sociologies of Disability and Illness: Contested Ideas in Disability Studies and Medical Sociology* (Basingstoke: Palgrave Macmillan).

Thomson, R. G. (1997) *Extraordinary Bodies: Figuring Physical Disability in American Culture and Literature* (New York: Columbia University Press).

Thomson, R. G. (2006) 'Ways of Staring', *Journal of Visual Culture* 5(2): 173–92.

Topliss, E. and Gould, B. (1981) *A Charter for the Disabled* (Oxford: Blackwell).

Tøssebro, J. and Kittelsaa, A. (2004) 'Studying the Living Conditions of Disabled People: Approaches and Problems', in J. Tøssebro and A. Kittelsaa, eds, *Exploring the Living Conditions of Disabled People* (Lund: Studentlitteratur) pp. 17–43.

Townsend, P. (1979) *Poverty in the United Kingdom* (Harmondsworth: Penguin).

Tremain, S. (2002) 'On the Subject of Impairment', in M. Corker and T. Shakespeare, eds, *Disability/Postmodernity: Embodying Disability Theory* (London: Continuum) pp. 32–47.

Tremain, S. (2005) 'Foucault, Governmentality and Critical Disability Theory: An Introduction', in S. Tremain, ed., *Foucault and the Government of Disability* (Ann Arbor: University of Michigan Press) pp. 1–24.

UN (1975) *Declaration on the Rights of Disabled Persons* (New York: United Nations); available online at http://www2.ohchr.org/english/law/res3447.htm (accessed 25 July 2011).

UN Enable (2003) *The Standard Rules on the Equalization of Opportunities for Persons with Disabilities* (New York: United Nations); available online at http://www.un.org/esa/socdev/enable/dissre00 (accessed 25 July 2011).

UN Enable (2009) *Convention on the Rights of Persons with Disabilities and Optional Protocol* (New York: United Nations); available online at http://www.un.org/disabilities/documents/convention/convotprot-e/pdf (accessed 25 July 2011).

UPIAS (1976) *Fundamental Principles of Disability* (London: Union of the Physically Impaired Against Segregation).★

Wates, M. (1997) *Disabled Parents: Dispelling the Myths* (Cambridge: National Childbirth Trust Publishing in association with Radcliffe Medical Press).

Watson, N. (2010) 'Can a Critical Realist Approach Help in Our Understanding of Disability?' Paper presented at the Lancaster Disability Studies Conference, Lancaster University, 8 September.

Weeks, J., ed. (1991) *Against Nature: Essays, On History, Sexuality and Identity* (London: Rivers Oram).

Wolfensberger, W. (1989) 'Human Service Policies: The Rhetoric Versus the Reality', in L. Barton, ed., *Disability and Dependence* (Lewes: Falmer) pp. 23–42.

WHO (1976) *International Classification of Disease*, 9th revision (Geneva: World Health Organization).

WHO (1980) *International Classification of Impairments, Disabilities and Handicaps* (Geneva: World Health Organization).

WHO (1999) *International Classification of Functioning and Health*, Beta-2 draft, short version (Geneva: World Health Organization).

WHO (2001) *Rethinking Care from the Perspective of Persons with Disabilities* (Geneva: World Health Organization).★

WHO (2002) *Towards a Common Language for Functioning, Disability and Health (ICF)* (Geneva: World Health Organization); available online at http://www3.who.int/icf/icftemplate.cfm?myurl=beginners.html&mytitle=Beginner%27s20Guide (accessed 25 July 2011).

WHO (2005) *ICF Introduction* (Geneva: World Health Organization).

Williams, G. (2001) 'Theorising Disability', in G. L. Albrecht, K. D. Seelman and M. Bury, eds, *Handbook of Disability Studies* (London: Sage) pp. 123–44.

Williams, S. (1999): 'Is Anybody There? Critical Realism, Chronic Illness and the Disability Debate', *Sociology of Health and Illness* 21(6): 797–819.

Williams, S. (2003) *Medicine and the Body* (London: Sage).

Yeo, R. (2005) *Disability, Poverty and the New Development Agenda* (Disability Knowledge and Research Programme); available online at http://www.dfid.gov.uk/R4D//PDF/Outputs/Disability/RedPov_agenda. pdf (accessed 25 July 2011).

Young, I. M. (1990) *Justice and the Politics of Difference* (Princeton: Princeton University Press).

Zarb, G. and Nadash, P. (1994) *Cashing In on Independence: Comparing the Costs and Benefits of Cash and Services* (Derby: British Council of Organisations of Disabled People).★

Zarb, G and Oliver, M. (1993) *Aging with a Disability: What Do They Expect After All These Years?* (Greenwich: University of Greenwich).★

★ Also available on the Disability Archive UK: http://www.leeds.ac.uk/disability-studies/archiveuk/index. html

3

CRITICAL DISABILITY STUDIES

Rethinking the conventions for the age of postmodernity

Margrit Shildrick

As one of the newer disciplines in academia, disability studies has seen a remarkable expansion and development in little more than two decades that has moved it decisively away from the rehabilitation studies that previously marked its effective limits to the status of an interdisciplinary subject that is as much at home with theory as with pragmatic solutions. It has become one of the places in which new ideas have evolved most rapidly, suggesting the kind of changes in ways of thinking that can have significant material effects in the everyday reality of people with disabilities. In recent years, the powerful emergence of what has come to be called critical disability studies (CDS) has added new force to the theoretical impetus already at the heart of the social model, taking it in innovative directions that challenge not simply existing *doxa* about the nature of disability, but questions of embodiment, identity and agency as they affect all living beings. As I understand it, CDS is of crucial importance, no longer as some kind of putatively marginal interest, but to scholarship as a whole. Just as feminism, post-coloniality and queer theory have all successfully pushed out the theoretical boat, CDS is now the academic site to watch. What is exciting about each of those areas is that they have forced us to rethink everything. It is no longer a case of just 'adding on' women or ethnic minorities to a pre-existing syllabus; the task is to ask how that changes our understanding of society in general. In the same way, a course on the philosophy or sociology of the body, for example, cannot simply consign disability issues to week 9, because any thoroughgoing consideration of the anomalous body introduces yet another arena of difference which once investigated has the capacity to change how we think about all sorts of other things. In short, our understanding of *all* bodies is affected once we take the difference of disability into account. CDS emphatically cannot be sidelined, then, as primarily the concern of those with disabilities: insofar as each of us, however we are embodied, is complicit in the construction and maintenance of normative assumptions, it challenges every one of us to rethink the relations between disabled and non-disabled designations – not just ethically as has long been the demand, but ontologically, right at the heart of the whole question of self and other.

My own involvement, working and writing in the field of disability studies on and off for about the last 15 years, has largely deployed what I term a postconventional analytic, which may seem somewhat unfamiliar to those who understand disability in terms of issues like rights, or who use the social model of disability as a starting point. The move towards postmodernism in CDS is often met with external scepticism, but just recently it has felt as though this is now the area where some of the most exciting new theoretical work is being done. The point is to deliberately shake up some of our assumptions about disability and its historical antecedents by employing critique, not just as a way of challenging external forces, but as a method that contests the apparent verities of disability studies itself. It is Judith Butler, I think, who best captures the exciting opportunities that are mobilized by the use of critique in disability studies:

> What [critique is] really about is opening up the possibility of questioning what our assumptions are and somehow encouraging us to live in the anxiety of that questioning without closing it down too quickly. Of course, it's not for the sake of anxiety that one should do it … but because anxiety accompanies something like the witnessing of new possibilities.
>
> *(quoted in Salih and Butler 2004: 331)*

Butler of course has a reputation of being difficult – too postmodernist, too abstract – to be of much use in the substantive field of disability, but what I want to suggest is that her approach, and that of other postconventional thinkers like her, offers a newly productive way of thinking that has significant material application. We ignore the developments of postconventional theory and the changing environment of postmodernity at our peril – not because older models of understanding (notably the social model of disability) are wrong and should be replaced, but because we need to maximize the ways in which we can confidently develop our own agenda for CDS. In moving away from practice-based rehabilitation studies, disability studies – together with disability activism – has already made huge advances. But the issue I want to consider is whether socio-political gains and an increased understanding of the history and material conditions of disability are sufficient to the extent that it could be said that there is nothing more to be done. My claim is not that the postmodernist enquiry of CDS could ever provide final answers, but that, as Butler indicates, the work of critique is to keep alive the very process in which questioning itself generates new potential.

The initial question that must concern all those engaged with disability issues is why in the era of postmodernity, when multiple geopolitical insecurities are writ large and our individual expectations of the future are at best ambivalent, the societies of the global north should be so unsettled by non-normative forms of embodiment. As I put it elsewhere, '[f]or such anxieties to persist in the face of apparently more weighty global concerns speaks not to an over-investment in the local and individual, a kind of displaced anxiety even … but to the extraordinary significance of human corporeality' (Shildrick 2009: 1). What is striking in such societies is that the continuing discursive and material exclusion of disability coexists with concerted – and often effective – programmes of change that move towards the *formal* integration of disabled people into the standard rights, obligations and expectations of normative citizenship. To be perceived as differently embodied, however, is still to occupy a place defined as exceptional, rather than to simply be part of a multiplicity of possibilities. Despite the endlessly differential forms of human embodiment, the dominant discourse continues to mark some people – but not others – as inherently excessive to normative boundaries. Rather than simply continuing to base interventions on exploring *how* this happens, we should try to understand *why* – what it is that underlies and motivates the move of excluding others, – and that will entail utilizing and, where necessary, pushing to new limits all sorts of theoretical resources that take apart discourse as well as practice.

My contention is that disabled people[1] continue to be the targets of widespread discrimination, oppression and alienation, not so much for their differences (both visible and hidden), but because their performitivity of embodied selfhood lays bare the psychosocial imaginary that sustains modernist understandings of what it is to be properly human.[2] Perhaps the very notion of 'properly human' alone should give pause for thought, for that designation is precisely one that is increasingly contested in the era of postmodernity. Nonetheless, given the challenged but enduring influence of the modernist logos, we should note that the valued attributes of person-hood are autonomy, agency – which includes both a grasp of rationality and control over one's own body – and a clear distinction between self and other. Clearly then, any compromise of mental or physical organization or stability, any indication of interdependency and material connectivity, grounds – for the normative majority – a deep-seated anxiety. The consequence, as we see in substantive effects every day in the lives of those who are anomalously embodied, is that difference is made other, rejected and devalued by those who are able to broadly align themselves with the illusory standards of the psychosocial imaginary. As such it is easier to see that the conventional demands for an extension and solidification of rights for disabled people, and for a more inclusive culture, fall short of a more radical move that that would shake up not just law, policy and socio-cultural relations, but would contest the very nature of the standards that underpin their normative operation. In order to move forward, it is necessary to investigate more deeply what it is that continues to impede the evolution of equitable conditions of possibility.

Such a mode of thinking marks what is often termed critical disability studies, a relatively recent development that is broadly aligned with a postconventional theoretical approach.[3] Its purpose is both to extend into new territory the existing achievements of more modernist paradigms of disability like the social model, and where necessary to productively critique the limitations of such models. While CDS should never lose sight of its own history, it must consciously engage with all the theoretical resources available to it, whether from feminism, postmodernism, queer theory, critical race theory or long-established perspectives like the phenomenology of the body and psychoanalysis. Such committed interdisciplinarity in a postconventional vein is still relatively unexplored in published work, particularly in the United Kingdom (UK), where the social model has long held sway but there are signs that it is beginning to open up. The way forward was in part evident in Corker and Shakespeare's edited collection *Disability/Postmodernism* (2002), which consciously set out to introduce new ways of thinking about the disabled body. Although not fully transdisciplinary, the book offered a whole-hearted endorsement of the value of, at least, a soft postmodernist lens in understanding the status, meaning and practices of disability. In the preceding years, many individual scholars had been developing their own contestation of the modernist paradigms that underlay disability studies, but the new collection represented a radical shift that greatly increased the range of critique whilst enthusiastically engaging with new theoretical models more suited, perhaps, to the fast-changing landscape of the twenty-first century. More recently, Dan Goodley's book *Disability Studies* (2011), which provides an introductory overview of the whole field that takes on board a much broader critique than usual, has made the case for non-specialists, while my own work – and especially *Dangerous Discourses* (Shildrick 2009) – attempts to stir up the interlinked issues of sexuality and subjectivity in the terms of such discourses as Lacanian psychoanalysis and Deleuzian assemblages. In turning to what I class as postconven-tional approaches, the elements to stress are a new focus on the significance of embodiment; an awareness of the workings of the cultural imaginary; a deconstruction of binary thought in favour of the fluidity of all categories; and a recognition that emotion and affect are as important as the material aspects of life.

Before looking into those aspects more closely, it is instructive to ask what comprises the category of disability, which marks out one major contemporary location of what I have referred to as anomalous embodiment (Shildrick 2002). Although some form of definitive answer is often called for, and given, it is one that those working within a postconventional framework are particularly reluctant to provide. The setting out of any fixed parameters or definitional bound-aries has long been resisted by disability scholarship as unnecessarily reductive – and perhaps only the medical model has attempted such a categorization – but for recent theorists, the demand would speak to a desire to close down and thus normalize what otherwise remains a shifting nexus of both physical and mental states that resists final domestication.[4] What qualifies as a disability in any case varies greatly according to the socio-historical and geopolitical context, and even in a single location the designation remains stubbornly multi-faceted and resistant to definition in terms of both its boundaries and meanings. As is clear from Rosemarie Garland Thomson's summary of just some of the considerations, conventional binary thinking – either this or that – cannot capture the rich interweaving of bodily states that constitute a more nuanced approach to the question of difference:

> Disability is an overarching and in some ways artificial category that encompasses congenital and acquired physical differences, mental illnesses and retardation, chronic and acute illnesses, fatal and progressive diseases, temporary and permanent injuries, and a wide range of bodily characteristics considered disfiguring, such as scars, birthmarks, unusual proportions, or obesity. … The physical impairments that render someone 'disabled' are almost never absolute or static; they are dynamic, contingent conditions affected by many external factors and usually fluctuating over time.
>
> *(Garland Thomson 1997: 13)*

For all its complexity, Garland Thomson's list outlines here solely physical as opposed to cognitive developmental disabilities. Moreover, what further and necessarily complicates the picture are the many other intersectional concerns – such as those of ethnicity, age, class, sexuality, gender and more – that impact on the experience and significance of any disabled state.

The self-evident reality of such complex variation, nonetheless, has not prevented the kind of reductive universalizing approach that speaks of disability as a single classification, although to a certain extent – where the simplification is internal to disability politics rather than imposed from the outside – there might be some strategic justification. In order to make the strong point that those with disabilities are 'othered', reference must clearly be made to the binary structures that support all modern societies of the global north. For that reason, 'the contestation of ableist attitudes, values and politics will often set aside intricate differential considerations in the face of strategic necessity' (Shildrick 2009: 3). The apparent strength to mount a socio-political challenge to existing normativities often resides in the extent to which an identity politics is adopted, signalling a self-defined and unified group identity and the capacity to voice a common cause, even at the expense of marginalizing actual internal differences. A period of identity politics is heavily associated with most movements that stand against the mainstream, and real changes are often procured; the drawback is that minority interests within – unconventional forms of sexual expression for example – are once again silenced. As Donna Haraway reminded feminists facing similar problems, the 'dream of a common language …, of perfectly faithful naming of experience, is a totalizing and imperialist one' (Haraway 1991: 173). What she recommended in place of identity politics was the pursuit of temporary and partial affinities, *ad hoc* alliances that would give leverage to socio-political claims without solidifying and policing the reductive coils of sameness and difference. The very diversity of disabilities demands a similarly sensitive temporal approach that recognizes broad overlapping interests but refuses the putative safety of naming oneself as a member of a fixed and bounded category. Speaking of disability in theoretical terms, then, must both respond to, and critique, the power and simplicity of binary thinking. To postmodernist thinkers, the dominance of the binary may be based on an illusion, but its operation is all too real. What matters is that we recognize that the essential challenge to the damaging *effects* of oppositional binaries is not the limit of what is either possible or necessary. Indeed, Haraway herself, although not writing of disability as such, indicates an alternative way forward based precisely on the extravagance of corporeal possibility. She writes:

> How can our 'natural' bodies be reimagined – and relived – in ways that transform the relations of same and different, self and other, inner and outer, recognition and misrecognition into guiding maps for inappropriate/d others? And inescapably, these refigurings must acknowledge the permanent condition of our fragility, mortality, and finitude.
>
> *(Haraway 1991: 3–4)*

The issues at stake here are twofold and ultimately related. The first is that while most of us concerned with disability studies may already have an enriched understanding of the multiple subdivisions of human morphology, the further point is that the parameters around all and any types of embodiment – and not just disabling conditions – are in any case uncertain. In the postconventional approach, all putative categories are slippery, unfixed, permeable, deeply intersectional, intrinsically hybrid and resistant to definition. Second, whilst recognizing that what exactly constitutes the 'otherness' of those assigned to the category of disability is hard to identify, we should remember that the binary distinction between disabled and non-disabled is itself vulnerable to deconstruction. Lennard Davis (2002), for example, catches one highly significant aspect of the issue when he points to the instability of disability as 'a subset' of the wider instability of all identities in the era of postmodernity, while Henri-Jacques Stiker points out that the disabled 'are the tear in our being that reveals its open-endedness, its incompleteness, its precariousness' (1999: 10). In short, although the boundary that separates those who count as able bodied from those who are marked as disabled is both deeply influential and taken for granted in modernist thought, neither of those terms is as self-evident as it appears. Indeed, I would argue that the separation and distinction between diverse forms of embodiment is at best an expediency, and at worst a violent imposition of epistemic and/or material power. The challenge of such a view is that it undermines the seductive lure of identity politics that has seemed to offer the most sociopolitical impact, not least to disability activism. By complicating the liberal humanist claim that, like other identifiable oppressed groups, disabled people should simply be afforded the same rights and benefits enjoyed by mainstream members of their society, critical theorists acknowledge *both* the notion of multiple irreducible differences, and the indistinction of boundaries in a way that problematizes the whole notion of categorical clarity. In other words, the status of both disabled and able bodied designations is at best provisional rather than marking a fixed identity.

At a superficial level, it is a truism that any individual may experience unexpected accidental trauma, the loss of capacity through illness, or simply the processes of ageing that can result in any one of us crossing the boundary between one category and another and acquiring the label of disability. The use of the term 'temporarily able bodied' (TAB) to express this insight has become ubiquitous in disability discourse. Nonetheless I find such an explanation of the limits of the central binary of disabled and non-disabled deeply inadequate, and scarcely likely to shake the epistemic certainty with which that binary is habitually deployed. What is more important is to uncover the imbrication *within* difference that destabilizes the normative notion that there is a clear distinction between forms of embodiment. The issue, for me, is not only that the mainstream model of TAB can only envisage an individual *falling away* from what remains a dominant, normative standard, but that it shows no recognition of either the material or psychic intercorporeality that underlies our relations with others. If we ask why disability should be so unsettling, so productive of anxiety, it is surely because it speaks not to some absolute difference between the experience of disabled and non-disabled forms of embodiment, but rather to a deeply disconcerting insinuation of commonality. Henri-Jacques Stiker puts it at its most provocative and personal when he comments: 'Each of us has a disabled other who cannot be acknowledged' (Stiker 1999: 8). Or as Thomas Couser notes: 'Part of what makes disability so threatening to the non-disabled then may be precisely the indistinctness and permeability of its boundaries' (Couser 1997: 178). As poststructuralism has made clear, the modernist confidence in the separation of self and other cannot hold.

The point arising from such an analysis is that, while there may be a strategic necessity, it cannot be sufficient to put in place formal structures of equality to ameliorate the discrimination and oppression that disabled people face worldwide. That is not to deny that many pragmatic aspects of living with a disability can and do benefit from an approach focused on changes in law and social policy, but rather to draw attention to the limits of the equality model in terms of both the embodiment of difference and the anxiety that disability is so clearly capable of generating.[5] In consequence, I have reservations about the efficacy of the social constructionist model of disability (SMD), and believe that an investigation into both the phenomenological experience of the disabled body and into the psychosocial dimensions of what mobilizes normative exclusions would yield a deeper understanding of the issues at stake. To summarize briefly, what the SMD importantly insists on is that the major 'problem' of disability is located not in the marginalized individual but within the normative structures of mainstream society. In relatively recent years, the North American and the UK disability movements have decisively rejected the biomedical discourse of disability as an individual pathology of physical or cognitive development and embraced an understanding that the condition is socially constructed. The determined promotion of the SMD has resulted in considerable material gains for disabled people insofar as many countries have passed dedicated legislation that undercuts discrimination and undoubtedly leads to a more inclusive organization of social life. Whilst grounding a revalorization of people with disabilities, however, the changes do not necessarily contest the underlying attitudes, values and subconscious prejudices and fears that ground a persistent, albeit often unspoken, intolerance. In other words, in the psychosocial imaginary, morphological imperfection is still disavowed. The response, then, must go beyond simply extending the *formal* framework in which disabled people can maximize their status as good citizens of the neo-liberal polity, but must seek ways of first critiquing and then transforming the nature of those entrenched and scarcely acknowledged obstacles to fundamental change. Insofar as each of us – whatever our individual form of embodiment – is complicit in the maintenance of the psychosocial imaginary, what is required is both a recognition of just why disability appear so threatening to the normative majority, and a re-imagining of the potentialities of bodily difference. Whether we choose to focus on who is to count as a subject or on something like the experience of sexuality, the ethical task is to mobilize both discursive analysis and substantive intervention, each of which can demonstrate the capacity of disabled embodiment to perform a radical queering of normative paradigms.

What, then, are the implications of such a perspective? The identification of any disruption to the perceived stability of normative expectations both mounts a direct challenge to the attitudes and values of mainstream society *and* constitutes a critique of the model of disability politics that primarily sets out to reform what is identified as an oppressive external social structure. What CDS intends is to unsettle entrenched ways of thinking on both sides of the putative divide between disabled and non-disabled, and to offer an analysis of how and why certain definitions are constructed and maintained. Given that none of us stand outside the discursive conventions of our specific time and place, this is no simple task; whatever our relation to disability, we are all deeply influenced at both conscious and subconscious levels by a characteristically modernist conception of the world. It is as though all knowledge and experience were grounded in binary opposites that would unproblematically figure a socio-politics of inclusion or exclusion, and that identification with one category rather than the other is an inevitable step that requires no further analysis. To be aligned with normative forms of embodiment automatically and *naturally* entitles one to a range of external goods, benefits and advantages, while to be named as disabled signals a marginalization that can only be countered by the strength of unified resistance and a claim to access what is denied. The struggle for equal opportunities in jobs, education, transport and so on, may be stubbornly resisted, but it is one in which the participants on either side of the have/have not divide 'know their place' in the binary hierarchy and can speak and act from it as though the problematic were wholly resolvable at the structural level. The losses and gains from any confrontation may entail some reformulation of categorical assumptions, but the fundamental binary of disabled/non-disabled is undisturbed. As Wendy Brown points out, 'rights are never deployed "freely", but always within a discursive, hence normative context' (2002: 422).

When it comes to experiential and affective issues like subjectivity and sexuality, moreover, it is even less possible to see the problematic in such clear-cut terms. Both areas are highly productive of anxiety precisely because they disorder normative assumptions and generate demands, not so much for structural reform as for a transformation in the meaning of selfhood, not only for those who are anomalously embodied but, by extension, for every one of us. As soon as the other moves beyond simple binary opposition and refuses to stay in place, the implications of change affect the whole relation. By and large, in seeing the negative status of disability as externally-based in the discriminatory social procedures, the SMD has been unconcerned with subjectivity, and slow to put sexuality on the agenda. A social constructionist understanding of disability simply assumes that there is some core pre-given subject waiting to be empowered. The argument is where disabled people have been treated in the past as passive objects of concern, rather than as autonomous subjects, the socio-political approach will be effective in demanding the recognition of independent agency. But just as feminism has painfully learned to question its own founding assumptions about equality, disability studies too needs to ask whether demands for recognition within the existing system – as though the problem were no more than one of material exclusion – is an adequate response. For poststructuralists, in any case, the subject is no longer seen as a stable, grounding category that can be taken for granted, but as a discursive construction, which indicates that all sorts of epistemic, ontological and ethical claims must be rethought (Shildrick 1997). In similar ways, the notion of sexuality has been problematized by critical cultural and queer theory to the extent that CDS acknowledges the need to complicate the socio-political assertion that disabled people have the same rights as others to sexual identity and expression. Given that unmanaged sexuality always already has the propensity to threaten the efficient organization of social relations – a threat greatly amplified in the context of the anxiety-provoking disabled body – then we need to uncover which psychosocial factors are in play and what is the nature of the boundaries that are vulnerable to transgression.

My argument is that all of us – regardless of our own individual morphology – are participants in the socio-cultural imaginary that pervasively shapes the disposition of everyday attitudes and values – and we all therefore have a responsibility to interrogate it. The implication is that the view that only disabled people themselves have a right to speak authoritatively with regard to disability must be rethought. The attraction of standpoint theory is that it openly privileges the lived experience and knowledge of those at the centre of a specific problematic, and gives a voice to those who may previously have been unheard, whether they be women, black people or people with disabilities. What standpoint theory promotes is a hierarchy of truth telling in which the oppressed uncover a suppressed reality while those who are dominant – effectively historic oppressors of all kinds – speak only a limited discourse that reflects their own ideological interests. This interpretation is in part supported by Foucault's assertion that power does indeed construct a very biased and incomplete form of knowledge but, as he (1980) also makes plain, the partiality of discourse does not imply the existence of some absolute truth that could, under the right conditions, be accessed. In contemporary feminist thinking, the implausibilities of standpoint theory have largely led to its demise as a mode of analysis, only for it to reappear in disability theory and practice. Clearly the promotion of voices that have been historically subjugated – what Foucault calls 'the great anonymous murmur of discourses' (Foucault 1989: 27) – is a good thing, but not to the extent of claiming a categorical authority that puts in question the validity of any account proposed by those who are defined as non-disabled. Indeed, I would argue strongly that they are the ones – and I include myself here – who have the weightiest responsibility in the matter, not to speak on behalf of, or to pre-empt the experience of, others unlike themselves, but to interrogate precisely their own cultural and psychosocial location as non-disabled (Marks 1999, Shildrick 2009).

To recap, what I understand by CDS is an approach marked by a true transdisciplinarity and an openness to a plethora of resources that are not commonly seen as relevant to the concerns of mainstream disability studies. Although simply conflating our specific parameters of inquiry with other arenas of difference, like those of race or gender, would be damagingly reductive, there are, I believe, sufficient overlaps in the respective discursive constructions to justify some strategic responses in common. If the aim is critique, then it calls for the utilization – and sometimes deliberate deformation – of multiple elements of feminist, queer, poststructuralist and postmodernist theory in order to disrupt the conventional meanings of the terms associated with disability, including those of subjectivity, and sexuality. Underlying each of those inherently resistant discourses is a retheorization of the question of difference that entails a radical shift from the modernist privileging of an autonomous and stable self to the postmodernist contention that the self is always embodied, dependent on its others, unsettled, and always in process. To mobilize such a critique signifies not the search for some successor theory, but a way of holding open theoretical conjunctions that are potentially contradictory in meaning and original intent. The goal is not to construct a universal theory, but to position disability as figuring an irreducible provocation to the normative desire, evident in the psychosocial imaginary, for stability and certainty about what it means to be human. The far from modest question that underlies the enterprise of CDS is: what it would mean, ontologically and ethically, to reimagine dis/ability as the very condition of human becoming? The task at the level of embodiment is to explore how and why the disabled *body* – the body that falls outside modernist conventions – already disorders the power of prevailing socio-cultural normativities. In place of modernist stereotypes that construct an insidious devaluation of bodily difference, and of disabled people, postconventional theories of embodiment expose the uncertain and vulnerable nature of all forms of embodied selfhood. Where once the post-Enlightenment sovereign subject, who relies on the exclusionary strategies separation and distinction, seemed secure, the emergence of first Merleau-Ponty's phenomenology and later the theory of performativity have been prominent in showing how the privileging of some forms of embodiment to the detriment of others might be productively disturbed.

My purpose is not to suggest that such disruption is a unique feature of postmodernity, although the particular theoretical framework of postmodernism embraces such disturbance as central to ontological and epistemological knowledge. As both Foucault (2003) and Henri-Jacques Stiker (1999) have shown, a genealogy of the disabled body will always disrupt the notion of a progressive and sequential development of ideas, and uncover instead a series of contradictory, splintered and non-teleological discourses firmly embedded in particular socio-historical locations. Where mainstream disability studies has relied on a narrative of progressive transformations of meaning – from early Judaic biblical models of impurity to a dominant biomedical approach that pathologizes the disabled body, and more recently to the SMD analysis that has politicized the problematic – CDS works with a far more messy, disorganized and insecure set of indicators. As Stiker shows, we can identify a thoroughgoing governmentality at the heart of policy initiatives – as with rehabilitation programmes or the use of prosthetics – that indicate they are never as positively progressive as they claim or may seem. Like the critical legal theory of Wendy Brown which shows how rights-based claims to equality arising from a liberal recognition of the exclusionary nature of the modernist model of sovereign selfhood are double-edged, holding out material gains only at the cost of assimilation to normative standards, Stiker is fully cognisant of the danger of normalization strategies that cover over difference. As he notes: 'Paradoxically, [disabled people] are designated in order to be made to disappear, they are spoken in order to be silenced' (Stiker 1999: 134). His warning has direct relevance to the recent claims to 'sexual citizenship', which have been strongly promoted within disability politics (Shakespeare *et al.* 1996; Siebers 2008; Rogers 2009). The issue of who counts as a sexual subject is highly cogent insofar as the sexuality of disabled people is both highly regulated *and* invalidated or silenced completely (Shildrick 2009), but it remains to ask whether sexual citizenship is an effective objective. As I understand it, the move neither radically contests nor transforms the current neo-liberal under-standing of sexuality, but simply attempts to buy into the normative order and thus fails to break with the devaluation of difference.[6]

We must not forget that beyond the insistent operations of governmentality that mark contemporary society, there is also a level of interior, even subconscious meanings given to disability. Where a Foucauldian analysis speaks to the ubiquitous forms of the self/other binary, a more specifically deconstructive approach reveals the other to be an interior element of the embodied self. Consequently, a more nuanced understanding of the materialization of normative constructions of disability supplements the Foucauldian approach by engaging with the psycho-social elements that constitute the western imaginary. With specific regard to the pleasure and danger of sexuality and erotic desire, for example, a psychoanalytic approach would ask what part the links between desire, lack and anxiety play in frustrating a positive model of disability and sexuality. Although many disability theorists have been justifiably wary of psychoanalysis and its use as a tool of oppression, others are increasingly turning to it in recognition that the perspective may offer an important and resistant mode of understanding (Wilton 2003; Shildrick 2009; Goodley 2011). At its heart is the conviction that our apparent psychic and bodily integrity is never given, but is an ongoing process, constantly open to disruptions from within in terms of both stable body image and self-identity, and always risking the irruption of anxiety, especially with regard to sexuality. Building in particular on Lacan's rereading of Freud, which traces the gradual emergence in the Symbolic of a putatively coherent (sexual) subject, we need to ask what has been repressed in order to achieve the illusion of unity and order, and which forms of embodied subjectivity cannot come into being because their antecedents in the Real are already too disruptive? The psychoanalytic approach offers some powerful insights into the socio-cultural denial of desire and sexual identity to people with disabilities, and more generally it provides a convincing account of the normative anxiety that surrounds the whole subject of disabled embodiment. As a tool for further understanding normative responses, psychoanalysis is extremely valuable and signals where resistance might lie, but what it cannot fully do is provide a positive model of disability in all its aspects. For that, queer theory, and particularly its extension into Deleuzian theory, is considerably more productive.

Contemporary disability scholars such as Tremain (2000), Sherry (2004) and McRuer (2006) increasingly deploy queer theory with the aim of opening up the question of how anomalous embodiment in all its forms can be seen as inherently transgressive. In place of a Foucauldian model of governmentality, or an alternative psychoanalytic model based on the notion of lack – each of which adds to our understanding of the challenge disability makes to normativity – a queer reading of the performativity of desire, especially in a Deleuzian sense, offers an affirmative account of disability. For Deleuze and Guattari (1984, 1987), the concept of desire is greatly extended to encompass its meaning, not just as a component of specifically sexual being, but as an element of *self-becoming* that permeates all aspects of what it means to live in the world. Desire enables a productive positivity that leaves behind the normal/abnormal binary to mobilize instead the ungovernable energies and intensities that emanate from a series of unrestrained and often unpredictable conjunctions. Where other models are engaged with the contested boundaries of self and other, the Deleuzian tool box facilitates a move beyond conventional distinctions and separations between whole and 'broken' bodies, or between the organic and non-organic. The conditions of possibility are transformed, and one immediate outcome is that neither the disabled body in general nor the prostheticized body are excluded from discourses of pleasure and desire. Rather the disabled body could be seen as paradigmatic, not of the autonomous subject at the heart of modernist discourse, but of the profound interconnectivity of all embodied social relations. In Deleuzian terms, we are all interdependent, and come together and break apart in unpredictable energies and flows of desire (Grosz 1995; Gibson 2006). To rely on a wheelchair for mobility, a prosthetic limb for balance, or a human assistant for daily tasks, is to be engaged in assemblages that always exceed the individual and her capacities. In the era of the postmodernity, where the liberal humanist subject is displaced by the posthuman, corporeal variation is an unlikely justification for devaluation or exclusion. The overriding point, however, is that indeterminacy and instability are not unique to the anomalous body but stand as the conditions of *all* corporeality in as much as the finality and integrity of the normative subject are merely features of a phantasmatic structure. As such, the 'disabled' body signals not some exceptional lack or failure, but simply one mode among multiple ways of becoming. Once corporeal integrity loses its privilege in the era of postmodernity, and is seen as no more than a provisional mode of embodiment, then modernist anxieties around non-normative morphology become signs of a pointless nostalgia.

In conclusion, I want to set out some ambitious claims for critical disability theory that highlight its efficacy and even its inevitability. Where feminism, postcolonial studies and queer theory have in the recent past all helped us to think and therefore act differently, I believe that CDS can now take up that task. Given the widespread oppression of disabled people perpetuated in many societies globally, it is clear that disability poses probing questions about the nature of those societies, not only with regard to their overt organization but also in terms of their psychosocial imaginaries. The responsibility for enquiry and analysis falls on all those who participate in the relevant structures, and just as racism has been identified as a problem of whiteness, so too (dis)ableism must be addressed both by those who are identified with normative standards, and by those who are excessive to them. By taking on a range of contemporary critical theories and asking what difference they can make to the othering of disabled people, no single perspective is privileged above others. At the same time, whole new areas, like that of sexuality, which had been previously sidelined as politically inessential, have been opened up to scrutiny, and deconstructive inquiry has been directed inward as well as engaging with external materialities. As I indicated at the beginning of the chapter, the key to the new scholarship is critique, not in the sense of the destruction of old certainties, but as a bold and risky enterprise that subjects all the conventions to potentially disruptive analyses. This is no empty scholarly game, but a necessary move that recognizes that as limit cases certain bodies – monstrous bodies and disabled bodies – clearly demonstrate the inadequacy of conventional models of embodied selfhood as self-sufficient and in control. To take the path of CDS and to rethink the operative conditions under the gaze of postconventional critique is bound to generate controversy, but ultimately it is a move of high ethical responsibility.

We are left, then, with an important ethical question: how can we engage with morphological difference that is not reducible to the binary of either sameness or difference?[7] What should be the response to those who cannot be assigned to either the category of those others who are absolutely not-like-us, or to the category of those who can be reclaimed or normalized, or made like us. As long as the anomalous body remains the absolute other, it is so distanced by its difference, its not-me-ness, that it is no threat. Once, however, it begins to resemble those who lay claim to the primary term of identity, or to reflect back aspects of ourselves that we don't usually acknowledge, then its indeterminate status – as neither wholly self nor absolutely other – becomes deeply disturbing. If we are to have an ethically responsible encounter with corporeal difference, then, we need a strategy of queering the norms of embodiment, a commitment to deconstruct the apparent stability of distinct and bounded categories. We need to remind ourselves that the embodied self is always vulnerable, and that the normative parameters of the embodied subject as defined within modernist discourse are based on an illusion. Perhaps if there were more recognition that there is no single acceptable mode of embodiment, and that all bodies are unstable and vulnerable, then rather than being labelled as deficient, the bodies that are further from normative standards would be revalued as simply different. The way forward is far from clear, but my hope and expectation is that, in its commitment to deepening conceptual frameworks, CDS has begun to engage with just the kind of critical thinking that throws new ontological, epistemological and ethical questions into relief.

Notes

1 The terminology around disability is highly contested, not least around the naming of those who putatively occupy the category. The current preference within both CDS, and some but no means all activists circles, is for 'disabled people' rather than 'people with disabilities', although even then, practice may vary between the UK and the United States. The term 'people with disabilities' was initially promoted to signal a break with older and more evidently stigmatizing terms such as handicapped, retarded, crippled, and so on. Other supposedly more positive designations such as differently-abled, physically challenged or special needs have fallen from favour, and the use of so-called *people-first* language forms is now seen as failing to encompass the significance of disability (Overboe 1999; Titchkosky 2006), treating it as more as a contingent add-on than a fundamental element in the production of identities. Nonetheless, 'people with disabilities' remains in widespread use among disabled and non-disabled people alike, and some academic journals make it mandatory. On either side such policing seems unnecessarily divisive, and in any case chases after the illusion of perfect terminology that will not in time become marked by ongoing prejudices and anxieties. Accordingly, although I prefer 'disabled person' as more adequate to denoting the process of embodiment, I use its alternative wherever it seems contextually more appropriate.

2 The imaginary is the fictive (non)location where multiple projections and identifications work to shape dominant corporeal, categorical and socio-cultural formations. It is the locus in which what count as normal and abnormal are held apart.

3 See Meekosha and Shuttleworth (2009) for their assessment of the significance of the term 'critical'. It is not entirely clear when the discipline of *critical* disability studies first appeared as such, but certainly York University, Toronto established an MA – and subsequently PhD – programme in it in 2003.

4 Even as I complete this chapter, the UK coalition government is attempting to reverse the gains of recent years and reimpose simple binary – and broadly medicalized – definitions of disability that better allow its management within a welfare system. In the neo-liberal state, the desire to domesticate – and thus eliminate the troublesome excessiveness of morphological anomaly – is reinvigorated in the service of socio-economic governance.

5 See Shildrick (1997) for a fuller analysis of the shortcomings of claiming equality in relation to any oppressed grouping.

6 This critique is more fully developed in Shildrick (forthcoming).

7 Given the hierarchies of difference that operate within disability, where those with physical conditions may feel superior to those with developmental and intellectual disabilities – not the mention the myriad subtle nuances within each form – the question concerns all of us, and not just the normative majority.

Bibliography

Brown, Wendy (2002) 'Suffering the Paradoxes of Rights', in Wendy Brown and Janet Halley, eds, *Left Legalism/Left Critique* (Durham: Duke University Press): pp. 420–35.

Corker, Marian and Shakespeare, Tom, eds (2002) *Disability/Postmodernism: Embodying Disability Theory* (London: Continuum).

Couser, Thomas (1997) *Recovering Bodies: Illness, Disability and Life Writing* (Wisconsin: University of Wisconsin Press).

Davis, Lennard (2002) *Bending over Backwards: Disability, Dismodernism and Other Difficult Positions* (New York: New York University Press).

Deleuze, Gilles (1987) *A Thousand Plateaus: Capitalism and Schizophrenia*, trans B. Massumi (Minneapolis: Minnesota University Press).

—— and Guattari, Félix (1984) *Anti-Oedipus: Capitalism and Schizophrenia*, trans. R. Hurley (Minneapolis: Minnesota University Press).

Foucault, Michel (1980) *Power/Knowledge. Selected Interviews and Other Writings 1972–1977*, ed., C. Gordon (Brighton: Harvester Press).

—— (1989) *Foucault Live (Interviews 1966–84)* ed. Sylvere Lotringer, trans. John Johnston (New York: Semiotexte).

—— (2003) *Abnormal*, trans. G. Burchell (New York: Picador).

Garland Thomson, Rosemarie (1997) *Extraordinary Bodies* (New York: Columbia University Press).

Gibson, Barbara E. (2006) 'Disability, Connectivity and Transgressing the Autonomous Body', *Journal of Medical Humanities* 27(3): 187–96.

Goodley, Dan (2011) *Disability Studies: An Interdisciplinary Introduction* (London: Sage).

Grosz, Elizabeth (1995) *Space, Time, and Perversion: Essays on the Politics of Bodies* (London: Routledge).

Haraway, Donna (1991) 'A Cyborg Manifesto', in *Simians, Cyborgs and Women: The Reinvention of Nature* (London: Free Association Books): pp. 149–83.

McRuer, Robert (2006) *Crip Theory: Cultural Signs of Queerness and Disability* (New York: New York University Press).

Marks, Deborah (1999) *Disability: Controversial Debates and Psychosocial Perspectives* (London: Routledge).

Meekosha, Helen and Shuttleworth, Russell (2009) 'What's so "Critical" about Critical Disability Studies?', *Australian Journal of Human Rights* 15(1): 47–75.

Overboe, James (1999) '"Difference in Itself": Validating Disabled People's Lived Experience', *Body and Society* 5(4): 17–29.

Rogers, Chrissie (2009) '(S)excerpts from a Life Told: Sex, Gender and Learning Disability', *Sexualities* 12(3): 270–88.

Salih, Sara and Butler, Judith, eds (2004) *The Judith Butler Reader* (Oxford: Blackwell).

Shakespeare, Tom, Gillespie-Sells, Kath and Davies, Dominic (1996) *The Sexual Politics of Disability: Untold Desires* (London: Cassell)

Sherry, Mark (2004) 'Overlaps and Contradictions Between Queer Theory and Disability Studies', *Disability & Society* 19(7): 769–83.

Shildrick, Margrit (1997) *Leaky Bodies and Boundaries: Feminism, Postmodernism and (Bio)ethics* (London: Routledge).

—— (2002) *Embodying the Monster: Encounters with the Vulnerable Self* (London: Sage).

—— (2009) *Dangerous Discourses of Disability, Subjectivity and Sexuality* (London: Palgrave Macmillan).

—— (forthcoming) 'Sexual Citizenship, Governance and Disability', in *Beyond Citizenship: Feminism and the Transformation of Belonging*, ed. Sasha Roseneil (due 2012 Palgrave Macmillan).

Siebers, Tobin (2008) *Disability Theory* (Ann Arbor: University of Michigan Press).

Stiker, Henri-Jacques (1999) *A History of Disability*, trans. William Sayers (Ann Arbor: University of Michigan Press).

Titchkosky, Tanya (2006) 'Policy, Disability, Reciprocity?', in M. A. McColl and L. Jongbloed, eds, *Disability and Social Policy in Canada* (Concord, ON: Captus Press): pp. 54–71.

Tremain, Shelley (2000) 'Queering Disabled Sexuality Studies', *Sexuality and Disability* 18(4): 291–99.

Wilton, Robert (2003) 'Locating Physical Disability in Freudian and Lacanian Psychoanalysis: Problems and Prospects', *Social and Cultural Geography* 4(3): 369–89.

4

MINORITY MODEL

From liberal to neoliberal futures of disability

David Mitchell and Sharon Snyder

Introduction

The coordinates of the theory underpinning the disability minority model developed in the 1970s and 1980s. Our task here is to identify developments in the foundational claims of this approach. The minority model gives primary positioning to disability as located in the environment rather than the person. It also solidifies a rights-based argument about the ability of people with disabilities to actively participate alongside able-bodied people as full citizens on the basis of equal access. In making this argument, the minority model forwards a concept of disability identity as mirroring the desires of those with normative embodiments that may no longer prove viable for a working politics.

Specifically, the analysis draws upon French disability historian Henri-Jacques Stiker's arguments in *A History of Disability* about the twentieth century as dominated by approaches to the normalization of disability within the rehabilitation sciences as a singular model of inclusion (Stiker 1997: 121–89). Stiker, in turn, followed Michel Foucault's analyses of the rise of disciplinary institutions in the nineteenth century that took up the study of 'natural Man' – that is, the organic materiality of the body – as their primary object in the creation of docile citizens (Foucault 1990: 155). Finally, we take up global queer theorist Jasbir Puar's arguments about the arrival of 'homonationalism' – her name for mapping the politicized normalization efforts taken up by gay rights movement activists in the effort to gain access to dominant social institutions (Puar 2007: 2). In turn we develop a parallel concept of ablenationalism that theorizes the ways in which some aspects of disability have entered into the discourse of American exceptionalism as a normative claim. This is a new representational mode that we refer to as the 'able disabled.'

Our thesis in joining these theorists is that we have moved some distance (in a cultural sense) from a eugenics-driven formula of disability as unassimilable pathology or deviance requiring radical sequestration; in its place we witnessed the ascendancy of a more neoliberal contemporary concept of disability as a paradigm for all bodies as lacking capacities that are in need of market-based solutions – particularly those pedaled within a new era of biopolitics (Rose 2006) by an increasingly globalized pharmaceutical industry. The goal is to try and show how disability minority rights models have strategically moved between: (1) advancing ideas of difference informed by disability as a material social condition requiring creativity of living and, therefore, a source of unique subjectivity in its own right; and (2) those more visible social reformist approaches based on advocacy of assimilation through social accommodation – that is, the entry of a normalized disabled body into the social sphere of active citizenship promoted by democratic social orders. This final turn in approaches to disability as an integrable difference is largely in line with the development of other civil rights-based movements that some see as now losing efficacy at the opening of the twenty-first century.

The micro-technologies of normalization

The opening montage of disability rights voices that comprise our 1995 disability documentary film, *Vital Signs: Crip Culture Talks Back*, captures disabled political scientist Harlan Hahn emphatically explaining a core precept of the disability minority model: 'We want all aspects of the environment changed. We want the architectural environment changed; we want the social environment changed; we want the attitudinal environment changed. All we want to do is change the world!' The interview was shot at the first North American conference on disability and the arts, held at the University of Michigan, which included, among others, presentations by disabled academics, artists and activists who were all working in their own separate scholarly geographies at the time. The meeting surprised all of its participants with the discovery of a tradition of like-minded individuals pursuing various aspects of disability as a socially contextual, rather than medicalized, phenomenon. It brought together survivors of the micro-technologies of normalization in rehabilitation, charity, education, psychology, social work and the social service industries: all disciplines that separate, measure, data collect, diagnose, train, correct, advocate and, most generally, normalize people with disabilities in order to improve and, ultimately, assimilate them.

In this context we employ the term 'normalization' for practices intended to mitigate the stigma assigned to disability through techniques of disguise, supplementation, masking, and, most importantly, the devising of strategies of passing. As Brad Rothbart, a disabled performer in *Vital Signs*, put it: 'in school to pass as non-disabled was the ultimate *ne plus ultra*.' Students with disabilities expend enormous amounts of energy hiding their disabilities in the effort to be included alongside their able-bodied peers. This expenditure requires so much attention that academic engagement takes a back seat and persons with disabilities (PWDs) sacrifice their education to the greater social task of concealing their differences.

The National Longitudinal Transition Study (NLTS) conducted by the Institute of Education Sciences on behalf of the United States (US) Department of Education researched outcomes for disabled students in public high schools in the late 1990s. The study underscored a critical finding: students who openly embrace their disability status as a defining aspect of their identity perform at a higher rate than those who spend time concealing their particular form of diverse embodiment. In contrast to the findings of this study, we also must grapple with the fact that a commitment to normalization requires an open willingness on the part of institutions to accept the power to manage people who share little in common with respect to their embodiment other than their experience of stigma. These are forms of exclusion that accompany a society that has fully normalized normalization itself (Stiker 1997: 168).

We would qualify what we have described thus far in terms of a relatively hostile environment in which PWDs find themselves only by explaining that subjection to operations of normalization are hardly the worst kind of social fate one can endure. However, PWDs serve as canaries in the coal mine of government-funded initiatives in that their situation as the objects of proliferating service provision opportunities expose their vulnerability within vulnerable social assistance systems: places where government cutbacks take away liberties with one hand while ultimately withdrawing support with the other.

During the last few months of 2010 there were protests mounted among PWDs and others threatened by service reductions in California regarding a street art performance satirically entitled 'Arnieville' after then Governor Arnold Schwarzenegger. 'Arnieville' was established in August 2010 and again in October as a tent city to demonstrate that the exchange of liberties for services as the requirement of receiving public assistance makes one vulnerable not only to a loss of liberty but, ultimately, the loss of service provision. Consequently, PWDs are often left only in a negative relation to the loss of liberty exchanged as a result of entering into government-funded service systems promising assistance.

Nevertheless, the gathering of so many PWDs at the North American conference (and ultimately convening in the imaginary space of the film *Vital Signs*) resulted in a mutual recognition of the knowing company that experiences of disability involve. A moment when participants realized that, while embodiments varied radically even within shared diagnostic categories, stigma reproduced itself with a fair amount of consistency. There is an ironic quotation that Foucault uses at the conclusion of *Discipline & Punish* to indicate the moment in 1840 when the carceral prison system completed its work and effectively became a place of belonging in exclusion. As expressed in the last words of a dying child who had been imprisoned in the penitentiary at Mettray: 'What a pity I left the colony so soon' (Foucault 1995: 293). What is surprising about this sentiment for Foucault is its condensation of a moment when a form of incarceration that integrated 'all the coercive technologies of behaviour' – those of the cloister, prison, school and regiment – became integrated into a punitive system that seemed increasingly to take shape for inmates as a way of life (Foucault 1995: 293).

These last words represent a similarly ironic claim often expressed by participants in disability culture. Despite all one's efforts to leave the institution behind and gain wider access to mainstream society, many PWDs re-find a community among other disabled people in their adulthood whose association they thought they were seeking to escape. The need to leave behind the kind of carceral life encountered in institutions and other cultural locations of disability suggests that segregation is not just a pursuit of a right to liberty; rather it is also an effort to diminish one's own degree of stigma by distancing oneself from other stigmatized people. Not only individualized stigma, but association with other stigmatized people becomes an all-engulfing medium that, as the sociological theorist of stigma Erving Goffman put it, threatens to nullify all other characteristics of one's humanity (1986: 41). As our colleague, Tobin Siebers, once remarked: 'two disabled people in a hallway results in a freak show.'

The point of *Vital Signs* was to explore, then, a nascent notion of disability culture – that is, crip culture – that sought not 'merely' inclusion, but rather a revision of exclusionary social networks based on disability as a foundational aspect of human diversity as opposed to deviancy. In taking up this utopian project, politicized PWDs adopted a radical, upstart position with respect to their social devaluation. The radical premise was that their bodies expressed natural human variations and only narrow social norms (largely aesthetic in derivation) precluded the realization of their full inclusion.

In defining the nature of their oppression, proponents of disability culture assailed – not medicine per se – but the insatiable appetite that medicine generates in nearly all other social institutions. One needs to turn again to Foucault at this point in order to further this way of thinking about the oversight of professions of deviancy – that which we have called 'the controlling professions' in another context (Snyder and Mitchell 2006: 175) – extant in the late 1970s when he was writing *Discipline and Punish: The Birth of the Prison* (Foucault 1977):

> The judges of normality are present everywhere. We are in the society of the teacher-judge, the doctor-judge, the educator-judge, the 'social-worker' judge; it is on them that

the universal reign of the normative is based; and each individual, wherever he may find himself, subjects to it his body, his gestures, his behaviors, his altitudes, his achievements.

(Foucault 1995: 304)

The key aspect of Foucault's formulation in this quote is that subjection to normalization results from mutual collaboration of the proliferation of professional domains of expertise based on body management as well as individual willingness to comply with such levels of subjection.

To explain the relative ease with which we subject ourselves to such practices Foucault argues that we do so willingly as a result of the social saturation of such practices into every nook and cranny of civil life (that which he defined as the essence of a neoliberal *biopolitcs*). The naturalization of normalization, so to speak, has occurred to such an extent that PWDs participate following a period of internalization where they become their own disciplinary agents. Disability marks one as subject to the extension of domains of oversight seeking to produce docility as their primary social operation. Additionally, the coercion involved in operating among these institutions achieves its primary goal: participation is voluntary and mandated expectations of compliance by disciplinary institutions are increasingly hidden.

Incapacity: the new social standard

It is in this recognition of the workings of a diffuse disciplinary network of power relations that disabled people assist us in realizing that all our bodies supply the raw material upon which contemporary disciplinary systems work their productive power. To secure this point we might think of the way commercial media is dominated by selling contemporary audiences products through the heightening of awareness of proliferating zones of bodily imperfection: incontinence, erectile dysfunction, uterine discomfort, back pain, menstruation relief, depression, reflux and body aches. Such ailments and embodied insufficiencies multiply across every surface, crevice and cavity of that which we imagine as our personal interior and exterior space. Increasingly, we come to knowledge of ourselves as embodied beings only through understanding our bodies within a binary system of the normal and the pathological, or what Georges Canguilhem called 'the experience of bodily breakdown' (1991: 209). Contemporary bodies find themselves increasingly colonized by what Nikolas Rose calls 'Big Pharma' through a process that segments body parts into insufficiencies in need of interventions.

Late capitalism produces bodies as languishing through excessive demands of labor productivity, exacerbated social anxiety and toxic environments in order to exploit new markets. Whereas a prior era celebrated autonomous bodies rich in capacity, our own era turns the corner and proliferates pathologies as opportunities for new product dissemination opportunities (that is, forms of addiction now promoted as solutions). Incapacitated bodies are now the standard to an increasing degree and corporations recognize them as rich veins of data for ailments that are largely social in their making. Such interventions can only be addressed through the active consumption of over-the-counter medications and other forms of body alleviating consumption. This shift to contemporary bodies as incapacitated rather than autonomous and independent marks a massive shift in the operations of a normalizing contemporary marketplace. The body is targeted as inherently lacking and the pharmaceutical industry promises not to remove but to mask social symptoms as individualized failing. Nowhere in this marketing scheme is there a direct address of inhospitable environments, workplaces or living arrangements as the appropriate objects of critique.

Disability discovers itself inserted into the fine-tuning of diagnostic classifications seeking to extend their power across all bodies. In fact, this situation can be interpreted as little more than the unveiling of a false specificity of abnormality – one that was used to underwrite the equally fictitious existence of normative embodiment. Our argument here is that beginning with a foundational concept of disability as prevalent, trans-historical, cross-cultural and not bound to observe the foundational borders of social identity such as race, class, gender, or sexuality produces an arbitrary experience of body difference as stigmatizing. Such an experience is largely an effect of historical forces that shift from fetishizations of full capacity to those of incapacity.

This ebb and flow of ideas of embodiment reveals the outlines of an artificially tailored infrastructure that excludes and then requires retro-fitting to a new market-driven formula. Two hundred years of institutionalization and/or isolation within one's home actively produces social unfamiliarity with embodied difference. The result is that this lack of shared space with PWDs has ill prepared social contexts for integrative life and results in a variety of inflexibilities that seem overly expensive to rectify. Educational segregation, over-zealous medicalization, ineligibility for govern-ment housing, consignment to rehabilitational programs that rarely return their charges to the social world, private business barriers, historic building preservation laws, economic disincentives to employment and consumer markets that resist recognizing PWDs as part of their consumer base – all result in corresponding levels of inaccessibility (architectural, social and attitudinal as disabled political scientist Harlan Hahn says in the quotation from *Vital Signs* with which we opened) that become naturalized and acceptable as a necessary product of PWDs' exclusion.

Ablenationalism: minority model normativities

Whereas most twentieth-century rights-based movements have argued on behalf of access to social privileges on the basis of human similarities distorted by ideological investments in false biological models of inferiority, disability cultures cannot effectively distance themselves from the quandary of material bodily variation. For instance, in her book, *Terrorist Assemblages*, global queer studies theorist Jasbir Puar argues that gender, sexuality and racial liberation movements have all pursued a rights-based rhetoric that opts to normalize differences across populations. In doing so, rights-based arguments have strategically promoted normatively oriented assimilationist models. Those strategies that rehabilitate a portion of a minority demographic in the likeness of a dominant majority while creating relations of 'homonormativity.' For Puar, homonormativity includes once-marginalized members of deviant communities most capable of, or willing to replicate, the norms of dominant communities as a strategy of integration.

> Homonormativity can be read as a formation complicit with and invited into the biopolitical valorization of life in its inhabitation and reproduction of heteronormative norms ... channeled through the optics of gender and class are the attendant attributes and valuations of longevity, illness, health, environment, fertility, and so on. Through the pining for national love, the temporality of minority model discourses is one of futurity, as endlessly deferred or deflected gratification, mirroring biopower's constant march forward, away from death, where the securitization for today funnels back through the guarantees of the quality of life for tomorrow.
>
> *(Puar 2007: 9, 27)*

Puar's critique of the minority model approach here centers on the ways in which civil rights-based models further solidify the normative practices of majority lifestyles. In particular her insights expose the degree to which concepts of health are linked to prevailing heteronormative choices. For instance, gay marriage as a fetishization of heteronormative social institutions of privilege largely available to white, middle class, gay men or, in an even more pressing racial assimilationist model, the Sikh American communities that sought to publically distance themselves from

Muslim identities by culturally rehabilitating themselves as hard working, patriotic and hetero-sexual Americans rather than terrorists. From this perspective, minority model approaches further entrench the very institutions and value systems that marginalize them in the first place.

At times PWDs have tried to mimic this strategy – particularly in the US – by arguing that their access to normative privileges and lifestyles is dependent upon opening up public spaces (what Hardt and Negri call 'the commons') to a wider variety of body types. So, for instance, curb cuts made wheelchair accessibility feasible, audible signals at intersections and Braille signage accom-modated those with visual impairments, and lighting-based signaling systems in the home or hotel provided those with hearing impairments with the means to more adequately respond to cues in a hearing world. Yet the emphasis in each of these instances did not necessarily result in a mean-ingful integration of differences. Rather, accommodation provided those bodies with levels of already integrable disability into normative frameworks that did not significantly upset or disrupt environments suited to a narrow range of abilities.

In following Puar, we might call this tactic *ablenationalism*: the degree to which treating people with disabilities as exceptions valorizes able-bodied norms of inclusion as the naturalized qualifi-cation of citizenship. One might be led to think that within rubrics of undervaluation, disabled populations find themselves marginalized at the outskirts of cultural power. Yet, recent ablena-tionalisms – those open rhetorical claims of a new era of inclusion for people with disabilities issued by the state and corporations – have situated some mutant bodies as effectively and normatively disabled. Disabled people now perform their representational work as a symbol of expansive neoliberal inclusion efforts: a largely rhetorical space that operates by what ethnic historian Susan Koshy defines as 'a simulacrum of inclusiveness even as it advances a political culture of market individualism that has legitimized the gutting of social services' and supports while retaining commitment to the integration of some of its most vulnerable citizens (2001: 193).

We may think of efforts in late January 2010, by the US, Britain and Canada, to send cast-off prosthetic items such as artificial legs and arms, wheelchairs, crutches and walkers to earthquake-decimated Haiti on behalf of the 'scores of newly disabled.' In the wake of an earthquake that resulted in massive social and structural upheaval, Cable News Network's (CNN) Dr. Sanjay Gupta, for instance, explained to audiences that the 'loss of a leg' was tantamount to a 'death sentence' in the post-earthquake aftermath. Such observations were obligatorily accompanied by off-hand editorials about the insufficiency of Haiti's healthcare system before the earthquake, as if a negligent healthcare infrastructure was ultimately to blame for the number of individuals experi-encing the devastation of crush wounds resulting in widespread amputations. Consequently, the donations of disabled people and families (presumably more than adequately taken care of in their own lands) would turn their excess equipment into the accoutrements of Haiti's regained mobility and the future ascendancy of a more modern, western-style, healthcare system. This display of disability largesse is an example of a kind of American exceptionalism whereby provisions are assumed to be excessive for disabled people living in western, industrialized nations. The inade-quacies of distribution of assistive technology and equipment are erased in Anglophone countries through a sort of Malthusian denial of the rampant rejection rates characteristic of insurance industries on behalf of people with disabilities.

Those of us who find ourselves living with significant levels of socially classified aberrancy, and over extended periods of a life-span, have metamorphosed into the equivalent of something no longer kin to a giant Kafkaesque beetle-like Gregor Samsa with more than adequate justification for our own self-loathing.

Gracing a poster for the Emotion Pictures' Disability Film Festival held in 2006 in Athens, Greece, was a photograph of the double-amputee, Amy Mullins, speeding across a beach with her artificial legs powered by resplendent coils. This kind of cultural inclusion, presumably indicative of a new era of disabled athleticism – buffed, muscular, yet technologically supplemented bodies – promises all of the transcendent capacity a hyper-technologized culture can offer. Within this approach some disabled bodies find a degree of acceptance while further marginalizing bodies not so easily integrated.

The Mullins image that year was paralleled by other forms of 'positive and affirming' kinds of disability popularly narrated in the cultural lineage of dystopian films such as *X-Men*. Members of the X-Men cohort have significant – even severe – incapacities but also harbor extra-human compensatory abilities. Compensation – or, rather, schemes of superpower overcompensation – rule the roost of neoliberal explanatory systems. Such systems enshrine those bodies different yet enabled enough to ask nothing of their crumbling, obstruction-ridden infrastructure, continually naturalized as environments made for most but (unfortunately) not all bodies. Enhanced super-crips are celebrated by capitalist commodity cultures and social democratic governments alike as symbols of the success of systems that further marginalize their 'less able' disabled kin in the shadow of committed researchers conjoined to 'creaming' practices for *the non-impaired impaired*.

As in race sociologist Paul Gilroy's identification of the black, buffed, hyper-athletic bodies of African American athletes now commodified and traded across the Atlantic in advertisements for unaffordable sneakers, the newly rehabilitated, fetishized disabled body comes replete with racialized, classed, gendered and sexualized characteristics of its own – features that seem to make the new inclusivism a radically individualist and ever-accomplishable horizon for disabled subjects (Gilroy 2002: 348). Following Puar's formula of 'upright homosexuals engaged in sanctioned kinship roles,' we need to undertake a fierce study of this new trans-national bolstering of crip normativities – *the able disabled* – in order to seek out, maintain and even challenge the transgressive alterities of former multicultural identities (Puar 2007: 20).

Neoliberal discourses of power involve the production of 'inclusive' lifestyles that provide opportunities for narratives of national exceptionalism based on a new era of humane treatment of people with disabilities. Such developments provide a sideways glance at the normativized disabled subject and an accompanying normalization of 'treatable' deviancies.

Furthermore, this normalization of some disabilities is created against other non-normative, less easy to accommodate differences (neuro-diverse people, mental retardation, intersexed people and those with communication-based disabilities). This process of the normalization of disability, referred to by Lennard Davis as 'dismodernism' – the idea that postmodernism entails a recognition that we are all disabled to some extent – undermines our ability to pay attention to abject populations peripheral to the project of living (Davis 2006: 239). There is not a level playing field that all bodies occupy, and calling for all to recognize levels of insufficiency will do little to accomplish meaningful systems change. This is the global underbelly of a disability phenomenon equivalent to what Mbembe calls 'necropolitics' with regard to the expendability of populations where race, class, sexuality, gender and disability intersect (2003: 13).

Conclusion: something other than becoming in order to be fixed

Let us conclude by returning to the impossible idealism of Harlan Hahn's statement in the video clip as the expressed purpose of the disability rights movement: 'All we want to do is change the world.' While one could read this declaration as meaning a relatively reductionist concept of accommodation – on the order of 'all is we want is access to what able-bodied folks have' – we would choose to read it as an affirmation of a world with disabled people in it that cannot yet be anticipated. At this time we continue to participate in a binary relationship of ability and disability –

we only know non-normativity through its specific deviation from normalcy (the unmarked and unremarkable term in the ability/disability dyad).

Instead we should imagine a future time in which people will wonder how our cultural movement spent so much time in the specification of aberrancy. How foreign those prior historical bodies of deviance look in contrast to vulnerable bodies definitively understood in this future time as those materialities that 'disobeyed "appropriate" bodily practices and the sanctity of the able body' (Puar 2007: 221). Perhaps there will be a time when people wonder how we could have spent so much time classifying modes of aberration as if this practice brought us into a greater familiarity with the particularities of bodies deemed disabled? How, one may wonder, could a period lasting a couple of hundred years and so fixated on not wasting time prove so fixated on answering the question 'what is disability?' We would suggest that there could be a time when disability comes to occupy the status of a misnomer – no more and no less than the variable body operating in flux; something more akin to a Deleuzian modality of propulsions, drives and multiplicities that come to comprise a more robust concept of difference.

Rather than fixing individuals in their disability label, disability would be allowed its status as movement, in Brian Massumi's terms, rather than an identity that locks individuals into a human synonym of their own eclipsing impairment:

> Position no longer comes first, with movement a problematic second, it is secondary to movement and derived from it. It is retro movement, movement residue. The problem is not to explain the wonder that there can be stasis given the primacy of process.
>
> *(Massumi 2002: 8)*

Within this formula we would dissolve the seemingly commonsensical bifurcation of ability and disability.

In their place, following Foucault's peroration at the conclusion of *The History of Sexuality: An Introduction, Volume 1* regarding the call to address 'bodies and pleasures,' we might insert something along the lines of *bodies and mutations* as a way of imagining materiality's constitutive multiplicities and potential resistances (1990: 160). Disability does not (only) upset the social landscape because we, too, may experience the vagaries of embodiment; rather, we worry over disability's ability to elude capture by the compliances we demand of bodies. In their place we might follow Foucault's peroration regarding the injunction to expose their variability to the impossible conformity of standardized functionalities, capacities and appearances. Instead, we would allow disability to reference a state of being without a coherent collective of affective experience – a denial of the extraordinary social effort to make disability an essence only of becoming in order to be fixed.

Bibliography

Canguilhem, Georges (1991) *The Normal and the Pathological* (New York: Zone Books).

Davis, Lennard (2006) 'The End of Identity Politics and the Beginning of Dismodernism: On Disability as an Unstable Category', in L. Davis, ed., *The Disability Studies Reader* (New York: Routledge): pp. 231–42.

Foucault, Michel (1990) *The History of Sexuality: An Introduction, Volume 1* (New York: Vintage Books).

—— (1995) [1977] *Discipline and Punish: The Birth of the Prison* (New York: Vintage Books).

Gilroy, Paul (2002) *Against Race: Imagining Political Culture Beyond the Color Line* (Cambridge: Belknap Press of Harvard University Press).

Goffman, Erving (1986) *Stigma: Notes on the Management of Spoiled Identity* (New York: Touchstone).

Hardt, Michael and Negri, Antonio (2005) *Multitude: War and Democracy in the Age of Democracy* (New York: Penguin).

Koshy, Susan (2001) 'Morphing Race into Ethnicity: Asian Americans and Critical Transformations of Whiteness', *Boundary 2* 28(1), February: 153–94.

Massumi, Brian (2002) *Parables for the Virtual: Movement, Affect, Sensation* (Durham: Duke University Press).

Mbembe, Achilles (2003) 'Necropolitics', *Public Culture* 15(1): 11–40.

Puar, Jasbir (2007) *Terrorist Assemblages: Homonationalism in Queer Times* (Durham: Duke University Press).

Rose, Nikolas (2006) *The Politics of Life Itself: Biomedicine, Power, and Subjectivity in the Twenty-First Century* (Princeton: Princeton University Press).

Snyder, Sharon and Mitchell, David (2006) 'Afterword – Regulated Bodies: Disability Studies in the Controlling Professions', in D. Turner, ed., *Social Histories of Deformity* (New York: Routledge): pp. 175–89.

—— (2010) 'Ablenationalism and the Geo-Politics of Disability', *Journal of Literary and Cultural Disability Studies* 4(2): 113–25.

Stiker, Henri-Jacques (1995) *Vital Signs: Crip Culture Talks Back*. Brace Yourselves Productions. Dir. by Sharon Snyder. Digital video. 48 mins.

—— (1997) *A History of Disability* (Ann Arbor: University of Michigan Press).

Wagner, Mary; Newman, Lynn and Cameto, Rene (2005) *Changes Over Time in the Early Postschool Outcomes of Youth with Disabilities. A Report of Findings from the National Longitudinal Transition Study (NLTS) and the National Longitudinal Transition Study-2 (NLTS2)* (Menlo Park, CA: SRI International).

5

THE INTERNATIONAL CLASSIFICATION OF FUNCTIONING, DISABILITY AND HEALTH AND ITS RELATIONSHIP TO DISABILITY STUDIES

Jerome E. Bickenbach

Introduction

The International Classification of Functioning, Disability and Health (ICF) (WHO 2001) occupies an intriguing place in disability studies. Although the ICF is now well entrenched as a standard epidemiological tool in many domains of health practice and research – from medicine and the rehabilitation therapies to public health, health systems and health policy – it is either ignored or heavily criticized by disability studies scholars who dismissively associate it with the medical model of disability. There are certainly many reasons to be sceptical about the ICF and its applications, but ignoring it and its increasing influence – foremost in the health sector, but increasingly in the labour and education sectors as well – is not, I want to argue, a sensible strategy. Once misunderstandings are removed and the flaws are honestly and plainly identified, the ICF should be acknowledged as an intellectual achievement and a scientifically valid and scholarly tool, but most importantly as an instrument of empowerment, especially in light of its potential role in national monitoring mechanisms mandated by the United Nations (UN) Convention on the Rights of Persons with Disabilities (CRPD 2006).

In what follows I present the ICF from a stance fully within disability studies, scrutinizing its theoretical foundations, philosophical and conceptual assumptions and potential value for disability studies scholarship, while skimming over many of the technical details of the ICF as an epidemiological, clinical and health systems tool and international standard. The technical details are fully accessible in the scientific literature; the ICF's conceptual foundations somewhat less so.

Barbara Altman has enriched disability studies by offering a helpful distinction between *definitions of disabilities* on the one hand and *models* (conceptualizations or conceptual frameworks) and *classification schemes* of disability on the other (Altman 2001). She argues that answering the question 'What is disability?', although intuitively a matter of providing a definition, is actually a complex scholarly and political enterprise that goes well beyond linguistics or semantics to deeper philosophical and political issues about the conceptualization of disability. Before turning to the ICF and its significance to disability studies, it is worthwhile reviewing the complex debate over the definition and conceptualization of disability.

Disability scholars could hardly be unaware of the debate over 'models of disability', as this discussion has been so entrenched in disability studies as to be almost emblematic of the discourse. Scholars of women's studies debate the conceptualizations of gender, to be sure, but not so much the relevance or existence of biological differences of sex. Disability studies is different because the conceptual debate has included the issue of whether it is legitimate even to posit a biological, medical or health dimension of disability. Whether early adherents of the British version of the 'social model' rejected the relevance of the biological phenomena of impairments in the conceptualization of disability out of purely political rather than strictly scholarly concern is open for debate (see Shakespeare 2006). But the fact remains that disability studies has both multidisciplinary academic and political activist roots, and the interaction between the two has been most evident in the conceptualization or model debate (I review the early history of this debate in Bickenbach 1993).

The issue of definition is importantly different from the model debate. Ultimately, a definition is a tool that must be 'fit for purpose', and there is no reason to think that there could, or should, be a single, all-purpose definition of a complex notion like disability. A lawyer will have specific requirements for definitions, and these will be quite different depending on the legal domain: a legal definition for an anti-discrimination law should be very inclusive and not at all tied to strict biological or medical criteria – which in part accounts for the politically counterproductive judicial interpretation of the Americans with Disabilities Act 1990 (ADA) that required the Americans with Disabilities Act Amendment Act 2008 (ADAAA). A legal definition to determine eligibility for funding support for assistive technology (AT), by contrast, should precisely define, in a clear and clinically grounded manner, the medical or rehabilitative criteria of who is eligible. Similarly, the definition of a policy-targeted group needs to fit the purposes of the policy – whether employment, education, transportation or health. Academics and researchers from different disciplines and methodological approaches should use definitions that are congenial to their discipline or theoretical approach and facilitate their research. Clinical definitions of disability, finally, can only be useful if they link disability to underlying health conditions (diseases, injuries, congenital disorders or ageing).

But the problem with definitions of disability is not that there are many of them; that is what we should expect and hope for. The problem is that we fail to see that our definitions are instruments designed for specific purposes and start to think of them as universal and all-purpose. This is to confuse definition with conceptualization, defining with theoretical modelling. To elevate a 'fit for purpose' semantic tool to a conceptual characterization of disability is to court disaster: a legal definition appropriate for a human rights treaty would be useless and unfair as a tool for setting criteria for AT eligibility, and a clinical definition for rehabilitative treatment planning would be – as the ADA history attests – a poor choice for a human rights document.

So what is a conceptualization or model? First, a conceptualization is a theoretical and a priori construction, not an empirical generalization. Models are recommended structures for making sense of complex phenomena, which then can be used to collect information and organize our thinking for a variety of applications: creating historical explanations of social reactions to people with disabilities; generating hypotheses about the nature and dynamics of disability experiences; explaining how people think about, and respond to, people with disabilities; creating statistical representations of prevalence and incidence of disability; providing testable accounts of causes and longitudinal trajectories of living with disabilities and so on (to the limits of our intellectual imaginations). As theoretical structures, conceptualizations or models are validated or invalidated, found useful or useless, determined to be internally coherent or compatible with other theoretical constructs, or not. To be blunt: conceptualizations are not facts that can be shown to be true or false; they are constructions for organizing our thoughts that are successful or not.

As Altman notes, although many of the definitions of disability found in scholarly research are actually models in disguise, a properly constructed model should the basis, not for a definition, but for a suite of definitions, fit for different purposes. Definitions grounded in models preserve their specificity for different purposes while being mutually consistent. This is a difficult balance to achieve and maintain, but it is optimal. The conceptualization, so to speak, can spin off different definitions that rely on essential components (or constituent concepts) and relationships between the components that make up the conceptualization or model.

The final step in this development is a full-blown classification scheme, and once again Altman clearly expresses the relationship: a classification scheme transforms a model into an empirical instrument by means of a multifaceted process called 'operationalization' that links concepts with observable phenomena (or facts) in the world. More specifically, a classification identifies categories or terms that exhaustively capture all empirical manifestations of the constituent concepts of the model, and arranges them in some format to ease application (typically in a hierarchical, 'genus-species' form – a classification that lacks this structure is more accurately called a 'terminology'). Each category is operationalized into observable criteria that, hopefully, distinguish it from closely related categories. If all goes well, the classification can then be used to collect and collate information, first in terms of the hierarchical structure and second in terms of the conceptual relationships that the model has created between the components of the classification.

In the case of disability, there have been only a small handful of models or conceptualizations proposed, and most of these models are very similar and rely on similar – or closely analogous – constituent concepts or components. With great appreciation to Altman for her compilation, Table 5.1 presents, with some modifications, her presentation of the basic models of disability, the names used to identify the components of these models and the meaning of the concept of disability (which was not proposed as a definition in the strict sense, but rather a description of the overall concept).

It is important to summarize this complex picture because it puts the ICF into context. First, the ICF embodies a conceptualization of disability, but unlike the others this conceptualization is grounded in the notion of human functioning: disability is parasitical on positive, multidimensional notions of human functioning. The centre of gravity of the ICF is the universal human experience of functioning across a spectrum from the most basic biological to the most complex, and socially constructed, domains of participation. Table 5.1 also makes clear that the ICF model fully includes environmental factors, which are features of the physical environment (climate and population density), the human-built world (streets, homes, public buildings), attitudes, values and beliefs, and complex social, cultural and political institutions and systems – anything in the world that, in interaction with the background health conditions, will yield some level and kind of functioning across the three dimensions.

Another reason to situate the ICF in this matrix is to show its family resemblance to other conceptualizations while noting that the ICF is the only fully worked-out, culturally and linguistically piloted, and evidence-based, classification of functioning and disability. In this context, the only other contender is the Quebec model, which has a rudimentary – though untested – classificatory scheme attached to its model (Bickenbach *et al.* 1999). The Nagi model – which is the basis for the Institute of Medicine models and the Verbrugge and Jette approach – although hugely influential in the United States (US) has never been worked out as a classification

Table 5.1 Models, components and conceptual meanings of 'disability'

Model of disability	Components of the model	Conceptual meaning of 'disability'
Nagi (1965, 1969, 1977, 1991)	• Pathology • Impairment • Functional limitation • Disability	Pattern of behaviour that evolves in situations of long-term or continued impairments that are associated with functional limitations
Social (UPIAS 1976; Oliver 1990, 1992, 1996)	• Impairment • Disability	Limit or loss of opportunities to take part in community life because of physical and social barriers
Verbrugge and Jette (1993)	• Pathology/disease • Impairment • Functioning limitation • Disability	Disability is experiencing difficulty doing activities in any domain of life due to a health or physical problem
Institute of Medicine (Pope and Tarlov 1991; Brandt and Pope 1997; Field and Jette 2009)	• Pathology • Impairment • Functional limitation • Disability	The expression of a physical or mental limitation in a social context – the gap between a person's capabilities and the demands of the environment
ICIDH (WHO 1993)	• Impairment • Disability • Handicap	In the context of health experience, any restriction or lack (resulting from an impairment) of ability to perform an activity in the manner or within the range considered normal for a human being
ICIDH-2 (WHO 1997)	• Body function and structure (impairment) • Activity (Activity limitation) • Participation (Participation restriction) • Contextual factors: environment and personal	Disability is an umbrella term comprising impairments as problems in body function or structure as a significant deviation or loss, activity limitations as difficulties an individual may have in the performance of activities, and participation restrictions as problems an individual may have in the manner or extent of involvement in life situations

Quebec (DCP) (Fougeyrollas 1989, 1995; Fougeyrollas et al. 1998)	• Risk factors
	• Personal factors:
	  – organic systems: integrity/impairment
	  – capabilities: ability/disability
	• Environmental factors:
	  – facilitator/obstacle
	  – life habits
	• Social participation/handicap
		No conceptualization of disability as such, rather a model of the 'disability creation process':
		'an explanatory model of the causes and consequences of disease, trauma and other disruptions to a person's integrity and development'

ICF (WHO 2001)	• Body function and structure (impairment) • Activity (Activity limitation) • Participation (Participation restriction) • Contextual factors: environment and personal	As in ICIDH-2. cf.: 'Disability is a difficulty in functioning at the body, person, or societal levels, in one or more life domains, as experienced by an individual with a health condition in interaction with contextual factors' (Leonardi et al. 2006)

(a process that might display some of its internal tensions). The ICF, in short, is a globally implemented statistical, clinical and scientific research tool – an international classification – as well as a conceptualization of functioning and disability. This is the short answer to the question why disability studies researchers should be familiar with and apply the ICF: it is the only game in town.

WHO, health professionals and the ICF

The World Health Assembly of the World Health Organization (WHO) endorsed the publication and global use of the ICF in May 2001. The ICF classification is the successor to the International Classification of Impairments, Disabilities and Handicaps (ICIDH), which was released for field trial purposes in 1980 and reissued in 1993. Responding to criticisms of the ICIDH, and the fact that it was little used, WHO initiated a seven-year international, collaborative revision exercise, with input from hundreds of health professionals, epidemiologists, health statisticians, health systems analysts and members of disability advocacy groups. To ensure cross-cultural and linguistic applicability of the ICF, after the first draft version was released (ICIDH-2 1997), it was piloted internationally using a set of innovative cultural applicability field tests (reported in Üstün *et al.* 2000 and Trotter *et al.* 2001).

The WHO's 1948 Constitution obliges this UN agency to collect, collate and make available international health statistics, principally to further its international public health mandate and to assist member states (who are in turn obliged to provide WHO with its health data). Such statistics would be useless unless comparable across regions of the world; hence the need for data standards.

The search for comparable data standards has a long history. A standard vocabulary for 'causes of death' – the most basic element of health statistics – was proposed as early as 1785, and with the urging of statisticians and epidemiologists led to the proposal of the International Statistical Institute for an 'International List of Causes of Death' in 1891. The need for mortality data was an agenda item for health organization proposed at the League of Nations in 1928, and was highlighted as a crucial bio-statistical tool by the US Committee on Joint Causes of Death in 1945. By the time the WHO was launched after the war, what came to be called the International Classification of Diseases, Injuries and Causes of Death was in its sixth international revision. Now in its tenth revision, the International Statistical Classification of Diseases and Related Health Problems (ICD) is again being revised for completion in 2015.[1]

WHO's entry into the debate over disability conceptualization was through this epidemiological-statistical back door. But, despite the simplistic perception (which persists) that the WHO approached disability as a purely medical phenomenon, the WHO's presumption was very different. The famous WHO definition of health found in its 1948 constitution ('Health is a state of complete physical, mental and social well-being and not merely the absence of disease or infirmity') committed it to reject the medical model of disability, as it had rejected the medical model of health. Arguably, the WHO's primarily statistical and epidemiological interest in disability was guided by an insight that sends a political message that is far clearer than the standard advocacy rhetoric of the 'social model' of disability: if you want to understand health, you need to know about more than just mortality and morbidity – what kills you and makes you sick; you also need to know about the lived experience of being in sub-optimal physical and medical and social functioning. In other words, you need to know about disability.

For physical and occupational therapists, and other allied health and rehabilitation professionals, taking into account the role of a person's context – both physical and social – was their very raison d'être. As a rehabilitation therapist you cannot prepare a person to return to work after an accident unless you know what the workplace is like: its expectations, its ambient social and psychological demands and the impact of this context on the functioning of the individual. To be sure, medical practitioners regularly ignore the environment since their focus, appropriately enough, is biomedical, if not physiological. But even for them, totally abstracting their patients from the world they live in would be a huge clinical and therapeutic mistake.

The ICF, in short, was a product of WHO's epidemiological and statistical role as the premier international public health organization not at all hostile to a person-environment interactive conception of health and disability.

The ICF: conceptualization and classification

The ICF conceptualizes – and provides an international language to describe – functioning and disability from the perspective of health. The ICF shares this with all of the other conceptualizations mentioned above except the original version of the social model in which impairments are decoupled from disability, which is understood as a 'socially constructed disadvantage'. Hence: 'disability has nothing to do with health' (Oliver 1990). The ICF, by contrast, requires the presence of a health condition of some sort – a disease, injury, disorder or syndrome, or a health problem that is congenital or associated with wholly natural processes, such as pregnancy and ageing. The move here is obviously not to turn ageing or pregnancy into a disease, but to highlight the obvious fact that these processes, albeit natural, have an impact on how the body functions.

The ICF conceptualization also follows the pattern of other models by distinguishing three dimensions or levels of human functioning: functioning that occurs at the body level (e.g., the functioning responsible for visual acuity, digestion or metabolism; as well as structurally, for example, missing limbs or spinal cord lesions); and functioning at the level of the whole person (the complex functioning responsible for thinking, communicating, walking, maintaining inter-personal relationships, attending school and working). These examples of functioning, simple and complex, identify basic bodily functions as well as human capacities to perform actions, behaviours and roles. When there are decrements in functioning at the body level, the ICF uses the term *Impairment*;[2] when there are problems at the level of whole-person capacities, the ICF uses the term *Activity Limitation*. The complete portrait of an individual's Body Functions and Structures, Impairments, Activities and Activity Limitations constitute that person's complete state of health in functioning terms.

A third level of functioning captures the 'lived experience of health' by characterizing functioning as an outcome of the (invariably complex) interaction between these body-level functionings and person-level capacities with the complete physical, human-built, social and attitudinal environment (Environmental Factors). This fully contextualized dimension is called Participation in the ICF. A person with problems or difficulties at this level is said to have a *Participation Restriction*. By virtue of an executive decision during the developmental stage of the ICF, Functioning was used as an 'umbrella term' encompassing all Body Functions and Structures, Activities and Participation, while Disability was similarly used for Impairments, Activity Limitations and Participation Restrictions. As it has turned out, and could have been anticipated, using Disability in this way has generated misunderstanding: since in the ICF an Impairment is a Disability, the ICF has been dismissed as WHO's 'medical model of disability'.

The ICF model, like the others, is both *multidimensional* and *interactive*, that is, the components of the model are related to each other. The well-known diagram of the ICF model (Figure 5.1) indicates as much, but it is open to being misconstrued. The problem is the arrows that link the

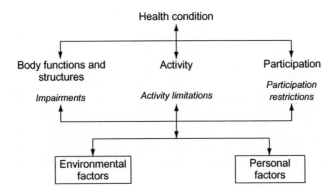

Figure 5.1   ICF model

components. It is tempting, but quite wrong, to automatically interpret these as arrows of causation, or temporal sequence. The ICF – in part to distance itself from its predecessor, the ICIDH, which was soundly criticized on just this ground – makes much of the fact that it offers an 'etiologically neutral' model that posits no a priori theory about how disability comes about. The ICF model does not rule out the possibility of causal links between any of the components; it merely insists that the model does not presume any and what causal links there may be must be independently determined by research and good evidence: 'Thus, ICF takes a neutral stand with regard to etiology so that researchers can draw causal inferences using appropriate scientific methods' (ICF 2001: 4).

The ICF conceptualization makes explicit two more conceptual features of functioning and disability that the other models gloss over. The first is *universality*: since the ICF is grounded in the neutral notion of human functioning, across three dimensions, it is intended for application to every human being, not to some pre-selected subset or minority group. Health – good or otherwise – is a universal feature of human beings; likewise functioning, at optimal or less than optimal levels, is part of the human condition. Epidemiologically, less than optimal functioning in one or more domains is universally prevalent among humans across the lifespan.

This is trivial from a scientific perspective, but potentially contentious socially and politically. The point of insisting that the ICF applies to every human being is that ICF-Disability is part of the human condition; it is not the mark or social indicator of a minority group. ICF-Disability does not share the logic of other, more or less dichotomous aspects of human life, such as race, gender and social status. Everyone is, or will be (if they survive long enough), a person with an ICF-Disability. To be sure, the impact of ICF-Disability is not evenly distributed across a population, but this is a different matter. A just society strives to distribute resources so that ICF-Disability does not invidiously or unfairly prejudice the lives and welfare of people.

The final conceptual feature of the ICF model reinforces universalism, but impacts more profoundly on the political and social dimension of disability, more broadly construed. In the ICF, Functioning and Disability are *continuous* rather than dichotomous concepts. Simplistically, Disability is a matter of more or less, not yes or no. Take visual acuity, the seeing function of being able, to quote the ICF, '[to sense] form and contour, both binocular and monocular, for both distant and near vision'. Plainly, this is a matter of degree that ranges from complete absence of functioning to some statistically generated, population-based standard of normal, to some extrapolated upper bound of hyper-normal functioning (e.g., the running ability of an Olympic athlete).[3] This feature of Disability language means that in the ICF it makes little sense to say that people are either Disabled or not – again, epidemiologically speaking, it is probably safe to assume that everyone, at some point in their life, will have or acquire some degree of Disability.

There are very good reasons that the ICF adopts the continuous approach, the principal being that a cut-off or threshold point cannot be determined a priori but needs to reflect, and be determined in light of, the purposes for creating the threshold. The ICF has nothing to say about where thresholds are set; that is not its role as a classification. Although scientifically motivated, this feature of the ICF has a salient political advantage: it makes it clear that, for example, eligibility criteria for disability pensions are not a priori legitimate or empirically determined but are, and should remain, political decisions that, in a just society, should be reasonable, fair and transparent.

The WHO's aim in creating the ICF was to standardize health and disability data collection by means of an 'international language of Functioning and Disability'. The importance of this aim ought not to be underestimated. For descriptive and research epidemiology, the effect of the ICF will be profound given how basic, prevalence and incidence information has long been collected. Disability data has traditionally been collected by means of censuses and population health surveys, or derived from administrative data collections, in terms of broad categories – blind, deaf, crippled and retarded are the traditional ones. Often, disease conditions are used as proxies for disability. The resulting prevalence information is of little use for resource allocation or public health planning because it is impossible to tease apart the various factors that are involved in the creation of the disability actually experienced by individuals. If evidence for this was needed, one only need consult the UN Statistics Division's Disability Statistics Database (DISTAT) website,[4] in which disability prevalence results from around the world have been assembled. A review of this data reveals a 60-fold difference in prevalence rates (from Norway at more than 30 per cent to Sierra Leone with some 2 per cent), demonstrating the wide variation, not in actual prevalence rates, but in definitions of disability and survey operationalizations of the notion around the globe. DISTAT is in the process of implementing the ICF as its standard data collection classification.

Because the ICF's model describes decrements of Functioning on a continuum, and the ICF classifications offer the language needed to describe this full spectrum of human functioning, the ICF greatly expands our ability to understand disability and the complex processes that create disability as a lived experience. As a clinical tool, ICF-structured data collection can be system-atically analysed for health administrative purposes. Insights into patterns of disabilities across populations can be analysed in terms of demographic factors and social determinants for a more complete picture of disability at the population level. The range of epidemiological uses for the ICF is extensive, and the ICF promises to become a powerful tool for epidemiology (Raggi *et al.* 2010). Needless to say, without valid and reliable statistics on disability, the basic social science of disability studies is undermined. Data drives policy agendas.

The ICF and disability studies

Should disability studies scholars use the ICF in their work, should they be interested in it, or are they justified in dismissing it as irrelevant? I strongly believe the latter would be a mistake, a missed opportunity. There are many reasons for this, but I have already hinted at the most pragmatic one: there is no viable competitor to the ICF. Political rhetoric mobilizes people, and that is often a very good thing. But at the end of the day, unless one is attracted to theories that deny the legitimacy of the scientific method or evidence-based policy, the only game in town is qualitative and quantitative scientific methodologies that informed the creation, testing and implementation of the ICF. Science and the judicious application of the scientific method are hardly immune from political manipulation; but if it is truth you are after there is no alternative.

This reason aside, the ICF has much to recommend it. As an epidemiological tool it structures data collection about disability in a manner that fully acknowledges, and operationalizes, the revolutionary kernel of truth that has always been at the core of the social model, namely that disability is the outcome of an interaction between features of the person and features of the person's physical, human-built, attitudinal and social environment. We are beginning to see in a few countries the revision of basic population-based disability information collection modalities – censuses, population household surveys and administrative records – that utilize the ICF model as a template for which kinds of information are relevant to understanding disability. Standard surveys and questionnaires that only asked about diseases and impairments are, in several countries, now being augmented by questions about levels of participation, and the presence or absences of environmental barriers and facilitators.[5] At present, the methodology only exists in standard data collection instruments to collect information about the environmental barriers and facilitators that impact at the individual level. As disability organizations correctly insist, the truly significant environmental barriers are those that are systematic and structural. Research is needed to find valid and reliable ways – beyond individual antedoctal evidence – of collecting information about these barriers. Once again, political rhetoric motivates progressive political change, but only a scientifically validated tool like the ICF can affect permanent change at the technical level, where the rubber hits the road (cf. Zola 1993).

No more relevant application of the ICF in this regard is that of its potential role in the mandate to monitor implementation of the CRPD (see Bickenbach 2011). This human rights treaty is a unique tool for empowerment and progressive policy because, although the rights enunciated in its substantive articles have been expressed many times before, the CRPD also requires states to live up to the responsibilities created by their ratification by instituting mechanisms that monitor the progress of implementation. Specifically, Article 31 requires States Parties to 'collect appropriate information, including statistical and research data, to enable them to formulate and implement policies to give effect to the present Convention'. This data is relevant to the obligation set out in Article 33 to 'maintain, strengthen, designate or establish within the State Party, a framework, including one or more independent mechanisms, as appropriate, to promote, protect and monitor implementation of the present Convention'.

This human rights mandate creates a role for disability studies scholars to provide the social scientific expertise needed to develop the data streams and indicators for an implementation monitoring mechanism. Using data and monitoring technology in this way transforms political rhetoric into evidence-based science. One indication of the importance of making this shift is the perplexing example of the academic debate involving the ADA and its effectiveness over two decades to improve the employment rate for persons with disabilities. Faced with challenges from the political right that anti-discrimination laws are counterproductive (Epstein 1992), ADA advocates found themselves at a loss since, in the absence of indicators of effectiveness and, more importantly, in the absence of relevant data, they found it difficult to factually support their position (National Council on Disability 2000; Krieger 2003). The importance of anti-discrimination law is orthodoxy; but orthodoxy without empirical evidence is empty. The CRPD offers the hope that good science and reliable data can come to the aid of human rights orthodoxy, but that can only happen if tools like the ICF can be brought to bear on the empirical challenge of making the case for the implementation of human rights.

More abstractly, the building blocks of the ICF model of Functioning and Disability described above – multidimensional, interactive, universal and continuous – capture the intellectual strands of the best of disability theorizing of the past several decades – and avoid some scientific and political pitfalls, admirably summarized in Shakespeare (2006). But, the ICF model operationalizes these abstract notions into a classification that can be implemented across sectors. In this way, the ICF potentially 'mainstreams' the experience of disability by acknowledging it to be a universal human experience. By shifting the focus from cause to the full range of lived experiences, it places all health conditions on an equal footing, allowing them to be compared using a common metric – a ruler of ICF-Disability. From emphasizing people's disabilities, and labelling people as 'disabled', we can now focus on the level of health and functional capacity of all people. This may be the most important, and politically significant, aspect of the ICF's model of Functioning and Disability.

It may be time for disability studies research to mature and leave behind its 'in your face' radical rhetorical stage and move into a research phase that is both more transparent and more systematic. It may be time as well to set aside talk of 'paradigm shifts' in favour of the development of indicators of progress towards feasible and progressive social goals. There remains a vast area of empirical research that also needs to be done: basic epidemiology, data comparability, outcome measurement, international data comparability, health and social systems research, and AT and personal assistant services (PAS) utilization and service delivery research. Moreover, there is surely no conflict between participatory, emancipatory research serving overtly progressive ends and data-driven, systematic, interdisciplinary research that meets all standards of social scientific rigour.

But to my mind the most persuasive argument for disability studies scholars to investigate the ICF's conceptual foundations and appreciate its potential progressive power in a wide variety of applications and policy sectors, is that their skills are required to craft even-handed critiques of the ICF that will not only reveal its inherent flaws but also provide a way to move beyond them so that the full potential of the ICF might be realized.

Disability studies and the critique of the ICF

During its development, and later, the ICF attracted criticism – some justified and some not. At the extreme were bizarre claims that the ICF was a precursor to eugenics and the elimination of people with disabilities (Pfeiffer 2000)[6] or the kneejerk claim that it reflected the 'medical model' of disability. Recently two disability scholars who attended the drafting sessions of the CRPD remarked that when the ICF was proposed as the basis for the treaty's definition section, 'in spite of its contemporary prominence as a statistical, analytical and planning tool, including within the UN and other multilateral agencies … the IDC [International Disability Caucus] vehemently opposed reference to the ICF on the basis that it reflected a medical model of disability' (Kayess and French 2008). As it happens, although never referenced and only paraphrased, the ICF conceptualization does surface in the preamble of the CRPD (cf. Leonardi *et al.* 2006).

These objections aside, rehabilitation practitioners and researchers have long objected to at least two aspects of the ICF as a clinical and research tool that are indeed quite problematic and can be traced to some dubious executive decisions by the WHO during the development period up to 2000.[7]

The first of these I will merely mention as it is somewhat technical. The ICF, like its predecessor the ICIDH, is a classification – a standard terminology or language for describing (and uniquely coding) the multidimensional features of Functioning and Disability. A classification is not an assessment instrument, let alone a measurement tool. Despite this, the descriptive qualifiers for Body Functions, Activities and Participation and Environmental Factors were scaled, both qualitatively (No problem, Mild, Moderate, Severe, Complete problem), but also in a quantitative manner in terms of arbitrary percentage scores (e.g., No problem = 0–4 per cent;

Mild problem=5–24 per cent and so on). Clinicians in the various rehabilitation professions and measurement theorists have developed assessment tools designed to measure specific Body Functions. Some of these have acceptable statistical properties, are reliable, and are widely accepted by professional communities worldwide. Other such tools have been developed for very local purposes – specific diseases, specialized clinical settings – often primarily designed to regularize professional remuneration or insurance pay-out in specific jurisdictions. Yet, being misled into thinking that there was actual science between the percentage scores, and hoping for an international, WHO-standard of assessment, rehabilitation professionals have either complained bitterly (and justifiably) about the scant justification for the WHO scaling, or have resorted to exotic statistical techniques, such as Rasch Analysis, to generate reliable measurement scaling from data from repeated clinical use of the WHO scale. The jury is still out on whether all of this will resolve into usable metrics.

The second problematic aspect of the ICF, and the source of much confusion about the underlying model, involves the distinction between the two dimensions of Activity and Performance. As Table 5.1 indicates, there has been a long tradition in disability modelling to identify three dimensions of disability phenomena.[8] The pattern is the same: disability is a matter of the body, the person and the person in society. Hence the triads: impairment, disability, handicap (ICIDH and Quebec); and impairment, functional limitation, disability (Nagi).

It stands to reason that in the ICF the pattern should be repeated, and it apparently is: Impairment, Activity Limitation, Participation Restriction. But there is a catch. The Activity and Participation classification 'merges' the two; or more correctly, the individual categories in that classification are both Activity and Participation categories. But how can Activity and Participation be *conceptually different*, but *identical* in terms of their list of categories? Marcel Dijkers, a leading researcher in the rehabilitation community, has put the point in precise language:

> Distinguishing between concrete, person-level, immediately-observable Activities and more abstract, community-society level Participation is an old tradition in rehabilitation, and has been the basis of fruitful research and efficient administration of services. However, to the degree that operationalization of the concepts involves the ICF in some fashion, the refusal of WHO as an authoritative source to make a split 'in practice' (in the taxonomy) as well as in theory (the famous ICF conceptual framework) creates problems.
>
> *(Dijkers 2008)*

Marcel Dijkers is quite correct. In practice, there is no difference in the categories of Activity and Participation, but in the ICF they are defined as if they were categorically different. Activity is 'the execution of a task or action by an individual' and Participation is 'involvement in a life situation'. Of course, one might point out that the definition of Participation is so broad and vague that it can easily apply to tasks and actions by an individual, but the problem is deeper than this. Roughly, the problem is, as Dijkers points out, the rehabilitation community is committed to a distinction between 'person-level' and 'community-social level' and, since these levels are apparently different, the classification items to which they apply should also be different. But a glance at the chapter headings in the ICF Activities and Participation classification (Table 5.2), seems to suggest that they are mixed up together.

One would have thought that up to, roughly, Chapter 6 the categories refer to 'person-level', immediately observable actions and tasks, whereas from that point on the categories are 'community-social level' relationships and roles. Although the Nagi-related models do not go

Table 5.2 Chapter headings of ICF Activity and Participation classification

Activities and participation	
Chapter 1	Learning and applying knowledge
Chapter 2	General tasks and demands
Chapter 3	Communication
Chapter 4	Mobility
Chapter 5	Self-care
Chapter 6	Domestic life
Chapter 7	Interpersonal interactions and relationships
Chapter 8	Major life areas
Chapter 9	Community, social and civic life

into sufficient classification detail to make it clear, the original ICIDH fully adopted this distinction: the 'person-level' ICIDH-Disability was 'any restriction or lack (resulting from an impairment) of ability to perform an activity in the manner or within the range considered normal for a human being', whereas the 'social level' ICIDH-Handicap was 'a disadvantage for a given individual, resulting from an impairment or a disability, that limits or prevents the fulfilment of a role that is normal (depending on age, sex and social and cultural factors) for that individual' (ICIDH 1980). What happened along the way to the ICF?

Very simply, the practical problem was this: over the course of nearly five years there was never an agreement, at the level of particular chapters or specific categories, where the 'person' level ended and 'community and social' level started up. No proposed line of demarcation between the proposed chapters, clearly distinguishing the personal and the social, ever attracted a consensus among the participants of the revision process. Cuts made in terms of 'simple *v.* complex' or 'done alone *v.* done with others' all failed once they were found in practice to be both ambiguous and arbitrary. Every professional group represented made the cut differently, depending on their focus or favoured theory. The other participants – mostly government representatives – expressed their intuitions, but these were as erratic as those of professionals.

At the same time, the revision process clearly wanted to distance itself from the ICIDH which, although it had its adherents, had been either ignored or condemned for its 'linear model' reflecting an underlying medical model (Heerkens *et al.* 1995 and Pfeiffer 1998). As a result, although ICIDH-Impairments remained uncontroversial (since they were, after all, acceptable biomedical categories), the ICIDH-Disability and Handicap distinction was rejected. In particular, the ICIDH notion of Handicap was rejected as a precondition for the revision process, in part because the word itself was thought to be insulting to persons with disabilities, but also because the theoretical underpinning of the notion relied entirely on Abraham Maslow's 1943 theory of human motivation in terms of a hierarchy of needs (Maslow 1943). It was thought that a concept less wedded to a single, somewhat contentious theory might be preferable as a foundation for an international epidemiological standard classification.

For several years the battle of 'splitting' Activities from Participation waged long and hard. In retrospect, it is plain that those who insisted that the conceptual distinction had to be reflected in the classifications, so that Activity categories would not overlap with Participation categories, were essentially those who were reluctant to leave ICIDH behind (Brown 1993; Whiteneck *et al.* 1992; Whiteneck 2006). The view was that the personal/social distinction, operationalized in terms of actions/social roles, was the best and only way to analyse the concept of disability in a manner that preserved the three-part distinction. Into the mix was the suggestion, most firmly expressed by the adherents of the Quebec model (see Bickenbach *et al.* 1999), that the third dimension (whether it was called Handicap or Participation) had to be conceptualized as a disadvantage wholly created by social forces of stigma and discrimination. Roles were compromised for persons with impairments, on this view, not because of any limitations on their part to perform them, but entirely because of society's active discrimination or failure to provide accommodation.

Obviously, the conceptual debate was fraught with political and professional issues. By late 1999, as the collaborative process – never stably funded or supported by the WHO administration – threatened to grind to a halt without a product, it was evident to those in charge of the revision process that there was no clear way out of the impasse. Rather than allow the process to end, ignominiously, it was decided to opt for a classic bureaucratic strategy: compromise. At a crucial meeting of collaborating partners, a proposal was suggested that, in essence, everyone could be right, and although the Activities and Participation classification would stay united, four options for structuring the relationship between Activities and Participation in terms of the list of categories were proposed (ICF, Annex 3), with the invitation that:

> It is expected that with the continued use of ICF and the generation of empirical data, evidence will become available as to which of the above options are preferred by different users. … Empirical research will also lead to a clearer operationalization of the notions of activities and participation.
>
> *(WHO 2001: 237)*

This is how the situation remains to this day. The compromise agreement has been secured with the peculiar promise that a *conceptual distinction* that demarks a fundamental difference between two models of disability will somehow be resolved empirically. Since 2001, it has become increasingly obvious that the underlying problem is that the personal *v.* social distinction is simply not conceptually robust enough to support the work intended for it, and that, as Marcel Dijkers correctly remarks, the distinction is purely heuristic, conventional and traditional. For most applications, certainly those involving purely clinical practice, the comforting distinction between the personal and the social makes very little difference. But for the collection of data, in which conceptual confusions can compound through iteration, the potential for disadvantageous impact on policy on behalf of persons with disabilities cannot be discounted.

A more fundamental and conceptual distinction – although one that requires a frank rethinking of the basic elements of the interactive model – is one that draws the conceptual distinction between the intrinsic health component of ICF-Disability, and the extrinsic environmental component that in interaction with the health component produces the level of Participation in various domains. This is one of the options found in Annex 3 of the ICF, and relies on the distinction between intrinsic capacity and actual, fully contextualized performance – a distinction operationalized as two qualifiers of the Activity and Participation classification. Whether, this distinction in turn can be made robust, defensible and, most crucially, usable, is another story. But it is a further development of the ICF that cries out for participation by the widest and most inclusive range of stakeholders, including, of course, those in disability studies. There is little doubt that the conceptual confusions remaining in the ICF could profit from disability studies scholars, if only they would turn their talents to this enterprise.

Notes

1 For a history of the ICD, see http://apps.who.int/classifications/apps/icd/icd10online/ (accessed 25 July 2011).

2 Disability conceptualization and definition is fraught with confusion created by the practice of using the same words in very different ways. When this is done explicitly, and care is taken to define how a term is being used, then confusion is usually kept at bay. But typically, different usages are wholly unexplained – as if everyone agrees (or should agree) with the author's particular usage – leading to rampant confusion. To avoid confusion here, I adopt the convention of capitalizing the ICF terminology (or even more carefully, use the term 'ICF-Disability'). Let the reader be aware that Impairment need not mean the same as impairment, Disability the same as disability, and so on.

3 Although it is silent on this point, it is arguable that the ICF range for all Functioning tops up at population normality, leaving the field open for super-functioning, as in athletic ability. The fact that this upper bound is dynamic and will likely change over time is easily accommodated in the operating model and classification and coding scheme of the ICF (see Bickenbach 2008).

4 The human functioning and disability section of the DISTAT website can be found at http://unstats.un. org/unsd/demographic/sconcerns/disability/disab2.asp (accessed 25 July 2011).

5 By way of example consider the Canadian Participation and Activity Limitation Survey (PALS 2002) http://www.statcan.gc.ca/pub/89-577-x/index-eng.htm, and the more recent Irish National Disability Survey (2006), details of which can be found on the Central Statistical Office website, http://www.cso.ie. Both surveys were explicitly based on the model of Disability found in the ICF.

6 Being privileged to know David Pfeiffer during this period I cannot help but think that many of his wild claims were tongue-in-cheek, or at least semi-serious.

7 It is appropriate at this juncture to mention that I was involved as a full or part-time employee of the unit at WHO responsible for the internationally collaborative ICIDH revision process, and the early implementation of ICF, from 1995 to 2002.

8 All of the models (except the Social model) recognize other components of disability as well, but 'pathology' (as in Nagi and Verbrugge and Jette and the Institute of Medicine) or 'risk factors' (as in the Quebec model) or 'contextual factors' (as in Quebec, ICIDH, ICIDH-2 and ICF) are properly speaking determinants of disability, not dimensions of disability.

References

Altman, Barbara M. (2001) 'Disability Definitions, Models, Classification Schemes, and Applications', in G. L. Albrecht, K. D. Seelman and M. Bury, eds, *Handbook of Disability Studies* (Thousand Oaks, CA: Sage): pp. 97–121.

Americans with Disabilities Act of 1990, Pub. L. No. 101–336, 104 Stat. 328.

Americans with Disabilities Act (ADA) Amendments Act of 2008, Pub. L. No. 110–325, 122 Stat. 3553.

Bickenbach, J. E. (1993) *Physical Disability and Social Policy* (Toronto: University of Toronto Press).

Bickenbach, J. E. (2008) 'Disability, Non-talent and Distributive Justice', in Kristjana Kristiansen, Tom Shakespeare and Simo Vehmas, eds, *Arguing About Disability: Philosophy Meets Disability Studies* (New York: Routledge): pp. 105–23.

Bickenbach, J. E. (2011) *Monitoring the United Nation's Convention on the Rights of Persons with Disabilities: Data and the International Classification of Functioning, Disability and Health* (BMC Public Health).

Bickenbach, J. E., Chatterji, S., Badley, E. M. and Üstün, T. B. (1999) 'Models of Disablement, Universalism and the International Classification of Impairments, Disabilities and Handicaps', *Social Science and Medicine* 48(9): 1173–1187.

Brandt, E. N. and Pope, A. M., eds (1997) *Enabling America: Assessing the Role of Rehabilitation Science and Engineering* (Washington, DC: National Academy Press).

Brown, S. C. (1993) 'Revitalizing "Handicap" for Disability Research: Developing Tools to Assess Progress in Quality of Life for Persons with Disabilities', *Journal of Disability Policy Studies* 4(2): 57–76.

Dijkers, Marcel P. J. M. (2008) 'Issues in the Conceptualization and Measurement of Participation: An Overview'. Paper presented at the symposium 'Participation: Conceptualization, Measurement and Application in Rehabilitation Research', annual meeting of the American Congress of Rehabilitation Medicine, October 14–19, Toronto, Canada.

Epstein, Richard A. (1992) *Forbidden Grounds: The Case Against Employment Discrimination Laws* (Cambridge MA: Harvard University Press).

Field, M. J. and Jette, A. M., eds (2009) *The Future of Disability in America* (Washington, DC: National Academies Press).

Fougeyrollas, Patrick (1989) 'Les implications de la diffusion de la classification internationale des handicaps sur les politiques concernant les personnes handicappées', *World Health Statistical Quarterly* 42: 281–88.

Fougeyrollas, Patrick (1995) 'Documenting Environmental Factors for Preventing the Handicap Creation Process: Quebec Contributions Relating to ICIDH and Social Participation of People with Functional Differences', *Disability and Rehabilitation* 17(3–4): 145–60.

Fougeyrollas, P., Cloutier, R., Bergeron, H., Cote, J. and St Michel, G. (1998) *The Quebec Classification: Disability Creation Process* (Quebec: International Network on Disability Creation Process (INDCP)/CSICIDH).

Heerkens, Y. F., van Ravensberg, C. D. and Brandsma, J. W. (1995) The Need for Revision of the ICIDH: An Example – Problems in Gait, *Disability and Rehabilitation* 17(3–4): 184–94.

Kayess, Rosemary and French, Phillip (2008) 'Out of Darkness into Light? Introducing the Convention on the Rights of Persons with Disabilities', *Human Rights Law Review* 8(1): 1–34.

Krieger, L. H., ed. (2003) *Backlash Against the ADA: Reinterpreting Disability Rights* (Ann Arbor: University of Michigan Press).

Leonardi, M., Bickenbach, J. E., Üstün, T. B., Kostanjsek, N. and Chatterji, S. (2006) 'The Definition of Disability: What's in a Name?', *The Lancet* 368(9543): 1219–21.

Maslow, Abraham (1943) 'A Theory of Human Motivation', *Psychological Review* 50(4): 370–396.

Nagi, S. Z. (1965) 'Some Conceptual Issues in Disability and Rehabilitation', in M. Sussman, ed., *Sociology and Rehabilitation* (Washington, DC: American Sociological Association): pp. 100–13.

Nagi, S. Z. (1969) *Disability and Rehabilitation: Legal, Clinical and Self-concepts and Measurement* (Columbus, OH: Ohio State University Press).

Nagi, S. Z. (1977) 'The Disabled and Rehabilitation Services: A National Overview', *American Rehabilitation* 2(5): 26–33.

Nagi, S. Z. (1991) 'Disability Concepts Revisited: Implications for Prevention', in A. M. Pope and A. R. Tarlov, eds, *Disability in America: Toward a National Agenda for Prevention* (Washington, DC: National Academic Press): pp. 309–27.

National Council on Disability (NCD) (2000) *Promises to Keep: A Decade of Federal Enforcement of the Americans with Disabilities Act* (Washington, DC: NCD).

Oliver, M. (1990) *The Politics of Disablement* (Basingstoke: Macmillan).

Oliver, M. (1992) 'Changing the Social Relations of Research Production?' *Disability, Handicap and Society* 7(2): 101–20.

Oliver, M. (1996) *Understanding Disability: From Theory to Practice* (Basingstoke: Palgrave).

Pfeiffer, D. (1998) 'The ICIDH and the Need for its Revision', *Disability & Society* 13(4): 503–23.

Pfeiffer, David (2000) 'The Devils are in the Details: The ICIDH2 and the Disability Movement', *Disability & Society* 15(7): 1079–82.

Pope, A. M. and Tarlov, A. R., eds (1991) *Disability in America: Toward a National Agenda for Prevention* (Washington, DC: National Academy Press).

Raggi, A., Leonardi, M., Caello, M. and Bickenbach, J. E., eds. (2010) 'Applications of ICF in Clinical Settings Across Europe', *Disability and Rehabilitation* 32 Suppl 1: S17–22.

Shakespeare, T. (2006) *Disability Rights and Wrongs* (London: Routledge).

Trotter, Robert T. II, Üstün, T. B., Chatterji, S., Rehm, J., Room, R. and Bickenbach, J. (2001) 'Cross-Cultural Applicability Research on Disablement: Models and Methods for the Revision of an International Classification', *Human Organization* 60(1): 13–27.

Union of the Physically Impaired Against Segregation (UPIAS) (1976) *Fundamental Principles of Disability* (London: UPIAS).

United Nations (2006) *Convention on the Rights of Persons with Disabilities*, G.A. Res. 61/106 (2007); available online at http://www.un.org/esa/socdev/enable/rights/convtexte.htm (accessed 2 October 2011).

Üstün, T. B., Chatterji, S., Bickenbach, J. E., Trotter II, R. T. and Saxena, S (2000) *Disability and Culture: Universalism and Diversity* (Bern: Hogrefe and Huber).

Verbrugge, L. and Jette, A. M. (1993) 'The Disablement Process', *Social Science and Medicine* 6(1): 1–14.

Whiteneck, Gale (2006) 'Conceptual Models of Disability: Past, Present, and Future', in M. J. Field, A. M. Jette and L. Martin, eds, *Workshop on Disability in America: A New Look – Summary and background papers* (Washington, DC: National Academies Press) pp. 50–66.

Whiteneck, G., Charlifue, S., Gerhart, K., Overholser, J. and Richardson, G. (1992) 'Quantifying Handicap: A New Measure of Long-term Rehabilitation Outcomes', *Archives of Physical Medicine and Rehabilitation* 73(6): 519–26.

WHO (World Health Organization) (1980) *International Classification of Impairments, Disabilities and Handicaps (ICIDH)* (Geneva: WHO).

WHO (World Health Organization) (1992) *International Statistical Classification of Diseases and Related Health Problems, tenth revision (ICD-10)* (Geneva: WHO).

WHO (World Health Organization) (1993) *The International Classification of Impairments, Activities and Participation (ICIDH-2)* (Geneva: WHO).

WHO (World Health Organization) (2001) *International Classification of Functioning, Disability and Health (ICF)* (Geneva: WHO).

Zola, I. K. (1993) 'Disability Statistics, What We Count and What It Tells Us: A Personal and Political Analysis', *Journal of Disability Policy Studies* 4(2): 9–15.

6

FEAR, PITY AND DISGUST

Emotions and the non-disabled imaginary

Bill Hughes

Introduction

For Sartre (1971), emotion springs from a transformation of the subject's perspective on the world. There is a kind of 'magic' in this transformation because the subject is spontaneously altering her attitude in the face of objective events. Emotion is an embodied experience. It involves physiological sensations like the pounding heart associated with love or fear, or the nausea – even retching – associated with disgust. This interpretation of emotions embeds them in *corporeal being in the world* but the element of magical transformation suggests that, at the same time, emotion may be either immersion in positivity or an attempt to escape from and disengage from the alienating objective reality that presents itself to us and is our perspective at that given moment in time. The link between emotion as an embodied perspective and as a mechanism for disengagement with certain aspects of the world has advantages in understanding the emotional relationships between disabled and non-disabled actors. In the phenomenological tradition emotions are the means by which consciousness apprehends objects and attaches value (or disvalue) to them. They are a source of – pre-reflective – judgement, and with respect to the basic aversive emotions (Kolnai 2004) – fear, hatred and disgust – there would seem to be little ambiguity about the value associated with objects that inspire and arouse aversion. It is clear that some forms of social inequality – for example the caste system – institutionalize disgust and contempt. This line of reasoning should help in the development of a 'critical social ontology for disability studies' (Hughes 2007) that both problematizes the hegemony of ableist sensibilities (Campbell 2010) and exposes the aversive emotions that populate the non-disabled imaginary.

This chapter owes its wider general frame of reference to what is sometimes described as 'the 'affective turn' (Clough and Halley 2007), a process that follows from the recognition that accounts of emotion cannot be reduced to individual feeling but should – following feminist and poststructuralist arguments – be explored in their economic, social, historical and cultural context. In sociology, the turn to emotions has followed logically from the growth in body studies and the recognition of the intensely somatic nature of contemporary society. Bruno Latour (2004) suggests that we should think about bodies, not as things or reified objects but as process – in terms, that is, of 'what a body can do': its reactions and impacts, its capacities and practices, and most fundamentally how it affects and is affected. One is reminded of Bergson's (1988: 225) vitalist view of the body as 'an instrument of action and of action only', and he continues, 'in no sense, under no aspect does it', the body, 'serve to prepare, far less explain a representation'. From this perspective, there is escape from the body as object but no escaping recognition of the currents of emotion that circulate our embodied social lives like the weather systems bombarding our experience with wind and rain and sun. Emotions are, of course, bodily forms of knowing, corporeal moments of sensation. The affects are 'enfleshed', even when they are shared and circulating in groups and communities.

This chapter is concerned with the ways in which circulating constellations of emotion both inform the non-disabled imaginary and invalidate disabled bodies. Ahmed (2004) offers insight into what she calls 'the sociality of emotions'. This idea comes to the surface at the confluence of a number of sociological questions, including how emotions are lived and experienced through bodies, how cultural politics implicate the affects in the stratification of society, and how the processes of othering and invalidation rest upon a psychic bedrock made from moral divisiveness, intolerance and firmly felt prejudice. Ahmed writes (2004: 10): 'it is through emotions, or how we respond to objects and others that surfaces and boundaries are made; the "I" and the "we" are shaped by and even take the shape of contact with others'. Object and other can be perceived as problematic or 'sticky', to use her glutinous term. The attribution of a viscid nature associates object and other with negative affective value which is the emotional basis for discrimination and exclusion.

Following Thomas (1999), disability studies has, of late, begun to explore the issue of 'psycho-emotional disablism' (Reeve 2004, 2006). In addition to structural disablism, including the ubiquitous barriers to full social participation, disabled people experience the 'socially engendered undermining' of their 'psycho-emotional wellbeing' (Thomas 1999: 60). In the quotidian spaces of everyday life, disabled people experience attacks on their existential security. The impact of discrimination and exclusion is augmented by a disablist interaction order in which people with impairments are patronized, ignored, abused and subjected to the subcutaneous violence of the intrusive, demeaning and disturbing non-disabled gaze (Garland-Thomson 2009). Undermined as mothers, fathers, workers, lovers and in a host of other capacities, disability is a life lived before a looking glass that is cracked and distorted by the vandalism of normality.

In this chapter I will examine the three emotions that I think are the major – though not the exclusive – building blocks of the emotional infrastructure of ableism. It is these emotions, as they collect in the non-disabled imaginary, that contribute, therefore, to the social distance between disabled and non-disabled people. These three emotions are fear, pity and disgust. The tendency in modernity to consign disabled people to segregated spaces or to try to make them identical to non-disabled people is an expression of the civilizing process (Elias 2000). In modernity the threshold of repugnance narrows and attitudes to bodily and intellectual difference – particularly bodies and minds that do not conform to the hygienic norms of somatic control and appearance – harden into aversive emotions like fear and disgust and into the conviction that impairment is a tragedy, its 'victims' deserving of benefaction and favour.

Fear

Dread (or *Angest* in Danish), in its philosophical sense, particularly in Kierkegaard's work refers principally to the existential anxiety that is produced by one's realization that freedom and choice is human destiny. Kierkegaard (1957), through the mouth of his character/pseudonym Vigilius Haufniesis in the *Concept of Dread* describes this subjective condition, compellingly, as 'the dizziness of freedom'. Dread is also to be understood in terms of the recognition of one's identity as a mortal, vulnerable, fleshy creature, at the juncture, as it were, between freedom and necessity. In twentieth century existentialism, angst and anguish are used more regularly to refer to the ontological insecurity that Kierkegaard described. 'Angst', philologists argue, has its roots in the Latin '*angar*' meaning 'choking' and '*anguista*' meaning 'tightness'. These forms of bodily comportment are the corporeal expression of fear and disgust and, in particular, the way in which these emotions combine as we experience or ponder the harsh inevitable realities of suffering, loss, pain and death. Ultimately, it is the fear of 'nothingness' and whatever suggests this possibility to us that makes us choke and feel constricted, heavy with the uncertainties of human finitude. A negative and aversive reaction to the presence of disability is, in part, fear for the precariousness of one's own being and the vulnerabilities of our ephemeral flesh. For Kierkegaard, fear is 'of' something in the world and anguish is horror of the self as freedom in the face of nothingness. The misrecognition and disrespect – not to mention segregation and oppression – that disabled people suffer at the hands of their non-disabled counterparts is a form of violence bred from our fear of and anguish about our alienation from the human condition where being human is simultaneously a facet of self and other. The feeling of anguish with respect to others is indivisible from the feeling of disgust for oneself but in an ableist culture these feelings become separated. The body beautiful creates its eugenic opposite and proceeds to tyrannize the forms of physical and mental difference that are products of its own existential insecurity.

The critique of modernity that we find in the work of philosophers like Kierkegaard and (especially) Nietzsche pivots on the view that modern persons are in denial when it comes to facing up to their own vulnerability. They fail to recognize, let alone celebrate, pain, loss and death. In these early powerful critiques of modernity, we hear of a culture that is being emptied of passion and overloaded with objectivity (Hughes 1996). The blight of objectivity is such that it empties life of meaning and purpose and replaces the candour of subjective culture with fear and denial about our carnal frailties. There are real losers in this process. In particular, those others who come to represent loss, pain, suffering and death become objects of fear and disgust. Fiedler (1978: 24) argued that the 'true freak' will 'stir both supernatural terror and natural sympathy'. This perspective suggests that encounters with the monstrous are emotionally powerful because they challenge the stable view of embodied self that is characteristic of non-disabled identity. Such encounters push at the walls of the architecture of ableism. In the context of such an encounter, non-disabled persons are most likely to attempt to resolve the element of fear manifest in the challenge of difference by erasure, by putting clear emotional, physical and social distance between themselves and the source of this kind of visceral identity shock. This can be achieved by an act of 'reclassification' that dehumanizes and objectifies the aberrant body. The sense of 'sympathy' that Fiedler describes may be treated as a confirmation of one's own humanity or may work itself out in a good deed or a philanthropic act, which is, as we will see, another mechanism for creating social distance between disabled and non-disabled people.

Fear implies a threat, so we need to clarify in what way disability constitutes a threat. The work of Margrit Shildrick (2005) is helpful in this respect. She argues for a 'specifically deconstructive approach' that 'seeks to uncover the other as an interior attribute of the embodied self' (Shildrick 2005: 755). Psychoanalytical and postmodernist ideas inform this approach to disability history and it also possesses affinities with the humanities tradition in the United States of America (USA), particularly its predilection to expose the 'social phantasms projected upon the disabled subject in history' (Mitchell and Snyder 1997: 3). Shildrick searches for the 'other within the same', the self that denies its own frailty and precariousness and projects it onto others who become the anomalous, the monstrous, the defective, the strange, the alien. We make hideous objects out of the very elements of self that we are too afraid of and too disgusted by to recognize, let alone celebrate. In this respect, modernity – with its penchant for solid separation and clear distinction – is particularly precarious (Hughes 2009):

> Given the explicit privileging of wholeness, independence and integrity demanded of the able bodied subject, the cultural imaginary is highly invested in fantasies of an invulnerable body. Yet, in the face of disability that threatens always to claim its identity in the selfsame, such fantasies generate a normative anxiety that cannot be allayed.
>
> *(Shildrick 2005: 757)*

The 'threat' of disability in the contemporary world is, according to Shildrick, considerable: 'It is the other that not only disturbs normative expectations but destabilizes self-identity' (ibid). The capacity of the disabled body to disturb individuals and cultures alike is, according to Shildrick, universal because it (disability) never fully submits to being either different or the same. She regards the anxiety that underpins disability as trans-historical because ancients and moderns, scientists and theologians alike share the doubt about a body that could be natural or not, human or not, unnatural or not, non-human or not.

Such a psychoanalytic deliberation fits well with the age of anxiety but seems too inclusive, even essentialist, to capture the emotional differences and complexities that cut through time and culture. It also seems – ironically – a little too much in tune with the modernist view in which the best of all possible worlds is one in which everything is clean, proper, separate and distinct. Shildrick's psychic reductionism brings disablism as close to the home of non-disability as it can get, placing it firmly in the delusion of perfection and the disavowals of frailty that characterize non-disabled life but human timidity in the face of its own precariousness is as good at explaining everything in general as it is at clarifying nothing in particular. The threat of disability is, in modernity, a threat to the comfortable settlements of civility, to absurdly narrow ableist notions about proper conduct and norms of bodily comportment (Hughes, forthcoming).

Fear encourages 'flight or fight'. It has manifest itself in the segregation of disability, its enclosure behind high walls; the anthropophagic strategy of early to mid modernity which put impairment out of sight and out of mind. The de-institutionalization of disability, the demand for inclusion and the appearance of impairment in the contemporary world as a 'spectacle' for non-disabled persons to psychically consider and accommodate has recast the relationship between disability and non-disability (Linton 1998). Perhaps the phenomenon of disability hate crime – both cyber and corporeal – (see, for example, Sherry 2010) can be explained – in socio-emotional terms – as a manifestation of fear of impairment, resentment and hatred actualized as virtual or visceral violence against disabled people.

Pity

Although philanthropy has been around since Prometheus gave humanity the gift of fire, some post-enlightenment approaches to disability seem to depend quite strongly on the mobilization of the emotions of pity and compassion. On this view, disabled people are cast as 'unfortunates', existing (and in most cases subsisting) in the dark throes of great suffering. Such persons are in need of and deserve sympathy and charity and it is the moral or religious duty of decent people to participate in the provision of alms. In the wake of the 'philanthropic bonanza' (Borsay 2005: 142) that spread across Britain from the 1780s, disabled people became the objects of the pathos of the charitable gaze.

Rousseau argues that sympathy for others (*pitie*) is a feature of man in the state of nature and that it is a characteristic that tempers and moralizes the instinct of self-preservation. However, in the real world (*amour propre*) people are driven to compare themselves with others and, in this context, the drive to seek domination over others transforms pity from a state of natural sympathy and compassion into a base symptom of social inequality. In this context, pity is 'accompanied by a certain kind of contempt' (Miller 1997: 25). The object of compassion and pity in 'the real world' is always a victim, the other whose shoes one does not want to be in, the one who invokes the pitying response, 'there but for fortune go I', the one whose invalidity is redemption and validation for the valid. The charitable attachment to the disabled other is saturated with selfishness because it sustains one's sense of ontological security and wholeness. Charitable giving also 'demonstrates the persistence of public virtue' and 'confirms to individual donors their possession of that virtue by distinguishing them from both takers and the invalidated' (Longmore 1997: 136). In his study of American telethons, Longmore (1997: 14) notes that, 'although they ostensibly seek the physical repair of those socially invalidated by disability' televized charitable bashes are, in essence, 'rituals of moral restoration for nondisabled communicants'.

Pity is a hierarchizing emotion in which superiority is at work in those who feel it and inferiority the projected status of those who are its target. Even if one is tempted, as many have been, to criticize or even laugh-off Rousseau's anthropology, one cannot disentangle pity from the social construction of inequality, particularly in disability politics where its role is constitutive in the demarcation of populations into the moral categories of the normal and the pathological. Charity 'requires a class of persons defined as "needy", as socially invalidated' (Longmore 1997: 140) and it is the 'pathological', those who deviate from a biological norm, who are a palpable, material, embodied and 'natural' manifestation of this needy class of persons. Pity – a recurrent experience for disabled people in their everyday dealings with their non-disabled counterparts – embodies negativity in a number of more or less obvious ways. Kreigel (1987) notes that, 'the cripple is threat and recipient of compassion, both to be damned and to be pitied – and frequently to be damned as he is pitied'. At the political level of charitable action 'damnation' takes two forms: The 'less fortunate' must be cast in the role of the subaltern, neither fully fledged citizens nor fully fledged persons. The generosity embodied in the charitable gift or donation is an attempt to ameliorate the personal and the socio-political deficits of the 'unfortunates'. In the act of giving the non-disabled person converts pity into social capital and confirms her status as a benevolent person-citizen who is independent and authentic. There is no reciprocation in the charitable gift; it is a pure act of 'othering'.

'Personal tragedy theory' has played an important role in the development of the social model of disability. Oliver (1990) argues that it is central to the medicalized, individualistic perspective on disability and that it underpins the charitable and compensatory social policy response to disabled people. The clear emotional correlate of 'personal tragedy theory' is pity. For the social model, it is pity, more than any other emotion, that informs the affect position that non-disabled people adopt as they seek to make what they regard as an appropriate emotional response to disability. Non-disabled people tend to read pity – as it is deployed in the context of the tragedy of impairment – in terms of compassion and philanthropy. It is – following Christianity – a virtue, perhaps the highest virtue.

Disabled people and the Disabled People's Movement in particular, tend to take a very different view. Their position is closer to that adopted by Nietzsche in his critique of Christianity where he argued: 'Nothing in our unhealthy modernity is more unhealthy than Christian pity' (Nietzsche 1968: 119). Far from being the 'highest virtue', the German philosopher argues that pity has 'a depressive effect'; it is a 'life denying' emotion, a 'depressive and contagious instinct' and a 'multiplier of misery … a conserver of everything miserable' (Nietzsche 1968: 118). One of the slogans of the disabled people's movement in the United Kingdom (UK) – 'piss on pity' – is a clear manifestation of the considerable emotional gap between a charitable and rights approach to Disability. In the non-disabled imaginary impairment/disability is equivalent to ruin, a blighted life, a life not worth living. Disability is a collapse in one's human currency, the destruction of one's social, emotional and cultural capital. It is an irretrievable stumble into a dark and negative existence, a gateway to ontological invalidation. All light and positivity is extinguished. However, disability for disabled people is frequently constructed in terms that embody affirmation (Swain and French 2000). The 'practical nihilism' (Nietzsche 1968: 118) of pity is something that disabled people can do without.

Although pity is not regarded in the literature as an aversive emotion, it does – like the aversive emotions – embody an orientation to its object that carries negative value. In the specific case of disability, the tragic object – the impaired body – is judged to be, relative to the non-disabled self, an unfortunate and broken being. The 'complete' non-disabled body is the comparator that confirms the tragedy and 'lack' of impairment. Pity (in some cases alongside fear and disgust) is the affect that both creates and takes up the emotional space between the valid and the invalidated subject. The brew that constitutes this emotional space will contain compassion but it is also brim full of the kind of well-intentioned, hierarchizing pathos that leads to the ontological demotion of those who are the target of its bountiful benefaction. The attribution of pity to impaired bodies by the normate community lies in the validating/invalidating consequences, the marking off of some bodies as authentic and others as not. The discriminatory distinction between the ablest body of normality and its 'inadequate' other is reproduced and consolidated by the charitable disposition. The legacy of pity and tragedy – not to mention guilt and shame – is manifest in the '*telos* of cure' that pervades non-disabled discourse about disability and is frequently evident in parental narratives about disabled children (Avery 1999: 112). Disability – in one of its many myths – is cast as the lead actor in the age-old narrative of suffering and its alleviation, triumph over hardship. The story bears no relationship to the reality of disabled people's lives but it has gone down well in modernity with the philanthropic classes moved by the fundraisers and marketers – in for example blind and deaf institutions in the nineteenth century – who, 'in marketing themselves to their public … hunted funds by stressing the horrors of sensory deprivation' (Borsay 2005: 95). Disabled people and especially disabled children are marked and marketed by the charitable sector – particularly through photographic imagery – as victims, as suffering, as patients, as pitiable (Hevey 1992). The view seems to be that the truths of representation matter little. If pathos pushes deepest into non-disabled people's pockets and turns their sympathies into cash, then so be it. Yet the feel good fanfare of the telethon is restricted to the donors. One does not detect the same level of pious enthusiasm in the recipients, even when 'they' are invited to express their gratitude.

Disgust

Disgust stems from fear of the messiness of our own intrinsic, organic human constitution (Kolnai 2004: 39) and from modern cultural sensibilities that require us to manage the animal orifices that threaten to despoil and defile (Elias 2000). And disgust is a moral tribunal that is used to judge others, to assign them to an inferior status and at the same time make a compelling case for 'our' superiority, 'our' place above the herd, 'our' purity. In its judgements, disgust is harsh and invalidating: 'It … judges ugliness and deformity to be moral offences' and 'it knows no distinction between the moral and the aesthetic, collapsing failures in both into an undifferentiated revulsion' (Miller 1997: 21).

The idea of disgust looms large in the philosophies of Søren Kierkegaard, Georges Bataille, Jean-Paul Sartre, Julia Kristeva and Aurel Kolnia. Sartre is of particular interest because disgust plays a key role in his particular brand of existentialism: existence itself is a concatenation of uncanny experiences. Insofar as we are 'condemned' to be free, disgust and anguish are the primary emotions through which we engage ontologically with ourselves and with the material objects that (are supposed to but do not) 'fix' our 'meaningless' being in this slimy, ignoble, world. We are also condemned to die and death – or nothingness – makes a mockery of freedom and being. In Sartre's world '*La Nausée*' is universal, embedded in the unfamiliarity and hostility of material objects, self and other. This unfamiliarity and hostility has its origins in '*le visqueux*', which translates as 'the slimy'. In *Being and Nothingness* (1969) Sartre offers an extended meditation on 'the slimy'. Slime disgusts and disgust is a reaction to 'something perceived as dangerous because of its' putative and perceived 'powers to contaminate, infect, pollute by proximity, contact or ingestion' (Miller 1997: 2). Slime fits this bill because it is neither one thing nor the other, neither liquid nor solid. It is 'the agony of water' (Sartre 1969: 607). It has no categorical place as an object and resists assimilation into the subjective system of meaning. It breaches the norms of ontology because it is an 'aberrant fluid' (1969: 609). Fear of the slimy is profound. We fear, foremost, having it attach itself to us, being sucked into it and yet it is in us, on our tongues in our all-consuming mouths, everywhere bubbling beneath our skin. It offends the modernist desire for ontological order and it is connected to 'human baseness' (1969: 605). It is connected to us, to our embodied and visceral selves, to the fact that 'we live and die and that the process is a messy one emitting substances and odours that make us doubt ourselves and fear our neighbour' (Miller 1997: 2).

Le visqueux – when it overflows into consciousness – compromises the integrity of being in the world. The slimy disgusts us because it invokes what is ambiguous and anomalous, just as: 'People with disabilities invoke anxiety and revulsion because they are defined as literally embodying … loss of control, loss of autonomy, at its deepest level, finitude, confinement within the human condition, subjection to fate' (Longmore 1997: 154). Stiker (1999) endorses a position in which disability pays a trans-historical and ontological role as a shadow that reminds the human community of its frailty. Disabled people are, he writes, 'the tear in our being that reveals its open-endedness, its incompleteness, its precariousness' (1999: 10). We wish to avoid reminders of our visceral, animal, messy selves and impairment and sickness provide us with these very reminders. The social process of the invalidation of disabled people is locked into the disavowal of the slimy self which is projected onto the other, palpably displaying the signs of breakdown and defilement of what I am and will be but refuse to face. Disgust in the presence of disability is a form of cowardice in the face of inevitability and a failure to recognize that mortality is not an enemy but simply the price one pays for life.

In effect, we are all slimy, 'leaky' (Shildrick 1997), gross and sticky, in the process of becoming, of being incomplete but only some are destined to be defined as such and therefore assigned to the chaotic world of the in-between, aberrant, anomalous. The power and tyranny of the normal world with its hegemonic ableist values and practices makes the scourge of sliminess stick to some; the some who become the in-between, the objects of castigation and who, thereby, justify appeasement and denial for all those who are known for their 'clean and proper' (Kristeva 1982) dispositions; those who are impaled upon the non-disabled imaginary and who have disavowed their excretory bodies, their vulnerabilities, their ultimate and inevitable demise, the cadavers they must become. Disgust is an emotion that derives, ultimately, from the mortal limits of our abject bodies (Kristeva 1982; Kolnai 2004) and from the leaky fluids that sometimes escape the boundaries of our corporeal selves (Lupton 1998a, 1998b) but it has a history in which it is muted or exacerbated by specific cultural sensibilities. The 'grotesque body' of the Feudal period is described by Bakhtin (1968: 26) as a body that 'transgresses its own limits', that is 'open to the outside world' that is defined by 'its apertures and convexities', its 'various ramifications and offshoots: the open mouth, the genital organs, the breasts, the phallus, the potbelly, the nose' not to mention 'copulation, pregnancy, childbirth, the throes of death, eating, drinking, defecation'. This volatile 'carnivalesque' body evident in medieval celebrations is open to *le visqueux*; its modern counterpart is not. The story of the civilization process (Elias 2000) is the story of the rise of the 'modern protestant body' (Mellor and Shilling 1997) with its marked intolerance towards leaki-ness and impairment; a story we will illustrate with respect to the recent history of saliva and drooling.

Elias (2000) refers to the good council of Erasmus in 1530 where the Dutch philosopher remarks that it is 'unmannerly to suck back saliva, as equally are those who we see spitting at every third word not from necessity but from habit'. Erasmus also advised that one should 'turn away when spitting, lest your saliva fall on someone' and recommended the use of 'a small cloth' – an object that later became known as a handkerchief (Elias 2000: 138). The decline of the use of the spittoon, the virtual elimination of this outlet for saliva after the flu epidemic in 1918 and the hygiene wars against expectoration because of its association with the (spread of) tuberculosis are important events that are indicative of the increased control exerted by contemporary societies in relation to expectoration and the externalization of saliva (Smith 1988). However, 'disgust and nausea at the ejection of saliva intensified and the taboos surrounding it increased, long before people had a clear idea of the transmission of certain germs by saliva' (Elias 2000: 134). It was the socialization of the affects into restraint around the release of bodily fluids in public, considerations of etiquette and civility, rather than scientific argument that inspired the tightening of prohibitions around spitting and drooling.

Saliva is not intrinsically problematic. If it stays in the mouth and does not become visible to others, it presents no problem. Likewise, both love and lust involve the exchange of bodily fluids including saliva but such reciprocity is not 'normally' a cause for complaint, at least for those directly involved in the process. Intimacy moderates disgust. However, etiquette suggests that one should keep one's mouth closed whilst eating. Conformity to this injunction keeps saliva and partly chewed food out of the public domain and in a place where it cannot cause offence. In escaping from the mouth, through dribbling or drooling, saliva becomes socially problematic and disabled adults who experience drooling (ptyalism to use the medical terminology) as a symptom of an impairment will be only too well aware of the disgust response that this invokes if it happens in the presence of others. In escaping from the container of the body, saliva becomes, as Mary Douglas (1966) put it 'dirt'; that is, 'matter out of place'. It becomes an anomalous substance. It is transformed into a pollutant or, more precisely, is interpreted by others as a potential pollutant or contaminant.

With respect to the disgust response, there is a further age-related complication. Ptyalism amongst babies is considered normal and generally does not elicit a negative emotional reaction. The disgust response is reserved for disabled adults for whom ptyalism is a symptom of impair-ment. The (discredited) biological logic of Ernst Haekel which claims that ontogeny replicates phylogeny seems to be at work here in a practical sociological way. When Elias wrote that 'the individual in his short history passes once more through some of the processes that his society has traversed in its long history' (2000: XI), he embraces a recapitulationist explanation for a normative, age-related approach to ptyalism in which the drooling of the child is forgiven because the impact of the civilizing process – on the infant – is only in its infancy. In this context there is no disgust response or, at best, it is muted. However, as time marches on; as the child becomes the adult; as expectations of emotional control and bodily comportment are raised and as thresholds of repugnance realign themselves to the mores of mature behaviour, then fluid excreted from the mouth is transformed into the abject, a slimy object of horror and revulsion. Indicative of a failure of self-control, the secreted saliva reminds non-disabled people of how they too might – in the course of time – fail to comport themselves in ways that conceal their vulnerability to decay, degeneration and infantalizing regression.

At a cultural level the 'problem' of ptyalism is related to the 'various folk and learned traditions', including Freudianism, that recognize 'homologies between mouths and anuses, mouths and vaginas' (Miller 1997: 94) to the appetites that promote both eating and fornication and more generally to the bodily orifice as a locus for disgust, a point at which bodily boundaries can be breached, letting in or letting out potentially contaminating substances that threaten ontological security. Saliva is such a substance and its central role in oral incorporation, specifically mastication, enhances its potential to repel because it is involved in the first stage of the production of faeces. It is the liquid at the ingress end of the 'canal' that assists in the passage and transformation of life-giving, ingested material into foul waste product. It mediates between the delights of appetite and the production of excrement and in so doing highlights the precariousness of the relationship between desire and disgust.

Ptyalism is also linked to 'idiocy', not only, therefore, to a potentially dangerous and contaminating body but to cognitive and intellectual deficit, to unreason, to the dark side of enlightenment and modernity. Drooling, particularly in the nineteenth and twentieth centuries – in the wake of the medicalization of 'idiocy' – was taken as a sign of 'feeble mindedness', 'imbecility' or 'mental retardation'. Eugenic thinking, which reached its height during the Edwardian period, conceived of 'feeble mindedness' as a 'social evil' (Jackson 1998), thereby enhancing the contaminating and polluting aura of its outward signs and de-humanizing those who manifest them. Idiocy was transformed into a menace, a threat to the social fabric, and became a source of moral panic exacerbating reproductive fears. In practice, this meant that the Victorian distinction between 'idiots and dangerous idiots', enshrined in a number of nineteenth century statutes, collapsed. All 'idiots' were potentially a threat to the integrity of the population and the lucidity of future generations. Droolers and dribblers were signifiers of degeneracy, of an aberrancy so contaminating that it might potentially take us all.

Conclusion

A central metaphor for our contemporary times is 'flow'. Body studies in the social sciences and the humanities has come, of late, to embrace the concepts of kinetics and movement (Sheets-Johnstone 2009; Manning 2007; Mussami 2002) as if to admit to the redundancy of the idea of the all too solid nature of the notion of the body as object. The term 'liquid' and the idea of liquidity are much in use to describe postmodern social formations and the sensibilities that they inspire (Bauman 2006). Feminists like Iris Marion Young (1990: 193) – impressed by the fluid and volatile features of women's bodies – have argued for a 'process metaphysic' in which 'movement and energy is ontologically prior to thingness'. Dipping into this relatively new metaphorical pond involves attributing epistemological currency to almost anything that is not fixed. In disability (and indeed feminist) studies, 'leakiness' is the fluid term that has had the most influence (Shildrick 1997). It is to be noted, however, that it is not quite the equivalent of its siblings in the wider cannons of contemporary discourse. The other metaphors suggest water *without the agony*. Leakiness, on the other hand, is mired in the abject – in the mess and waste of human bodies (Hughes *et al.* 2005), the taboos of civilizing modernity (Hughes, forthcoming). The time may have come – so argue the proponents of *écriture féminin* – to celebrate mess, waste and excess. It is an argument that can only bring benefit to disabled people and to everyone who is subjected to the body fascism of ableist culture.

If one was to construct, as a purely intellectual exercise, the other, who was the opposite of the (unattainable, normative, perfect) self of ableist mythology, the emotional arsenal that one would most likely deploy in the characterization of such a figure would include fear, pity and disgust. These are the aversive and hierarchizing emotions deployed in the bowels of intolerance to depict enemies, outliers, strangers – the embodied portents of defilement. Such sentiments depict an alterity that is evil, sinister, threatening, contemptible, repulsive and pitiable. All the moral deficits heaped on top of one another make up what the conceited 'we', most certainly, is not. But – and here is the rub – the perfect self is fictive and the empirical self that lives in the real world with its ableist myths and abstraction will always have a small window through which – despite denial and disavowal – s/he will always be able to see, to some extent, a refracted reflection of self in the despised other. The vulnerability, mortality, monstrosity assigned to others involves a particular kind of failure to see. It fails to contend with the perspective that, 'to perceive any object whatsoever as horrible is to perceive it on the basis of a world which reveals itself as *already* being horrible' (Sartre 1971: 89). That which the non-disabled world cannot come to terms with – its own slime and visceral embodiment – 'is a revelation of the meaning of the world' (Sartre 1971: 75). In the *Anatomy of Disgust*, William Miller (1997: 90) argues that 'the stare of the dead, the blankness of idiocy, the possession of madness … have the capacity to horrify' and horror is 'a particular blend of fear and disgust'. Pity too invites itself into this family of affects in order to make up the ensemble of emotions that constitute the tabloid of ableist sentiments.

References

Ahmed, S. (2004) *The Cultural Politics of Emotion* (Edinburgh: Edinburgh University Press).

Avery, D. M. (1999) 'Talking Tragedy: Identity Issues in the Parental Story of Disability', in M. Corker and T. Shakespeare, eds, *Disability Discourse* (Buckingham: Open University Press): pp. 116–126.

Bakhtin, M. (1968) *Rabelais and His World* (Cambridge, MA: MIT Press).

Bauman, Z. (2006) *Liquid Fear* (Cambridge: Polity Press).

Bergson, H. (1988) *Matter and Memory*, trans. by N. Paul and W. Palmer (New York: MIT Press).

Borsay, A. (2005) *Disability and Social Policy in Britain Since 1750* (Basingstoke: Palgrave).

Campbell, F. K. (2010) *Contours of Ableism: The Production of Disability and Abledness* (Basingstoke: Palgrave Macmillan).

Clough, P. and Halley, J., eds, (2007) *The Affective Turn: Theorizing the Social* (Durham: Duke University Press).

Douglas, M. (1966) *Purity and Danger: An Analysis of the Concept of Pollution and Taboo* (London: Routledge).

Elias, N. (2000) *The Civilizing Process* (Oxford, Blackwell).

Fiedler, L. (1978) *Freaks: Myths and Images of the Secret Self* (New York: Simon and Schuster).

Garland-Thomson, R. (2009) *Staring: How we Look* (New York: Oxford University Press).

Hevey, D. (1992) *The Creatures that Time Forgot: Photography and Disability Imagery* (London: Longman).

Hughes, B. (1996) 'Nietzsche: Philosophizing with the Body', *Body and Society* 2(1): 31–44.

Hughes, B. (2007) 'Being Disabled: Towards a Critical Social Ontology for Disability Studies', *Disability & Society* 22(7): 673–84.

Hughes, B. (2009) 'Wounded/Monstrous/Abject: A Critique of the Disabled Body in the Sociological Imaginary', *Disability & Society* 24(4): 399–410.

Hughes, B. (forthcoming) 'Elias: Disability, Modernity and Cultures of Exclusion', in D. Goodley, B. Hughes and L. Davis, eds, *Social Theories of Disability: New Developments* (Basingstoke: Palgrave).

Hughes, B., McKie, L., Hopkins, D. and Watson, N. (2005) 'Loves Labour's Lost: Feminism, the Disabled People's Movement and an Ethic of Care', *Sociology* 39(2): 259–75.

Jackson, M. (2000) *The Borderland of Imbecility: Medicine, Society and the Fabrication of the Feeble Mind in Late Victorian and Edwardian England* (Manchester: Manchester University Press).

Kierkegaard, S. (1957) *The Concept of Dread*, trans. by W. Lowrie (Princeton: Princeton University Press).

Kolnai, A. (2004) *On Disgust* (edited and introduced by B. Smith and C. Korsmeyer) (Chicago and La Salle, Illinois: Open Court).

Kreigel, L. (1987) 'Disability as a Metaphor in Literature', in A. Gartner and T. Joe, eds, *Images of the Disabled: Disabling Images* (New York: Praeger): pp. 31–46.

Kristeva, J. (1982) *Powers of Horror: An Essay on Abjection*, trans. by L. Roudiez (New York: Columbia University Press).

Latour, B. (2004) 'How to Talk About the Body? The Normative Dimensions of Science Studies', *Body and Society* 10(2–3): 205–30.

Linton, S. (1998) *Claiming Disability: Knowledge and Identity* (New York: New York University Press).

Longmore, P. (1997) 'Conspicuous Contribution and American Culture – Telethon Rituals of Cleansing and Renewal', in D. Mitchell and S. Snyder, eds, *The Body and Physical Difference* (Ann Arbor: University of Michigan Press): pp. 134–58.

Lupton, D. (1998a) 'Going with the Flow: Some Central Discourses in Conceptualizing and Articulating the Embodiment of Emotional States', in S. Nettleton and J. Watson, eds, *The Body in Everyday Life* (London: Routledge): pp. 82–99.

Lupton, D. (1998b) *The Emotional Self* (London: Sage).

Manning, E. (2007) *The Politics of Touch: Sense, Movement, Sovereignty* (Minneapolis: University of Minnesota Press).

Mellor, P. and Shilling, C. (1997) *Re-forming the Body: Religion, Community and Modernity* (London: Sage).

Miller, W. I. (1997) *The Anatomy of Disgust* (Cambridge, Mass.: Harvard University Press).

Mussami, B. (2002) *Parables for the Virtual: Movement, Affect, Sensation* (Durham: Duke University Press).

Nietzsche, F. (1968) *The Twilight of the Idols and the Anti-Christ*, trans. by R. J. Hollingdale (Harmondsworth: Penguin).

Oliver, M. (1990) *The Politics of Disablement* (Basingstoke: Macmillan).

Reeve, D. (2002) 'Psycho-emotional Dimensions of Disability and the Social Model', in C. Barnes and G. Mercer, eds, *Implementing the Social Model of Disability: Theory and Research* (Leeds: The Disability Press): pp. 83–100.

Reeve, D. (2006) 'Towards a Psychology of Disability: The Emotional Effects of Living in a Disabling Society', in D. Goodley and R. Lawthom, eds, *Disability and Psychology: Critical Introductions and Reflections* (London: Palgrave): pp. 94–107.

Sartre, J. P. (1969) *Being and Nothingness: An Essay on Phenomenological Ontology*, trans. by H. E. Barnes (London: Methuen).

Sartre, J. P. (1971) *Sketch for a Theory of the Emotions*, trans. by P. Mairet (London: Methuen).

Sheets-Johnstone, M. (2009) *The Corporeal Turn: An Interdisciplinary Reader* (Charlottesville Virginia: Imprint Academic).

Sherry, M. (2010) *Disability Hate Crimes: Does Anyone Really Hate Disabled People?* (Farnham: Ashgate).

Shildrick, M. (1997) *Leaky Bodies and Boundaries: Feminism, Postmodernism and (Bio)ethics* (London: Routledge).

Shildrick, M. (2005) 'The Disabled Body, Genealogy and Undecidability', *Cultural Studies* 19(6): 755–70.

Smith, F. B. (1988) *The Retreat of Tuberculosis 1850–1950* (London: Croom Helm).

Stiker, H.-J. (1999) *A History of Disability*, trans. by W. Sayers (Ann Arbor: University of Michigan Press).

Swain, J. and French, S. (2000) 'Towards an Affirmative Model of Disability', *Disability & Society* 15(4): 569–82.

Thomas, C. (1999) *Female Forms: Experiencing and Understanding Disability* (Buckingham: Open University Press).

Young, I. M. (1990) *Throwing Like a Girl and Other Essays in Feminist Philosophy and Social Theory* (Bloomington: Indiana University Press).

7

PSYCHO-EMOTIONAL DISABLISM

The missing link?

Donna Reeve

Introduction

Although early disability writers such as Paul Hunt (1966) documented the impact of stigma and internalized oppression on the psyche of disabled people, these problems have largely remained a difficulty for the individual to manage whilst the disabled people's movement addressed the more material forms of disadvantage such as exclusion from employment, education and the built environment. It was the naming of these personal experiences as *psycho-emotional disablism* which has allowed for a sociological analysis of these aspects of social oppression, rather than leaving them in the hands of psychologists and other professionals 'who would not hesitate to apply the individualistic/personal tragedy model to these issues' (Thomas 1999: 74).

This chapter has two aims. First, it provides a description of psycho-emotional disablism and the different forms it can take. Second, it explores what the phenomenological concept of the 'dys-appearing' body offers to an analysis of psycho-emotional disablism. As well as enabling the concept of 'internalized oppression' to be unpacked into its two components, the chapter also highlights the relevance of impairment via cultural prejudices when looking at the experience of psycho-emotional disablism. Whilst mentioning impairment is taken by some in disability studies to be equivalent to reinforcing an *individual* model of disability (such as Barnes and Mercer 2010: 96–97), the continued silence means that:

> disability theory withholds moral recognition from (the wrong kinds of) disabled people as effectively as anyone who actively stereotypes them or denies that some kinds of disability identity exist.
>
> *(Scully 2008: 175)*

Similarly Wendell (2001) has argued that disability studies needs to take more account of disablism faced by those with chronic illness – the so called 'unhealthy disabled' who do not represent the 'paradigmatic person with a disability [who] is healthy disabled and permanently and predictably impaired' (Wendell 2001: 21).

Finally, I would like to be explicit about the scope of this chapter, which draws predominantly on disability studies work based in the United Kingdom (UK). Therefore my analysis of psycho-emotional disablism and the forms it may take is very UK-centric and it would be expected that psycho-emotional disablism would look very different in other cultures, particularly those in the Majority world which are outside my area of expertise. In addition, the chapter draws on data collected as part of my doctoral thesis where participants with physical impairments talked about their experiences of disablism (Reeve 2008b). Whilst this means my conclusions can only be partial, I present this chapter to continue the discussions that are needed within disability studies to broaden the empirical and theoretical study of psycho-emotional disablism (Thomas 2004).

Psycho-emotional disablism

The concept of psycho-emotional disablism was first introduced by Carol Thomas in her book *Female Forms* (1999); whilst initially the term 'psycho-emotional dimensions of disability' was used, more recently this has been changed to 'psycho-emotional disablism' (Thomas 2007) to make connections with other forms of social oppression such as hetero/sexism, ageism and racism. In order to redress the balance between recognition of the public and more private forms of oppression, Thomas reformulated the Union of the Physically Impaired Against Disability (UPIAS) definition of disability (UPIAS 1976) to produce an extended social relational definition of disablism:

> Disablism is a form of social oppression involving the social imposition of restrictions of activity on people with impairments and the socially engendered undermining of their psycho-emotional well-being.
>
> *(Thomas 2007: 73)*

In other words, disablism can be experienced as two forms of social oppression: structural disablism and psycho-emotional disablism. Structural barriers are those that operate from outside the individual such as inaccessible environments, physical and social forms of exclusion, discrimination and the like, or in other words, the usual forms of social oppression acting on a person with impairments which are *implied* by a social model definition. What differentiates this extended social relational definition of disablism from the traditional social model definition is the *deliberate* inclusion of psycho-emotional disablism, disabling barriers which operate on the psycho-emotional well-being of people with impairments. Whilst the original UPIAS-informed social model definition of disability did not exclude these 'inner' barriers, their specific omission meant that they were often overlooked in analyses of the lived experience of disability in favour of the more visible 'outer' barriers. However, recently there has been increasing interest within disability studies on the psychological impact of disablism which is discussed further by Goodley elsewhere in this book.

As well as the differentiation between structural and psycho-emotional disablism, it is also possible to identify two sources of this latter kind of disablism (Reeve 2008b). *Direct* psycho-emotional disablism arises from relationships that the disabled person has with other people or themselves and is the most important form of psycho-emotional disablism. However, it is also possible to identify examples of *indirect* psycho-emotional disablism which emerge alongside the experience of structural disablism. I will now discuss some examples of these two forms of psycho-emotional disablism using data collected as part of my doctoral research involving people with physical impairments (Reeve 2008b).

Direct psycho-emotional disablism

Hughes (2007) argues that the 'disavowal of disability' can be found in the 'most mundane everyday words or deeds that exclude or invalidate' (Hughes 2007: 682). Invalidation can take various forms: common examples include being stared at by strangers, having jokes made about your impairment or having to deal with the thoughtless comments of others (Reeve 2006, 2008a). Related to being stared at is the opposite – that of being actively avoided because of a prejudice that 'disability is catching'. Adinuf – self-named because he'd 'ad enough – had a chronic illness called Reflex Sympathetic Dystrophy (RSD) and he described how friends would wave when they saw him in the street, but then cross over to avoid talking to him. Once he started using a wheelchair it got worse. Adinuf said:

> They see me coming along in a wheelchair and they're even more frightened. They are literally frightened to death to talk to me then, because they think that they're going to catch something.

Adinuf talked a lot about the hurt he felt at being treated as if he were contagious and being avoided. This prejudice had not been helped by a neighbour spreading the rumour that Adinuf had Acquired Immune Deficiency Syndrome (AIDS). But Adinuf also experienced the reverse of contagion, when a stranger would ask invasive questions about his condition. Ginny, his wife, described how she would try to tread the thin line between remaining polite yet retaining personal control over what was revealed to others. So Ginny described how she would respond to that inevitable question, 'What's wrong with him?'

> 'He's just got a bit of a nerves disease.' 'But what is it?' and I'll say [RSD], 'I've never heard of that!' And I'll go, 'No, well never mind' and I'll walk off and I won't talk to them. 'But what does it *do* to you?'

It can be seen how the questioner keeps on pressing until they get to the 'real' question they want to ask which could be summed up by the 'But what does it *do* to you?' question. The questioner needs to be reassured that Adinuf is not contagious, that it won't happen to them and is a good example of how wheelchair users in particular can 'generate[s] dis-ease in the fully mobile' (Shildrick and Price 1999: 439).

In addition, though, to this psychological 'disavowal of disability' – that is, the projection of the unwanted fears about mortality, dying and physicality onto disabled people (Shakespeare 1994: 298) – Hughes argues that there is an ontological invalidation of disability as a 'worthwhile existential status' (Hughes 2007: 681). So, for example, Laura, who has multiple sclerosis (MS) and who uses a wheelchair, described an all too-common experience on the street:

> Then like a guy walking past me on the street, saying, 'I'd rather be dead than be in one of those' – Well, where do these people get off? All those sort of things can be very disturbing, can't they?

This ontological invalidation undermines psycho-emotional well-being. It is a comment informed by the tragedy myths of disability in our society, and is also seen in the current debates about assisted suicide in the UK. As can be seen here, it was also a comment which Laura found disturbing and difficult to deal with because of the hugely negative value accorded to her life as a wheelchair user – which was in stark contrast to how she saw herself.

In these examples, direct psycho-emotional disablism is experienced at the point that the stranger reacts to the disabled person – either saying something inappropriate or avoiding the disabled person altogether. Being subject to these kinds of comments from strangers can be difficult to deal with and can undermine psycho-emotional well-being. But it is not just the encounter itself that is disabling, there is also the 'existential insecurity' associated with the uncertainty of not knowing how the next stranger will react. This uncertainty further compounds this example of psycho-emotional disablism (see Thomas 2004: 38 for more discussion about existential security).

How people respond to direct psycho-emotional disablism varies with time and place. Although for many people with visible impairments, the experience of being stared at because of a failure to match the cultural 'normate' body/mind can be stigmatizing and judgemental (Garland-Thomson 2009: 87), others are able to resist the normative gaze and to manage the social encounter in productive ways. Sue, who also had MS, used a Zimmer frame to walk outside the house and described how she used her interactions with strangers as a means of education, by challenging assumptions about what disabled people *looked like*. For example, Sue said:

> I don't feel that I am stared at – I don't know, probably I am. I sometimes feel that with my walker, yes, I do feel people watching there. But I don't mind, I think it's something, yes I sort of feel, 'Well it's good for people to see younger people with one'.

In this respect, Sue's pragmatic approach to seeing herself as educating people about what 'disabled people look like', is a way of returning the gaze. For her, it is one way of retaining control over the interaction, refusing to be rendered vulnerable to the stares of strangers. Not all disabled people can respond in this way as it takes a degree of self-worth and self-confidence, as well as energy, to be able to adopt this approach. It is likely that other aspects of Sue's life, such as being in paid employment, contributed to this ability to return the gaze.

One of the difficulties facing disabled people within social interactions is that there is a lack of culturally 'agreed' rules of engagement about how strangers should treat disabled people (Keith 1996: 72). There are cultural rules about commenting on someone's size: it is acceptable to remark how slim someone is, but not to comment that they are fat. When it comes to people with visible impairments, there is often no such restraint as was seen in the case of Adinuf's persistent questioner. Another consequence of the lack of rules of engagement is that, all too often, fear of 'doing the wrong thing' results in avoidance rather than interaction. So often it will be the disabled person who has to 'manage' the interaction with other people by undertaking 'emotion work', be it educating or reassuring the person that they won't catch anything (Reeve 2006, 2008a) – the alternative would be to remain excluded and 'Other'.

A final important example of direct psycho-emotional disablism is that of internalized oppression which arises from the relationship someone has with themselves (Marks 1999). It happens when a disabled person internalizes prejudices about disability, thereby effectively 'invalidating them-selves'. It is not just people who grow up with impairment who find themselves surrounded by a world in which they are not represented as disabled parents, disabled workers or disabled sexual beings. Non-disabled people also internalize norms about disability and so for those people who become disabled in later life one consequence is that they have to overcome their own prejudices about disability, now that they have moved from the included to the excluded group in society. For example, Adinuf described how he 'fought' for two years not to use a wheelchair because of the negative connotations he had internalized about the kinds of people who used wheelchairs – in other words, 'the disabled'. It was only when he fell over in town and people assumed that he was drunk that he started using a wheelchair – being seen as disabled was preferable to being seen as drunk. I will discuss internalized oppression in more detail later in this chapter.

Indirect psycho-emotional disablism

Whilst all these acts of invalidation are examples of *direct* psycho-emotional disablism because they arise from a relationship that the disabled person has with other people or themselves, *indirect* psycho-emotional disablism can arise from the experience of structural disablism. So the experience of being faced with an inaccessible building can evoke an emotional response such as anger or hurt at being excluded. Therefore the act of exclusion operates at both a material and psycho-emotional level because of the message being given to disabled people that reminds them that "'you are out of place", "you are different"' (Kitchin 1998: 351).

Spatial barriers affect disabled people's lives at all levels: inaccessible schools affect education, poor housing restricts choice of where someone lives, lack of transport impacts on employment options, inaccessible public spaces reduce social contact with others. Laura had eventually given up work with the local council because of the environmental barriers she faced at the building where she worked, once her MS had progressed to the point where she needed to use a wheelchair. She described how she got 'flashbacks' about times when she was trying to get into the building when it was raining:

> And not being able to open the doors, waving to people to try and get them to come and open the doors, and you're getting soaking wet. It was amazing how things like that would really – I mean, now I don't let that bother me, but it was all so new then, and distressing, it was really distressing.

The practicalities of learning how to use a wheelchair in everyday life were made more difficult by these access issues and caused her a lot of distress. Laura is describing how her experience of being excluded (structural disablism) also has a psycho-emotional part (indirect psycho-emotional disablism).

Whilst these different examples of (in)direct psycho-emotional disablism may appear as relatively harmless one-off incidents, it needs to be borne in mind that for many disabled people these are experienced on a daily basis. Psycho-emotional disablism impacts on a person's emotional well-being and sense of self and so can have a cumulative negative impact over time on someone's self-esteem and self-confidence (Reeve 2006). However, it is not an inevitable consequence of having an impairment because of the interconnection with other aspects of identity including class, gender, ethnicity, sexuality and age, as well as other life experiences.

Phenomenology and the dys-appearing body

Phenomenological approaches have been central to the development of the sociology of the body, which seeks to overcome the Cartesian mind/body divide by viewing the body instead as both subject/object (Merleau-Ponty 2005 [1962]). The world is perceived through the body; as embodied subjects, experience is not simply an 'inner' phenomenon but is at the same time related to involvement in a world that exists independently of someone's experience of it. In other words, there is a 'lived body' which 'simultaneously experiences and creates the world' (Paterson and Hughes 1999: 601). In *The Absent Body* (1990) Leder uses phenomenological ideas to develop the concept of the 'dys-appearing' body, showing how bodily awareness is absent most of the time (it *dis*appears) and it is only when one experiences pain or stumbles, for example, that the body is suddenly brought to the foreground. The hyphenated term 'dys-appear' is used quite deliberately; although the *dys* part comes from the Greek for 'bad', 'hard' or 'ill' as in 'dysfunctional', in Latin *dys* can mean instead to pull 'away, apart, asunder' (Leder 1990: 87). At times of dys-appearance, whether due to illness or as the result of a changing body during puberty, the body returns to the foreground of awareness at the same time as being experienced as *away or apart* from the self:

> In experiential terms, one becomes aware of the recalcitrant body as separate from and opposed to the 'I'.... The self that takes note of the body remains a moment of the organism, an *embodied* self.
>
> (Leder 1990: 88, emphasis in original)

Leder identifies two different ways that the body can dys-appear. The onset of pain, which is an *intracorporeal* phenomenon, is a reminder of the physicality of our bodies – if I have twisted my ankle I will need to pay attention to how I walk. In contrast, *intercorporeal* phenomena include ways in which the body dys-appears in interactions with the social world – be they people, environments or institutions; for example, wearing the wrong clothes to a social gathering or feeling that one is too thin or too fat.

In addition, the dys-appearance of the body is associated with a 'demand' for attention; looking at one's reflection in the mirror or concentrating on the body during a yoga session are to some extent optional activities whereas the onset of pain or feeling overdressed at a social event brings the body *sharply* into focus. As well as an attentional demand, dys-appearance also disrupts at the existential level because of the way that the body is tied up with self-interpretation.

It is Leder's discussion of social dys-appearance, intercorporeal interactions between the body and the social world, which are of most interest here. Acknowledgement is made of the ways that dys-appearance is linked to aesthetic judgements which in turn are located in particular times and places. The loving look of a partner is different to the hardened stare in the street by a stranger:

> As long as the Other treats me as a subject – that is, experiences *with* me to the world in which I dwell, mutual incorporation effects no sharp rift. But it is different when the primary stance of the Other is highly distanced, antagonistic, or objectifying.
> *(Leder 1990: 96, emphasis in original)*

Like many other phenomenologists, Leder does tend to assume the 'normal and healthy body' (Leder 1990: 86) and therefore to see illness and injury as dys-appearance. (For a thorough critique of phenomenology and impaired bodies, see chapter five in Scully 2008.) However, recognition is made about how ideology and power relations can influence where/when bodies dys-appear. In the case of disabled people, Leder observes that:

> biological dysfunction may inaugurate social dys-appearance, such as is frequently experienced by the handicapped and disabled. The body is at once a biological organism, a ground of personal identity, and a social construct. Disruption *and healing* take place on all these levels, transmitted from one to another by intricate chiasms of exchange.
> *(Leder 1990: 99, my emphasis)*

It is this concept of social dys-appearance and how it is revealed in the everyday lives of disabled people that will feature in the rest of this chapter.

The 'dys-appearing' body: embodied disablism and/or sociology of impairment?

Hughes and Paterson (1997) have turned to phenomenology as a way of retaining the body as a fleshy object. This carnal sociology theorizes 'the body as *the* place where self and society interact' (Goodley 2010: 56, emphasis in original). For some disability studies scholars this represents a way out of the impairment/disability dualism, allowing for an account of an impaired body that has agency and activity and is not simply an object which is acultural and ahistorical (Paterson and Hughes 1999). Subsequently, as part of their continuing project to understand the 'carnal politics of everyday life', Paterson and Hughes (1999) have drawn on the phenomenological concept of the dys-appearing body to add further weight to their arguments, advocating a sociology of impairment.

Paterson and Hughes (1999) provide examples of how disabling barriers of all kinds cause the impaired body to 'dys-appear' – to become the thematic focus of (unwanted) attention.

One can argue – applying Leder – that the disablist and disabling sociospatial environment produces a vivid, but unwanted, consciousness of one's impaired body. Here, the body undergoes a mode of 'dysappearance' which is not biological, but social. For example, in the context of the ubiquitous disabling barriers of the spatial environment, one's impaired body 'dys-appears' – is made present as a thematic focus of attention. When one is confronted by social and physical inaccessibility one is simultaneously confronted by oneself; the external and the internal collide in a moment of simultaneous recognition. When one encounters prejudice in behaviour or attitude, one's impaired body 'dys-appears'.

(Paterson and Hughes 1999: 603)

The examples the two authors give here refer to what I have termed indirect and direct psycho-emotional disablism respectively; therefore the 'dys-appearing' body is also highly pertinent to a discussion of psycho-emotional disablism. At the moment of dys-appearance there is also a psycho-emotional response – which can include feelings of anger, frustration, shame, embarrassment, awkwardness. The previously-absent body comes to the foreground of attention because of the apparent dis-ease in the mind of the stranger, based on myths fuelled by the cultural 'tyranny of perfection' (Glassner 1992, cited in Hughes 1999: 159).

The experience of inaccessible buildings or the thoughtless comments of others can both cause the impaired body to dys-appear and are clearly examples of intercorporeal phenomena. The problem lies with a social and physical world which is set up to accommodate certain kinds of normate bodies; Paterson and Hughes suggest that part of the quest for citizenship is based around creating new environments which are more inclusive of diversity, so that people with impairments are no longer reminded that they are 'Other' each time their bodily difference fails to find a fit. In other words, 'a world in which their bodies do not 'dys-appear' (Paterson and Hughes 1999: 604), a world free from disabling barriers.

Paterson and Hughes use the concept of the dys-appearing body presented in Leder's particular version of phenomenology to support their call for a sociology of impairment which is linked to, but still separate from, disability. This separation has surprised Thomas who points out that:

given their desire to transcend dualisms, Hughes and Paterson present this line of thinking as a route to developing a *social model (or sociology) of impairment* rather than as a route to developing a unified or integrated theorisation of impairment and disability/disablism.

(Thomas 2007: 129, emphasis in original)

Drawing on the examples which Paterson and Hughes use to support a sociology of impairment, I have shown that these can also be described as forms of psycho-emotional disablism. The dys-appearing body can reveal ways in which 'disability is embodied *and* impairment is social' (Hughes and Paterson 1997: 336, my emphasis); this involves considering both disablism and impairment together (rather than either/or), which I will discuss later in this chapter.

Internalized oppression unpacked

I now want to discuss some further examples of psycho-emotional disablism that expand on the points raised by Paterson and Hughes (1999) in their discussion of the dys-appearing body. So far I have considered examples that looked at the dys-appearing body within *intercorporeal* encounters between the disabled person and other people – the invalidating stare or comment. As I indicated earlier, direct psycho-emotional disablism can also occur within the relationship someone has with themselves, in the form of internalized oppression which is very difficult to challenge; it is often only through contact with other disabled people that one sees alternatives to the mainstream cultural lexicon that equate disability with loss and lack. I have written elsewhere (Reeve 2006) about the long-term impact that internalized oppression can have on someone's psycho-emotional well-being, directly restricting the choices about who they can be, such as potential parent, lover, worker, student. This 'false consciousness', to use the Marxist term, represents a state in which the body never dys-appears because the individual has wholly internalized the stereotype, believing that is 'normal' that people like them don't have children for example.

Whilst not advocating that false consciousness is politically desirable for disabled people as a way of life because it is still a form of psycho-emotional disablism, it does have the benefit that one is living in 'blissful ignorance'. The next step towards enlightenment, which in my case was being introduced to the social model of disability, is that of moving into 'double consciousness'. Although this transition marks the first important step towards identifying disabling barriers, it can be quite traumatic:

> While the subject desires recognition as human, capable of activity, full of hope and possibility, she receives from the dominant culture only the judgement that she is different, marked, or inferior.
>
> *(Young 1990: 60)*

The experience of double consciousness, where one is defined by both a dominant and sub-ordinate culture in this way, is what Young calls 'cultural imperialism' (Young 1990: 58–61). This is one of the five faces of oppression faced by people marked as Other (for more information, see chapter two in Young 1990).

In comparison to false consciousness, the experience of double consciousness is associated with *chronic* dys-appearance because of the *continual* 'presence-as-alien-being-in-the-world' (Paterson and Hughes 1999: 603) associated with cultural imperialism. Whereas Paterson and Hughes discuss what I would consider to be forms of direct psycho-emotional disablism that are inter-corporeal and *intersubjective* events, these are discrete – albeit frequent – occurrences. Instead, here I am referring to an experience that is both intercorporeal and *intrasubjective*. A good example of this is provided by Lucy, who had become disabled following a car accident. When she came to marry for the second time she described how she did not feel able to wear a white dress:

LUCY: Because I didn't want to walk down the aisle again, all in my perfect white dress, whatever I chose to wear, realising that I wasn't perfect anymore. Because on your wedding day – I had been married before and it was such a special day and you feel all – and I didn't feel I could do it this time – walk down the aisle and look special, because of my new-found disability.

DONNA: So it wasn't because you were marrying for the second time –

LUCY: No. And I didn't feel perfect anymore, as you do when you're going down the aisle. That was quite an important thing I thought. [cut] I wanted a red dress. I went round everywhere, [friend] went with me – [city name], [city name] – everywhere, couldn't find a red dress.

DONNA: Why red?

LUCY: Because I wanted to be shocking. If everyone was going to look, bloody look at my red dress.

Lucy now walks with a limp and she talked a lot about dealing with people staring at her; so 'walking down the aisle' will be different now that she has an impairment. Lucy has also internalized the prejudice that disabled women are *imperfect* women and she does not feel that she can match up to the image in UK society about brides in long white dresses gliding effortlessly down the aisle. This illustrates a gendered dimension of psycho-emotional disablism because she feels of less value than non-disabled women simply because she now has an impairment. Her solution – or reaction – to this problem is to choose a red dress to shock people, so that they have something else to stare at instead of her limp. Lucy has challenged the conventional image of the blushing bride by choosing a colour which is more usually associated with a brothel than a church, which is her way of dealing with feeling imperfect. Lucy is also using the colour as a way of concealing her impairment, so this is an example of how impairment can interact with psycho-emotional disablism (in this case internalized oppression) and influence the way that someone challenges their internalized oppression.

I would suggest that the red wedding dress can be seen as a form of resistance because Lucy has deliberately stepped outside the social 'norm' that brides wear white by creating her own rules about bridal gowns. Her red dress made her body disappear so that it no longer dys-appeared when seen by others. The red dress as a productive outcome to psycho-emotional disablism can also be seen as an example of how dys-appearance can produce healing rather than disruption (Leder 1990: 99). Similarly, the way in which Sue described earlier how she used her encounters with strangers as a way to educate them about what about what disabled people 'look like' could also be considered as a healing outcome of dys-appearance.

The term 'internalized oppression' tends to incorporate both these understandings of oppression – false consciousness and 'double consciousness' – which I have tried to untangle here as part of the process of understanding the different actions of direct psycho-emotional disablism. In reality one may experience false consciousness in some areas of life and be troubled by double consciousness in others. I would also suggest that people who seek to educate people with impairments about disablism need to remain alert to the emotional distress double consciousness can cause. Whilst disability equality training can be empowering, the 'road to Damascus' is not an easy path to take. In the same way that an abused child finds it easier to blame themselves than their parent (Miller 1991), it can be easier to believe that exclusion from the social world is because of personal impairment rather than a society that makes normative bodies and minds the necessary passport for full inclusion. Finally, it could be argued that the term 'internalized ableism' is a better term than 'internalized oppression' because it specifically draws attention to the ableist stereotypes impacting on the lives of people with impairments (for more information, see chapter two in Campbell 2009).

(Re)producing the disabled subject

Up to this point I have been discussing examples where the dys-appearing body was related to finding oneself 'out of place' when failing to meet the carnal norms of an ableist world. I now want to consider the creation of disabled bodies when claiming disability related benefits and other concessions such as disabled parking badges (Porter 2000; Shildrick 1997). Disability Living Allowance (DLA) provides money for helping disabled people with their mobility and personal care needs. As part of the application process the claimant is required to report in detail how their body fails to meet the 'norm' and a successful claim is more likely if the language used matches that recognized by the government agency (Daly and Noble 1996). The claimant is (re) producing the disabled subject and consequently only certain bodies and minds are considered as 'disabled' and eligible for benefits. Similarly, when using accessible toilets and parking spaces that are marked with the universal wheelchair symbol, those who fail to match the stereotypical image of disability can be challenged by others over their right to use these reserved facilities. It has been argued that the current wheelchair symbol is problematic as a representation for disability because it reinforces a very narrow view of what disabled people 'look like' and ends up separating wheelchair users from other people with impairments who also need to use these facilities (Bichard *et al.* 2007).

As part of the process of creating culturally recognizable 'disabled bodies', the disabled person is required to foreground their impairment, to make their own body dys-appear. So, for example, someone may 'limp worse' in order to prove their right to park in an accessible space and to avoid being challenged by a passing stranger. Lucy explained:

> I limp worse when I get out the car than I do normally [laughs] just to show people that I have got a disability, I can park in the bay. [cut] That's deliberate. It's probably subconscious now, but in the beginning [after the accident] it was deliberate. Because my husband's noticed it – because he says, 'What's the matter with you today?' And I say, 'Nothing'. 'Oh, alright then'. And then I forget and start walking then, once I've passed the bay, and people look [laughs].

Here Lucy is describing a deliberate performance that she undertakes to assert her identity and rights as a 'real' disabled person; however, this performance is 'leaky' and incomplete when she fails to maintain the limp until she gets into the shop and she becomes re-subject to the judgemental gaze of others. Similarly, when claiming sickness benefit one has to reproduce the incapable body/mind and to identify as a disabled person incapable of work (Price and Shildrick 1998). It can be psychologically difficult to have to describe oneself in terms of the medical and deficit discourses which underscore the application process.

As I indicated above, being forced to define oneself in terms of what one is *unable* to do, impacts on psycho-emotional well-being. In some cases being forced to describe the details of impairment can make it temporarily worse as the person becomes what they have described (Reeve 2008b); this is particularly true for some people with mental health difficulties who have been advised to be positive about what they *can* do in order to manage their symptoms. Mental health difficulties are often fluctuating and are much more complicated to 'measure' than physical or sensory impairment. The stress and anxiety of going through the benefit application process can make mental health worse, particularly as the new Work Capability Assessment (which forms part of the Employment Support Allowance that has replaced Incapacity Benefit since 2008) has been described as being:

> so riven with faults that it's hard to see what kind of mental illness would, under its terms, actually qualify someone for help.
>
> *(Williams 2011: np)*

Having to reconstruct oneself as disabled can therefore make impairment temporarily worse as one is forced to produce the dys-appearing body/mind within a harsh welfare system situated in a culture which labels disabled people as lazy or fraudulent.

(Re)producing the 'normal' subject

Finally, another example of how the dys-appearing body can be more consciously foregrounded occurs when passing – adopting 'norms' of behaviour and movement and 'passing' as non-disabled. In this example of social dys-appeance the body:

incorporates an alien gaze, away, apart, asunder, from one's own, which provokes an explicit thematization of the body.

(Leder 1990: 99)

In other words, the body is behaving according to cultural norms of able-bodiedness rather than being free to adopt any mode of behaviour and movement that is 'normal for them'. This can protect someone with invisible impairments from experiencing the kinds of invalidation that those with visible impairments (and/or impairment effects (Thomas 2007: 135–7)) experience, such as being avoided or stared at. However, there is always the risk that their disability status will be revealed, in turn risking psycho-emotional disablism when their body dys-appears as they become subject to the prejudiced comments of strangers. This gives rise to the 'negative psycho-emotional aspects of concealment' (Thomas 1999: 55). Similarly, Lingsom (2008) argues that people with invisible impairments occupy a highly vulnerable position because they are continually managing whether to conceal or disclose information about their impairment. If someone chooses to pass as 'normal' then they will be expected by others to conform to conventional norms of behaviour and stamina – which can be particularly difficult if an invisible impairment is fatigue.

There can be difficulties disclosing an invisible impairment; for example a young person with a stroke may be disbelieved because this is 'seen' as an impairment affecting only older people. It can also be difficult to convince others about the reality of some impairments such as pain and fatigue, a problem faced particularly by people with chronic illness (Wendell 2001). As mentioned previously, people with invisible impairments may also be challenged when attempting to use facilities reserved for disabled people because they do not match the stereotypical image of someone who is elderly and/or a wheelchair user. Therefore, like Lucy who will 'limp worse', they may choose to use a stick, to adopt a visible marker of impairment, in order to use these facilities without harassment – but this may also have an emotional cost in publicly identifying as disabled (Reeve 2002).

Leder (1990) argues that dys-appearance makes demands on both the attention and existential levels because of the way in which the body is tied up with self-interpretation. So it could be suggested that passing and exposure are both forms of dys-appearance because of the impact they have on self-identity as disabled, non-disabled or something in between. In addition, when someone adopts a visible marker of impairment without seeing themselves as a disabled person, this act risks producing a conflicted self because:

[t]he deployment of the denotation of disability strategically cannot be undertaken without some incorporation of internalised ableism, either at a conscious or at an unconscious level.

(Campbell 2009: 28)

So whether someone is describing themselves in terms of the medical format of benefit application forms or will 'limp worse' when using an accessible parking space, then they risk internalizing the culturally informed 'disabled' identity that they are performing.

The role of impairment in experiences of psycho-emotional disablism

Although someone needs to have (or have had) a perceived impairment in order to experience disablism, the social model of disability otherwise cleaves the experience of disability from that of impairment. The original UPIAS statement which underpins the conventional social model understanding of disability clearly states that:

[d]isability is something imposed *on top of our impairments* by the way we are unnecessarily isolated and excluded from full participation in society.

(UPIAS 1976: 14, my emphasis)

This has been politically very useful for challenging structural disablism by 'fixing' society, not the individual. Another consequence of the clear separation of disablism from impairment has been the assumption that 'disabled people share a common experience of oppression, regardless of impairment' (Shakespeare 2006a: 31). However, disabled people do not share a common experience of disablism: factors including class, age, sexuality, gender and ethnicity all impact on the consequences of impairment and therefore on the social and economic experience of disability (Shakespeare 1996).

Within disability studies, the impaired body has been receiving more attention from a variety of theoretical angles (for a more detailed discussion, see other chapters in this book as well as chapter five in Thomas 2007). For the remainder of this chapter I want to consider the interplay between psycho-emotional disablism and impairment. This is an initial attempt to respond to the following statement:

I have come to recognise that psycho-emotional disablism – both its enactment and its effects – should be thought about as fully embodied. This form of disablism should not be treated as one that operates simply at the level of mind or consciousness.

(Thomas 2007: 152)

I have used the dys-appearing body to illustrate how psycho-emotional disablism is embodied as well as social and political, that 'disability is embodied' (Hughes and Paterson 1997: 336). The accounts of people like Lucy and Adinuf reveal how impairment/impairment effects and the experience of disablism are intertwined and can impact on each other. I have shown how the experience of psycho-emotional disablism can make impairment worse. Similarly the physical difficulties caused by negotiating an inaccessible environment (structural disablism) can also make impairment worse (Crow 1996).

I now want to take a step further by suggesting that psycho-emotional disablism allows an insight into the ways that impairment and disablism can be interconnected in more subtle ways. I need to stress that I am *NOT* suggesting that impairment *causes* disablism, but I want to suggest that the manner in which psycho-emotional disablism is enacted – the kinds of disablist comments and treatment that someone receives – is often associated with the type of impairment and impairment effects that are visible/known to the other person. (This is not denying that someone with an invisible impairment can also experience psycho-emotional disablism if they find themselves, for example, in a group of people who are making jokes about that particular impairment.) Psycho-emotional disablism is critically associated with the cultural representations of disability within the media and wider society. I discussed earlier how fears of contamination or beliefs about the inability or undesirability of impaired bodies underpin the invalidating responses of others towards people with impairments. The strong connection between cultural stereotypes and oppression was discussed earlier with reference to cultural imperialism, which is kept in place by stereotypes that are so embedded in culture that they go unnoticed and unchallenged (Young 1990). For example, the ubiquitous wheelchair symbol ends up reinforcing the hegemony of particular kinds of impaired bodies which will be accommodated and recognized as 'disabled'.

Watson (2003) highlights the importance of understanding the processes whereby prejudice, and therefore oppressive stereotypes, are maintained and reproduced within contemporary culture, society and practices. As I discussed earlier, it is in the everyday interpersonal interactions that much psycho-emotional disablism is enacted, based on prejudice and stereotypes. If psycho-emotional disablism is embodied, then it could be predicted that prejudice (which leads to disablism) is influenced by perceived impairment – that psycho-emotional disablism takes different forms depending on what is known/visible to the other (non) disabled person. For example whilst I am stared at by people because I walk differently with two sticks, I am not subject to the kinds of 'souvenir photography' that Shakespeare (2006b) experiences – because we have very different impairments.

Analysis of the 2009 British Social Attitudes Survey showed that the assumption that people hold either 'negative' or 'positive' attitudes towards disabled people was not borne out by the data. Instead, attitudes were related to the perceived impairment:

> Respondents' demographic characteristics interact with both the situation in which a disabled person is encountered, and *the impairment that they have*, in influencing the attitudes people hold.
>
> *(Staniland 2011: 72, my emphasis)*

People were much more likely to be prejudiced towards people with learning difficulties or mental health difficulties than those with physical or sensory impairments. Similarly, the former two groups of disabled people experience a disproportionately higher rate of disablist hate crime compared to other groups of disabled people (Sin *et al.* 2009); this is not surprising if disablist hate crime is seen as an extreme form of direct psycho-emotional disablism. Prejudices about disabled people are based around hierarchies of impairment which are rooted in cultural myths about disability (Tregaskis 2003). This differentiation of the relative value of disabled people by impairment type is also reflected in the prejudices held by disabled people (Deal 2003). Deal points out that disabled people need to acknowledge their own prejudices before they can demand a wholly inclusive society because hierarchies of impairment end up further isolating and oppressing those disabled people perceived to be towards the bottom end of the hierarchy. This process can be complicated because people who acquire impairments in adulthood have to deal with the shift from being 'normal' to 'Other', which entails shifting internalized stereotypes and dealing with guilt when they reflect on how they themselves used to view disabled people in the past (Reeve 2008b).

Conclusion

In this chapter I have provided an introduction to psycho-emotional disablism and showed how it can impact on the emotional well-being and self-identity of disabled people. As psycho-emotional disablism is enacted at the inter/intra-personal level, it is beneficial to locate the analysis at the point where the 'cultural constructions of disability and impairment are played out within and through the body' (Goodley 2010: 56). To that end I have explored how the phenomenological concept of social dys-appearance highlights the embodied nature of psycho-emotional disablism and the manner in which it is mediated by impairment and impairment effects via the operation of cultural prejudices about disability.

Whilst the 'arid materialism of disability studies' (Paterson and Hughes 1999: 599) has been very effective at challenging structural disablism, it quite deliberately does not engage with impairment and so does not allow for any theoretical engagement with the lived body. In response, some would argue that phenomenology has little to offer disability studies because it only provides interactionist accounts of living with impairment (Barnes and Mercer 2010). The continued 'stubbornness of the "real" body' (Thomas 2007: 128) cannot be ignored when analysing psycho-emotional disablism because of the way in which impairment and prejudice are interlinked within the cultural lexicon. Therefore, I have used phenomenology as a way of providing insight into psycho-emotional disablism which retains an interconnection with the realities of living with physical impairment and experiencing disablism.

Although much progress has been made in removing sources of structural disablism, the prevalence of prejudice about disability in mainstream society and culture means that psycho-emotional disablism will be much harder to eradicate. For example, disabled people are reporting increased rates of discrimination and harassment which are directly linked to the rhetoric about disability benefits in the media (Scope 2011); psycho-emotional disablism, like the fleshiness of the lived body, is still very much alive and kicking. This is not surprising given that cultural imperialism is a key component of psycho-emotional disablism. Therefore even when legislation and policy exist to protect disabled people, oppression continues to operate via:

> informal, often unnoticed and reflective speech, bodily reactions to others, conventional practices of everyday interactions and evaluation, aesthetic judgments and the jokes, images, and stereotypes pervading the mass media.
>
> *(Young 1990: 148)*

This goes someway to explaining why psycho-emotional disablism is still a problem facing disabled people in the UK even after more than 15 years of the Disability Discrimination Act. Therefore psycho-emotional disablism is important – it is not just a 'personal trouble' but needs to be seen as a public issue caused by the ableism endemic in our society.

References

Barnes, C. and Mercer, G. (2010) *Exploring Disability: A Sociological Introduction*, 2nd edn (Cambridge: Polity Press).

Bichard, J.-A., Coleman, R. and Langdon, P. (2007) 'Does My Stigma Look Big in This? Considering Acceptability and Desirability in the Inclusive Design of Technology Products', *Universal Access in Human Computer Interaction: Coping with Diversity, Part 1* 4554: 622–31.

Campbell, F. A. K. (2009) *Contours of Ableism: The Production of Disability and Abledness* (Basingstoke: Palgrave Macmillan).

Crow, L. (1996) 'Including All of Our Lives: Renewing the Social Model of Disability', in J. Morris, ed., *Encounters with Strangers: Feminism and Disability* (London: Women's Press): pp. 206–26.

Daly, M. and Noble, M. (1996) 'The Reach of Disability Benefits: An Examination of the Disability Living Allowance', *Journal of Social Welfare and Family Law* 18(1): 37–51.

Deal, M. (2003) 'Disabled People's Attitudes Toward Other Impairment Groups: A Hierarchy of Impairments', *Disability & Society* 18(7): 897–910.

Garland-Thomson, R. (2009) *Staring: How We Look* (Oxford: Oxford University Press).

Glassner, B. (1992) *Bodies: The Tyranny of Perfection* (Los Angeles: Lowell House).

Goodley, D. (2010) *Disability Studies: An Interdisciplinary Approach* (London: Sage).

Hughes, B. (1999) 'The Constitution of Impairment: Modernity and the Aesthetic of Oppression', *Disability & Society* 14(2): 155–72.

Hughes, B. (2007) 'Being Disabled: Towards a Critical Social Ontology for Disability Studies', *Disability & Society* 22(7): 673–84.

Hughes, B. and Paterson, K. (1997) 'The Social Model of Disability and the Disappearing Body: Towards a Sociology of Impairment', *Disability & Society* 12(3): 325–40.

Hunt, P., ed., (1966) *Stigma: The Experience of Disability* (London: Geoffrey Chapman).

Keith, L. (1996) 'Encounters with Strangers: The Public's Responses to Disabled Women and How this Affects Our Sense of Self', in J. Morris, ed., *Encounters with Strangers: Feminism and Disability* (London: Women's Press): pp. 69–88.

Kitchin, R. (1998) '"Out of Place", "Knowing One's Place": Space, Power and the Exclusion of Disabled People', *Disability & Society* 13(3): 343–56.

Leder, D. (1990) *The Absent Body* (Chicago, IL: University of Chicago Press).

Lingsom, S. (2008) 'Invisible Impairments: Dilemmas of Concealment and Disclosure', *Scandinavian Journal of Disability Research* 10(1): 2–16.

Marks, D. (1999) *Disability: Controversial Debates and Psychosocial Perspectives* (London: Routledge).

Merleau-Ponty, M. (2005 [1962]) *The Phenomenology of Perception*, trans. C. Smith (London: Routledge).

Miller, A. (1991) *The Drama of Being a Child*, trans. R. Ward (London: Virago Press).

Paterson, K. and Hughes, B. (1999) 'Disability Studies and Phenomenology: The Carnal Politics of Everyday Life', *Disability & Society* 14(5): 597–610.

Porter, A. (2000) 'Playing the "Disabled Role" in Local Travel', *Area* 32(1): 41–8.

Price, J. and Shildrick, M. (1998) 'Uncertain Thoughts on the Dis/abled Body', in M. Shildrick and J. Price, eds, *Vital Signs: Feminist Reconfigurations of the Bio/logical Body* (Edinburgh: Edinburgh University Press): pp. 224–49.

Reeve, D. (2002) 'Negotiating Psycho-emotional Dimensions of Disability and their Influence on Identity Constructions', *Disability & Society* 17(5): 493–508.

Reeve, D. (2006) 'Towards a Psychology of Disability: The Emotional Effects of Living in a Disabling Society', in D. Goodley and R. Lawthom, eds, *Disability and Psychology: Critical Introductions and Reflections* (London: Palgrave): pp. 94–107.

Reeve, D. (2008a) 'Biopolitics and Bare Life: Does the Impaired Body Provide Contemporary Examples of Homo Sacer?' in K. Kristiansen, S. Vehmas and T. Shakespeare, eds, *Arguing about Disability: Philosophical Perspectives* (London: Routledge): pp. 203–217.

Reeve, D. (2008b) *'Negotiating Disability in Everyday Life: The Experience of Psycho-Emotional Disablism'*, PhD thesis (Lancaster: Lancaster University).

Scope (2011) *Deteriorating Attitudes Towards Disabled People*, available online at http://www.scope.org.uk/news/attitudes-towards-disabled-people-survey (accessed 25 July 2011).

Scully, J. L. (2008) *Disability Bioethics: Moral Bodies, Moral Difference* (Lanham, MA: Rowman & Littlefield Publishers).

Shakespeare, T. (1994) 'Cultural Representation of Disabled People: Dustbins for Disavowal?' *Disability & Society* 9(3): 283–99.

Shakespeare, T. (1996) 'Disability, Identity, Difference', in C. Barnes and G. Mercer, eds, *Exploring the Divide: Illness and Disability* (Leeds: The Disability Press): pp. 94–113.

Shakespeare, T. (2006a) *Disability Rights and Wrongs* (Abingdon: Routledge).

Shakespeare, T. (2006b) *Snap Unhappy*; available online at http://www.bbc.co.uk/ouch/features/snap_unhappy.shtml (accessed 27 July 2011).

Shildrick, M. (1997) *Leaky Bodies and Boundaries: Feminism, Postmodernism and (Bio)ethics* (London: Routledge).

Shildrick, M. and Price, J. (1999) 'Breaking the Boundaries of the Broken Body', in J. Price and M. Shildrick, eds, *Feminist Theory and the Body* (Edinburgh: Edinburgh University Press): pp. 432–44.

Sin, C. H., Hedges, A., Cook, C., Mguni, N. and Comber, N. (2009) *Disabled People's Experiences of Targeted Violence and Hostility (Research Report 21)* (Manchester: Office for Public Management).

Staniland, L. (2011) *Public Perceptions of Disabled People: Evidence from the British Social Attitudes Survey 2009* (London: ODI).

Thomas, C. (1999) *Female Forms: Experiencing and Understanding Disability* (Buckingham: Open University Press).

Thomas, C. (2004) 'Developing the Social Relational in the Social Model of Disability: A Theoretical Agenda', in C. Barnes and G. Mercer, eds, *Implementing the Social Model of Disability: Theory and Research* (Leeds: The Disability Press): pp. 32–47.

Thomas, C. (2007) *Sociologies of Disability and Illness: Contested Ideas in Disability Studies and Medical Sociology* (Basingstoke: Palgrave Macmillan).

Tregaskis, C. (2003) *Constructions of Disability: Researching Inclusion in Community Leisure* (London: Routledge).

UPIAS (1976) *Fundamental Principles of Disability* (London: Union of the Physically Impaired Against Segregation and The Disability Alliance).

Watson, N. (2003) 'Daily Denials: The Routinisation of Oppression and Resistance', in S. Riddell and N. Watson, eds, *Disability, Culture and Identity* (London: Longman): pp. 34–52.

Wendell, S. (2001) 'Unhealthy Disabled: Treating Chronic Illnesses as Disabilities', *Hypatia* 16(4): 17–33.

Williams, Z. (2011) 'It's the Tests that Deceive, Not the People Claiming Benefits, *The Guardian*, 10 March; available online at http://www.guardian.co.uk/commentisfree/2011/mar/10/tests-deceive-benefits-mental-illness (accessed 25 July 2011).

Young, I. M. (1990) *Justice and the Politics of Difference* (Princeton, NJ: Princeton University Press).

8

RESEARCHING DISABLEMENT

Nick Watson

Introduction

Disability studies in the United Kingdom (UK), North America and elsewhere was founded not in wonder or out of curiosity but in anger by disabled people who were dissatisfied with the way that society treated them and the limited opportunities that they were afforded. Importantly, this anger was directed not just at society and its exclusionary practices but also at the way that the social sciences in general and medical sociology in particular constructed disability and disabled people, the way that the social sciences researched disability and the way that they presented the problems faced by disabled people. The emergence of disability studies as a discipline in its own right and the research activities and practices associated with the topic, in particular emancipatory research (Oliver 1992), suggest that this is an area where a sound research base has been developing hand in hand with the subject. However, as this chapter will argue, if the research task of disability studies is to emerge as more than evaluation of policy and practice for disabled people and as more than sociology, social policy, politics or economics with a disability theme or angle, and make a contribution to the emancipation of disabled people, then considerable practical and theoretical problems arise. In, for example, work on direct payments or employment for disabled people it is sometimes difficult to identify meaningful research (as against evaluation) questions (Kelly 1989).

This chapter aims to present an overview of how disability studies has developed its research agenda and what has influenced this development. It starts out with a very brief overview of where disability studies first engaged with research on disability. It then moves on to examine emancipatory research – the research agenda most strongly linked with disability studies and participatory research. The next section presents a critique of the emancipatory research paradigm and the chapter finishes with suggestions for further development of research on disability, drawing on the ideas of critical realism.

Background: researching disability

One of the most influential texts on researching disabilities, albeit unwittingly, was Eric Miller and Geraldine Gwynne's study of life in residential homes, *A Life Apart: A Pilot Study of Residential Institutions for the Physically Handicapped and the Young Chronic Sick*, first published in 1972. The research on which the book is based was initially instigated at the behest of Paul Hunt and other residents from the Le Court Home, a care home run by the Leonard Cheshire Foundation. Hunt and his colleagues were unhappy at the lack of choice and control in their lives and their denial of representation on the management of the home. They cited these issues when they persuaded Miller and Gwynne, two academics from the Tavistock, London, of the need for this research (Hunt 1981). They hoped that the research would provide an insight into what it was like to live in a residential institution for physically disabled people and be segregated from the mainstream of society, and to present their side of the argument – a perspective that they felt was lacking in much of the available literature at the time. Their hope was that Miller and Gwynne, as experts in group dynamics, would be sympathetic to their wish for more control in their lives and support their desire for greater involvement in the management of the Home. What they got was a report that, in an attempt to present a 'balanced', 'objective' and 'detached' account, failed to endorse their perspective. Whilst Miller and Gwynne suggested that the institutional life was a 'living death' (p. 13), rather than challenge this they felt that one of the key roles of the care home was to prepare the residents for their actual death. Hunt and others in the home saw *A Life Apart* as biased and a betrayal of their trust (1981).

Miller and Gwynne, as Marks (1999) among others has argued, adopted the approach of many social scientists, health and social care professionals and those from the psychology profession. Namely, they used their research and the experience of those they researched not to help empower those they worked with, but rather to support their own professional interests. Furthermore, they justified their approach by arguing that any other conclusions would not be scientifically valid and would be open to challenge on the grounds of academic rigour.

The book and its findings were widely disputed by many of those who lived in the care sector and by disabled people from across the UK. So Barton writes:

> Criticisms of such research included their misunderstanding of the nature of disability, their distortion of the experience of disability, their failure to involve disabled people and the lack of any real improvements in the quality of life of disabled people that they have produced.
>
> *(Barton 1992: 99)*

Hunt and his colleagues responded to the book both politically and intellectually and the publication became a mobilizing device that played its part in the founding of the Union of the Physically Impaired Against Segregation (UPIAS). In their document *The Fundamental Principles of Disablement*, not only did UPIAS set in place the ideas for the social model of disability, they also laid the foundations for what Mike Oliver later came to call the *Emancipatory Research Paradigm*. In this document they argued:

> Any scientist, seeking to deal effectively with a problem, knows that the cause must first be identified. Therefore, if disability is a social condition then an analysis of the ways in which society actually disables physically impaired people is obviously required before the condition can be eliminated. To persist in concentrating on the effects, on the other hand, is to divert attention from the real problems; and in fact it entrenches disability even further by seeking its remedy in the opposite direction from the social cause by concentrating on the assessment of the individual.
>
> *(UPIAS 1976: 13)*

It is to a brief discussion of this paradigm that this chapter now turns.

Emancipatory research

Drawing on and developing the ideas of Hunt and his colleagues in UPIAS, Oliver (1992), Barnes (1990) and others from within disability studies in the UK and beyond (Rioux and Bach 1994) challenged not only the way that disability itself is theorized but also the methods employed in academic research on disability. They argued that previous research had failed to fully capture the experiences of disability from the perspectives of disabled people, that it had not provided policy makers with ideas that could improve the material conditions under which disabled people lived and had failed to acknowledge the struggles of disabled people themselves. At the root of this was the belief that disability was a political as well as a medical or welfare issue.

Scholars in disability studies pointed to the divide between those who are researched ('the subjects'), and those who research ('the researchers'), and the power imbalance that this creates. They argued that researchers are able to control the design, the implementation, the analysis and the dissemination of their work and highlighted disabled people's lack of control and involvement in the overall research process (Barnes and Mercer 1997). This serves to promote an epistemology that reasserts an essentialist divide between disabled and non-disabled people, between the researched and the researcher. They questioned the usefulness of research and the motives of academics (Oliver 1992; Barnes and Mercer 1997). In a controversial and acerbic attack on research into disability, Oliver (1992) condemned much previous mainstream research on disability as a 'rip off'.

In this paper Oliver directly challenged the work of Miller and Gwynne and in doing so laid down the terms for emancipatory research. He argued that Miller and Gwynne and others' research had failed to address the social oppression faced by disabled people or to establish an alternative social policy that might bring about an improvement in the lives of disabled people. For Oliver:

> Disability research should not be seen as a set of technical objective procedures carried out by 'experts' but part of the struggle by disabled people to challenge the oppression they currently experience in their lives.
>
> *(Oliver 1992: 102)*

Oliver combined the ideas of Hunt and his colleagues with the evolving 'critical social research' paradigm of feminist writers such as Lather (1987) and Ribbens (1990) and developed a model of research that argued for an emancipatory approach. So he wrote:[1]

> The development of such a paradigm stems from the gradual rejection of the positivist view of social research as the pursuit of absolute knowledge through the scientific method and the gradual disillusionment with the interpretative view of such research as the generation of socially useful knowledge within particular historical and social contexts. The emancipatory paradigm, as the name implies, is about the facilitating of a politics of the possible by confronting social oppression at whatever level it occurs.
>
> *(Oliver 1992: 110)*

These developments mirrored similar moves in research on ethnicity and on other oppressed groups which emerged at roughly the same time (Truman *et al.*, 2000).

The emancipatory research paradigm has become, after the social model, the second clarion call of the discipline. Rules setting out what constitutes acceptable practice for disability research have been laid down. For example, Stone and Priestley identified six core principles:

1   the adoption of the social model of disability as the ontological and epistemological basis for research production;
2   the surrender to falsely premised claims to objectivity through overt political commitment to the struggles of disabled people for self-emancipation;
3   the willingness only to undertake research where it will be of some benefit to the self-empowerment of disabled people and/or the removal of disabling barriers;
4   the devolution of control over research production to ensure full accountability to disabled people and their organisations;
5   the ability to give voice to the personal whilst endeavouring to collectivise the commonalty of disabling experiences and barriers; and
6   the willingness to adopt a plurality of methods for data collection and analysis in response to the changing needs of disabled people.

(1996: 706)

Similarly Barnes (2003), in a review of emancipatory research ten years after its development, argued that that for research to be emancipatory it had to:

1   Be accountable to disabled people and their organisations
2   Place the social model at the heart of the research agenda
3   Be politically committed to the emancipation of disabled people
4   Be relevant and produce research that has a meaningful practical outcome for disabled people.

Whilst Oliver (1997, 1999) became increasingly critical of the emancipatory research paradigm towards the end of his career, and others such as Shakespeare (2006) and Danieli and Woodhams (2005) have been questioned its suitability as a research methodology, emancipatory research still holds sway in disability research today. For example recently writers have argued that an emancipatory paradigm is still needed and that it enables the use of innovative research methods (Hodge 2008) and ensures that research is accessible (Garbutt 2009), whilst Priestley *et al.* (2010) have restated its centrality to research on disability policy.

Participatory research

Participatory research, sometimes referred to as inclusive research, action research or co-production, has also played a central part in disability studies, particularly in research with people with a learning disability. The aim of this paradigm is to include people as more than just subjects or objects of research and according to Walmsley (2004) it can be traced back to the work of Margaret Flynn (1986) and Dorothy Atkinson (1989). These were among the first researchers to actually include the testimony of people with a learning disability in their research and to document the methodological implications of their work. Whilst participatory research has been seen by some as part of the move towards emancipatory research (Zarb 1992), others have argued that its use reflects the difficulty of realizing emancipatory research with people with a learning difficulty (Walmsley 2010). There are, according to Stalker (1998), three main assumptions common to both emancipatory and participatory approaches to research:

first, that conventional research relationships, whereby the researcher is the 'expert' and the researched merely the object of investigation, are inequitable; secondly, that people have the right to be consulted about and involved in research which is concerned with issues affecting their lives; and thirdly, that the quality and relevance of research is improved when disabled people are closely involved in the process.

(Stalker 1998: 6)

In participatory research the actual process of research is seen as more than just a means of collecting data; taking part in research becomes a source of validation for those who participate (Reason and Heron 1986). There are many examples in the literature to support these claims (see for example Docherty *et al.* 2006).

Participatory research has been criticized by some researchers within disability studies for reinforcing the researcher/researched divide and failing to challenge, confront or change oppressive structures and practices. It has also been criticized for its potential to open up those who are researched to even greater surveillance (Baistow 1994).

Having examined briefly the main ideas that have driven disability research in the last 20 or so years this chapter now moves on to address some of the problems with research on disability. The structure of this next section draws heavily on a paper published by Mike Kelly in 1989 called *Some Problems with Health Promotion Research* and the debt owed to that paper is acknowledged here.

Some problems with disability research

In its attempts to engage with the demands of the disabled people's movement and to align itself with disability activists and meet the demands laid down by the emancipatory research paradigm, disability studies has adopted a largely idealistic, ideological and programmatic approach to research on disability. The focus of disability studies has become one of challenging and removing the barriers that disabled people face and ensuring that disabled people have equal access to, for example, housing, income, education, employment, social justice and equity. Under the influence of the emancipatory research paradigm, research has been directed at achieving these aims. The principle means of achieving them are, as Oliver (1990) Barnes and Mercer (2010) and others make clear, political. Disability must be seen as a political and social rather than medical issue; the problems faced by disabled people can be solved through the development of appropriate policies that allow for enablement through which disabled people can achieve their fullest potential. Anti-discrimination legislation that aims to remove the barriers faced by disabled people is seen as central to any such approach, as is the creation of policies such as those promoted by the Independent Living Movement (ILM) that support disabled people and enable their participation in the mainstream of society (Morris 2006). These ideals of improvement and change, along with a political programme, are juxtaposed to provide a *de facto* definition of what constitutes disability research.

The agenda has become one where the aim is to highlight and provide evidence for the multiple and significant social inequalities that exist between disabled and non-disabled people and the systematic and institutional discrimination they face in their day-to-day lives (Barnes and Mercer 2010). However, disability research goes further than just documenting these discriminatory practices, attitudes and structures; it is about working with disabled people and aiding in their politicizing and mobilizing, providing evidence for altering the *status quo* and pointing hopefully to some future better state.

These aims are, of course, worthy and important and are hard to disagree with. However, they do create problems and their sheer scope makes the translation of such ideals into a research agenda problematic, as Oliver has acknowledged (1997, 1999). Furthermore, they make a huge demand for disability related research in a wide variety of domains and the question posed by Barnes' and others' writings on discrimination is whether disability studies can meet the demands of research in all these disparate areas. One of the underlying themes that is seen as identifying disability studies research is that the work should be of practical benefit to disabled people as opposed to purely theoretical and that the involvement of disabled people is essential.

The difficulties inherent in transforming political objectives into researchable issues have not been confined to disability studies. For example in their review of emancipatory research, Danieli and Woodhams (2005), citing the work of Acker *et al.* (1991), argue that feminist research has questioned the usefulness of emancipatory research as a research paradigm. In his review of health promotion research, Kelly (1989) identified three key problems: translating ideals into research questions, the role of social science and the involvement of people in the setting of priorities. All of these are equally applicable to emancipatory research and are taken up in the next section of this chapter.

First, ideals and demands of the disabled people's movement, for example the removal of disabling barriers, do not translate easily into research questions. This problem is highlighted by research carried out in the early 1990s by Barnes and Zarb, who undertook a research project, Measuring Disablement in Society. This project aimed to provide a systematic empirical analysis of the barriers faced by disabled people and it ran into many difficulties which both Barnes (1995) and Zarb (1997), in their overviews of the project, are quick to acknowledge. Barnes concluded that whilst, for example, physical access can be measured, other issues, which Thomas (1999) later came to call psycho-emotional disabalism, cannot. The research also bracketed differences found between different groups of disabled people, and the intersection of disability with, for example, ethnicity, sexuality, gender and the different ways disabled people experience capitalism was also difficult to research.

Further research under this paradigm has the potential to become a self-fulfilling prophecy and there is a danger that disability research stops looking at what people are saying and looks instead for evidence that supports the social model. Finkelstein (1996), for example, has argued that unless the focus of research is on 'dismantling the real disabling barriers "out there"' (p. 34), a 'discredited and sterile approach to understanding and changing the world' is produced. He suggests that any other approach diverts attention from the causes of disablement, confining political action to personal experience and preventing disabled people from forming alliances with other oppressed groups (p. 36). If this method is adopted there is a real danger of what Kelly (1989) describes as the 'is' and the 'ought to be' becoming conflated with the answers to the research questions predetermined by ideological beliefs.

Second, disability studies covers the whole range of the social sciences. Other social and political scientists do write on disability and the question is what defines disability studies research and what defines sociology and politics. Furthermore, if sociologists and other social scientists can do this, is there any special need for disability studies? There is much debate within disability studies about what constitutes the subject, as Goodley (2010) has recently argued, and there is a danger that we will reject some of these important ideals out of hand because they do not follow the tightly held beliefs laid down by the emancipatory research paradigm.

Third, while participation by disabled people is held up as a cornerstone of disability studies, the obvious question is to what extent have disabled people been consulted in the setting up of priorities put forward in disability research? The answer is they have not and instead disability scholars and activists have assumed that role (Kitchen 2000). This problem is further muddied by the fact that it is difficult to define who disabled people are; many people who are disabled do not see themselves as disabled (Watson 2002) and research shows that in the UK many people covered by the Disability Discrimination Act (DDA) do not consider themselves to be covered by that Act (Hurstfield *et al.* 2004). The DDA and Americans with Disabilities Act (ADA) now include cover for people with cancer, but are they part of the disability community? Many will be discriminated against and many will be disabled in the social model sense, but are they disabled people and if they are have they been consulted about the disability research agenda? This problem links to the previous point on the broad nature of disability research. For example, in his critique of disability studies, the medical sociologist Bury (1996) has asked where does chronic illness end and disability begin? We need, as a discipline, to answer this question rather than just finesse it by simply referring to the social model. Setting the criteria for research, deciding on the priorities and obtaining consensus from the disability community is a difficult task, and there is a danger that this has become lost in definitions of what constitutes disability research and how disability research should be conducted.

These three problems are expanded and further developed in the next sections of the chapter, where the focus is shifted to examining how research can produce change and the relative roles of structure and agency.

Change, development and improvement

With its focus on barrier removal and the emancipation and empowerment of disabled people, emancipatory research is at its roots transformative and the role of the researcher is to establish a research agenda that can help to realize these goals (Barnes 2003). This focus on change, development and improvement assumes, of course, that research can identify changes to include disabled people, that researchers have the capacity to generate such an agenda and that such changes are always desirable. It assumes that we can tackle the exclusion and oppression that disabled people face simply by social change and that the focus of research should be on the means of achieving that social change. On the face of it, this is a not unreasonable, perhaps even self-evidently true, argument.

There are, however, important researchable issues here. The social model is at its roots normative; it implies judgments of good and bad, of what ought and what ought not to be. This normative dimension is barely acknowledged and unless it is, linked as it can be to the Marxian idea of false consciousness, it has the potential to be seen as being illiberal and paternalist. The approach can silence those who do not support its underlying principles (Danieli and Woodhams 2005). The right to intervene on, for example, an individual's housing, employment or educational opportunities is a political decision and how these decisions are made and who makes them are themselves researchable questions. One large unresolved problem is that while certain discriminatory practices can be can be removed or blocked, it is sometimes difficult to think of or find less discriminatory or oppressive factors to replace them with. For example, in promoting access to work it is often difficult to see how barriers to employment for some disabled people can be removed to enable participation leading to what Abberley (1996) termed the Utopic ideals of the disability movement.

Disability studies has also, to a large extent, ignored research on behaviour or attitude change. The idea of changing behaviour and attitudes to disabled people, and through this changing the social and physical environment, should be an integral part of disability studies but is one that is rarely approached. Reeve's (2004) work on psycho-emotional disablism highlights how detrimental imagery, cultural representations and interactions with others can be for disabled people. This neglect comes against a backdrop of many such campaigns, for example the 'Save Me Campaign', which have aimed to tackle the stigma associated with having an impairment (Pilgrim and Rogers 2005). The assumption within much of the writings in disability studies has been that such psycho-emotional disablism can be challenged through a social model approach and there has been no attempt to unpack or examine the models of social or behavioural change that may be operating. There have also been very few attempts to engage with some of the recent developments in this area (see for example Sniehotta 2009). Current approaches are based on a very simplistic notion of behaviour change, namely that through knowledge, attitudes will be changed and as a result of attitudinal change, behaviour will be altered.

Much disability studies research focuses on the structures that disable rather than individual capacity to challenge or alter those structures, and it is to an examination of these that the chapter now turns.

Agency–structure problem

The agency–structure debate has been at the centre of social science research since its inception (Carter 2003). In its analysis of the disability problem, disability studies has to a large extent ignored agency and, driven by the social model, argued that disability can only be challenged through changes in structure. There is a danger that in this approach agency has been removed from disabled people and they have again been presented as victims – albeit this time as victims of society rather than victims of the body. Disabled people are active agents and are able to challenge the structures and practices that disabled them. Simulation exercises, for example in which people are blindfolded or are placed in wheelchairs so they can experience what it is like to be a disabled person, have been heavily criticized because they do not allow for agency (French 1992). However, agency is rarely part of the research agenda.

The disabled people's movement has long recognized that the ideas of empowerment and enablement lie alongside anti-discrimination policy in tackling the discrimination experienced by disabled people. Many of the debates within the discipline straddle this agency and structure divide, yet this has rarely been theorized. The ILM, for example, whilst emphasizing disabled people's right to make decisions about their lives and to full participation in the mainstream community, living on a equal footing with their non-disabled peers, also places great emphasis on the development of skills and knowledge that allow individual disabled people to exercise these choices (Morris 1993). Providing people with the knowledge and power to act and take control enables people to express their agency and at the root of this is the possession of the skills necessary to facilitate empowerment (Kelly and Glover 1987).

Furthermore, despite this recognition by the ILM that there is a need to help disabled people develop knowledge about their rights to housing, to employment and to funding for personal assistance, disability studies has to a large extent ignored one other major area of knowledge – the right to knowledge about one's own body and healthcare. To do so is perhaps dangerous because it does acknowledge that disabled people have health problems and that issues that might concern disabled people may, at times, be individual in origin, but to deny research attention to such areas will surely only result in further exclusion. There is a danger that by downplaying these very real issues we can open the way for reactionary ideologies or programmes (Birke 1986).

By not engaging with health at this level and not taking on health as an issue, disability studies has allowed programmes such as Kate Lorig's Chronic Disease Self-Management Program (2006) and the Expert Patient Programme, also developed from the work of Lorig and based on ideas developed at the Stanford Patient Education Research Centre, to emerge unchallenged. All of these programmes have failed to engage with the disability studies agenda; the underlying philosophy of these and other similar courses is the promotion of self-efficacy – they suggest that disabled people can be best helped by encouraging self-management through which individuals are taught to live with their condition and given confidence to deal with health service professionals. They are also instructed about role management and the emotional management of their condition. The programmes aim to move patients from being passive recipients of care to agents actively involved in the self-management of their care. They aim to empower participants to take responsibility for the management of their condition and to work in partnership with health and social care professionals and so take greater control over their lives. Typically the course content includes sections on disease-related problem solving, managing emotions, exercise, relaxation, nutrition, communication skills, as well as advice on managing medication and using the health care system (Richardson *et al.* 2007).

All these programmes individualize the problems that disabled people face; they are very medical in their outlook with a focus on symptom management, presenting disability as a medical rather than a social issue and to a large extent they ignore the wider determinants of health (Taylor and Bury 2007). Yet, because disability studies as a discipline has failed to engage in this area of research it has allowed this programme to emerge unchallenged.

There is also an inherent contradiction in that by deciding that disabled people are in need of or would benefit from research programmes that aim to promote their emancipation, a funding body or similar organization has already decided that disabled people have special problems and that they need assistance. The reasoning behind the very establishment of a project may be at odds with its intentions (Kelly 1989). For example, the very fact that the concept of participation as a research paradigm emerged suggests that somebody decided that people with a learning disability were not currently participating on an equal footing with non-disabled people and would not be able to do so unless such an approach was developed. These decisions were not taken by people with a learning disability. The study of such a tension, as Kelly (1989) argues, is important, not because it allows a sociological or theoretical examination of the agency–structure debate, but because it allows for an exploration of how involved disabled people are in the assessments of need and demand and in the development of appropriate organizational responses. The agency–structure debate therefore has a strong practical application and disability studies must develop ways of engaging at this level.

Research within disability studies should explore and examine the interface between agency and structure, and this tension should be built into research questions. It is to an examination of such alternative research paradigms that this chapter now turns.

Alternative approach to disability research – Towards a critical realist agenda

Disability research is a difficult and contested area. Disability studies has argued for research that promotes the emancipation of disabled people and much of the thrust of the discipline has been directed towards that aim. However, no matter how laudable this aim may be it does require adequate theory and, whilst a desire for emancipation is important political rhetoric, no matter how engaged it may cannot be used to justify a theory. To do so would be a teleological error (Kelly 1989). Research needs to be politically engaged so as not to return to the earlier approach adopted by medical sociology so rightly criticized by Hunt and his colleagues, but it also it needs to allow for an exploration of change, of agency and of individual experience. A social understanding of disability is necessary and research should focus on and engage with societal attitudes and structural and experiential factors and not only document but also explain, criticize and, if appropriate, provide a means to undermine and challenge oppressive or discriminatory factors. If the research starts out with a pre-existing commitment to a particular understanding it will prevent reflexivity, and an exploration of who defines and controls the research questions and how they do it can become blurred.

Drawing on the ideas of Roy Bhaskar (1997) and others (Archer *et al.* 1998, Sayer 1999, Williams 1999, Scambler 2005), this next section argues that these aims can best be achieved through a critical realist approach. Bhaskar is clear that critical realism is committed to human emancipation (Collier 1998), demanding a focus that combines the 'social processes of structure and agency that shape and reshape one another over time' (Williams 1999: 809). In critical realism, social science research is concerned with exploring how agency is influenced by structures and vice versa, without overemphasizing either agency or structure.

Put simply, critical realism argues that phenomena exist whether or not we have concrete knowledge of them, and that the existence of phenomena should not be confused with knowledge about them. It is not reality per se that is socially constructed, rather it is our theories of reality and the methods we use to explore and investigate it (Pilgrim and Bentall 1999). A critical realist agenda enables us to move beyond debates about what is disability and how it should be defined and what is or is not an impairment and what is the relationship between impairment and chronic illness and disablement. It also permits an examination of the experiential basis of impairment and an exploration of the day-to-day problems associated with living with a condition without reducing the disease to a social construction or creation (Scambler 2005). By 'bringing the body back in' (Williams 1999) and theorizing impairment and its lived experience as part of human embodiment it allows for the reclamation of impairment, which under the emancipatory research paradigm is left to medicine (Hughes and Paterson 1997). By focusing on both structural barriers to inclusion and individual agency, critical realism allows for an approach that gives appropriate weight to the different dimensions of the disability experience (Shakespeare 2006). Critical realism also allows an engagement with different methodologies, including quantitative and qualitative approaches. It enables an analysis that can accommodate both material causation and, at the same time, a critical analysis of the way that people with impairment are treated. It can achieve this without resorting to either the reductionist tendency found in the social model or the individualism found in traditional medical sociology.

A further strength of the approach is its use of what Collier (1998) has termed a stratified or laminated system. This concept has been used by Bhaskar and Danermark (2006), who have pointed the way towards the development of a critical realist agenda for research within disability studies. They argue that research on disability can be explored at the following levels:

- physical;
- biological;
- psychological;
- psychosocial and emotional;
- socio-economic;
- cultural;
- normative.

Traditional medical approaches have tended to focus more on the first three, whilst emancipatory research has placed emphasis on the latter three. All of these layers are 'essential to the understanding of the phenomena in fields such as disability research' (*Ibid.* p. 289). We live our lives in interacting and inter-arching spheres and processes and procedures which interact simultaneously and it is this that critical realism allows us to access (New 2005). All these levels intermesh, interrelate and interplay and need to be examined if we are to develop an approach that fully incorporates the lived experience of disablement and impairment and avoids both 'biological reductionism' and 'contextual essentialism' (Shakespeare and Watson 2010).

Few would dispute that capitalism is an important determinant of the cultural and socio-political life of disabled people, and in fact how they tend to think about disablement and the disability experience is profoundly marked by the specific concepts highlighted in the social model; what is in question is rather the apparently exclusive and reductive focus on discrimination and oppression.

This chapter has argued that emancipatory research, whilst an excellent basis for a political movement, provides an inadequate grounding for a social theory. Its materialist and Marxist foundation has meant that much of the disability experience has not been explored and that debate and analysis has been curtailed. If it is to develop, disability studies must learn from and incorporate new theoretical perspectives, particularly those from within critical realism. An approach that incorporates both individual agency and allows an analysis of the experience of living with an impairment will provide a far-reaching and important insight into disablement and will enable the development of new ideas that will have major implications for medical and social intervention in the twenty-first century.

Note

1 It is important to note that Oliver's attack is an attack on both positivist and interpretivist research.

References

Abberley, P. (1996) 'Work, Utopia and Impairment', in L. Barton, ed., *Disability and Society: Emerging Issues and Insights* (Harlow: Longman): pp. 61–80.

Acker, J., Barry, K. and Esseveld, J. (1991) 'Objectivity and Truth, Problems of Doing Feminist Research', in M. M. Fonow and J. A. Cook, eds, *Beyond Methodology: Feminist Scholarship as Lived Research* (Bloomington: Indiana University Press): pp. 133–53.

Archer, M., Bhaskar, R., Collier, A., Lawson, A. and Norrie, A., eds, (1998) *Critical Realism: Essential Readings* (London: Routledge).

Atkinson, D. (1989) 'Research Interviews with People with a Mental Handicap', in A. Brechin and J. Walmsley, eds, *Making Connections* (Hodder and Stoughton).

Baistow, K. (1994) 'Liberation and Regulation?: Some Paradoxes of Empowerment', *Critical Social Policy* 14(42): 34–46.

Barnes, C. (1990) *Cabbage Syndrome: The Social Construction of Dependence* (Lewes: Falmer).

Barnes, C. (1995) *Measuring Disablement in Society: Hopes and Reservations*; available online at http://www.disability-archive.leeds.ac.uk/authors_list.asp?AuthorID=8&author_name=Barnes%2C+Colin (accessed 27 July 2011).

Barnes, C. (2003) 'What a Difference a Decade Makes: Reflections on Doing "Emancipatory" Disability Research', *Disability & Society* 18(1): 3–17.

Barnes, C. and Mercer, G. (1997) *Doing Disability Research* (Leeds: The Disability Press).

Barnes, C. and Mercer, G. (2010) *Exploring Disability* (Cambridge: Polity).

Barton, L. (1992) 'Introduction', *Disability, Handicap and Society* 7(2): 99.

Bhaskar, R. (1997) *A Realist Theory of Science* (London: Verso).

Bhaskar R. and Danermark, B. (2006) 'Metatheory, Interdisciplinarity and Disability Research: A Critical Realist Perspective', *Scandinavian Journal of Disability Research* 8(4): 278–97.

Birke, L. (1986) *Women, Feminism and Biology: The Feminist Challenge* (London: Wheatsheaf).

Bury, M. (1996) 'Defining and Researching Disability: Challenges and Responses', in C. Barnes and G. Mercer, eds, *Exploring the Divide: Illness and Disability* (Leeds: The Disability Press): pp. 18–38.

Carter, B. (2003) 'What Race Means to Realists', in J. Cruickshank, ed., *Critical Realism: The Difference it Makes* (London: Routledge).

Collier, A. (1998) 'Explanation and Emancipation', in M. S. Archer, R. Bhaskar, A. Collier, T. Lawson and A. Norrie, eds, *Critical Realism: Essential Readings* (London: Routledge): pp. 444–72.

Danieli, A. and Woodhams, C. (2005) 'Emancipatory Research Methodology and Disability: A Critique', *International Journal of Social Research Methodology* 8(4): 281–96.

Docherty, A., Harkness, E., Eardley, M., Townson, L. and Chapman, R. (2006) 'What They Want – Yes, But What We Want – Bugger Us!', in D. Mitchell, R. Traustadottir, R. Chapman, L. Townson, N. Ingham and S. Ledger, eds, *Exploring Experiences of Advocacy by People with Learning Disabilities: Testimonies of Resistance* (London: Jessica Kingsley): pp. 100–7.

Finkelstein, V. (1996) 'Outside. Inside Out', *Coalition*, April: 30–36.

Flynn, M. (1986) 'Adults Who are Mentally Handicapped as Consumers: Issues and Guidelines for Interviewing', *Journal of Mental Deficiency Research* 30: 369–77.

French, S. (1992) 'Simulation Exercises in Disability Equality Training: A Critique', *Disability, Handicap and Society* 7(3): 256–66.

Garbutt, R. (2009) 'Is There a Place Within Academic Journals for Articles Presented in an Accessible Format?' *Disability & Society* 24(3): 357–71.

Goodley, D. (2010) *Disability Studies: An Interdisciplinary Introduction* (London: Sage).

Hodge, N. (2008) 'Evaluating Lifeworld as an Emancipatory Methodology', *Disability & Society* 23(1): 29–40.

Hughes, B. and Paterson, K. (1997) 'The Social Model of Disability and the Disappearing Body: Towards a Sociology of Impairment', *Disability and Society* 12(3): 325–40.

Hunt, P. (1981) 'Settling Accounts with the Parasite People: A Critique of *A Life Apart* by E. J. Miller and O. V. Gwynne', *Disability Challenge* 1: 38.

Hurstfield J., Meager, N., Aston, J., Mann, K., Mitchell, H., O'Regan, S. and Sinclair, A. (2004) *Monitoring the DDA 1995: Part 111* (London: Department for Work and Pensions).

Kelly, M. (1989) 'Some Problems with Health Promotion Research', *Health Promotion International* 4(4): 317–33.

Kelly, M. and Glover, I. (1987) 'Sociology for Technik', *Higher Education Review* 19(3): 24–36.

Kitchen, R. (2000) 'The Researched Opinions on Research: Disabled People and Disability Research', *Disability and Society* 15(1): 25–47.

Lather, E. (1987) 'Research as Praxis', *Harvard Educational Review* 56(3): 257–73.

Lorig, K. (2006) *Living a Healthy Life with Chronic Conditions: Self-management of Heart Disease, Arthritis, Diabetes, Asthma, Bronchitis, Emphysema and Others*, 3rd edn (Boulder, CO: Bull Publishing Company).

Marks, D. (1999) *Disability: Controversial Debates and Psychosocial Perspectives* (London: Routledge).

Miller, E. and Gwynne, G. (1972) *A Life Apart: A Pilot Study of Residential Institutions for the Physically Handicapped and the Young Chronic Sick* (London: Tavistock Publications).

Morris, J. (1993) *Independent Lives* (Tavistock: Macmillan).

Morris, J. (2006) 'Independent Living: The Role of the Disability Movement in the Development of Government Policy', in C. Glendinning and P. Kemp, eds, *Cash and Care* (Bristol: The Policy Press): pp. 235–48.

New, C. (2005) 'Sex and Gender: A Critical Realist Approach', *New Formations* 56: 54–70.

Oliver, M. (1990) *The Politics of Disablement* (London: Palgrave Macmillan).

Oliver, M. (1992) 'Changing the Social Relations of Research Production', *Disability, Handicap and Society* 7(2): 101–114.

Oliver, M. (1997) 'Emancipatory Disability Research: Realistic Goal or Impossible Dream?', in C. Barnes and G. Mercer, eds, *Doing Disability Research* (Leeds: The Disability Press): pp. 15–31.

Oliver, M. (1999) 'Final Accounts with the Parasite People', in M. Corker and S. French, eds, *Disability Discourse* (Buckingham: Open University Press): pp. 183–91.

Pilgrim, D. and Bentall, R. (1999) 'The Medicalisation of Misery: A Critical Realist Analysis of the Concept of Depression', *Journal of Mental Health* 8(3): 261–74.

Pilgrim, D. and Rogers, A. (2005) 'Psychiatrists as Social Engineers: A Study of an Anti-stigma Campaign', *Social Science & Medicine* 61(12): 2546–56.

Priestley, M., Waddington, Li and Bessozi, C. (2010) 'Towards an Agenda for Disability Research in Europe: Learning from Disabled People's Organisations', *Disability & Society* 25(6): 731–46.

Reason, P. and Heron, J. (1986) 'Research with People: The Paradigm of Co-operation Experiential Enquiry', *Person-Centred Review* 1(4): 456–76.

Reeve, D. (2004) 'Psycho-emotional Dimensions of Disability and the Social Model', in C. Barnes and G. Mercer, eds, *Implementing the Social Model of Disability: Theory and Research* (Leeds: The Disability Press): pp. 83–100.

Ribbens, J. (1990) 'Interviewing – An "Unnatural Situation"?', *Women's Studies International Forum* 12(6): 579–92.

Richardson, G., Kennedy, A., Reeves, D., Bower, P., Lee, V., Middleton, E., Gardiner, C., Gaitely, C. and Rogers, A. (2007) 'The Cost Effectiveness of the Expert Patients Programme (EPP) for Patients with Chronic Conditions', *Journal of Epidemiology and Community Health* 62(4): 361–67.

Rioux, M. and Bach, M., eds (1994) *Disability is not Measles* (Ontario: L'Institut Roeher).

Sayer, A. (1999) *Realism and Social Science* (London: Sage).

Scambler, S. (2005) 'Exposing the Limitations of Disability Theory: The Case of Juvenile Batten Disease', *Social Theory and Health* 3: 144–64.

Shakespeare, T. (2006) *Disability Rights: Disability Wrongs* (London: Routledge).

Shakespeare, T. and Watson, N. (2010) 'Beyond Models: Understanding the Complexity of Disabled People's Lives', in S. Scambler and G. Scambler, eds, *New Directions in the Sociology of Chronic and Disabling Conditions: Assaults on the Lifeworlds* (Basingstoke: Palgrave Macmillan): pp. 57–77.

Sniehotta, F. F. (2009) 'Towards a Theory of Intentional Behaviour Change: Plans, Planning, and Self-regulation', *British Journal of Health Psychology* 14(2):261–73.

Stalker, K. (1998) 'Some Ethical and Methodological Issues in Research with People with Learning Difficulties', *Disability & Society* 13(1): 5–19.

Stone, E. and Priestley, M. (1996) 'Parasites, Pawns and Partners: Disability Research and the Role of Non-Disabled Researchers', *British Journal of Sociology* 47(4): 699–716.

Taylor, D. and Bury, M. (2007) 'Chronic Illness, Expert Patients and Care Transition', *Sociology of Health & Illness* 29(1): 27–45.

Thomas, C. (1999) *Female Forms: Experiencing and Understanding Disability* (Milton Keynes: Open University Press).

Truman, C., Mertens, D. M. and Humphries, B. (2000) *Research and Inequality* (London: UCL Press).

UPIAS (1976) *Fundamental Principles of Disability* (Union of the Physically Impaired Against Segregation) available online at http://www.leeds.ac.uk/disability-studies/archiveuk/UPIAS/UPIAS.pdf (accessed 27 July 2011).

Walmsley, J. (2004) 'Involving Users with Learning Difficulties in Health Improvement: Lessons from Inclusive Learning Disability Research', *Nursing Inquiry* 11(1): 54–64

Walmsley, J. (2010) 'Research and Emancipation: Prospects and Problems', in G. Grant, P. Ramcharan, M. Flynn and M. Richardson, eds, *Learning Disability: A Life Cycle Approach*, 2nd edn (Maidenhead: McGraw Hill/Open University Press): pp. 489–501.

Watson, N. (2002) 'Well, I Know This is Going to Sound Very Strange to You, but I Don't See Myself as a Disabled Person: Identity and Disability', *Disability & Society* 17(5): 509–27.

Williams, S. J. (1999) 'Is Anybody There? Critical Realism, Chronic Illness and the Disability Debate', *Sociology of Health & Illness* 21(6):797–819.

Zarb, G. (1992) 'On the Road to Damascus: First Steps Towards Changing the Relations of Disability Research Production', *Disability, Handicap and Society* 7(2): 125–38.

Zarb, G. (1997) 'Researching Disabling Barriers', in G. Mercer and C. Barnes *Doing Disability Research* (Leeds: The Disability Press): pp. 49–66; available online at http://www.disability-archive.leeds.ac.uk/authors_list.asp?AuthorID=191&author_name=Zarb%2C+Gerry (accessed 27 July 2011).

PART 2

Disablement, disablism and impairment effects

9

DEAF IDENTITIES IN DISABILITY STUDIES

With us or without us?

Jackie Leach Scully

> Many disabled people see Deaf people as belonging with them outside the mainstream culture. We, on the other hand, see disabled people as 'hearing' people in that they use a different language to us, from which we are excluded.
>
> *(Ladd and John 1991: 15)*

As is now widely acknowledged, and as the quote from Ladd and John indicates, disabled and D/deaf people[1] can have quite divergent views of the place of deafness within disability. In this chapter I want to look at how the experiences of deafness are contained, or not, within disability theory. There are several reasons why the particularities of deafness might be of interest to the academic understanding of disability in general. First, the question of where to place deafness within the spectrum of physical variation does not have a simple answer, and that alone makes it worth a closer look. But second, the fact that situating *deafness* within disability theory is problematic points to the persisting inadequacies of our thinking about disability and impairment *as a whole*: deafness tests the coherence of current disability theory, and frequently finds it wanting.

The areas that have seen most debate concern the ontological status of deafness and, by implication, of disability, and its normative status, or whether being deaf can ever be anything other than 'damaged'. In real life, beliefs and claims about ontology and normativity are played out through beliefs and claims about identities. In this chapter, then, I focus on questions of deaf identities and identifications as they lie at the heart of disability theory's difficulties with deafness. First, I consider how disability theory has approached the idea of *disability* identity. Then, I examine why deafness might need to be considered differently, especially in view of the existence of the Deaf community and the processes through which it has been formed. I look at the emergence of the model of 'Deaf culture', which has been profoundly important to the evolution of a strong Deaf identity, but also question whether the model is able to incorporate the genuine diversity of deaf experiences. Finally I argue that deafness and disability may better be examined in terms of phenotypic variation, rather than social structures or cultural identities.

The contested idea of disability identity

There are well-rehearsed accounts of the evolution of different models of disability, especially the rise of what has been called the (bio)medical or individual tragedy model, to the development of the strong social model from the 1970s onward, and I will not repeat them here (e.g., Barnes *et al.* 1999; Campbell and Oliver 1996; Shakespeare 2006; Oliver 2006; Thomas 2007). All models of disability indirectly provide a concept of the relationship between disability and either personal or collective identity, differing in the extent to which each model configures disability as either constitutive of or damaging to an 'authentic' personal identity, or whether it sees disability as a possible basis for a political identity (Swain and French 2000; Scully 2008).

Contemporary identity politics organizes around the idea that marginal groups have been subjected to injustice because of unique features that mark them out – so the group's members must share some features to start with (Kenny 2004). Hence a frequent objection to the notion of a collective disability identity, whether taken in a political or in a broader sociocultural sense, is that it is simply meaningless because there is a lack of consensus within disability theory about what constitutes disability, and if we can't say what disability *is*, how can we identify what disabled people might share as identity-forming? A medical/individual tragedy model, for instance, would see impairment (the physical or mental deviation from an accepted norm) as the common feature. The problem here lies in unambiguously defining physical or mental normality, and providing a compelling reason why it should be this and not something else. For the strong social model, on the other hand, the common feature of a disability identity is not the *nature* or *extent* of the impairment, but the political *experience* of oppression (Oliver 1990; Barnes 1996). At this point, second wave disability theorists are inclined to express some scepticism that oppression is really that all-encompassing or ubiquitous (Crow 1996; Shakespeare and Watson 2001; Watson 2002; Shakespeare 2006). Disabled people, they say, undergo a wide range of experiences as the direct result of their impairment, and some identity-forming experiences may better be described as exclusion, rejection or isolation, or may actually be positive rather than negative. If the expression of oppression is not universal, then it cannot be the basis of a general theory of disability.

Thinking about disability in terms of identity is also contested because of the lack of agreement about its normativity. I don't mean here the moral or political status of disabled people, but the question of whether disability is intrinsically always problematic, a state something less than ideal, or whether it only becomes a problem if other factors operate as well. (This is what distinguishes disability from analogous categories of gender, class or race. Theories of gender, class or race are not theories *of a problem*; but some theories of disability are exactly that.)

As a result, not everyone is convinced that disabled people share enough elements of experi-ence, and enough sense of fundamental difference from non-disabled people, for *any* kind of meaningful shared identity to exist. There may be an identification with others with related impairments, especially if they also share experiences of special schools, clubs, clinics and so on, but this is not something that is shared with *all* other disabled people. What empirical evidence there is suggests that disabled people's own sense of common identity is quite varied: while some consider themselves part of a disability community or political movement, others may reject any notion of there being such a community at all, or acknowledge its existence but still assert that they themselves are not part of it (see Watson 2002; Ville *et al.* 2003).

Yet notwithstanding these theoretical and empirical problems, some disabled people and disability scholars do hold that there is *something* about the experience of disability that is distinctive enough to speak meaningfully of a disability identity (Peters 2000). Ultimately, there is also the pragmatic observation that collective self-identification around the idea of disablement has probably been the key driver of improvements in the social and economic status of disabled people over the last half-century. When Vic Finkelstein asks rhetorically, 'why now, when there is much greater awareness of our desire to be fully integrated into society, do we suddenly want to go off at a tangent and start trying to promote … our separate identity?' he answers it by saying that having 'a cultural identity will play a vital role in helping us to develop the confidence necessary for us to create the organisations which we need to promote the social change we want' (1996: 111). Overall, then, *disability* identity remains a concept that is contested, troublesome and yet still extremely useful, both theoretically and practically.

Deafness and why a D/deaf identity might be special

The concept of *deaf* identity is equally contested and troublesome, but for rather different reasons. Deafness is understood by the majority of hearing people, and by many deaf people as well, as a purely audiological state in which someone's range of usable hearing is significantly more restricted than most other people's. Having a hearing capacity 'below the norm' is clearly an impairment, and for those who take this view it will seem obvious that to be deaf is to be disabled and that deaf people are part of the disability community. If there is a collective disability identity to be claimed, then deaf people can and should claim it.

The extraordinary strengthening of a distinct self-consciousness and politicization among deaf people since the 1980s, especially among the signing, culturally Deaf community, challenges this. An increasing number of people – primarily members of the signing Deaf community, but some other deaf and hearing people as well – now argue that being deaf has little in common with other impairments like being blind or having constrained mobility. Instead, they see deaf people as occupying a distinct 'Deaf world' or as members of 'Deaf culture' (Corker 1996; Padden and Humphries 2005). The term culture is used to capture the distinctive beliefs and practices of Deaf people that have been shaped by the dominance of visual over auditory interaction with the world. Although 'the central role of sign language in the everyday lives of the community' (Padden and Humphries 2005: 1) is taken for granted, Deaf culture is not just about a peculiarity of language form; it refers to a rich background of distinctive social practices, a shared past and a network of social organizations ranging from schools for the deaf and D/deaf social clubs, to today's virtual D/deaf groups operating online and through video blogs. While similar institutions exist for other kinds of impairment, for example schools for the blind, claims to a distinct community or culture have never been made for these impairments in the way they have for Deaf people.

The existence of Deaf culture is far from universally accepted, and even its proponents agree it differs in important ways from other linguistically and ethnically based cultures to which it is compared. A culture that arises out of the fact of deafness is one that for much of its history was, and for the majority of people still is, premised on a fundamental *defect*. This is not the case for cultures generated through geography or language. If deafness is primarily about audiological impairment then it cuts right across spatial or linguistic borders, again unlike other cultural identities. However, the view that defect provides the basis of Deaf culture is rejected by those who see it as emerging from a more complex interaction of language difference and social marginality, not just because of ears that don't work like other people's.[2] As Padden and Humphries say, 'Being Deaf [is] not a consequence of not hearing. Being Deaf [is] an existential experience, complete in itself and not a consequence of broken bodies but the outcome of biological destiny' (Padden and Humphries 2005: 156). By this view of Deaf culture it is closer to some other cultural identities that have also arisen because of language difference and exclusion from mainstream society. Additionally, this model is open to the way that the experience of Deaf culture is not universal but is inevitably modulated by other cultural identities and identifications with which it interacts, such as ethnicities (see for example Foster and Kinuthia 2003; Smiler and McKee 2007).

Deaf culture is also unusual because of the processes through which it is handed on in the community. Most cultures are transmitted vertically, from parent to child. For Deaf people this happens relatively rarely, when both parents have the same genetic basis for their deafness and therefore have a high probability of having deaf children. Because most hearing impairment is not genetic, in over 90 per cent of cases deaf children will have hearing parents (Nance 2003). Transmission of audiological deafness, and so of Deaf culture, are thus both usually disrupted in each generation. While Deaf families are rare, they have been peculiarly significant within the Deaf world, providing a repository of cultural knowledge to pass on to deaf children from hearing families (Preston 2001: 71). In the past this led to the sociological novelty that the chief conduits for Deaf identity were institutional, such as schools for the deaf or Deaf clubs (Harris 1995: 121–40), rather than familial, and there is anecdotal evidence that until quite recently Deaf people would tend to name their school as the point of entry into their self-identification as Deaf, as the place where they 'came from'.[3]

The identification of culturally Deaf people with the Deaf world and Deaf culture is undoubtedly strengthened by the fact that even today, for most deaf people, the Deaf world is a *found* community. Many Deaf memoirs are structured around a narrative of 'coming home' after years of isolation and frustration because of the impossibility of hearing speech. In addition, the dispiriting history of 'oralist' attempts to suppress signed languages and to encourage/force deaf children and adults to communicate through speech instead has also, paradoxically but predictably, fostered a strong group identity in response (Lane 1984).

The 'biological destiny' that Padden and Humphries mention is an audiological difference. The question of the normativity of D/deaf identity depends on whether this is considered an impairment, or alternatively as a difference falling within the range of normal human variation (Padden and Humphries 1988, 2005). When Ladd and John say that 'Labelling us as "disabled" demonstrates a failure to understand that we are not disabled in any way within our own community' (Ladd and John 1991: 14–15) they reflect the view that, at least in that context, Deaf people can acknowledge that they embody a physical difference from the norm, without having to consider themselves to be impaired (Lane 1992; Harris 1995). This stance is distinct from the strong social model of disability, which would still view audiological deafness as an *impairment* while arguing that the *disablement* of deafness is caused by communication and other barriers that prevent deaf people participating fully in society. By contrast, some (although by no means all) culturally Deaf people prefer to think of their audiological deafness purely as difference, or at most a trivial impairment, rather than a significant problem. While the available evidence suggests that this is a minority stance within the adult deaf population, it is also true that the group Corker called the Deaf elite, 'deaf people ... who distance themselves from notions of deafness as hearing impairment and disability' (Corker 1998: 6) have been extremely influential in transforming the sense of self-conscious identity, and outsider perceptions, of deaf people.

The deaf community: boundaries and diversity

It is worth repeating here that, just as with disability identity, the various concepts of D/deaf identity, culture, world, community and so on are all contested ones. Some people, including some deaf people, reject the idea of a (relatively) homogeneous Deaf culture; other deaf people will agree that it exists but do not see themselves as belonging to it, and others will consider themselves fully paid-up members. There remains considerable debate about what a 'Deaf culture' actually is, what its boundaries are, who belongs to it or can claim to belong to it, and why (Padden and Humphries 1988; Corker 1996, 1998; Lane 1992; Woll and Ladd 2003).

What makes it harder to provide definitions or delineate boundaries around Deaf culture is the growing diversity of members or potential members of the deaf community.[4] As Padden and Humphries note (2005: 150), in the 1950s the question of 'Who is deaf?' was easily answered:

'Deaf people are those who attend schools for the deaf and go to Deaf clubs'. But by the 1970s these distinctive spaces for affirming deaf identity were in decline, and the more abstract notion of Deaf culture called for a socially and culturally detailed account of what constitutes deaf identity. And this in turn raised unprecedented questions about the kind of deaf identity that could be considered an authentic part of the community and of Deaf culture. If deaf people are not defined by the pragmatic criteria of schools or clubs, or according to audiological status or the age at which they became deaf, what exactly are the criteria for belonging to this community? Are certain experiences, leading to a particular sense of self, absolutely necessary? How many 'different pathways of experience' (ibid p. 155) can be included? If deaf people undergo a variety of different experiences, which are the most formative in terms of Deaf identity? And who has the authority to define which kinds of D/deaf identities are authentic? Inevitably, this leads to the question of just how much diversity of experience, identity and identification the idea of deafness as a culture can tolerate. Diversity within a supposed coherent group may be feared as being equivalent to fragmentation, compromising the group's claim to the outside world to be recognized *as* a group.

Mairian Corker was one of the first scholars to subject the cultural processes at work in the establishment of a 'Deaf identity' as part of a 'Deaf culture' to critical scrutiny, and was particularly alert to the consequences that the need to articulate a coherent Deaf identity could have for the real-life diversity of deaf experiences. In her discussion of how novel social, cultural and political identities are generated, she notes the general tendency to set up a binary opposition between those inside and those outside the group, to define oneself over and against the other 'in order to justify the creation of a different concept of "purity"', with the risk of ossifying the boundaries between identities that might in reality be more fluid (Corker 1998: 22). In the case of deafness, Corker is concerned that constructing Deaf identity in terms of a cultural minority encourages the rigid dichotomization of experience into just two categories of deaf and hearing, inside and outside the group. If this taxonomy is maintained too rigidly there will be no place for the experiences that fall outside it (Appiah 1994).

When drawing the boundaries of deaf identity, it might seem axiomatic that the first line to be drawn is between deaf people and hearing people. But the simplicity of this is deceptive. We've already seen that there is basic disagreement over whether the 'deafness' that matters to being part of Deaf culture is a primarily audiological or a sociocultural trait. The audiological criterion appears to be more straightforward and objectively measurable. Yet even then, if 'deaf people' is taken to include everyone with any kind of not-quite-standard-model hearing, that label must still encompass the distinct experiences and identities of:

- people who consider themselves fully culturally Deaf, notably those who have been born or raised within Deaf families, and who often (but not always) use signed languages as their primary means of communication;
- those culturally Deaf people who identify themselves as having an impairment, *and* those who reject the idea that they are in any way impaired, except by social barriers and attitudes;
- culturally Deaf people who are happy to use hearing aids or cochlear implants (CIs), *and* those who reject them as unnecessary or even as threats to the integrity of their identification as Deaf;
- partially deaf, hard of hearing, and late-deafened people, who continue to identify themselves as hearing people with an impairment, who function primarily in the phonocentric world (Corker 2003), and who depend to a greater or lesser extent on the technologies of hearing aids or CIs rather than using sign and non-auditory supports in their daily lives;
- partially deaf and late-deafened people who have become (or tried to become) part of the culturally Deaf community;

- those whose hearing impairment is fixed and stable, *and* those for whom it fluctuates or is in periodic decline.

As Corker and others (e.g., Leigh 2009) have demonstrated, then, considerable oversimplification is involved when deafness is treated as the homogeneous opposite of hearing. The categories of deaf and hearing are analytically useful constructions, but they may not have much to do with the real complexity of deaf experience. Deaf people who prefer to use sign but who, by choice or circumstance, function predominantly within the hearing world, or moderately hearing impaired people who can sign but also function well in hearing contexts, or non-signing audiologically deaf people who can use hearing aids or CIs to participate fully in phonocentric society – all fall outside a neat framework of 'deaf' vs 'hearing' or 'Deaf' vs 'deaf'.

Technology and D/deaf identity

In addition to the complexities already outlined, D/deaf identities are also evolving in response to technology (Chorost 2005). New modes of communication such as texting, email, instant messaging and so on offer alternatives to the phonocentric dominance of communication in the hearing world, as a result shifting the experiences of both deaf and hearing people in their interactions with each other. For example, no one using these modes of communication need know that their interlocutor is deaf unless he or she chooses to say so, and in principle this makes it easier for deaf and hearing people to interact on a more equal footing.

A rather more contentious example of technology's effects on deaf identities can be found in the use of CIs. The culturally Deaf community's initial response to CIs in the early 1980s and 1990s was dominated by anxiety and sometimes outright hostility, particularly as the CI industry moved towards favouring implants for very young children (Lane and Bahan 1998; Nunes 2001; Christiansen and Leigh 2002/2005; Sparrow 2005; Ladd 2007). In retrospect, it is possible to see this hostility as fuelled by the (over)zealous promotion by the CI industry of the implants as total 'cures' for deafness (Goggin and Newell 2003). The idea that CIs cure deafness was and is especially appealing to late-deafened adults and to culturally hearing parents who find themselves with a deaf infant; it promises to restore deaf children to the parents' hearing world. From the point of view of culturally Deaf people, on the other hand, the same promise of cure effectively obliterates the future of the Deaf community. With the passage of time, however, both deaf and hearing people seem to be moving towards a more moderate and realistic view as a growing number of Deaf adults take up the technology, and ironically as it becomes clearer that CIs, despite the hype, do not eradicate deafness either as an audiological trait or as a culture. Children and adults whose hearing impairment is severe enough to warrant CI implantation do not miraculously become hearing post-implant. They will always have a significant audiological difference from the 'norm', and their experiences and therefore their identities and identifications reflect this (see for example Christiansen and Leigh 2002/2005; Doe 2007; Leigh *et al.* 2008).

Hence the debate around CIs today is not so much about whether they will cause the extinction of the Deaf community. The question has become whether CI users represent a new way of living deafness, one that as yet does not fit easily within familiar models of Deaf culture or identity (Most *et al.* 2007). Drawing on Grosjean (1996), Leigh has discussed the experiences of some CI users, particularly young people who have grown up with the technology as a routine part of their own deaf lives, as illustrating a trend towards 'biculturalism' (Holocomb 1997; Most *et al.* 2007; Hintermair 2008; Leigh 2009: 49–53) within D/deaf communities. While recognizing the positive potential of being able to inhabit both Deaf and hearing cultures without being forced to choose between them, Leigh does not downplay the stresses of moving between cultures, and the flexibility of identifications and behaviours that this demands, especially when one culture is disvalued by the other, or when one or both cultures may reject the possibility of a bicultural identity. These issues have of course been extensively examined in the context of ethnic or racial biculturalism; at the moment, it is not clear how far those models can be applied to deafness, in part because deaf biculturalism is a relatively new phenomenon, and also because there is as yet only a small (although growing) body of empirical evidence about how CI users, of different ages, make use of the technology, and how they negotiate identification within and without Deafness (see for example Wheeler *et al.* 2007).

Deaf and/or disabled?

The Deaf cultural construction of deafness, not as impairment but as membership of a minority linguistic group, is a powerful one for deaf identity. Clearly, it also presents some difficulties for both the disability movement and disability theory. Part of the incompatibility of approach lies in the fact that neither the political disability movement nor disability studies is primarily concerned with the *normative status* of the physical or mental variation that ends in disability. For both activism and theory, there is generally less interest in how 'normal' a visual or mobility impairment might be than in understanding or eliminating the social and political disadvantage that follows from it. Disability activists and theorists alike have worked to get across the message that disabled people are 'just like anyone else', except for the disadvantage that follows from their impairment; that disabled people have the same value, civil and political rights, and can hold the same positions in society, as their non-disabled peers. Similarly, those deaf people whose identity is as people 'just like anyone else' but with a hearing impairment can join with the disability movement in arguing that removal of social barriers will go a long way towards removing the disablement caused by an audiological impairment.

But the alternative view of deafness as a *normal human variation* – not a failure of function, but a state of being, supported by a distinct culture that currently is not accommodated within main-stream society – is rather different. Those who hold this view are saying that the kind of barriers they face are simply not analogous to the ones encountered by other disabled people (that is, hearing people with other kinds of impairment). The major barrier of language difference divides them from other disabled people as much as from the non-disabled, hearing majority. As Corker says, while disabled people want to be incorporated into the non-disabled world, the Deaf culture view implies that Deaf people do not want to be part of the hearing world in the same way but want the right to exist as a minority group. Not surprisingly, this has caused tensions between a Deaf cultural consciousness and the political disability movement, since 'for disabled people [it] implies social and, more importantly, political fragmentation, because Deaf people conceptualize oppression and their relationship to the oppressor differently' (Corker 1998: 137).

An additional, less obvious, difficulty is that strict adherence to the cultural minority group model also raises difficulties for those Deaf people who wish to disavow an identity as hearing impaired, but at the same time also want/need access to various accommodations such as sign language interpreters or financial support to obtain hearing aids or CIs to bypass their audiological deafness in a hearing world. It is problematic to assert that one is not disabled because of one's deafness and yet still claim to need the kind of support that is made available through *disability* discrimination legislation.

Reproductive technologies and deaf identity

The question of the ontological status of deafness – whether some kind of normative deaf identity is a reality or just special pleading by deaf people trying to raise their self-esteem – is particularly salient at a time when various techniques of prenatal, preimplantation and even preconception diagnosis of heritable deafness are becoming routine (Arnos 2003; Smith *et al.* 2010). As genes associated with genetic forms of deafness are found, genetic testing of embryos or fetuses for deafness is likely to be offered both to 'at-risk' families and potentially as part of population-wide screening programmes. In most countries, these highly sophisticated (and expensive) reproductive diagnostic technologies are also highly regulated, and as a result, there is considerable pressure from regulators and healthcare providers to define which conditions may or may not be tested for, and which tests will be reimbursed by insurers. The diagnostic possibilities coupled with the need for regulation mean that the question of 'defining deafness' (and other disabilities) is introduced into public and policy discussions. Crucially this has meant that confusions and disagreements about the nature of deafness and disability are exposed to greater public scrutiny.

A recent example occurred in the United Kingdom (UK) during the 2008 revision of the Human Fertilization and Embryology Act. Revision of the original law was felt to be necessary because of the technical advances that had been made since 1990, including preimplantation genetic diagnosis (PGD) of various traits. In the event, one of the most disputed changes was the introduction of a clause prohibiting the clinics that provide PGD or gamete (sperm or egg) donation from using embryos or gametes carrying genes for known serious genetic disorders, *if* there are alternatives that do not carry those genes. So for example, if a deaf couple is using IVF services because of the woman's infertility, and wants to use a donated egg, the new law in principle prevents them from selecting an egg donor known to have genetic deafness if 'non-deaf' donor eggs are available. While the draft law itself mentioned disability only in general terms, in the ensuing debates it became obvious that the clause had been introduced in response to one or two high profile cases of culturally Deaf people expressing a preference for having deaf rather than hearing children (Levy 2002; Spriggs 2002; Bauman 2005; Scully 2008). The subsequent parliamentary and media discussion (see Emery *et al.* 2010) also revealed significant misunderstanding and misrepresentation of why (some) Deaf people should want to have, or at least not exclude the possibility of having, a deaf child. It was usually presented as a case of Deaf people wanting 'to have children like themselves'; in other words allowing their need to identify with their child, or their ideological convictions about populating a future Deaf community, to override their obligation to safeguard the child's best interests. This misses the point that, if the Deaf cultural perspective is that deafness is an identity, not an impairment (Anstey 2002), then the question of whether it is ethically permissible to inflict impairment on the child is not salient – although other ethical queries remain.

Commentators also failed to grasp that for the most part, Deaf people were not arguing for the right to select for (or to increase the chances of having) a deaf child. Suppose a woman undergoes IVF and PGD to produce six embryos, three of which have a gene associated with heritable deafness, and three of which do not. Opting to transfer the three 'hearing' ones expresses a preference to have hearing children. Opting for the three 'deaf' ones expresses a preference for deaf children (which is what the UK law is designed to prevent). An alternative possibility, however, is not to have a preference for either, or to want not to express a preference for either, if you believe there is no difference between deaf and hearing that would matter to you or to the child. (This need not entail holding the strong culturally Deaf position, but could also include the more moderate position that audiological deafness is an impairment, but not enough of a disadvantage that an alternative must always be preferred.)

The new clause blocks both the positive choice in favour of a child with genetic hearing impairment ('choosing a deaf child'), *and* the negative choice of not wanting to make any selection ('leaving it up to chance'). Although the debate has focused on the rights and wrongs of the positive choice, that is, expressing a preference for a deaf child, the people most likely to be affected are those who would prefer not to make any selection. Through its regulation of access to reproductive technology, the new Act embeds in law the conviction that deafness (and any of the other serious genetic conditions the law covers) is undesirable enough that an alternative embryo or gamete donor must *always* be preferred. Essentially this is a rejection of the possibility that a Deaf identity can ever be normative. The designers of the law clearly felt that this conviction was incontestable, although the subsequent public debate meant that it was challenged by a variety of stakeholders, including some disability groups.

The ethical importance of self-definition

the discourse of culture [is] a process involving a concerted focus on self-definition rather than being defined by hearing observers as had previously been the case.

(Leigh 2009: 15)

I have been arguing that the crucial fissure between disability and Deaf culture is to do with the contested meaning of deafness and whether it should be seen as impairment, or as a neutral but identity-forming characteristic. The lack of unanimity here is important for the reasons outlined above: the difficulty that the Deaf cultural understanding presents for disability studies' attempts to produce a coherent theory of disability, and the effect that the exclusion of Deaf people has on the movement's political authority. Disability theory needs to address the theoretical tension, because as an academic discipline it is required to analyse and understand the phenomenon of disability in all its manifestations and through all its consequences. If the empirical evidence about the lives of deaf and disabled people, and their own statements about identity or belonging, sit uneasily with the theory, then the theory needs to be modified.

If accounting for a culturally Deaf identity is problematic for disability theory, one approach would be to accept the difficulties as insurmountable: disability theory just does not give an adequate account of Deaf experience. That still leaves us with the problem of a theory that is unable to account for an awkward observation. Another possibility would be to say that Deaf identity is not, and cannot be, a cultural minority; that the claim is quite simply mistaken. But for disability theory to do that would be to take away from Deaf people their authority to define who they are. The contemporary politics of identity holds that recognition is as much about processes of self-definition as it is about creating political entities (Taylor 1994; Honneth 1996; Lloyd 2005). If so, then refusing to accept a group's self-definition is wrong for two reasons: first, because it compromises the group's ability to disavow the negative characterizations created by others, and second, and more fundamentally, because it fails to respect the individuals concerned as autonomous agents. To respect the autonomy of a deaf woman, for example, means crediting her with the epistemic and semantic capacity to articulate her selfhood to others in ways that are in keeping with her own experience, rather than the hearing world's understanding – or the culturally Deaf world's, if her experience happens not to fit that. To say that her claim to a Deaf identity is meaningless, or conversely to say that she is not 'authentically' deaf because she sees her deafness as an impairment and not as a neutral variation, effectively denies her capacity for self-definition. It inflicts moral harm by holding her to a reduced mode of being (Taylor 1994: 25).

Concluding comments

D/deaf identities present disability studies with some serious difficulties in terms of theorizing disability, the relationship between disability, impairment and 'normal' variation, and in framing the relationship between disability and identity. These difficulties are not just of interest to disability scholars, as deaf identities are also problematic for the political disability movement, bringing anxieties about fragmentation and weakened political and ethical claims. Such anxieties raise broader questions about the nature of collective identity and the politics of recognition that cannot be given detailed examination here (but see Scully 2008; Leigh 2009). What *can* be said is that in the D/deaf world, 'reliance on a single and primary unifying identity is giving way to the plurality of identities/self-labels' (Leigh 2009: 166), and that within both the disability and deaf worlds there seems now to be greater acceptance that diversity of experience is an empirical reality that cannot be glossed over for the sake of ideological neatness (Corker 1998; Padden and Humphries 2005; Fernandes and Myers 2010). Attempting to do so runs the risk not just of being theoretically untrue but of losing political credibility, as the rhetoric starts to diverge from the realities of deaf people's lives.

It could be argued that having a deaf identity, in which one is a person disabled by social or attitudinal barriers, is fully compatible with the theories of disability that see physical impairments leading to disablement because of disabling social structures. But because it does not refer to impairment at all, a model of Deaf identity based on a culturally Deaf view of deafness as normative is hard if not impossible to contain within existing disability theory. For Corker, the main difference is that the disability movement focuses on social structures and sees identity emerging from socially structured difference; Deaf people on the other hand make identity claims based on cultural difference (Corker 2003). For its part, Deaf studies also has problems accommodating the growing diversity of experiences of deafness. As I've said, this diversity is likely to increase with the social acceptance and presence of deaf people in wider society, and as technological aids increase the range of ways in which deaf people can engage with the phonocentric world and perhaps also the fluidity of identities that can be maintained. The difficulty here is to account for the full range of experiences and deaf identities they generate, while remaining as theoretically consistent as possible.

I have detailed elsewhere (Scully 2008) why I consider that it may be helpful to shift the explanatory framework away from the language of either impairment or of a neutral identity-forming characteristic, and from Corker's binary of socially versus culturally generated differences, towards the examination of phenotypic variations in context. Deafness and disability should be understood as instances of embodied human diversity that cannot be evaluated if displaced from the specific familial, cultural and social context in which they will be lived. The varied accounts of D/deaf identities indicate that the *same* phenotypic variation can have very different meanings to different deaf people. The features that determine whether deafness is lived as a damaged or a normative identity are partly intrinsic (type and stability of hearing impairment, age of onset, association with other impairments), but the most decisive factor in the formation of a culturally Deaf identity may well be simply the degree to which the normality of deafness is endorsed by family and community.

Interestingly, some recent legal discourse on disability gives indications of moving towards the idea that (at least some kinds of) disability are the consequence of a general societal intolerance of the possibilities of human diversity. For example, the United Nations Convention on the Rights of Persons with Disabilities, which came into force in May 2008, contains a statement of eight General Principles in Article 3 that guided the thinking behind the Convention and that should guide how it is interpreted in the future. General Principle (d) is given as *Respect for difference and acceptance of persons with disabilities as part of human diversity and humanity*. Many of the key terms in this principle are open to interpretation; but it is possible to understand the phrase 'acceptance of persons with disabilities as part of human diversity and humanity' to mean that disability is not *necessarily* an undesirable anomaly in human life, and that at least some forms of disability may be considered as human variations that, in the right context, can be trivially or not at all disadvantageous.

While this is not the only possible interpretation of General Principle (d), the move towards a discourse of disability 'diversity' rather than 'impairment' or 'anomaly' is significant, and one that may offer a more fruitful way of including Deaf culture and disability within the same theoretical and political language (Scully 2011, in press).

Ultimately then the difficulties faced by both disability and Deaf studies are potentially creative, forcing the re-examination of inadequate theory, based sometimes on equally inadequate empirical knowledge. Deaf scholars such as Corker (1998), Leigh (2009) and Scully (2008), and disability scholars such as Watson (2002), Shakespeare (2006) and Thomas (2007), have all drawn attention to the need for models of deafness and of disability respectively to be more faithful to the empirical evidence that experiences of both deafness and of disability are highly contextual and result from different kinds of mismatch between cultural expectations of normality and the realities of a person's embodiment. An empirical approach that focuses on exploring the details of the mismatch between embodiment and expectation, rather than on the nature of the impairment or on the sociopolitical label of D/deaf or disabled, is also more in accord with contemporary views of identity as dynamic, contextual and intersubjective. In this way is possible to see the 'problem' of D/deaf identity as beginning to open up a theoretical space that enriches both Deaf and disability studies.

Notes

1 Throughout this chapter I use the convention by which audiological deafness is indicated with a lowercase d and cultural Deafness with an upper case D. Where I want to refer generally to both, I use deaf; when I want to emphasize that I'm referring to both, I use D/deaf.
2 Indeed, it has been suggested that it is not necessary to be audiologically impaired in order to be considered Deaf by the Deaf world.
3 The significance of the Deaf school to the perpetuation of the community lies behind the resistance of many Deaf activists to mainstreaming in education – that is, the policy of prioritizing the integration of children with impairments into standard schools. From the Deaf point of view the result is further dilution and fragmentation of the sites of Deaf culture.
4 There are clearly problems with referring to 'the deaf community' in a discussion that emphasizes the plurality of identifications of deaf people. Throughout this chapter I am using 'community' in a loose sense, to indicate deaf people generally, without making any strong claims to community coherence or uniformity, and without denying that, in a very real sense, multiple communities of deaf people exist.

References

Anstey, K. W. (2002) 'Are Attempts to Have Impaired Children Justifiable?', *Journal of Medical Ethics* 28(5): 286–8.

Appiah, K. A. (1994) 'Identity, Authenticity, Survival: Multicultural Societies and Social Reproduction', in A. Gutmann, ed., *Multiculturalism* (Princeton, NJ: Princeton University Press): pp. 149–64.

Arnos, K. S. (2003) 'The Implications of Genetic Testing for Deafness', *Ear and Hearing* 24(4): 324–31.

Barnes, C. (1996) 'Theories of Disability and the Origins of Oppression of Disabled People in Western Society', in L. Barton, ed., *Disability and Society: Emerging Issues and Insights* (London: Longman): pp. 43–60.

Barnes, C., Mercer, G. and Shakespeare, T. (1999) *Exploring Disability: A Sociological Introduction* (Cambridge: Polity Press).

Bauman, H.-D. L. (2005) 'Designing Deaf Babies and the Question of Disability', *Journal of Deaf Studies and Deaf Education* 10(3): 311–15.

Campbell, J. and Oliver, M. (1996) *Disability Politics: Understanding Our Past, Changing Our Future* (London: Routledge).

Chorost, M. (2005) *Rebuilt: How Becoming Part Computer Made Me More Human* (New York: Houghton Mifflin).

Christiansen, J. B. and Leigh, I. (2002/2005) *Cochlear Implants in Children: Ethics and Choices* (Washington, DC: Gallaudet University Press).

Corker, M. (1996) *Deaf Transitions: Images and Origins of Deaf Families, Deaf Communities and Deaf Identities* (London: Jessica Kingsley Publishers).

Corker, M. (1998) *Deaf and Disabled, or Deafness Disabled?* (Buckingham: Open University Press).

Corker, M. (as Scott-Hill) (2003) 'Deafness/disability – Problematising Notions of Identity, Culture and Structure', in S. Riddell and N. Watson, eds, *Disability, Culture and Identity* (Harlow: Pearson Education Ltd): pp. 88–104.

Crow, L. (1996) 'Including All of Our Lives: Renewing the Social Model of Disability', in J. Morris, ed., *Encounters With Strangers: Feminism and Disability* (London: Women's Press): pp. 206–22.

Doe, L. (2007) 'Cochlear Implants: Are They Really a Threat to the Deaf Community?' *Deaf Worlds* 23(1): 1–17.

Emery, S. D., Middleton, A. and Turner, G. H. (2010) 'Whose Deaf Genes are They Anyway? The Deaf Community's Challenge to Legislation on Embryo Selection', *Sign Language Studies* 10(2): 155–69.

Fernandes, J. K. and Myers, S. S. (2010) 'Inclusive Deaf Studies. Barriers and Pathways', *Journal of Deaf Studies and Deaf Education* 15: 17–29.

Finkelstein, V. (1996) 'Interview', in J. Campbell and M. Oliver, *Disability Politics: Understanding Our Past, Changing Our Future* (London: Routledge): p. 111.

Foster, S. and Kinuthia, W. (2003) 'Deaf Persons of Asian American, Hispanic American, and African American Backgrounds: A Study of Intraindividual Diversity and Identity', *Journal of Deaf Studies and Deaf Education* 8(3): 271–90.

Goggin, G. and Newell, C. (2003) *The Social Construction of Disability in New Media* (Lanham: Rowman & Littlefield).

Grosjean, F. (1996) 'Living with Two Languages and Two Cultures', in I. Parasni, ed., *Cultural and Language Diversity and the Deaf Experience* (New York: Cambridge University Press): pp. 20–37.

Harris, J. (1995) *The Cultural Meaning of Deafness* (Aldershot: Avebury).

Hintermair, M. (2008) 'Self-esteem and Satisfaction with Life of Deaf and Hard of Hearing People – A Resource-oriented Approach to Identity Work', *Journal of Deaf Studies and Deaf Education* 13(2): 278–300.

Holocomb, T. K. (1997) 'Development of Deaf Bicultural Identity', *American Annals of the Deaf* 142(2): 89–93.

Honneth, A. (1996) *The Struggle for Recognition: The Moral Grammar of Social Conflict* (Cambridge, MA: MIT Press).

Kenny, M. (2004) *The Politics of Identity: Liberal Political Theory and the Dilemmas of Difference* (Cambridge: Polity).

Ladd, P. (2007) 'Cochlear Implantation, Colonialism, and Deaf Rights', in L. Komesaroff, ed., *Surgical Consent* (Washington, DC: Gallaudet University Press): pp 1–29.

Ladd, P. and John, M. (1991) *Deaf People as a Minority Group: The Political Process, Course 251: Issues in Deafness* (Milton Keynes: Open University Press).

Lane, H. (1984) *When the Mind Hears: A History of the Deaf* (New York: Vintage).

Lane, H. (1992) *The Mask of Benevolence: Disabling the Deaf Community* (New York: Knopf).

Lane, H. and Bahan, B. (1998) 'Ethics of Cochlear Implantation in Young Children: A Review and Reply from a Deaf-World Perspective', *Otolaryngology – Head and Neck Surgery* 119(4): 297–313.

Leigh, I. (2009) *A Lens on Deaf Identities* (Oxford: Oxford University Press).

Leigh, I., Maxwell-McCaw, D., Bat-Chava, Y. and Christiansen, J. B. (2008) 'Correlates of Psychosocial Adjustment in Deaf Adolescents With and Without Cochlear Implants: A Preliminary Investigation', *Journal of Deaf Studies and Deaf Education* 14(2): 244–59.

Levy, N. (2002) 'Deafness, Culture and Choice', *Journal of Medical Ethics* 28(5): 284–5.

Lloyd, M. (2005) *Beyond Identity Politics: Feminism, Power and Politics* (London: Sage).

Most, T., Wiesel, A. and Blitzer, T. (2007) 'Identity and Attitudes Towards Cochlear Implant Among Deaf and Hard of Hearing Adolescents', *Deafness and Education International* 9(2): 68–82.

Nance, W. E. (2003) 'The Genetics of Deafness', *Mental Retardation and Developmental Disabilities Research Reviews* 9(2):109–19.

Nunes, R. (2001) 'Ethical Dimension of Paediatric Cochlear Implantation', *Theoretical Medicine and Bioethics* 22(4): 337–49.

Oliver, M. (1990) *The Politics of Disablement* (Basingstoke: Macmillan).

Oliver, M. (2006) *Understanding Disability: From Theory to Practice* (London: Palgrave Macmillan).

Padden, C. and Humphries, T. (1988) *Deaf in America: Voices from a Culture* (Cambridge, MA: Harvard University Press).

Padden, C. and Humphries, T. (2005) *Inside Deaf Culture* (Cambridge, MA: Harvard University Press).

Peters, S. (2000) 'Is There a Disability Culture? A Syncretisation of Three Possible World Views', *Disability & Society* 15(4): 583–601.

Preston, P. (2001) *Mother Father Deaf: Living between Sound and Silence* (Cambridge, MA: Harvard University Press).

Scully, J. L. (2008) *Disability Bioethics: Moral Bodies, Moral Difference* (Lanham: Rowman & Littlefield).

Scully (2011, in press) 'Disability and the Pitfalls of Recognition', in J. McLaughlin, P. Phillimore and D. Richardson, eds, *Contesting Recognition: Culture, Identity and Citizenship* (Palgrave).

Shakespeare, T. (2006) *Disability Rights and Wrongs* (Abingdon: Routledge).

Shakespeare, T. and Watson, N. (2001) 'The Social Model of Disability: An Outdated Ideology? Exploring Theories and Expanding Methodologies', *Research in Social Science and Disability* 2: 9–28.

Smiler, K. and McKee, R. L. (2007) 'Perceptions of Maori Deaf Identity in New Zealand', *Journal of Deaf Studies and Deaf Education* 12(1): 93–111.

Smith, R. J. H., Hildebrand, M. and Van Camp, G. (2010) [1999] 'Deafness and Hereditary Hearing Loss Overview', *Gene Reviews*; available online at http://www.ncbi.nlm.nih.gov/books/NBK1434/ (accessed 29 July 2011).

Sparrow, R. (2005) 'Defending Deaf Culture: The Case of Cochlear Implants', *Journal of Political Philosophy* 13(2): 135–52.

Spriggs, M. (2002) 'Lesbian Couple Create a Child Who is Deaf Like Them', *Journal of Medical Ethics* 28(5): 283.

Swain, J. and French, S. (2000) 'Towards an Affirmation Model of Disability' *Disability & Society* 15(4): 569–82.

Taylor, C. (1994) 'The Politics of Recognition', in A. Gutmann, ed., *Multiculturalism* (Princeton, NJ: Princeton University Press): pp. 22–73.

Thomas, C. (2007) *Sociologies of Disability and Illness* (Basingstoke: Palgrave Macmillan).

Ville, L., Crost, M., Ravaud, J.-F. and Tetrafig Group (2003) 'Disability and a Sense of Community Belonging. A Study Among Tetraplegic Spinal-cord-injured Persons in France', *Social Science and Medicine* 56(2): 321–32.

Watson, N. (2002) 'Well I Know This is Going to Sound Very Strange to You, But I Don't See Myself as a Disabled Person: Identity and Disability', *Disability & Society* 17(5): 509–27.

Wheeler, A., Archbold, S., Gregory, S. and Skipp, A. (2007) 'Cochlear Implants: The Young People's Perspective', *Journal of Deaf Studies and Deaf Education* 12(3): 303–16.

Woll, B. and Ladd, P. (2003) 'Deaf Communities', in M. Marschark and P. E. Spencer, eds, *Oxford Handbook of Deaf Studies, Language, and Education* (Oxford: Oxford University Press): pp. 51–63.

10

THEORIZING THE POSITION OF PEOPLE WITH LEARNING DIFFICULTIES WITHIN DISABILITY STUDIES

Progress and pitfalls

Kirsten Stalker

Introduction

From the 1960s through to at least the 1990s, the dominant theoretical framework within the academic study of learning difficulties, and within policy-making and service delivery for people with learning difficulties, was normalization: arguably this is still the case (Yates *et al.* 2008; Walmsley 2010). Normalization has been roundly critiqued by writers within and outside disability studies (DS), for example because it fails to explain the oppression of people with learning difficulties or to offer a means of liberation (Oliver 2009). On the other hand, Race *et al.* (2005) suggest that academic differences between DS and normalization are ideological rather than substantive, pointing to similarities between their respective analyses of devaluation that would repay closer examination.

Nevertheless, there have been few attempts to theorize the position of people with learning difficulties in DS. Some writers have asserted that DS has ignored people with learning difficulties (Chappell 1997; Walmsley 1997, 2010) or that the social model of disability fails to address the barriers facing them (Aspis 2000). Others have gone further, arguing that this has resulted in a 'discursive othering' (Dowse 2001) or disempowerment (Roets *et al.* 2004) of people with learning difficulties, many of whom do not find the social model accessible (Docherty *et al.* 2010). DS has also been charged with failing to take researchers with learning difficulties seriously (Bjornsdottir and Svensdottir 2008; Aspis 2000).

People with learning difficulties were certainly missing from the definition of disability coined by UPIAS (tellingly, the Union of the *Physically* Impaired against Segregation), which formed the basis of the social model of disability, namely:

> Disability is the disadvantage or restriction caused by a contemporary social organisation which takes no or little account of people who have physical impairments and thus excludes them from the mainstream of social activities.
>
> *(UPIAS 1976: 20)*

Although the word 'physical' was later removed, Shakespeare (2006) suggests that a broader definition of impairment might have led to a richer understanding of disability.

Most 'key' DS texts make little reference to people with learning difficulties. Oliver's seminal *Politics of Disablement* (1990), which sets out the main theoretical framework for the social model, makes little mention of people with learning difficulties – an omission which he later defended on the grounds that disabled people should not be divided into impairment groups. A notable exception is *Another Disability Studies Reader? Including people with learning difficulties* (Goodley and van Hove 2005), which specifically aims to develop a better understanding of people with learning difficulties within DS, and includes several writings by and with people with learning difficulties. Goodley (2004a) also edited a Special Issue of the *British Journal of Learning Disabilities* along similar lines.

In the United Kingdom (UK), where DS has been dominated by the social model of disability, there has been a steady trickle of work about people with learning difficulties by academics, researchers and, increasingly, people with learning difficulties themselves since the 1990s. Some of this thinking focuses on developing an inclusive social model of disability, some centres around inclusive research and how to do it, and some of it draws on social constructionism, post-structuralism and/or post-modernism. In the United States (US), where for several decades interpretivism and, particularly, social constructionism have been key perspectives in understanding the position of people with learning difficulties, inquiries into their social, cultural and political situation are more firmly grounded within DS (Taylor 1996). Goodley (2004a) reports that DS in Belgium, France, Scandinavia, Croatia and Australasia closely reflects the agendas of people with learning difficulties.

This chapter aims to give an overview of how far, in what ways and how effectively learning difficulties has been theorized within DS. It includes an examination of the concept of impairment – a highly contested area, but key to different ways of understanding the experiences of people with learning difficulties. The chapter concludes with some suggestions for future directions of travel. I am using the term 'people with learning difficulties' because that is the preferred term of the self-advocacy movement.

How far and in what ways does the social model account for the experiences of people with learning difficulties?

Experiences people with learning difficulties share with other disabled people

Some writers have argued that the social model *does* have the potential to account for the experiences of people with learning difficulties but that it has not as yet been fully applied to them and that further theorization is needed to include them.

As various DS commentators have pointed out, there are a number of dimensions on which the social model appears to fit very well with the position of people with learning difficulties. First, the model rests on a Marxist analysis of the impact of capitalism and industrialization on people with impairments: this applies equally to those with learning difficulties (Ryan and Thomas 1987). The rise of the long-stay institution, eugenics and the emergence of professionals further contributed to their oppression (Chappell 1997). Today, new forms of governance associated with increasing globalization, neo-liberalism and the 'risk society' present new challenges at both a personal and political level for people with learning difficulties (Dowse 2009).

Second, like other disabled people, those with learning difficulties experience exclusion and discrimination in many areas of their lives – for example, in the health service (Disability Rights Commission 2006), education (National Institute of Adult Continuing Education 1998), employment (Berthoud and Blekesaune 2007), housing (Edgar and Muirhead 1997) and transport (Jolly *et al.* 2006). There are proportionally higher rates of poverty among disabled people, including those with learning difficulties (Emerson *et al.* 2005), than the non-disabled population. Simpson (1999) argues that people with learning difficulties must demonstrate competence before being given liberty – the opposite of what applies to other citizens. Often they are not listened to, not respected and subject to other people's judgements and decisions.

Third, numerous studies have shown that people with learning difficulties face attitudinal barriers that range from being patronized or pitied to harassment and hate crime. As children and adults they may be subject to high levels of abuse and neglect. These experiences are not so well addressed in the so-called 'strong' social model but are addressed in Thomas's (1999, 2007) concept of 'psycho-emotional disablism', meaning:

> The intended or 'unintended' 'hurtful' words and social actions of non-disabled people (parents, professionals, complete strangers, others) in interpersonal engagement with people with impairments. ... The effects of psycho-emotional disablism can be profound.
>
> *(2007: 72)*

The cumulative impact of psycho-emotional disablism can lead to 'barriers to being', meaning restrictions on who an individual feels they can be or become, their inner world, sense of self and social behaviours being negatively shaped by these experiences. Thomas further argues that psycho-emotional disablism interacts with restrictions imposed on disabled people in various areas of their lives including employment and education. Given that psycho-emotional disablism is a common occurrence for people with learning difficulties, it is surprising that this concept has been little explored in relation to this group.

Finally, while people with learning difficulties may be less likely to face the material barriers experienced by those with physical or sensory impairments (although some people with learning difficulties have other impairments as well), they often face barriers in terms of information provision, including inaccessible formats, use of jargon and complex language (Stalker and Lerpiniere 2008). Current developments in communication such as texting, the internet and emails create additional barriers for some (Docherty *et al.* 2010).

In short, people with learning difficulties have similar experiences to other disabled people on several dimensions that are addressed by the social model of disability. The concept of psycho-emotional disablism is also relevant. However, there are other ways in which the position of people with learning difficulties may be seen as distinctive.

Experiences which may be distinctive to people with learning difficulties

First, a potential difficulty for the inclusion of people with learning difficulties in the social model has been the latter's focus on the body as 'the site of impairment' (Chappell 1997). Boxall (2002) suggests that the experiences of people with learning difficulties may have more in common with other minorities' experiences of marginalization than with other disabled people's experiences of impairment (pain, fatigue and so on). On the other hand, Shakespeare (2006) argues that disablism differs from sexism or racism in that there is nothing intrinsically disadvantageous in having black skin or being female, whereas there are real drawbacks to having an impairment. I will return to the question of embodiment towards the end of the chapter.

Second, an important feature of DS is its stance on disability as part of a positive collective identity, reflected in the concept of 'disability pride' within the Disabled People's

Movement. In contrast, people with learning difficulties – as represented in the self-advocacy movement – generally reject being labelled as disabled, preferring to focus on their shared humanity with fellow citizens (Taylor 1996). The slogan of the international People First movement, as many writers point out, is 'label jars, not people'. There are isolated examples of individuals with learning difficulties celebrating their impairment (e.g., de Souza's positive statement, quoted in Goodley (2001: 217), about having 47 rather than 46 'cells': her father called this 'Up Syndrome' rather than Down's syndrome). However, it is more common for people to distance themselves from the traits and stigma typically associated with learning difficulty and sometimes for relatively 'able' individuals to differentiate themselves from those with more severe impairments (McVittie *et al.* 2008).

Third, although this is a contested area, the 'strong' social model downplays the role of personal experience in understanding disability and oppression. Personal experience is very important to many individuals with learning difficulties who tend to focus on their own stories – concrete examples drawn from day to day life – in discussion (Walmsley 1997). Partly for this reason, many studies with people with learning difficulties have used life history methods. On the other hand, there have been many calls for the social model to recognize the significance of personal experience (e.g., Morris 1991, Crow 1996, Shakespeare and Watson 2002). The issue therefore may be how to support people to move from anecdotal accounts to more generalized analysis of shared experiences, as discussed below.

Lastly, there is an argument that the widespread prejudice and discrimination faced by people with learning difficulties also obtain within DS. Aspis (quoted in Campbell and Oliver 1996) suggests other disabled people are frightened of being labelled 'stupid' if they associate with people with learning difficulties or include them in DS. Docherty *et al.* (2010) perceive a hierarchy of impairments within the Disabled People's Movement, in which people with learning difficulties and those with mental distress are at the bottom, 'like the doormat of disability' (p. 438).

These problems indicate a need for more theorization. However, more attention has been paid to *who* is, or should be, developing theory rather than to actually doing it. The next section reviews these arguments because they have implications for theory development.

Who should theorize about 'learning disability' – and how?

There has been increasing criticism of writing and research about people with learning difficulties that does not involve them in the process,[1] mirroring earlier calls for the withdrawal of non-disabled people from DS. Townson *et al.* (2004) describe any research that does not actively include people with learning difficulties in planning/executing it as 'rejecting research': this includes work that involves people with learning difficulties in some but not *all* aspects of a study. Aspis (2000) believes that people without learning difficulties deliberately exclude those with learning difficulties from research, for example by choosing not to fund proposals written by the latter or engage them in analysis, because to do so would diminish non-disabled researchers' power.

DS promotes emancipatory research in which disabled people are in control. A number of researchers have noted that most people with learning difficulties need support to conduct research and develop ideas. On the basis of many years' experience of conducting inclusive research, Walmsley (2010) suggests emancipatory research is 'more difficult' for most people with learning difficulties to achieve. Increasingly, there are published accounts of work under-taken by researchers with learning difficulties and their non-disabled supporters. Walmsley has critiqued this literature in terms of the power relations involved and how transparently – or not – these are represented. Most of this work is either very applied research – evaluations of services, investigations of how support could be improved – or life stories. Docherty *et al.* (2006), for example, describe how they have become increasingly assertive in standing up for their rights and discuss the improvements they would like to see in lifelong learning and transport provision. Spedding *et al.* (2002) recount parts of their life stories and reflect on what they have learnt while, in the same text, Chapman, a non-disabled volunteer with this group, argues that supporters have a role in facilitating a shift in perspective from the personal to the political aspects of self-advocacy, which 'links directly into the social model of disability'. They can assist self-advocates to understand that their individual experiences of oppression have common threads that relate to wider attitudes, structures and history. Boxall (2002) notes that some theorizing about people with learning difficulties within DS is 'complex' but adds that with support some individuals can gain an understanding of the basic principles of the social model. They may conceptualize their oppression as unfair treatment. Boxall *et al.* (2004) later give an account of a learning disability studies course at Manchester University which aims to contribute to the development of the social model by supporting people with learning difficulties to articulate their ideas.

One consequence, or perhaps symptom, of the tension between research conducted by academics alone and that carried out by self-advocates is a strain of what could be seen as anti-intellectualism or 'anti-theory' evident in some writings. Bjornsdottir and Svensdottir (2008), a PhD student and her co-researcher with learning difficulties, reject the notions of 'academic authority' and 'complex theory', stating that the latter is equally impenetrable to them both. Chapman and McNulty (2004) condemn the use of 'complicated methods' and academic concepts which 'reject people from so much they could be part of'. Boxall *et al.* (2004) refer to non-disabled researchers' 'vicarious interpretations' of the experiences of people with learning difficulties and criticize 'negative and disabling objective knowledge about people with learning difficulties produced by dominant group researchers' (p. 108).

Walmsley (2001) agrees that researchers should develop accessible ways to engage people with learning difficulties in theorizing but notes that the 'often complex, nuanced and difficult' nature of theory is not debated within DS. She admits she has been challenged by the ethical dilemma of how to support without 'taking over' and for this reason has on several occasions 'held back' from developing the theoretical implications of a study because to do so would have excluded her colleagues with learning difficulties. This leads her to pose some difficult questions regarding theoretical development, including: should we avoid theorizing if people with learning difficulties are not or cannot be included? If so:

> There is a risk that learning disability studies may remain the untheorised experience-based poor relation of its intellectually wealthier cousins in disability studies, feminism and black studies.
>
> *(Walmsley and Johnson 2003: 186)*

'Doing the social model'

A different view is that, while most people with learning difficulties may not be theorizing in the conventional sense or using academic methods to do so, some self-advocates are engaging with ideas inherent in the social model through everyday acts of resistance and resilience. However, the political nature of their actions often goes unrecognized and therefore untheorized (Chappell *et al.* 2001; Chapman and McNulty 2004).

Goodley (2001) gives some examples of people with learning difficulties 'doing' the social model in this way. One concerns Elaine, a self advocate who is driven to self-advocacy meetings by taxi because she has been assessed as unable to travel independently, including crossing roads, and never able to learn. Once the taxi has dropped her off and is out of sight, Elaine looks right and left then walks across the road to buy milk and biscuits for the meeting. The clinical psychologist's assessment of Elaine as incompetent is contrasted with the responsibility invested in her by the self-advocacy group for whom she is 'shopping manager'. Goodley concludes:

> She demands that we start asking how we see people with the label of learning difficulties, while alerting us to the contexts (real or imagined) in which we do the seeing.
>
> *(p. 221)*

Arguably, however, this incident is open to different interpretations and Goodley does not report having discussed his interpretation of Elaine's behaviour with her.

Those individuals with learning difficulties who have become successful researchers and commentators are sometimes described as atypical and unrepresentative of the wider population of people with learning difficulties. The implication is that their work is in some way invalid and the majority of people with learning difficulties could not be expected to produce work at a similar level. Bogdan and Taylor (1982) anticipated a similar response to the life stories of Ed Murphy and Pattie Burt, who were labelled as 'mentally retarded' and spent many years in institutions yet relate their histories with great insight and articulacy. Certainly, it is unfair to apply tests of representativeness to people with learning difficulties that are not generally applied to other groups. On the other hand, 'learning difficulties' is a blanket term applied to people with a very wide range of abilities, which brings us to the thorny issue of impairment.

Impairment – the contested issue

Although the original UPIAS (1976: 20) definition described impairment as 'lacking all or part of a limb, or having a defective limb, organism or mechanism of the body', the early social model did not on the whole discuss impairment. Abberley (1987) was unusual in proposing that a theory of disability as oppression must recognize the social *origins* of impairment, although he is sometimes cited as arguing for the social *construction* of disability which is an over-simplification of his position. For instance, he gave the example of phenylketournia (PKU) as a 'real' impairment leading to learning disability which can now be seen as 'socially determined' since diagnostic tests can detect and resolve the condition. However, the focus in the social model, at least in its early days, was very much on the socially constructed nature of *disability*, with impairment and its implications receiving little attention. The emphasis was on disabled people's shared experiences of oppression: considering impairment was tantamount to a return to the individual or medical model. Over the years, however, it has become a contested issue. Some DS theorists see impairment as socially constructed, others would argue it has a material or organic basis.

Impairment as a social construction

The social construction of learning difficulties has been traced across centuries. Historically people with learning difficulties have been ascribed many different identities – often opposing, contradictory identities, not of their making or choosing. They have been portrayed as asexual and as sexually promiscuous; as dangerous/innocent; in league with the devil/a gift from the angels and so on (Ryan and Thomas 1987; Simpson 1999; McClimens and Richardson 2010). In these examples, impairment itself may not be questioned; the focus is on its perceived meaning and significance.

In a study of eight Bengali mothers whose children had 'limited speech, challenging behaviour and severe impairments', Rao (2006) records how the women perceived their sons and daughters as competent, able, 'normal' (a word the mothers used) and intelligent, despite acknowledging their weak academic abilities. In this community, the most important skills for children to master were, first, understanding and fulfilling appropriate social roles and relationships within the family and, second, abiding by the tenets of 'good conduct'. These children were able to do both to their mothers' satisfaction. Their differences were seen as 'part of the normal range of human diversity' illustrating that, in Rao's words, 'while impairment is a human constant, how it is perceived depends on the social and cultural milieu of which it is part' (p. 160).

Other theorists argue that 'impairment' is a socially constructed category with little useful meaning but acknowledge that *difference*, including varying forms and levels of intelligence, exists. In their seminal life history work with Ed and Pattie, two former residents of long-stay institutions in the US, Bogdan and Taylor (1982) assert:

> The phrase 'mental retardation' does point to a state of mind – not the state of mind of the people who are alleged to have it, but the state of mind of those who use the concept in thinking about others. Mental retardation is a misnomer, a myth.
>
> *(p. 7)*

Bogdan and Taylor highlight the flawed nature of IQ testing, which remains a key determinant of a 'diagnosis' of learning difficulty today. They suggest that the existence of people with lower levels of intellectual ability does not prove the existence of 'mental retardation' any more than, in the Middle Ages, the existence of people who disturbed or upset their neighbours proved the existence of witchcraft. In a later paper, Taylor (1996) argues that 'learning difficulties' is a social phenomenon resulting from educational systems that assess, test and classify children (see also Dowse 2001 and Aspis 1999). A similar argument can be made in relation to welfare benefits systems. Individuals' disability status can change overnight when new definitions of disability or new eligibility criteria for benefits are introduced.

Goodley and colleagues in a series of texts (Goodley 2001, 2004b; Goodley and Rapley 2002; Goodley and van Hove 2005) go further, apparently arguing that impairment, or at least learning difficulties, is totally socially, linguistically and discursively constructed and that no *real* differences exist between those labelled with learning difficulties and the rest of the population. Goodley (2001: 217) refers to the 'absurdity of genetically oriented notions of personhood and the associated assumptions of inability'. He argues that:

> social structures, practices and relationships naturalise the subjectivities of people with 'learning difficulties', conceptualising them in terms of some a priori notion of 'mentally impaired'.
>
> *(p. 211)*

At times using a postmodernist analysis, these writers reject the dualisms of impairment/disability, mild/severe learning difficulty and the individual/society. Goodley (2001) proposes that a theory of disability which should include and explain the experiences of people with learning difficulties, by recognizing what he calls the social origins of impairment, would have four elements. The first involves a 'deconstruction of impairment', analysing relevant literature to show the social basis of diagnostic criteria. The second is 'impairment as storied': this would draw upon the life histories of people with learning difficulties to highlight their own definitions and accounts of themselves, thus challenging those ascribed by traditional labelling and diagnostic categories. The third element, 'reculturizing impairment', focuses on people's resistance to imposed definitions and restrictions, citing individual examples. The fourth, 'epistemological impacts', involves an examination of the ways that understandings of 'learning difficulties' affect those who are given the label. For example, people who make assumptions about the low competence of others will interpret the latter's actions in that light and miss other explanations which contradict their belief.

While each element promises interesting material and has validity (e.g., other research has shown the socio-cultural determinants of certain medical diagnoses), the proposed theory would not tell the 'whole story' of learning difficulties, 'disprove' the existence of an organic basis in some cases nor explain variations in people's intellectual abilities. Nonetheless, Goodley concludes:

> It is no good theorising impairment in relation to learning difficulties if biological assumptions direct (aspects of) analysis. The only theory left would be one shot through with the ideology of individualism and pathology.
>
> *(p. 225)*

I will return to this particular dualism later.

Drawing on interpretivist conceptualizations, Goodley argues that people with 'learning difficulties' [sic] are 'voluntaristic individuals engaged in constructing identities and negotiating roles'. In a later paper, Goodley and Rapley (2002) argue that the 'phenomenon known as learning difficulties' would be better understood as aspects of social interaction. They suggest that acquiescence bias, sometimes attributed to people with learning difficulties as 'evidence' of the unreliability of their spoken accounts, is brought about through 'psy-complex practices' and that closer examination, for example of interview data, shows an interactional resilience that often goes unrecognized.

Yates *et al.* (2008) takes up Goodley's call to challenge accepted epistemologies by drawing on Foucault and discourse analysis. They highlight what they see as a conceptual problem in the notion of a pre-social being designated as having learning difficulties who does not respond actively to negative socialization. From this perspective, essential attributes of the human subject cannot be separated from the social domain, the very notion of learning difficulties arising only within certain systems of knowledge:

> A subject is both constituted as an object of thought within systems of knowledge (power) and at the same time actively engaged in their own projects of selfhood and struggling with the ways their subjectivities are constituted and power takes hold of them.
>
> *(p. 256)*

Similarly, Roets *et al.* (2008) draw on postmodernist feminist thought to argue that learning difficulties has been naturalized as impairment through the mechanisms of truth, power and knowledge. They question 'essentialist rhetoric' – the idea that reality exists independent of cultural and historical circumstances – which they argue constructs categories and subject positions which become accepted as pre-given, universal and immutable. However, they do not explain why some individuals – and not others – come to be labelled with learning difficulties. This complex theoretical paper is co-authored by two people with learning difficulties. It is not clear what the various authors' respective contributions were.

Impairment as a reality

Other DS theorists take a different view about the nature of impairment. Various commentators (Morris 1991; Crow 1996; Shakespeare and Watson 2002) have called for DS to pay greater attention to impairment and its implications. Thomas's (1999, 2007) concept of 'impairment effects' refers to restrictions of activity imposed on people as a direct consequence of having an impairment (e.g., a dyscalculiac person struggles with mathematical concepts and may have difficulty with financial accounting) as opposed to restrictions imposed on people with impairments as a result of other people's disabling actions. In Thomas's (2007) view, it is 'nonsensical' to suggest that learning difficulties are entirely socially constructed, while Vehmas and Mäkelä (2009) opine that some postmodernist thinking in this area is 'peculiar, confusing and even unhelpful'. Baron *et al.* (1998), Riddell *et al.* (2001), Walmsley and Johnson (2003) and Shakespeare (2006) all express similar reservations. Oliver (2009) – although sometimes charged with neglecting the implications of impairment – nevertheless declared that having one was a necessary condition of being a disabled person. Abberley (1987), while arguing for a recognition of the social origins of impairment, also described himself as having a 'very obvious collection of impairments' as a result of polio: in other words, not all impairments are exclusively social all of the time. Marks (1999) warns against denying the real problems faced by an individual with organic brain damage, reasoning that it is important to acknowledge and respect difference rather than seek to erase it. A practical consequence of the latter may be that people will not receive the support to which they are entitled, resulting in further exclusion.[2]

Boxall *et al.* (2004) argue that if people with learning difficulties are to benefit from the social model, then there is a need to focus on their similarities to other disabled people rather than the differences. They further state their 'commitment' not to attribute any problems or difficulties people experience to individual deficit but rather to external barriers. This suggests a selective approach to considering evidence and implies that if all material and social barriers were removed, people with learning difficulties would face no limitations – a position Walmsley and Johnson (2003) and Shakespeare (2006) consider untenable. Perhaps the challenge this poses to the wider social model is one reason why few disability scholars have explored the issue in depth.

Race *et al.* (2005) suggest that viewing impairment as 'perceived' or 'accredited' obviates the need to consider the truth or legitimacy of the impairment. This is not dissimilar to Goodley and Rapley's (2002) argument that impairment is linguistically constructed and could not even be discussed if language did not exist. However, in an analysis of the ontology of impairment and disability, Vehmas and Mäkelä (2009) reject the notion that impairments are simply matters of representation and discourse which can be done away with through a process of de- and reconstruction. These authors distinguish between 'brute facts' and 'institutional facts', the latter resting on language and representation, the former on 'brute physics and biology' (p. 45). They suggest that DS is dominated by social constructionism because of its political usefulness but propose that an ontology which recognizes the material origins of impairment, as well as the relational nature of disability, may prove more powerful in eradicating both organic and social causes of individual and collective distress. Similarly, Bhaskar and Danermark (2006), arguing for the use of critical realism in DS, comment:

> To weak constructionism, which involves the idea that there is a necessarily interpreted element in the construction of any theoretical understanding and any social object, a critical realist has no objection. However if this is taken to imply that the phenomenon investigated is *just* a theoretical interpretation or cognitive construction, or that a social phenomenon such as some specific form of disability exists *only* as an idea or belief, then it is clearly false.
>
> *(283–4)*

Several writers – including some who see learning difficulties as at least partly socially constructed – acknowledge that people with severe or profound impairments will always need some level of support (e.g., Simpson 1999; Richardson 2000). Klotz (2004: 98), writing about people with severe and profound learning difficulties, asserts that 'intellectual disability' is 'an ontological reality which makes a real difference to one's experience of being in the world'. She is critical of sociocultural approaches, including the work of Bogdan and Taylor, which 'ignore the implications of difference as *both* productive of the sociocultural world and the product of it' (p. 98). Indeed, there are some genetic conditions that involve both physiological and cognitive features, such as Down's syndrome, Prader Willi syndrome or Rett syndrome, where it is hard to see how difference can be viewed as totally socially constructed.

Summary and conclusions

This chapter has examined how far and in what ways the position of people with learning difficulties has been theorized in DS. It is difficult to avoid concluding that, in the UK, theorizing has been limited, in some respects flawed and is in danger of reaching an impasse. Several factors are involved. First, the social model, particularly in its early years, neglected people with learning difficulties. A number of reasons can be identified for this, including the dominance of normalization and the social model's emphasis on the body as the locus of impairment. While the social model may account for some of the experiences of people with learning difficulties, such as unjust treatment and communication barriers, other aspects fit less well or not at all. The implications for DS can be seen in different ways. It could become more inclusive, for example, by taking greater cognizance of personal experience while supporting individuals with learning difficulties to make links between their own lives and collective oppression, structural and historical factors. Alternatively, the position of people with learning difficulties could be seen as highlighting the inadequacies of the social model more widely. For example, if all physical and social barriers were taken away, would people with impairments still be at a disadvantage compared to those without?

More attention has been paid to people with learning difficulties within British DS in the last 10–15 years. Nevertheless, a second factor undermining theoretical development is that this has involved a relatively small group of people taking very different approaches. There has been little cumulative work with one team building on the work of another. Furthermore, some (including those who have pioneered inclusive research) have at times avoided theoretical work because of perceived barriers in involving people with learning difficulties. Others, including some who discount impairment, have produced complex texts likely to be inaccessible to most people with learning difficulties.

Third, ownership of learning difficulties research and, to a lesser extent, of theorizing has become a contested area. Much effort has gone into this contesting and less into advancing theory. There has been increasing research activity by people with learning difficulties, which is much to be welcomed. They have a unique perspective and valuable insights, as many studies have shown. However, work undertaken by/with people with learning difficulties generally takes the form of applied research or life histories rather than theory. It has been claimed that self-advocates are 'doing' the social model in their everyday lives, especially through acts of resistance and resilience. It is not always clear, however, if this interpretation has been raised with or claimed by the individuals concerned nor how far it helps advance theoretical development. Walmsley and Johnson (2003) argue that participatory rather than emancipatory research is more achievable for people with learning difficulties. These authors helpfully set out options for creative partnerships between researchers and people with learning difficulties.

Fourth, DS has been experienced as excluding and inaccessible by some in the learning disability field, but 'counter calls' for a blanket rejection of theoretical work, or of research which does not involve people with learning difficulties fully in the process, may restrict future development. This stance is somewhat disingenuous when coming from academics themselves. A more reflexive approach might recognize the academy's power to universalize ideas and values but, following Bourdieu (1990), be active in challenging *which* values and ideas are universalized and how.

Future directions of travel

At a conceptual level, it seems perverse for those who reject dualisms to then set up a binary opposition between a wholly social constructionist viewpoint on the one hand and 'an ideology shot through with individualism and pathology' (Goodley 2001: 205) on the other. Such polarization gives no space for a more nuanced position capable of capturing the considerable diversity, complexity, contingency and relationalism which, I would argue, characterize the position of people with learning difficulties.

To do this, DS could turn to critical realism, which offers the possibility of explaining a phenomenon in terms of 'a multiplicity of mechanisms, potentially of radically different kinds … corresponding to different levels or aspects of reality' (Bhaskar and Danermark 2006; see also Shakespeare 2006 and Watson, forthcoming 2012). From this perspective, neither nature nor non-human reality is socially constructed, but what we know about them is. Bhaskar and Danermark argue that each of the meta-theories informing DS, which they characterize as naive realism/empiricism, social constructionism, neo-Kantianism and hermeneutics, has valuable insights to offer but that none alone sufficiently explains disability. Critical realism is presented as 'doubly inclusive' because it embraces all causally relevant levels of reality – helping us understand material relations with nature, social interactions between agents, social structures and the stratification of agents' 'embodied personalities' (p. 289) – while at the same time accommodating the insights of the meta-theoretical positions mentioned above.

If DS adopted critical realism as a 'grand theory', then Thomas's proposed 'sociology of impairment' (1999, 2007) offers a complementary mid-range or substantive theory. Her concept of 'impairment effects', referred to earlier, recognizes the implications of specific impairments on people's day to day lives. However, this is an interaction, not a one-way process, since 'impairments and impairment effects are thoroughly enmeshed with the social conditions that bring them into being and give them meaning' (p. 151). Thomas argues that an impairment and its effects are both contingent on social context, and that impairment is influenced by social features and circumstances. Thus, neither an impairment nor its effects can be seen as purely biological; rather, they are 'complex bio-social phenomena'. This is reminiscent of Marks (1999), who emphasized the importance of biological, emotional, relational and unconscious levels of analysis in relation to theorizing learning difficulties, arguing that bodily, emotional and social differences are mutually constitutive.

In addition, I have suggested that the concept of psycho-emotional disablism appears to speak to the experiences of people with learning difficulties although it has been little explored in relation to them. Importantly, Thomas's model allows the impact of specific impairments to be acknowledged without detracting from the central role and significance of disablism.

This perspective has potential to fit with themes reviewed earlier in this chapter, including the social and cultural meaning of impairment, the impact of economic, administrative, health and welfare systems, the availability of support, the practical implications of specific impairments, the genetic or organic basis of some conditions – and how various aspects of these different dimensions may interact. It may offer a fruitful way forward for future work in this field.

Acknowledgements

Thanks to Jan Walmsley for helpful comments on this chapter.

Notes

1 Some readers will be critical of my decision not to invite a person with learning difficulties to co-author this chapter.
2 This is particularly concerning at a time of savage financial cuts in public services; for example, promoting the idea that people with learning difficulties can take on a wide range of paid work may result in their disability benefits being removed. Similarly, the personalization agenda, which has been so liberating for people with physical or sensory impairments, could carry significant risk for those with learning disabilities if their particular vulnerability is not addressed (Walmsley 2011, personal communication).

References

Abberley, P. (1987) 'The Concept of Oppression and the Development of a Social Theory of Disability', *Disability & Society* 2(1): 5–19.

Aspis, S. (1999) 'What They Don't Tell Disabled People with Learning Difficulties', in M. Corker and S. French, eds, *Disability Discourse* (Buckingham: Open University Press): pp. 173–82.

Aspis, S. (2000) 'Researching Our History: Who is in Charge?', in L. Brigham, D. Atkinson, M. Jackson, S. Rolph and J. Walmsley, eds, *Crossing Boundaries: Change and Continuity in the History of Learning Disability* (Kidderminster: British Institute for Learning Disability): pp. 1–5

Baron, S., Riddell, S. and Wilkinson, H. (1998) 'The Best Burgers? The Person with Learning Difficulties as Worker', in T. Shakespeare, ed., *The Disability Reader: Social Science Perspectives* (London: Cassell): pp. 94–109.

Berthoud, R. and Blekesaune, M. (2007) *Persistent Employment Disadvantage*, Research Report no. 416 (Leeds: Department for Work and Pensions).

Bhaskar, R. and Danermark, B. (2006) 'Metatheory, Interdisciplinarity and Disability Research: A Critical Realist Perspective', *Scandinavian Journal of Disability Research* (8)4: 278–97.

Bjornsdottir, K. and Svensdottir, A. S. (2008) 'Gambling for Capital: Learning Disability, Inclusive Research and Collaborative Life Histories', *British Journal of Learning Disabilities* 36(4): 256–62.

Bogdan, R. and Taylor, S. (1982) *Inside Out: The Social Meaning of Mental Retardation* (Toronto: University of Toronto Press).

Bourdieu, P. (1990) 'The Scholastic Point of View', *Cultural Anthropology* 5(4): 380–91.

Boxall, K. (2002) 'Individual and Social Models of Disability and the Experiences of People with Learning Difficulties', in D. G. Race, ed., *Learning Disability – A Social Approach* (London: Routledge): pp. 209–26.

Boxall, K., Carson, I. and Docherty, D. (2004) 'Room at the Academy? People with Learning Difficulties and Higher Education', *Disability & Society* 19(2): 99–112.

Campbell, J. and Oliver, M. (1996) *Disability Politics: Understanding Our Past, Changing Our Future* (London: Routledge).

Chapman, R. and McNulty, N. (2004) 'Building Bridges? The Role of Research Support in Self-advocacy', *British Journal of Learning Disabilities* 32(2): 77–85.

Chappell, A. L. (1997) 'From Normalisation to Where?', in L. Barton and M. Oliver (1997) *Disability Studies: Past, Present and Future* (Leeds: The Disability Press): pp. 45–61.

Chappell, A. L., Goodley, D. and Lawthom, R. (2001) 'Making Connections: The Relevance of the Social Model of Disability for People with Learning Difficulties', *British Journal of Learning Disabilities* (29) 2: 45–50.

Crow, L. (1996) 'Including All Our Lives: Renewing the Social Model of Disability', in C. Barnes and G. Mercer, eds, *Exploring the Divide: Illness and Disability* (Leeds: The Disability Press): pp. 55–73.

Disability Rights Commission (DRC) (2006) *Equal Treatment: Closing the Gap – A Formal Investigation into Physical Health Inequalities Experienced by People with Learning Disabilities and/or Mental Health Problems*; available online at http://www.leeds.ac.uk/disability-studies/archiveuk/DRC/Health%20FI%20main.pdf (accessed 14 September 2011).

Docherty, A., Harkness, E., Eardley, M., Townson, L. and Chapman, R. (2006) 'What They Want – Yes, But What We Want – Bugger Us!', in D. Mitchell, R. Traustadottir, R. Chapman, L. Townson,

N. Ingham and S. Ledger, eds, *Exploring Experiences of Advocacy by People with Learning Disabilities: Testimonies of Resistance* (London: Jessica Kingsley): pp. 100–7.

Docherty, D., Hughes, R., Phillips, P., Corbett, D., Regan, B., Barber, A., Adams, M., Boxall, K., Kaplan, I., Izzidien, S. (2010) 'This is What We Think', in L. J. Davis, ed., *The Disability Studies Reader* (London: Routledge): pp. 432–40.

Dowse, L. (2001) 'Contesting Practices, Challenging Codes: Self-advocacy, Disability Politics and the Social Model', *Disability & Society* (16)1: 123–41.

Dowse, L. (2009) 'Some People are Never Going to Be Able to Do That: Challenges for People with Intellectual Disability in the 21st Century', *Disability & Society* 24(5): 571–84.

Edgar, B. and Muirhead, I. (1997) 'Tenancy Rights for Community Care Client Groups in Supported Accommodation in Scotland', *Integrate News* 64, May: 7–9.

Emerson, E., Malam, S., Davies, I. and Spencer, K. (2005) Adults with Learning Disabilities in England 2003/04 (National Statistics, and NHS Health and Social Care Information Centre); available online at http://www.lancs.ac.uk/staff/emersone/FASSWeb/Emerson_05_ALDE_Main.pdf (accessed 1 August 2011).

Goodley, D. (2001) '"Learning Difficulties", The Social Model of Disability and Impairment: Challenging Epistemologies', *Disability & Society* 16(2): 207–31.

Goodley, D. (2004a) 'The Place of People with "Learning Difficulties" in Disability Studies and Research: Introduction to this Special Issue', *British Journal of Learning Disabilities* 32(2): 49–51.

Goodley, D. (2004b) 'Who is Disabled? Exploring the Scope of the Social Model of Disability', in J. Swain, S. French, C. Barnes and C. Thomas, eds, *Disabling Barriers, Enabling Environments*, 2nd edn (London: Sage): pp. 118–24.

Goodley, D. and Rapley, M. (2002) 'Changing the Subject: Postmodernity and People with "Learning Difficulties"', in M. Corker and T. Shakespeare, eds, *Disability/ Postmodernity: Embodying Disability* (London: Continuum): pp. 127–42.

Goodley, D. and van Hove, G., eds (2005) *Another Disability Studies Reader: Including People with Learning Difficulties* (Antwerp: Garant).

Jolly, D., Priestley, M. and Matthews, B. (2006) *Secondary Analysis of Existing Data on Disabled People's Use and Experiences of Public Transport in Great Britain* (Disability Rights Commission); available online at http://www.leeds.ac.uk/disability-studies/archiveuk/jolly/DRC%20transport%20research%20report%20-%20August%202006%20final.pdf (accessed 14 September 2011).

Klotz, J. (2004) 'Sociocultural Study of Intellectual Disability: Moving Beyond Labelling and Social Constructionist Perspectives', *British Journal of Learning Disabilities* 32(20): 93–104.

McClimens, A. and Richardson, M. (2010) 'Social Constructions and Social Models: Disability Explained?', in G. Grant, P. Ramcharan, M. Flynn and M. Richardson, eds, *Learning Disability: A Life Cycle Approach*, 2nd edn (Maidenhead: McGraw Hill/ Open University Press): pp. 19–32.

McVittie, C., Goodall, K. E. and McKinlay, A. (2008) 'Resisting Having Learning Disabilities by Managing Relative Abilities', *British Journal of Learning Disabilities* 36(4): 256–62.

Marks, D. (1999) 'Dimensions of Oppression: Theorising Through the Embodied Subject', *Disability & Society* 14(5): 611–26.

Morris, J. (1991) *Pride Against Prejudice: Transforming Attitudes to Disability* (London: The Women's Press).

National Institute of Adult Continuing Education (1998) *Continuing Education and Equal Opportunities for Adults with Learning Difficulties* (York: Joseph Rowntree Foundation).

Oliver, M. (1990) *The Politics of Disablement* (Basingstoke: Macmillan).

Oliver, M. (2009) *Understanding Disability: From Theory to Practice*, 2nd edn (Basingstoke: Palgrave Macmillan).

Race, D., Boxall, K. and Carson, I. (2005) 'Towards a Dialogue for Practice: Reconciling Social Role Valorisation and the Social Model of Disability', *Disability & Society* 20(5): 507–22.

Rao. S. (2006) 'Parameters of Normality and Cultural Constructions of "Mental Retardation": Perspectives of Bengali Families', *Disability & Society* 21(2): 159–78.

Richardson, M. (2000) 'How We Live: Participatory Research with Six people with Learning Difficulties', *Journal of Advanced Nursing* (32) 6: 1383–95.

Riddell, S., Baron, S. and Wilson, A. (2001) *The Learning Society and People with Learning Difficulties* (Bristol: Policy Press).

Roets, G., Reinaart, R., Marie Adams and Geert Van Hove, G (2008) 'Looking at Lived Experiences of Self-advocacy Through Gendered Eyes: Becoming *Femme Fatale* With/out "Learning Difficulties"', *Gender and Education* 20(1): 15–29.

Roets, G., Van de Perre, D., Van Hove, G., Schoeters, L. and de Schauwer, E. (2004) One for All – All for One! An Account of the Joint Fight for Human Rights by Flemish Musketeers and Their Tinker Ladies', *British Journal of Learning Disabilities* 32(2): 54–64.

Ryan, J. and Thomas, F. (1987) *The Politics of Mental Handicap*, revised edn (London: Free Association Books).

Shakespeare, T. (2006) *Disability Rights and Wrongs* (London: Routledge).

Shakespeare, T. and Watson. N. (2002) 'The Social Model of Disability: An Outdated Ideology?', *Research in Social Sciences and Disability* 2: 9–28.

Simpson, M. (1999) 'Bodies, Brains, Behaviours: The Return of the Three Stooges in Learning Disability', in M. Corker and S. French, eds, *Disability Discourse* (Buckingham: Open University Press): pp. 148–56.

Spedding, F., Harkness, E., Townson, L., Docherty, A., McNulty, N. and Chapman, R. (2002) 'The Role of Self Advocacy: Stories from a Self-advocacy Group Through the Experiences of its Members', in B. Gray and R. Jackson, eds, *Advocacy and Learning Disability* (London: Jessica Kingsley): pp. 137–51.

Stalker, K. and Lerpiniere, J. (2008) 'It's Against Our Law, Never Mind Anyone Else's: The Disability Discrimination Act 1995 and Adults with Learning Disabilities', *Disability & Society* 24(7): 829–43.

Taylor, S. (1996) 'Disability Studies and Mental Retardation', *Disability Studies Quarterly* 16(3): 4–13.

Thomas, C. (1999) *Female Forms: Experiencing and Understanding Disability* (Buckingham: Open University Press).

Thomas, C. (2007) *Sociologies of Disability and Illness* (Basingstoke: Macmillan).

Townson, L., Macauley, S., Harkness, E., Chapman, R., Docherty, A., Dias, J., Eardley, M. and McNulty, N. (2004) 'We Are All in the Same Boat: Doing "People-led" Research', *British Journal of Learning Disabilities* 32(2): 72–6.

UPIAS (1976) *The Union of the Physically Impaired Against Segregation and The Disability Alliance Discuss Fundamental Principles of Disability* (London: Union of the Physically Impaired Against Segregation); available online at http://www.leeds.ac.uk/disability-studies/archiveuk/UPIAS/fundamental%20principles.pdf (accessed 1 August 2011).

Vehmas, S. and Mäkelä, P. (2009) 'The Ontology of Disability and Impairment: A Discussion of the Social and Natural Features', in K. Kristiansen, S. Vehmas and T. Shakespeare, eds, *Arguing About Disability: Philosophical Perspectives* (Abingdon: Routledge): pp. 42–56.

Walmsley, J. (1997) 'Including People with Learning Disabilities: Theory and Practice', in L. Barton and M. Oliver, *Disability Studies: Past, Present and Future* (Leeds: The Disability Press): pp. 62–77.

Walmsley, J. (2001) 'Normalisation, Emancipatory Research and Inclusive Research in Learning Disability', *Disability & Society* 16(2): 187–215.

Walmsley, J. (2010) 'Research and Emancipation: Prospects and Problems', in G. Grant, P. Ramcharan, M. Flynn and M. Richardson, eds, *Learning Disability: A Life Cycle Approach*, 2nd edn (Maidenhead: McGraw Hill/Open University Press): pp. 489–502.

Walmsley, J. and Johnson, K. (2003) *Inclusive Research with People with Learning Disabilities: Past, Present and Future* (London: Jessica Kingsley).

Watson, N. (forthcoming 2012) 'How Can Disability Theory Help Our Understanding of the Lives of Disabled Children?', *Children & Society*.

Yates, S., Dyson, S. and Hiles, D. (2008) 'Beyond Normalisation and Impairments: Theorising Subjectivity in Learning Difficulties – Theory and Practice, *Disability & Society* 23(3): 247–58.

11

LONG-TERM DISABLING CONDITIONS AND DISABILITY THEORY

Sasha Scambler

Introduction

Long-term conditions (also known as chronic illnesses) have been defined as conditions that require management over a period of years or decades, affect multiple areas of daily life and, at the present time, have no cure (Turk 1979). As such, they can include anything from cancer to arthritis, multiple sclerosis, Parkinson's disease or Batten disease. There are a huge range of conditions or diseases that fall under the umbrella of long-term disabling conditions and vary according to diagnosis, trajectory and prognosis as well as the number and general profile of people living with the condition. This said, commonalities include the requirement to live with the condition on an ongoing basis, the effect on daily life, the impact of the associated disability/ disabilities associated with the condition and the lack of a 'cure'.

Long-term disabling conditions are the most common cause of disability in the developed world, and the most common disability in the United Kingdom (UK) is arthritis. To put this in context, in a population of 60+ million, there are approximately 17.5 million people in the UK with long-term conditions (Department of Health 2004). In spite of this, disabilities that occur as the result of long-term conditions are often relegated to the sidelines in mainstream disability studies texts. A token chapter on chronic illness can be found in the main textbooks but these lack the depth of discussion, research and theorizing that surrounds other forms of disability. If we want to explore the experiences of people living with long-term disabling conditions and the implications of these conditions on multiple areas of daily life, we need to move into medical sociology where there is a long tradition of research in the sociology of chronic illness. This offers insight into experiences of people living with a range of disabling conditions on a daily basis and includes explorations of coping strategies, stigma, narrative disruption/reconstruction, economic impact and illness/disease narratives but rarely focuses on the wider issues of political oppression and discrimination faced by these groups.

In this chapter I am going to make the case that more attention should be paid to long-term disabling conditions within disability studies. The case could be made simply on the prevalence of people living with these conditions, but I will also argue that an understanding of the nature of disabilities that emerges from the study of these types of conditions offers both consideration of a different 'type' of disability and a fresh insight into ongoing debates within disability studies. I start, then, with a selective outline or summary of key work within the sociology of long-term conditions before seeking to locate this work within a disability studies perspective. The second part of the chapter then takes two case studies of empirical work to illustrate the value of research in this area in addressing existing challenges and creating new ones. The first case study explores the emergence of 'empowerment' as a concept within healthcare policy and practice and the impact of this on people living with diabetes, positing this as a medicalization of the oppression approach. In the second case study the debate around the presence and relative importance of impairment, biology and the body is revisited with the aid of work on Batten disease: a long-term, life-limiting condition resulting in multiple disabilities. I finish with some thoughts about possible future directions for disability studies and how and why long-term disabling conditions should be an integral part of this future.

The sociology of long-term disabling conditions (chronic illness)

There is little disagreement about the definition of chronic illness, but a variety of approaches to the sociological study of chronic illness have developed, focusing specifically, in later decades, on the day-to-day experiences of living with a condition of this type. The sociology of chronic illness emerged in the 1950s when the American sociologist Talcott Parsons (1951) first focused sociological attention on health and illness. There is insufficient space here for a comprehensive review of the vast theoretical and empirical literature that has developed in this area over the past six decades but a selective overview of key approaches and themes is enough to demonstrate the relevance and importance of the inclusion of those with long-term life-limiting conditions in wider disability studies debates. Five broad theoretical approaches to sociological study in this area can be identified along with six key themes of daily life.

- Functionalist
- Interactionist
- Conflict
- Interpretative
- Social constructionist.

The functionalist approach

The sociology of chronic illness developed through the realization that the biomedical model of health does not adequately account for the significant effect that chronic illness has on the lives of the sufferers and their families. Parsons (1951) looked at health and illness and the maintenance of social roles, suggesting that health is the norm and that a person who is unwell is, therefore, deemed deviant. People who are unable to work through illness need legitimization for their inability to perform their 'normal' social roles and so take on a 'sick-role' for a temporary period until they are able to revert to their usual roles. Parsons sees the 'sick-role' as a form of 'sanctioned deviance'. Medical power provides legitimation for the temporary withdrawal from mainstream society. Parsons' work has been widely criticized as failing to take into account people with long-term or chronic conditions who remain in the 'sick-role' for extended periods of time, if not permanently, and for whom the 'sick-role' becomes their normal state (Kassebaum and Baumann 1965). In addition, Friedson (1970) challenges the idea that the 'sick role' is accepted by society, and suggests that the level of acceptance depends on whether the illness is seen as serious, the individual is seen as responsible for causing the illness and the illness is accepted as a legitimate one. Gordon (1966) posited the idea of an 'impaired role' that is permanent and extremely difficult to move out of, and forces people into an identity as a 'second class citizen' (Sieglar and Osmond 1974). This view can be seen to be perpetuated through the focus on adaptation and normalization and the biomedical approach to the treatment of impairment and chronic illness (Barnes *et al.* 1999) Barnes *et al.* suggest further that people with chronic illnesses are 'treated more as objects than as active participants in the treatment process' (Barnes *et al.* 1999: 42).

The interactionist approach

The idea of illness as deviance was developed by sociologists working from a symbolic interactionist perspective who devised the labelling theory looking at the processes through which a person is labelled as ill and deviant and the impact of this label. Goffman (1968) studied the categorization of people as 'normal' or 'abnormal' in society through interaction. He identified three classes of stigma covering: 'abominations of the body – the various physical deformities', including things like homosexuality, paraplegia and dwarfism; 'blemishes of individual character'; and 'the tribal stigma of race, nation and religion'. The negative image that these groups carry is contagious and is transferable to family and friends who are said to acquire 'courtesy stigma' (p. 44). In addition, management of the condition depends on the visibility of the symptoms. People with conditions that are visible and immediately apparent on interaction are 'discredited' and focus on managing the tension of the reactions of 'normals', whilst people with conditions that are not immediately apparent (such as controlled epilepsy) focus on managing information and disclosure or non-disclosure of the diagnosis. Coping strategies are dependent on the management of interactions, and three coping strategies were identified as 'passing', 'covering' and 'withdrawal'. 'Passing' is when a discreditable person focuses on management of information, 'covering' is when a discredited person focuses on the management of tension and 'withdrawal' is removal from any interaction with 'normal' people to avoid problems of interaction. Goffman suggests, further, that the stigmatized person is then forced into a role as an 'abnormal' person and all other aspects of their life have to fall within this role.

The use of stigma roles can be seen as a way of maintaining control of people who do not fit neatly into norms of broader society. It is expected that the stigmatized people should make a concerted effort to 'fit' back into society in their new roles and if they are seen to adjust well then they are acknowledged. 'This means that the "good adjustment" of the handicapped is actually a quality granted to them by others. Then people say about them things like, "he's very brave", or "she's always so cheerful"' (Radley 1994: 154). The inevitability of a stigmatized role has been challenged, however.

> For critics, Goffman's account is obsessed with the defensive, anxiety-ridden and largely doomed manoeuvrings of stigmatised individuals, and of their acceptance of the negative label.
>
> *(Barnes et al. 1999: 47)*

Higgins (1981) studied the management of stigma by a group of deaf people. He found that the emphasis was placed on maintaining everyday functioning rather than managing their stigmatized identity. A number of studies looking at the effects of stigma on people with learning disabilities also found that the negative images were actively discarded (Bogdan and Taylor 1989; Booth and Booth 1994). Goffman's focus on negative stigmatization was further challenged through research on epilepsy (Scambler and Hopkins 1986; Scambler 1989) which found that actual occurrences of negative stigmatization – 'enacted' stigma – were relatively rare, and that the fear of 'enacted' stigma – 'felt' stigma – was significantly more common.

The conflict approach

Conflict theorists focus on power relations between the medical profession and the lay population. Waitzkin (1989) suggests that the relationship between the doctor and the patient is a medical interaction but can also play an important role within the wider social context. He states that often when people with a chronic illness or disability consult a doctor it is for non-medical reasons, such as a doctor examining an employee for authorization of benefits or sick leave. Silverman (1987) suggests further that chronically ill patients with an expertise acquired through experience are one of the groups that are beginning to challenge the power of the medical profession. This ties in with work on the development of an 'Expert Patient' programme (Bury 2010) and empowerment (Asimakopoulou *et al.* 2010) which are explored later in the chapter.

The interpretative approach

Interpretative studies focus on the ways in which people understand health and illness and the concomitant interactions between the individual and society (Radley 1994). The social disadvantage accredited to people with a long-term disabling condition is seen as a result of the ways in which the individual interacts with society and vice versa (Williams and Wood 1988). The interpretative approach focuses on the complexities of the subjective experience of long-term conditions in everyday life for the individual and those within their social network. Experiential research looks at interaction and negotiation (Roth 1963), coping strategies, the cultural and organizational demands placed on the family and the social factors that may influence the experience such as gender, ethnicity, age and stage in the life cycle. All aspects of life with a long-term disabling condition are assessed from the perspective of the individual and the family, looking at the subjective responses to constraints at home, at work and in all other aspects of life experience. The final focus of this approach is to look at the long-term impact of long-term conditions on people's lives and the way in which priorities, problems and strategies change as the disease process progresses.

Advocates of this approach suggest that broad studies on disablement often fail to look at the subjective experiences of the people with the disabling conditions (Anderson and Bury 1998), leading to a body of research focusing on the experiences of people living with a range of long-term disabling conditions; for example, epilepsy (Schneider and Conrad 1983; Scambler and Hopkins 1986; Scambler 1989), multiple sclerosis (Strauss 1984; Robinson 1988, 1998), Parkinson's disease (Singer 1973, 1974; Pinder 1998), rectal cancer (Macdonald 1998), psoriasis (Jobling 1998), arthritis (Bury 1997), tuberculosis (Roth 1963), motor neurone disease (Locock *et al.* 2009), diabetes (Balfe 2007) and HIV and AIDS (Aggleton *et al.* 1989; Ridge *et al.* 2008; Harris 2009). The findings of these studies led to the development of the key themes.

The social constructionist approach

Stemming from the work of Foucault (1965, 1976), the social constructionist approach looks at the changing nature of disease through the different ways in which the body has been understood throughout history. This approach to the study of long-term disabling conditions focuses on the increased importance of the 'body' in a consumer culture, the emphasis on looking good and the implications of this for the disabled body:

> The rise of commodity culture to prominence in western societies has resulted in the ageing body and the disabled body becoming sources of great anxiety. A body that does

not function 'normally' or appear 'normal', that is confined to a wheelchair or bed, is both visually and conceptually out-of-place, as evidenced by the lack of public facilities for people with disabilities or the elderly.

(Lupton 1994: 38)

At the same time the body, now required to be perfect, is provided with all kinds of opportunities for improvement from medical technology to an endless stream of diet and fitness regimes.

Implicit throughout this literature is the idea that weak, unattractive or disabled bodies are rejected or avoided as distasteful. Healthy, 'able' bodies are seen as morally superior (Elias 1978). Nettleton (1995) highlights the implications of this in overcoming shame and embarrassment both for disabled people and those who assist them with intimate or personal care. In addition, the work of Sacks (1984), Charmaz, (1987) and Mathieson and Stam (1995) identify the effect that the onset of illness has on body consciousness and the awareness that the body is not functioning in the way that is expected of it. Barnes *et al.* (1999) see the social constructionist approach as disregarding the biomedical view of the body and refocusing on the way in which the body is created through discourse and language. Thus, the impairment becomes secondary to the effect it has on discourse.

Key themes within a sociological understanding of chronic illness

A broad spectrum of features are common to the experience of chronic illness in everyday life. As identified by Turk (1979), these features provide a common framework of understanding around what it is to have a chronic illness.

All chronic illnesses represent assaults on multiple areas of functioning, not just the body. Patients with various chronic illnesses may face separation from family, friends, and other sources of gratification; loss of key roles; disruption of plans for the future; assault on self-images and self-esteem; uncertain and unpredictable futures; distressing emotions such as anxiety, depression, resentment and helplessness; as well as such illness related factors as permanent changes in physical appearance or in bodily functioning.

(Turk 1979: 291)

These features appear in the many studies that have been carried out and can be condensed into four key areas: uncertain and unpredictable futures; impact on social relations; assaults on self-image and self-esteem; and biomedical concerns.

Uncertain and unpredictable futures

Uncertainty in relation to the disease aetiology, trajectory and the future of the person with the diagnosis are common to many long-term conditions. The dual uncertainty of aetiology and trajectory can be found in the experiences of people with multiple sclerosis (Robinson 1998) and arthritis (Anderson 1998) where it is difficult to know from day to day how symptoms will affect people and what activities they will and will not be able to undertake. With Parkinson's disease there is the added uncertainty relating to whether symptoms are disease or drug related (Pinder 1990). Uncertainty also plays a large part in the management of HIV/AIDS where affected people do not know how long they will remain asymptomatic before they develop AIDS or if they will indeed develop AIDS, and if they do there is uncertainty about how long they will have the syndrome before they die (Aggleton and Thomas 1988). Where uncertainty is rife prior to diagnosis, the diagnosis may even be welcomed as a legitimization of experiences (Robinson

1988). The legitimization of the sick-role can also alleviate the guilt over not being able to perform everyday tasks (Badura and Waltz 1984; Mayou 1986; Brown *et al.* 1981). In addition, it is suggested that, even where the end result of the condition – slow degeneration and death – are known, there may still be a great deal of uncertainty about when and how degeneration will occur (Hobbs and Perrin 1985).

Impact on social relations

It is widely recognized that chronic long-term conditions affect the whole family and not just the person who has the illness. Care and rehabilitation are the main roles undertaken by families (Smith 1979; Anderson 1998) and can result in exhaustion, social isolation, depression and financial hardship when intensive or full-time care is needed (Fitzpatrick 1990). Anderson and Bury suggest, further, that a chronic illness can have a more significant effect on family life and roles if the woman is ill because this can cause changes in traditional domestic roles and have a huge impact on the life of the family unit (1998). In addition to this, chronically ill women are more likely to be abandoned and more likely to live longer and be alone (Anderson and Bury 1998). It is widely recognized that long-term disabling illness has an impact on finances and employment, affecting both immediate costs and long-term employment prospects (Conover 1973; Townsend 1979; Whitehead 1987). Interestingly, and unlike the literature on parent carers and disability more widely, positive aspects of having family members with long-term conditions rarely appear in the literature.

Another effect of chronic illness on social relations can be seen in the work on stigma. It has been suggested that the potential spoiling of identity through the negative reactions of others to changes in normal bodily or behavioural experiences is at the centre of much of the perceived misery of long-term disabling conditions (Anderson and Bury 1998). The very act of being labelled as epileptic was reported as distressing in one study, with acquisition of the label challenging people's image of themselves as 'normal' (Scambler 1989). Here, the fear of stigma – 'felt' stigma – was far more predominant than actual acts of stigmatization – 'enacted' stigma. Private fear and public enactment were also themes in the work of Kelly (1992a, 1992b) who identified difficulties in managing the private and public identity in people who had undergone illeostomies. The challenge of coping with private changes in bodily function and image along with public perceptions and stigmatizing attitudes were highlighted. This ties in to a perceived link between health and 'moral worth' (Cornwell 1984), which is prevalent in early work on the experiences of people with HIV/AIDS (Aggleton and Thomas 1988; Aggleton *et al.* 1989; Green and Platt 1997). In her work on 'dread diseases', Susan Sontag (1991) highlights the public perceptions of diseases in society and the moral judgements associated with different conditions, such as fear, pity and contempt. A number of studies suggest that the negative perceptions held about certain illnesses exacerbate the already problematic and unpleasant experiences of people with some long-term disabling conditions (Scambler and Hopkins 1986; West 1979; Schneider and Conrad 1983). Albrecht and Higgins (1982) also found that people distinguished between symptoms affecting the mind and those affecting the body, suggesting that more stigma was faced by those with mental symptoms than physical ones.

Assaults on self-image and self-esteem

Biographical disruption, on diagnosis, can affect the self-image and public image of a person diagnosed with a long-term disabling condition, causing them to rethink their past, present and future (Bury 1997). Bury suggests a need to construct an account of what has happened and why and to seek legitimization for the condition and the lifestyle changes it necessitates. In contrast, Bloom, through his analysis of the experience of a woman with kidney disease and cancer (1992), charts a progression from the 'dys-embodied self' through reflexive self-awareness to a re-alignment. On a cautionary note, such negotiated settlements can be temporary and fragile (Williams 1996) and temporal, changing over time (Pinder 1998). Biographical and social disruption can occur simultaneously on diagnosis (Locker 1983) and may also lead to a rewriting of previous experiences in light of a new diagnosis (Anderson and Bury 1998).

Biomedical concerns

Diagnosis of a long-term condition often necessitates close contact with doctors, hospitals and the biomedical world. This can take the form of direct medical interventions or the need for information. The difficulties posed by direct medical interventions and the importance of managing a complex medical regime is explored in relation to Parkinson's disease, where there is the need to balance the control of symptoms with the management of complex drug regimes and the need to cope both with the symptoms caused by the disease and the additional symptoms caused by the drugs taken to control the disease (Pinder 1998). In his work on psoriasis, Jobling (1998) goes on to describe the way in which the treatment regime can come to dominate the everyday lives of people living with the condition and the need to balance the benefits and costs of treatment. He also highlights the need for negotiation between doctors and patients as to the regime followed and how it should be managed. Time spent on managing a complex medical regime cannot be spent on other, more enjoyable things (Locker 1983). Research suggests that people with long-term disabling conditions are less satisfied with their doctor/patient relationships than with any other aspect of care (Fitzpatrick 1990). In addition, there is dissatisfaction with information provided by doctors (Patrick *et al.* 1983; Macdonald 1998), communication skills and approachability (Harding and Modell 1985; Cooper and Huitson 1986) and a recognition that patients should be partners in care (Schneider and Conrad 1983). The recent emergence of 'empowerment' as a form of patient/doctor partnership is critiqued later in the chapter.

What can be seen from this brief and selective summary of the sociological literature on long-term disabling conditions is that the everyday experiences of people living with a vast range of different conditions have been explored in some detail and from a variety of perspectives. It is also apparent, however, that the focus of the vast majority of this work is on the negative implications of long-term disabling conditions and the 'coping' skills necessary in dealing with them. There is little evidence here of the type of political or oppression-based approach that is more familiar in disability studies. This has led to the allegation that sociology has fallen in to the medicalization trap; whilst purporting to challenge the dominance of biomedicine there is a widespread, if unintentional, view of long-term disabling conditions as negative. This said, the reverse may be true in that, whilst purporting to champion the cause of disabled people, disability studies has largely focused on relatively static, non-disease linked disabilities and has sidelined the huge numbers of disabled people who are disabled through long-term, often degenerative, conditions.

Locating chronic illness in disability studies

Many of the themes highlighted in relation to the literature on long-term disabling conditions can also be found within the wider disability literature. The concepts of 'normalization', 'identity' and 'stigma', for example, play key roles in current debates around disability politics and the identity of disabled people. This said, it has been suggested that the political aim for equality, whilst clearly justified, has led to a failure to acknowledge the feelings of loss and pain experienced by some (Scambler 2005; Watermeyer 2009) in favour of the positive experiences (Morris 1989; Oliver 1990; Finkelstein *et al.* 1993) of others. As Watermeyer (2009) suggests:

> Of concern is the possible extent to which such constructions – politically highly necessary – require a purging of accounts of disability which do carry aspects of loss and struggle. As has oft been pointed out, the question of whether such struggles are construed as attributable to impairment or disabling barriers remains of key political significance. However, disability research which expressly eschews loss serves to collude with the perpetuation of the false binary opposition, which, again, embodies a silencing of real lives.
>
> *(pp. 97–8)*

Clearly there are studies looking at the experiences of people with long-term conditions from a disability studies perspective (see for example Blackford 1999; Moss *et al.* 2004; Dyson *et al.* 2007; Kendall and Rogers 2007; Allred 2009). These disabilities are still hugely under-represented in the wider literature. Finding a place for these types of disabilities requires a move to bridge the gap between the 'coping/loss' and 'oppression' paradigms, often presented as binary opposites.

There is a growing awareness within both sociology and disability studies of the possible merits of these opposing traditions alongside long-standing disputes over the political implications of each approach, and recent work from both sides of the divide has sought to challenge existing orthodoxies. The most obvious example here is the work of Carol Thomas (2007) where she seeks to lay out a systematic argument for a more oppression aware approach to the sociological study of disabled people (see also Thomas 2004, 2010). Again, from a disabilities studies perspective, Shakespeare (2006) sought to openly acknowledge that the importance of pain, loss and negative experiences in the daily lives of disabled people related directly to the particular impairments that they live with rather than as a result of oppression they experience. Examples can also be found from a sociological perspective where, in a re-theorization of stigma, for example, Scambler (2009) suggests that a reframing of relations of stigma as 'cultural norms of shame or blame' may be more helpful in integrating rival paradigms of sociology and disability studies and allowing for coping and oppression. In a recent book (Scambler and Scambler 2010a), I also sought to draw together experts from the sociological and disability studies perspectives to open a dialogue between the disciplines and move towards a resolution of differences in approach (Scambler and Scambler 2010b).

Challenging questions

So what can the study of long-term disabling conditions add to our understanding of disability and the lives of disabled people? As previously stated, it would be relatively simple, and justifiable, to make the argument that these types of disabilities should take on a more significant role within disability studies simply through prevalence. I want to suggest further, however, that the study of long-term disabling conditions and the people who live with them on a daily basis can offer fresh insights into existing debates within the field of disability studies. To illustrate this point, two case studies are presented. The first explores the concepts of empowerment and self-management within healthcare policy and practice and the impact of this on the provision of care for people living with diabetes, positing this as a medicalization of anti-oppression approaches. The second revisits the debate on the relative importance of impairment, biology and the body with the aid of work on Batten disease, a long-term, life-limiting condition resulting in multiple disabilities.

Empowerment, diabetes and the medicalization and state sponsorship of 'anti-oppression' measures

Empowerment can be defined as a process of education and skill development which enables people with long-term conditions to take responsibility for the daily management of their illness. The formal idea of self-management was introduced into the National Health Service (NHS) with the NHS Improvement Plan (Department of Health 2004). This document laid out a model of care based on a Californian plan to provide healthcare for people with long-term conditions. The 'Kaiser' model incorporated three levels of care, with high-risk patients receiving professional care, a 'shared-care' approach for those in the middle and self-management for the low-risk majority (Bury 2010). This model was deemed successful in California and 'Chronic Disease Self-Management' programmes were put in place with the aim of 'giving patients the knowledge and skills to manage their illness daily' (Lorig 2002: 814).

The self-management/empowerment approach to the provision of care for people with long-term conditions has been adopted across the NHS, at least in principle. One example of the model in practice can be found in the development of diabetes care. In Kaiser model style, high-risk patients and those with complications are seen in the diabetes clinic; patients who – for whatever reason – are not achieving good symptom control are seen by diabetes nurse specialists to develop a shared-care plan, set targets and be 'empowered'; and low-risk patients attend, or are invited to attend, education courses and access community services as and when needed. A collaborative of NHS organizations (The DESMOND Collaborative 2008) have put together a series of education programmes for people with diabetes, 'Diabetes Education and Self-Management for Ongoing and Diagnosed' (DESMOND), and nurses and other allied health professionals are being trained in how to do DESMOND. Empowerment is widely seen as a positive move within diabetes care as it heralds a move away from the patriarchal notion of 'compliance' to a more patient-centred notion of self-management (Asimakopoulou 2007). This ties in with the ideological shift towards consumer healthcare and patient choice that were championed by the New Labour government. This can be seen as a positive move in recognizing the knowledge and skills which develop over the course of living with a long-term condition and prioritizing experiential expertise in daily life over medical interventions.

The problem with empowerment in diabetes care emerges when we try to define 'successful empowerment'. If empowerment is about giving people the skills to manage their disease then how do we judge whether the empowerment has been successful? What becomes clear if you look at the literature on empowerment in diabetes is that there is confusion and disagreement not only about how success should be measured in relation to empowerment but about what the term empowerment actually means (Asimakopoulou 2007; Asimakopoulou *et al.* 2010; Anderson 2007; Adolfsson *et al.* 2004). In a recent study I looked at professionals' understandings of and attitudes towards empowerment in practice. In this qualitative study 13 professionals involved in the specialist provision of care for people with diabetes, across practical and organizational roles in acute and primary practices within a discrete location, were interviewed. What emerged from the interviews was that there was no clarity of shared understanding about what empowerment is and what it involves. In addition, there was disagreement about the level of freedom that patients should have in making choices: practice ranged from actively leading patients to the 'correct' choice to an acceptance that a patient can make a conscious and informed decision not to make the 'correct' choice. There was no formal consensus on the definition or measure of 'successful' empowerment but biochemical targets were used as the main tool in ascertaining success. In this study the rhetoric started with talk of giving patients the tools with which to manage their own illnesses and ended with acknowledgement that in practice patients were coached in how to meet biochemical targets (Scambler *et al.* 2010). Patient choice and control turns to disease management and biochemical symptom control.

The debate around empowerment and self-management illustrates the tension between policy initiatives and the lived experience of long-term conditions. Evidence suggests that these programmes are less effective than was hoped in managing long-term conditions (Newbould *et al.* 2006; Newman *et al.* 2004) and have not reduced the demand for health services. This brings into question the continued state support for empowerment and self-management programmes. Building on his categorization of an ideological shift to patient-centred rhetoric as a means of disguising the failure of biomedicine in dealing with long-term conditions, Bury (2010) suggests that the rhetoric has changed. He illustrates how terms and concepts that were initially used to challenge the state sponsored dominance of biomedicine have been colonized by the very system they sought to challenge: 'where once the "new age" rhetoric of personal growth, autonomy, empowerment and the like were used by social movements to challenge state controlled bureaucratic structures and systems, today they have become part and parcel of state activity itself' (Bury 2010: 176). He goes on to suggest that this kind of rhetoric can be seen as a way of placing the patient at the centre of care or as a way of glossing over the complexities of living with conditions of this kind over an extended period of time and the very real need for quality healthcare.

I would go further and suggest that the promotion of the self-management and empowerment agendas conceals a deeper agenda. By promoting the idea that patients are in control and make choices over their care that affect the likelihood of achieving symptom control (self-management), whilst maintaining control over the mechanisms through which the 'success' of this self-management is measured, the power of the patient choice/shared decision-making/empowerment agenda is neutralized. Empowerment cannot be used as a way to fight the oppression of the power of biomedicine over the lives of people with long-term disabling conditions if the very measures used to judge the success or failure of empowerment are biomedical. The social power of these concepts is negated.

Batten disease and the primacy of the biological

A second case study to illustrate the role that research on long-term conditions can play in furthering disability debates concerns the interface between disability, impairment, biology and the body. Batten disease is the common name for the group of rare, genetic, neurodegenrerative, metabolic diseases that can be found in both children and adults across the world. At present, nine different forms of Batten disease have been identified with four main types, four variants and a congenital form of the disease (Batten Disease Family Association 2008). Whilst age at onset, life expectancy, progress of symptoms and genetic causes vary by disease type, the group of diseases share broadly similar symptoms which include: epilepsy, visual impairment, cognitive and motor degeneration (including the loss of the ability to walk, eat and talk) and a shortened life expectancy (Scriver *et al.* 2001). This said, people with the juvenile form of the disease can live for more than 20 years post-diagnosis. The last two decades have seen significant changes in the care available for children and young people with Batten disease. The mechanisms through which these conditions are diagnosed, the drugs available for seizures and other symptom control and nutritional management strategies have all evolved. Work is well underway to develop gene therapies for some variants of Batten disease; however, 'at present there is no cure or treatment that makes a significant impact on the progressive decline in bodily functions and inevitable early death' (Batten Disease Family Association 2008).

I have previously argued that the reality of Batten disease poses a challenge to arguments around the social construction of disability (Scambler 2005) and the separation of impairment and disability (Scambler and Newton 2010). The physical reality of the symptoms of Batten disease are such that they cannot be less significant than the social reality of living with the disease. In later stages of the disease process it would not be unusual to meet a young adult with the juvenile form of the disease who is unable to walk or talk, has a gastrostomy, is doubly incontinent, with little control over facial expression, a very limited short-term memory, and who has epilepsy and terrifying hallucinations. The impaired body cannot be separated from the lived experience of the disease. The social reality of living on a daily basis with this disease is an embodied experience that is significantly shaped and curtailed by the nature and functioning of the body in which it is experienced. The role of the physical body and the impairments at the heart of people's experiences of disabilities also need to be taken into account. There is a multifaceted and multilayered effect that can be causally attributed to the biological attributes of the disease but is biological, social and psychological in its impact. The biological impact of the disease is both direct in its determination of the symptoms of the disease itself and the nature of the trajectory, and indirect in its impact on every, or almost every, aspect of daily life. Even the direct biological impact of the disease spreads far beyond the affected, diagnosed individual. The hereditary nature of Batten disease spreads the direct biological impact to siblings and extended family members as well as potentially to future generations through a network of carrier, post and prenatal testing (Scambler and Newton 2010).

The impairment/disability or biology/oppression debate is one that is currently being explored by writers such as Hughes (2004), who charts the, often contrary, relationship between medical sociology and disability studies, focusing on the role of impairment as a way of making a valuable connection between the two disciplines. Hughes makes the argument that, at the very point where sociologists were moving to develop an understanding of the embodied nature of social action, disability studies was moving to exclude the body and impairment from the discourse around disability and focus solely on the social construction of disability. He suggests we need to move towards a 'post-Cartesian' position where the somatic nature of society is accepted and we come to see disability as embodied and impairment as social.

This thesis extends possibilities for a shared understanding and synthesis between the bodies of knowledge developed through disability studies and medical sociology and strengthens the case for the importance of long-term disabling conditions in adding to our understanding of this debate. This is a position that reiterates the need, as articulated by Corker and French (1999), for more work, such as that by Hughes, examining the permeable boundary between the physical embodied experience of disability and the social experience of disability, and the ways in which the two impact on one another. It is a challenge that has been taken up by writers such as Sherry (2002, cited in Shakespeare 2006) who drew on interviews with people with acquired brain injury to suggest that a range of experiences are presented that cannot be classified as 'either' impairment 'or' disability. He proposed that these categories are best conceptualized as a fluid continuum rather than a dichotomy. A similar conclusion was reached by (Lock *et al.* 2005) in their work on the experiences of stroke survivors. Shakespeare (2006: 37) suggests that 'any qualitative research with disabled people will inevitably reveal the difficulty of distinguishing impairment and disability'.

I have added to this debate in a study which uses the theory of Bourdieu to encapsulate the inherently biological assault on the lifeworld caused by chronic disabling conditions that result in profound and/or multiple disabilities. To use the more traditionally fought dichotomy between impairment and disability, I suggest that, in these extreme conditions, both impairment and social oppression play a role in the assault on the lifeworld, but that the impairment is predominant and shapes even the experiences of social oppression (Scambler and Newton 2010). Shakespeare suggests that there are two important features of impairment which need to be addressed when looking at the wider picture.

First, there is a hierarchy of impairment: different impairments have different impacts, and the same impairment can have different effects. Second, mild to moderate impairment may not be a difficulty for anyone, given supportive and flexible environments prepared to respect and value difference. However, severe forms of impairment will often cause considerable problems and limitations and sometimes suffering and distress for individuals and their families. The goal of promoting cultural respect and social acceptance for people with impairment should not distract us from the importance of mitigating or preventing impairment via individual medical or psychological therapies.

(Shakespeare 2006: 116)

I contend that Batten disease is one such 'severe form of impairment' and would go so far as to suggest that the social effects of the oppression are, in this case, secondary to the biological effects of the disease itself.

Future directions and collaborations

Long-term disabling conditions are the main cause of disability in the developed world and yet, as illustrated in the first part of this chapter, are largely absent from mainstream disability theory. The specific, empirically based, examples cited above illustrate the important contribution that the study of long-term disabling conditions can make to our understanding of disability and the social/oppression/disability theory approach to disability. Small, but increasing, numbers of medical sociologists and disability theorists are making the case for a collaboration between the disciplines (Thomas 2004, 2010; Scambler and Scambler 2010a; Shakespeare 2006) with the aim of mutual learning and a more multi-dimensional view of the disability/society/biomedicine divide.

The examples cited in this chapter give a very brief glimpse of the depth of sociological research exploring the experiences of people living with long-term conditions. In recent work looking to move the disability debate beyond a focus on models and towards acceptance of the role of impairment in the lives of disabled people, Shakespeare and Watson (2010) call for research that focuses on 'what disabled people say and think, not what we might wish they should say and think'. They elaborate: 'Accusing disabled people of false consciousness, or waiting for them to see the light of the social model, is not adequate or appropriate' (2010: 72). The sociological tradition focuses on exploring what people with long-term disabling conditions think and how they experience daily life. A wealth of research that explores what disabled people say and think already exists and needs acknowledgement and incorporation into the wider debates. At the same time, as Thomas (2010) suggests, sociologists working in the field of long-term conditions need to be more aware of the prevailing deviance paradigm within medical sociology and to incorporate the social oppression paradigm.

References

Adolfsson, E. T., Smide, B., Gregeby, E., Fernstrom, L. and Wikblad, K. (2004) 'Implementing Empowerment Group Education in Diabetes', *Patient Education and Counselling* 53(3): 319–24.
Aggleton, P. and Thomas, H. (1988) *Social Aspects of AIDS* (London: Falmer).
Aggleton, P., Hart, G. and Davies, P. (1989) *AIDS, Social Representations, Social Practices* (London: Falmer).
Albrecht, G. and Higgins, P. (1982) *Understanding Deviance* (New York: McGraw Hill).
Allred, S. (2009) Reframing Asperger Syndrome: Lessons From Other Challenges to the *Diagnostic and Statistical Manual* and ICIDH approaches', *Disability & Society* 24(3): 343–55.
Anderson, R. (1998) 'Stroke', in R. Anderson and M. Bury, eds, *Living with Chronic Illness: The Experience of Patients and their Families* (London: Unwin Hyman).

Anderson, R. M. (2007) 'When We Assume. A Commentary on the Assumptions Underlying the Empowerment Approach to Diabetes Care and Education', *European Diabetes Nursing* 4(3): 98.

Anderson, R. and Bury, M., eds (1998) *Living with Chronic Illness: The Experience of Patients and their Families* (London: Unwin Hyman).

Asimakopoulou, K. G. (2007) 'Empowerment in the Self-Management of Diabetes: Are We Ready to Test Assumptions?' *European Diabetes Nursing* 4(3): 94–7.

Asimakopoulou, K. G., Newton, P., Scambler, S. (2010) 'First Do No Harm: The Potential Shortfalls of Empowerment in Diabetes', *European Diabetes Nursing* 7(2): 79–81.

Badura, B. and Waltz, M. (1984) 'Social Support and Quality of Life Following Myocardial Infarction', *Social Indicators Research* 14: 295–311.

Balfe, M. (2007) 'Diets and Discipline: The Narratives of Practice of University Students with Type 1 Diabetes', *Sociology of Health & Illness* 29(1): 136–53.

Barnes, C., Mercer, G. and Shakespeare, T. (1999) *Exploring Disability: A Sociological Introduction* (Cambridge: Polity Press).

Batten Disease Family Association (2008) *About Batten Disease*; available at http://www.bdfa-uk.org.uk (accessed 25 July 2011).

Blackford, K. A. (1999) 'A Child's Growing Up with a Parent Who Has Multiple Sclerosis: Theories and Experiences', *Disability & Society* 14(5): 673–85.

Bloom, L. R. (1992) '"How Can We Know the Dancer from the Dance?" Discourses of the Self-Body', *Human Studies* 15(4): 314–34.

Bogdan, R. and Taylor, S. (1989) 'Relationships with Severely Disabled People: The Social Construction of Humanness', *Social Problems* 36(2): 135–48.

Booth, T. and Booth, W. (1994) *Parenting Under Pressure: Mothers and Fathers with Learning Difficulties* (Buckingham: Open University Press).

Brown, J., Rawlinson, M. and Hilles, N. (1981) 'Life Satisfaction and Chronic Disease: Explanation of a Theoretical Model', *Medical Care* 19(2): 1136–46.

Bury, M. (1997) *Health and Illness in a Changing Society* (London: Routledge).

Bury, M. (2010) 'Chronic Illness, Self-management and the Rhetoric of Empowerment', in G. Scambler and S. Scambler, eds (2010) *New Directions in the Sociology of Chronic and Disabling Conditions: Assaults on the Lifeworld* (London: Palgrave Macmillan).

Charmaz, K. (1987) 'Struggling for Self: Identity Levels of the Chronically Ill', in J. A. Roth and P. Conrad, eds, *Research in the Sociology of Healthcare, vi: The Experience and Management of Chronic Illness* (Greenwich, CT: JAI Press).

Conover, P. (1973) 'Social Class and Chronic Illness', *International Journal of Health Sciences* 3(3): 357–67.

Cooper, G. and Huitson, A. (1986) 'An Audit of the Management of Patients with Epilepsy in 30 General Practices', *Journal of the Royal College of General Practitioners.* 36(286): 204–11.

Corker, M. and French, S., eds (1999) *Disability Discourse* (Buckingham: Open University Press).

Cornwell, J. (1984) *Hard Earned Lives: Accounts of Health and Illness from East London* (London: Tavistock).

Department of Health (2004) *The NHS Improvement Plan: Putting People at the Heart of Public Services* (London. Department of Health).

The DESMOND Collaborative (2008) *Developing Quality Structured Education in Diabetes*; available online at http://www.desmond-project.org.uk (accessed 1 August 2011).

Dyson, S. M., Atkin, K., Culley, L. A., Dyson, S. (2007) 'The Educational Experiences of Young People with Sickle Cell Disorder: A Commentary on the Existing Literature', *Disability & Society* 22(6): 581–94.

Elias, N. (1978) *The Civilising Process*, vol. I (Oxford: Blackwell).

Finkelstein, V., French, S., Oliver, M., eds (1993) *Disabling Barriers, Enabling Environments* (London: OUP/ Sage).

Fitzpatrick, R. (1990) 'Social Aspects of Chronic Illness', in J. Hasler and T. Schofield, ed., *The Management of Chronic Disease*, 2nd edn (New York: Oxford University Press): pp. 47–63.

Foucault, M. (1965) *Madness and Civilisation: A History of Insanity in the Age of Reason* (London: Tavistock).

Foucault, M. (1976) *The Birth of the Clinic* (London: Tavistock).

Friedson, E. (1970) *Profession of Medicine: A Study of the Sociology of Applied Knowledge* (New York: Harper and Row).

Goffman, I. (1968) *Stigma: Notes on the Management of Spoiled Identity*, (Harmondsworth: Penguin).

Gordon, C. (1966) *Role Theory and Illness: A Sociological Perspective* (New Haven: Connecticut College and University Press).

Green, G. and Platt, S. (1997) 'Fear and Loathing in Health Care Settings Reported by People with HIV', *Sociology of Health and Illness* 19(1): 70–92.

Harding, J. and Modell, M. (1985) 'How Patients Manage Asthma', *Journal of the Royal College of General Practitioners* 35(274): 226–8.

Harris, M. (2009) 'Troubling Biographical Disruption: Narratives of Unconcern About Hepatitis C Diagnosis', *Sociology of Health and Illness* 31(7): 1028–42.

Higgins, P. (1981) *Outsiders in a Hearing World* (London: Sage).

Hobbs, N. and Perrin, J. M., eds (1985) *Issues in the Care of Children with Chronic Illnesses* (San Francisco and London: Jossey-Bass Publishers).

Hughes, B. (2004) 'Disability and the Body', in J. Swain, V. Finkelstein, S. French and M. Oliver, eds, *Disabling Barriers–Enabling Environments* (London: Sage): pp. 63–9.

Jobling, R. (1998) 'Treating Psoriasis', in R. Anderson and M. Bury, eds, *Living with Chronic Illness: The Experience of Patients and Their Families* (London: Unwin Hyman).

Kassebaum, G. and Baumann, B. (1965) 'Dimensions of the Sick-Role in Chronic Illness', *Journal of Health and Social Behaviour* 6: 16–25.

Kelly, M. P. (1992a) 'Self-Identity and Radical Surgery', *Sociology of Health and Illness* 14(3): 390–415.

Kelly, M. P. (1992b) *Colitis* (London: Routledge).

Kendall, E. and Rogers, A. (2007) 'Extinguishing the Social? State Sponsored Self-care Policy and the Chronic Disease Self-management Programme', *Disability & Society* 22(2): 129–43.

Lock, S., Jordan, L., Bryan, K. and J. Maxim (2005) 'Work After Stroke: Focussing on Barriers and Enablers', *Disability & Society* 20(1): 33–47.

Locker, D. (1983) *Disability and Disadvantage: The Consequences of Chronic Illness* (London: Tavistock).

Locock, L., Ziebland, S., Dumelow, C. (2009) 'Biographical Disruption, Abruption and Repair in the Context of Motor Neurone Disease', *Sociology of Health and Illness* 31(7): 1043–58.

Lorig, K. (2002) 'Partnerships Between Expert Patient and Physicians', *Lancet* 359(9309): 814–5.

Lupton, D. (1994) *Medicine as Culture* (London: Sage).

Macdonald, L. (1998) 'The Experience of Stigma: Living with Rectal Cancer', in R. Anderson and M. Bury, eds (1998) *Living with Chronic Illness: The Experience of Patients and Their Families* (London: Unwin Hyman).

Mathieson, C. M. and Stam, H. J. (1995) 'Renegotiating Identity: Cancer Narratives', *Sociology of Health and Illness* 17: 263–306.

Mayou, R. (1986) 'The Psychiatric and Social Consequences of Coronary Artery Surgery', *Journal of Psychsomatic Research* 30: 255–71.

Morris, J. (1989) *Pride Against Prejudice. A Personal Politics of Disability* (London: Women's Press).

Moss, B., Parr, S., Byng, S., Petheram, B. (2004) '"Pick Me Up and Not a Down Down, Up Up": How are the Identities of People with Aphasia Represented in Aphasia, Stroke and Disability Websites?', *Disability & Society* 19(7): 753–68.

Nettleton, S. (1995) *The Sociology of Health and Illness* (Cambridge: Polity Press).

Newbould, J., Taylor, D., Bury, M. (2006) 'Lay-led Self-management in Chronic Illness. A Review of the Evidence', *Chronic Illness* 2(4): 249–61.

Newman, S., Steed, L., Mulligan, K. (2004) 'Self-management Interventions for Chronic Illness', *Lancet* 364(9444): 1523–37.

Oliver, M. (1990) *The Politics of Disablement* (Basingstoke: Macmillan).

Parsons, T. (1951) *The Social System* (New York: Free Press).

Patrick, D., Scrivens, E., Charlton, J. (1983) 'Disability and Patient Satisfaction with Medical Care', *Medical Care* 21(11): 1062–75.

Pinder, R. (1990) *The Management of Chronic Illness: Patient and Doctor Perspectives on Parkinson's Disease* (London: Macmillan Press).

Pinder, R. (1998) 'Striking Balances: Living with Parkinson's Disease', in R. Anderson and M. Bury, eds, *Living with Chronic Illness: The Experience of Patients and their Families* (London: Unwin Hyman).

Radley, A. (1994) 'The Elusory Body in Social Constructionist Theory', *Body and Society* 1(2): 179–207.

Ridge, D., Williams, I., Anderson, J. and Elford, J. (2008) 'Like a Prayer: The Role of Spirituality and Religion for People Living with HIV in the UK', *Sociology of Health and Illness* 30(3): 413–28.

Robinson, I. (1988) *Multiple Sclerosis* (London: Routledge).

Robinson, I. (1998) 'Reconstructing Lives: Negotiating the Meaning of Multiple Sclerosis', in R. Anderson and M. Bury, eds, *Living with Chronic Illness: The Experience of Patients and their Families* (London: Unwin Hyman).

Roth, J. (1963) *Timetables: Structuring the Passage of Time in Hospital Treatment* (New York: Bobbs-Merrill).

149

Sacks, O. (1984) *A Leg to Stand On* (New York: Summit Books).

Scambler, G. (1989) *Epilepsy* (London: Tavistock).

Scambler, G. (2009) 'Health Related Stigma', *Sociology of Health and Illness* 31(3): 441–55.

Scambler, G. and Hopkins, A. (1986) 'Being Epileptic: Coming to Terms with Stigma', *Sociology of Health and Illness* 8(1): 26–43.

Scambler, G. and Scambler, S., eds (2010a) *New Directions in the Sociology of Chronic and Disabling Conditions: Assaults on the Lifeworld* (London: Palgrave Macmillan).

Scambler, G. and Scambler, S. (2010b) 'Assaults on the Lifeworld: The Sociology of Chronic Illness and Disability', in G. Scambler and S. Scambler S, eds, *New Directions in the Sociology of Chronic Illness and Disability: Assaults on the Lifeworld* (Palgrave Macmillan).

Scambler, S. (2005) 'Exposing the Limitations of Disability Theory: The Case of Juvenile Batten Disease', *Social Theory and Health* 3: 144–64.

Scambler, S. and Newton, P. (2010) 'Where the Biological Predominates: Habitus, Reflexivity and Capital Accrual within the Field of Batten Disease', in G. Scambler and S. Scambler, eds (2010) *New Directions in the Sociology of Chronic and Disabling Conditions: Assaults on the Lifeworld* (London: Palgrave Macmillan).

Scambler, S., Newton, P. and Asiakopoulou, K. G. (2010) *Health Care Professionals' Understanding and Practice of Empowerment*. Research Report for Diabetes UK.

Schneider, I. and Conrad, P. (1983) *Having Epilepsy. The Experience and Control of Illness* (Philadelphia: Temple University Press).

Scriver, C. R., Beaudet, A. L., Sly, W. S., Childs, B. and Vogelstein, B., eds (2001) *The Neuronal Ceroid Lipofuscinoses* (New York: McGraw Hill).

Shakespeare, T. (2006) *Disability Rights and Wrongs* (London: Routledge).

Shakespeare, T. and Watson, N. (2010) 'Beyond Models: Understanding the Complexity of Disabled People's Lives', in G. Scambler and S. Scambler, eds (2010) *New Directions in the Sociology of Chronic and Disabling Conditions: Assaults on the Lifeworld* (London: Palgrave Macmillan).

Sherry, M. (2002) '"If I Only Had a Brain": Examining the Effects of Brain Injury in Terms of Disability, Impairment, Identity and Embodiment'; University of Queensland PhD. Unpublished. Cited in T. Shakespeare (2006) *Disability Rights and Wrongs* (Routledge: London).

Sieglar, M. and Osmond, M. (1974) *Models of Madness: Models of Medicine* (London: Collier Macmillan).

Silverman, D. (1987) *Communication and Medical Practice: Social Relations in the Clinic* (London: Sage).

Singer, E. (1973) 'Social Costs of Parkinson's Disease', *Journal of Chronic Disease* 26: 243–54.

Singer, E. (1974) 'Premature Social Ageing: The Socio-Psychological Consequences of Chronic Illness', *Social Science and Medicine* 8: 143–51.

Smith, R. T. (1979) 'The Rehabilitation of the Disabled: The Role of Social Networks in the Recovery Process', *International Rehabilitation Medicine* 1: 63–72.

Sontag, S. (1991) *Illness as a Metaphor. AIDS and its Metaphors* (London: Pelican).

Thomas, C. (2004) 'How is Disability Understood? An Examination of Sociological Approaches', *Disability & Society* 19(6): 569–83.

Strauss, A. L. (1984) *Chronic Illness and the Quality of Life*, 2nd edn (Chicago: Mosby).

Thomas, C. (2007) *Sociologies of Disability and Illness: Contested Ideas in Disability Studies and Medical Sociology* (London: Macmillan).

Thomas, C. (2010) 'Medical Sociology and Disability Theory', in G. Scambler and S. Scambler, eds (2010) *New Directions in the Sociology of Chronic and Disabling Conditions: Assaults on the Lifeworld* (London: Palgrave Macmillan).

Townsend, P. (1979) *Poverty in the United Kingdom* (London: Allen Lane).

Turk, D. C. (1979) 'Factors Influencing the Adaptive Process with Chronic Illness', in A. Sarason and C. D. Spielberger, eds, *Stress and Anxiety*, volume 6 (Washington, DC: Halstead Press).

Waitzkin, H. (1989) 'A Critical Theory of Medical Discourses', *Journal of Health and Social Behaviour* 30: 220–39.

Watermeyer, B. (2009) 'Claiming Loss in Disability', *Disability & Society* 24(1): 91–102.

West, P. (1979) 'An Investigation into the Social Construction of Consequences of the Label Epilepsy', *Sociological Review* 27(4): 719–41.

Whitehead, M. (1987) *The Health Divide: Inequalities in Health in the 1980s* (London: Health Education Council).

Williams, G. and Wood, P. (1988) 'Coming to Terms with Chronic Illness: The Negotiation of Autonomy in Rheumatoid Arthritis', *International Disability Studies* 10: 128–32.

Williams, S. J. (1996) 'Medical Sociology, Chronic Illness and the Body: A Rejoinder to Michael Kelly and David Field', *Sociology of Health and Illness* 18(5): 699–709.

12

PSYCHIATRIC SYSTEM SURVIVORS

An emerging movement

Peter Beresford

The late twentieth century witnessed the emergence of collective action on the part of mental health service users internationally. The modern mental health service users' or survivors' movement is a very recent development. Its history is usually traced to the 1980s, with early beginnings in about 1970. It has not only developed a presence in North America, the Scandinavian countries, the United Kingdom (UK) and other parts of Europe, but also in South America, Australasia and the 'developing' or majority world. The 'survivor' movement has developed its own international, European and global organizations, as well as local, regional and national groups (Stone 1999; MindFreedom 2009; Campbell 1996, 2009). The movement tended to emerge later than the disabled people's movement and has frequently sought to draw a distinction between itself and disability politics and struggles (Campbell and Oliver 1996; Plumb 1994). Indeed this tendency, its implications for the future and how these should be considered are a central issue for this chapter.

In 1978, Judi Chamberlin, a pioneer of the United States' (US) survivor movement, first published the key text *On Our Own*, which gained international importance among mental health service users/survivors and their organizations. Building particularly on US experience and ideas, but also taking into account wider developments, it offered a radical service user critique of both existing understandings and responses to mental health issues and survivor ideas and alternatives (Chamberlin 1988). Then Mary O'Hagan, a survivor activist from New Zealand, offered an early account of her visits to survivor organizations in the US, UK and Netherlands in which she sought to offer an honest and critical account of service user developments based on talking directly to activists involved (O'Hagan 1994). A groundbreaking UK survey of service user organizations published in 2003 concluded that 'the service user/survivor movement exists and a large number of people see themselves as belonging to it (Wallcraft *et al.* 2003: v). It stressed the inadequacy and insecurity of the movement's funding while highlighting its wide-ranging role in providing mutual support, taking part in decision-making and providing information, education and training, creative activities, campaigning and services.

A large and growing number (albeit a small proportion overall) of mental health service users/survivors have become involved in service user groups and organizations at local, regional, national and international levels. The mental health service user/survivor movement is concerned not only with self-help and mutual support, but also with collective action to reform the service system and make wider changes. There are now black and minority ethnic organizations as well as organizations for people hearing voices, with eating distress and who self-harm. As well as developing their own organizations, service users/survivors have had a growing involvement in and influence on traditional charitable organizations. In the UK, this includes organizations such as Mind. In some cases such organizations have become user controlled; for instance, MDF – the bipolar organization (formerly the Manic Depressive Fellowship) (Campbell 1999).

Some key international issues

While the emergence of the mental health service user/survivor movement represents an international development, with its own significant internal variations, it has also taken place in the context of a broader framework of mental health policy, practice and conceptualization, which is itself enormously varied internationally. It is difficult, and not necessarily helpful, to consider service user/survivor organizations and their movements in advanced western societies and traditional cultures and societies in the majority world in a monolithic way – as raising the same issues and reflecting the same circumstances. At the same time, globalizing trends in health, international aid and mental health discourse and policy do highlight some common international themes and problems which service users and their movements face across continents. It is worth highlighting these because they have such general significance for both service users and policy internationally. Here we consider three particularly important and influential issues.

Dominance of the medical model

While western understandings of disability have been subjected to fundamental reassessment in recent years, the medicalized individual model of 'mental illness' continues to dominate mental health policy and practice internationally. It still shapes public understanding of 'mental health' and governs the lives and experience of many mental health service users. Such western models and their associated emphasis on physical treatments/interventions and drug therapy have been exported globally, as well as being reinforced in former Eastern Bloc countries since the collapse of the Soviet Union. In different cultures and historically, madness has been interpreted and understood in many different ways. It has been associated with magical powers, the supernatural, divine intervention, possession by the devil, violence, irrationality, spirituality and special gifts and insight. Western models, however, have increasingly overlaid local traditional and different cultural and social understandings of mental health issues, imposing their own inequalities (Rogers and Pilgrim 2003). If anything, such 'mental illness' understandings of people's experience seem to be gaining ground. They have been exported to the majority world. As will be discussed further below, they have also been reinforced by the introduction of a new 'recovery' model for mental health services, first developed in the US (Rogers and Pilgrim 2010).

The number and range of psychiatric diagnostic categories has continued to mushroom. These increasingly cast broader socially related issues in medicalized terms, for example 'Attention Deficit Hyperactive Disorder' (ADHD) and 'post-traumatic stress disorder' (PTSD). The needs of a growing range of groups, notably children and young people and older people, are increasingly being framed in psychiatric terms. While making clear that it cannot 'treat' them, psychiatry has also categorized a growing range of people and behaviours under the heading of 'personality disorder'. Some of these are closely associated with violence and homicide. This has reinforced traditional associations of mental health service users with dangerousness, which has resulted in pressure for increasing restrictions on their rights, notably in North America and the UK. A growing focus on and recent developments in genetics, the neurosciences and pharmacology seem to have confirmed the ascendancy of the natural sciences in this field as the key source for understanding, interpretation and 'treatment' of 'mental disorder'(Coppick and Hopton 2000; Rogers and Pilgrim 2001, 2010; Ferguson *et al.* 2003). Doctors are still the most powerful professionals operating in this area. Understanding mental disorder in terms of physical processes fits with the large-scale use of drugs as the main and routine response to people's difficulties. The dominance of psychiatry in the field, in terms of status, legitimacy and power, continues, even though it may be argued that it has been subjected to increasing managerialist and political pressures in recent years. It still plays a dominant role in shaping provision as well as individual mental health service users' experience and outcomes, and its influence has been felt by all related mental health professions and occupations to a greater or lesser extent.

Over-reliance on chemo-therapy

Current over-reliance on chemo-therapy is both a consequence and a reinforcement of the dominance of the medical model in mental health policy, practice and understanding. In 1994, the New Zealand survivor activist Mary O'Hagan commented on a prevailing treatment approach:

> which claims that mental problems are physical illnesses which need to be treated by physical means such as drugs. This is the most dominant model in the mental health system. The medical model places a lot of power at the hands of experts and because it is so deterministic, can put survivors in a very passive, disempowered role.
>
> *(O'Hagan 1994: 14–15)*

Drugs are still by far the most common psychiatric treatment. Psychotherapy is usually more readily available to people with money and less debilitating problems; however, many survivors in the movement believe much psychotherapy can be as oppressive as physical treatments. Mental health service users/survivors express concern that there has been an increase in biological psychiatry in the last 20 years. They worry that drugs are seen as offering a cheap, fast-acting and often sedating approach to 'treatment'. While people are often left feeling that drugs are the only way of dealing with their difficulties, they also create their own problems. They may not only have short-term damaging 'side' effects, but also do lasting damage in the long term, as well as create problems of psychological and physical dependence. Drugs, however, continue to be a major area of spend in mental health and the focus of much if not most research expenditure (Newnes *et al.* 2001). While, as Mary O'Hagan says, service users can expect to be told that drugs are 'the only thing that could help you' (O'Hagan 1994: 7), they point to other helpful responses. They stress the importance of addressing social factors and of social interventions in enabling them to live better, less difficult lives. They highlight the importance of supportive loving and friendship relationships for their well-being; of being able to flourish through employment, training and education, of hobbies and constructive occupation and contributing more to society, the value of complementary therapies and holistic approaches to psychological difficulties (Faulkner 1997; Faulkner and Layzell 2000; O'Hagan 2009).

Increased emphasis on dangerousness and control

Beginning in the 1960s and 1970s, there was an international policy shift to de-institutionalize mental health policy and provision. There were many reasons for this shift, both positive and negative. These included concerns about poor conditions in institutions and the denial of service users' rights, as well as a desire to save money by getting rid of and selling off rather than maintaining rundown old buildings – maintaining people instead by prescribing newly developed major tranquilizers and other neuroleptic drugs (often associated with damaging (side) effects). Care in the community was based on a philosophy of people being able to stay in their own homes or live somewhere nearby in their 'neighbourhood' and have suitable support to do so (Rogers and Pilgrim 2001).

This coincided and connected with economic and ideological changes resulting in a shift to the marketization of welfare, with an increasing emphasis on private provision in health and welfare and the reduction of state intervention and expenditure. What this tended to mean in practice was that such reforms were frequently poorly implemented and while traditional institutional services closed, replacement community-based provision was often inadequate, under-funded, of poor quality and poorly coordinated (Coppick and Hopton 2000; Rogers and Pilgrim 2001).

As a result, with more mental health service users decarcerated, fears were raised by politicians and the media regarding patients who presented a risk. This had an international reaction, with an increasing emphasis on control, the stigmatizing of service users, their association (generally without supporting evidence) with violence and homicide, often presented in racialized terms and crucially the extension of provisions for control, particularly from hospitals, into the community (Taylor and Gunn 1999). It has resulted in government prioritizing of the concept of 'public safety' in mental health policy. This can now be seen in many countries, including, for example, the UK, US, Australia and Canada, in a greater or lesser switch from support to controlling and forensic services and an increase in numbers and proportions of people in forensic and restricted services.

Issues of language and terminology

There is no agreed language in the field of madness and mental health which provides a basis for consensus, nationally or internationally. The title of this chapter, 'psychiatric system survivors' has been chosen specifically because it probably represents the most explicitly political term used by mental health service users/survivors to describe themselves and their movement. The term is deliberately used to frame survivors in terms of the psychiatric system. They do not mean by it that they see themselves as survivors of madness or mental health problems as, for example, survivors of childhood abuse might describe themselves. In this sense, the term does not mean mental health survivors. Rather they seek to emphasize that they see themselves a people who have or are seeking to survive the *psychiatric system*. Thus it is this system that is seen as the problem, the underlying issue, rather than any psychological or psychiatric difficulty that the person might be seen as having. Organizing and campaigning is thus framed in terms of challenging the problematic nature of the psychiatric system. The early radical UK user controlled organization Survivors Speak Out highlighted this term and extended its popular usage in the UK, although it has also developed internationally (Beresford 2000).

Traditional formal language used about mental health service users/survivors has largely been rejected by service user activists. The terms used have either followed from their role in the psychiatric system as *patients*, or been associated with the diagnostic categories in which they have been placed. Thus the most commonly used term has been 'patient', or 'psychiatric' or 'mental' patient. Many service users/survivors reject such terms because they feel they emphasize their passivity and frame them narrowly in terms of services that they frequently dislike and reject. People are also described in terms of diagnostic categories as 'schizophrenics', 'manic-depressives' or 'bi-polars'. Such labels are frequently experienced as demeaning, reducing people to a set of symptoms, framing them in narrow medical terms. They are especially problematic because the diagnostic categories attached to people frequently change, overlap and do not seem to be consistently applied. Such labels are especially felt to objectify and reduce the people they are attached to.

It is also important to address the widespread use of derogatory, stigmatic and abusive language that is used about distress and mental health service users in popular and media discussion. A wide and growing range of such terms continue to be used and developed. They include words like 'nutter', 'loony', 'nut case', 'mental case', 'mental', 'mentalist', 'psycho', 'community care case' and 'crazy'. Some can be seen as leftovers from previous ages. Others have much more recent origins. They are part of a broader environment of stigma and exclusion which mental health service users routinely encounter and which connects them with the experience of disabled people defined more broadly.

From the time that they started to develop their own groups and organizations in the 1980s, mental health service users/survivors have sought to develop their own alternative terminology. Three terms internationally have been at the heart of their attempts to describe themselves. These are *survivor*, *service user* and *consumer*, the latter developing particularly in North America. In this discussion, the term mental health service user/survivor will be used (although both these words – user and survivor – have come in for some criticism), as being the least contentious and the least tied to any external ideology (Beresford 2005).

Service users have also sought to move beyond prevailing medical models to describe the experiences they have. Thus they have tended to talk much more about 'distress' – emotional and mental distress – than mental health or mental health problems. Some also talk about madness. Service users have not only worked to develop their own terminology; they have also sought to re-appropriate and reclaim existing language. Thus they have used the term 'madness' to describe differences and extremes of emotion and perception. They have used the word in a non-pejorative way. This can be seen as part of a broader development, where mental health service users/survivors like other oppressed groups and minorities, including black and minority ethnic people, women, gay men, lesbians, bi-sexuals and transsexuals, seek to reclaim oppressive language used against them, particularly in their communication with each other. Thus 'Mad Pride' has emerged in the UK and North America as a badge for campaigning and activism committed to challenging the devalued position of mental health service users/survivors (Wallcraft *et al.* 2003; Beresford and Campbell 2004).

Mental health not disability

While terms like mentally disabled and psychiatric disability are used in some countries and in some contexts, this has not been the general way in which service users/survivors have described themselves or been described. This avoidance of the use of disability terminology reflects a broader history of, and emphasis on, separate development by survivors. This has extended widely. Service users/survivors have self-consciously developed their own movement internationally. They have developed their own organizations, groups and networks, as we have seen at all levels. They refer to their own history, culture, arts and struggles. While some organizations like my own – the UK-based Shaping Our Lives – have sought to work across different 'user' and impairment groups, this has tended to be the exception rather than the rule.

There is significant evidence to indicate that mental health service users frequently do not or do not wish to associate themselves with disability or disabled people (Plumb 1994; Beresford 2000). There seem to be multiple and complex reasons for this. While this seems to be an international issue, the UK offers a helpful case study where such collective action and state-led participation are relatively well developed.

Survivors, disability and disabled people

It appears from the evidence that many people with experience as mental health service users do not want to be linked with disability (Beresford *et al.* 1996). While they may be included in official categorizations as disabled people, while they may receive disability benefits and come within the remit of disability legislation and services, nonetheless they do not classify or count themselves as 'disabled'. This seems primarily to be due to their reluctance to have what they see as another stigmatizing identity imposed upon them in addition to that as 'mentally ill' people or mental health service users. It also appears to relate to their – and indeed other people's – tendency to see disability narrowly in terms of people with physical or sensory impairments.

Similarly, many mental health service users/survivors do not seem to relate particularly to or identify with disabled people (Plumb 1994). They do not necessarily see themselves as facing common issues or having common concerns. It also needs to be said that just because one individual or group faces discrimination or oppression does not mean that it understands or is supportive of another. Basically many survivors seem reluctant to be associated with what they see as the negative identity of being disabled. Yet we also know that mental health service users/ survivors are at particular risk of acquiring impairments and becoming disabled people. This can result from both difficulties they encounter in their lifestyle, as well as damaging (side) effects from long-term medication.

At the same time there also seems to be a strong tendency for people with physical and sensory impairments to be reluctant to identify with mental health service users. Yet we know that, whether as the result of the oppression and discrimination that they face or for other reasons, many people with physical and sensory impairments have their own experience of madness and distress and their own involvement in the psychiatric system. Similarly, many people with learning difficulties seem to come into contact with the psychiatric system, perhaps through being identified as having 'challenging behaviour' or as a result of institutionalization, abuse or neglect.

Thus, while there has been a tendency for survivors (and indeed other disabled people) to emphasize their differences, both individually and collectively, there are clearly significant overlaps between the two. This is further reflected in the different philosophies underpinning these different movements. It probably makes most sense to start with those associated with the disabled people's movement

The social model of disability

As we would expect in a book concerned with disability studies, there is much discussion elsewhere in this publication of the social model of disability. It is nonetheless still helpful to touch on it in this chapter, since it is so central to its focus. The social model of disability was developed by the disabled people's movement. It has had a major impact on public policy and understanding in the UK and internationally, leading to major new legislation, new policies, new support roles and new approaches to service provision. It challenged traditional western medicalized individualistic understandings of disability. These focused on the individual disabled person, seeing disability as located within them and resulting from some inherited or acquired disability that restricted what they could do and could result in them being dependent and unable to live a 'normal' life. During the twentieth century, individualized understandings of disability were overlaid by the medicalized thinking of emerging medical professions which appropriated disability as an area of their expertise. The disabled people's movement saw this as resulting in a medicalized individual model of disability which conceived of disability as pathological and disabled people as requiring institutionalization, rehabilitation and welfare support (Oliver 1996; Oliver and Barnes 1998; Thomas 2007).

The social model of disability, which disabled activists developed instead, drew a distinction between the physical, sensory or intellectual impairment or perceived impairment affecting an individual disabled person and the negative societal reaction to it. It is the latter which they conceived of as disability. Thus disability was understood as a discriminatory and oppressive response to people seen as having an impairment, rather than a characteristic attached to the individual. Discussion of the social model of disability among disability activists and in disability studies has been lively and fast-moving (Thomas 2007). For disabled people, it has been a groundbreaking idea, shifting blame and responsibility for disability from the individual to society and exploring the complex inter-relationship between the two. The social model of disability highlights the oppressive nature of the dominant social response to impairment, which excludes, segregates and stigmatizes disabled people, creates barriers to their equality and participation and discriminates against them, restricting their human and civil rights. This approach to understanding has encouraged disabled people to highlight the problems they face as primarily a civil and human rights (rather than welfare) issue. There is no doubt that the social model of disability has influenced public understanding of disability, as well as many disabled people's own perceptions of themselves.

The social model of disability is a radical shift in understanding because it does not just take account of social factors while retaining an essentially medical approach to disability. It challenges such a medical approach because it highlights the way that societal responses generate both understandings of disability and responses to it. It goes beyond the traditional 'nature' versus 'nurture' approach to understanding people's situation as disabled people.

The social model of disability helps us to understand:

- the many barriers disabled people still face in society – these include social, economic, political and cultural barriers;
- the discrimination that they face – the negative attitudes they encounter both from individuals and more broadly in society;
- the oppressive way in which they can expect to be treated in society;
- the way their human and civil rights tend to be restricted and undermined (Oliver 1996).

At the same time, the social model has come in for criticism on a number of fronts. These include its failure adequately to address the complex interactions of disability and impairment and the potentially disabling effects of impairment (Shakespeare 2006; Barnes and Mercer 2005; Thomas 2007). Also highlighted has been a tendency to focus the social model narrowly on people with physical and visual impairments, taking inadequate account of and failing to explore the model with people with learning difficulties, mental health service users/survivors and Deaf people who identify as a linguistic minority. Its application in majority world settings has also been criticized (Stone 1999). At the same time it can be argued that as each such criticism has emerged, efforts have been made to address it.

The philosophy of independent living

This philosophy follows from the social model of disability and again was originally inspired by the disabled people's movement. It is based on a belief that disabled people should be enabled to live their lives on as equal terms as possible alongside non-disabled people. It says that disabled people should have the same choices as anyone who is not disabled. It turns traditional notions of 'independence' on their head. It is not preoccupied with the individual, or narrow ideas of personal autonomy, although its use of the term 'independent' means that it is sometimes challenged (wrongly) for understating people's 'inter-dependence'. It does not mean 'standing on your own two feet' or 'managing on your own'. Instead of seeing the service user as having a defect or deficiency requiring 'care', it highlights the need to ensure that they have the support they need to live their lives as fully as possible, on equal terms and interdependently with others (Morris 1993). This support is not expected to come from family members required to be unpaid or informal 'carers'. The philosophy rejects the concept of care and replaces it with the idea of support. It sees independence as being in a position to make your own decisions rather than having to do everything for yourself (Campbell and Oliver 1996; Morris 2004). Instead of people being assessed for 'care' on the basis of what they cannot do, to qualify for 'care', under this model, support is provided to enable them to live their lives as fully as possible, as they wish to. There are two inter-related and key aspects to the philosophy of independent living, which are:

- ensuring people have the support that they need under their control to be able to live their lives as fully as they can, on as equal terms as possible, with non-disabled people;
- equalizing their access to mainstream policy, services and amenities, like housing, health, education, employment and recreation.

These two ideas – the social model of disability and the philosophy of independent living – have been very influential in the field of disability internationally. While they are not universally accepted, while both as we have seen have come in for criticism and their achievement should not be overstated, they have been a basis for change in societal understandings of disability, for the making of policy, practice and legislation and for disabled people's own identity, discourses and collective action.

Mental health service user/survivor thinking

What is interesting is how limited the impact of ideas like the social model of disability and independent living have so far been on mental health service users/survivors, their organizations and movements. As has been indicated, there seems generally to have been a process of separate development at work between the two movements in their philosophy and theory-building. Historically, the issue seems less that mental health service users/survivors have rejected ideas from the disabled people's movement, more that they have adopted a different approach to developing their own. Again the UK situation offers an interesting and advanced case study that also seems to reflect many aspects of the wider international situation.

A very wide range of people with experience of mental health services were involved in the survivor movement's founding and development. This includes people who had spent a long time in psychiatric hospitals, people who had spent much of their lives in and out of such hospitals, people identified as having the most serious or severe diagnoses, who had tried to kill themselves, who had ongoing problems of depression, self-harm and eating distress. It has also included people who have been politically active as well as others who have never got involved before, people from many different black and ethnic communities, men and women, older and younger people, lesbians, gay, bisexual and transgender people as well as heterosexuals. As Peter Campbell, who is one of the founders of the UK movement, also helpfully makes clear, there is not one single position or view among people who are active in service user/survivor organizations and the survivor movement. They may focus on different issues, have different priorities and see things in different terms (Campbell 2009: 48). What has unified them has been the personal experience of mental distress, madness and/or using mental health services. It is this direct experience, or as is it is sometimes called 'experiential knowledge', which they have in common and which is their unifying force (Wallcraft *et al.* 2003).

However, the survivors' movement has not developed explicit philosophies or theories comparable to those of the social model of disability or independent living, developed by the disabled people's movement. At the same time, there can be no question that its members are generally critical of the dominant medicalized individual model operating in the psychiatric system. The survivor movement has tended to operate more closely than the disabled people's movement within the prevailing service system. It has based its approach much more on a partnership than a separatist approach to collective action. Much energy has been expended in participatory processes, seeking to reform existing services, although activists seriously question how much has been achieved (Campbell 2009). The UK disabled people's movement, for example, focused more on developing disabled people's own ideas and models for policy, services and support, critiquing rather than seeking to reform traditional medicalized disability services. While the campaigning and objectives of the disabled people's movement in the UK, for example, flowed from its key theoretical developments, this was not the case with the survivor movement.

It would, however, be a mistake to suggest that there is no set of shared values and beliefs underpinning the survivor movement. The survivor movement and its associated organizations are very conscious of 'the social' in their thinking and activities. Service user/survivor discourses address both material and spiritual issues; the personal as well as the political. However, this still has not led to the widespread development of any equivalent of the social model of disability. There are signs that there is a wariness about doing this, both for fear of imposing another orthodoxy, or of coming in for attack for being seen as denying people's personal difficulties and distress (Beresford 1999; Beresford and Campbell 2004). Survivors and their organizations have nonetheless developed new ideas and approaches that challenge traditional understandings of 'mental illness', generating new ideas and thinking about self-harm, eating distress and hearing voices (Beresford and Campbell 2004; Romme *et al.* 2009). As with other user movements, they have also prioritized the right of service users to speak for themselves, to be treated as equals and to be respected for who they are. It is these general principles, rather than any more specific theory or philosophy, which have underpinned and guided survivors' thinking and objectives.

The survivors' movement, operating more closely within the service system, has been much less successful in developing a counter to the medical model of mental illness and the drug-based treatments that continue to predominate in the psychiatric system. Much energy has been expended in participatory processes, seeking to reform existing services, but activists seriously question how much has been achieved (Campbell 2009).

Recovery

However, if the survivor movement has been unable or unwilling to develop its own equivalent of the social model of disability, it has given significant support to another model, which has gained international importance in recent years. This is the 'recovery' model. The idea of recovery has recently gained major interest in UK mental health policy and practice. Survivor commentators like Mary O'Hagan from New Zealand have also talked in terms of recovery (http://www. maryohagan.com/publications.php). There is talk of a 'recovery movement' (Pilgrim 2008). Many service users value the idea of recovery because it does not write them off as irreparably damaged or defective, as pathologizing medical approaches often have done historically. Instead it seems to offer hope and the possibility of positive outcomes for their lives (Turner-Crowson and

Wallcraft 2002). Other survivors, however, are highly critical of the concept's essentially medicalized basis and the associated emphasis on 're-ablement' and moving people into employment. Framed in medical terms of 'getting better', it has offered the medical model a new lease of life. While the philosophy of independent living developed by disabled people emphasizes people's potentially continuing need for support to live their lives to the full, recovery instead implies that such support may become unnecessary and be withdrawn as people 'recover'. For this reason, some survivors see recovery as at least consistent with and in some cases supportive of the neo-liberal agenda of cuts, integration into the labour market and increasing reliance on self-help and people 'looking after themselves'.

The contradiction facing survivors and their movement

It is interesting that mental health service users/survivors and their organizations do not yet seem to have drawn significantly on the social model of disability or developed their own equivalent, given the many issues and concerns that they share with other disabled people. There are not only many overlaps between the two groups, as we have seen, but they also face many shared difficulties in relation to society and other people. These include experiencing social barriers and restrictions on their human and civil rights; stigma and negative stereotyping, discrimination and other forms of oppression, poverty and material disadvantage.

However, the inability of the survivor movement to develop its own social model does not mean that mental health service users/survivors feel comfortable with the medical model, even if they have failed to throw it off. This has been highlighted by new evidence from a UK research project (Beresford *et al.* 2010).

Valuing social approaches

This research explored service users'/survivors' views about the conceptualization of mental health issues. There was significant agreement that a medicalized individual model of mental illness still predominated. This medical model was seen as very powerful among professionals, in society generally and also among service users, shaping understanding and attitudes. It was seen as almost entirely negative in effect. This was strongly reflected in people's comments, for example:

> the problems I think it creates is that it's a predominately negative way of looking at people's lives, to think in terms of illness … it focuses on the individual rather than the situation in which the individual's living. It tends to apologise … it individualises problems, but it tends to make people feel negative I think, about themselves … and it doesn't actually remove the blame … the blaming aspect.

> It's a deficit deviant model, that there is definitely something wrong with the individual … it's definitely a biological perspective, they don't see it as a social issue, it's a biological thing full stop. And they respond by giving you drugs, giving you electric treatments, whatever they call it, that kind of stuff. It's an individualistic approach.
>
> *(Beresford et al. 2010: 12–13)*

There was strong support for a social understanding of mental health issues. This reflects a broader renewal of such interest (Tew 2005; Ramon and Williams 2005). A common view was that people's mental health was affected by and a response to broader social and environmental factors. Service users/survivors said, for example:

I understand mental health as essentially the outcome of a personal and social relation between an individual and her/his environment (physical/spiritual/social/cultural) overtime.

I think more of a social [approach]. I think pressure comes from society and pressure comes from what's actually happening in your life.

(*Beresford et al.* 2010: 15)

Major concerns about the social model of disability

Such a social approach, it was felt, did need to take account of people's individual and different needs as well as shared social circumstances and barriers. While there was strong support for such social approaches, and while most participants felt that they experienced barriers as mental health service users/survivors, their views of the social model of disability were complex and divided. While some could see it as potentially offering a helpful basis for understanding mental health issues, others saw it as more problematic. Problems of terminology in mental health created additional difficulties, because many people were uncomfortable with non-medicalized terminology like 'madness'. A particular issue which creates concerns for people was the concept of 'impairment' (even where this was presented in terms of 'perceived impairment') as part of the social model of disability. Some mental health service users/survivors felt that they and other mental health service users might not have an impairment and that it could therefore be unhelpful to apply this framework to them.

I don't know, I think it's very complex. … The word impairment, I'm not that happy with the word impairment, because, you know, it's about limits isn't it?

I not sure that it's a fixed … and permanent the way some impairment are fixed, like visual impairment, or hearing impairment, because somebody with a mental health [problem] can fluctuate, whereas somebody with a sensory impairment.

(*Beresford et al.* 2010: 27)

Continuing concerns about being identified as 'disabled' also again surfaced:

I'm not sure I wanna be called disabled.

The problem with [associating it with] disability is once again the fact that it is making it seem to be permanent and irrecoverable, that's what I don't like about it. It certainly should help people making policies more careful about how they're structured and, you know, help people to become more included, but the basic idea that there is something pertinently wrong with you I don't like at all, or that you're inadequate in some way.

(*Beresford et al.* 2010: 19)

As a result, this led some service users/survivors to think that more thought was needed about the social model of disability, a possible social model of madness and distress and the relationship there might be between the two.

A worsening time to be isolated?

While we know that the social model of disability is not universally accepted by disabled people and the international disabled people's movement, its approach and influence have had an internationally powerful effect in highlighting disability as an empowerment and rights issue and in mobilizing collective action and public and political support of these. While mental health service users/survivors internationally have achieved much more than even they could probably have expected from their own collective action, with many mental health service users/survivors gaining new confidence and understanding about themselves, we also know that their circumstances in society and the barriers and exclusions that they face have in many cases increased rather than diminished. Thus we have a situation where there is an overlapping group of disabled people and mental health service users/survivors facing many common issues of oppression, exclusion and discrimination, barriers and restricted rights. But it continues to be divided philosophically and both constituencies are arguably weakened and diminished by this. The potential gains from unity and solidarity are not achieved. Certainly the current history of separate development does not seem to offer a profitable road ahead for mental health service users/survivors who continue to be one of the most stigmatized and marginalized groups of disabled people. It also needs to be said that this situation is likely to get worse, as external pressures through global economic difficulties make the economic and social position of all disabled people more difficult and tenuous.

The key question this raises here is: is this a helpful situation in an increasingly uncertain and potentially hostile international environment, either for mental health service users/survivors or other disabled people? Is it time to move on from a tradition of movements subject to separate development to one which is not only committed to building stronger links and networks, but also to exploring ways of building more inclusive and appropriate underpinning models and philosophies as a basis for shared identity and collective action? Clearly any steps to unity would have to ensure that the integrity and independence of different identities and movements were retained. At the same time further work on the relation between disabled people's and mental health service user/survivor movements seems like a helpful step.

Next steps

The research study on service user/survivor perceptions of models of mental health (Beresford *et al.* 2010) set out a series of recommendations for next steps and these are perhaps helpful as part of a process of sharing ideas and increasing understanding between movements. These recommendations included:

- sharing the findings more widely among mental health service users/survivors, disabled people and the wider disabled people's movement;
- facilitating further opportunities for mental health service users and their organizations to discuss these findings and explore their implications;
- from such discussions identifying priorities for action, particularly in relation to the negative effects associated with current dominating medical models of mental health issues and the negative media presentation of mental health matters;
- for existing proponents of the social model of disability to explore how it might be made more accessible, particularly for mental health service users, so that they are able to gain a better understanding of it in relation to themselves;
- for survivor leaders and activists, particularly those concerned with the movement's value base and philosophy, to explore the social model of disability in more depth, considering if and how it might be developed better to address and include mental health issues;
- providing opportunities for mental health service users to become more aware of disability issues generally and the social model of disability specifically and how these might be relevant to them;

- supporting mental health service users/survivors and their organizations to learn more about the work of the disabled people's movement and legislation/rights issues that they can benefit from – this will help them to secure rights and work together with disabled people's groups on common issues like, for example, direct payments, individual budgets, personalization and self-directed support;
- creating more opportunities for different groups of service users to come together and explore ideas like the social model and independent living together, thinking through possible similarities and differences;
- challenging negative labels attached to mental health service users/survivors. Labelling and stigma again emerge as major barriers for mental health service users. Some, however, have begun to challenge negative labels and identities imposed on them. It will be helpful to explore how mental health service users might be able to challenge the negatives attached to them and take greater pride in who they are, possibly reclaiming language which has been attached to them for negative and hostile reasons (Beresford *et al.* 2010).

Taken together these may help in building a positive agenda for rethinking the social model of disability in relation to the survivor movement and developing stronger, more strategic and unifying relations between psychiatric system survivors and disabled people and their movements.

References

Barnes, C. and Mercer, G., eds (2005) *The Social Model of Disability, Europe and the Majority World* (Leeds: The Disability Press).

Beresford, P. (1999) 'Making Participation Possible: Movements of Disabled People and Psychiatric System Survivors', in T. Jordan and A. Lent, eds, *Storming the Millennium: The New Politics of Change* (London: Lawrence and Wishart): pp. 34–50.

Beresford, P. (2000) 'What Have Madness and Psychiatric System Survivors Got to Do with Disability and Disability Studies?', *Disability & Society* 15(1): 168–72.

Beresford, P. (2005) '"Service User": Regressive or Liberatory Terminology? Current Issues', *Disability & Society* 20(4): 469–77.

Beresford, P. and Campbell, P. (2004) 'Participation and Protest: Mental Health Service Users/Survivors', in M. J. Todd and G. Taylor, eds, *Democracy and Participation: Popular Protest and New Social Movements* (London: Merlin Press): pp. 326–42.

Beresford, P., Gifford, G. and Harrison, C. (1996) 'What Has Disability Got to Do with Psychiatric Survivors?', in J. Reynolds and J. Read, eds, *Speaking Our Minds: Personal Experience of Mental Distress and its Consequences*. Open University reader for Open University course, 'Mental Health: Issues, Skills and Perspectives' (Basingstoke: Palgrave): pp. 209–14.

Beresford, P., Nettle, M. and Perring, R. (2010) *Towards a Social Model of Madness and Distress? Exploring What Service Users Say* (York: Joseph Rowntree Foundation).

Campbell, P. (1996) 'The History of the User Movement in the United Kingdom', in T. Heller, J. Reynolds, R. Gomm, R. Muston and S. Pattison, eds, *Mental Health Matters: A Reader* (Basingstoke: Macmillan): pp. 218–25.

Campbell, P. (1999) 'The Service User/Survivor Movement', in *This is Madness: A Critical Look at Psychiatry and the Future of Mental Health Services* (Ross-on-Wye: PCCS Books): pp. 195–209.

Campbell, P. (2009) 'The Service User/Survivor Movement', in J. Reynolds, R. Muston, T. Heller, J. Leach, M. McCormick, J. Wallcraft, M. Walsh, eds, *Mental Health Still Matters* (Basingstoke: Palgrave Macmillan): pp. 46–52.

Campbell, J. and Oliver, M. (1996) *Disability Politics: Understanding Our Past, Changing Our Future* (London: Routledge).

Chamberlin, J. (1988) *On Our Own: User Controlled Alternatives to the Mental Health System* (London: Mind).

Coppick, V. and Hopton, J. (2000) *Critical Perspectives on Mental Health* (London: Routledge).

Faulkner, A. (1997) *Knowing Our Own Minds: A Survey of How People in Emotional Distress Take Control of Their Lives* (London: Mental Health Foundation).

Faulkner, A. and Layzell, S. (2000) *Strategies for Living: A Report of User-led Research into People's Strategies for Living with Mental Distress* (London: Mental Health Foundation).

Ferguson, I., Barclay, A., and Stalker, K. (2003) *'It's a Difficult Life to Lead': Supporting People with Personality Disorder: Service User and Provider Perspectives* (Stirling: Department of Applied Social Science, University of Stirling).

MindFreedom (2009) 'Psychiatric Survivor Movement History'; available online at http://www.mindfreedom.org/kb/act/movement-history (accessed 2 August 2011).

Morris, J. (1993) *Independent Lives?: Community Care and Disabled People* (Basingstoke: Macmillan).

Morris, J. (2004) 'Community Care: A Disempowering Framework', *Disability & Society* 19(5): 427–42.

Newnes, C., Holmes, G. and Dunn, C., eds (2001) *This is Madness Too: Critical Perspectives on Mental Health Services* (Ross-on-Wye: PCCS Books).

O'Hagan, M. (1994) *Stopovers On My Way Home From Mars: A Journey into the Psychiatric Survivor Movement in the USA, Britain and the Netherlands* (London: Survivors Speak Out).

O'Hagan, M. (2009) *Making Sense of Madness from the Inside*; available online at http://www.outoftheirminds.co.nz/?p=222 (accessed 6 October 2011).

Oliver, M. (1996) *Understanding Disability: From Theory to Practice* (Basingstoke: Macmillan).

Oliver, M. and Barnes, C. (1998) *Disabled People and Social Policy: From Exclusion to Inclusion* (Harlow: Longman).

Pilgrim, D. (2008) '"Recovery" and Current Mental Health Policy', *Chronic Illness* 4(4): 295–304.

Plumb, A. (1994) *Distress or Disability? A Discussion Document* (Manchester: Greater Manchester Coalition of Disabled People).

Ramon, S. and Williams, J. E., eds, (2005) *Mental Health at the Crossroads: The Promise of the Psychosocial Approach* (Aldershot: Ashgate).

Rogers, A. and Pilgrim, D. (2001) *Mental Health Policy in Britain*, 2nd edn (Basingstoke: Palgrave).

Rogers, A. and Pilgrim, D. (2003) *Mental Health and Inequality* (Basingstoke: Palgrave Macmillan).

Rogers, A. and Pilgrim, D. (2010) *A Sociology of Mental Health and Illness* (Basingstoke: Palgrave Macmillan).

Romme, M., Escher, S., Dillon, J., Corstens, D. and Morris, M. (2009) *Living with Voices: 50 Stories of Recovery* (Ross-on-Wye: PCCS Books).

Shakespeare, T. (2006) *Disability Rights and Wrongs* (London: Routledge).

Stone, E., ed. (1999) *Disability and Development: Learning from Action and Research in the Majority World* (Leeds: The Disability Press).

Taylor, P. and Gunn, J. (1999) 'Homicides by People with Mental Illness: Myth and Reality', *British Journal of Psychiatry* 174: 9–14.

Tew, J., ed. (2005) *Social Perspectives in Mental Health: Developing Social Models to Understand and Work with Mental Distress* (London: Jessica Kingsley).

Thomas, C. (2007) *Sociologies of Disability and Illness: Contested Ideas in Disability Studies and Medical Sociology* (Basingstoke: Palgrave Macmillan).

Turner-Crowson, J. and Wallcraft, J. (2002) 'The Recovery Vision for Mental Health Services and Research: A British Perspective, *Psychiatric Rehabilitation Journal* 25(3): 245–54.

Wallcraft, J., Read, J. and Sweeney, A. (2003) *On Our Own Terms: Users and Survivors of Mental Health Services Working Together for Support and Change* (London: Sainsbury Centre for Mental Health).

13

IT'S ABOUT TIME! UNDERSTANDING THE EXPERIENCE OF SPEECH IMPAIRMENT

Kevin Paterson

The opportunity to communicate – impart to another person or persons opinions, ideas, thoughts, feelings and emotions – plays a central part in social life and the defining of a 'social being' (Jordan and Kaiser 1996; Rae 1993). Although many disabled people are excluded from such opportunities to communicate and find it difficult to have their voices heard and understood, disability studies has little to say about this exclusion and issues of communication remain theoretically underdeveloped from a social model perspective. Drawing upon the proposition of a sociology of impairment (see Paterson and Hughes 1999) and the idea of 'temporal barriers' to communication (see Parr *et al.* 2003b), this chapter seeks to develop an understanding of 'communication disablement' from the standpoint of a person with speech impairment.

The phenomenology of Maurice Merleau-Ponty (1962) is crucial to a sociology of impairment. He grounded perception in the experienced and experiencing body. The world as perceived through the body is the ground level of all knowledge, for it is through the body that people have access to the world. Our perception of everyday reality depends upon a 'lived body' (Williams and Bendelow 1998), that is, a body that simultaneously experiences and creates the world. Crossley's (1995) suggestion that the physical, cultural and social world is carnally formed and informed by bodily activity facilitates an understanding of the everyday embodied reality of being disabled. The body acts and by its actions it builds a world of intersubjective and intercorporeal relations. In the context of these relations, however, it is acted upon. Disabled people's everyday embodied experience of the lifeworld is one of 'dys-appearance' (Leder 1990). Unlike the non-impaired body, which is customarily 'unaware' of itself until it is confronted by pain or discomfort, the impaired body can also be stunned into its own recognition by the disablism that permeates everyday life. This experience is produced because social space is fashioned for and reflects the needs of non-impaired carnality and the impaired body is not recognized or valued in social space. The objectification marked by 'dys-appearance' is, in itself, a manifest form of oppression which is 'felt' in a variety of ways by the disabled people who experience it (Paterson and Hughes 1999; see also Imrie 2000, 2004; Edwards and Imrie 2003).

Disability studies is dominated by a topography/geography of oppression. Its structural account of disability fails to interrogate the everyday world. The social model tells us little or nothing of the ways in which disability is produced in the lifeworld, how oppression and discrimination become embodied and become 'felt'. Oppression is not simply produced by structural barriers – it is a question of intercorporeal norms and conventions. It is about the extent to which 'competence' is negotiated in the everyday world and how this negotiation hinges on carnal factors. It is about how social encounters can go astray within the taken-for-granted (spatio) temporal relations and how these relations can produce the experience of 'dys-appearance'.

In contemporary society, where our lives are governed by the maxim 'time is money', time is conceived as a precious resource – it is not passed but spent. However, we rarely consider how this reckoning of time impacts on our everyday lived experience. Adam (1995) describes time as the 'backcloth' to our lives, a taken-for-granted reckoning that she wants to make visible. This chapter will consider how this essentially 'hidden' temporal mediation of the everyday world impacts on disabled people (see Parr *et al.* 2003b; Corker 1998; French 1992). I will argue that, with respect to taken-for-granted and negotiated choreography of everyday life, temporal norms disadvantage people with speech impairment. The ableist nature of temporal norms means that people with speech impairment find it nigh impossible to acquire and sustain the physical and cultural capital necessary to participate in everyday social encounters. The choreography of the (spatio) temporal domains tends, therefore, to reinforce the exclusion and estrangement of people with speech impairment.

The concept of 'choreography' denotes an intersection between embodied action, space and time. 'Choreography' is the sequence of scripted bodily movements set within a specific tempo and space. It emphasizes the importance of (socially coded) bodily actions and signs in mediating and distorting everyday interactions and encounters (Crossley 1997). I want to demonstrate that compliance with the notations of intercorporeal encounters has exchange value: it accords communicative capital. The choreography of communication has produced a context for embodied action in which people with speech impairment are framed as being 'out of time' and 'out of step' and so credited with little or no communicative capital.

Time and the social model of disability: a critique

Although the spatial disciplines have, by and large, ignored the issue of disability until recently (Gleeson 1999; Imrie and Edwards 2007), the production of social space is the central concern of disability studies (Kitchin 1998; Freund 2001). Within the social model, disability is the relationship between the impaired body and the organization of social space. It is concerned with spotlighting 'restrictions', 'barriers' and 'obstructions' that produce disability. Although this analysis does not deny the importance of attitudinal barriers, the power of language or everyday embodied experience, such issues are viewed as secondary and marginal (Corker and French 1999) in comparison to the concrete terrain of social structure and organization. This reliance on a structural account of disability does not adequately explain the oppressive nature of intercorporeal and intersubjective relations (Paterson and Hughes 1999). It is also important to identify the ways in which estrangement and marginalization are produced by the choreography of everyday life.

Embodied norms of communication are oppressive to people with speech impairment (Robillard 1994; Lenney and Sercombe 2002) as they are exclusively informed by and reflect the needs of non-impaired bodies. This oppression is 'felt' as bodily 'dys-appearance'. Both time and proprioception are central to communication, indeed central to success, or for that matter failure, in the everyday world. The social model offers an understanding of disabled people's experience of oppression, most explicitly in terms of society's production of structural barriers and access to social, cultural and physical space. This has largely been the outcome of the collapse of the meaning of impairment into a 'homogeneous notion' in which mobility is the key term and in which mobility has been regarded as a problem of getting into and getting around public and domestic spaces. For example, when issues of 'communication disablement' are touched upon they are framed as being the result of structural barriers, and it is argued that such barriers to social participation can be removed by the 'proper' provision of augmentative and alternative communication technology and human facilitators. There are two problems here: there is a temporal dimension to the oppression of people with mobility impairments which is largely ignored in the literature and, second – and more central to the concerns of this chapter – there are other forms of oppression that cannot be reduced to spatial access. People with speech impairment, for example, are regularly excluded from everyday social encounters by the temporal conventions that structure communication. While the social model allows the disabling contours of the spatial environment to be mapped and defined, it is theoretically underdeveloped with respect to patterns of oppression that are constituted predominantly by temporal factors.

The development of a politics of space has been and remains a central vehicle for the emancipation of disabled people. However, just as the spatial disciplines appear to have failed to recognize this point, so disability studies has missed the 'temporal turn' within the spatial disciplines and wider social theory (Adam 1995). Attention has been turned to the interwoven nature of space and time and their social determinants. Disability studies might so move in the direction of a social analysis of time (Adam 1995) and map out the place of temporality in the relations of oppression which mark the embodied experience of disability. Just as concern is given to revealing 'restrictions', 'barriers' and 'obstructions' in the spatial environment that disable people with impairments, regard must also be given to exposing patterns of exclusion that are constituted predominantly by the 'tempo', 'pace' and 'rhythm' of everyday life (Parr *et al*. 2003b).

Parr *et al*. (2003b) have pointed out that social model writers have never completely ignored the importance of the reckoning of time in the production of disability. For example, Gleeson, (1999), Oliver (1990) and Finkelstein (1980) highlight how the change in tempo and pace of social and economic life enacted by the Industrial Revolution is a significant factor in the exclusion of people with impairments. The pace of factory-based work and the discipline of production norms were a stark contrast to the slower and more self-determined methods of agrarian and cottage-based work into which people with impairments had been integrated (Ryan and Thomas 1980). The feudal understanding of temporality was conceived through the turning of the seasons, the passage of the day and nature's life cycles rather than mechanical clock time. Within this temporal framework the reckoning of labour time was task orientated: work lasted as long as the job required (Thompson 1974). The body was itself a powerful source of temporality, mediating the extent and duration of tasks undertaken. Gleeson (1999: 85) asserts that this 'self-determination of tasks meant that individuals could match work rhythms with their corporeal abilities'. Moreover, 'Feudal temporality was a significant contributor to "somatic flexibility" in the peasant labour process.'

As industrialization developed, time and money became virtually synonymous (Weber 1987). The new process of production demanded a form of somatic flexibility that was determined by the pace and rhythm of the mechanized factory floor rather than the individual worker. Individuals with all types of impairments were pushed outside the labour market and into the workhouse and the asylum (Oliver 1990; Finkelstein 1980).

Adam (1995) has criticized this dualistic analysis which associates 'non-western' or pre-industrial societies with cyclical, task-orientated time and 'western' or industrialized societies with linear, clock time. Customarily, social science has tended to keep apart the different conceptions of time and grant supremacy to rationalized clock time. What is important for Adam is to question that which is taken for granted: the hegemony of clock/commodified time.

However, there is no doubt that traditional dualistic analyses denote changes in the organization of time resulting from industrialization. There is also no doubt that the social model is helpful with respect to the ways in which time is determined by epochal changes. Its structural approach illustrates the way temporal changes between modes of production impact on the exclusion of people with impairments. However, just as the social model of disability is not the best vehicle for discussing the embodied nature of everyday spatial relations, so too it can be argued that it ignores the everyday embodied reality of commodified time. This is where a phenomenological sociology of impairment could fill the gap.

One of the consequences of the hegemony of clock time/commodified time is what has been called 'the valourization of speed' (Adam 1995). One can argue that the reckoning of western time is soma-centric and the soma that underpins the reckoning is non-impaired. In other words, the organization and orchestration of time is formed and informed by the carnal needs of non-disabled people.

In (post)industrialized societies efficiency, profitability and competitiveness all have a positive value. Processes that take a long time, procedures and actions the duration of which cannot be accurately estimated and calculated, are cast out as 'waste' and 'delay'. To be typified as 'slow' in the performance of (most) tasks is to be seen as 'deficient' and 'incompetent'. Moreover, the terms 'slow' and 'a bit slow' have been used to ascribe an impairment. Such valourization of speed tells the tale of rationalization of time: time as calculable, as quantitative measurement, work as paid employment and the money-efficiency-profit link are irrevocably interwoven into a culture that lives off the energy of time consumed as quick as reason and resources will allow (Adam 1995).

However, timescapes based on the desire for speed carry their toll. Not only does our 'need for speed' place a heavy burden on the planet, it also mitigates against equality between peoples, both globally and locally. If individuals cannot comply with the reckoning of time in relation to money, efficiency, competition and profit, then they face discrimination and exclusion. As Adam (1995: 101) argues, 'the link between speed, economics and clock time operates against the principle of equal opportunity, whether this be in relation to different sexes, occupational groups, cultures or categories of people'. Disabled people palpably find themselves as such a category of people (French 1992; Wendell 1996; Parr *et al.* 2003b).

Commodified time not only restricts access to and within the workplace (French 1992), it also encroaches into the everyday world, structuring intercorporeal and intersubjective relations and producing the 'dys-appearance' experienced by people with speech impairment. 'Formalized' temporal rules marginalize and estrange a variety of social groups when negotiating health and welfare services. Bureaucratic time pressures can limit the possibilities for the appropriate flow and exchange of information for people whose first language is not English for example, hampering the services received (Warin *et al.* 2000). People with speech impairment are obviously disadvantaged by such time pressures. While family, friends and partners may 'have the time' to communicate, this is not often the case for individuals working in the health and social care professions (see Robillard 1994; Higginbotham and Wilkins 1999; Hemsley *et al.* 2001). People who face communication barriers are very sensitive to non-disabled people's levels of investment in interactions with them (Parr *et al.* 2003b) and a lack of investment is 'felt' as 'dys-appearance'.

From a phenomenological standpoint, people with speech impairment are not only policed by the 'formal' organization of time, they are also policed by 'informal' everyday temporal rules into unsatisfactory interactions (Parr *et al.* 2003b). Everyday 'codes of conduct' have schedules and rhythms that are required to be met. Speedy communication is valued since time should not be wasted. People with speech impairment are marginalized because they are framed as a threat to the fast and 'easy' flow of communication. Durations of participation are exclusively informed by and reflect the carnal needs of non-disabled people. People with speech impairment are pre-disposed to appear wanting in the face of these norms of communication. If a person is viewed as 'undisciplined' or 'lax' in respect to these temporal conventions then they are judged 'inarticulate' and their voice is unheard. A person with speech impairment 'dys-appears' because there is 'no slack' when negotiating the choreography of everyday life. One must keep 'in time' and 'in step' with the tempo of communication because slowness is the embodiment of failure and 'deficiency'. Disruptions (and distortions) arise in communicative encounters between people with and without speech impairment because the choreography of everyday life demands an exclusionary form of bodily performance and 'style' which does not reflect the carnal information of the former.

It is often suggested that disruptions and distortions to communication are created through an interlocutor's apprehension and anxiety about speech impairment and their fear of not being able to interpret what a person with speech impairment is saying (Robillard 1994; Lenney and Sercombe 2002). The social model of disability emphasizes that negative attitudes towards disabled people are embedded in and are a product of the structures and social relations of contemporary society. However, one must also seek to understand how these attitudes are played out in the everyday world, how discrimination and prejudice is 'felt' and becomes embodied in everyday encounters.

Often when a person with speech impairment encounters an unfamiliar interlocutor the latter decides they have 'no time' for the former. The assumption is that the person with speech impairment is and will be a 'waste of time' and therefore the stranger frequently looks for some competent other to address. This judgement is made and these taken-for-granted assumptions accepted because the scripts from which non-disabled people bestow 'competence' are devoid of impaired carnality. When the person with speech impairment speaks, the stranger's assumptions are confirmed because their ears are already closed. Their limited time is elapsing and the disabled person has become a barrier to the efficient spending of it. The stranger does not want to devote 'more time' to listening to what is being said or to ask for misheard words to be repeated. The person with speech impairment *disappears* for the stranger because they are a 'waste of time' and the person with speech impairment 'dys-appears' (for themselves) because they are in an immanent moment of obvious and palpable exclusion in which their social worth has been denied.

It is not uncommon for people with speech impairment when out with non-disabled companions to be approached by strangers who ask if they are siblings or related in some other way. This again reflects a denial of disabled people's socio-temporal corporeal worth. The stranger sees and hears the interaction and seeks to interpret why a non-disabled person would spend their invaluable time talking to a person with speech impairment. The stranger seeks a way to perceive this experience – which undermines the 'normal' notion of social interaction – and stabilize its unfamiliarity by drawing on scripts which place the disabled person firmly on the sidelines of 'social competence'. There seems to be no return for the non-disabled companion's temporal investment and the assumption is made that they must be acting out of 'family duty'. The stranger sometimes expresses 'admiration' for the non-disabled companion when they learn that this is not the case. The person with speech impairment disappears (for the stranger) because they are guesting as a player in the game of social interaction and 'dys-appears' (for themselves) because they are 'reminded' that their corporeal status casts them as a fraudulent 'social being'.

One can argue that non-disabled people's anxieties and fear about speech impairment might not be a problem in itself if they were prepared to take the time to listen and to exercise the 'patience' with respect to interpretation. However, non-disabled people are products of the conventions of communication, the intercorporeal relations which reflect their carnal peculiarities. Their apprehension and embarrassment arises in the context of the disruption to a set of verbal utterances and non-verbal bodily queues and gestures which are scripted and sequenced by hegemonic non-impaired carnality. These embodied notations and protocols are central to participation in the lifeworld, but which are also pre-disposed to the exclusion of those who do not dance the same dance. A person with speech impairment, viewed as being 'out of time' and 'out of step' and therefore anticipated as a 'distortion', is a barrier to successful communication and is confronted as such. This temporal estrangement is a palpable constituent in bodily 'dys-appearance'.

Interlocutors sometimes attempt to anticipate what people with speech impairment are saying when they plainly do not know. This is a common 'coping mechanism' that many people use in unfamiliar interactions, such as a conversation where the individuals are not fluent in the other's first language. It is a clear example of the powerful mediating influence of temporal relations in communicative encounters: interpretation must be instantaneous or not at all. Such encounters go astray and the person with speech impairment 'dys-appears' not because her interlocutor mis-understands what is being said but because the interlocutor is policed by temporal norms of communication into declining to take the time to ascertain what is being said.

People with speech impairment do not expect their interlocutors to always understand them. It takes time for people to 'acquaint' themselves with non-conformist 'styles' of communication and familiarity eases communication. However, if the choreography of communication was carnally re-informed to reflect the corporeal status of people with speech impairment, social interaction could afford the time and the room to iron out any misunderstandings.

Speech impairment and communicative capital

Speech and language therapy and the social model are both concerned (in opposing ways) with assisting people with speech impairment to 'get into' social interaction. Their goals and philoso-phies about facilitating 'competent' communication may be different in the extreme. However, both seek to 'tool up' people with speech impairment with the resources – either technical or bodily – to allow them to successfully negotiate the choreography of everyday life. Neither speech and language therapy nor the social model seek to confront the everyday, mundane 'meshes of microauthority' which estrange and exclude disabled people. The goal of an emancipatory politics of disability is not just about disabled people 'getting in' and 'getting around' social space, it is also about creating a 'sense of belonging' (see Marks 2000). Consider the access needs of disabled people. It is not only that their access needs should be met, it is also that their needs should be viewed as legitimate (Marks 2000). This not only relates to the access requirements of disabled people being 'tacked onto' the spatial environment as an after-thought, it also relates to the extent to which disabled people are recognized as 'social beings' through having the time and the room to participate fully in the everyday world. Adopting a phenomenological sociology of impairment, one does not seek to 'tool up' disabled people to allow them to 'keep pace' with everyday life, or to implore non-disabled people to 'grant' the time and the room to allow the social participation of disabled people; one seeks to fuel a struggle to carnally re-inform the (spatio) temporal rules which structure participation so that disabled people are valued, included and legitimized in the choreography of everyday life, and so do not 'dys-appear'.

As I stated earlier, issues of communication have been overlooked within disability studies. It is true that a social model approach within speech and language therapy is beginning to take shape, with important work focusing on Aphasia (see Jordan and Kaiser 1996; Jordan and Bryan 2001; Parr *et al.* 2003a; Byng and Duchan 2005). Despite these welcome developments, a social model approach to 'communication disablement' remains limited. It is not my intention to argue that the social model of disability has not offered any notion of liberation for people who face commu-nication barriers – far from it. Neither do I wish to disavow the importance of speech and language therapy. My intention is to seek an approach that understands that communication barriers are constituted by intercorporeal and intersubjective relations as well as by structural relations.

Claims for better communication aids and resources are vital and consistent with the materialist emphasis of the social model but do not challenge the carnally informed notations and protocols of communication. Such claims embrace technical solutions but do not challenge the hegemony of non-disabled norms in the everyday world. Technological fixes not only leave ableist norms of communication unchallenged, they reinforce them. Such fixes also mean that non-disabled people do not have to and are not expected to make adjustments to how they use time. Oliver (1990) has pointed out that technology itself will not necessarily produce or equally deliver benefits. New technology can have a liberating effect on the lives of disabled people. However, disabled people may be further excluded if they are not enabled to take full advantage of new technological opportunities because of educational, financial, attitudinal and administrative barriers (Cornes 1991; Thornton 1993; Hodge 2007). Moreover, new technology offers individual solutions that are not going to be universally available because of resource allocation and supply. The social model promotes collective solutions and views the benefits of new technology as existing in its potential to rehabilitate the disabling environment (Roulstone 1998). Disability studies is right to be wary of technological determinist ideas, to not fall for the technology-equality falsehood that suggests that technology is the panacea to every disabling situation (French 1992; Corker 1998). However, it has not formulated this position with regard to issues of communication.

New technology can facilitate access to social encounters but one must highlight the fact that everyday intercorporeal relations exclude people with speech impairment. Communication aids facilitate (or are supposed to facilitate) access to social encounters. However, the choreography of social encounters does not always accommodate such facilitation. Thus, people with speech impairment are de-legitimized as 'social beings', which in turn produces their bodily 'dys-appearance'. As Albert Robillard (1994) points out, alphabet boards are only enabling if his interlocutors are ready to step outside the dominant tempo, pace and rhythm of communicative encounters and dance to his dance. Furthermore, the use of assistive technology involves the inevitable technical glitch which creates further temporal estrangement (see Corker 1998; Hodge 2007).

The social model structural account of disability tells us little or nothing of the ways in which disability is produced in the everyday world, nor about the ways in which this process is limited to reactions to impairment or the 'embodied experiences' (of impaired people) that are associated with it. 'Communication disablement' is not a problem of 'botching' a carnal performance (giving the wrong verbal or non-verbal cue). It is matter of being estranged by the dominant choreography of everyday life. The body-subject disappears in the everyday interactions between non-disabled people and people with speech impairment because subjectivity and speech are so closely articulated and because the desire for successful interactions is a moving force in the choreography of everyday life. People with speech impairment become pure body-objects, in the negotiation of everyday encounters, because they are perceived as being in-deficit, culturally. They do not belong to the same (communicative) culture. Exclusion takes the form of 'gestures' and movements: the gestural rejection of the speech impaired body by the non-disabled body is a commonplace method of ending encounters. The ideology of tragedy plays itself out in gestures of rejection or appeals to others to mediate or interpret. In many cases, the only way to deal with the disabled subject is to deny their subjectivity by way of 'unusual' civil inattention or over-attention (Robillard 1994; Lenney and Sercombe 2002).

Drawing on the work of Pierre Bourdieu (1984), one can argue that physical and cultural capital is accorded to bodies that perform to the embodied norms of communication and withheld from those that do not. Bourdieu views the body as an unfinished project which develops in association with a range of social forces and is central to the maintenance of social inequalities. The body is conceptualized as a form of physical capital (Shilling 1993). According to Bourdieu (1984), bodies bear the imprint of social class and status through the interrelation between an individual's social location (the material conditions that shape everyday life and the development of the body), habitus (the formation of habitual class-based skills, such as bodily performance and presentation) and taste (the processes whereby individuals appropriate as voluntary choices and preferences, lifestyles that are shaped by material constraints). Bodies develop through the interrelation of social location, habitus and taste, which serves to shape as a marker of distinction. This interrelation locates the body in what he terms as a 'body schema' (Bourdieu 1984: 218), a hierarchical network organized according to social status.

Bourdieu's analysis can be applied to other social identities to take account of the ways social differences are 'naturalized' and viewed as pre-social (Shilling 1993; Hancock and Tyler 2000). This naturalization of the body is important to Boudieu's theory of social reproduction as he argues that there are substantial inequalities in the symbolic value accorded to particular bodily forms. Crucial to the value of different forms of physical capital and to their veneration is the ability of dominant groups to specify their bodily forms and presentation as proper, worthy of reward and as 'the embodiment of class' (Shilling 1993: 140). It is not only social class but other social identities – such as gender, 'race', sexuality, age and disability – that shape such embodied hierarchies, as the body acts as an important bearer of value in contemporary culture (Hancock and Tyler 2000). Bodily attributes and differences such as skin colour, anatomy and performance acquire and symbolize specific value and such differences are translated into social differences which mediate one's life chances (Crossley 2001; see also Young 1990).

Bourdieu recognizes that acts of labour are needed to turn bodies into social entities and that this 'body work' influences how people develop and hold their body shape, and learn how to present their bodies through expressions of speech, demeanour, gesture and dress (bodily performance and aesthetics). Bourdieu argues that the bodily forms produced by the working classes constitute a form of physical capital that has less exchange value than that developed by the dominant classes. By less exchange value, Bourdieu means that particular forms of physical capital have value not only within their own social spheres, but also across social spheres. Bourdieu applies this to inequalities in the education system. He argues that children from working class families are 'low attainers' because working class speech and bodily demeanour – valued within their socio-familial sphere – is interpreted less favourably by school teachers and the school system. Conversely, middle class children are 'high attainers' because middle class speech and demeanour has little or no differential value between their socio-familial sphere and school system. Schooling validates a middle class 'style of being'.

Applying Bourdieu to disability, one can take account of the ways in which socio-structural inequalities between disabled and non-disabled bodies are 'naturalized' and viewed as pre-social. Physical and cultural capital is accorded to the bodies that are constructed as 'normal' through the modalities of function and aesthetics. The bodily forms of disabled people are credited with less exchange value than non-disabled bodies, and this reproduces the view that their 'inabilities' and 'deficiencies' are natural rather than socially produced. This distribution of physical and cultural capital is symbolic of the distinction between 'normal' and 'abnormal' corporeal status (see Allen 2004; Edwards and Imrie 2003).

One could argue that the remit of speech and language therapy is to increase the physical and cultural capital of people with speech impairments. Although the social model of disability has gained influence within speech and language therapy, communication difficulties are predominately framed as an individual or family problem rather than a social problem (Jordan and Kaiser 1996). Therapy is centred on the 'improvement' of speech and language function and competence and encourages individuals in-deficit to become 'practised' in the embodied protocols of communication. The individual is encouraged to work towards a 'legitimate' bodily performance and style of communication, which is regarded as a basic building block of social participation. Focus is on the correct presentation, rather than recognizing the legitimacy of other 'styles' of communication, or on identifying the problem as one that is related to the disablist choreography of everyday social encounters.

George Bernard Shaw's *Pygmalion* is the archetypical representation of the aims of speech and language therapy. The proper way of speaking is associated with the received pronunciation, diction and grammatical idiosyncrasies of the ruling class and those who do not live up to those standards may, if they are lucky enough to have an appropriate benefactor, make some progress towards the manner of speech that is recognized as appropriate in polite circles. The traditional goal of speech and language therapy is to determine ways in which (carnal) performance of a person with speech impairment might be restored to something approximating the orderliness of 'proper communication'. The approach or 'treatment' seeks to adjust an individual's performance to facilitate 'social competence'. Ironically, speech and language therapists advise people with speech impairment to 'speak slowly' and 'take their time' in order for their voice to be heard and their words to be discerned. However, the choreography of communication is not 'free style' and the 'default settings' for communicative encounters do not provide such temporal accommodation.

This therapeutic approach relates to what Bourdieu sees as struggles over the power to develop, define and appropriate bodily forms that embody most value in society at a particular time. Such struggles over the corporeal are amplified in importance when they encompass definitions of what is a legitimate body, and the legitimate use of the body in contemporary society (Shilling 1993). These struggles are associated with the production and attainment of physical capital. However, they also extend beyond (mere) resources issues. They relate to the very structure of what Bourdieu terms 'social fields' (e.g., education, health care and rehabilitation) which make judgements about the merit of certain bodies or bodily practices. Those who exert power over fields that concern themselves with the corporeal include: 'moralists and especially the clergy, doctors (especially health professionals), educators in the broadest sense' (Bourdieu 1978, in Shilling 1993: 145). These groups of 'body experts' play a part in educating bodies and labelling as legitimate or deviant particular ways of managing or experiencing our bodies. This mediates the way we recognize our own bodily practices and performances and the bodily practices and performances of others, as 'right' and fitting or in need of governance and improvement (Shilling 1993).

Definitions of the legitimate body and legitimate bodily performances are clearly evident in the field of therapy and rehabilitation. Speech and language therapy aims to invest the impaired body with physical and cultural capital through its 'prescription' of the legitimate performance of speech, timing and movement. The disabled person would then be able to comply with the protocols of 'competent communication' and thus be able to participate in social encounters. The assimilationist values embedded in this approach (which prioritizes the performance of non-disabled people rather than disabled people) have been clearly delineated in social model critiques of rehabilitation yet these values are themselves carnally informed and arise from the ways in which non-disabled bodies leave their imprint on the world.

One cannot discuss communication and not mention Jurgen Harbermas. Crossley (1997) draws on both Bourdieu and Merleau-Ponty in his attempt to bring a sense of embodiment into Habermas's theory of communicative action. He claims that attending to the corporeal in the theory of communication illuminates a key Habermasian concern: 'systematically distorted communication'. Our embodiment is one of the key modes for the introduction of distortions into communication. In fact, only embodied discourses are susceptible to distortions (Crossley 1997). This position offers an understanding of the distortions that arise in communicative encounters between disabled and non-disabled people.

One of Habermas' central concerns regarding the systematic distortion of communication is that the opportunity for open exchange is negated through the influence of socio-structural factors such as social class, status and power (Crossley 1997). Crossley's argument, following Bourdieu (1977, 1984, 1992), is that these factors often intrude into communication through the mediation of our embodiment, for example speech, comportment, gesture, demeanour, bodily attitude. Moreover, it is clear that they trigger a corresponding bodily attitude or a Merleau-Pontyian 'style of being' (Crossley 1997: 31). For example, Crossley states that a middle class accent may elicit deference or arouse animosity in a working class interlocutor, shaping the way in which they both listen and respond and thereby distorting a social encounter. Moreover, the (socially coded) embodied signs of gender or 'race' may produce a range of prejudicial patterns of behaviour, with similar consequences (see Young 1990). Similarly, the (socially coded) embodied markers of impaired bodies can trigger disablist attitudes and reactions which distort and disrupt social interactions.

Bodily markers will 'comment' upon whatever else is being said, either positively or negatively (Crossley 1997). A public school accent and self-assured demeanour may be a considerable asset in some contexts of political debate. However, such a bodily performance is less of an asset when attempting to extol the virtues of working class solidarity, appearing less than convincing because such an accent would imply that the speaker is unacquainted with the manual labour s/he lionizes. Through these corporeal markers the social status of the speaker infiltrates their communication and comments upon it. Social encounters are framed by bodily markers (Crossley 1997) and such bodily markers are drawn from white, middle class, male, non-disabled bodies.

With the aestheticization of contemporary culture (Featherstone 1992), a person's appearance and embodied action comments upon what it is that they say and thus may detract from and distort it (Crossley 1997). The aesthetics, sound and comportment of bodies is relevant to having one's voice heard (Crossley 1997, 2001). Bodily markers also frame what is viewed as 'legitimate' social interaction. For example, sign language is often perceived as aggressive, inappropriate or sexualized bodily performance (Sutherland 1981; Davis 1995; *The Observer* 1998). Here, the timing and proprioception which constitutes this form of social interaction is viewed as the antithesis of physical and cultural capital. The 'style' of communication is seen as an 'affront' – and literally a threat – to 'good' intercorporeal relations. This relates to what Bourdieu sees as struggles over the power to define what is a legitimate or deviant body, and what are legitimate bodily practices and performances in contemporary society (Shilling 1993; Edwards and Imrie 2003).

Drawing all these threads together, it is my contention that the (spatio) temporal norms and conventions of the everyday world mean that people with speech impairment find it difficult to reveal themselves as 'social beings' and 'articulate bodies'. They are prevented from acquiring and sustaining the physical and cultural capital necessary to participate in everyday social encounters. The choreography of everyday life reinforces the exclusion and estrangement of people with speech impairment.

Compliance with the embodied norms and conventions of communication has exchange value: it accords communicative capital. People with speech impairment are estranged and marginalized by the dominant choreography of communication and hence communicative capital is bestowed principally on the corporeal status of non-disabled people. It is symbolic of the distinction between the 'articulate body' and the 'inarticulate body'. People with speech impairment's 'style of being' and 'style' of communication is seen to comment negatively upon what it is that they wish to express and thus detracts from and distorts it.

It is not only that people with speech impairment are prevented from having the time and the room to talk because of the norms of negotiation that structure the choreography of communication. It is that their embodied action, their proprioception is constituted as temporal 'incompetence' and casts them out as 'inarticulate bodies'. When a person with speech impairment is in public spaces and places, they are reacted to in relation to the institutional disablism that structures society. However, they are further excluded and marginalized because the notations and protocols of intercorporeal relations prevents the bodily performance of disabled people from being credited with physical or cultural capital. Every time they are out in the street, visit a pub, a shop, a restaurant or other social gathering, they are framed as having speech and body language 'indiscipline' as scripted by the disablist choreography of everyday life. Disabled people fracture the (spatio) temporal rules of bodies passing by each other, congregating with each other and communicating with each other and non-disabled people are jolted out of the 'usual' dance of civil attention or inattention. A person with speech impairment is cast as someone who cannot play the game of social interaction and so will 'botch' the everyday embodied norms of communication.

The ability to engage in 'conversation' is perceived as a key to defining 'social competence' (Jordan and Kaiser 1996). This perception of 'social competence' is central to gaining access to the everyday world. It is this defining of a 'social being' and its linkage with communication (or rather the norms of speech, timing and proprioception) that informs the withholding of communicative capital. It is not enough to suggest that communication barriers can be dismantled by the proper provision of augmentative and alternative communication technology and human facilitators. The ingrained norms and discourses about what constitutes 'communication' need also to be tackled and deconstructed. Phenomenology offers a way to critically interrogate the norms and values that propagate the notion of 'communication' and so delineate their disabling effects.

Conclusion

The struggle to overcome 'communication disablement' has long been overlooked as a serious issue within the disabled people's movement. The movement has understandably underplayed the differing realities of different impairments, and since communication is its principal weapon it is not surprising that people who face communication barriers tend to be under-represented (Jordan and Kaiser 1996; Parr *et al.* 2003a). Thus there is a need for the movement to incorporate what is required to empower people with speech impairment into its ideas and activities. The theoretical position of the social model sustains this marginalization of people with speech impairment because it has collapsed the meaning of impairment into a 'homogeneous notion' in which an emancipatory politics of disability is associated with getting into and getting around social space.

There is awareness within the disabled people's movement about issues relating to 'communication disablement'. However, communication barriers need to be addressed collectively and openly by people who experience them (Rae 1993; Parr *et al.* 2003a). The discussion must be a reflection of their carnal position. It is for people with speech impairment to claim and clarify the issues for themselves. Mike Oliver acknowledges as much in his forward to Jordan and Kaiser's (1996) book. He states that people with speech impairment – empowered by their own collective self-organization – should become much more centrally involved in the disabled people's movement. This will enable their individual and collective voice to be registered. This chapter has attempted to show how a phenomenological sociology of impairment can facilitate people with speech impairment in their struggle to have their voice acknowledged and legitimized. I have offered an alternative understanding of 'communication disablement' by asserting that the ableist nature of temporal norms make it difficult for people with speech impairment to acquire and sustain the physical and cultural capital necessary to participate in everyday social encounters. The choreography of the (spatio) temporal domains tends, therefore, to invigorate the exclusion and estrangement of people with speech impairment.

References

Adam, B. (1995) *Timewatch. The Social Analysis of Time* (Oxford: Polity).

Allen, C. (2004) 'Bourdieu's Habitus, Social Class and the Spatial Worlds of Visually Impaired Children', *Urban Studies* 41(3): 487–506.

Bourdieu, P. (1977) *Outline of a Theory of Practice* (Cambridge: Cambridge University Press).

Bourdieu, P. (1978) 'Sport and Social Class', *Social Science Information* 17: 819–40.

Bourdieu, P. (1984) *Distinction: A Social Critique of the Judgement of Taste* (London: Routledge).

Bourdieu, P. (1992) *Language and Symbolic Power* (Oxford: Polity).

Byng, S. and Duchan, J. (2005) 'Social Model Philosophies and Principles: Their Applications to Therapies for Aphasia', *Aphasiology* 19(10–11): 906–22.

Corker, M. (1998) *Deaf and Disabled, or Deafness Disabled?* (Buckingham: Open University Press).

Corker, M. and French, S., eds (1999) *Disability Discourse* (Buckingham: Open University Press).

Cornes, P. (1991) 'Impairment, Disability, Handicap and New Technology', in M. Oliver, ed., *Social Work. Disabled People and Disabling Environments* (London: Jessica Kingsley Publishers): pp. 98–114.

Crossley, N. (1995) 'Merleau-Ponty, the Elusive Body and Carnal Sociology', *Body & Society* 1(1): 43–63.

Crossley, N. (1997) 'Corporeality and Communicative Action: Embodying the Renewal of Critical Theory', *Body & Society* 3(1): 17–46.

Crossley, N. (2001) *The Social Body: Habit, Identity and Desire* (London: Sage).

Davis, L. J. (1995) *Enforcing Normalcy: Disability, Deafness and the Body* (London/New York, Verso).

Edwards, C. and Imrie, R. (2003) 'Disability and Bodies as Bearers of Value', *Sociology* 37(2): 239–56.

Featherstone, M. (1992) 'Postmodernism and the Aestheticization of Everyday Life', in S. Lash and J. Friedman, eds, *Modernity and Identity* (Oxford: Blackwell).

Finkelstein, V. (1980) *Attitudes and Disabled People: Issues for Discussion* (New York: World Rehabilitation Fund).

French, S. (1992) 'Equal Opportunities? The Problem of Time', *New Beacon* 76(1): 97–8.

Freund, P. (2001) 'Bodies, Disability and Spaces: The Social Model of Disabling Spatial Organisations', *Disability & Society* 16(5): 689–706.

Gleeson, B. (1999) *Geographies of Disability* (London: Routeldge).

Hancock, P. and Tyler, M. (2000) 'Working Bodies', in P. Hancock, B. Hughes, E. Jagger, K. Paterson, R. Russell, E. Tulle-Winton, M. Tyler *The Body, Culture and Society: An Introduction* (Buckingham: Open University Press): pp. 84–100.

Hemsley, B., Sigafoos, J., Balandin, S., Forbes, R., Taylor, C., Green, V. A. and Parmenter, T. (2001) 'Nursing the Patient with Severe Communication Impairment', *Journal of Advanced Nursing* 35(6): 827–35.

Higginbotham, J. and Wilkins, D. (1999) 'Slipping Through the Timestream: Social Issues of Time and Timing in Augmented Interactions', in D. Kovarsky, J. Duchan and M. Maxwell, eds, *Constructing (In)competence: Disabling Evaluations in Clinical and Social Interaction* (Mahwah, NJ: Lawrence Erlbaum): pp. 49–82.

Hodge, S. (2007) 'Why is the Potential of Augmentative and Alternative Communication Not Being Realized? Exploring the Experiences of People Who Use Communication Aids', *Disability & Society* 22(5): 457–71.

Imrie, R. (2000) 'Disability and Discourses of Mobility and Movement', *Environment and Planning A* 32(9): 1641–56.

Imrie, R. (2004) 'Disability, Embodiment and the Meaning of the Home', *Housing Studies* 19(5): 745–63.

Imrie, R. and Edwards, C. (2007) 'The Geographies of Disability: Reflections on the Development of a Sub-discipline', *Geography Compass* 1(3): 623–40.

Jordan, L. and Kaiser, W. (1996) *Aphasia – A Social Approach* (Cheltenham: Stanley Thomes).

Jordan, L. and Bryan, K. (2001) 'Seeing the Person? Disability Theories and Speech and Language Therapy', *International Journal of Language and Communication Disorders* 36, Suppl: 453–8.

Kitchin, R. (1998) '"Out of Place", "Knowing One's Place": Space, Power and the Exclusion of Disabled people', *Disability & Society* 13(3): 343–56.

Leder, D. (1990) *The Absent Body* (Chicago: Chicago University Press).

Lenney, M. and Sercombe, H. (2002) '"Did You See That Guy in the Wheelchair Down the Pub?" Interactions Across Difference in a Public Place', *Disability & Society* 17(1): 5–18.

Marks, D. (2000) 'A Secure Base? Attachment Theory and Disabling Design', in L. McKie and N. Watson, eds, *Organizing Bodies: Policy, Institutions and Work* (Basingstoke: Macmillan): pp. 42–54.

Merleau-Ponty, M. (1962) *The Phenomenology of Perception*, trans. C. Smith (London: Routledge).

Observer, The (1998) 'Deaf People Barred From London Pubs', 12 July.

Oliver, M. (1990) *The Politics of Disablement* (London: Macmillan).

Parr, S., Duchan, J. and Pound, C., eds (2003a) *Aphasia Inside Out* (Buckingham: Open University Press).

Parr, S., Paterson, K. and Pound, C. (2003b) 'Time Please! Temporal Barriers in Aphasia', in S. Parr, J. Duchan and C. Pound, eds *Aphasia Inside Out* (Buckingham: Open University Press): pp. 127–43.

Paterson, K. and Hughes, B. (1999) 'Disability Studies and Phenomenology: The Carnal Politics of Everyday Life', *Disability & Society* 14(5): 597–610.

Rae, A. (1993) 'Communication – Whose Issue?, *Coalition*, June: 31–4.

Robillard, A. B. (1994) 'Communication Problems in Intensive Care Units', *Qualitative Sociology* 17: 383–95.

Roulstone, A. (1998) *Enabling Technology: Disabled People, Work and New Technology* (Buckingham: Open University Press).

Ryan, J. and Thomas, F. (1980) *The Politics of Mental Handicap* (Harmondsworth: Penguin).

Shilling, C. (1993) *The Body and Social Theory* (London: Sage).

Sutherland, A. (1981) *Disabled We Stand* (London: Souvenir Press).

Thompson, E. P. (1974) 'Time, Work-Discipline and Industrial Capitalism', in M. W. Flinn and T. C. Smout, eds, *Essays in Social History* (Oxford: Clarendon Press): pp. 39–77.

Thornton, P. (1993) 'Communications Technology – Empowerment or Disempowerment', *Disability, Handicap & Society* 8(4): 339–49.

Warin, M., Baum, F., Kalucy, E., Murray, C. and Veale B (2000) 'The Power of Place: Space and Time in Women's and Community Health Centres in South Australia', *Social Science and Medicine* 50(12): 1863–75.

Weber, M. (1987) *The Protestant Ethic and the Spirit of Capitalism* (London: Unwin Paperbacks).

Wendell, S. (1996) *The Rejected Body. Feminist Philosophical Reflections on Disability* (New York/London: Routledge).

Williams, S. and Bendelow, G. (1998) *The Lived Body: Sociological Themes, Embodied Issues* (London: Routledge).

Young, I. (1990) *Justice and the Politics of Difference* (New York: Princeton University Press).

14

VISUAL IMPAIRMENT AND DISABILITY

A dual approach towards equality and inclusion in UK policy and provision

Karen Beauchamp-Pryor

Debates about the polarization of the social and medical model divide have dominated discussions within disability studies in the United Kingdom (UK). Arguments for each perspective are well rehearsed, with the social model attributing disability to socially produced inequality and dependency (Oliver 1996; Barnes and Mercer 2003), and the medical model treating disability as a result of individual 'inability' and 'abnormality': a division based upon 'society' and 'the individual'; 'disability' and 'impairment'; and 'the political' and 'the personal'.

The dichotomy is perceived as oversimplified, because it is argued that disability is not a single unity that can be neatly presented as socially or individually caused (Schillmeier 2008). Disabled people are not a homogeneous social group, and the social model is criticized for neglecting experiences of disablism based on gender, ethnicity, sexuality, age and class (Morris 1991, 1992, 1993; French 1993; Wendell 1996; Priestley 2003). The onset and type of impairment will also impact on an individual's outlook and experience: some disabled people will have grown up with impairments and others will be propelled from being 'able-bodied' to disabled through accident or illness. Other issues around identity include whether individuals (impaired, chronically ill, or even 'cured') view themselves as disabled or not (Shakespeare 1996; Watson 2002; Beauchamp-Pryor 2011). Additionally, understanding the significance of impairment effects (the experience of living with impairment) and the psycho-emotional impact of disablism (e.g., issues around self-esteem and personal confidence), as detailed by Carol Thomas (1999, 2007), is key to understanding the relationship between individual and social factors.

I was in my late thirties and studying for a degree in social policy when I was first introduced to the social model of disability by my lecturer, Robert Drake. He encouraged me to explore the disability studies literature and I was inspired by his research in the field. The accounts of Colin Barnes and Sally French were significantly influential in developing my understanding and because of the shared experience of visual impairment I was able to relate to their experiences:

> the visually-impaired person is not disabled by lack of sight, but by lack of Braille, cluttered pavements and stereotypical ideas about blindness.
>
> *(French 1994: 11)*

I understood that external causes could en-able or dis-able me, but at the same time I questioned the exclusion of individualized factors. For instance, my sister who was blind and used a guide dog seemed more confident in travelling and finding her way from 'A' to 'B' than I was. My lack of confidence and ability became particularly evident when my vision deteriorated further during my thirties. In an account given by Don, a fourth year university student interviewed by Rod Michalko (2002: 121–8), he commented that whilst he had developed skills to get around, not all visually impaired people were able to do so. Don relied on his senses of hearing and touching, which were enabling. However, other factors such as the fear of disorientation can prove disabling. Reginald Golledge discussed this fear in terms of 'panic': 'when uncertainty dramatically increases, self-confidence falls and, in all but the strongest individuals, some panic can occur' (1994: 371). Golledge's paper *Geography and the Disabled* (1993) was critiqued by Ruth Butler (1994), Rob Imrie (1996) and Hester Parr (1997) and criticized for its focus on 'theoretical orientations, terminologies, lack of inclusion of individual, subjective viewpoints and failure to acknowledge wider social structures of oppression' (Parr and Butler 1999: 20). Whilst the views of Golledge and Butler reflected the divide between the individual/society, impairment/disability and the personal/political, both authors approached the discussion from a personal position of visual impairment.

Colin Low is also visually impaired and in 2006 was made a life peer for his work as a high-profile campaigner. He holds a number of prominent positions across a range of organizations and charities representing disabled people, which include president of the European Blind Union and vice-president of the Royal National Institute of Blind People (RNIB). His views are therefore influential and, notably, in a divisive and controversial lecture, 'Have Disability Rights Gone Too Far?', he argued that the social model failed because it 'has nothing to do with the individual' (2001: 13) and, consequently, the complexity of disability was not understood:

> It is the central contention of this lecture that monolithic or one-dimensional analyses and prescriptions are inherently unable to do justice to the complexities of the phenom-enon that is disability ... it throws whole orphanages out with the bath-water, and its excoriation of alternative perspectives leads to error in its policy prescriptions.
>
> *(Low 2001: 4)*

Arguably, Low's concentration on the individual also reflects a 'one-dimensional' analysis, and fails to understand the impact of disabling barriers.

The inequality that stems from focusing on the individual was identified by Michalko (2002) in his discussion about his experience of visual impairment, in terms of society's expectations and the requirement to conform; dominant perceptions about ability; and the significance and power of difference. In conforming to everyday expectations Michalko drew on the 'language of sight': 'I "walked the walk and talked the talk" that was sightedness' (2002: 169). When teaching he complied with expected 'standards of normalcy', moving about the classroom and using body gestures. He strived to 'convince' his colleagues and those around him that he was capable, 'despite' his blindness, to teach at university. He concluded: 'some believe this, most do not' (2002: 80). The need to conform is about challenging the visible indicator of difference, which identifies behaviour as other than 'normal'. Michalko contended that visually impaired people are able to do things, but not in the same way as sighted people: 'we do them differently. Inability and ability become collapsed under this rubic of difference' (2002: 149). Being different and doing things differently are perceived as 'abnormal', and as Martha Minow reasoned, difference is about power: 'categories for organizing perceptions assign differences to some but not others and thus perpetuate or increase disparities of power between groups' (1990: 111–12). Don exemplified the way an onlooker may interpret difference as 'abnormal' (Michalko 2002: 124): in an environment constructed for sighted people, Don 'looked around' with his stick, veering from side to side of the pathway. Michalko noted that Don was 'in touch' with what others 'looked at', but to the onlooker Don's body and behaviour visibly lacked control. Michalko, within the context of 'rights' and 'equality', argued for a different way of thinking about disability:

> Everyone, including every society, has practical issues that require practical solutions and disability is no different. Disabled people (like everyone else) have many practical things to do and must find ways (often different from nondisabled ways) to do them, and this is what makes them 'like everyone else.' But, this practicality, while being part of disability, is not the whole of it. Yet, this is what contemporary society does with disability – *it confuses the part for the whole.*
>
> *(2002: 168)*

The political and policy response within the UK has been built upon the division between individual and social causes, with policies either based upon impairment and individual solutions targeting the 'needy' (e.g., care, concern and compensation), or as more recently observed, policies based on social structures and processes targeting inequality and exclusion and based on 'rights'. Growing recognition and understanding of the inequality experienced by disabled people is evident within legislation (Department for Work and Pensions 2005), with the government endorsing the social model in *The Duty to Promote Disability Equality: Statutory Code of Practice (England and Wales)*:

> The poverty, disadvantage and social exclusion experienced by many disabled people is not the inevitable result of their impairments or medical conditions, but rather stems from attitudinal and environmental barriers. This is known as 'the social model of disability', and provides a basis for the successful implementation of the duty to promote disability equality.
>
> *(Disability Rights Commission 2005: 1.6)*

The focus on social causes raises an important issue: will such an approach work to exclude discussion about the relationship between individual and social factors and will this impact on achieving equality and inclusion for disabled people? It is, therefore, important to determine the relationship between individual and social factors in challenging inequality and exclusion. Concentrating on visual impairment, I revisit empirical data that explored the experiences of disabled students in Welsh higher education (Beauchamp-Pryor 2008).[1] As part of the research process, six visually impaired students were interviewed and their varied experiences were explored. The chapter initially provides an overview of the methodological approach, before introducing the six participants whose personal histories consisted of many similarities and differences. Drawing on their views, I discuss the influence of individual and social factors in achieving inclusion, reflecting on their transition to university, development of friendships and socializing. The remainder of the chapter details dominant approaches within higher education policy and practice: first, a dual approach towards disabled students is considered, based on social and individual factors, but set within a 'rights' context; and second, an individualized approach centred on impairment.

Methodological approach

The purpose of my study was to evaluate the impact of legislation and policy on the experiences of disabled students studying at a higher educational institution in Wales and, importantly, to identify those factors that led to inequality and exclusion. Initially, a survey of Welsh higher educational institutions was carried out, with questionnaires sent to each of the 13 institutions in Wales. Eight questionnaires were completed and returned by disability support staff. The questionnaire was designed to ascertain the steps being taken by institutions to comply with legislation and to determine dominant perceptions and approaches towards disability. A case study university was selected, which was chosen mainly because of the high level of provision offered to disabled students. The university provided extensive support for visually impaired students and attracted students from schools for visually impaired young people (e.g., New College Worcester, a school for blind and partially sighted children and young people). Questionnaires were sent to the 491 disabled students registered with Disability Support Services, and 115 were completed and returned. The number of visually impaired students at the university totalled 19 and nine completed questionnaires. This questionnaire was designed to gather information across a wide range of support, with additional space included for student comments. The questionnaire also identified those students who were willing to participate further in the research. Twenty-three students were chosen to reflect a cross-section of impairment categories and of these six visually impaired students were interviewed. Students represented a range of backgrounds and character-istics such as gender, ethnicity, age, experience of different courses and subject areas, and levels of study. Interviews were carried out between 2001 and 2003 and were largely unstructured (an approach which provided students with the opportunity to discuss the issues that were important to them) and as a result, the data covered many aspects of university life. Students welcomed the opportunity to share their views and experiences and were keen to participate in the research. Their identities were protected throughout the research and subsequent publications, with each student allocated a fictitious name. Managerial, administrative and support staff, working in a wide range of departments such as planning, estates, admissions and marketing, equal opportunities, widening participation, staff development, disability services, examination support, the interna-tional office and accommodation, were also interviewed. Questions were structured to determine dominant perceptions about disability; understanding of disability legislation; and the application of legislation. In addition, six disability co-ordinators in academic departments were interviewed and questions were similarly structured to ascertain the impact of legislation; the co-ordinator's knowledge of legislation; and their views about disability.

The participants

The visually impaired students who agreed to participate in the study represented a range of backgrounds, interests and experiences, and this section briefly introduces each student.

Carol was a full-time undergraduate student in the School of Arts and Humanities. She was interviewed in the first year of her degree when completing modules in American studies, anthropology and politics, and re-interviewed in her second year. She was a mature student who had a range of hidden and visible impairments, which included partial sightedness, speech difficulties, mobility difficulties, aphasia, dysphasia and epilepsy. Carol had previously attended university as a non-disabled student and her views about impairment and disability were insightful:

> I feel when you are a disabled student you have to prove to them that you are actually able, more if you understand. It's horrible. The relationship with tutors was on a more equal standing [in the past], whereas as soon as you raise with them that you have a disability, well I then feel I am put in a position where I have to kind of say '*look, you know, but I'm kind of, I'm ok, I'm safe*'. It's that power discrepancy. It's the way in which

you are viewed and of course the way you view yourself, but more as to how you handle the disability, and your ability is now determined by your disability. [sic]

Christine was a part-time postgraduate student participating in a Masters programme in early childhood studies in the School of Human Science. She had completed a degree at the university, but found the support provided lacked continuity and, as a consequence, was often reliant on individual responses within departments. She was a partially sighted mature student and was interviewed in her second year of postgraduate studies. Throughout her life she felt she had been disadvantaged, particularly within education.

Dawn was a full-time undergraduate student studying social policy in the School of Human Science. Due to the stress she experienced in her first year because of the initial lack of support (e.g., delays in the appointment of note takers and in the provision of equipment), she decided to defer her studies for a year. I interviewed Dawn during the second year of her degree scheme. She was a blind student whose vision had deteriorated at the age of 15. She continued her education in mainstream schooling, but felt that she had to learn to 'fight for [her] needs to be met' and 'to be treated equally by both students and staff'.

Justine was a full-time undergraduate student in early childhood studies in the School of Human Science and was interviewed in the second year of her degree. Whilst at school she received no additional support and consequently struggled, but her university experiences were much more positive. However, she disliked having to inform individual lecturers about her visual impairment.

Lee was a full-time undergraduate student in the School of Arts and Humanities and was studying modules in history, politics and psychology. Due to the lack of support (similar to Dawn) he decided to repeat his first year of study and I interviewed Lee in his repeat year. Lee was a blind student, who was also hearing impaired and had mental health difficulties. He had attended a school for blind and visually impaired students and prior to university had never met a sighted person of his own age. During his first year he had found it difficult to socialize, but had begun to participate more in his repeat year.

Sue was a full-time undergraduate student in the School of Human Science. In her first year she completed modules in psychology, American studies, politics and history, and at the time of the interview she was in her second year. Sue was a blind student who also had mental health difficulties. Although she enjoyed university life, she too had experienced delays in the organization of support. She was reluctant to make a complaint about the delays due to the possible impact on future support.

Included, but not inclusive

Student accounts illustrated the importance of understanding the influence of both individual and social factors in achieving inclusion. Significantly, individual factors in many instances stemmed from inequality directly attributed to social causes (e.g., inequality within the education system in support provided or as a result of attitudes towards them), which impacted on their independence, self-esteem and confidence. In other instances the effects of visual impairment directly influenced their experience of inclusion (e.g., the inability to cope in a large crowd of students). The relationship between equality and social and individual influences is illustrated in Figure 14.1.

To exemplify the relationship further, three areas discussed by the students are drawn upon: the transition to university; developing friendships; and socializing.

The transition to university is a challenging process for most students and involves new experiences and opportunities. Whilst the transition may be daunting for some students, it is

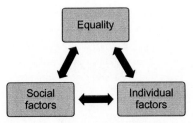

Figure 14.1   Towards an equality framework

most likely to be considered as a positive experience. In a study by Houston Lowe and Anthony Cook (2003), it was clear that whilst personal problems and difficulties in the early months at university were often anticipated by students, problems were more widely expected than experienced. Little is known about the experience of disabled students and how comparable their experiences are with non-disabled peers. Notably, for the visually impaired students in my study, the transition was more than a challenging hurdle and more of a leap into the unknown.

Previous educational experience was a significant factor for each of the students in their transition to higher education. Five of the students had attended mainstream schools and, although they discussed their 'struggle' in a mainstream setting, they felt that because of their experiences they were prepared to 'fight' for their 'rights' in moving into higher education. However, it was evident that Lee, who notably had received a high level of academic support at a residential school for blind and visually impaired children, was ill-equipped and unprepared for the move:

> it was a great school in the academic sense of the word, but like all those kind of institutions it was very insular, and like I had never met before I came here, it sounds really bad, but I'd never met any sighted person of my own age. So I came here and had to get used to people's different reactions and I didn't know how to combat them. [sic]

During Lee's first year he spent the majority of his time alone in his room. His lack of confidence was compounded by the lack of mobility training, which meant he was unable to find his way around campus on his own.

The interview data identified that growing up visually impaired influenced the development of friendships: a finding which was substantiated by the RNIB's 'Shaping the Future' research project, which reported on the experiences of blind and partially sighted children and young people between the ages of five and 25 in the UK (Cole-Hamilton and Vale 2000). The RNIB study found that one in three visually impaired children (within the category 'around average learning ability') wished they had more friends, which compared to one in ten of the National Society for the Prevention of Cruelty to Children survey (Ghate and Daniels 1997, quoted in Cole-Hamilton and Vale 2000: 56). The visually impaired students at the case study university discussed the difficulty of making friends more extensively than any other impairment group. They felt that non-disabled students did not want to include them. As Dawn explained:

> You never get any of the other students coming to say hello or anything, or we are going for coffee, do you fancy coming? ... and you try, I had a seminar and I tried to make conversation with the person next to me, but you can tell either by the way they are talking to you or the tone of their voice, they don't really know what to say.

The attitude of non-disabled students towards disabled students (according to disabled students) appeared to reflect widely held attitudes within the university towards disability, which were based on perceptions about ability, compensatory measures and sympathetic responses. The understanding of *all* students was also likely to be influenced by past experience. However, the process of developing friendships demonstrated the potential of increasing awareness and general understanding, as Lee discussed:

> I had problems last year, but people on my floor [residence rooms] knew I had problems, but couldn't really identify, you know, to them I sit here and talk about mobility training, and they are like '*err, what's that?*' So it's difficult. I'm lucky this year, because I've got a really good floor, they are really nice people, and if they don't understand they will try their best to understand.

Where visually impaired students had developed friendships, they found their friends to be supportive, both practically and emotionally. Developing good relationships between disabled and non-disabled students results in a feeling of 'togetherness' (Taylor and Palfreman-Kay 2000) and is an important step in challenging inequality and exclusion experienced by disabled students.

An important aspect of the student experience is being able to participate in student activities. For the visually impaired students it was often difficult to socialize or participate in activities due to issues around lack of confidence, lack of friends, pressures of study, access issues, and reliance on family members to help with transport and personal assistance. The RNIB study also highlighted that over half of the students (aged 16 to 25 in further and higher education) reported difficulties participating in activities due to inadequate facilities, lack of support, poor access or poor lighting (RNIB 2000).

Clearly, to achieve equality and an inclusive environment, a relationship between the under-standing of individual and social factors is necessary. The remainder of the chapter discusses two approaches within policy and practice at the case study university, which exemplify, first, a dual approach based on social and individual factors and, second, an individualized approach focusing on impairment.

Dominant approaches in policy and practice

A dual approach

Throughout my research the dominant response within policy and practice reflected an indivi-dualized approach towards disabled students based on meeting individual 'need'. However, examples of inclusive approaches were evident and the most striking example concerned the provision of support for visually impaired students by the university's Transcription Centre. The Transcription Centre provided material for students in a range of formats, which included audio recordings, Braille and large print. Staff also offered advice and support to both students and academic staff. Whilst provision was set within an equality framework (based on an understanding of disability as a 'rights' issue), the focus was not solely on social factors, but also individual factors. Many individual issues stemmed from the inequality experienced as a result of social causes; for example, during my fieldwork the lack of mobility training meant that individuals were dependent on others in moving around campus.

The Transcription Centre spent time with students and supported them with any issues or concerns that arose:

We know it's hard, we do all kinds of things like helping people over the road, helping to get them to where they need to be, and being understanding. So if somebody comes and has a problem, we'll listen or help and do what we can for them and we won't say *'look sorry but if you were to disappear we could get on with the Braille that you want'* ... we realise there's no point in us just churning out Braille and tapes and being just a Transcription Centre. If the student can't get from 'A' to 'B', or if the student has major problems as well [we will help].

(Centre Co-ordinator)

Providing support was time consuming for staff, but they recognized how essential this was for the students in terms of inclusion. The staff listened to students and it was clear that they were prepared to assist students wherever they could. For example, the lack of mobility training meant that students were unable to find their way to and from lectures and two of the students interviewed (Sue and Lee) discussed contacting the Transcription Centre's staff for assistance, as Sue explained:

We had no training for a while, so we had real problems getting to lectures at the beginning of term. We didn't really have anybody to show us for a few weeks. ... the ladies in the Transcription Centre are really nice and I kind of phone them up at 9 o'clock in the morning saying *'will you take me to this lecture?'*

Whilst this example illustrates the failure to implement provision aimed at securing the independence of students, it demonstrates the importance of listening to students and responding to individual concerns. The Transcription Centre was active in seeking student views and used questionnaires and regular meetings to do this: openness in views was evident. The meetings provided students with an opportunity to discuss policy, the quality of provision and any area of concern. Sharing experiences increased the understanding of both the Centre's staff and the students and, importantly, reduced the isolation often felt by the students.

Close working relationships between the Transcription Centre and academic departments were also evident, which enabled the Centre's staff to offer advice and disseminate models of good practice. Moreover, staff often mediated on behalf of students with academic staff. At interview, Dawn highlighted the difficulties she had encountered with one of her lecturers over a mix-up with coursework and explained how the staff at the Centre had helped:

I approached this particular lecturer about getting some work for one of my essays and she replied *'oh yes I will send some text books over to the Transcription Centre'*. A week had gone by and I asked the Centre if they had received anything from the lecturer and they hadn't. So I sent an email to this lecturer and said nothing had been sent over and she sent me a really stroppy email back saying *'yes I have'* and for me to organise myself and sort myself out. I was really quite upset. So I said to the Centre, *'you just deal with it'*. So they did and this lecturer replied and said *'oh I am sorry it was this book'*.

The Transcription Centre understood that students often found it difficult to talk directly with academic staff over support and were prepared to assist:

It depends on the department, it is hard for a student to be nagging a lecturer, please send your notes in advance ... it's humiliating, it is much easier if an email comes from us saying that.

(Centre Co-ordinator)

The process of approaching lecturers, as discussed by students, was often demeaning and whilst stigma persists based on perceptions of 'inability' students will feel awkward and embarrassed approaching lecturers. However, the inclusive approach of the Transcription Centre demonstrated ways in which initiatives could be implemented to challenge inequality experienced.

A singular approach

The previous example identified the importance of both social and individual factors in the achievement of inclusivity. In the following two examples of policy and practice (admissions and examinations), the focus shifts to a concentration on individual factors, which further illustrates why a dual approach in challenging inequality and exclusion is necessary.

Admissions

Central to the admissions process was a medical approach, with impairment highlighted early on in the application process. A candidate's suitability for admission was not only determined by their academic ability, but also by an evaluation undertaken by an educational psychologist or medical practitioner (Admission Policy 2007). Disabled applicants who received an offer of a place were informed by the Admissions Office that their offer was subject 'to the arrangement of suitable systems' being in place. Applications were then passed to the Disability Office for a full assessment, which in the case of the six visually impaired students required them to attend a medical evaluation. Several disabled students had been rejected at this juncture due to concerns over guaranteeing a support system:

> I am able to turn around and reject somebody on grounds of disability. I have done it a handful of times ... there is no benefit to the student, to the institution or to us personally, by having a student who is going to have a lousy time.
>
> *(Senior Manager, Disability Office)*

Carol had initially been rejected on this basis: her application was prior to the Special Education Needs and Disability Act (DfEE 2001), and on reapplying in 2002 she was, subsequently, accepted. She had been informed by the Disability Office that the university was unable to guarantee a support system for her and, therefore, her application was rejected. Similarly, Riddell *et al.* identified that whilst English and Scottish institutions asserted admissions were based purely on academic grounds, this was not the case in practice:

> Institutions all maintained that admission was based on academic grounds alone. However, ... senior managers acknowledged that institutions could operate a 'cooling out' effect, stressing the difficulties which the student would encounter at the university and urging them to consider taking up a place elsewhere.
>
> *(2005: 75)*

Concentrating on impairment worried the students interviewed, due to concerns over being rejected from their choice of university or course. However, they welcomed the opportunity to establish an open dialogue in which support systems could be addressed. Whilst decisions about choice of university, department and course were influenced by factors relevant to all students, such as an interest in the subject area, previous study, career prospects and employment, decisions for the visually impaired students were also based on a range of other factors which included: their experience when visiting the university and in particular the attitude of staff towards disability issues; their knowledge of how other visually impaired students had fared; and the support systems offered. For instance, prior to his application, Lee had been in regular contact with a blind student who had left his school and was completing a history degree at the case study university.

The admissions process is central to securing inclusion and, whilst admissions tutors at the case study university were instructed to reach a decision about an applicant irrespective of any information about impairment, it was evident that negative attitudes towards disabled applicants existed. In addition, the suitability of studying a particular course was not only influenced by the admissions tutor, but also by the applicant's own perception of suitability. Statistical analysis by impairment category in two departments at the case study university (English and Engineering) highlighted the likelihood of perceptions about aptness of subject choice (Table 14.1). Both departments had a higher percentage of disabled students when compared with the average across all departments. However, students with a range of impairments were more likely to study English than Engineering, with the exception of dyslexic students who were more likely to study Engineering.

It is difficult to draw any firm conclusions from recent statistical analysis of Higher Education Statistical Agency (HESA) datasets (2008a) about the subject choices of visually impaired students when compared with all students, because of the low participation rates (Table 14.2).[2] A similarity in popularity of subject choice existed between 'all' students (includes both non-disabled and disabled) and visually impaired students. However, when the percentage of visually impaired students studying each subject area was calculated, the analysis highlighted higher participation rates on less popular courses (based on percentage alone, the top 20 choices for visually impaired students exceeded 0.28 per cent). For example, the subject choice of 'imaginative writing' attracted 5,305 students ('all' students) and 25 visually impaired students (0.47 per cent). Therefore, whilst popularity between subject choices existed, attracting high numbers of 'all' students and high numbers of visually impaired students, none of the top 20 subject choices had a high percentage rate.

It is also worth noting that whilst the percentage of visually impaired students may appear exceptionally low, the prevalence of visual impairment in the population is difficult to ascertain. In a report commissioned by the RNIB, the lack of consistency in estimates of visual impairment within the population aged 16–64 differed more than two-fold from 0.8 per cent to 2.0 per cent (Tate *et al.* 2005). Moreover, visual impairment increases with age, and of the estimated 370,000

Table 14.1 Comparison of participation rate by impairment category (all levels of study)

Impairment	English %	Engineering %
Dyslexia	0.52	3.73
Visually impaired	0.26	0.10
Hearing impaired	0.52	0.29
Wheelchair/mobility	0.26	0.00
Personal care	0.00	0.00
Mental health	0.26	0.00
Unseen disability	1.04	0.69
Multiple disabilities	0.78	0.00
Disability not listed	1.55	0.59
Total percentage of disabled students	5.19	5.40

Source: Case study university statistics (October 2002).

Table 14.2 Top ten most popular subject choices for all students 2007/8

Subject choice	All students	VI students	% VI
Nursing	164,420	165	0.10
Business studies	117,725	160	0.14
Combined	117,130	115	0.10
Teacher training	94,830	150	0.16
Academic studies in education	79,830	90	0.11
Psychology	70,435	135	0.19
Management studies	65,740	75	0.11
Computer science	61,910	170	0.27
English studies	59,705	105	0.18
Social work	58,310	150	0.26

Source: HESA Student Record (2008a).[3]

people (0.6 per cent of the population) registered as blind and partially sighted (RNIB 2011), 75 per cent were recorded over the age of 70 (Department for Work and Pensions 2011).

Statistics held at the case study university indicated that more than half of the students registered as disabled did not declare a disability prior to commencing their studies: worryingly, it was clear that students were reluctant to be identified as disabled during the admissions process. The findings clearly showed that the dominant approach based on individual factors proved detrimental and worked against the open dialogue that students sought.

Examinations

During the study a working group was set up to develop a policy for dealing with students with extenuating circumstances and/or special needs in terms of assessments and examinations. The policy initially appeared to be all-encompassing with no specific reference to impairment; however, the focus on 'special needs' implied that disability was something other than normal, requiring special treatment. It is now over a decade since Lea Myers and Viv Parker claimed that the term 'special needs' was perceived as 'simplistic, pejorative, and patronising' (1996: 67). Although concerns about the term were raised with the working group by the Student Union, the final document continued to concentrate on 'special needs'. Definitions are powerful and maintain discrimination, inequality and oppression (Thompson 1998). As discussed by Fowler *et al.*:

> A major function of sociolinguistic mechanisms is to play a part in the control of members of subordinate groups by members of dominant groups. The control is effected both by regulation and by constitution: by explicit manipulation and by the creation of an apparently 'natural world' in which inequitable relations and processes are presented as given and inevitable. Power differential provides the underlying semantic for the systems of ideas encoded in language structure.
>
> *(Fowler et al. 1979: 2, quoted in Manning 1985: 6)*

Discussions about 'special needs' reinforced dominant perceptions about disability based on 'inability'. Similarly, the terms of reference were compensatory in nature as opposed to recognizing the need to equalize opportunity, which was a further concern of students at interview. The lack of power experienced by disabled people was evident, with their views excluded from the process.

A lack of flexibility by the working group was also observable. For instance, the policy stipulated that students were unable to apply for retrospective adjustments:

> Once the Disability Office has made an assessment and recommended compensatory measures, students in receipt of them may not be granted any further relief or aid in respect of this assessed need.

Ensuring academic standards were maintained was obviously a priority of the working group and as part of this process all students are required to be assessed against an academic benchmark. However, to achieve equality of opportunity, flexibility is also needed in demonstrating this achievement. During the interview process, it was evident that initial assessments and recommendations had proved inadequate and subsequently required amendment. For example, the allocation of time allowed for dictating examination answers in one instance proved inadequate and was readjusted for future examinations. This example demonstrates the importance of individual responses within policy and provision. Whilst concerns over the policy approach were evident, students found the examination staff approachable and flexible. Each of the visually impaired students discussed how examination staff listened to their anxieties, which were wide-ranging and concerned issues of using a scribe, computer equipment and software: listening to individual accounts enabled implementation of appropriate support.

The working group also lacked understanding about the inequality experienced by disabled students at university. For instance, the guidelines stipulated that disabled students were required to inform relevant staff within their department/school of any disability. The Student Union advised the working party that the responsibility of informing relevant staff (with the permission of the student) was the duty of the institution (Disability Rights Commission 2002: 5.13), but the final document was not amended to reflect this. Students explained the difficulty of approaching individual members of staff, which often proved demeaning and disempowering. Said Carol:

> There should be a way in which the onus is taken off the student to go round begging lecturers and informing individual lecturers of their problems.

The importance of including the views of disabled students in the development of policy and provision was evident, but also the importance of listening to individual students' situations to ensure equality and inclusive practice.

Interestingly, HESA data (2008b) identified that visually impaired graduates outperformed 'all graduates' (total graduate figure for disabled and non-disabled students) in the achievement of a first class and second class honours degree and were less likely to receive a third class honours/pass or to fail (Table 14.3). Whilst some may argue that these results suggest that policy and provision is

Table 14.3 Degree classification marks 2007/8

Degree classification	All graduates %	Visually impaired graduates %
First class honours	12.41	12.45
Upper second class honours	44.51	45.13
Second class honours	28.13	30.69
Third class honours/pass	6.94	5.96
Unclassified	8.01	5.78

Source: HESA Student (Qualifiers) Record (2008b).

positively supporting visually impaired students, or even that they are over-compensated, the interview data revealed that other factors such as personal ambition and motivation to succeed, persistence and strength, the support of family and close friends, and previous educational support and encouragement were influential in student achievement. Likewise, Eva Magnus (2006) similarly identified that disabled students were ambitious and dedicated to their studies. There is a wide range of theoretical discussion indicating that family support, parental involvement, friendships, educational experience and personal ambition are often attributable to student attainment (see for example, Schmidt and Padilla 2003).

Conclusion: towards equality and inclusion

The examples illustrated the importance of developing a dual approach within policy and provision, which included an understanding of both social and individual factors. Importantly, a growing awareness within public bodies of inequality resulting from social causes is evident, although as identified in the experiences of visually impaired students, dominant perceptions persisted within policy and practice, which centred on individualized responses. However, findings discussed identified the importance of ensuring individual experiences and accounts were included in policy and practice to ensure equality and inclusion. In a report commissioned by the RNIB the importance of including individual accounts in the development of support was evident:

> The needs of people who lose their sight are many and varied and the support provided for people who lose their sight, and for family members, must be personalised if it is to meet individual needs.
>
> *(2009: 4)*

Whilst the focus of the RNIB report reiterated the importance of the personal perspective, the approach remained on meeting 'needs' as opposed to ensuring 'rights'. It is important that discussions about individual factors are firmly set within a 'rights' context. As previously argued, definitions are powerful and, therefore, discussions about impairment must be associated with achieving equality. Furthermore, as identified in the examples discussed, the exclusion of personal experience is likely to result in inequality and exclusion.

Inequality and exclusion stem from the categorization of individuals; therefore, valuing the differences of each person on whatever basis is the pathway to equality and inclusion. Failing to recognize the inequality that stems from difference is an exclusionary process and reflects the lack of power experienced based on difference. Consequently, 'rights' is about recognizing and valuing differing individual experiences.

Acknowledgements

My sincere gratitude is extended to Professor Anne Borsay for her perceptive comments on the initial draft of my chapter and also to the editors of the volume for their helpful and constructive guidance in developing my ideas.

Notes

1 The findings from my study will be available in a forthcoming book, *Disabled Students in Welsh Higher Education: A Framework for Equality and Inclusion*, to be published by Sense.

2 Data did not include statistics for London Metropolitan University and University College Birmingham (due to a request for individual-level data not to be released) and the University of Central Lancashire (due to technical issues with the submission of data).
3 HESA data rounded: 0, 1, 2 are rounded to 0, and all other numbers rounded to the nearest multiple of 5.

References

Admission Policy (2007) Anonymized as part of case study data.
Barnes, C. and Mercer, G. (2003) *Disability* (Cambridge: Policy Press).
Beauchamp-Pryor, K. (2008) *A Framework for the Equality and Inclusion of Disabled Students in Higher Education*. PhD thesis, Swansea University.
Beauchamp-Pryor, K. (2011) 'Impairment, Cure and Identity: "Where Do I Fit in?"', *Disability & Society* 26(1): 5–17.
Butler, R. (1994) 'Geography and Vision-impaired and Blind Populations', *Transactions of the Institute of British Geographers* 19(3): 366–8.
Cole-Hamilton, I. and Vale, D. (2000) *Shaping the Future: The Experiences of Blind and Partially Sighted Children and Young People in the UK* (summary report) (London: RNIB).
Department for Education and Employment (DfEE) (2001) *Special Educational Needs and Disability Act (SENDA)* (London: HMSO).
Department for Work and Pensions (DWP) (2005) *Disability Discrimination Act (DDA)* (London: HMSO).
Department for Work and Pensions (DWP) (2011) *Visual Impairment*; available online at http://www.dwp.gov.uk/publications/specialist-guides/medical-conditions/a-z-of-medical-conditions/vision/visual-impairment-vision.shtml (accessed 6 October 2011).
Disability Rights Commission (DRC) (2002) *Code of Practice: Post-16 Education and Related Services* (Stratford-upon-Avon: DRC).
Disability Rights Commission (DRC) (2005) *The Duty to Promote Equality: Statutory Code of Practice (England and Wales)* (Stratford-upon-Avon: DRC).
Fowler, R., Hodge, B., Kress, G. and Trew, T. (1979) *Language and Control* (London: Routledge and Kegan Paul).
French, S. (1993) 'Disability, Impairment or Something in Between?', in J. Swain, V. Finkelstein, S. French and M. Oliver, eds, *Disabling Barriers – Enabling Environments* (London: Sage): pp. 17–25.
French, S. (1994) 'What is Disability?', in S. French, ed., *On Equal Terms* (Oxford: Butterworth-Heinemann Ltd): pp. 3–16.
Ghate, D. and Daniels, A. (1997) *Talking About My Generation: A Survey of 8–15 Year-Olds Growing Up in the 1990s* (London: NSPCC).
Golledge, R. G. (1993) 'Geography and the Disabled: A Survey with Special Reference to Vision Impaired and Blind Populations', *Transactions of the Institute of British Geographers* 18(1): 63–85.
Golledge, R. G. (1994) 'A Response to Ruth Butler', in *Transactions of the Institute of British Geographers* 19(3): 369–72.
Higher Education Statistics Agency (HESA) (2008a) *HESA Student Record 2007/08* (Cheltenham: HESA).
Higher Education Statistics Agency (HESA) (2008b) *HESA Student (Qualifiers) Record 2007/08* (Cheltenham: HESA).
Imrie, R. F. (1996) *Disability and the City* (London: Paul Chapman).
Low, C. (2001) *Have Disability Rights Gone Too Far?* Insight Lecture at City University, London, 3 April. Reprinted in *Disability World* 7, March–April; available online at http://www.disabilityworld.org/03-04_01/news/low.shtml (accessed 2 August 2011).
Lowe, H. and Cook, A. (2003) 'Mind the Gap: Are Students Prepared for Higher Education?', *Journal of Further and Higher Education* 27(1): 53–76.
Magnus, E. (2006) *'Disability and Higher Education – What are the Barriers to Participation?'*, conference paper presented at the Disability Studies Association Conference, Lancaster University, 18–20 September.
Manning, N. (1993) [1985] *Social Problems and Welfare Ideology* (Aldershot: Gower).
Michalko, R. (2002) *The Difference That Disability Makes* (Philadelphia: Temple University Press).
Minow, M. (1990) *Making All the Difference: Inclusion, Exclusion, and American Law* (New York: Cornell University Press).
Morris, J. (1991) *Pride Against Prejudice* (London: The Women's Press Ltd).
Morris, J. (1992) 'Personal and Political: A Feminist Perspective on Researching Physical Disability', *Disability, Handicap and Society* 7(2): 157–66.

Morris, J. (1993) 'Gender and Disability', in J. Swain, V. Finkelstein, S. French and M. Oliver, eds, *Disabling Barriers – Enabling Environments* (London: Sage): pp. 85–92.

Myers, L. and Parker, V. (1996) 'Extending the Role of the Co-ordinator for Disabled Students', in S. Wolfendale and J. Corbett, eds, *Opening Doors: Learning Support in Higher Education* (London: Cassell): pp. 66–83.

Oliver, M. (1996) *Understanding Disability: From Theory to Practice* (Basingstoke: Macmillan Press).

Parr, H. (1997) 'Naming Names: Brief Thoughts on Disability and Geography', *Area* 29(2): 173–6.

Parr, H. and Butler, R. (1999) 'New Geographies of Illness, Impairment and Disability', in R. Butler and H. Parr, eds, *Mind and Body Spaces: Geographies of Illness, Impairment and Disability* (London: Routledge): pp. 1–24.

Priestley, M. (2003) *Disability and the Life Course: Global Perspectives* (Cambridge: Cambridge University Press).

Riddell, S., Tinklin, T. and Wilson, A. (2005) *Disabled Students in Higher Education: Perspectives on Widening Access and Changing Policy* (Abingdon: Routledge).

Royal National Institute for the Blind (RNIB) (2000) *Shaping the Future: Blind and Partially Sighted Children and Young People Aged 16 to 25 in Further and Higher Education* (mini-conference summary) (London: RNIB).

Royal National Institute of Blind People (RNIB) (2009) *Understanding the Needs of Blind and Partially Sighted People: Their Experiences, Perspectives and Expectations*. Executive summary prepared by Surrey Social Market Research at the University of Surrey (London: RNIB).

Royal National Institute of Blind People (RNIB) (2011) *Key Information and Statistics*; available online at http://www.rnib.org.uk/aboutus/Research/statistics/Pages/statistics.aspx (accessed 6 October 2011).

Schillmeier, M. (2008) '(Visual) Disability – From Exclusive Perspectives to Inclusive Differences', *Disability & Society* 23(6): 611–23.

Schmidt, J. A. and Padilla, B. (2003) 'Self-esteem and Family Challenge: An Investigation of Their Effects on Achievement', *Journal of Youth and Adolescence* 32(1): 37–46.

Shakespeare, T. (1996) 'Disability, Identity and Difference', in C. Barnes and G. Mercer, eds, *Exploring the Divide: Illness and Disability* (Leeds: The Disability Press): pp. 94–113.

Tate, R., Smeeth, L., Evans, J., Fletcher, A., Owen, C. and Woflson, A. R. (2005) *The Prevalence of Visual Impairment in the UK* (a review of the literature). Report commissioned by the RNIB (London: RNIB).

Taylor, G. and Palfreman-Kay, J. M. (2000) 'Helping Each Other: Relations Between Disabled and Non-disabled Students on Access Programmes', *Journal of Further and Higher Education* 24(1): 39–53.

Thomas, C. (1999) *Female Forms: Experiencing and Understanding Disability* (Buckingham: Open University Press).

Thomas, C. (2007) *Sociologies of Disability and Illness: Contested Ideas in Disability Studies and Medical Sociology* (Hampshire: Macmillan).

Thompson, N. (1998) *Promoting Equality, Challenging Discrimination and Oppression in the Human Services* (Basingstoke: Palgrave).

Watson, N. (2002) 'Well, I Know This is Going to Sound Very Strange to You, But I Don't See Myself as a Disabled Person: Identity and Disability', *Disability & Society* 17(5): 509–27.

Wendell, S. (1996) *The Rejected Body: Feminist Philosophical Reflections on Disability* (London: Routledge).

PART 3

Social policy and disability
Health, personal assistance, employment and education

15

DISABILITY AND NEOLIBERAL STATE FORMATIONS

Karen Soldatic and Helen Meekosha

Disability and state formations

Some people can't conceive of what it is like to have the policies of politicians – who have little concept of living with a disability – continually threatening to erode your already meagre standard of living.

(Women with Disabilities Australia 1999)

The historical state categorization of disability, as a mechanism for delineating the so-called 'deserving poor' from the 'undeserving poor' for state poor relief, is evidence of the complex set of social and economic relations of disability. Stone (1981) was one of the first disability studies scholars to reveal the extent to which the emergence of the modern capitalist state relies on the categorization of the human body. The modern nation state and the capitalist political economy operate jointly not only in harnessing a multiplicity of state regulatory measures for regulating internal populations within the nation state but also external populations attempting to enter its borders (Jakubowicz and Meekosha 2002).

While such measures have historically been expressed via socio–legal administration beginning with the Speenhamland system (1795) and the English Poor Laws (1834), and more recently with immigration and anti-terrorist legislation, the resultant practices and institutional structures 'constitute subjects in socially distinctive ways' (Peck 2001: 57) marking bodies with symbolic meaning, practices and capital. Here, the disabled body is deemed to be a health and financial risk to the general citizenry and a burden on the state (see Gothard 1998).

The maintenance of social order requires the state to continually create broad social consent to emergent political/economic structures and it is here that the state regulation of bodies through a plethora of sophisticated classification regimes is necessary (Foucault 1977). Bodies marked out as 'exceptional' are powerfully held out as a moral deterrent to other citizens from resisting the ideals of the prevailing social order (Peck 2001). Disability's social meanings have been central to this process.

Historically fluid, social classification regimes contribute to particular ideological, political and economic projects. The remaking of social categorization therefore becomes pivotal to maintaining the hegemony of the historical moment, where the state formation is set in time and space. Shifting state formations, in turn with emergent material structures, as Gleeson (1999: 70) suggests, 'signal a potentially profound change in the course of social embodiment, involving new forms of freedom, prestige and wealth for some, and new types of restraint, discrimination and deprivation for others'. Disabled people can attest to the fluidity of these state regulatory structures as their bodies continually undergo a process of re-classification, stratifying their disability status into new hierarchical formations and, in turn, diminishing their access to a raft of social rights to which they previously had access (see Grover and Piggott 2010; Soldatic and Pini 2009).

Accordingly, in this chapter we examine the constitutive mechanisms that seek to sustain hegemonic constructions of disability. With the emergence of the neoliberal nation state, new meanings of disability emerge. Neoliberalism, as ideology, political economy and state formation, is an inimitable 'theory of political economic practices' (Harvey 2005: 2), coupled with a unique regime of state regulating practices (Biyanwila 2010: 66). Key areas of concern include the restructuring of social rights with emergent authoritarian social policies, the remapping of disability labour-market programming and the rise of the informal 'care economy' and ideologies of 'care'. These areas all fall under neoliberal welfare state restructuring in line with its ideological commitment to workfare, re-regulating the welfare/labour market nexus, co-opting some disabled bodies as 'work able', while re-positioning others as 'truly deserving of state welfare'. We draw upon the case of Australia to exemplify our arguments and to demonstrate the radical implications for disabled people's well-being within with the rise of neoliberalism as political hegemony. We specifically include an analysis that examines gender difference in the experience of workfare.

The ideological, political and economic landscape: defining neoliberalism

Neoliberalism has multiple interpretations and meanings, 'depending upon one's vantage point' (Ong 2006: 1), and as Willis *et al.* (2008: 3) rightly suggest 'it is not a coherent or homogenous ideology'. As a governing ideology, political economy and state formation, neoliberalism is spatially differentiated, and the historicity of spaces and places mediate its sweeping force (Leitner *et al.* 2007: 1). Neoliberalism's central tenets surround the primacy of the free market as the key organizing principle of society, the elevation of the individual as a free autonomous agent, and the winding back of the prior Keynesian welfare state consensus (Harvey 2005; Willis *et al.* 2008; Peck 2001).

The ascendency of neoliberalism as a hegemonic world view first emerged in the 1980s with the arrival of what has become known as the 'New Right' through parliamentary elections in the United Kingdom (UK) and United States of America (USA) respectively (Harvey 2005). British Prime Minister Margaret Thatcher and the American President Ronald Reagan, as the vanguard of the global New Right, undertook a process of revolutionary change in positioning the state, the market and society (Maddison and Martin 2010: 103). The unfettered workings of the market were signalled as paramount and the role of the state was radically restructured to ensure that the market was given free rein from all social constraints (Willis *et al.* 2008: 2).

This process of 'market liberalization' within lay discourse is generally known as 'free trade' and, increasingly, citizens expect their governments to create a set of optimum conditions for the market to 'work' through the provision of capital-friendly policies that attract foreign capital investment. As Leys (2001) argues, states and the realm of representative politics have become subsumed to the realm of the market as the public interest is framed only within market terms. More poignantly, Giroux (2004: xiii) has argued, 'Wedded to the belief that the market should be the organizing principle for all political, social and economic decisions, neoliberalism wages an incessant attack on democracy, public goods, and non-commodified values.' These market orthodoxies have thus become central to state–citizen relations, elevating the individual 'as a *market* agent, pursuing advantage in competition with others' (Connell 2008: 247, emphasis in original). The emphasis on individual responsibility has become endemic in western liberal democracies. States have undergone a radical process of transformation to normalize this discourse within the polity, actively promoting the virtues of performing competitive individualism as a daily practice (Rose 1996).

Merging the ideologies of the 'free individual' with the 'free market' is of critical importance to neoliberal understandings of the self, as the individual is represented as an active autonomous agent, free from all constraint in pursuing their own individual interests. The free market individual, freed from all social and moral restraint, is empowered to make their own individual choices and, consequently, free to experience their own individual failings (Beck and Beck-Gernsheim 2002). This unfettered 'capacity for self-realisation' (Leitner *et al.* 2007: 4) is premised upon a set of government technologies that reposition the individual as a self-defining entrepreneur, engaging in a range of activities to build their human capital so that they are an effective resource, highly sellable, within the marketplace. The role of the neoliberal state is therefore to propel the 'willing', and coerce the 'unwilling', into adopting, practising and regulating their *individual* behaviour in favour of 'free' market competition.

Given this ideological commitment to the free, autonomous, competitive individual, it is not surprising then that collective structures of social organization are largely delegitimized. As Maddison and Martin (2010) have argued, neoliberal states have mounted a range of authoritarian campaigns to undermine the collective claims of social movements struggling for rights, recognition and state strategies for redistribution. They unleash severe measures to silence dissent (Hamilton and Maddison 2007). While locally distinct, these authoritarian state structures are part of the globalization of neoliberal regulation (Tickell and Peck 2003).

Social movements, particularly the labour movement, have been actively targeted as they are seen to undermine the individual's potential to self-realize their full capacities in line with neoliberal economic norms and to impede market efficiencies (Biyanwila 2010). The disability movement has not been exempt from these state campaigns (Chouinard and Crooks 2008; Soldatic and Chapman 2010). The imposition of state contracts explicitly enacting measures to curtail collective social action has been the most damaging where neoliberal states have imposed a range of silencing strategies as a condition of state funding (Frohmader and Meekosha, forthcoming).

To survive this assault Mladenov (2009) suggests that disability advocacy organizations have been forced to engage in state partnerships, which, in turn, have diminished their capacity to engage in radical collective politics for issues of social justice. 'A major challenge for Non-Government Organisations (NGOs) remains one of relationships with government. Can we have meaningful relationships with governments when we are challenging their authority?' (Frohmader and Meekosha, forthcoming). To both bypass and curtail the growing authoritarianism of neoliberal nation states, segments of the disability movement have engaged in practices of resistance via the international realm. This broader global identity became critically important for the movement around the formation of the United Nations Convention on the Rights of Persons with Disabilities. International recognition has forced some neoliberal states to be more amenable to the movement's broader demands for participation, representation and inclusion.

Despite the rise of transnational advocacy around disability in both the Global North and the Global South, being forced into service provision within the realm of work has disempowered many disabled people's collectivities. Furthermore, the neoliberal state has actively co-opted the disability movement's collective demands for the right to work through harnessing individual 'employability'. This state strategy for de-collectivization has been particularly compelling for many within the disability movement, as the site of the labour market has been integral to both their collective and individual struggles for equality, respect and recognition. However, the gendered relations of disability mean that women are less employable than men. In Australia far more disabled men are in full-time employment (21 per cent) than disabled women (9 per cent) (Australian Bureau of Statistics 2004).

Inclusion within the labour market has been and remains high on the disability movement's agenda for social change. While many of the disability movement's demands around work have been met within the Global North, such as legislation that prevents discrimination in employment, the emergence of the neoliberal state strategies to propel disabled people into the labour market to curtail growing social security costs undermines these more progressive moves. While espousing normative values of social recognition, disability discrimination legislation, when seen in this context, is compatible with states eager to give the neoliberal market legitimacy. Across western liberal democracies, as we document in the following sections, state co-option of the right to work as an individualizing discourse, has had detrimental consequences in real terms, where a segment of the disability population has been extensively targeted and is now forced to look for work in low waged and unskilled labour markets to maintain access to a range of social entitlements (see Soldatic and Chapman 2010). Disabled women, in particular, when they do obtain employment are more likely to be in low paid, part-time, short-term casual jobs.[1]

More significantly, the positioning of the fit and competitive individual as the optimum form of embodiment has major ramifications for disabled people's collective potentiality to demand change to exclusionary and discriminatory structures. As legitimizing discourses, neoliberal state measures not only individualize, but also directly blame, those who are suffering from structural disadvantage (Grover and Piggott 2010; Haylett 2001; Sayer 2005; Skeggs 2004; Soldatic and Pini 2009), by harnessing moral discourses of individual responsibility (Goodin 2002). This is particularly onerous for disabled women, who often have caring roles that limit their employment opportunities. Structural and systemic disadvantage remains hidden, discrimination in the workplace often remains covert; disabled people are considered less 'able' and less reliable.

State responsibilities in enacting citizenry rights and entitlements that are essential to being human (see Nussbaum 2004) are relegated to the moral worth of the individual (Sayer 2005). Moral worth is associated with competence and ability – concepts that have been strongly contested and problematized by disability studies scholars. For example, Campbell uses the term ableism to describe 'an attitude that devalues or differentiates dis-ability through the valuation of able-bodiedness equated to normalcy' (Campbell 2009: 5). As discussed in the next section on neoliberal workfare, disabled people are highly targeted under these regimes, with state campaigns encompassing a full gamut of strategies that clearly position marginalization as the responsibility of the disabled individual. Disabled women, as both receivers and providers of 'care', are rapidly becoming the most disadvantaged under these regimes (Magna *et al.* 2008).

The rise of the free market and the reign of the self-interested individual, as Harvey (2005: 82) notes, result in an ungovernable situation, which is 'inherently unstable'. To counter these tendencies, western liberal democracies have entrenched pre-existing neoconservative ideologies of the heterosexual family as a means to maintain social order (Maddison and Martin 2010: 104). For women with disabilities and, in particular, disabled mothers, this process is mutually constitutive, as their identities as disabled women and disabled mothers with care responsibilities become highly regulated by a range of state technologies. Disabled mothers endure a high level of surveillance under neoliberal state regimes (see Malacrida 2009), fixating on their individual performance as 'good mothers' and their ability to economically participate in the polity, albeit part-time, via low wage casualized labour markets (Soldatic and Meekosha, forthcoming).

Thus, the emergence of neoliberalism as political and economic orthodoxy results in a range of tensions, contradictions and inconsistencies for disabled people. As outlined in the following sections on workfare, ideologies of care and, finally, the privatization of support structures, the delegitimization of structural disadvantage within neoliberal state formations compounds existing social inequalities. These new regulating practices, while locally distinct, are driven by the over-riding rationality of neoliberalism, which remains consistent across national scales. State regulating regimes are paramount to these processes.

From the Poor Laws to workfare

The boundary between welfare and work, is, socially constructed and perpetually reconstructed.

(Peck 2001: 49)

The relationship between disability, state formations and the labour market has been central to the capitalist political economy (Abberley 2002; Oliver 1990; Roulstone and Barnes 2005). By the nineteenth century craft workers in England were unable to compete with industrialization and the growing capitalist economy. This precipitated a vast displacement of the population from rural to urban areas where they were forced to sell their labour in the textile factories, cotton mills and mines of the growing cities and towns. 'The success of the Victorian economy was accompanied by high unemployment, poverty, urban squalor and harsh working and living conditions' (Hudson 2010).

State regulatory technologies and, in particular, the *Poor Law Amendment Act 1834*, endorsed the establishment of workhouses where conditions were extremely harsh (Clear and Gleeson 2001; Gleeson 1997; Oliver 1990). Disabled people, especially those labelled 'mentally abnormal' or 'idiots', were incarcerated in the workhouses or asylums. It is in this context that disability became an important socio-political category, given the capitalist imperative to separate those bodies 'unable' to work from those who were defined as just 'unwilling' (Oliver 1990; Stone 1981). The sorting of fit, productive bodies for the labour market meant that those identified as 'disabled' gained access to poor relief through the workhouse (Oliver 1990). Being socially constituted as disabled became a two-edged sword; a deeply stigmatized social privilege (Stone 1981), which forced a person to swap the discipline of the capitalist market for the harsh conditions of the workhouse (Thompson 1963).[2]

The institutional architecture of the workhouse comprised permanent structures of exclusion for those impaired bodies transformed by the disabling political economy of capitalist social relations (Gleeson 1997). Medical science had access to a range of bodies relegated to the status of a dependent class (Clear and Gleeson 2001; Oliver 1990). The passage of the *Anatomy Act 1832* legally 'transferred the dissection of the murderer to the pauper' (Powell 2007: 35). The emergent state form drew upon the hegemony of medicine to stratify bodies into classes of citizens marked by their exclusion from the capitalist labour market. In turn, the social classification of the body through socio-medical technologies became an important mechanism of social, moral and economic regulation.

While these regulatory structures have undergone extensive transformation since their inception, the internal logic of regulating social forms of embodiment via the welfare/labour market nexus remains paramount (Shragge 1997). Systems of poor relief are integral to the social, political and moral legitimation of the capitalist economy despite the gamut of inconsistencies, tensions and contradictions that are inherent in this relationship (Offe 1984). The ongoing reorganization of state structures of relief, or welfare, is to 'reinforce work norms' (Piven and Cloward 1993: 366).

With the emergence of neoliberalism as the prevailing social order, new welfare structures have become established, socially regulating a range of bodies for 'the brave new world of work' (Beck 2000) and powerfully *re*-regulating social, moral and political understandings of the individual citizen and their claims upon the polity (Peck 2001). Thus, the logic of dividing, sorting and classifying bodies into distinct classes of the 'deserving and undeserving' has remained unchanged, albeit in different forms.

Neoliberal welfare is often defined as *workfare*, encompassing a newly defined set of citizenship norms (see Peck 2001). Embodying notions of exchange in state–citizen relations (Moss 2006), access to state-funded social security entitlements is tied to participation in a range of state-sponsored labour market programmes that which were previously defined by 'need or necessity' under the prior Keynesian order (Carney 2006; Peck 2001; Peck and Theodore 2000). Participation in the labour market has become the hegemonic citizenship discourse (Bessant *et al.* 2006: 106–07), and is largely reflected in the populist slogan of 'no rights without responsibilities' (Fiske and Briskman 2007: 52). Thus, the core of the neoliberal argument is that any job is a job worth having, regardless of its conditions, hours or pay (Peck and Theodore 2000: 123). This affects men and women differentially. Disabled women are not able to take any job, as their role as child carers and carers of other family members may prevent them from doing so. However, these roles are not recognized, being relegated to the private realm.

> Women with disabilities report being depressed and demoralised by the job search process. Rejections are frequent. ... They reported being 'grateful' to get any job. Many have neither the will, nor the skill, nor the self-esteem to bargain with employers. Some have concerns that contracts are being signed without informed consent on the part of the employee. This leads to unsatisfactory and in some cases unsafe outcomes both for employers and employees. Both skilled professional and unskilled women with disabilities find it difficult to enter the workforce. Graduates remain unemployed long after their peers have entered the workforce.
>
> *(National Foundation for Australian Women 2007)*

In Australia, the neoliberal restructuring of welfare is articulated in the policy of 'mutual obligation' (Goodin 2002), positing citizen relations as one of *absolute* exchange (Soldatic 2009), a form of socio-political conscription (Bessant 2000). Qualifications for disability entitlements have been central to the global restructuring of neoliberal workfare (Barnes and Mercer 2005; Chouinard and Crooks 2006; Hyde 2000; Roulstone and Barnes 2005; Russell 1998). Across the Global North, there has been a remarkable similarity of nation states embarking upon disability restructuring programmes to curtail expenditure and, as a means to create public consent, to withdraw state social provisioning measures. Australia has been both leader and follower in these global trends; indeed, since the early 1990s there has been a surplus of strategies implemented to reduce the number of people accessing the central disability payment – the Disability Support Pension (Galvin 2004a).

In the early 1990s, access to disabled social entitlements underwent dramatic change. Disability social entitlements became directly linked to labour market participation and a new work test was institutionalized through disability legislative frameworks. Being defined as 'disabled' and gaining access to a range of disability state social provisioning measures was premised upon a maximum work capacity of 30 hours of work per week. Following the passage of key pieces of legislation in late 2005, the disability temporal work test was slashed in half to just 15 hours of work per week (Meekosha 2005), propelling many disabled people off disability entitlements and into lower unemployment benefits and entitlements which do not account for costs associated with impairment. The passage of this disability classification regime occurred within 24 hours of national legislation to de/re-regulate the broader labour market. Thus, the new temporal classification regime, while underpinned by medical science, embraced advancing neoliberal labour market structures as its central criterion, where part-time, casualized work within contingent labour markets has become the norm.

Australia's adoption of new temporal technologies for the classification of disabled bodies, while globally consistent, is locally distinct. While similar strategies have been consistently rehearsed across the Global North, including Canada, the USA and more recently, the UK under the Cameron Government, state classification regimes are spatially differentiated. Local state forms draw upon a vast range of technologies, reflective of local contingencies and historical welfare structures, but all aim to curb access to the state disability classification regimes and associated entitlements that disability status brings. Peck (2001) articulates a typology of neoliberal workfare structures, identifying the historical contingencies of state welfare formations, and the local permutations that have emerged in turn . Drawing upon Esping-Andersen's (1990) seminal work *The Three Worlds of Welfare Capitalism*, Peck depicts neoliberal workfare restructuring in the manner shown in Table 15.1.

As identified by Peck, western liberal state formations such as Australia, the UK, the USA and Canada have developed the harshest measures for the re-regulation of the labour market/welfare nexus. Structural unemployment, discrimination and marginalization are reframed as 'welfare dependency' where the lack of a job signifies a private moral failure (Grover and Piggott 2010; Skeggs 2004; Sayer 2005). Recent studies, particularly within the UK (Grover and Piggott 2010)

Table 15.1 Peck's analysis of workfare states

	Corporatist welfare states	*Liberal welfare states*	*Social democratic welfare states*
Orientation	Statist Emphasis on labour market adjustment and skilling Emphasis on work values Tackling structural unemployment	Market Individualist approach: behaviour modification and 'incentives' Countering 'welfare dependency'	Social Labour market adjustment through social democratic means Continuing commitment to universalism and social redistribution
Workfare model	Labour market reintegration approach Residual commitment to active labour market policies Differentiated strategy	Labour-force-attachment approach Restriction of welfare entitlements and benefits	Human-capital approach Incorporation of labour-market partners in policy formulation and program delivery
Ideology/ discourse	Work values with continuing commitment to class/status rights	Moral regulation: family values and work disciplines	Structural reorientation of welfarist approach
Regulatory dilemmas	Reluctance to commit to large-scale, comprehensive workfare programs Between laissez-faire and adjustment	Contradiction between costs of workfare and objective of reducing social expenditures 'Unfunded' workfarism Between social control and laissez-faire	Paternalism Tension between labour-market objectives and individual autonomy Between adjustment and social control

Source: Peck (2001: 76, Table 2.3).

and Australia (Soldatic and Pini 2009), reveal the ways in which elite state actors, including national politicians, have engaged in social practices of individual moralization of a segment of the disability population accessing welfare payments. The principal aim of this moral repudiation is to create public consent for the re-stratification of 'disability', enabling active state withdrawal of disability social provisioning measures for a new class of disability that is 'more work-able', or the more 'able of the disabled'.

This class of disabled people have become a group of people 'living in between' (Lightman *et al.* 2009: 2), not disabled enough to be 'deserving' of state welfare, nor 'able-bodied enough' to be considered fully able-bodied by the labour market. This is a highly precarious existence as it further entrenches disabled people's structural position of poverty, which is more pronounced for women with disabilities (Horvath-Rose *et al.* 2006; Salthouse 2005).

In Australia:

> The raft of legislation which accompanied the *Workplace Relations Amendment (Work Choices) Act 2005* radically changed the industrial landscape. The major change was to individualise employment relations. This disproportionately affected women with disabilities who now had to rely on their individual bargaining power to negotiate work contracts. Because of the barriers to obtaining work in the first place, women with disabilities reported that they were not willing risk their employment by asking for any improvements in pay and conditions. They thus tended to be victims of this legislation and were progressively pushed into the more low paid positions. Even though this legislation has been repealed, it has had a negative long-term effect on their economic well being.
>
> *(Women with Disabilities Australia 2009)*

Lack of accessible transport, personal assistance support within the workplace and measures to facilitate disabled people's employment participation all constitute forms of discrimination that prevent disabled people from engaging in meaningful work, but are rarely acknowledged in workfare debates (Wilton and Schuer 2006). Under neoliberal workfare, the new state-sanctioned class of disabled people, deemed as 'really disabled' and 'deserving of state welfare', have in turn witnessed a diminishing range of labour market programmes and supports to facilitate their participation and inclusion within the world of work (Soldatic 2009). In turn, there has been a remapping of disability labour market programmes and employment supports to reflect the regulatory logic of neoliberal workfare as discussed in the following section.

Re-shaping the workhouse: spaces of workfare

Many disabled people who had previously qualified for state disability entitlements have been propelled into disability workfare programmes. As Chouinard and Crooks (2006) note, these programmes are disciplining regimes where disabled people are forced to participate as a means to maintain access to diminished social entitlements. Many of these programmes emerged from the disability movement's collective demand for the right to work at its pinnacle period of activism during the 1980s and are formally suggestive of Harvey's (2000) spaces of hope and places of transformative solidarity. These programmes, however, have now been reconfigured to reflect neoliberal spatial relations following the advent of neoliberal governance. The remapping of these programmes has been integral to neoliberal workfare restructuring (Peck 2001; Schram *et al.* 2008; Fording *et al.* 2007).

New state-contractual relations, embodying New Public Management discourses and the privatization of welfare have been implemented across most of these spaces (McDonald and

Chenoweth 2009). These programmes have all undergone a process of radical reform with neoliberal intensification, with state funding restructured to reflect neoliberal workfare orthodoxies (see Chouinard and Crooks 2006; Magna *et al.* 2008). To concur with Roulstone and Morgan (2009), there has been a precarious convergence of neoliberal state regimes and the disability movement's struggles for self-directed support via individualized funding structures.

Workfare restructuring of disability employment programming has mostly co-opted the movement's language on this issue, where there has been a realignment of collective-based provision, commonly referred to as a 'block grant model', to a highly competitive individualized funding model where fiscal resources are allocated to services premised upon individualized contractual programme outcomes. These individualized models, while espousing the aims of the movement's claim for self-directed individualized support, are formulated against a highly medicalized classification regime pinned against labour market structures (Soldatic and Chapman 2010: 143). The focus on individualized outcomes constitutes a deliberate strategy to disguise structural processes of exclusion and inequality (Skeggs 2004: 82). Disabled people, in turn, have almost no control over their workfare funding as the provision of funding is directly targeted towards services' management of disabled people's welfare-to-work transition.

> extremely high percentages of women with disabilities are in the hidden unemployment bracket because they face barriers to participation or cannot find suitable Disability Employment support agencies. Support agencies themselves report that they do not have capacity to assist all the women who present for help. Moreover, these agencies are finding it progressively more difficult to secure employment positions for women with disabilities. The annual report of a Canberra agency[3] shows that in 2007/08, 1200 potential employers were contacted in order to secure 154 interviews. The proportion of job placements was even lower.
>
> *(Women with Disabilities Australia 2009)*

Disability labour market services are thus now contracted by the state to 'case manage' welfare-to-work transitions, and accordingly an associated range of new governing technologies has been trialled, tested and implemented in these spaces (McDonald *et al.* 2003). Many of the strategies, such as the use of individual compacts, utilize individual behaviour modification (see Martin 2007). Aimed at disabled citizens living on welfare-to-work benefits, these strategies have become more pronounced as state–citizen workfare relations have largely undergone what Schram *et al.* (2008) refer to as 'second-order devolution'. This process of 'second-order devolution' shifts sanctioning responsibilities down to the street level.

Across the Global North, frontline case workers are now required to observe, monitor and sanction disabled people in workfare programmes for a full range of individual misdemeanours and non-compliance (see Chouinard and Crooks 2006; Thornton and Marston 2009). In Australia, caseworker discretion has lead to a raft of mistakes in which disabled people were cut off from their payments (Commonwealth Ombudsman's Report 2007). Recent international research highlights this growing trend across neoliberal workfare states (Fording *et al.* 2007; Magna *et al.* 2008; Schram *et al.* 2008), signifying the changing relations of place, where frontline case workers are effectively adopting new practices of moral boundary drawing in their frontline work (Haylett 2003).

Practices of moral boundary drawing have been encouraged by neoliberal states' contractual relations with the shift to individualized outcomes based funding. Here, with the imposition of the 'contract', disability employment services actively engage in practices of 'creaming', where the targeting of labour market support is intentionally aimed at the most 'able of the disabled' (Soldatic

2009). This group of disabled people, assumed to be more easily amenable to open, casualized, flexible, contingent labour markets, assure services of their state-contractual targets. In turn, many disabled people walk a tightrope: being 'disabled enough' and thus entitled to workfare labour market support, but 'not too disabled' and risk losing access to disability labour market supports (Soldatic and Meekosha, forthcoming). Thus, neoliberal workfare programming and the social practices of case workers within them, have the power to deny disabled people access to the resources they most need for participation in the labour market.

The broader structural changes direct labour market support, resources and opportunities to those disabled people who are viewed as the most resource efficient. In turn, those disabled people, deemed 'truly deserving' of state welfare, now assessed as not 'work-able' not only lose access to labour market supports and opportunities, but increasingly are relegated to the private sphere of the household, with little access to state social provisioning measures for social, cultural and political participation. In the final section, we highlight the ways in which new ideologies of care have been effectively harnessed by the state to further workfare restructuring in this regard.

Neoliberal workfare restructuring and ideologies of care

The centrality of work within neoliberal workfare citizenship debates is constructed on able-bodied, masculine notions of care, work and productivity. 'Care' has become a dominant ideology with the privatization of welfare and the emergence of the neoliberal workfare state (Player and Pollock 2001). Within workfare debates, the construction of care is highly contradictory (Mink 1998), where it is both espoused as a legitimate form of social embodiment for middle-class mothers within the heterosexual family, while simultaneously delegitimized as a valued social practice for other groups of women including working-class mothers providing care to their children (Gillies 2007). In the UK, state discourses of care have been particularly pervasive with workfare restructuring, where working-class mothers living on welfare have been morally repositioned as the 'chav mum' (Tyler 2008), as Haywood and Yar (2006: 16) suggest: 'a term [that is] of intense class-based abhorrence'. Thus, this differential reading of neoliberal discourses of care has become central to workfare restructuring. Neoliberal discourses of care are increasingly used as a technology of control, to both reify normative constructions of the heterosexual middle-class family and to morally, socially and culturally regulate poor people with care responsibilities, for themselves and others, under workfare structures and programmes.

For disabled people there are numerous tensions with the harnessing of care by neoliberal workfare state restructuring. As Hughes *et al.* (2005: 264) have argued elsewhere, the disability movement has sought 'to control care by transforming it into a formal contractual relationship'. For many within the disability movement, this has been a central strategy to re-assert their autonomy within a key relationship of power where the rights and needs of disabled people, as the recipients of care, have often been relegated to the realm of gratitude (Galvin 2004b).

Thus, the disability movement's contestation of 'care' is embedded in a historical context where 'care' captures the paternalism and oppression inherent in much of the asymmetrical relations of power embedded in informal relations of care (Hurst 2001). The disability movement's resistance to the re-evaluation of 'care' by feminist scholars is set within this history, although there have been several attempts by disability activists and scholars to reconcile these differences (see Hughes *et al.* 2005; Watson *et al.* 2004). The feminist perspective on care calls for integrating care into citizenship rights and as part of a platform of social justice (Sevenhuijsen 1998).

Yet in many ways the neoliberal co-option of feminism's re-evaluation of care reinforces the historical normative positioning of disabled people. First, informal carers, within the domestic sphere are increasingly gaining access to a range of supports and legislative measures to support their role as an informal carer of a disabled people. The carers' rights movement, which has an overwhelming female membership and leadership, across western liberal democracies has welcomed these measures as it provides for 'carers within their own right' (Lloyd 2000: 141).

However, such strategies have largely been incorporated in state plans to reduce public expenditure on disability social provisioning measures. Largely low cost and short term, these measures targeted at informal carers seek to privatize the right of disabled people to personal support assistance, thus absolving the state of its responsibilities to a class of citizens. Typically, the discursive positioning of disabled people within this framework is largely that of 'burden', where carers are seen as 'suffering' in their caring role. This not only reinforces disabled people's historical oppression, but also stigmatizes disabled people's subjective experience of the self and the body. They are made to feel inferior because of lack of success in the labour market, and at the same time the negative re-evaluation of their impairment is repeated throughout public discourse.

Second, the restructuring of workfare harnesses discourses of care and is principally associated with the privileging of informal care over formal care relations. Here, the aim is to 'naturalize' disabled people's care within the private realm. The relegation of disabled people to the private realm is normalized and the withdrawal of state social provisioning measures that enable disabled people's broader participation in society remains unchallenged.

This second move also delegitimizes disabled people's broader claims within the polity for social provisioning measures such as personal assistance support. This is particularly heightened for the diminishing class of disabled people who qualify for disability entitlements with the onset of strict disability classification regimes. Thus, the normative framing of this class of disabled people as 'deserving' is also underpinned by a normative re-positioning as 'waste' (Hughes *et al.* 2005) and therefore unworthy of state support beyond the realm of 'care'. This is most clearly expressed via the Cameron Government in the UK and proposals to cut mobility allowance to this class of disabled people, bounding their bodies into the private sphere of the home and charitable institutions (see Gentleman 2011).

Third, workfare discourses of care reinforce the normative framing of the able-bodied hetero-sexual 'good' and respectable mother. This stands in contrast to the situation where the productive sphere for disabled women remains tightly controlled by nation states through a raft of legislative measures (Dowse *et al.* 2010). Disabled mothers living on welfare endure heightened levels of surveillance as a segment of the population with neoliberal workfare restructuring. As Magna *et al.* (2008) report, disabled mothers are required to endure a round of surveillance through workfare regimes that assess their capacity to provide ongoing care, while simultaneously assessing their employability for precarious labour markets.

This is primarily due to the moral evaluation of their performance as the good mother, coupled with their general precarious economic positioning within the labour market. Deemed both unable to care and unable to work leaves them in an insecure position. Accessing disability entitlements, despite the centrality of care for *others* within their lives, is a highly stigmatizing experience.

Conclusion

The state is neither monolithic nor universal and the relationship between disability and work remains as complex as ever. Access to citizenship rights and entitlements is now predicated on a raft of conditions, restrictions and strict specifications. We have identified throughout this chapter that disability has been particularly targeted, even though all state-citizen relations have undergone this dramatic moral, political and economic process of reframing. The overall intent has been to re-imagine notions of disability public welfare and directly tie the access to welfare rights to the neoliberal restructuring of labour market, albeit part-time, casualized and contingent. As a set of state practices, neoliberal regulating regimes entrench disability relations of poverty, marginalization and exclusion.

We learn from the neoliberal turn the 'ambiguity' of disability, as a class of citizenship. While medical science wishes us to imagine that disability is predicated on a concrete and stable measuring of the body, in fact, the historical specificity of disability and its meaning as a class of citizenship is continually moving. The fluidity of state definitions of disability is revealed through its historical location within the broader political, economic and moral power dynamics of state relations. The state, of course, is not monolithic; however, the general tendencies we have mapped out in this chapter in relation to disability appear to be consistent across the vast majority of neoliberal state forms. While the practices of neoliberal state regulating regimes vary dependent upon the temporal-spatial historicity of the nation state, the underlying ideological, moral and political commitment to re-regulating, re-dividing, re-classifying and re-sorting 'disability' is globally coherent.

Thus the state plays a central role in creating social, moral and political understandings of disability, and therefore we need to 'bring the state back in' (Jessop 2001) to our analysis. In any examination of disability, we need to articulate the ways in which changing state formations impinge upon disabled people's struggles for equality, respect and recognition. Regulatory practices that enable the state to legitimate its power and control are integral to understanding how disabled people experience not only their daily lives but also their lived experience of discrimination, marginalization and stigmatization.

An alternative valuation of disability requires accepting a legitimate diversity of bodies. But this will not become a reality until state policies address continuing structural social inequalities. There is growing scepticism in civil society about the ability of the state and the market capitalism to deliver equality. The disability movement, along with other social movements, is rethinking strategies to reduce inequalities and discrimination.

This entails arguing for a radical shift away from 'blaming the individual' and the moral discourses of individual responsibility. Strategies for social and political change include rethinking the concept of individual contracts and how they may be replaced with social contracts, funding local initiatives by disabled people's organizations and continuing to demand substantial investments in removing barriers to work. Given that employment of disabled people does not necessarily lead to greater participation in society, the new discourse of workfare throws up challenges to activists, allies and intellectuals. Moreover individualized funding structures, which underpin the rights discourse and emerged from demands by disabled people for more control over their lives, will not lead necessarily lead to greater self-determination, especially when these structures fit within the orthodoxy of neoliberalism. Thus, we expect the hegemony of neoliberalism will continue to be contested and demands for different and greater participation in the decision-making apparatus of the state will continue to emerge in both the Global North and the Global South.

Acknowledgements

We would like to thank Carolyn Frohmader and Linda Briskman for their support throughout the development of this chapter.

Notes

1 See Women with Disabilities Australia, 2008, Submission to the Parliamentary Inquiry into pay equity and associated issues related to increasing female participation in the workforce. Available online at http://www.wwda.org.au/wwdapesub1.htm.
2 This is not to negate the harsh reality of the workhouse, but to acknowledge the deeply contradictory nature of its operation for those who were incarcerated behind its walls (see Stone (1981) for a brief discussion of this point) and the 'moral bodily boundaries' emerging with, and integral to, the functioning of the capitalist political economy.
3 Advance Personnel (2008) *Annual Report 2007/2008.*

References

Abberley, P. (2002) 'Work, Disability, Disabled People and European Social Theory', in C. Barnes, M. Oliver and L. Barton, eds, *Disability Studies Today* (Cambridge: Polity Press): pp. 12–138.

Australian Bureau of Statistics (2004) 'Disability, Ageing and Carers, Australia: Summary of Findings'. Cat. No. 4430.0. Disaggregated data purchased from the Australian Bureau of Statistics by Women with Disabilities Australia.

Barnes, C. and Mercer, G. (2005) 'Disability, Work, and Welfare: Challenging the Social Exclusion of Disabled People', *Work, Employment and Society* 19(3): 527–45.

Beck, U. (2000) *The Brave New World of Work* (Oxford: Polity Press).

Beck, U. and Beck-Gernsheim, E. (2002) *Individualisation* (London: Sage).

Bessant, J. (2000) 'Civil Conscription or Reciprocal Obligation? The Ethics of "Work-for-the-Dole"', *Australian Journal of Social Issues* 35(1): 15–33.

Bessant, J., Watts, R., Dalton, T. and Smyth, P. (2006) *Talking Policy: How Social Policy is Made* (Sydney: Allen & Unwin).

Biyanwila, S. J. (2010) *Trade Unions in the Global South* (London: Routledge).

Campbell, F. K. (2009) *Contours of Ableism: The Production of Disability and Abledness* (New York: Palgrave Macmillan).

Carney, T. (2006) 'Neoliberal Welfare Reform and "Rights" Compliance Under Australian Social Security Law', *Australian Journal of Human Rights* 12(1): 223–53.

Chouinard, V. and Crooks, V. (2006) '"Because *They* Have All the Power and I Have None": State Restructuring of Income and Employment Supports and Disabled Women's Lives in Ontario, Canada', *Disability & Society* 20(1): 19–32.

Chouinard, V. and Crooks, V. (2008) 'Negotiating Neoliberal Environments in British Columbia and Ontario, Canada: Restructuring of State–Voluntary Sector Relations and Disability Organisations' Struggles to Survive', *Environment and Planning C: Government and Policy* 26(1): 173–90.

Clear, M. and Gleeson, B. (2001) 'Disability and Materialist Embodiment', *Journal of Australian Political Economy* 49(1): 34–55.

Commonwealth Ombudsman's Report (2007) *Application of Penalties Under Welfare to Work, report no. 16* (Canberra: Commonwealth of Australia).

Connell, R. (2008) 'A Thousand Miles from Kind: Men, Masculinities and Modern Institutions', *Journal of Men's Studies* 16(3): 237–52.

Dowse, L., Frohmader, C. and Meekosha, H. (2010) 'Intersectionality: Disabled Women', in P. Eastreal, ed., *Women and the Law in Australia* (Sydney: LexisNexis): pp. 249–68.

Esping-Andersen, G. (1990) *The Three Worlds of Welfare Capitalism* (Cambridge: Polity Press).

Fiske, L. and Briskman, L. (2007) 'Rights and Responsibilities: Reclaiming Human Rights in Political Discourse', *Just Policy* 43(April): 50–4.

Fording, R., Schram, S. and Soss, J. (2007) 'Devolution, Discretion and the Effect of Local Political Values on TANF Sanctioning', *Social Services Review* 81: 285–316.

Foucault, M. (1977) *Discipline and Punish* (London: Penguin).

Frohmader, C. and Meekosha, H. (forthcoming) 'Recognition, Respect and Rights: Women with Disabilities in a Globalized World', in D. Goodley, B. Hughes and L. Davis, eds, *Disability and Social Theory* (London: Palgrave Macmillan).

Galvin, R. (2004a) 'Can Welfare Reform Make Disability Disappear?', *Australian Journal of Social Issues* 39(3): 343–53.

Galvin, R. (2004b) 'Challenging the Need for Gratitude: Comparisons Between Paid and Unpaid Care for Disabled People', *Journal of Sociology* 40(2): 137–55.

Gentleman, A. (2011) 'Disability Living Allowance Cuts Could Confine Disabled to Homes, Say Charities', *Guardian*, 12 January; available online at http://www.guardian.co.uk/society/2011/jan/12/disability-living-allowance-cuts-charities (accessed 21 September 2011).

Gillies, V. (2007) *Marginalised Mothers: Exploring Working Class Experiences of Parenting* (London: Routledge).

Giroux, H. (2004) *The Terror of Neoliberalism: Authoritarianism and the Eclipse of Democracy* (Boulder, CO: Paradigm).

Gleeson, B. (1997) 'Disability Studies: A Historical Materialist View', *Disability & Society* 12(2): 179–202.

Gleeson, B. (1999) *Geographies of Disability* (London: Routledge).

Goodin, R. (2002) 'Structures of Mutual Obligation', *Journal of Social Policy* 31(3): 579–96.

Gothard, J. (1998) 'Burden on the State: The "Unfit" Immigrant', in E. Richards and J. Templeton, eds, *The Australian Immigrant in the 20th Century: Searching Neglected Sources* (Canberra: Australian National University): pp. 38–64.

Grover, C. and Piggott, L. (2010) 'Disgusting! Understanding Financial Support for Disabled People in the UK'. Paper presented at the Disability Studies fifth bi-annual conference, Lancaster University, Lancaster, 7–9 September.

Hamilton, C. and Maddison, S., eds (2007) *Silencing Dissent* (Sydney: Allen & Unwin).

Harvey, D. (2000) *Spaces of Hope* (Berkeley, CA: University of California Press).

Harvey, D. (2005) *A Brief History of Neoliberalism* (Oxford: Oxford University Press).

Haylett, C. (2001) 'Illegitimate Subjects?: Abject Whites, Neoliberal Modernisation and Middle-class Multiculturalism', *Environment and Planning D: Society and Space* 19(3): 351–70.

Haylett, C. (2003) 'Remaking Labour Imaginaries: Social Reproduction and the Internationalising Project of Welfare Reform', *Political Geography* 22(7): 765–88.

Haywood, K. and Yar, M. (2006) 'The "Chav" Phenomenon: Consumption, Media and the Construction of a New Underclass', *Crime, Media, Culture* 2(1): 9–28.

Horvath-Rose, A., Stapleton, D. and O'Day, B. (2006) 'Effects of Welfare Reform on Statistics for Young Women with Disabilities', *Journal of Disability Policy Studies* 17(3): 166–79.

Hudson, P. (2010) *The Workshop of the World*; available online at http://www.bbc.co.uk/history/british/victorians/workshop_of_the_world_01.shtml (accessed 21 September 2011).

Hughes, B., McKie, L., Hopkins, D. and Watson, N. (2005) 'Love's Labours Lost? Feminism, the Disabled People's Movement and an Ethic of Care', *Sociology* 39(2): 259–74.

Hurst, R. (2001) 'Rethinking Care from a Rights Perspective', in WHO Disability and Rehabilitation Teams, eds, *'Rethinking Care' from Different Perspectives*; available online at http://www.leeds.ac.uk/disability-studies/archiveuk/WHO/rcpapers.pdf (accessed 6 October 2011).

Hyde, M. (2000) 'From Welfare-to-Work? Social Policy for Disabled People of Working Age in the United Kingdom in the 1990s', *Disability & Society* 15(2): 327–41.

Jakubowicz, A. and Meekosha, H. (2002) 'Bodies in Motion: Critical Issues Between Disability Studies and Multicultural Studies', *Journal of Intercultural Studies* 23(3): 237–52.

Jessop, B. (2001) 'Bringing the State Back in Yet Again: Reviews, Revisions, Rejections and Redirection', *International Review of Sociology* 11(2): 149–73.

Leitner, H., Sheppard, E., Sziarto, K. and Maringanti, A. (2007) 'Contesting Urban Frontiers: Decentring Neoliberalism', in H. Leitner, J. Peck and E. Sheppard, eds, *Contesting Neoliberalism: Urban Frontiers* (New York: The Guildford Press) pp. 1–25.

Leys, C. (2001) *Market-driven Politics: Neo-liberal Democracy and the Public Interest* (London: Verso).

Lightman, E., Vick, A., Herd, D. and Mitchell, A. (2009) '"Not Disabled Enough": Episodic Disabilities and the Ontario Disability Support Program', *Disability Studies Quarterly* 29(3): 1–9.

Lloyd, L. (2000) 'Caring About Carers: Only Half the Picture?', *Critical Social Policy* 20(1): 136–50.

McDonald, C. and Chenoweth, L. (2009) '(Re)Shaping Social Work: An Australian Case Study', *British Journal of Social Work* 39(1): 144–60.

McDonald, C., Marston, G. and Buckley, A. (2003) 'Risk Technology in Australia: The Role of the Job-seeker Classification Instrument in Employment Services', *Critical Social Policy* 23(4): 498–525.

Maddison, S. and Martin, G. (2010) 'Introduction: Surviving Neoliberalism: The Persistence of Australian Social Movements', *Social Movement Studies* 9(2): 101–20.

Magna, S., Parish, S. and Cassiman, A. (2008) 'Policy Lessons from Low-income Mothers with Disabilities', *Journal of Women, Politics and Policy* 29(2): 181–206.

Malacrida, C. (2009) 'Gendered Ironies in Home Care: Surveillance, Gender Struggles and Infantilisation', *International Journal of Inclusive Education* 13(7): 741–52.

Martin, S. (2007) *Welfare Reform, the Underclass Thesis and the Process of Legitimising Social Divisions* (Melbourne: The Australian Centre, University of Melbourne).

Meekosha, H. (2005) 'A Feminist/Gendered Critique of the Intersections of Race and Disability: The Australian Experience'. Paper presented at the University of British Columbia, British Columbia, 23 June.

Mink, G. (1998) *Welfare's End* (Ithaca, NY: Cornell University Press).

Mladenov, T. (2009) 'Institutional Woes of Participation: Bulgarian Disabled People's Organisations and Policy-making', *Disability & Society* 24(1): 33–45.

Moss, J. (2006) '"Mutual Obligation" and "New Deal": Illegitimate and Unjustified', *Ethical Theory and Moral Practice* 9(1): 87–94.

National Foundation for Australian Women (2007) *'What Women Want': Consultations on Welfare to Work and Work Choices* (New South Wales: National Foundation for Australian Women).

Nussbaum, M. (2004) *Hiding from Humanity: Disgust, Shame and the Law* (Princeton: Princeton University Press).

Offe, C. (1984) *Contradictions of the Welfare State* (Cambridge, MA: MIT Press).

Oliver, M. (1990) *The Politics of Disablement* (London: Macmillan).

Ong, A. (2006) *Neoliberalism as Exception: Mutations in Citizenship and Sovereignty* (Durham, NC: Duke University Press).

Peck, J. (2001) *Workfare States* (New York: The Guildford Press).

Peck, J. and Theodore, N. (2000) '"Work First": Workfare and the Regulation of Contingent Labour Markets', *Cambridge Journal of Economics* 24(1): 119–38.

Piven, F. and Cloward, R. (1993) *Regulating the Poor: The Functions of Public Welfare*, 2nd edn (New York: Vintage Books).

Player, S. and Pollock, A. (2001) 'Long-term Care: From Public Responsibility to Private Good', *Critical Social Policy* 21(2): 231–55.

Powell, F. (2007) *The Politics of Civil Society: Neoliberalism or Social Left?* (Bristol: The Policy Press).

Rose, N. (1996). 'Governing "Advanced" Liberal Democracies', in A. Barry, T. Osborne and N. Rose, eds, *Foucault and Political Reason: Liberalism, Neoliberalism and Rationalities of Government* (London: ECL Press): pp. 37–64.

Roulstone, A. and Barnes, C. (2005) *Working Futures? Disabled People, Policy and Social Inclusion* (Bristol: Policy Press).

Roulstone, A. and Morgan, H. (2009) 'Neo-liberal Individualism or Self-directed Support: Are We All Speaking the Same Language on Modernising Adult Social Care?', *Social Policy and Society* 8(3): 333–45.

Russell, M. (1998) *Beyond Ramps: Disability at the End of the Social Contract* (Monroe: Common Courage Press).

Salthouse, S. (2005) 'Jumping through Hoops: Welfare and Industrial Relations Reform Implications for Women with Disabilities'. Paper presented at the What Women Want Workshop on behalf of Women with Disabilities Australia; available online at http://www.wwda.org.au/w2wjuly05.htm (accessed 21 September 2011).

Sayer, A. (2005) *The Moral Significance of Class* (Oxford: Oxford University Press).

Schram, S., Fording, R. and Soss, J. (2008) 'Neo-liberal Poverty Governance: Race, Place and the Punitive Turn in US Welfare Policy', *Cambridge Journal of Regions, Economy and Society* 1(1): 17–36.

Sevenhuijsen, S. (1998) *Citizenship and the Ethics of Care: Feminist Considerations on Justice, Morality and Politics* (London: Routledge).

Shragge, E., ed. (1997) *Workfare: Ideology for a New Underclass* (Toronto: Garamond Press).

Skeggs, B. (2004) *Class, Self, Culture* (London: Routledge).

Soldatic, K. (2009) 'Disability and the Australian Neoliberal Workfare State'. Unpublished PhD thesis, University of Western Australia.

Soldatic, K. and Pini, B. (2009) 'The Three Ds of Welfare Reform: Disability, Disgust and Deservingness', *Australian Journal of Human Rights* 15(1): 76–94.

Soldatic, K. and Chapman, A. (2010) 'Surviving the Assault? The Australian Disability Movement and the Neoliberal Workfare State', *Social Movement Studies* 9(2): 139–54.

Soldatic, K. and Meekosha, H. (forthcoming) 'The Place of Disgust: Disability, Class and Gender in Spaces of Workfare', *Gender, Place and Culture*.

Stone, D. (1981) *The Disabled State* (Philadelphia: Temple University Press).

Thompson, E. P. (1963) *The Making of the English Working Class* (New York: Vintage Books).

Thornton, S. and Marston, G. (2009) 'Who to Serve? The Ethical Dilemma of Employment Consultants in Nonprofit Disability Employment Network Organisations', *Australian Journal of Social Issues* 44(1): 73–89.

Tickell, A. and Peck, J. (2003) 'Making Global Rules: Globalisation or Neoliberalisation?', in J. Peck and H. Wai-chung Yeung, eds, *Remaking the Global Economy: Economic-Geographical Perspectives* (London: Sage): pp. 163–81.

Tyler, I. (2008) 'Chav Mum Chav Scum', *Feminist Media Studies* 8(1): 17–34.

Watson, N., McKie, L. Hughes, B., Hopkins, D. and Gregory, S. (2004) '(Inter)Dependence, Needs and Care: The Potential for the Disability and Feminist Theorists to Develop an Emancipatory Model', *Sociology* 38(2): 331–50.

Willis, K., Smith, A. and Stenning, A. (2008) 'Introduction: Social Justice and Neoliberalism', in A. Smith, A. Stenning and K. Willis, eds, *Social Justice and Neoliberalism: Global Perspectives* (London: Zed Books): pp. 1–15.

Wilton, R. and Schuer, S. (2006) 'Towards Socio-spatial Inclusion? Disabled People, Neoliberalism and the Contemporary Labour Market', *Area* 38(2): 186–95.

Women With Disabilities Australia (WWDA) (2009) Submission to the Australian NGO Beijing+15 Review. Prepared by Carolyn Frohmader, Margie Charlesworth and Sue Salthouse for WWDA; available online at www.wwda.org.au/subs2006.htm (accessed 21 September 2011).

16

DISABLED PEOPLE, WORK AND EMPLOYMENT

A global perspective

Alan Roulstone

Introduction

The barriers faced by disabled people globally in accessing paid work are a profound social challenge. Many reasons are provided as to why these barriers exist and new policy visions offered up. Any analysis that does not include issues of impairment type and severity, social barriers, welfare regimes, cultural expectations and wider social and economic systems underestimates the complexity of the factors involved. There are a number of conundrums that lie at the heart of our understanding of disability, work and employment. First, how is it that, given the major efforts being invested in trying to get disabled people into paid employment in the 'developed' world, progress is so slow – encouraging one key writer to state that there are no easy or enduring fixes for disabled people and paid work, and that many programmes are doomed to fail or under-shoot their target (Marin in Marin *et al.* 2004)? The second key conundrum is why, given the historically low expectations and assumptions that disabled people cannot work, have some disabled people actually gone on to obtain and retain paid work (Burchardt 2005; Roulstone and Barnes 2005)? However, whilst disabled people are increasing their presence in the contractual labour market there is much evidence of continued labour market disadvantage.

The employment position of disabled people in a global context

Across the globe disabled people find it difficult overcoming barriers to the workplace. If we look at all Organisation for Economic Co-operation and Development (OECD) countries (Scherer in Marin *et al.* 2004: 131–2), we can see that disabled people are half as likely to be in paid work as their non-disabled counterparts (averaged across the OECD member countries). Barriers to paid work are not simply an issue in certain countries or even continents. In both 'advanced' economies and largely poor rural majority world contexts, disabled people are disadvantaged in both accessing and sustaining work and other forms of economic activity. It is axiomatic that in a world where work is valorized as an important social contribution, as a defence (however limited) against poverty, and as a source of self-validation, the lack of paid work or wider economic activity is a significant social disadvantage. Indeed, the lack of access to paid work and wider economic activity helps maintain the link between poverty and disability in many country contexts in both the majority and minority worlds (World Health Organization 2011). Disability in some societies continues to be constructed as inimical to a wide variety of economic activity in the mainstream. There is clearly also a vicious circle operating in some majority world contexts – that poverty and poor healthcare and assistive support actually lead to greater risk or severity of impairment, which in turn perpetuates and confirms a disabled person's economic position (Yeo and Moore 2003). Disability can be seen to be a 'problem' in capitalist, communist and post-communist contexts (Mete 2008). Any simple connection between broad socio-economic systems and the specific exclusions of disabled people from economic activity are likely to have limited explanatory and theoretical value. Economic and cultural assumptions can also be seen to merge to exclude disabled people where religious or ritualistic practices converge with economic exclusion to further exclude disabled people from constructions of work-ability (Ingstad and Reynolds-Whyte 1995; Sena-Martins 2010). The planning of disability and employment are made more difficult by the absence of reliable data that links disability and employment in many world countries (International Labour Organization 2007).

The minority world: who is excluded, who is supported to gain work?

The minority or 'first' world is characterized as having substantial mediating factors between a person with an impairment and the otherwise raw realities of an economic wage labour system. The development of worker protections, a welfare state to support health and economic stability and specialist employment support providers all feature in these mediating factors (Lunt in Roulstone and Barnes 2005). In this sense the relationship between objective impairment and employment options is complex; indeed a person with a more minor impairment with significant barriers to economic, transport and social capital may struggle to enter paid work. Conversely significant impairment need not of itself limit a person where wider social capital and resource make employment possible (Zola 1982).

Whilst there is no predictive model that allows a shorthand reading of the relations between impairment, disability, dis/advantage and opportunity, we do have a growing body of evidence on the factors that intervene between the state and the market in a given society and the level of effectiveness in aiding disabled people's employment and work status in the minority world. What we know about disability, un/employment and the benefits system from OECD research is that more generous disability benefits (earnings replacement and wider disability support) correlate with lower rates of employment (Andrews in Marin *et al.* 2004: 257–9). It is important not to take strong inferences from this and to impute a causal relationship between generous benefits and worklessness. Simply reducing benefit levels may not straightforwardly benefit disabled people; although they may be more likely to leave lower-rated benefits and seek economic activity, such work may often offer poor reward that is little better than out-of-work or poverty relief transfers (Burchardt 2000). High income replacement benefits may lead to a two-way disincentive effect but, longer term, such rates might also be a historical recognition that employment may be unobtainable for disabled people, thus necessitating compensatory benefit levels.

There are also shared and divergent facts about disabled people's un/employment in the minority world. For example, although disabled people are generally less likely to be employed than their non-disabled counterparts, across all OECD countries disabled people over 50 are less likely to be in work and to receive vocational training and support. Those with more significant impairments and more limited educational attainments are also least likely to obtain paid work (Marin *et al.* 2004). People with mental health problems and people with learning disabilities are also more likely to be outside of paid work and economically inactive (not looking for paid work) in most minority world contexts. However, in the industrialized former state socialist countries, people with mobility impairments are those most disadvantaged in formal labour markets. This may reflect the relatively poor environmental infrastructure in some of these contexts (Mete 2008). Those with congenital impairments fare worse in these labour markets than those with adventitious impairments. This may point to the role of cumulative disadvantage in labour market exclusion. In the rapidly developing former state socialist countries, for example Moldova, Uzbekistan and Romania, poor health care intersects with disability to limit labour market opportunities:

> As a result, some health conditions that today do not have much impact on the daily functioning of individuals in industrialised countries may still be cause for concern in some (post communist) transition economies.
>
> *(Mete 2008: 9)*

At the other end of the age spectrum, disabled people going through the transition to early adulthood in the minority world are also prey to very disparate vocational and training provision, often low expectations, low attainments and 'failed' education set against the increasingly academic thresholds established for the background population (Philip and Velche 2010). Specifically, disabled people are much less likely to attain 'level two' qualifications and to be encouraged into less academic routes to educational success. Disabled people are more likely to drop out of or receive insufficient support in their advanced education and training. Perhaps the most worrying fact is that many disability employment programmes simply do not work in making major in-roads into the world of paid work in more developed countries (Marin *et al.* 2004). We know that most of the programmes in OECD countries are largely not that effective – these include financial incentives for disabled people, employer sweeteners and sanctions against disabled people perceived to be closer to the labour market. Disabled people are more likely to be supported into paid work where they are already close to the labour market. In other words, these disabled people may well have entered work without such interventions and the apparent effect of a programme is artifactual (Arthur *et al.* 1999). The most effective national welfare schemes in supporting disabled people are those that afford a more flexible build-up of hours, protected re/entry and exit from paid work where periods of illness supervene, where wider benefit claw-backs are least severe on re-entering paid work and where flexible and adjusted working are well supported by fiscal and local disability support measures (Marin *et al.* 2004; Roulstone and Barnes 2005).

Disabled people who are some distance from the labour market in minority countries and who may have been out of work for longer or never worked are very rarely helped to get closer to the labour market. An incorrect assumption is that such distance from the labour market is evidence of lack of interest in paid work and ingrained economic inactivity. For example, we know that some minority world countries make access to the protections of paid work difficult (e.g., in Holland) but once in work provide very strong work retention and protection. Conversely, the Danish labour market is more porous, with disabled people getting more ready access, but people are also less protected and exit is as easy for employers of disabled people as access (Hogelund 2003). This suggests that over-personalizing non-activity may be a major error of behavioural attribution in failing to read a labour market and benefits context for disabled jobseekers. Some employment programmes, for example sheltered work, are actually seen to reinforce negative attitudes and the continued segregation of disabled people (Hyde 1996). However, supported employment seems to have more success in its modern guise of mainstream jobs and unsubsidized pay, but often supported by workplace mentors and 'natural supports' (Drake *et al.* 1996; Crowther *et al.* 2001). We know for example that, overall, 'place and train' approaches to vocational support are far more effective than 'preparation' models, which have witnessed disabled young people in a 'revolving door' of training and vocational preparation abstracted from any real job opportunities (Corrigan and McCracken 2005). However, these schemes are mainly focused on post-school but pre-45 year-old disabled people.

Demographic and regional economic factors are also very important in limiting the opportunities available to disabled workers. For example, there is strong evidence that high levels of work 'incapacity' type benefits are evident in areas of post-industrial decline (Beatty *et al.* 2002). The accretion of industrially acquired impairment adds to the challenge, as does the growth in young women who are entering incapacity type benefits with mental health problems (Labour Force Survey UK 2008). In these contexts more minor impairments often translate into significant labour market disadvantage where opportunities are very limited and 'healthy' labour very plentiful. The degree to which governments acknowledge the link between regional context and disabled people's employment disadvantage is a moot point. Recent attempts to make access to incapacity type benefits more difficult arguably fails to take into account the wider labour market context and the often very disparate regional development of an 'advanced' economy (HM Treasury 2010). There is also evidence that attempts to support disabled people back to work in these areas often takes the form of 'cherry picking' those closest to the labour market. The following sums up the challenge:

> It is surely no surprise that the areas hardest hit by industrial decline … are also the ones most likely to see high levels of inactivity.
>
> *(Wise Group 2009)*

Any crude attempt to connect the best opportunities with the 'best' people in these contexts often overlooks the complex interplay between impairment, self-identity, aspirations and labour market realities. Recent critical discourses attempting to separate out the 'genuinely disabled' from benefit malingerers (commonly referred to as the 'bad backs') can be seen to misunderstand the complex relationship between opportunity, identity, impairment and state activity. These efforts are showing evidence of reducing the flow onto incapacity benefits but more typically they are simply moving claimants onto unemployment benefits or even into the informal economy.

Across Europe and North America a highly confusing array of discourses has been attached to unemployed disabled people and to the best policy and practice responses. Discourses include legal exhortations to adhere to anti-discrimination legislation (Cooper 2000; Lawson 2007), to moral duties to employ those that struggle to maintain a foothold in the labour market (Doyle 1993), and business cases for employing disabled people based on assumptions that disabled people are more productive than non-disabled workers or add value to an organization's image (Zadek and Scott-Parker 2003). Taken together with harsher, more frustrated policy discourses around wasted talent and the need to break cycles of dependency this makes for a very dizzying combination of discourses and underpinning diagnoses of the problem. If we reflect on academic theories of disabled people's worklessness (detailed below), identifying industrial standardization, credentialism and cultural assumptions of disabled people as not work-able, then we see a dramatic mismatch between academic and policy constructions of the 'disability employment problem'. In sum, the business case holds some water for some disabled people, with research pointing to job and ontological insecurity provoking extra outputs from workers who may in reality have less energy and stamina than their non-disabled counterparts. The downside here is that disabled people who do not display additional productivity to their non-disabled colleagues may be seen to 'break the model' and give the lie to these hyperproductivity type business case approaches. A more nuanced business case attaches to disabled people's role in adding diversity to an organization that adds value to its processes, imagery and self-image as an inclusive, reflexive organization. The argument seems to adhere to the logic that being responsive to disability diversity amongst staff makes an organization more responsive to the breadth of customer/client needs. There is limited empirical evidence to support the claims being made, whilst critiques argue that disabled people are being used as confection in some organizations wanting to be seen to 'do the right thing'. Alternatively, it could be argued that if employment is on equal terms and enduring, any justification ought to suffice in supporting disabled people's working lives.

The approach that has gone out of fashion somewhat of late is the moral impulse to recruit and retain disabled people. This approach was arguably always least explicit in its conceptual under-pinnings but assumed it is good to include the formerly excluded in the workplace. Certainly if we look at broader institutional practices, whilst assumptions have been made that work should not be available to some disabled people in a categorical sense due to the adverse costs involved, this has never been applied in the education field in outright terms, but has taken the form of segregation. In this sense reaching adulthood does take some disabled people into an era of heightened jeopardy where outright exclusion is quietly sanctioned.

Understanding wider reasons as to why disabled people are less likely to be in paid employment we can build on a range of more specific insights and theories, all of which are useful, whilst none of which provide a uni-dimensional explanation of these barriers. First, we know that, despite their increasing presence in the workplace in the late twentieth century and their improved educational position, disabled people face generally low expectations regarding their capacity to do paid work and specifically to achieve a 'normal' rate of productivity. Evidence has consistently attempted to challenge this assumption (Knapp *et al.* 2008). Academic theories that better capture the historical position of disabled people revolve around labour market segmentation and segregation theory. The former points to dual or segmented labour markets which, in reserving the 'core' labour market opportunities for the most privileged employees with key organizational capital, tend to restrict access of lower status work groups to peripheral positions (Doeringer and Piore 1971).

Historically women, older workers and disabled workers have been seen to occupy these positions. Whilst this approach may hold some water theoretically, the fact that some disabled people have entered what are clearly 'core' labour market positions invites questions as to the depth of explanatory value of this approach. Are such phenomena the exception that proves the rule or is the dual labour market theory itself limited? In fact, such achievements do not necessarily deny the inherent value of this approach as a generalizing framework – that disabled people are generally more likely to be out of work or in peripheral work – as this seems broadly to be the case since more disabled people are in casual, part-time and temporary work (Labour Force Survey UK 2008; OECD 2003). Some writers have asserted that disabled people are in such a chronically disadvantaged labour market position that this equates their position to that of a 'reserve army of labour' (Hyde 2000). Once again, whilst wartime and immediate post-war events provide some evidence for this approach, the longer-term advancement of those disabled people in mainstream employment in the second half of the twentieth century seems to challenge this assumption. Indeed recent evidence by Rigg (2005: 10) suggests that once in employment, some disabled people, particularly those disabled women in mid-career, advance through organizational structures in a broadly similar manner to their non-disabled counterparts.

However, overall progress for disabled people lags behind non-disabled people, although not nearly as dramatically as dual or segmented labour market theories might suggest. What is striking from major longitudinal United Kingdom (UK) research is that disabled people are more likely to enter low paid work and never to transcend that – this is especially true of disabled men. All disabled workers, especially those with more obvious impairments, are likely to leave the labour market earlier than their non-disabled counterparts (Rigg 2005: 27). Disabled people are seen to enter paid employment at times of labour growth and shrinkage, although relative rates of entry are disadvantageous to disabled people in both economic boom and slump (Lonsdale 1980).

What the evidence does show, however, is that younger and older disabled workers seem to face greater barriers to career advancement despite anti-discrimination legislation in many English-speaking contexts (Lawson 2007). There is much evidence of a glass ceiling (Wilson-Kovacs *et al.* 2008), glass cliff (Ryan and Haslam 2005) and latterly a glass partition effect (Roulstone, forthcoming) operating for disabled people which limits their access to more senior positions. The glass ceiling effect is well rehearsed in pointing to the apparent upper limits of disadvantaged labour groups. The glass cliff effect points to previously excluded workers – women and disabled workers – being afforded risky career advancements. The glass partition effect is beginning to emerge as an idea in economies where labour opportunities are limited and where disabled workers are reluctant to move jobs or roles and lose organizational capital or support that they have accrued (Roulstone, forthcoming). The situation for younger disabled people is particularly stark; recent research by Burchardt points to the quite dramatic erosion of young disabled people's job aspirations as they move from age 16 to 21 in the UK. At 16 career aspirations are largely similar for disabled and non-disabled young people; by 21 aspirations are considerably different for these comparator groups, with evidence pointing to the role of employment rejection in depleting young disabled people's career ambitions (Burchardt 2005). The collection of essays from Europe and Canada on young disabled people's experiences of paths to paid employment points up the cross-national challenges of obtaining and retaining paid employment. The lack of access to higher level qualifications, the concentration of rehabilitation and training on entry level and often low skilled manual occupations themselves help position disabled young people into a rather stereotyped range of jobs, where employment is possible at all (Philip and Velche 2010).

Disabled people in the minority world traditionally prefer work in the public sector. The reasons for this are unclear, but the sector has historically been seen to be more open to employing disabled people and can be seen to implicitly challenge pure productivity models associated with marketized work. The reality is more complex, with the third sector in some countries out-performing the public sector (Danieli 2006; Hirst *et al.* 2004). Anecdotally, disabled people are generally chosen for and preferred in 'backroom' functions. In an age where image and perfor-mativity are key features of much front of house work, the challenge of accepting difference in 'front of house' roles is as yet under-researched. The current threat to many backroom public sector jobs due to the fiscal crises of many western economies is a concern here, as the small number of employment shelters may come under increasing threat with the proposed public cuts (HM Treasury 2010).

Wider evidence suggests that disabled people have lower educational qualifications, are expected to achieve less educationally, and leave the labour market at an earlier age than their non-disabled comparators (Rigg 2005). However, the public sector continues to be the largest most adaptive employment context for disabled people despite its recent transformations. Reasonable adjustments were largely, if not exclusively established in these contexts (Roulstone *et al.* 2003); whilst in the UK the duty to promote the rights of disabled people (at work and beyond) was deliberately pitched as a public sector duty (Equality and Human Rights Commission 2009). In the United States (US), the undue hardship clause of the reasonable accommodations guidance would not likely excuse most larger public bodies from making a range of workplace accommodations (United States Equal Employment Opportunities Commission 2002). In this sense the enhanced duties reflect the spirit of section 504 of the Rehabilitation Act 1973 in the US linking the public domain with the leading edge of enabling policies (Friedman 1993). The wider educational role and the impact of keynote disability discrimination cases do point to the impact – albeit more limited than public expectations – on employer behaviour in the UK, Canada, US and Australasia (Lawson 2007; West 1996). The earlier 'great hope' in legislative support for disabled people in the form of quota systems now seems to have largely withered on the vine across the globe. The failure to enforce, employer exclusions and the repeal of quotas with some later anti-discrimination legislation (ADL) developments have all served to detract from the original aims of the quota system. Daniel Mont's World Bank study of OECD country quota compliance suggests levels varying between 50–70 per cent (Mont 2004). Compliance tends to be better in the minority world, although as stated above quotas are being withdrawn in some countries where full-blown ADL is being introduced, for example the UK.

Disabled people and employment: towards a more historically situated understanding

To date much disability employment policy activity can best be described as atheoretical and pragmatic in nature. To understand disabled people and employment requires a deeper understanding of the changing construction of ideas as to just what disability is taken to mean in the context of paid work. The earliest and most culturally pervasive notions of disability as they applied to employment derive from broader understandings that disability is a negative and limiting condition of the individual – one that requires medical and wider professional attention to get disabled people closer to the world of normality, economic opportunity and the position of citizenship.

Here citizenship is premised strongly on an ability to contribute to paid work and thus form part of an active social system that values and valorizes paid work (Prideaux and Roulstone 2011). Conversely, those people whose bodies or intellects fail to live up to expected norms of productivity, agility and strength will likely fall into the social category of dependency. Social disapprobation or protection may then attach to a disabled person, depending on the context and historical period under examination. The unwritten social codes that accompany assessments of disability and socially sanctioned exclusion from work have nowhere been fully appraised in the way that, for example, short term illness is captured in Parsons' formulation of the sick role (Parsons 1951). We can begin to move towards such a formulation based on historic assumptions as laid out below.

Work and the disability role

- Disabled people have 'conditions', usually long-term, that inhere in themselves and that may limit their absolute or relative ability to contribute to paid work.
- Although some contribution is not ruled out, they will always likely present a problem in employment terms as minimum standards and performances are required in the domain of paid work.
- Disabled people's role, therefore, is to orientate themselves to a life without work where their condition is severe enough to justify that in statutory excusal systems from paid work.
- Where disabled people have some capacity to work they are expected to make available that portion of themselves that can reasonably be applied to the world of paid work. They are excused involvement where their 'disability' or the wider economic circumstances disallow paid work, but should be available to enter paid employment where the state judges conditions of body/or society to fit with paid work opportunities.

As with the sick role, the assumptions behind the above formulation are both abstract and at times clumsy in comprehending disability, rights, responsibilities and opportunities. Unlike the sick role, the constant shifting of the 'disability role', according to policy imperatives (Stone 1984), means it is inherently less stable a term and evaluations need to contextualize the 'role' in the changing matrix of social, economic and policy conditions and constructions of a given era. Whilst the construction of disability has until the last 40 years been wrapped up with notions of personal deficit, tragedy and loss, and to some extent still is, the exact mix of social sentiments and expectations around disabled people and paid work varies enormously depending upon the economic position of a given society, the degree of state support to make entry to paid employment possible and the broader labour market position (Ingstad and Reynolds-Whyte 1995). For example, at times of labour shortage during the two world wars, disabled people and notions of dis-ablement were reappraised, some might say conveniently, to afford disabled people greater access to paid work. This mirrors the experiences of women who had new-found serendipitous opportunities during the two world wars.

Like women more generally, disabled people – many of whom were of course women – entered non-stereotyped work that had previously been seen as inimical to disabled people's perceived personal deficits (Humphries and Gordon 1992). The ability to shift just how disability and opportunity are constructed in a given social context tells us much about the wider challenges of supporting disabled people into work in conditions of scarcity of paid work (Morris and Butler 1972). However, the world wars, especially World War Two, did witness a major shift in what seemed to be genuine attempts to enhance disabled people's opportunities even beyond the war itself. This involved notions of the rehabilitation of the individual through health and social interventions to support longer term labour activity. The extent to which enlightened state constructions filtered through to everyday employer practice and changing family values towards disabled people and paid work is, however, hard to determine from the records of the time.

By the 1960s and 1970s very new constructions started to influence disability studies, the nascent disabled people's movement and ultimately some features of social policy. The work of Charlton (1999) in the US and Finkelstein and Davis in the UK (Davis 1990; Finkelstein 1980) began to fundamentally challenge the constructions of disability as a loss and deficit. Ideas began to cohere around the reappraisal of disability as the resulting failure of society to take account of difference and variety that are actually 'normal'. The realization that previous naturalized notions of normality were actually hegemonic constructions that were reified over time into scientific discourses of inadequacy was important. The new focus then was exclusionary environmental design, organizational practices and personal disablist behaviour. Although some have argued that the early disabled peoples movement was less concerned with paid work than, for example, the broader notion of independent living (Morris 1994), clearly this new social model of disability afforded very different insights as to the labour market exclusion of many disabled people – a way of thinking that influenced wider ideas about social barriers amongst thinkers who had previously been suspicious of the model (Walker 1981). In focusing on the social barriers that limited disabled people, debates around employment exclusion were enriched to afford a new language of exclusion. Over time, alternative histories of disability and employment emerged informed by the social model of disability (Finkelstein 1980; Ryan and Thomas 1980).

These insights highlighted the nature of employment in capitalist society rather than treat unemployment and labour market exclusion as random events attaching to people with personal employment limitations. These histories teased out the 'inner logic' of industrial capitalism, its focus on the standardization of production in and beyond the factory system, the link between accountancy, capitalism and notions that time had become an economic commodity alongside human labour (Thompson 1967). These histories have since been criticized for being too schematic (Landes 2003; Roulstone 2002). Indeed a careful reading of the industrialization process does point to greater variety of forms of economic activity from small-scale artisan craft working, small workshop and family businesses which survived the factory system and which offered inadvertent shelters (Borsay 2004) for disabled people and diverse bodies. In the same way as capitalism was not consciously devised to exclude disabled people, nor were its relative shelters a product of enlightened reinterpretations of a 'just life' for disabled people.

The fact that industrial capitalism developed in parallel to not as a blanket successor to agricultural capitalism afforded continued options on some small-holdings and family run farms. These are useful and important correctives to social model critiques of periodized histories which risk overlooking those forms of economic activity that allowed disabled people to continue contributing to the economic and social life of their community. Likewise the evidence emerging from the former state socialist countries points to very similar dynamics in the overall shift to industrialization in the former Soviet Union (Allen 1998). Indeed the idolization of Schmidt, the perfect worker in a capitalist economy (Taylor 1910), is closely mirrored in the Stakhanovite construction of the apotheosis of productive prowess in communist worker mythology (Shlapentokh 1988). There is no space here for an extensive comparison of the two contexts, but what we can say is that workplace disablism may likely emanate from a broader set of values that structure the complex organization of labour in 'advanced' industrial societies of various forms. This has implications for some social model writings that seem to suggest that the fundamental exclusionary forces in a disabling society emanate in their purest form from a capitalist society. This is clearly not borne out by the evidence.

However, the assertion that capitalism's calculative logic seems to hold within it values that are particularly inimical to an enabling society has to be taken seriously. In being largely concerned with profit maximization, capitalism has little interest in markets that relate to disabled people who are poor and on the margins of society. Put simply, there are few market opportunities in those people that arguably have been excluded by the broader social system. Some writers point to the convergence of capitalism and communist societies as Lenin acknowledged he was impressed by Fordist production line systems. The shocking images of the treatment of disabled people in some former Soviet satellite states, most especially Romania, Albania and Bulgaria, suggest that wider cultural dynamics also have a powerful role to play in mediating attitudes to disabled people (UNICEF 2006). The role of the state in intersecting with the dynamics of industrial capitalism *and* industrial communism have perhaps been underestimated – their power to shape market and command economy principles in a way that afford disabled people some opportunities. The shift towards a service economy and new requirements for performativity and new emotional economies of the contemporary workplace add further complexity to these debates. These latter, however, clearly help explain why despite structures that might otherwise systematically exclude do witness some disabled people entering the world of paid work.

Disability, employment and work: a majority world perspective

The work situation of disabled people in the majority world, whilst diverse, is largely very challenging, with most countries that collect reliable statistics suggesting that for the most part people deemed disabled are not likely to be in work (Brouliette 1995; Coleridge in Roulstone and Barnes 2005; Mitra and Sambamoorthi 2006). One major problem with many evaluations of disabled people, work and employment is the attempt to transpose western notions of work as employment into majority world contexts. These arguments tend to assume that employment (as paid work) and work are the same thing. This is a very important distinction as in much of the majority world work is a broad spectrum of non-contractual economic activity which can range over (and be a mix of) barter, small commodity production, hawking, provisioning (from waste land and tips) begging and wider exchanges of labour which include goods, services and promissory activity which are not based on contractual arrangements. In this way an attempt to graft minority (or advanced) world perspectives on to majority world contexts can be hugely problematical. For example, the attempt to instigate formal legal rights to holidays, healthcare, legal protection against discrimination at work and workplace harassment all hold little credence in informal economic contexts.

Unlike the minority world where complex protective factors mediate between the market and disabled person, these structures are often startlingly absent. For many disabled people the economy and realities of 'making out' may have caused or contributed to their impairment. This lack of formal structures has mixed implications – the more localized, particularistic (Parsons 1951) arrangements for producing, exchanging and using goods in many rural, agrarian and even some rapidly industrializing contexts can involve people with a range of impairments where calculative, globalized labour output standards have not taken hold. However, work in the majority world can be a very bleak context in which to scrape a living, with local prejudices against difference merging with exploitative labour conditions that some disabled workers would simply not be considered for or where they may already have developed impairments as a result of very poor labour protections. Indeed to return to earlier appraisals of the relationship between impairment and disability, in some poorer majority world contexts impairment rapidly translates into disability in the absence of mediating structures.

The above forms of making out and economic 'shelters' are also accompanied by some largely successful state and non-governmental organization (NGO) sponsored (regional and national) work activities such as home-based enterprises which allow production to take place at home using labour input which is often contracted out and where disabled people can work alongside their wider family members. The role of micro-finance initiatives, whilst not definitive (Brau and Woller 2004) in supporting these more localized often family-based enterprises may prove to be an important counter to development from above (World Health Organization 2011), which tends to leave disabled people out of development related employment opportunities. The downside to home-based enterprises is that contractual arrangements for home work (as they are across the globe) are often very exploitative and mirror the social arrangements characteristic of the European Mediaeval putting out system. Perhaps the most welcome governmental and non-governmental (NGOs) supported economic activities are developments towards Community Based Rehabilitation (CBR). Here economic activity is fostered for disabled people by tapping into the natural social and economic context in a way that aims to use wider community dynamics to better integrate disabled people into work activities. Here the scarce resources that do characterize many majority world contexts are accompanied by strong familial, community and localized resource environments that make inclusion possible. Most these projects are fostered by NGOs to build on naturally available resources and community dynamics to provide 'appropriate' work options for disabled people. This model contrasts sharply with assumptions that formal, contractual western solutions will benefit majority world contexts. The following sums up the aims and motivations of the CBR approach:

> The goal of CBR is to demystify rehabilitation and to give responsibility back to the individual, the family and the community. It draws on existing organisations and infrastructure for the provision of services, by recruiting and training local supervisors from the community. ... Simple rehabilitation techniques are delegated to auxiliaries and volunteers ... CBR attempts to involve the community in the planning,

implementation and evaluation of the programme. ... The intention is that rehabilitation is perceived as an integral part of the community's own development efforts. Only when a community takes responsibility for the integration of its disabled people can the process be truly called community-based rehabilitation.

(O'Toole and Maison-Hills 1994: 25)

As with understandings of disabled people and employment in the majority world, notions of unemployment and under-employment are also fairly meaningless in that context (Coleridge in Roulstone and Barnes 2005: 176), as these terms only make sense read alongside background employment data based on contractual arrangements. We do know, however, that where majority world economies are exposed to formal wage labour systems, disabled people are much less likely to be in paid contractual work or to access training than their non-disabled counterparts. Urban economies are less likely to offer opportunities than rural economies in the majority world (International Labour Organization 2007). People with mental health problems are at a particular disadvantage in some of these contexts, whilst ritual, religion and taboo continue to play a large part in constructions of normality and economic contributions. We have also to be very careful – the continent of Africa and each constituent country holds significant internal diversity despite being seen as squarely within the majority world. For example in urban Kenya, there is a discernible if sluggish disability and employment infrastructure, with a 5 per cent reserved occupation standard (Coleridge in Roulstone and Barnes 2005); whereas in Malawi there is no similar infrastructure, significant poverty and with very low per capita incomes, impairment rapidly translates into disablement. The current lack of clarity as to very different forms of work for disabled people, ranging from local informal self-provisioning through to highly structured labour contexts, leads to a recent typological development in thinking about work in its many guises and how it impinges upon disabled people. Prideaux *et al.* (2009) posit the following reframing of disability and work typology:

- **Industrial Work Typology**
  Work is largely seen as paid work. That paid work is that series of economic and social exchange for gain between two or more people, that is socially and economically valorised as 'real' work and which is motivated by gain and/or survival.
- **Progressive Work Typology**
  Work can be understood as the paid and unpaid transactions without which social and economic activity, integration and cohesion would be severely restricted, this would include unpaid care and household maintenance for which both formal and informal transaction may take place. This clearly has to include contractual paid work.
- **Majority World Work Typology**
  Those economic and social exchanges transacted in cash, kind, barter or promissory understanding (or which is socially unacknowledged: foraging, scavenging) that forms a diverse matrix of formal and informal activity from begging through to paid contractual work and all of which function as ways of 'making out'.
- **Post Welfarist Work Typology**
  Modes of economic and social activity in 'advanced' industrial society that take account of all forms of paid and unpaid activity including employees, employers, unpaid care and new social and economic arrangements such as direct payment recipients acting as employers and which questions assumed ideas around welfare dependency and non-working constituencies.

(Prideaux et al. 2009)

Prideaux *et al.* are as much concerned here with developing a critique of contemporary assumptions of work and welfare, one which positions work as the antithesis of welfare, with all the attendant assumptions that those in receipt of welfare either cannot or will not move closer to work-based social activities. The typology makes clear that disabled people contribute in diverse ways and in forms that are currently comprehended in often simplistic statutory and academic formulations which interpret economic costs and benefits in a very narrow sense. They take their cue from the development in direct payments in some European countries – a situation which places disabled people at the welfare recipiency *and* employer ends of a spectrum of activity-positions that are historically devalued and valorized respectively. The melding of employer and welfare recipient begs new questions as to how we frame disabled people's wider civic, economic and social contributions. Prideaux *et al.* acknowledge this is simply a starting point in any such re-evaluation and there is more work required to fully comprehend the range of social values disabled people contribute to. Indeed, there remain many barriers for the majority of disabled people across the world in meeting even their most basic aspirations in gaining and keeping paid employment.

Conclusions

Disability, work and employment are a complex triad which require very complex interpretations to avoid misplaced inferences in explaining disabled people's unemployment and under-employment. Personal constructs, identity, impairment effects, familial influences, religious beliefs, networks of support, education, economic opportunities, labour market policies – all intersect to afford or stop off such opportunities. In the minority world, education, statutory support, a degree of employer attitude change and wide social support all play their part. Disabled people are still, however, disadvantaged in availing themselves of many of these resources and forms of capital. In the majority world the work is construed to be a broad spectrum of economic activities and shelters that make impairment and economic opportunities possible for a small number of disabled people. For some, the absence of infrastructure, regulations and globalized productivity norms make for more opportunities, whilst some majority world contexts, particularly urban and the urban fringes, can be especially bleak for disabled people. Solutions in the majority world require more creative, often non-western, solutions to supporting disabled people to 'make out', such as appropriate microfinance and bottom-up community-based activities to support opportunities close to the natural supports of families and wider networks. Health care is a major issue in many majority world and rapidly transitional post-communist contexts.

References

Allen, R. C. (1998) 'The Standard of Living in the Soviet Union, 1928–1940', *The Journal of Economic History* 58(4): 1063–89.

Andrews, E. S. (2004) 'How Should Disability Benefits be Structured? A World Bank View', in B. Marin, C. Prinz and M. Queisser, eds, *Transforming Disability Welfare Policies* (Aldershot: Ashgate).

Arthur, S., Corden, A., Green, A., Lewis, J., Loumidis, J., Sainsbury, R., Stafford, B., Thornton, P. and Walker, R. (1999) *New Deal for Disabled People: Early Implementation*. DSS Research Report No. 106 (Leeds: CDS).

Beatty, C., Fothergill, S., Gore, T. and Green, A. (2002) *The Real Level of Unemployment 2002* (Sheffield: Centre for Regional Social and Economic Research, Sheffield Hallam University).

Borsay, A. (2004) *Disability and Social Policy in Britain Since 1750* (Basingstoke: Palgrave).

Brau, J. and Woller, G. M. (2004) 'Microfinance: A Comprehensive Review of the Existing Literature', *Journal of Entrepreneurial Finance and Business Ventures* 9(1): 1–26.

Brouliette, J. (1995) *Overcoming Obstacles to the Integration of Disabled People*. UNESCO-sponsored report as a contribution to the World Summit on Social Development Copenhagen, Denmark, March.

Burchardt, T. (2000) *The Dynamics of Being Disabled*. Case Paper 036 (London: LSE).

Burchardt, T. (2005) *The Education and Employment of Disabled Young People: Frustrated. Ambition* (Bristol: Policy Press and Joseph Rowntree Foundation).

Charlton, J. (1999) *Nothing About Us Without Us: Disability, Oppression and Empowerment* (Berkeley, CA: University of California Press).

Coleridge, P. (2005) 'Disabled People and "Employment" in the Majority World: Policies and Realities', in A. Roulstone and C. Barnes, eds, *Working Futures? Disabled People and Social Inclusion* (Bristol: Policy Press): pp. 175–92.

Cooper, J. (2000) *Law, Rights and Disability* (London: Jessica Kingsley).

Corrigan, P. W. and McCracken, S. G. (2005) 'Place First, then Train: An Alternative to the Medical Model of Psychiatric Rehabilitation', *Social Work* 50(1): 31–9.

Crowther, G., Marshall, M., Bond, G. and Huxley, P. (2001) 'Helping People with Severe Mental Illness to Obtain Work: Systematic Review', *BMJ* 322(7280): 204–8.

Danieli, A. (2006) *The Business Case for the Employment of Disabled People* (Warwick: Warwick Business School).

Davis, K. (1990) 'The Crafting of Good Clients', *Coalition*, September.

Doeringer, P. B., and Piore, M. J. (1971) *Internal Labor Markets and Manpower Analysis* (Massachusetts: D.C. Heath and Company).

Doyle, B. (1993) 'Disabled Workers, Employment Vulnerability and Labour Law', *Employee Relations* 9(5): 20–9.

Drake, R. E., McHugo, G. J., Becker, D. R., Anthony, W. A. and Clark, R. E. (1996) 'The New Hampshire Study of Supported Employment for People with Severe Mental Illness', *Journal of Consulting Clinical Psychology* 64(2): 391–9.

Equality and Human Rights Commission (2009) *The Disability Equality Duty – Impact and Outcomes So Far* (London: Equality and Human Rights Commission); available at http://www.equalityhumanrights.com/advice-and-guidance/public-sector-duties/what-are-the-public-sector-duties/the-disability-equality-duty-impact-and-outcomes-so-far/ (accessed 21 September 2011).

Finkelstein, V. (1980) *Attitudes and Disabled People* (New York: World Rehabilitation Monograph).

Friedman, S. (1993) 'Accommodation Issues in the Workplace for People with Disabilities: A Needs Assessment in an Educational Setting', *Disability & Society* 8(1): 3–23.

Hirst, M., Thornton, P., Dearey, M. and Maynard-Campbell, S. (2004) *The Employment of Disabled People in the Public Sector: A Review of Data and Literature* (London: Disability Rights Commission).

HM Treasury (2010) Budget statement by the Chancellor of the Exchequer, the Rt. Hon. George Osborne MP, 22 June.

Hogelund, J. (2003) *In Search of Effective Disability Policy: Comparing the Developments and Outcomes of Dutch and Danish Disability Policies* (Amsterdam: Amsterdam University Press).

Humphries, S. and Gordon, P. (1992) *Out of Sight: The Experience of Disability 1900–1950* (Plymouth: Northcote House).

Hyde, M. (1996) 'Fifty Years of Failure: Employment Services for Disabled People in the UK', *Work, Employment and Society* 10(4): 683–700.

Hyde, M. (2000) 'From Welfare to Work? Social Policy for Disabled People of Working Age in the United Kingdom in the 1990s', *Disability & Society* 15(2): 327–41.

Ingstad, B. and Reynolds-Whyte, S., eds, (1995) *Disability and Culture* (Berkeley, CA: University of California Press).

International Labour Organization (2007) *The Employment Situation of Disabled People: Towards Improved Statistical Information* (Geneva: ILO).

Knapp, M., Perkins, M., Beecham, J., Kumar Dhanasiri, S., Rustin, C. and King, D. (2008) 'Transition Pathways for Young People with Complex Disabilities: Exploring the Economic Consequences', *Child: Care, Health and Development* 34(5): 512–20.

Landes, D. (2003) *The Unbound Prometheus: Technological Change and Industrial Development in Western Europe from 1750 to Present* (Cambridge: Cambridge University Press).

Lawson, A. (2007) *Disability and Equality Law in Britain* (Oxford: Hart Publishing).

Lonsdale, S. (1980) *Work and Inequality* (London: Longman).

Lunt, N. (2005) 'Disability and Employment: Global and National Policy Influences in New Zealand, Canada and Australia', in A. Roulstone and C. Barnes, eds, *Working Futures? Disabled People, Policy and Social Inclusion* (Bristol: Policy Press): pp. 165–74.

Marin, B., Prinz, C. and Queisser, M., eds, (2004) *Transforming Disability Welfare Policies* (Aldershot: Ashgate).

Mete, C., ed., (2008) *Economic Implications of Chronic Illness and Disability in Eastern Europe and Former Soviet Union* (Washington, DC: The World Bank).

Mitra, S. and Sambamoorthi, U. (2006) 'Unemployment of Persons with Disabilities: Evidence from a National Sample Survey', *Economic and Political Weekly* 41(3): 199–203.

Mont, D. (2004) *Disability Employment Policy*. Discussion Paper 412 (Washington, DC: The World Bank).

Morris, A. and Butler, A. (1972) *No Feet to Drag: Report on the Disabled* (London: Sidgewick and Jackson).

Morris, J. (1994) *Independent Lives, Community Care and Disabled People* (London: Macmillan).

OECD (2003) *Transforming Disability into Ability* (Paris: OECD).

O'Toole, B. and Maison-Hills, G. (1994) 'Community-based Rehabilitation and Development', *Development in Practice* 4(1): 23–34.

Parsons, T. (1951) *The Social System* (London: Routledge and Kegan Paul).

Philip, A. and Velche, D. (2010) 'Formation et Insertion Professionelle', *La Nouvelle Revue de L'adaptation et de la Scolarisation* 48(4). Special edition on young disabled people and the labour market in the EU and Canada.

Prideaux, S. and Roulstone, A. (2011) *Understanding Disability Policy* (Bristol: Policy Press).

Prideaux, S., Roulstone, A., Harris, J. and Barnes, C. (2009) 'Disabled People and Self Directed Support Schemes: Re-Conceptualising Work and Welfare in the 21st Century', *Disability & Society* Special Edition 24(5): 557–69.

Rigg, J. (2005) *Labour Market Disadvantage Amongst Disabled People: A Longitudinal Perspective*. Case paper 103 (London: LSE).

Roulstone, A. (2002) 'Disabling Pasts, Enabling Futures: How Does the Changing Nature of Capitalism Impact on the Disabled Worker and Jobseeker?' *Disability & Society* 17(6): 627–42.

Roulstone, A. (forthcoming) 'Disabled Managers and the Glass Partition Effect', *Equal Opportunities International*.

Roulstone, A. and Barnes, C. (2005) *Working Futures: Disabled People and Social Inclusion* (Bristol: Policy Press).

Roulstone, A., Gradwell, L., Price, J. and Child, L. (2003) *Thriving and Surviving at Work: Disabled Peoples' Employment Strategies* (Bristol: Policy Press).

Ryan, J. and Thomas, F. (1980) *Politics of Mental Handicap* (New York: Free Association Books).

Ryan, M. K., and Haslam, S. A. (2005) 'The Glass Cliff: Evidence that Women are Over-represented in Precarious Leadership Positions', *British Journal of Management* 16(2): 81–90.

Scherer, P. (2004) 'The OECD Perspective on Mutual Obligations', in B. Marin, C. Prinz and M. Queisser, eds, (2004) *Transforming Disability Welfare Policies* (Aldershot: Ashgate).

Sena-Martins, B. (2010) 'Blindness in Mozambique: Cultural Experiences of Disability'. *Paper presented at Lancaster Disability Studies Conference*, September; abstract available online at http://www.lancs.ac.uk/fass/events/disabilityconference_archive/2010/documents/Book%20of%20Abstracts%20260710.pdf (accessed 21 September 2011).

Shlapentokh, V. (1988) 'The Stakhanovite Movement: Changing Perceptions over Fifty Years', *Journal of Contemporary History* 23(2): 259–76.

Stone, D. (1984) *The Disabled State* (Philadelphia: Temple University Press).

Taylor, F. W. (1910) *The Principles of Scientific Management* (New York: Harper and Row).

Thompson, E. P. (1967) 'Time, Work Discipline and Industrial Capitalism', *Past & Present* 38(1): 56–97.

UNICEF (2006) *Monitoring the Rights of Mentally Disabled Children and Young People in Public Institutions. Report of Monitoring Project 2005–2006* (New York: UNICEF).

United States Equal Employment Opportunities Commission (2002) *Enforcement Guidance: Reasonable Accommodation and Undue Hardship Under the Americans with Disabilities Act* (Washington, DC: USEEOC).

Walker, A. (1981) *Unqualified and Underemployed: Handicapped Young People and the Labour Market* (London: Macmillan).

West, J., ed., (1996) *Implementing the Americans with Disabilities Act* (Massachusetts: Blackwell).

Wilson-Kovacs, D., Ryan, M., Alexander-Haslam, D. and Rabanovich, A. (2008) '"Just Because You Can Get a Wheelchair in the Building Doesn't Necessarily Mean that You Can Still Participate": Barriers to the Career Advancement of Disabled Professionals', *Disability & Society* 23(7): 705–17.

Wise Group (2009) *Wise Group Response to Work and Pensions Committee Inquiry into Management and Administration of Contracted Employment Programmes* (London: Wise Group).

World Health Organization (2011) *World Report on Disability and Rehabilitation* (Geneva: WHO).

Yeo, R. and Moore, K. (2003) 'Including Disabled People in Poverty Reduction Work: Nothing About Us Without Us', *World Development* 31(3): 571–90.

Zadek, C. and Scott-Parker, S. (2003) *Unlocking Potential: The New Disability Business Case* (London: Employers' Forum on Disability).

Zola, K. E. (1982) *Missing Pieces: A Chronicle of Living with a Disability* (Philadelphia: Temple University).

17

DISABILITY STUDIES, INCLUSIVE EDUCATION AND EXCLUSION

Michele Moore and Roger Slee

The worst of times

Many will be familiar with the opening sentence of Charles Dickens's novel, *A Tale of Two Cities*:

> It was the best of times, it was the worst of times, it was the age of wisdom, it was the age of foolishness, it was the epoch of belief, it was the epoch of incredulity, it was the season of Light, it was the season of Darkness, it was the spring of hope, it was the winter of despair, we had everything before us, we had nothing before us, we were all going direct to Heaven, we were all going direct the other way – in short, the period was so far like the present period, that some of its noisiest authorities insisted on its being received, for good or for evil, in the superlative degree of comparison only.
>
> *(Dickens 2007)*

Perhaps Dickens's comparison of the London and Paris of 1775 with his own world in the middle of the nineteenth century holds. However, from the present vantage point of marginalized and disadvantaged people in England, and beyond, the vista sheds little light, offers no wellspring of hope. As we reflect on the vulnerability of disabled children and their families in an age of inclusive education, we observe the simultaneous advance of national human rights legislation and international conventions on the rights of disabled people and the systematic growth of exclusion under the liberal veneer of inclusion discourse.

In England, the unfolding of a number of factors intensifies our concern about encroaching exclusion. First was the backlash against inclusive education invited by the pronouncement by Baroness Warnock in 2005, in her pamphlet written for the Philosophy of Education Society of Great Britain (Warnock 2005), that inclusion was a disastrous legacy of her celebrated, yet essentially conservative,[1] *Special Educational Needs* report (Warnock 1978). Second was a declaration by then leader of the Conservative Party opposition David Cameron of the importance of the provision of a range of educational options to entitle parents of disabled children choice. As a parent of a disabled boy his argument was compelling and seldom deconstructed in its reportage. Third was the fact that although the Labour Party government had endorsed the United Nations Convention on the Rights of Persons with Disabilities and the Optional Protocol, it lodged its reservation on Article 24 concerning the education of people with disabilities. Fourth is the rapid withdrawal of the state signified by the Conservative/Liberal Democrat coalition government from the protection of public education. The dismantling of the welfare state sets a devastating backdrop for disabled people.

> Before it announced the results of its Public Spending Review, the coalition govern-ment insisted that disabled people had no reason to fear cuts to the welfare system. But disability organisations have said that the cuts to benefits and local authority spending risk pushing disabled people further into poverty.
>
> *(Peck 2011: 1)*

Richard Hawkes, the chief executive of Scope, a disabled people's advocacy organization, directs attention to the proposed cessation of the mobility allowance for people living in residential care:

> This assault on the most vulnerable is characterised by the callous removal of the mobility component of Disability Living Allowance (DLA) for people living in residential care, which will simply increase dependency and mean many people will literally become prisoners in their own homes.
>
> *(Peck 2011: 1)*

These factors are recent events that impact on English education policy. They must be added to the extant context of exclusion in order to explain the foundations of our concerns and our call for different approaches to what has been offered as inclusive education. At the centre of our call is a requirement for disability studies in education as a foundation for constructing inclusive schooling.

In this chapter we will:

- explore the foundations of educational exclusion and consider emerging patterns of exclusion; and
- establish the case for disability studies in education as a strategy pursuant to inclusive education.

Special education and the progress of collective indifference

In a gesture of exasperation Slee (2010) offered the notion of *the irregular school* as a counterpoint to debates about whether disabled students should be educated in the segregated special school or the neighbourhood regular school. As Danforth (2009) reminds us, these debates seldom acknowl-edge the symbolic complexity of the questions concealed within seemingly self-evident proposi-tions. Benevolent humanitarianism (Tomlinson 1982) is expressed as the special needs of students with impairments who are at risk in the regular school. In order to do our best for these 'needy' children a choice from a range of special schools, units, centres and classrooms is reaffirmed (Farrell 2006). Segregated special schooling, together with the range of so-called choices for the place-ment of disabled children, is a symbol of both the intransigence of the fortressed regular school and a measure of the simultaneous professional interest and disinterest in children who are a risk to a school's performance on national examination results-driven league tables. Let us explain this proposition. First, there is an intensification of a long-standing anxiety about the way in which students with poor academic prognoses represent a threat to the rating and ranking of schools (Slee 1998; Gillborn and Youdell 2000; Ball 2008). Responding to the challenge of improving results, schools have looked at ways of jettisoning difficult and hard-to-teach children. Second, and conveniently, there has been a steady expansion of categories of diagnosis of childhood disorders and impairments and a corresponding increase in professional interventions (Graham and Sweller 2010; Underwood 2008).

Collective indifference

Richard Sennett published his 2004 Castle Lecture series at Yale University in a book entitled *The Culture of New Capitalism* (Sennett 2006). Sennett (2006) depicts a modern social imaginary (Taylor 2004) of competitive individualism where community is fractured, as towns resemble commuter hubs. It is a world where people, living under a spectre of uselessness, scramble to adapt – a world where the craftsman is expendable, where the fragmentation of the short term is prized over vocational fidelity. New geographies of injustice emerge (Harvey 1996; Sibley 1995) and the fault lines of poverty and prejudice are etched deeper (Kozol 1991, 2005).

Detachment drives the neo-liberal ethic. Kevin McDonald (2006) observes the replacement of solidarity with fluidarity. Zygmunt Bauman (2004), in his book *Wasted Lives*, traces the production of the despised flawed consumer. These people are the collateral damage of the competition state (Jessop 2002; Cerny 1990). This wastage of people is described in a benignly impersonal language. The 'currency crisis', 'the terms of trade', 'a market adjustment', 'the downsizing or rightsizing' cast aside increasing numbers of redundant people. Competition increases and neighbours turn on each other. Most feared is the stranger, the alien, and the person who is different, for they represent a threat in a contracting labour market. Paradoxically, the liberal discourse of multiculturalism, diversity and inclusion struggles to conceal our growing *mixaphobia* (Bauman 2004).

Against this backdrop grows our condition of collective indifference (Slee 2010). We feel encouraged and able to turn away from the other. The hand of cooperative interdependence is extended to our equals and most particularly to those who may contribute to our trajectory of success. How this condition of collective indifference emerged and is sustained is complex and has expended rivers of ink. Let us point to two factors relevant to this discussion. First, bestowed understandings; second, professional knowledge and interest (Slee 2010).

Bestowed understandings

Bestowed understandings build oppressive epistemologies that disable. How do we come to understand disability? Stiker (1999) provides a meticulous history of disability and the development of powerful and oppressive forms of knowledge of disability. Knowledge is formed through the building blocks of expert discoveries and explanatory frames – typically medical – religious pronouncements, cultural representations and cultural bricolage. Nursery rhymes make way for novels, plays, films, television and art to build a composite knowledge. This knowledge is mediated by and may augment expert statements and personal biography. Accordingly we can see the collision and fusion of different perspectives of disability as catalogued by scholars and activists such as Michael Oliver (1990, 2009), Colin Barnes *et al.* (2002), Carol Thomas (1999), Tom Shakespeare (2006) and Tanya Titchkosky (2003). It is important to identify the hierarchies of knowledge and the subjugation of disabled people's contribution to building official accounts and popular understandings of disability. These different perspectives or disability discourses may be summarized as shown in Table 17.1.

While it may be tempting to assign these discourses to a historical chronology, linear representations are misleading. Notwithstanding our liberal sensibilities, observations of contemporary society across the globe readily reveal each of these ways of thinking about and representing disability. In this way we can observe policy contradictions where inclusive education is supposedly advanced through the practice of segregation.

Table 17.1 Summation of disability discourses

Disability discourse	Explanation	Responses
Fear and loathing	Disability is seen as an abhorrent defect. Impairments are often explained in religious terms, as God's punishment for the sins of the parents. Disabled people are accordingly characterized as representing danger.	Genocide. Eugenics. Institutionalization. Segregation. Ridicule. Ignorance. Isolation and hiding.
Pity and charity	Disability is perceived as a personal tragedy and disabled people are seen as being in need of charity.	Institutionalization. Begging as an acceptable social role. Expectation of individual heroism to overcome impairments. Segregated schooling. Sheltered workshops. Shame.
Medical	Disability is seen as a consequence of defective or disordered individual pathology. This results from genetic disorder, accident or disease.	There is a requirement for expert diagnosis, intervention and treatment with a view to cure, rehabilitation or normalization.
Rights	Disability is a measure of the barriers generated from the social response. In other words, disability is the burden people must carry, the barriers they will encounter because of society's inability to deal with difference. This is the social model of disability (Oliver 1990).	Changes to architectural, legislative, political, economic, social and cultural structures and relations of society in order to enable people to assume their rights of citizenship and participation.

In their analysis of global education policies Rizvi and Lingard (2009) draw on the political scientist David Easton to lay the foundations of public policy. 'The essence of policy', argues Easton (1953: 129–30), 'lies in the fact that through it certain things are denied to some people and made accessible to others. Policy … consists of a web of decisions that allocates values.' Education policy follows the neo-liberal moral compass. Competitive individualism is both ethos and practice. This ethic is manifest in current education policy practices (we deliberately do not call them educational practices). The imposition of a national curriculum that embraces particular cultural, class and gender values excludes many of the students destined to experience it. These students are at an immediate disadvantage. Overlay this curriculum with a series of high stakes tests that have serious flaws as instruments of assessment (Stobart 2008) and which obstruct our thinking about using assessment for learning (Wiliam *et al.* 2004) and we erect more barriers to students' participation in schooling. On top of this comes a rigid system of inspection that undermines the professional decision-making of teachers. Publishing league tables that rank schools on the basis of students' performance in GCSE examinations intensifies schools as sites of performativity (Ball 2008) and failure. In this climate there is increased latitude for student disengagement and teachers' professional alienation.

Caught within these policy strictures schools become apprehensive about those students who may lower their rankings. As we have already noted, Gillborn and Youdell (2000) describe the way in which schools practise a form of educational triage as they determine which students could be pulled through and those who aren't worth the effort. In Australia, Bob Lingard (2011) observes schools asking students to stay away from school when the national tests in literacy and numeracy in Years 3, 5, 7 and 9 take place.[2] The availability of an expanding range of categories of special educational needs and the availability of special classes and units inside and outside of school becomes highly seductive for schools looking to improve their academic profile. In this way, policy enables and disables; it allocates those who have value and those who are invalids.

Professional knowledge and interest

Nikolas Rose returns to Foucault's (1973) *Birth of the Clinic* to suggest that:

> the epistemological, ontological, and technical reshaping of medical perception at the start of the nineteenth century came about through the interconnections of changes along a series of dimensions, some of which seem, at first sight, rather distant from medicine.
>
> *(Rose 2007: 9)*

To understand the biopolitics of the twenty-first century Rose employs a number of lines of inquiry. He traces the movement of medical focus to the molecular level and with it the amalgam of disparate disciplines including computational engineering, mathematics, systems biology and pharmaceutical engineering. This new focus on the genome project has valorized 'technologies for optimisation'. People are reduced to their molecular elements, to their genetic predisposition. Accordingly we advance technology to intervene in what were once considered the natural patterns of life. Decisions are made about the optimums of health which themselves have significant impact upon a new ethics. Decisions about the value of life forms and population characteristics have shaped a new ethics and the formation of consumer eugenics (Rose 2001).

In an era of new somatic knowledge and tastes we have become health consumers and regulators. This is particularly interesting in the subjective area of behaviour and mental health. Norms are established globally through contestable (Kutchins and Kirk 1997) diagnostic manuals such as the one published by the American Psychiatric Association (2000). There exists a union of interest around the discovery, diagnosis and treatment of behavioural disorders. A new political economy of behaviour is apparent where large and powerful health identity lobby groups such as CHADD (Children and Adults with Attention Deficit/Hyperactivity Disorder) in America coalesce with the medical fraternity, the pharmaceutical industry and education organizations to effectively lobby for a rapidly and unevenly growing group of children who are hard to manage in schools (Slee 1994, 2010).

Our point here is not to deny the existence of attention deficit disorder. We do not have the evidence to make such a judgement. The concern we have, based on the rapid escalation of diagnosis, conflicting expert opinion about the science of attention deficit hyperactivity disorder (Rose 2005) and highly disproportionate incidence (Graham 2010), is that more children are at risk of being categorized as having special educational needs and experiencing an attenuated experience of schooling. Where students are seen as the bearers of results, the temptation for classroom teachers to refer children out becomes irresistible. The abundance of experts and special educators convinces teachers that certain children are not theirs to teach. Or if they are to stay in the classroom, their presence is conditional on the provision of a minder or teacher aide who all too often becomes the de facto teacher (Rutherford, in press).

In this climate the condition of collective indifference flourishes. The racialization of special educational needs is an enduring feature of the educational landscape where in England we witness a disproportionate consignment of Caribbean boys to special education (Tomlinson 1981; Gillborn 2008). In America this finds its parallel in the overrepresentation and underrepresentation of African American and Latino students in special education (Parrish 2002; Ferri and Connor 2006).

Education reform and disability studies in education

In the space of this short chapter it is not possible to provide a comprehensive blueprint for reform. Any attempt would be memorable for its reductive conceit. Instead what we offer is a general acknowledgement of the requirement for a fundamental reform to schooling if it is going to move beyond the rhetoric of inclusion. We affirm a commitment to the neighbourhood school as the site of education for all children in the neighbourhood. Building community based on the representation of its rich diversity should be more than an exercise in absorption of assimilation (Bernstein 1996). The educational mission of schooling should incorporate an apprenticeship in democracy (Knight 1985; Touraine 2000). Slee (2010: chapter 9) considers elements and tasks for the education reform project. Rather than restate that work, let us consider the place of disability studies in education in the general reform agenda.

Faced with the rising clamour for teacher education programmes to train teachers knowledgeable about inclusive education, the usual strategy adopted by faculties of education internationally was to charge special educators with this responsibility. The result has been an impossible union of different epistemologies in courses that are often called special and inclusive education. These courses tend to escort trainee teachers through a programme that contains the following elements:

- an introduction to the concepts of special and inclusive education;
- a history of special and inclusive education with attention to legislation and its implications for schools and teachers;
- instruction in the recognition of students with special educational needs and in testing for special needs;
- instruction in categories of special educational needs – sensory impairments; behavioural differences (including mental illness); physical impairments; intellectual impairments (still referred to as retardation in some programmes);
- an introduction to differentiated curricula and instruction in inclusive classrooms;
- understanding protocols, including the development of individual education plans and cross-agency work.

This is an indicative description and may be incomplete.

Such courses are not an adequate introduction to inclusive education for a number of reasons. These include, but are not limited to:

The reductive reflex – Inclusive education has become default vocabulary for 'special education needs' (Slee 1996, 2010). Social and educational exclusion is ubiquitous, affecting more than just disabled people. Exclusion proceeds through the intersection of a number of social phenomena and unequal power relations. Building teachers' understanding of exclusion and inclusion requires them to engage with the political economy of education and to understand the intersections between curriculum, pedagogy, assessment and school organization and diverse student identities. For so long as inclusive education is reduced to special education needs, disabled people will be seen as a problem to be fixed.

Irreconcilable epistemologies – Conveying traditional special education theory and practice within an inclusive discourse is flawed and soon unravels. Based upon notions of defectology, special education presents a pastiche of medical, psychological and rehabilitation traditions, understandings and practices. Where attempts are made at holistic analysis based on, for example, Bronfenbrenner's (2005) ecological theory (Cooper 2008), the dominant discourse represents medical utilitarianism.

Failure to address institutional causes of exclusion – Embracing the importance of institutional equilibrium, insufficient scrutiny is applied to policy frameworks, the structure of power or the implications of a social model of disability for schooling. The voices of disabled people are seldom enlisted in the production of theories and practices of inclusive education (Barton 2003; Moore 2000, 2010; Oliver 2009).

The incorporation of inclusive education in teacher education programmes demands a more considered approach. Two features are essential. First is the saturation of the whole programme with considerations of exclusion and inclusion so that inclusive education is a part of the orientation of teacher knowledge, skills and dispositions. This requirement assumes that teacher students will engage with critical race theory, gender studies and critical pedagogy to enable them to understand the formation of barriers to access, participation and success in education. Second is a requirement for the development of an understanding and critical application of disability studies in education.

Disability studies in education and the development of inclusive educational epistemologies, skills and dispositions

It is not our intention to rehearse a history of disability from a disability studies perspective. Such studies are readily available elsewhere, most notably in the work of scholars such as Stiker (1999), Potts and Fido (1991), Foucault (1965), Mitchell and Snyder (1997) and Bogdan (1988). Instead we will demonstrate the ways in which the fledgling field of disability studies in education supports the ethical project of inclusive education (Allan 2005).

The American Education Research Association's Special Interest Group (SIG) in Disability Studies in Education states its purpose and mission:

> The mission of the Disability Studies in Education SIG is to promote the understanding of disability from a social model perspective drawing on social, cultural, historical, discursive, philosophical, literary, aesthetic, artistic, and other traditions to challenge medical, scientific, and psychological models of disability as they relate to education.
>
> *(American Education Research Association 2011)*

This is indeed an ambitious agenda as the hegemony of traditional special education is manifest in teacher education and in policy-making. This is made more complex by the recent adoption by special education of a more liberal discourse of inclusion. This process has been observed over the years by a number of researchers (Slee 1993; Brantlinger 2006). Brantlinger (2004) surveys the way in which the large glossy college textbooks for students of special education have been updated with the addition of a chapter on inclusive education. Some even opt for oxymoronic titles such as special and inclusive education.

Notwithstanding this liberal turn, the deep epistemological antimony occasionally erupts, sometimes descending into vitriolic debate. In 1995 Kauffman and Hallahan's book, *The Illusion of Full Inclusion: A Comprehensive Critique of a Current Special Education Bandwagon*, was published. The book comprised a number of essays by prominent traditional special educators who argued that the bandwagon of inclusive education detracted from the achievement of special education research and practice. The claims of inclusive education couldn't be registered as research as they proceeded from an ideological position, namely full inclusion. By implication, research only counted as such if it embraced the positivist tradition of experimental design, replicating the laboratory work pursued in the so-called 'natural' or 'hard' sciences.

In response, Ellen Brantlinger (1997) published a paper in the American Education Research Association's journal, *Review of Educational Research*, that examined the claims collectively issued by Kauffman and Hallahan and their colleagues. First she examined claims that we can work in an ideological vacuum. This proposition has been repeatedly discarded as, at best, naïve or more typically mischievous. In an interview conducted by Julie Allan and Roger Slee (Allan and Slee 2008) with Dave Gillborn and Deborah Youdell the latter declared that for some researchers 'ideology was like sweat; you smell everybody else's, but not your own'. Foucault calls for circumspection in considering ideology, and as Zizek (1994: 4) puts it: 'When some procedure is denounced as "ideological par excellence" one can be assured that its inversion is no less ideological.'

Anti-racist education researchers like Barry Troyna have also encountered this struggle over the presence of ideology in research. Troyna (1995) took up the challenge from his detractors who denounced his notion of 'partisan research' as an oxymoron. Racism, he argued, had tended to 'be refracted through the lens of educational research' and that critical social research, in applying transparency and tests of scholarship, presented a form of integrity not apparent in the work of the so-called methodological purists.

Brantlinger's 'Using Ideology' paper is particularly instructive for researchers as she then went on to apply a forensic twist to her critique. Brantlinger considered 18 key works of traditional special educators in their critiques of inclusive education against Mick Dunkin's (1996) analysis of types of errors in synthesizing research in education. The errors Dunkin refers to include:

- the exclusion of relevant literature;
- unexplained selectivity of sources;
- lack of discrimination between sources;
- wrongly reporting details;
- erroneously summarizing positions;
- suppressing contrary findings;
- stating unwarranted conclusions and generalizations;
- non-recognition of faulty author conclusions;
- consequential errors;
- failure to marshal all evidence relevant to a generalization.

The consequences of such errors are serious, observes Dunkin (1996: 87). Syntheses of research found in systematic literature reviews are influential in regard to subsequent research, policy and practice. According to Brantlinger, the risk is intensified by the seniority or prominence of the authors she identifies in their field. Her analysis of the 18 documents is presented in a series of tables that reveal the failures of the authors to adhere to their own minimum expectations for scientific research.

Brantlinger's paper should not be read or dismissed as a methodological challenge to the dominance of empiricism and experimental design in traditional special education research. While she does recognize and advocate the incorporation of post-positivism in research, the paper progresses a political struggle about the purpose and form of schooling. In particular, it lays bare a deeply political struggle between the opposing views of disability and segregated education. For paradoxically the new inclusive discourse of special education still advocates for choice of segregation and a 'cascade' of provision down, from which children tumble to the margins of educational academic and social life.

There was no direct response from traditional special education to Brantlinger's paper. Perhaps this was a result of her rigour. However, antagonism smouldered and later combusted in the conservative special education journal *Exceptionality* in 2006. Herein Kauffman and Sasso (2006) attacked the 'intellectually bankrupt' 'postmodern fashionable nonsense' of Gallagher (2004, 2006) and Biklen and Cardinal (1997).

In some respects debates over methodological purity and ideology deflect from the essential epistemological fissure between traditional special education and disability studies in education. The former is founded upon understanding as a reflection of defective individual pathology. The response to such an assumption is that the task of the special educator is to diagnose the nature and severity of the pathological defect and then, armed with that knowledge, devise special interventions, placements and programmes for that child with special education needs.

Disability studies in education takes a different view. Following Barton (1988), 'special education need' is seen as a euphemism for the inability or unwillingness of schools to educate all children. Disability is contingent on the response to impairment or difference. The challenge for disability studies in education is that of identifying and removing barriers to educational access, participation and success. Such work recognizes schooling as a site for the 'politics of disablement' (Oliver 1990). Axiomatically, schooling holds the potential to be a theatre for enablement.

It is important to acknowledge that disability studies in education, though a relatively recent arrival to the education research arena, has a long intellectual lineage. Gabel (2005: 2) credits the Union of the Physically Impaired Against Segregation, Vic Finkelstein and other disability activists for the 'social model of disability'. More importantly she reminds us that Finkelstein had preferred his original usage of the term 'social interpretation' of disability. Interpretation allows for historical-materialist analysis of the power relations that construct disability as is at the heart of the first generation of disability studies scholars. Equally it allows us to recognize the intersections of other social phenomena that form the constellation of relationships of disablement and enablement. In this agency the individual experience of impairment and disability may be brought into the analytic frame. Moreover, a range of analytic traditions assists in building a more nuanced understanding of the messy reality of disability politics.

In this respect the field of disability studies is transdisciplinary and exhibits contesting and difficult debates about understanding disability. This is reflected in the positions struck in, for example, Tom Shakespeare's *Disability Rights and Wrongs* (2006) on the one hand, and Mike Oliver's second edition of *Understanding Disability* (2009) on the other. Post-structural theory, post-modernism, gender studies, post-colonial theory, actor network theory, critical discourse analysis, critical race theory and queer theory are among a range of analytic paradigms that are brought to disability studies in education.

Most particularly disability studies establishes a platform for the voices of disabled researchers and activists in recognition of the history of the subjugation of their voice, and as a necessary step in changing the political relations of research (Oliver 1992; Barton 2003). Martha Nussbaum (2004) stresses the urgent need for social analysis by disabled people. She observes that through the increasing publication of scholarship of disabled people about their social situation, 'it is possible to take measure of the isolation and marginalisation imposed upon them, and the extent of their routine humiliations' (Nussbaum 2004: 305). In education Moore (2000, 2010), Barton (2003) and Tregaskis (2004) urge for insider perspective in the construction both of analyses of exclusion and developing inclusive education initiatives.

Disability studies in education: lessons for inclusive education

Compiling a list of lessons for inclusive education that we could draw from disability studies in education would exceed the limits of this chapter. We will commence the discussion under three organizing themes:

- establishing authenticity;
- educating teachers; and
- building community.

Establishing authenticity

As we have noted the term inclusive education has been appropriated by special education. Inclusive education has become a casualty to a form of 'eduspeak' characterized by reductionism and disconnection and devoid of its original political intent. Reference to an essay by Edward Said (2000) called *Travelling Theory Reconsidered*, from his collection of essays published under the title of *Reflections on Exile and Other Literary and Cultural Essays*, illustrates our point. Said (2000: 426) discusses the way in which 'theories sometimes "travel" to other times and situations, in the process of which they lose some of their original power and rebelliousness'. He draws upon Georg Lukacs's theory of reification to make his point. Originally reification was a powerful critique of hegemonic discursive instruments of oppression. At the time of writing, Lukacs delivered a set of conceptual tools for better understanding historically specific sets of social relations as a lever for political agency. Said's argument is clearest in his own words:

> the first time a human experience is recorded and then given a theoretical formulation, its force comes from being directly connected to and organically provoked by real historical circumstances. Later versions of the theory cannot replicate its original power; because the situation has quieted down and changed, the theory is degraded and subdued, made into a relatively tame academic substitute for the real thing, whose purpose in the work I analyzed was political change.
>
> *(Said 2000: 436)*

Said follows the pathway of the theory of reification:

> The point I made about all this was that when they were picked up by late European students and readers of Lukacs (Lucien Goldmann in Paris, Raymond Williams in Cambridge), the ideas of this theory had shed their insurrectionary force, had been tamed and domesticated.
>
> *(Said 2000: 437)*

Stretched to adhere to changed political circumstances, the newfound elasticity subverted the original intent. Add to this the fact that as theories such as reification are 'picked up' and popularized, inside and outside the academy, they attract respectability and prestige. Subsequently there arises the clamour for orthodoxy and dogma is established.

Where established epistemological authority and professional interest are at play little wonder that this kind of appropriation occurs. Paul Gilroy reflects on the resilience of *raciology* despite its scientific refutation through the discovery of DNA.

> Raciology has saturated the discourses in which it circulates. It cannot be readily resignified or de-signified, and to imagine that its dangerous meanings can be easily re-articulated into benign, democratic forms would be to exaggerate the power of critical and oppositional interests.
>
> *(Gilroy 2000: 12)*

Our argument is that following the establishment of disability discrimination legislation across a range of nation states, the ratification of international conventions on the rights of children and persons with disabilities and the saturation of inclusive education discourse through international organizations such as the Organisation for Economic Co-operation and Development (OECD), the United Nations Educational, Scientific and Cultural Organization (UNESCO), UNICEF and The World Bank, there has been a rush to apply the rhetoric of inclusive education. Sadly the practice that it describes is often less than inclusive. Moreover, as Gilroy counsels, dismantling the epistemology of special education demands more than linguistic revisions. Powerful interests are at stake and change will be difficult. Disability studies in education teaches us to be vigilant. It invites us to distinguish between experts and expertise as we seek a correction to unequal power relations. More specifically we must continually strive to ensure that inclusive education reforms provide a platform for disabled people and their advocates to exert their leadership in changing educational structures, practices and cultures.

Educating teachers

Jurisdictions around the world have responded to disability discrimination legislation by mandating that pre-service teacher education and continuing professional development of qualified teachers equip teachers to provide an inclusive education. Universities and teachers' colleges around the world have responded positively to this request. Most often this has translated into the passing of the responsibility for inclusive education to departments of special education. These special education departments then seek accreditation for new modules or courses in 'inclusive and special needs education'. Many of these courses are framed according to the sequence of revised glossy special education textbooks (Brantlinger 2004). Accordingly student teachers, together with experienced teachers, are given a series of classes that acquaint attendees with a range of different student pathologies that reflect physical, intellectual and sensory impairments, syndromes and disorders. Courses also include introductions to the ever-growing 'spectrum' of behavioural, emotional and attention disorders. There is also the need for teachers to learn about the symptoms and aetiology of specific learning difficulties. Additionally such programmes will provide students with a chronology of the development of special education needs policies.

Less frequently are students invited to think of inclusive education as a political response to the problem of exclusion, or of the many and changing forms of exclusion. Were this the case, courses would need to interrogate the complex relationships between schooling and failure and the overlapping intersections of race, language, poverty, gender, sexuality, ethnicity, disability and schooling. Such courses would need to dissect the assumptions behind and the effects of pedagogies, forms of assessment, curriculum choices, the physical environment of schools, the structure of the workforce, the culture of schools and so the list proceeds.

Rarely are teachers offered disability studies in education as a means for critically engaging with dominant and oppressive epistemologies or for encountering the voices of disabled researchers and their allies. The need for this is obvious to us, but simply not on the radars for others. Suzanne Carrington and her colleagues have approached this through the development of a core Service Teaching programme (Carrington and Saggers 2008). Within this programme students engage with socio-cultural theories to understand diversity through the interrogation of readings and their own journals as they work in a variety of community settings. In New Zealand the Inclusive Education Alliance has brought teacher educators together with teachers, parents, disabled people and advocates to consider what reforms are required to enhance teachers' knowledge, skills and dispositions pursuant to inclusive schooling.

At the core of our call for radical approaches to teacher education is the premise that teaching is a political activity. Teachers are instrumental in the determination of social futures. As Ball (2008) and Apple (2006) remind us, teachers operate within policy frameworks and their agency is structurally constrained. There remains the possibility for finding spaces for change (Jordan and Goodey 2002; Slee 2010). Making this possible assumes an education in critical thinking rather than just instrumental training.

Building community

We have suggested that schools have embraced a neo-liberal ethic of competitive individualism. This is apparent in high stakes testing programmes (Johnson and Johnson 2006; Stobart 2008), national league tables (Ball 2008) and international indicators and testing programmes such as the OECD's Programme for International Student Assessment (Rizvi and Lingard 2009). Where schools are pitted against each other to demonstrate ever-improving test scores an increasing number of students become vulnerable to failure and rejection by their schools. Parents with the material means to do so become savvy education consumers and set out in search of the best school for their child. Children are on the move; schools often do not reflect the composition of the communities of their geographic location.

Researchers such as Jonathan Kozol (2005) in the United States (US) and Gillborn and Youdell (2000) in the United Kingdom (UK) have reflected upon the racialization of school failure. Kozol (2005) has also noted the way in which schools in the US where the majority of children enrolled are African American (greater than 95 percent) are described as multicultural schools. The growing trend to diagnose children for behavioural disorders and for education authorities to create alternative settings for 'troubling and hard-to-teach children' further fractures community.

Segregated special education has historically narrowed the education of children. Children educated in the neighbourhood school have little understanding of the diverse nature of the world when they emerge. Opportunities are missed to learn new forms of communication, to learn from others and to appreciate that interdependence and cooperation make for stronger social bonds. Moreover, the absence of disability studies in the school curriculum seriously attenuates knowledge, promotes ignorance and poor social relations.

Conclusion

This chapter has argued for disability studies as a necessary step in the authentication of inclusive education. We take as a given that inclusive education is a precondition for an apprenticeship in democracy (Pearl and Knight 1998). In 2000 the French social theorist Alain Touraine posed the question: Can we live together? He suggested that the spirit of a society was reflected through its juridical and education systems. If this is the case, then an examination of the plight of disabled children leads us to surmise that we live in a mean-spirited world. Like Bernstein (1996) before him, Touraine (2000) offers democratic education as the first step in reparation. Understanding disadvantage and oppression demands an education in disability studies and a decoupling of inclusive education from the archaic notion of special education needs (Slee 2010).

Notes

1 When compared with *Integration in Victorian Education* (also known as the Collins Report) (Victorian Ministry of Education 1984), which proceeded from principles of rights, the 1978 *Special Education Needs* report is a more conservative text.
2 For more information on Australia's National Assessment Programme – Literacy and Numeracy (NAPLAN), see http://www.naplan.edu.au (accessed 30 August 2011).

Bibliography

Allan, J. (2005) 'Inclusion as an Ethical Project', in S. Tremain, ed., *Foucault and the Government of Disability* (Ann Arbor: University of Michigan Press): pp. 281–97.

Allan, J. and Slee, R. (2008) *Doing Inclusive Education Research* (Rotterdam: Sense Publishers).

American Education Research Association (2011) Disability Studies in Education Special Interest Group; available online at http://www.aera.net/Default.aspx?menu_id=162&id=1297 (accessed 23 August 2011).

American Psychiatric Association (2000) *Diagnostic and Statistical Manual of Mental Disorders: DSM-IV-TR*, 4th edn (Washington, DC: American Psychiatric Association).

Apple, M. W. (2006) *Educating the 'Right' Way: Markets, Standards, God, and Inequality* (London: Routledge).

Ball, S. (2008) *The Education Debate* (Bristol: Policy Press).

Barnes, C., Oliver, M. and Barton, L. (2002) *Disability Studies Today* (Cambridge: Polity Press in association with Blackwell Publishers).

Barton, L. (1988) *The Politics of Special Educational Needs* (Lewes: Falmer Press).

Barton, L. (2003) *Inclusive Education and Teacher Education: A Basis for Hope or a Discourse of Delusion?* (London: Institute of Education, University of London).

Bauman, Z. (2004) *Wasted Lives: Modernity and its Outcasts* (Oxford: Polity).

Bernstein, B. (1996) *Pedagogy, Symbolic Control and Identity: Theory, Research, Critique* (London: Taylor & Francis).

Biklen, D. and Cardinal, D. N. (1997) *Contested Words, Contested Science: Unraveling the Facilitated Communication Controversy* (New York: Teachers College Press).

Bogdan, R. (1988) *Freak Show: Presenting Human Oddities for Amusement and Profit* (Chicago: University of Chicago Press).

Brantlinger, E. (1997) 'Using Ideology: Cases of Non-recognition of the Politics of Research and Practice in Special Education', *Review of Educational Research* 67(4): 425–59.

Brantlinger, E. (2004) 'Ideologies Discerned, Values Determined: Getting Past the Hierarchies of Special Education', in L. Ware, ed., *Ideology and the Politics of (In)exclusion* (New York: Peter Lang): pp. 11–31.

Brantlinger, E. A. (2006) *Who Benefits from Special Education? Remediating (Fixing) Other People's Children* (New Jersey: Lawrence Erlbaum Associates).

Bronfenbrenner, U. (2005) *Making Human Beings Human: Bioecological Perspectives on Human Development* (Thousand Oaks: Sage Publications).

Carrington, S. and Saggers, B. R. (2008) 'Service-learning Informing the Development of an Inclusive Ethical Framework for Beginning Teachers', *Teaching and Teacher Education* 24(3): 795–806.

Cerny, P. G. (1990) *The Changing Architecture of Politics: Structure, Agency, and the Future of the State* (London: Sage).

Cooper, P. (2008) 'Like Alligators Bobbing for Poodles? A Critical Discussion of Education, ADHD and the Biopsychosocial Perspective', *Journal of Philosophy of Education* 42(3–4): 457–74.

Danforth, S. (2009) *The Incomplete Child: An Intellectual History of Learning Disabilities* (New York: Peter Lang).

Dickens, C. (2007) [1859] *A Tale of Two Cities* (London: Penguin).

Dunkin, M. (1996) 'Types of Errors in Synthesizing Research in Education', *Review of Educational Research* 66(2): 87–97.

Easton, D. (1953) *The Political System, an Inquiry into the State of Political Science* (New York: Knopf).

Farrell, M. (2006) *Celebrating the Special School* (London: Routledge).

Farrell, M. (2008) *Educating Special Children: An Introduction to Provision for Pupils with Disabilities and Disorders* (London: Routledge).

Ferri, B. A. and Connor, D. J. (2006) *Reading Resistance: Discourses of Exclusion in Desegregation and Inclusion Debates* (New York: Peter Lang).

Foucault, M. (1965) *Madness and Civilization: A History of Insanity in the Age of Reason* (New York: Pantheon Books).

Foucault, M. (1973) *The Birth of the Clinic: An Archaeology of Medical Perception* (London: Tavistock Publications).

Gabel, S. L. (2005) *Disability Studies in Education: Readings in Theory and Method* (New York: Peter Lang).

Gallagher, D., ed., (2004) *Challenging Orthodoxy in Special Education: Dissenting Voices* (Denver: Love Publishing).

Gallagher, D. (2006) 'If Not Absolute Objectivity, Then What? A Reply to Kauffman and Sasso', *Exceptionality* 14(2): 91–107.

Gillborn, D. (2008) *Racism and Education: Coincidence or Conspiracy?* (Abingdon: Routledge).

Gillborn, D. and Youdell, D. (2000) *Rationing Education: Policy, Practice, Reform, and Equity* (Buckingham: Open University Press).

Gilroy, P. (2000) *Against Race: Imagining Political Culture Beyond the Color Line* (Cambridge, Mass.: Harvard University Press).

Graham, L., ed., (2010) *(De)constructing ADHD: Critical Guidance for Teachers and Teacher Educators* (New York: Peter Lang).

Graham, L. J. and Sweller, N. (2010) 'The Inclusion Lottery: Who's In and Who's Out? Tracking Inclusion and Exclusion in New South Wales Government Schools', *International Journal of Inclusive Education*.

Harvey, D. (1996) *Justice, Nature, and the Geography of Difference* (Oxford: Blackwell Publishers).

Jessop, B. (2002) *The Future of the Capitalist State* (Oxford: Polity).

Johnson, D. D. and Johnson, B. (2006) *High Stakes: Poverty, Testing, and Failure in American Schools* (Lanham: Rowman & Littlefield Publishers).

Jordan, L. and Goodey, C. (2002) *Human Rights and School Change: The Newham Story* (Bristol: Centre for Studies in Inclusive Education).

Kauffman, J. M. and Hallahan, D. P. (2005) *The Illusion of Full Inclusion: A Comprehensive Critique of a Current Special Education Bandwagon* (Austin, Texas: Pro-Ed).

Kauffman, J. and Sasso, G. (2006) 'Toward Ending Cultural and Cognitive Relativism in Special Education', *Exceptionality* 14(2): 65–90.

Knight, T. (1985) 'An Apprenticeship in Democracy', *The Australian Teacher* 11(1): 5–7.

Kozol, J. (1991) *Savage Inequalities: Children in America's Schools* (New York: Crown Publishers).

Kozol, J. (2005) *The Shame of the Nation: The Restoration of Apartheid Schooling in America* (New York: Crown Publishers).

Kutchins, H. and Kirk, S. A. (1997) *Making Us Crazy. DSM: The Psychiatric Bible and the Creation of Mental Disorders* (New York: Free Press).

McDonald, K. (2006) *Global Movements: Action and Culture* (Oxford: Blackwell).

Mitchell, D. T. and Snyder, S. L. (1997) *The Body and Physical Difference: Discourses of Disability* (Ann Arbor: University of Michigan Press).

Moore, M. (2000) *Insider Perspectives on Inclusion: Raising Voices, Raising Issues* (Sheffield: Philip Armstrong).

Moore, M. (2010) 'Inclusion, Narrative and Voices of Disabled Children in Trinidad and St Lucia', in J. Lavia and M. Moore, eds, *Decolonizing Community Contexts: Cross-cultural Perspectives on Policy and Practice* (London: Routledge).

Nussbaum, M. C. (2004) *Hiding from Humanity. Disgust, Shame and the Law* (Princeton: Princeton University Press).

Oliver, M. (1990) *The Politics of Disablement* (London: Macmillan Education).

Oliver, M. (1992) 'Changing the Social Relations of Research Production?', *Disability, Handicap & Society* 7(2): 101–14.

Oliver, M. (2009) *Understanding Disability: From Theory to Practice* (Basingstoke: Palgrave Macmillan).

Parrish, T. (2002) 'Racial Disparities in the Identification, Funding and Provision of Special Education', in D. Losen and G. Orfield, eds, *Racial Inequality in Special Education* (Cambridge, MA: Harvard Education Press).

Pearl, A. and Knight, T. (1998) *The Democratic Classroom: Theory to Inform Practice* (Cresskill: Hampton Press).

Peck, S. (2011) 'Welfare Cuts Mean Hard Times Ahead', *Disability Now*, available online at http://www.disabilitynow.org.uk/latest-news2/welfare-cuts-mean-hard-times-ahead (accessed 23 August 2011).

Potts, M. and Fido, R. (1991) *'A Fit Person to be Removed': Personal Accounts of Life in a Mental Deficiency Institution* (Plymouth: Northcote House Publishers Ltd).

Rizvi, F. and Lingard, B. (2009) *Globalizing Education Policy* (London: Routledge).

Rose, H. (2001) 'Gendered Genetics in Iceland', *New Genetics and Society* 20(2): 119–138.

Rose, N. (2007) *The Politics of Life Itself. Biomedicine, Power and Subjectivity in the Twenty-first Century* (New Jersey: Princeton University Press).

Rose, S. (2005) *The 21st Century Brain. Explaining, Mending and Manipulating the Mind* (London: Vintage).

Rutherford, G. (in press) 'In, Out, or Somewhere in Between? Disabled Students' and Teacher Aides' Experiences of School', *International Journal of Inclusive Education*.

Said, E. W. (2000) 'Travelling Theory Reconsidered', in E. W. Said, ed., *Reflections on Exile and Other Literary and Cultural Essays* (London: Granta Publications): pp. 436–52.

Sennett, R. (2006) *The Culture of the New Capitalism* (London: Yale University Press).

Shakespeare, T. (2006) *Disability Rights and Wrongs* (London: Routledge).

Sibley, D. (1995) *Geographies of Exclusion: Society and Difference in the West* (London: Routledge).

Slee, R. (1993) 'The Politics of Integration: New Sites for Old Practices?', *Disability, Handicap & Society* 8(4): 351–60.

Slee, R. (1994) *Changing Theories and Practices of Discipline* (London: Falmer Press).

Slee, R. (1996) 'Clauses of Conditionality', in L. Barton, ed., *Disability and Society: Emerging Issues and Insights* (London: Longman).

Slee, R. (1998) 'High Reliability Organisations and Liability Students – the Politics of Recognition', in R. Slee, G. Weiner and S. Tomlinson, eds, *School Effectiveness for Whom?* (London: Falmer Press): 101–14.

Slee, R. (2005) 'Education and the Politics of Recognition: Inclusive Education – An Australian Snapshot', in D. Mitchell, ed., *Contextualizing Inclusive Education* (Abingdon: Routledge): 139–65.

Slee, R. (2010) *The Irregular School: Exclusion, Schooling and Inclusive Education* (London: Routledge).

Stiker, H.-J. (1999) *A History of Disability* (Ann Arbor: University of Michigan Press).

Stobart, G. (2008) *Testing Times: The Uses and Abuses of Assessment* (London: Routledge).

Taylor, C. (2004) *Modern Social Imaginaries* (Durham: Duke University Press).

Thomas, C. (1999) *Female Forms: Experiencing and Understanding Disability* (Buckingham: Open University Press).

Titchkosky, T. (2003) *Disability, Self, and Society* (Toronto: University of Toronto Press).

Tomlinson, S. (1981) *Educational Subnormality: A Study in Decision-making* (London: Routledge and Kegan Paul).

Tomlinson, S. (1982) *A Sociology of Special Education* (London: Routledge and Kegan Paul).

Touraine, A. (2000) *Can We Live Together? Equality and Difference* (Cambridge: Polity Press).

Tregaskis, C. (2004) *Constructions of Disability: Researching the Interface Between Disabled and Non-disabled People* (London: Routledge).

Troyna, B. (1995) 'Beyond Reasonable Doubt? Researching "Race" in Educational Settings', *Oxford Review of Education* 21(4): 395–408.

Underwood, K. (2008) *The Construction of Disability in Our Schools. Teacher and Parent Perspectives on the Experience of Labelled Students* (Rotterdam: Sense Publishers).

Victorian Ministry of Education (1984) *Integration in Victorian Education (The Collins Report)* (Melbourne: Victorian Government Printer).

Warnock, M. (1978) *Special Educational Needs: Report of Enquiry into the Education of Handicapped Children and Young People* (London: Her Majesty's Stationery Office).

Warnock, M. (2005) *Special Educational Needs: A New Look* (Keele: Philosophy of Education Society of Great Britain).

Wiliam, D., Lee, C., Harrison, C. and Black, P. (2004) 'Teachers Developing Assessment for Learning Impact on Student Achievement', *Assessment in Education: Principles, Policy and Practice* 11(1): 49–66.

Zizek, S. (1994) *Mapping Ideology* (London: Verso).

18

INDEPENDENT LIVING

Charlotte Pearson

Introduction

This chapter explores how the philosophy of independent living has emerged over the last 30 years and, in turn, has been reflected in policy for disabled people. As Morris (2005) explains, local and national disability organizations have had some significant successes in promoting independent living, with research conducted using the social model of disability and involving disabled people and their organizations playing a key role in influencing policy development. However, there remains a limited understanding across the political spectrum of what independent living means and what is necessary to achieve it. Discussion in this chapter, therefore, seeks to show how independent living has been represented on the policy agenda. It begins by outlining the development of independent living in the US and its infiltration to encourage a network of independent living services, structures and policy initiatives in the UK. Alongside these changes, the chapter moves on to highlight broader policy through community care, direct payments and other cash payment schemes both in the UK and across North America and Europe. Whilst shifts to cash payment models have undoubtedly improved the choices for and the lives of many disabled people, commentary shows that their position in a service-led and resources-poor system of social care has restricted independent living options for much of the disabled population. The chapter concludes by looking at the prospects for independent living in an era of economic downturn.

Activism and independent living: the emergence of an agenda for change

The term 'independent living' refers to all disabled people having the same choices, control and freedom as any other citizen – at home, at work and as members of the community. As Brisenden (1989: 9) notes, this does not necessarily mean that any practical assistance required should be under the control of disabled individuals but that 'independence is created by having assistance when and how one requires it'. The Independent Living Movement is, therefore, based on four key assumptions:

- that all human life is of value;
- that anyone, whatever their impairment, is capable of exercising choices;

- that people who are disabled by society's reaction to physical, intellectual and sensory impairment and to emotional distress have the right to assert control over their lives; and
- that disabled people have the right to fully participate in society.

(Morris 1993: 21)

The concept of independent living originated in the US in the early 1970s. Then, three disabled students at the University of Berkeley successfully campaigned to employ personal assistants and to live in self-managed accommodation. As a result of this, the students had more direct control over how their support needs were met and were therefore able to participate more fully in university life. The appeal of their experiences led to a marked increase in the number of disabled people in the area seeking this type of support and ultimately triggered the establishment of the first Centre for Independent Living (CIL) in Berkeley, in 1972 (Barnes and Mercer 2006). Drawing on the model of personal assistance support favoured by the students, the CIL's goals were to facilitate the integration of disabled people into the community by providing a comprehensive system of support services (Centre for Independent Living 1982). The success of these services also attracted considerable interest from the UK, and small groups of disabled people in residential care began to ask questions about the type of support they were receiving. Important successes came in areas such as Derbyshire, where disabled activists played a pivotal role in the development of user-controlled services in the UK (Barnes and Mercer 2006). Notably, the Grove Road integrated housing scheme in Sutton-in-Ashfield was conceived and developed by disabled people. It took four years to develop and involved often difficult negotiations with housing associations, the district council, the local authority social services department, architects and planners. As Barnes and Mercer (2006) describe, the Grove Road development was a direct reaction to the dire experiences of institutional living and provided an opportunity for disabled and non-disabled people to live in the community in housing specifically designed to promote inclusion.

Another important development involved disabled people living at the Le Court Cheshire Home in Hampshire. In 1979, 'Project 81: Consumer Directed Housing and Care' was set up with a view to highlight 1981 as the United Nations' International Year of Disabled People (see Barnes and Mercer 2006). Following three years of intensive discussions with the county council and support from key managers, a pioneering system of indirect payments was set up. This allowed the local authority's funding of an individual's institutional 'care' to be paid into a trust fund and used, on behalf of the user, to purchase personal assistance. As discussion later in this chapter shows, this became an important starting point in the campaign for a formal policy of direct payments in the UK.

In the UK, the matter of group control became a defining issue in transforming attitudes towards disability throughout the 1980s (Oliver 2009). This period saw the beginning of a challenge to existing impairment-specific organizations which relied on charitable fundraising activities to provide services for disabled people. Indeed by 1990, the representation of disabled people had been established at a number of levels. On an international scale, Disabled Peoples' International had been set up and national coordination was facilitated through the British Council of Disabled People (BCODP). This was matched by the emergence of over a hundred constituent BCODP organizations, most of which were local coalitions of disabled people or CILs.

As a network of CILs emerged in the US, it was clear that the working ethos of these organizations drew strongly on notions of consumerism and self-help. As Shakespeare (1993) observes, this working ethos integrated US traditions of self-reliance and individual rights. In contrast, early attempts to establish independent living projects in the UK met with only limited success and were often not under the control of disabled people themselves. However, by the early 1980s real change began to be achieved through the struggles of disabled people themselves, with the emergence of the type of independent living projects described earlier in Derbyshire and Hampshire, alongside similar initiatives in Edinburgh and Rochdale. As Priestley (1999) suggests, these early projects not only provided tangible lived experiences of barrier removal but also demonstrated the potential for an alternative mode of self-organized welfare production (see also Prideaux *et al.* 2009).

Significantly for Shakespeare writing in the early 1990s (Shakespeare 1993), the development of CILs and the wider disability movement in the UK tended to focus on the notions of political autonomy and democratic participation. This contrasted with the more individualized and market-oriented US approaches. Whilst the growth of CILs in the UK has been seen as significant in the *collective* representation of disabled people, implementation of individualized budget schemes to facilitate independent living, such as direct payments over the past decade and a half, have pursued a more consumerist route.

Independent living by the backdoor? Reforming social security and the birth of the Independent Living Fund

As detailed so far, the 1980s saw small groups of disabled people begin to challenge the service structure in the UK. This occurred within the context of a broader policy framework which rendered opportunities for independent living amongst the disabled population to be highly restricted. However, from the mid-1980s reforms instigated through the then Conservative government's review of the welfare state began to make some important changes which, by default, introduced some significant opportunities for independent living. This shift emerged from two areas of policy change: a move from the means-tested Supplementary Benefit to a more restrictive system of Income Support and the subsequent introduction of the Independent Living Fund (ILF).

At this time, payments made to many disabled people through the social security benefits system came under threat from the then Conservative government's broader ideological goals of reducing the role of the state and 'targeting' welfare towards the poorest and most 'deserving'. Whilst earlier analysis traditionally placed disabled people in this category (see Drake 1999), the Conservative reforms of the mid-1980s instigated a long-term process of narrowing eligibility that has been maintained by successive New Labour and Coalition administrations.

Significantly, the reforms saw the removal of the 'additional requirement' payments as means-tested supplementary and housing benefits were changed to Income Support. Although the then Secretary of State for Health and Social Security, Norman Fowler, had claimed that this review of social security was not specifically targeting benefits for disabled people (Department of Health and Social Security 1985), the established link between low income and disability meant that it was inevitable that disabled people would be affected by these changes to means-tested benefits (Glendinning 1992). Furthermore, the 'additional requirement' payments covered provision such as extra heating and the costs of private domestic assistance – a provision used by an estimated 300,000 disabled people (Glendinning 1992). Although these extra payments were consolidated into fixed weekly 'disability' and 'severe' disability premiums, even by the government's own figures it was estimated that around 80,000 'sick and disabled' people would lose out by this shift (Glendinning 1992). Therefore, a temporary solution was set up in the form of the ILF.

The establishment of the ILF in 1988 was intended to enable a small number of disabled people to receive a cash benefit to buy in personal assistance to support their needs. At the time it was envisaged that the number of recipients would be low and payments from the ILF would only be made for a five-year period (Barnes and Mercer 2006). Although the ILF assumed a 'service'-based rationale, its position differed from mainstream local authority provision of services for disabled people in that it was a national charity, covering the entire UK. At the time of its introduction, the

ILF attracted criticism from a number of disability groups and opposition MPs angered by the replacement of legal entitlements to benefits with discretionary awards from a charity (Wood 1991). However, implementation proved to be remarkably successful – with take-up significantly overtaking government expectations – as well as revealing many benefits of a personal assistance scheme for the users (Kestenbaum 1992).

The success of the ILF resulted in its extension in 1993 and a new revised scheme was set up to run alongside services provided by local authorities. As well as providing users with a cash payment to buy in their services of choice, the scheme's appeal for many local authorities has been that it provides a top-up resource for services not covered by council budgets for persons with the highest support needs. Recipients can therefore access an ILF payment as well as a direct payment from the local authority (if their services would otherwise exceed the cost of residential care). However, more recent changes to the scheme implemented in the last months of the Brown government have greatly restricted its capacity as an enabler of independent living. This will be returned to later in the chapter.

Cash, care and routes to independence: policy change in the 1990s

In the post-war era, community care services established to support many disabled people lacked a cohesive framework. For the Conservative government this was accentuated by an escalation in the costs of the care throughout the 1980s. The main contributor to these rising costs was a ruling by the then Department of Health and Social Security which made it easier for residents of private and voluntary homes in receipt of Supplementary Benefit to claim their fees from the social security system. This meant that public subsidy of individual support was based solely on an assessment of financial entitlement and not a need for such care. Although provision focused largely on residential care for older people (see Means *et al.* 2008), it added considerable impetus to policy change across all user groups. For younger disabled people, the closure of long-stay institutions and the gradual emergence of independent living projects at this time contributed to broader changes in support (Priestley 1999). As a result, the government commissioned a series of reports to examine why community care policy had remained so disjointed over such a long period of time.

These government reports highlighted a range of problems with the existing provision of community care. Notably, *Making a Reality of Community Care* (Audit Commission 1986) showed that whilst successive governments had aimed to promote a system of community care, local authority services were still highly dependent on institutional and hospital-based resources. There followed a report commissioned by the Secretary of State to be carried out by Sir Roy Griffiths, the then chief executive of the supermarket chain Sainsbury's, to develop proposals for reorganizing community care. Publication of Griffiths's findings in 1988 signified an important departure in the direction of local authority service provision for disabled people. By addressing the long-term mismatch between community care services and resourcing, Griffiths argued that local-level responsibilities between health authorities, social (work) service authorities, housing authorities, the voluntary and private sectors were poorly coordinated. Central to his proposals was the creation of local mixed economies of care, whereby services were to be provided through private and voluntary sectors. Whilst promoting voluntary and private groups as integral service providers, a key role was also given to informal care – a focus that was problematic for many disabled people seeking to promote services based on the principles of independent living (Morris 1993).

A formal policy of community care was eventually set out in the 1990 NHS and Community Care Act. The focus of the act drew on a number of areas highlighted by Griffiths. Primarily, it was envisaged that there would be a closer link between health and social services and private and voluntary sectors. This, in turn, would be facilitated through Griffiths's notion of 'local care markets', where it was envisaged that the local authority's role would be transformed from that of a service provider to simply an enabling role. In these terms, packages of care would be organized by a care manager and developed in accordance with an individual's needs and circumstances (involving an assessment of impairment-related functional limitations, family situation and financial resources) (Barnes and Mercer 2006). Central to this shift to a more marketized system of 'care' services was the promotion of the user as a consumer of services. This was underpinned by a new rhetoric of empowerment and involvement, in which it was envisaged that disabled people and other user groups would have more choice, control and ultimately independence through their service provision. The election of Labour in 1997 reiterated support for the market in social care through a modernization agenda across the public services (Cabinet Office 1999).

Much has been written on the impact of the reform of community care in the 1990s (see, for example, Bornat *et al.* 1993; Wistow *et al.* 1994; Clark and Lapsley 1996). However, looking at community care's role in the promotion of independent living, commentators such as Morris (1993, 2004) have been particularly critical of its impact on disabled people. Central to her critique is that:

> The ideology of caring which is at the heart of current community care policies can only result in institutionalisation within the community unless politicians and professionals understand and identify with the philosophy and the aims of the independent living movement.
>
> *(Morris 1993: 45)*

Morris (2004) outlines five fundamental problems with the legislative framework for community care. First, she argues that it places duties on local authorities to provide services rather than give rights to individuals to receive support. Second, therefore, disabled people have no entitlement to live at home instead of in residential care. As Priestley (2005) explains, the rigidity of the care assessment at the heart of the community care process defines disabled people's needs in a very particular way. Consequently, the third problem highlighted by Morris is that legislation fails to adequately cover assistance to participate in leisure activities, work, have relationships or look after children or other family members. The final two areas focus on issues of redress, whereby Morris argues that the absence of entitlement to advocacy serves to contribute to inaccessibility to the legal system, with inadequate support for anyone seeking to make a challenge.

Both Morris and Priestley therefore show how the community care legislation has focused resources on personal care and limited domestic chores at the expense of support for social integration. The limits of a service-led structure which restricted choice and control in accordance with the availability of limited services formalized through the 1990 Act simply reinforced the lack of choice and control available to disabled people. Therefore, as the possibility of direct payments emerged from the mid-1990s, there appeared to be, at last, a move towards substantive changes in service provision for many disabled people. The following section explores the impact of these changes on the independent living agenda.

Cash for care: the arrival of direct payments and pursuing the goal of independent living

Discussion earlier in this chapter showed how independent living projects in different parts of the UK began to emerge during the 1980s. As these developed, so too did calls from the wider movement for a formal system of direct payments in the UK which would allow disabled people to choose when support services were provided and by whom. A key example of indirect payments – where a compliant local authority was willing to facilitate the equivalent cash value of direct services through a third party – was shown earlier through the work of activists in Hampshire, and others from different parts of the UK are documented elsewhere (see, for example, Priestley 1999; Pearson 2000). However, by the early 1990s although some local authorities were happy to proceed with making indirect payments as an innovative form of service delivery, nationally the Conservative government was less convinced. The already ambiguous legal position of the payments was worsened in 1992 when the then Minister for Health, Virginia Bottomley, issued a circular to local authorities running schemes stating that direct payments were illegal. Consequently, many existing schemes were withdrawn by local authorities.

Yet these localized initiatives clearly formed an important part of the campaign for direct payments. Likewise, the experiences of those in receipt of ILF monies were highlighted in research commissioned by the BCODP (Zarb and Nadash 1994) and were used to secure the U-turn by the Major government and eventual adoption of legislation through the Community Care (Direct Payments) Act 1996. The positioning of legislation as an appendix to the Community Care Act meant that direct payments were framed as an alternative mode of provision to that of directly provided services. Access to a direct payment was, therefore, to be organized by local authority social service departments through the same care assessment.

For the disabled people's movement, a system of direct payments to enable the employment of personal assistants at the control and discretion of individual users had always been seen as critical in challenging service-led care structures and pursuing independent living (Kestenbaum 1992). For the Conservative and subsequent New Labour administrations, support for direct payments drew strongly on market discourses (Pearson 2000), whereby the empowerment value of cash rather than services helped promote the model of consumerism in social care. Indeed, the BCODP research (Zarb and Nadash 1994) found that cash payment schemes could be up to 40 per cent cheaper than directly provided services, and this was evidently attractive to administrations seeking to cut public spending. Although this model was clearly important in securing governmental support for the policy, it has also undoubtedly contributed to the 'postcode lottery' which has seen take-up for direct payments vary acutely throughout different parts of the UK (see Priestley *et al.* 2010; Riddell *et al.* 2005). Whilst many local authorities in the south of England have embraced direct payments, in Scotland, Wales and Northern Ireland they have been viewed far more suspiciously. This has resulted in resistance to policy from many Scottish care workers and trade unions groups, as direct payments have been seen as a form of 'backdoor privatisation' of local services (Pearson 2004a).

Aside from the political difficulties in securing access to direct payments across the UK, their implementation over the past 15 years has also highlighted shortcomings in facilitating independent living. Although direct payments have been presented as an important tool in enabling independent living, it is clear that they are not enough on their own to achieve this goal. Much has been written about the problems within the system of direct payments that have prevented the realization of meaningful involvement of users in their services, which was espoused as a key driver of policy (see, for example, Dawson 2000; Leece 2000; Witcher *et al.* 2000; Ellis 2007). These reflect both the need for attitudinal change from frontline staff, alongside broader structural and resource shifts.

Indeed one of the fundamental problems with direct payments relates to their position in a cash-strapped social care system. As Morris (2004, 2005) and Priestley's (2005) critiques of community care set out earlier in this chapter show, care assessments generally fail to take into account wider social needs or costs which allow the individual to achieve real independence. Furthermore, the requirements of monitoring processes developed by local authorities have made many users feel uneasy about taking on a direct payment (see, for example, Pearson 2000). This certainly has not helped facilitate a positive environment about direct payments as a mainstream service option.

For disability-led organizations, the implementation of direct payments has brought with it mixed fortunes. On the one hand, many local areas have utilized user-led groups (often CILs) in a formal supporting role for new and existing direct payment users. In many cases, this has enabled organizations to expand and develop this supporting role (see d'Aboville 2006). However, this has often been at the expense of offering more innovative independent living services. It has also helped negate a broader campaigning because contract agreements with local authorities to support direct payment users prioritize other roles. In other instances, local authorities have opted to develop their own support services 'in-house' or to tender them to another organization that does not embrace user-led/independent living values (Pearson 2004b). Arguably, therefore, this has contributed to a feeling that the radical edge of direct payments as a facilitator of independent living has been lost.

International approaches to cash payment models

As indicated at the outset of this chapter, the cash payment model originated in the US in the 1970s. Indeed, as in the UK, there has been a gradual international shift towards individualized budgeting over the last 20 years. This section briefly explores how the cash payment model has developed both in the US and Canada, alongside its impact across European countries.

In the US and Canada, local initiatives have been critical in securing change. This has resulted in a reduced role for policy frameworks set out by government and instead a more independent and non-bureaucratic approach for self-funding initiatives. As Hutchinson *et al.* (2006) explain, change has been underpinned by values and principles that reflect self-determination and community participation. Consequently, these local initiatives had an important impact on the promotion of disabled people, the promotion of human rights and the broader independent living agenda, whereby 'individualized planning and direct funding [have] evolved as corner-stones of a new paradigm of disability supports for citizenship and inclusion' (Hutchinson *et al.* 2006: 49).

Across Europe, the development of cash payment models has been more recent, with change in most countries occurring from the late 1990s onwards. Research by Townsley *et al.* (2009) reviewed how these approaches supported the principle of independent living for disabled people in 26 European countries. Whilst the majority of the countries had policies with clear statements supporting independent living, progress was highly varied and did not always cover all groups. Notably in many cases, persons with learning difficulties were excluded from these policy statements. In addition, the research found that – like in the UK – few European countries have realized their strategic commitment to independent living, with schemes limited by local resources, an absence of a policy lead and a focus on a medical assessment rather than meeting individual needs. This reiterates earlier findings set out by Poole (2006), whose summary of European individualized budget schemes in 1997 showed that there was a clear focus on the provision of payments for a restricted number of social care or health roles rather than a broader interpretation of independent living. For example in Austria, payments were low with the expectation that anyone requiring more than four hours' support per day will live in an institution. Likewise in Germany, the scheme in place was found to be highly medicalized, with disabled people receiving less money if they chose to receive payments directly rather than selecting support from approved providers. In contrast, Sweden showed a clearer commitment to the principles of independent living, whereby personal assistance has been established as a right since 1994 and is now seen as the norm (Townsley *et al.* 2009).

Independent living, individualization and the modernization of services

Despite the slow and often lacklustre implementation of direct payments in the UK, successive governments have made it clear that it is a model of support they wish to proceed with. Following on from their initial emergence in the final months of the Major administration, New Labour embraced direct payments in a number of key policy documents. This began in their blueprint for the modernization of public services (Cabinet Office 1999). Elsewhere across the UK, the devolved administration in Scotland, first led by Labour and subsequently by the Scottish National Party (SNP), also maintained interest in the policy. Attempts to increase user access have been made since the introduction of direct payments through initiatives such as the Direct Payment Development Fund – a £9 million initiative established in 2003 by the Department of Health to pay for voluntary organizations, in partnership with local authorities, to set up additional information and support services in England (Hasler 2006). In Scotland, Direct Payments Scotland was established with an initial allocation of £530 million from the then Scottish Executive. Like the Development Fund in England, this had a clear remit to help establish support organizations and promote awareness of direct payments (Pearson 2006).

Around the same time, the cash payment model was extended to the idea of personal budgets or individualized budgets. As Glasby and Littlechild (2009) explain, direct payments and personal/individual budgets are often confusingly seen as the same idea, with similar goals in terms of promoting more choice, control and flexibility in service provision. However, there are key differences. Whilst personal budgets build on the history of independent living originating from the disabled peoples' movement, their inception is much more recent. They have been based around allies of the disability movement working within services for people with learning difficulties, rather than disabled people themselves (Glasby and Littlechild 2009). Individual budgets (also known as self-directed support) allow a person to know how much money is available for their support and then give them maximum choice over how the funds are spent. This could mean that a person takes the full personal budget as a direct payment or it could involve a more complex approach where, for example, a social worker or appointed third party manages the full amount on the individual's behalf. So money may not actually change hands, but critically the individual knows how much is available to be spent on their own needs and chooses how this is organized. Another important difference between direct payments and individual budgets is that the individual/personal budget can be spent on anything that can be shown to be meeting a person's assessed needs, which may include a combination of public, private and voluntary sector services. This differs from direct payments, which cannot be spent on public sector services. However, for Glasby and Littlechild, the fundamental difference is that although direct payments have undoubtedly transformed the lives of many users, their means of access remains the same – through a highly restrictive community care assessment. Conversely they argue that the more inclusive means of forming support packages that personal budgets seem to offer integrate all of the advantages of direct payments, but with a transformative potential of challenging more rigid care structures as a whole.

Another significant cash payment scheme emerging in the last few years is the In Control programme. This was launched in 2003 and aims to work with local authorities to develop systems of self-directed support for people with learning difficulties. Like individual budgets, In Control helps local councils develop a resource allocation system through which service users are again told how much money is available to them to fund their support arrangements (Rabiee *et al.* 2009). Service users are then helped to devise individualized support plans to meet their self-assessed needs (Poll *et al.* 2006). However, unlike individualized budgets, the scheme is focused primarily on persons with learning difficulties and includes only local authority social care resources.

Whilst these approaches underlined the position of cash payment models in social care markets, there was also some evidence to suggest that the government was willing to look more carefully at how an independent living agenda might be taken forward. By the mid-2000s, two significant policy documents emerged that reflected strongly on the principles of independent living: first, in England, the Green Paper *Independence, Well-being and Choice* (IWC) (Department of Health 2005) and second the cross-government publication *Improving the Life Chances of Disabled People* (ILCDP) (Cabinet Office 2005). From the outset, IWC implied that independence was desirable for all members of society, stating that 'the principle [is] that everyone in society has a positive contribution to make to that society and that they should have a right to control their own lives (Department of Health 2005: 9). However, as Barnes and Mercer (2006) noted, the tools to achieve this change were limited to the endorsement of direct payments and individual budgets. Furthermore, they argued that, 'The Green Paper is replete with the language of "care" rather than rights and there is no mention whatsoever of a social model analysis of disability nor, indeed, a definition of independent living' (Barnes and Mercer 2006: 175).

In contrast, ILCDP set out a comprehensive strategy to transform the structure of services for disabled people and their families across the life course, stating that by 2025 'disabled people should have full opportunities and choices to improve their quality of life and be respected and included as equal members of society' (Cabinet Office 2005: 4). Rather than restricting reform to discrete policy areas, ILCDP's strength lay in its definition of independent living. This acknowledged the need to focus reform across key policy areas of social care, health, housing, transport and education (Pearson 2006). Also, unlike the Green Paper, which was based on services in England, the cross-departmental emphasis of ILCDP meant that reform was intended to cover all parts of the UK.

ILCDP was also unusual as a policy document in that it was largely welcomed by the disability community. The BCODP described it as 'one of the most positive documents to come from government, relating to disabled people, in many years'. Indeed, its consultation and development drew on extensive research and consultation with a variety of disabled people and disabled representatives of organizations (Barnes and Mercer 2006) and it was framed around a social model analysis of disability.

Central to ILCDP's focus on promoting independent living was a move to plan and deliver services for disabled people through a model of individualized budgets. One of the main problems with the system of support for disabled people that has developed in the post-war era is that it has emerged in an entirely ad hoc fashion, with little coherence between the tiers and government departments that allocate monies (see Berthoud 1998). By moving to individualized budgets, it is envisaged that the various pools of support would be brought together and allocated on the basis of assessed need. The individual would then be able to decide how to use the money – either through a cash payment or service equivalent – thereby facilitating independent living.

As described, this type of budgetary model has been promoted in a number of guises and piloted in different areas of the UK. One recent example of this came in the last months of the New Labour administration through the launch of the Right to Control programme in early 2010. The programme aims to encourage personalized support envisaged in ILCDP by integrating different services, including housing, employment and community care (Dudman 2010). Like individualized budgets, this gives users a pool of cash from these different funding streams from which they can organize their support. The scheme is currently being piloted across eight English local authorities and will run until 2012.

In Scotland, the poor take-up of direct payments over the last decade has led to a refocus on cash-based payment models by the SNP administration. This has resulted in direct payments being widened and rebranded as 'self-directed support' to operate in a similar way to individualized budgets and incorporate pools of funding from social care, housing and the ILF. At the time of writing (September 2011), the Scottish government included the Self Directed Support (Scotland) Bill in its 2011–12 legislative session. The Bill was developed with the specific aim to promote policy as the mainstream social care service option in Scotland over a ten-year period. The Bill was also part of a wider strategy to promote independent living in Scotland. This included the Independent Living in Scotland Project – an initiative funded by the Scottish government and run by disabled people and their organizations to 'strengthen and develop the Independent Living Movement in Scotland and to support the involvement of disabled people in shaping the Scottish Government's approach' (ILiS 2010). The project was hosted by the Equalities and Human Rights Commission and will run until March 2012.

Alongside the model of individualized budgets set out in ILCDP was the pledge to establish a user-led organization in every local authority by 2010. The proposed model drew on a number of functions adopted by direct payment support organizations, notably the provision of advocacy, peer support, assistance with self-assessment, support in using individualized budgets and the provision of support to recruit and employ personal assistants. In addition, broader tasks relating to independent living, such as disability equality training, were cited (Cabinet Office 2005).

Despite this support for user-led organizations, there remain a number of barriers which, in turn, have compromised the realization of the 2010 deadline. As Woodin (2006) and Barnes and Mercer (2006) have highlighted, there has been no additional funds from local or national government to realize this pledge. Indeed, long-term under-investment has produced a severe shortfall in the capacity of CILs and other user-led organizations to meet the growing demand for independent living support services. Woodin also contends that support for user-led organizations from local authorities has often been ambivalent and hostile.

Likewise, the pledge in both the Green Paper and ILCDP to develop individualized budgets was set out on the understanding that independent living could be achieved within the existing budget constraints. Whilst early research findings from pilots of individualized budgets in England (Rabiee *et al.* 2009) showed favourable responses to the scheme and many advantages over more conventional forms of support – including direct payments – social care systems will need to move from a service-led model to one that is individualized and based on self-assessment (see Roulstone and Morgan 2009). As well as a need for a fundamental change in the organizational culture of social care, it is difficult to see a successful shift to this model without increased resources. It is in this context that discussion moves to explore how the independent living agenda has fared within the economic crisis.

Independent living in an era of austerity

Even before the announcements from the Coalition Government's Comprehensive Spending Review, 2010 was not shaping up to be a good year for promoting independent living in the UK. In the last months of the Brown administration, two important changes to the ILF were announced, which had a great impact on its access and provision. The ILF is clearly seen as costly, and its 21,000 users recorded in 2009–10 with a budget of £351m (Carson 2010) have made it vulnerable to reform. Therefore, it was announced that from May 2010, applications would be limited to disabled people receiving a minimum of £340 a week in local authority funding and working at least 16 hours a week. Within two months of this announcement, the ILF received around 2,600 applications – equivalent to 60 per cent of its annual average. This prompted a further change to the system, resulting in a cap of only 600 payments. Furthermore, all applications for the rest of 2010 were refused, alongside meeting the rising costs of existing users' care packages.

Inevitably these changes have caused great concern for users and the wider movement. The Right to Control programme described earlier includes ILF monies and, given that the Coalition has pledged its support to the initiative, it would appear that the ILF remains safe for the two-year duration of the Right to Control programme. However, its long-term future remains unclear.

Indeed the impact of the Chancellor of the Exchequer George Osborne's spending review on disabled people has been disproportionate. This has seen a limit of one year placed on claims for the contributory element of the Employment Support Allowance (ESA). ESA was brought in under New Labour to replace Incapacity Benefit and is intended to support people who are unable to work because of their ill health or impairment. Prior to this change, there was no time limit and people could claim ESA until they found another job. After one year, people with assets, savings or partners who work will no longer receive benefits. Single people with no assets may be able to qualify for the means-tested element of Job Seekers' Allowance, but everyone else will have to rely on their spouse's salary or use any savings they may have (Bawden 2010).

Other changes set out in the spending review will also impact on 380,000 disabled people living in care homes through the removal of the mobility component of Disability Living Allowance. This money is paid to help recipients with transport costs to undertake social activities outside their home environment. It is perhaps ironic that a policy that is based around the needs of individuals in care homes is presented as part of a discussion on independent living, but its removal will undoubtedly trap an already marginalized group.

In Europe, governments have also announced austerity measures which directly target disabled people. Notably, the Dutch government is removing personal budgets from 90 per cent (117,000) of disabled people who have been organizing their own support. From 2014, only persons classified as needing residential care will be eligible for a personal care budget (DAA News Network 2011).

Discussion and concluding comments

This chapter has sought to unravel how the philosophy of independent living, developed over 30 years ago, has manifested into policy and practice for disabled people. It shows that whilst there have been important victories and some policy shifts, the pace of change has remained slow and support for disabled people in the UK remains largely wedded to a cash-limited system of social care and a residualized benefit system. It is also evident that when looking at the overall picture of independent living on an international scale, there is not one single model, and approaches vary considerably from country to country (Townsley *et al.* 2009).

Clearly recent changes set out in the UK towards individualized/personal budgets are important in that they allow funding to be pooled, and thereby maximize choice and control, but this type of reform is not enough on its own. As Glasby and Littlechild (2009) argue, the move to individual budgets represents an important shift in the relationship between the state and the individual in that it moves the provision of support for disabled people away from the patchwork of benefits and initiatives towards a more coherent policy framework. However, there remain inconsistencies, and access to any of the cash payment models discussed in this chapter is largely dependent on where the disabled person lives. As such, any realization of independent living can only be achieved if it is taken out of the existing system of community care and controlled by disabled people themselves. In the UK, Barnes and Mercer (2006) argue that this could be achieved through the development of separate agencies in England, Scotland, Northern Ireland and Wales to support national networks of user-led initiatives that are sensitive and responsive to impairment, ethnic and cultural diversity within the disabled population and at a local level. Indeed Hutchinson *et al.*'s (2006) review of personal assistance in North America showed that the role of community support has been critical in facilitating a broader shift to cash payments, whilst at the same time promoting the citizenship rights of disabled people. In contrast, where European independent living schemes were found to be lacking in progress, insufficient community support was cited as a factor (Townsley *et al.* 2009).

Whilst successive governments over the past decade have pledged their support to the concept of independent living, there remains a gap between the rhetoric of reform and the vulnerability of even current spending on disability. Across Europe, Townsley *et al.*'s research (2009) showed that independent living was perceived by governments as an expense in the current economic climate, and the recent dramatic cuts to personal budgets in the Netherlands serve to underline this. Indeed, the targeting of key areas of funding for many disabled people in the UK's 2010 Comprehensive Spending Review suggested that independent living is also not a serious consideration for the Coalition Government. Likewise the narrowing of ILF eligibility in the last months of the Brown government also indicated that even maintaining existing support will be a challenge for the disability movement. From the outset, the grassroots activism of disabled people has been vital in ensuring that independent living remains on the political agenda. However, until the government adequately resources reform, the realization of independent living will not be achieved.

References

Audit Commission (1986) *Making a Reality of Community Care* (London: HMSO).

Barnes, C. and Mercer, G. (2006) *Independent Futures: Creating User-led Disability Services in a Disabling Society* (Bristol: Policy Press).

Bawden, A. (2010) 'A Safety Net is Taken Away', *The Guardian*, 21 October.

Berthoud, R. (1998) *Disability Benefits: A Review of the Issues and Options for Reform* (York: Joseph Rowntree Foundation).

Bornat, J., Pereira, C., Pilgrim, D. and Williams, F. (1993) *Community Care: A Reader* (Basingstoke: Macmillan).

Brisenden, S. (1989) 'A Charter for Personal Care', in Disablement Income Group (DIG) *Progress London*, No. 16 (London: DIG).

Cabinet Office (1999) *Modernising Government*; available online at http://www.archive.official-documents. co.uk/document/cm43/4310/4310.htm (accessed 21 September 2011).

Cabinet Office (2005) *Improving the Life Chances of Disabled People* (London: Cabinet Office).

Carson, G. (2010) 'What Future for the Independent Living Fund?', *Community Care*, 2 July; available online at http://www.communitycare.co.uk/Articles/2010/07/02/114826/what-future-for-the-independent-living-fund.htm (accessed 21 September 2011).

Centre for Independent Living (1982) 'Independent Living: The Right to Choose', in M. Eisenburg, C. Griggins and R. Duval, eds, *Disabled People as Second Class Citizens* (New York: Springer Publishing Company): pp. 247–60.

Clark, C. and Lapsley, I., eds, (1996) *Planning and Costing Community Care* (Melksham: Cromwell Press).

DAA News Network (2011) 'The Netherlands: Personal Budgets Decimated by Cuts'; available online at http://www.daa.org.uk/index.php?mact=Blogs,cntnt01,showentry,0&cntnt01entryid=423&cntnt01 returnid=98 (accessed 16 September 2011).

D'Aboville, E. (2006) 'Implementing Direct Payments: A Support Organisation Perspective', in J. Leece and J. Bornat, eds, *Developments in Direct Payments* (Bristol: Policy Press).

Dawson, C. (2000) *Independent Successes: Implementing Direct Payments* (York: Joseph Rowntree Foundation).

Department of Health (2005) *Independence, Well-being and Choice* (London: HMSO).

Department of Health and Social Security (1985) *Reform of Social Security, cmd 9517* (London: HMSO).

Drake, R. (1999) *Understanding Disability Policies* (Basingstoke: Macmillan).

Dudman, J. (2010) 'Right to Control: Trailblazer Councils Test Disabled Access', *The Guardian*, 10 March.

Ellis, K. (2007) 'Direct Payments and Social Work Practice: The Significance of "Street Level Bureaucracy" in Determining Eligibility', *British Journal of Social Work* 37(4): 405–22.

Hasler, F. (2006) 'The Direct Payment Development Fund', in J. Leece and J. Bornat, eds, *Developments in Direct Payments* (Bristol: Policy Press).

Hutchinson, P., Lord, J. and Salisbury, B. (2006) 'North American Approaches to Individualised Planning and Direct Funding', in J. Leece and J. Bornat, eds, *Developments in Direct Payments* (Bristol: Policy Press).

Glasby, J. and Littlechild, R. (2009) *Direct Payments and Personal Budgets* (Bristol: Policy Press).

Glendinning, C. (1992) 'Residualism versus Rights: Social Policy and Disabled People', in N. Manning and R. Page, eds, *Social Policy Review 4* (Canterbury: Social Policy Association).

ILiS (2010) 'About the ILis Project', available online at http://www.ilis.co.uk/about-the-ilis-project/ (accessed 15 September 2011).

Kestenbaum, A. (1992) *Cash for Care: The Experience of Independent Living Clients* (Nottingham: Independent Living Fund).

Leece, J. (2000) 'It's a Matter of Choice: Making Direct Payments Work in Staffordshire', *Practice* 12(4): 37–48.

Means, R., Richards, S. and Smith, R. (2008) *Community Care* (Basingstoke: Macmillan).

Morris, J. (1993) *Independent Lives? Community Care and Disabled People* (London: Macmillan).

Morris, J. (2004) 'Independent Living and Community Care: A Disempowering Framework', *Disability & Society* 19(5): 427–42.

Morris, J. (2005) 'Independent Living: The Role of Evidence and Ideology in the Development of Government Policy'. Paper delivered at 'Cash and Care Conference', Social Policy Research Unit, University of York, 12–13 April.

Oliver, M. (2009) *Understanding Disability: From Theory to Practice* (Basingstoke: Palgrave Macmillan).

Pearson, C. (2000) 'Money Talks?: Competing Discourses in the Implementation of Direct Payments', *Critical Social Policy* 20(4): 459–77.

Pearson, C. (2004a) 'Keeping the Cash Under Control', *Disability & Society* 19(1): 3–14.

Pearson, C. (2004b) 'The Implementation of Direct Payments: Issues for User-led Organisations in Scotland', in C. Barnes and G. Mercer, eds, *Implementing the Social Model of Disability: Theory and Research* (Leeds: Disability Press).

Pearson, C. (2006) *Direct Payments and the Personalisation of Care* (Edinburgh: Dunedin Academic Press).

Poll, C., Duffy, S., Hatton, C., Sanderson, H. and Routledge, M. (2006) *A Report of In Control's First Phase 2003–2005* (London: In Control Publications).

Poole, T. (2006) *Direct Payments and Older People* (London: King's Fund).

Prideaux, S., Roulstone, A., Harris, J. and Barnes, C. (2009) 'Disabled People and Self-Directed Support Schemes: Re-conceptualising Work and Welfare in the 21st Century', *Disability & Society* 24(5): 557–69.

Priestley, M. (1999) *Disability Politics and Community Care* (London: Jessica Kingsley).

Priestley, M. (2005) 'Tragedy Strikes Again!: Why Community Care Still Poses a Problem for Integrated Living', in J. Swain, S. French, C. Barnes and C. Thomas, eds, *Disabling Barriers – Enabling Environments* (London: Sage).

Priestley, M., Riddell, S., Jolly, D., Pearson, C. and Williams, V. (2010) 'Cultures of Welfare at the Front Line: Implementing Direct Payments for Disabled People in the UK', *Policy and Politics* 38(2): 307–24.

Rabiee, R., Moran, N. and Glendinning, C. (2009) 'Individual Budgets: Lessons from Early Users' Experiences', *British Journal of Social Work* 39(5): 918–35.

Riddell, S., Pearson, C., Jolly, D., Barnes, C., Priestley, M. and Mercer, G. (2005) 'The Development of Direct Payments in the UK: Implications for Social Justice', *Social Policy and Society* 4(17): 75–85.

Roulstone, A. and Morgan, H. (2009) 'Neo-Liberal Individualism or Self-directed Support: Are We All Speaking the Same Language on Adult Social Care?', *Social Policy and Society* 8(3): 333–45.

Shakespeare, T. (1993) 'Disabled People's Self-organisation: A New Social Movement?', *Disability, Handicap and Society* 8(3): 249–64.

Townsley, R., Ward, L., Abbott, P. and Williams, V. (2009) *The Implementation of Policies Supporting Independent Living for Disabled People in Europe: Synthesis Report* (Utrecht: Academic Network of European Disability Experts).

Wistow, G., Knapp, M., Hardy, B. and Allen, C. (1994) *Social Care in a Mixed Economy* (Buckingham: Open University Press).

Witcher, S., Stalker, K., Roadburg, M. (2000) *Direct Payments: The Impact of Choice and Control for Disabled People* (Edinburgh: Scottish Executive Central Research Unit).

Wood, R. (1991) 'Care of Disabled People', in G. Dalley, ed., *Disability and Social Policy* (London: Policy Studies Institute).

Woodin, S. (2006) *Mapping User-led Organisations: User-led Services and Centres for Independent/Integrated/Inclusive Living: A Literature Review Prepared for the Department of Health*; available online at http://www.leeds.ac.uk/disability-studies/archiveuk/woodin/v2%20user%20led%20-%20CIL%20Literature%20Review%203.pdf (accessed 21 September 2011).

Zarb, G. and Nadash, P. (1994) *Cashing in on Independence: Comparing the Costs and Benefits of Cash and Services* (Derbyshire: BCODP).

19

DISABLEMENT AND HEALTH

Eric Emerson, Brandon Vick, Hilary Graham, Chris Hatton,
Gwynnyth Llewellyn, Ros Madden, Boika Rechel and Janet Robertson

In this chapter we address what is known about the nature and determinants of the health inequalities faced by disabled people. First, we discuss the nature of the association between health and disability. Second, we briefly review what is known about the (poorer) health status of disabled people. Third, in the main part of this chapter, we discuss some of the processes that may link disability and health. Finally, we conclude by identifying the implications of this knowledge for policy and future research. Selected references are included in each section; a fuller set is available in the two reports on which this chapter draws. The first (Emerson *et al.* 2009) was commissioned in the context of a strategic review of health inequalities in the United Kingdom (UK) (Marmot Review 2010). The second (Emerson *et al.* 2011b) was commissioned in the context of a strategic review of health inequalities in Europe undertaken by the World Health Organization's (WHO's) Regional Office for Europe (World Health Organization Regional Office for Europe 2010).

Health and definitions of disability

Disability is universally defined in relation to (among other things) the presence of a health condition or impairment that is considered in some way salient. In this chapter we will consider disability from the perspective of the 'biopsychosocial' model that underlies the WHO's International Classification of Functioning, Disability and Health (ICF) (World Health Organization 2001, 2007). In the ICF, functioning and disability are conceptualized in terms of the complex interplay between bodily functions (and the immediate impairment effects of these), activities (and activity limitations), participation (and participation restrictions) and environmental factors. Environmental factors (such as living conditions, social attitudes and practices, services systems and policies) are explicitly recognized as having a crucial effect on a person's functioning and social participation (or social inclusion). As such, disability arises when people with health conditions or impairments are confronted by social conditions (or environmental barriers) that reduce their everyday activities and/or social participation (World Health Organization 2001). Disability is not seen as a characteristic of a person. Neither is it seen as an inevitable consequence of a particular disease or health condition. Rather, it is viewed as a socially determined outcome resulting from the operation of disabling and discriminatory cultural, social and environmental conditions. It is an outcome of being a particular person in a particular society at a particular point in time, who experiences a particular health condition or impairment. Given that all disabled people (by definition) have a health condition or impairment, it is necessarily true that disabled people (as a group) will have poorer health than non-disabled people. Our interest, however, is in attempting to understand why disabled people have poorer health than non-disabled people in areas of health that have no known biological link with the health condition or impairment associated with their disability.

The health of disabled people

There is extensive evidence that people with disabilities experience significantly poorer health outcomes than their non-disabled peers (Australian Institute of Health and Welfare 2010; Disability Rights Commission 2006). It is important to note that these negative outcomes extend to aspects of health that have no biological link to the *specific* health condition or impairment associated with the person's disability. For example, when compared with their non-disabled peers, people with intellectual disabilities or long-standing physical illness have significantly higher rates of mental health problems (Einfeld *et al.* 2006; Emerson and Hatton 2007c; Honey *et al.* 2011; Parkes *et al.* 2008; Scott *et al.* 2009), obesity (Australian Institute of Health and Welfare 2010; Ells *et al.* 2006; Lidstone *et al.* 2006; Melville *et al.* 2007) and oral health problems (Owens *et al.* 2006). Poorer health outcomes are also experienced by the family carers of disabled children and adults (Hawley *et al.* 2003; Hirst 2005; Ones *et al.* 2005; Pervin *et al.* 2006; Singer 2006).

Figures 19.1 and 19.2 illustrate these relationships using data on two indicators of health status (obesity and oral health) extracted from the World Health Surveys 2002–4. The operational definition of disability used was developed by the WHO to inform the WHO/The World Bank Group *World Report on Disability* (2011). Based on the ICF, the World Health Surveys asked about levels of difficulty on eight domains of health: mobility, self-care, pain/discomfort, cognition, interpersonal relationships, vision, sleep/energy and depression/anxiety. The response scale for each item ranged from no difficulty (a score of 1) to extreme difficulty/cannot do (a score of 5). The two indicators of health status were selected on the basis of the availability of data within the World Health Surveys and either the significance of the health condition to population health (obesity) (World Health Organization Regional Office for Europe 2007) or the low probability that the health condition was itself primarily associated with the identification of disability in the survey (oral health).

Across these European countries as a whole, rates of obesity and rates of oral health problems were higher for disabled adults (at 21 per cent for obesity, 50 per cent for oral health problems) than non-disabled adults (14 per cent and 33 per cent). Looking within countries, rates of health problems were also generally higher among disabled adults. For obesity, in 14 countries the difference in rates between disabled and non-disabled adults was statistically significant. For oral health problems, in 21 countries the difference in rates between disabled and non-disabled adults was statistically significant. These patterns held true across poorer and richer countries and the probability of these imbalances in health status occurring by chance alone is extremely remote.

The determinants of health inequalities experienced by people with disabilities

Four general factors are relevant to understanding the poorer health experienced by disabled people.

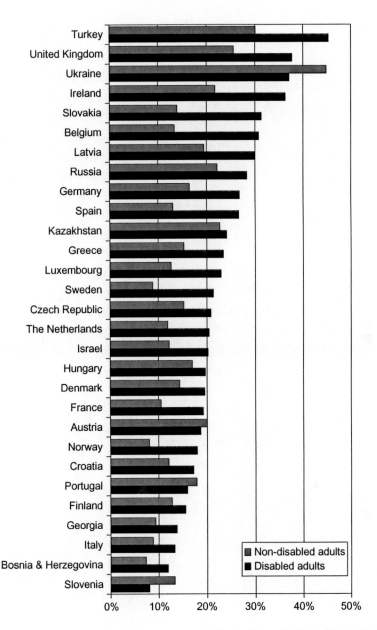

Figure 19.1 Age-adjusted prevalence of obesity among disabled and non-disabled adults in 29 European countries, 2002–4

- Some health conditions or impairments associated with disability involve increased risk of biologically linked secondary health conditions or impairments.
- Exposure to well-established social determinants of (poorer) health independently increases the risk of both health conditions or impairments associated with disability *and* poor health.
- Disablism increases the risk of exposure to well-established social determinants of (poorer) health.
- Disablism reduces access to timely and effective health care.

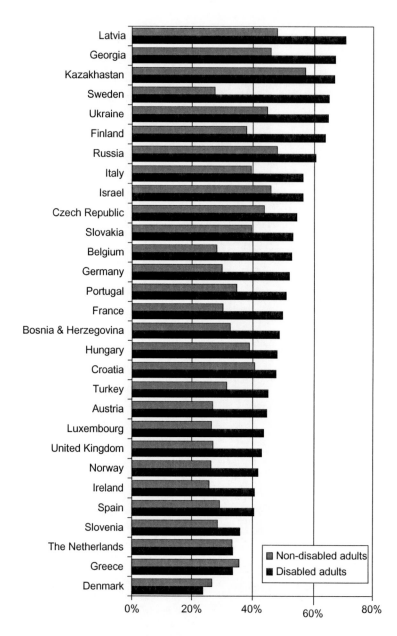

Figure 19.2 Age-adjusted prevalence of oral health problems among disabled and non-disabled adults in
29 European countries, 2002–4

'Secondary' health conditions or impairments

A number of the health conditions or impairments associated with disabilities appear to be
biologically linked to additional (or 'secondary') health risks. To give two examples:

- Disabled people with Down's Syndrome (the most common genetic cause of intellectual
  disability) are more likely than their non-disabled peers to experience congenital heart

disease, impaired hearing and early onset dementia (Einfeld and Emerson 2008; Einfeld and Brown 2010; Harris 2005);

• Disabled people with obesity are more likely than their non-disabled peers to experience a range of additional health conditions including cardiovascular diseases, various types of cancer, type 2 diabetes and insulin resistance, end-stage kidney disease, fatty liver disease, osteoarthritis, pulmonary embolism and deep vein thrombosis (Sassi 2010; World Health Organization 2002; World Health Organization Regional Office for Europe 2007).

In other instances, however, the link between 'primary' and 'secondary' health conditions or impairments is clearly mediated by social processes. For example, impairments in either cognition or communication are likely to reduce a person's independent capacity to understand health promotion advice, recognize symptoms of ill health and negotiate their way through most (if not all) health care systems. To the extent that the link between 'primary' and 'secondary' health conditions or impairments is mediated by social processes, issues of disablism come to the fore. We will return to these issues later.

'Selection': health conditions or impairments associated with disability and health status are independently influenced by common social determinants of health

As we have seen the incidence and prevalence of many of the health conditions and impairments associated with disability are socially patterned; the higher a person's position in the social hierarchy, the lower the risk of acquiring health conditions and impairments associated with disability (Blackburn *et al.* 2010; Breeze and Lang 2008; Dolk *et al.* 2001; Emerson in press; Gissler *et al.* 1998; Guralnik 2006; Huss *et al.* 2008; Kalff *et al.* 2001; Kubba *et al.* 2004; Lang 2008; McMunn *et al.* 2009; Melchior *et al.* 2006; Minkler *et al.* 2006; Newacheck and Halfon 1998; Parish *et al.* 2008; Salm and Schunk 2008; Schneiders *et al.* 2003; Spencer 2000; Strømme and Magnus 2000; Sundrum *et al.* 2005; Varela *et al.* 2009; Yang *et al.* 2007). The same is, of course, true of health in general (Marmot Review 2010; World Health Organization 2008; World Health Organization Regional Office for Europe 2010).

As a result, we would expect people with disabilities to have poorer health than their peers simply as a result of a process of 'selection'. That is, they are more likely to have been exposed to social conditions that *independently* lead to both the onset of health conditions and impairments associated with disability *and* to poorer health in general. For example, exposure to social and material deprivation in early childhood is known to be associated with (among other things) increased risk of intellectual disability (Einfeld and Emerson 2008; Emerson in press; Harris 2005) and to increased mortality and morbidity in later life (Cohen *et al.* 2010). As a result, we would expect people with intellectual disabilities to have poorer heath than their peers simply because as children they are more likely to have been exposed to conditions that are damaging to their future health. This would be expected *regardless* of any effects that having an intellectual disability may have on health (the latter effects will be addressed in the following section).

Few studies have attempted to estimate the extent to which the poorer health outcomes experienced by disabled people may be attributable to their increased risk of exposure to socio-economic disadvantage (rather than 'disability-specific' factors). However, the results of this nascent literature suggest that increased risk of exposure to socio-economic disadvantage may account for 20–50 per cent of the risk of poorer mental and physical health among children with general intellectual impairments (Emerson and Einfeld 2010; Emerson and Hatton 2007a, 2007b, 2007c) and most or all of the risk of poorer mental health and low rates of well-being among mothers of children with disabilities or general intellectual impairments (Emerson *et al.* 2006; Emerson and Llewellyn 2008; Emerson *et al.* 2010).

Disablism increases the risk of exposure to 'social determinants' of (poorer) health

Disablism ('the social beliefs and actions that oppress/exclude/disadvantage people with impairments') (Thomas 2007) also increases the risk of poor health. Two interrelated processes are likely to be important here: downward social mobility and discrimination.

First, disablism may lead to downward social mobility consequently increasing the risk of exposure to common social determinants of health associated with lower socio-economic position. There is abundant evidence that disabled people are significantly disadvantaged with regard to key factors that promote upward social mobility and defend against downward social mobility. These include education, employment and labour market experiences, social and cultural capital, health and well-being (Graham 2007; Nunn *et al.* 2007).

Education has been identified as one of the most important factors influencing social mobility (Graham 2007; Nunn *et al.* 2007). Disabled children have more unauthorized school absences, are more likely to be bullied and to have poorer academic attainment than their peers (Burchardt 2005; Department for Children, Schools and Families 2008; Department for Education 2010; Williams *et al.* 2008). Disabled children are also at risk of placement in segregated special schools, including residential special schools – settings that may significantly impede children's social inclusion (Audit Commission 2007; UNESCO 1994; UNICEF 2005). Figure 19.3 uses our analyses of the 2002–4 World Health Surveys to illustrate these inequalities in education in 28 European countries. Across these countries, disabled adults had received fewer years of education (11.4) than non-disabled adults (12.4). In 14 of these countries the difference was statistically significant.

Disabled adults have significantly reduced *employment and labour market opportunities* (Berthoud 2006; Burchardt 2005; Emerson *et al.* 2005; Shima *et al.* 2008; Williams *et al.* 2008). Figure 19.4 uses our analyses of the 2002–4 World Health Surveys to illustrate these inequalities in employment for disabled and non-disabled adults in 27 European countries in 2002–4.

Across these countries, disabled adults were less likely to be employed (40 per cent) than non-disabled adults (53 per cent). In 20 countries this difference was statistically significant. In some European countries (e.g., Belgium, Italy, Spain) people with disabilities who are employed are most likely to be employed in 'sheltered' settings (Shima *et al.* 2008). When in work, these same groups are more likely to be in low-paid, poor-quality jobs with few opportunities for advancement, often working in conditions that are harmful to health (Marmot Review 2010). The onset of disability among people in employment is associated with increased risk of subsequent unemployment and reduced earnings (Burchardt 2000, 2003; Jenkins and Rigg 2004).

Social and cultural capital. Socio-economically more advantaged families tend to have access to a wider range of social networks and cultural capital that facilitate upward mobility and protect against downward mobility than socio-economically more disadvantaged families. Disabled people, as well as experiencing socio-economic disadvantage, also tend to have more restricted social capital as a result of prejudicial and discriminatory practices (Emerson *et al.* 2005; Shakespeare 2006; Williams *et al.* 2008).

Health and well-being. Ill health can lead to a decline in socio-economic status. As noted above, there is extensive evidence that people with disabilities experience significantly poorer health outcomes than their non-disabled peers, including in aspects of health that are unrelated to their *specific* health conditions or impairments.

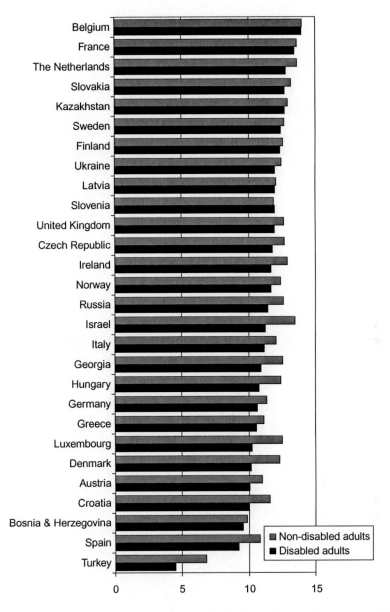

Figure 19.3 Age-adjusted mean years of education received by disabled and non-disabled adults in 28 European countries, 2002–4

Second, exposure to acts of disablist discrimination in everyday life is likely to have a negative impact on health status. A parallel may be drawn here with the research investigating the determinants of the health inequalities experienced by people from minority ethnic groups. Here, a growing body of research has highlighted the association between exposure to overt acts of racism and poorer health outcomes (Dressler *et al.* 2005; Gee *et al.* 2009; Krieger 1999; Mays *et al.* 2007; Myers 2009; Nazroo 2003; Pascoe and Richman 2009; Williams and Mohammed 2009). Exposure to overt acts of disablism is a relatively common experience for many people with

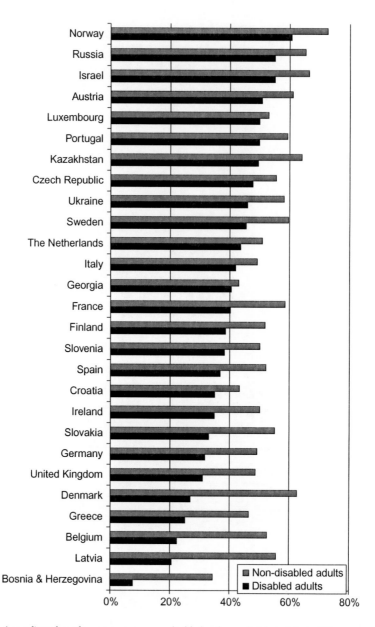

Figure 19.4 Age-adjusted employment rates among disabled and non-disabled adults in 27 European countries, 2002–4

disabilities (Emerson *et al.* 2005; Mencap 2007; Norwich and Kelly 2004; Sheard *et al.* 2001; White *et al.* 2003; Williams *et al.* 2008) and may plausibly be related to poorer health outcomes (Emerson 2010).

The impact of disablism (when combined with increased risk of exposure to poor socio-economic circumstances in childhood for other reasons [see above]) is likely to significantly disempower people with disabilities. Figure 19.5 uses our analyses of the 2002–4 World Health Surveys to illustrate these inequalities in feelings of empowerment and control among disabled and

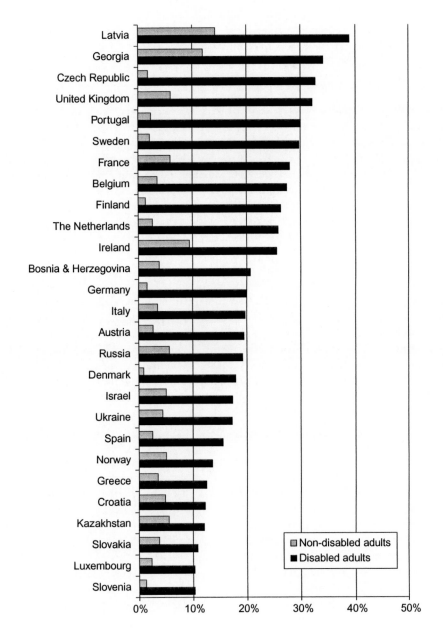

Figure 19.5 Age-adjusted rates of disempowerment among disabled and non-disabled adults in 27 European countries, 2002–4

non-disabled adults in 27 European countries in 2002–4. Across these countries, 20 per cent of disabled adults were more likely to report 'fairly often' or 'very often' being unable to control important things in their life, compared with 3 per cent of non-disabled adults. In 26 of the 27 countries this difference was statistically significant. These differences are of particular concern given both the magnitude of the differences and evidence that reported control (or disempowerment) may be an important psychosocial pathway through which the impact of environmental adversity on health is mediated (Matthews *et al.* 2010). These data suggest that 45 per cent of all disempowered adults in these European countries are also disabled.

Disablism reduces access to timely and effective health care

Finally, disablism in health care systems is evident in the range of organizational barriers that have been identified that prevent people with disabilities from accessing timely and effective health care (Alborz *et al.* 2003, 2005; Disability Rights Commission 2006; Giraud-Saunders 2009; Kwok and Cheung 2007; Michael 2008). These include: scarcity of services; physical barriers to access; failure to make 'reasonable adjustments' in light of the literacy and communication difficulties experienced by people with cognitive impairments; and disablist attitudes among health care staff. Barriers are evident in relation to health screening and health promotion (Alborz *et al.* 2005; Davies and Duff 2001; Emerson *et al.* 2005; Reynolds *et al.* 2008; Willis *et al.* 2008), primary health care (Kerr *et al.* 1996; Piachaud *et al.* 1998; Whitfield *et al.* 1996) and secondary health care (Beecham *et al.* 2002; Bernal 2008; Morgan *et al.* 2000; Tuffrey-Wijne *et al.* 2007).

The experience of disablism in health care is likely to be reflected in both reported rates of not receiving treatment when needed and overall satisfaction with health care. We have used our analyses of the 2002–4 World Health Surveys to illustrate these inequalities in Figure 19.6 (for reported rates of not receiving treatment for oral health problems) and Figure 19.7 (for overall satisfaction with health care). Across these countries, 27 per cent of disabled adults reported not receiving treatment for oral health problems compared with 20 per cent of non-disabled adults. In nine countries this difference was statistically significant. Similarly, 29 per cent of disabled adults reported being 'fairly' or 'very' dissatisfied with the way health care is run, compared with 17 per cent of non-disabled adults. In 16 countries this difference was statistically significant.

Implications for policy and research

In this chapter we have described and quantified the extent of health inequalities faced by disabled people in Europe and summarized what is known about the determinants of these health inequalities. We have drawn attention to four general factors, each of which is amenable to intervention:

- Some health conditions or impairments associated with disability involve increased risk of secondary health conditions or impairments.
- Exposure to well-established social determinants of (poorer) health independently increases the risk of health conditions or impairments associated with disability and poor health.
- Disablism increases the risk of exposure to well-established social determinants of (poorer) health.
- Disablism reduces access to timely and effective health care.

Our analysis underlines the importance of tackling material disadvantage directly. For children, while the socio-economic backgrounds of parents, as measured by their educational attainment and occupational status, are important, income, poverty and material hardship have a powerful additional effect on children's developmental health. Our analysis therefore argues for policies to improve and protect the living standards of families supporting disabled children. This evidence also suggests that the effects of exposure to socio-economic adversity on child development are mediated through the impact such exposure has on parental mental health, family dissolution and relationship quality, parenting practices and reduced capacity to positively invest in developmental

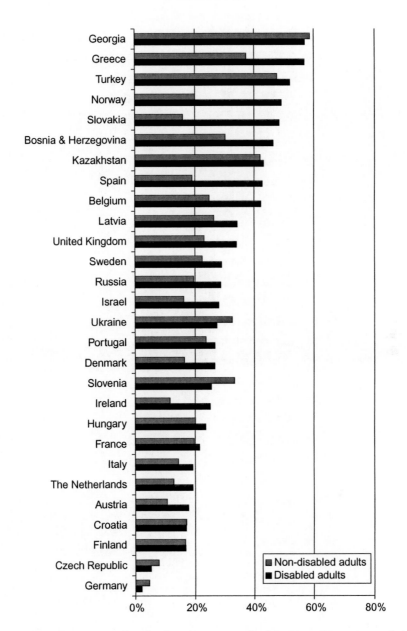

Figure 19.6 Age-adjusted rates of reported non-treatment of oral health problems among disabled and non-disabled adults in 28 European countries, 2002–4

opportunities (Conger and Donnellan 2007). Fiscal policy is the most powerful lever through which to reduce the chances of exposure to income poverty and material hardship in childhood. However, compared with many other high-income countries, the UK tax and benefit system is much less effective in lifting children out of poverty and reducing inequalities in living standards between poorer and richer families (Graham 2007; Ritakallio and Bradshaw 2006).

There exist a plethora of more specific policies that seek to reduce health inequalities. All too often, however, the discussion of strategies to reduce health inequalities pays little or no attention

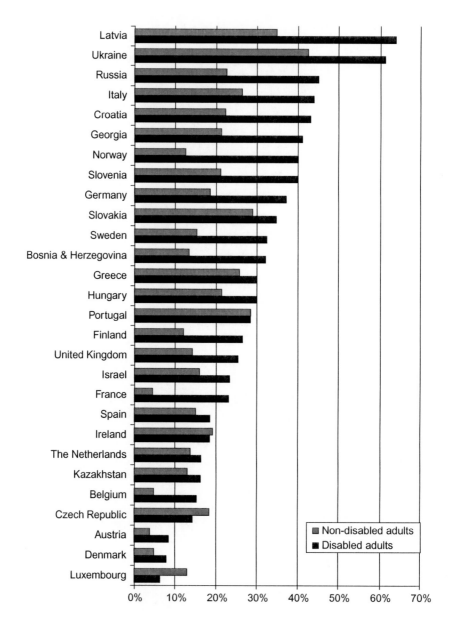

Figure 19.7   Age-adjusted rates of dissatisfaction with health care services among disabled and non-disabled adults in 28 European countries, 2002–4

to the situation of disabled people. For example, the interim statement of the WHO Commission on the Social Determinants of Health did not mention disability *at all* in any of its 53 pages (Emerson *et al.* 2011a).

Perhaps it is assumed that the benefits of population-level interventions or interventions targeted at deprived areas or families will accrue equally across all social groups. There is considerable evidence, however, that behaviour change interventions (whether 'upstream' or 'downstream') aimed at reducing health inequalities are likely to be more effective if they are tailored to the specific social and cultural contexts experienced by 'high risk' groups (National Institute for Health and Clinical Excellence 2007). Without such attention to the specific situation of disabled people, there is a real risk that they may either fail to benefit from the 'trickle down' effects of 'generic' social policies or become more disadvantaged (Disability Rights Commission 2007). For example, welfare to work policies based on increasing access to free childcare are likely to increase the relative disadvantage experienced by families of disabled children unless childcare provision is sensitive and attuned to the needs of such children and their families. It will be important for such policies to consider the importance of providing *additional* support for children and adults with disabilities if they are to access the opportunities – to escape poverty, gain educational qualifications, get and retain a rewarding job – available to non-disabled people (Sen 1992). Indeed, as has recently been pointed out in relation to reducing health inequalities: 'For specific groups who face particular disadvantage and exclusion, additional efforts and invest-ments and diversified provisions will be needed to reach them and to try to reduce the multiple disadvantages they experience' (Marmot Review 2010).

Finally, our analysis highlights the importance of directly addressing disablism in general and, more specifically, in the operation of health care systems. This is, of course, the primary focus of the UN Convention on the Rights of Persons with Disabilities (United Nations 2006). At the time of writing 147 countries have signed (of which 99 have ratified) the convention. Achieving the fundamental aims of the convention, 'to promote, protect and ensure the full and equal enjoy-ment of all human rights and fundamental freedoms by all persons with disabilities, and to promote respect for their inherent dignity', will require action on many fronts. In relation to health, these are likely to include:

1   The enactment and enforcement of disability discrimination legislation that places a require-ment on agencies to adjust their practices to take account of the specific situation and capabilities of disabled people;
2   Combating prejudicial public attitudes and acts towards disabled people (e.g., through public education campaigns, promoting active social inclusion); and
3   The ongoing monitoring of the nature and extent of social exclusion and disadvantage faced by disabled people.

In all of these areas there will be lessons to be learned from the success and failures of recent and current attempts to address inequality on the basis of gender, race and religion (Nelson 2009; Oskamp 2000; Plous 2003; Thornicroft *et al.* 2008; Tropp and Mallett 2011).

References

Alborz, A., McNally, R. and Swallow, A. (2003) *From the Cradle to the Grave: A Literature Review of Access to Health Care for People with Learning Disabilities Across the Lifespan* (London: National Co-ordinating Centre for NHS Service Delivery and Organisation).

Alborz, A., McNally, R. and Glendinning, C. (2005) 'Access to Health Care for People with Learning Disabilities in the UK: Mapping the Issues and Reviewing the Evidence', *Journal of Health Services Research & Policy* 10(3): 173–82.

Audit Commission (2007) *Out of Authority Placements for Special Educational Needs* (London: Audit Commission).

Australian Institute of Health and Welfare (2010) *Health of Australians with Disability: Health Status and Risk Factors* (Canberra: Australian Institute of Health and Welfare).

Beecham, J., Chadwick, O., Fidan, D. and Bernard, S. (2002) 'Children with Severe Learning Disabilities: Needs, Services and Costs', *Children & Society* 16(3): 168–81.

Bernal, J. (2008) 'Telling the Truth – or Not: Disclosure and Information for People with Intellectual Disabilities Who Have Cancer', *International Journal on Disability and Human Development* 7(4): 365–70.

Berthoud, R. (2006) *Employment Rates of Disabled People* (London: Department for Work and Pensions).

Blackburn, C., Read, J. and Spencer, N. (2010) 'Prevalence of Childhood Disability and the Characteristics and Circumstances of Disabled Children in the UK: Secondary Analysis of the Family Resources Survey', *BMC Pediatrics* 10: 21.

Breeze, E. and Lang, I. A. (2008) 'Physical Functioning in a Community Context', in J. Banks, E. Breeze, C. Lessof and J. Nazroo, eds, *Living in the 21st Century: Older People in England* (London: Institute for Fiscal Studies).

Burchardt, T. (2000) *Enduring Economic Exclusion: Disabled People, Income and Work* (York: Joseph Rowntree Foundation).

Burchardt, T. (2003) *Being and Becoming: Social Exclusion and the Onset of Disability*. Case report 21 (London: Centre for Analysis of Social Exclusion, London School of Economics).

Burchardt, T. (2005) *The Education and Employment of Disabled Young People: Frustrated Ambition* (Bristol/ York: Policy Press/Joseph Rowntree Foundation).

Cohen, S., Janicki-Deverts, D., Chen, E. and Matthews, K. A. (2010) 'Childhood Socioeconomic Status and Adult Health', *Annals of the New York Academy of Sciences* 1186(1): 37–55.

Conger, R. D. and Donnellan, M. B. (2007) 'An Interactionist Perspective on the Socioeconomic Context of Human Development', *Annual Review of Psychology* 58: 175–99.

Davies, N. and Duff, M. (2001) 'Breast Cancer Screening for Older Women with Intellectual Disability Living in Community Group Homes', *Journal of Intellectual Disability Research* 45(3): 253–7.

Department for Children, Schools and Families (2008) *Bullying Involving Children with Special Educational Needs and Disabilities* (London: Department for Children, Schools and Families).

Department for Education (2010) *Children with Special Educational Needs 2010: An Analysis* (London: Department for Education).

Disability Rights Commission (2006) *Equal Treatment – Closing the Gap* (London: Disability Rights Commission).

Disability Rights Commission (2007) *Bringing an End to Child Poverty* (London: Disability Rights Commission).

Dolk, H., Pattenden, S. and Johnson, A. (2001) 'Cerebral Palsy, Low Birthweight and Socio-economic Deprivation: Inequalities in a Major Cause of Childhood Disability', *Paediatric and Perinatal Epidemiology* 15(4): 359–63.

Dressler, W. W., Oths, K. S. and Gravlee, C. (2005) 'Race and Ethnicity in Public Health Research: Models to Explain Health Disparities', *Annual Review of Anthropology* 34: 231–52.

Einfeld, S. and Emerson, E. (2008) 'Intellectual Disability', in M. Rutter, D. Bishop, D. Pine, S. Scott, J. Stevenson, E. Taylor and A. Thapar, eds, *Rutter's Child and Adolescent Psychiatry* (Oxford: Blackwell).

Einfeld, S. L. and Brown, R. (2010) Down Syndrome – New Prospects for an Ancient Disorder, *JAMA* 303 (24): 2525–6.

Einfeld, S. L., Piccinin, A. M., Mackinnon, A., Hofer, S. M., Taffe, J., Gray, K. M., Bontempo, D. E., Hoffman, L. R., Parmenter, T. and Tonge, B. J. (2006) 'Psychopathology in Young People with Intellectual Disability', *JAMA* 296(16): 1981–9.

Ells, L., Lang, R., Shield, J., Wilkinson, J., Lidstone, J., Coulton, S. and Summerbell, C. (2006) 'Obesity and Disability – A Short Review', *Obesity Reviews* 7(4): 341–5.

Emerson, E. (2010) 'Self-reported Exposure to Disablism is Associated with Poorer Self-reported Health and Well-being Among Adults with Intellectual Disabilities in England: Cross-sectional Survey', *Public Health* 124 (682–9).

Emerson, E. (in press) 'Household Deprivation, Neighbourhood Deprivation, Ethnicity and the Prevalence of Intellectual and Developmental Disabilities', *Journal of Epidemiology and Community Health*.

Emerson, E. and Hatton, C. (2007a) 'The Contribution of Socio-economic Position to the Health Inequalities Faced by Children and Adolescents with Intellectual Disabilities in Britain', *American Journal on Mental Retardation* 112(2): 140–50.

Emerson, E. and Hatton, C. (2007b) 'Poverty, Socio-economic Position, Social Capital and the Health of Children and Adolescents with Intellectual Disabilities in Britain: A Replication', *Journal of Intellectual Disability Research* 51(11): 866–74.

Emerson, E. and Hatton, C. (2007c) 'The Mental Health of Children and Adolescents with Intellectual Disabilities in Britain', *British Journal of Psychiatry* 191: 493–9.

Emerson, E. and Llewellyn, G. (2008) 'The Mental Health of Australian Mothers and Fathers of Young Children at Risk of Disability', *Australian & New Zealand Journal of Public Health* 32(1): 53–9.

Emerson, E. and Einfeld, S. (2010) 'Emotional and Behavioural Difficulties in Young Children with and without Developmental Delay: A Bi-national Perspective', *Journal of Child Psychology and Psychiatry* 51(5): 583–93.

Emerson, E., Vick, B. and Rechel, B. (2011b) 'Health Inequalities and People with Disabilities in Europe', in J. Popay, ed., *Disadvantage, Social Exclusion and Vulnerability Task Group Report* (in press).

Emerson, E., Malam, S., Davies, I. and Spencer, K. (2005) *Adults with Learning Difficulties in England 2003/4* (Leeds: Health and Social Care Information Centre).

Emerson, E., Hatton, C., Blacher, J., Llewellyn, G. and Graham, H. (2006) 'Socio-economic Position, Household Composition, Health Status and Indicators of the Well-being of Mothers of Children with and without Intellectual Disability', *Journal of Intellectual Disability Research* 50(12): 862–73.

Emerson, E., Madden, R., Robertson, J., Graham, H., Hatton, C. and Llewellyn, G. (2009) *Intellectual and Physical Disability, Social Mobility, Social Inclusion and Health*, background paper for the Marmot Review (Lancaster: Centre for Disability Research, Lancaster University).

Emerson, E., McCulloch, A., Graham, H., Blacher, J., Llewellyn, G. and Hatton, C. (2010) 'The Mental Health of Parents of Young Children with and without Developmental Delays', *American Journal on Intellectual and Developmental Disability* 115: 30–42.

Emerson, E., Madden, R., Graham, H., Llewellyn, G., Hatton, C. and Robertson, J. (2011a) 'The Health of Disabled People and the Social Determinants of Health', *Public Health* 125: 145–7.

Gee, G. C., Ro, A., Shariff-Marco, S. and Chae, D. (2009) 'Racial Discrimination and Health Among Asian Americans: Evidence, Assessment, and Directions for Future Research', *Epidemiologic Reviews* 31: 130–51.

Giraud-Saunders, A. (2009) *Equal Access? A Practical Guide for the NHS: Creating a Single Equality Scheme that Includes Improving Access for People with Learning Disabilities* (London: Department of Health).

Gissler, M., Rahkonen, O., Järvelin, M.-R. and Hemminki, E. (1998) 'Social Class Differences in Health Until the Age of Seven Years Among the Finnish 1987 Birth Cohort', *Social Science & Medicine* 46: 1543–52.

Graham, H. (2007) *Unequal Lives: Health and Socioeconomic Inequalities* (Maidenhead: Open University Press).

Guralnik, J. M. (2006) 'Childhood Socioeconomic Status Predicts Physical Functioning a Half Century Later', *Journals of Gerontology: Series A: Biological Sciences and Medical Sciences* 61A(7): 694–701.

Harris, J. C. (2005) *Intellectual Disability: Understanding Its Development, Causes, Evaluation, and Treatment* (Oxford: Oxford University Press).

Hawley, C. A., Ward, A. B., Magnay, A. R. and Long, J. (2003) 'Parental Stress and Burden Following Traumatic Brain Injury Amongst Children and Adolescents', *Brain Injury* 17: 1–23.

Hirst, M. (2005) 'Carer Distress: A Prospective, Population-based Study', *Social Science & Medicine (1982)* 61(3): 697–708.

Honey, A., Emerson, E. and Llewellyn, G. (2011) 'The Mental Health of Young People with Disabilities: Association with Social Conditions', *Social Psychiatry & Psychiatric Epidemiology* 46: 1–10.

Huss, M., Hölling, H., Kurth, B.-M. and Schlack, R. (2008) 'How Often are German Children and Adolescents Diagnosed with ADHD? Prevalence Based on the Judgment of Health Care Professionals: Results of the German Health and Examination Survey (KiGGS)', *European Child & Adolescent Psychiatry* 17: 52–8.

Jenkins, S. P. and Rigg, J. A. (2004) 'Disability and Disadvantage: Selection, Onset and Duration Effects', *Journal of Social Policy* 33(3): 479–501.

Kalff, A. C., Kroes, M., Vles, J. S., Hendriksen, J. G., Feron, F. J., Steyaert, J., van Zeben, T. M., Jolles, J. and van Os, J. (2001) 'Neighbourhood Level and Individual Level SES Effects on Child Problem Behaviour: A Multilevel Analysis', *Journal of Epidemiology & Community Health* 55: 246–50.

Kerr, M. P., Richards, D. and Glover, G. (1996) 'Primary Care for People with a Learning Disability – A Group Practice Survey', *Journal of Applied Research in Intellectual Disability* 9: 347–52.

Krieger, N. (1999) 'Embodying Inequality: A Review of Concepts, Measures, and Methods for Studying Health Consequences of Discrimination', *International Journal of Health Services* 29(2): 295–352.

Kubba, H., MacAndie, C., Ritchie, K. and MacFarlane, M. (2004) 'Is Deafness a Disease of Poverty? The Association Between Socio-economic Deprivation and Congenital Hearing Impairment', *International Journal of Audiology* 43: 123–25.

Kwok, H. and Cheung, P. W. H. (2007) 'Co-morbidity of Psychiatric Disorder and Medical Illness in People with Intellectual Disabilities', *Current Opinion in Psychiatry* 20: 443–9.

Lang, I. A. (2008) 'Neighbourhood Deprivation and Incident Mobility Disability in Older Adults', *Age & Ageing* 37(4): 403–10.

Lidstone, J. S. M., Ells, L. J., Finn, P., Whittaker, V. J., Wilkinson, J. R. and Summerbell, C. D. (2006) 'Independent Associations Between Weight Status and Disability in Adults: Results from the Health Survey for England', *Public Health* 120: 412–17.

Matthews, K. A., Gallo, L. C. and Taylor, S. E. (2010) 'Are Psychosocial Factors Mediators of Socioeconomic Status and Health Connections? A Progress Report and Blueprint for the Future', *Annals of the New York Academy of Sciences* 1186: 146–73.

McMunn, A. M., Nazroo, J. and Breeze, E. (2009) 'Inequalities in Health at Older Ages: A Longitudinal Investigation of the Onset of Illness and Survival Effects in England', *Age and Ageing* 38: 181–7.

Mays, V. M., Cochran, S. D. and Barnes, N. W. (2007) 'Race, Race-based Discrimination, and Health Outcomes Among African Americans', *Annual Review of Psychology* 58: 201–25.

Melchior, M., Lert, F., Martin, M. and Ville, I. (2006) 'Socioeconomic Position in Childhood and in Adulthood and Functional Limitations in Midlife: Data from a Nationally-Representative Survey of French Men and Women', *Social Science & Medicine* 63: 2813–24.

Melville, C., Hamilton, S., Hankey, C., Miller, S. and Boyle, S. (2007) 'The Prevalence and Determinants of Obesity in Adults with Intellectual Disabilities', *Obesity Reviews* 8: 223–30.

Mencap (2007) *Bullying Wrecks Lives: The Experiences of Children and Young People with a Learning Disability* (London: Mencap).

Michael, J. (2008) *Healthcare for All: Report of the Independent Inquiry into Access to Healthcare for People with Learning Disabilities* (London: Independent Inquiry into Access to Healthcare for People with Learning Disabilities).

Minkler, M., Fuller-Thomson, E. and Guralnik, J. M. (2006) 'Gradient of Disability Across the Socioeconomic Spectrum in the United States', *New England Journal of Medicine* 355: 695–703.

Morgan, C. L., Ahmed, Z. and Kerr, M. P. (2000) 'Health Care Provision for People with a Learning Disability: Record-Linkage Study of Epidemiology and Factors Contributing to Hospital Care Uptake', *British Journal of Psychiatry* 176: 37–41.

Myers, H. F. (2009) 'Ethnicity- and Socio-economic Status-related Stresses in Context: An Integrative Review and Conceptual Model', *Journal of Behavioral Medicine* 32: 9–19.

National Institute for Health and Clinical Excellence (2007) *Behaviour Change at Population, Community and Individual Levels* (London: National Institute for Health and Clinical Excellence).

Nazroo, J. (2003) 'The Structuring of Ethnic Inequalities in Health: Economic Position, Racial Discrimination and Racism', *American Journal of Public Health* 93(2): 277–84.

Nelson, T. D. (2009) *Handbook of Prejudice, Stereotyping, and Discrimination* (New York: Psychology Press).

Newacheck, P. W. and Halfon, N. (1998) 'Prevalence and Impact of Disabling Chronic Conditions in Childhood', *American Journal of Public Health* 88(4): 610–17.

Norwich, B. and Kelly, N. (2004) 'Pupils' Views on Inclusion: Moderate Learning Difficulties and Bullying in Mainstream and Special Schools', *British Educational Research Journal* 30: 43–65.

Nunn, A., Johnson, S., Monro, S., Bickerstaffe, T. and Kelsey, S. (2007) *Factors Influencing Social Mobility* (London: Department of Work and Pensions).

Ones, K., Yilmaz, E., Cetinkaya, B. and Caglar, N. (2005) 'Assessment of the Quality of Life of Mothers of Children with Cerebral Palsy (Primary Caregivers)', *Neurorehabilitation and Neural Repair* 19: 232–7.

Oskamp, S. (2000) *Reducing Prejudice and Discrimination* (Mahwah, NJ: Lawrence Erlbaum Associates Publishers).

Owens, P. L., Kerker, B. D., Zigler, E. and Horwitz, S. M. (2006) 'Vision and Oral Health Needs of Individuals with Intellectual Disability', *Mental Retardation and Developmental Disabilities Research Reviews* 12: 28–40.

Parish, S. L., Rose, R. A., Andrews, M. E., Grinstein-Weiss, M. and Richman, E. L. (2008) 'Material Hardship in US Families Raising Children with Disabilities', *Exceptional Children* 75(1): 71–92.

Parkes, J., White-Koning, M., Dickinson, H. O., Thyen, U., Arnaud, C., Beckung, E., Fauconnier, J., Marcelli, M., McManus, V., Michelsen, S. I., Parkinson, K. and Colver, A. (2008) 'Psychological Problems in Children with Cerebral Palsy: A Cross-sectional European Study', *Journal of Child Psychology and Psychiatry* 49(4): 405–13.

Pascoe, E. A. and Richman, L. S. (2009) 'Perceived Discrimination and Health: A Meta-analytic Review', *Psychological Bulletin* 135: 531–54.

Pervin, K., Iseri, P. K., Ozten, E. and Aker, A. T. (2006) 'Posttraumatic Stress Disorder and Major Depressive Disorder is Common in Parents of Children with Epilepsy', *Epilepsy & Behavior* 8: 250–5.

Piachaud, J., Rohde, J. and Pasupathy, A. (1998) 'Health Screening for People with Down's Syndrome', *Journal of Intellectual Disability Research* 42: 341–5.

Plous, S. (2003) *Understanding Prejudice and Discrimination* (New York: McGraw-Hill).

Reynolds, F., Stanistreet, D. and Elton, P. (2008) 'Women with Learning Disabilities and Access to Cervical Screening: Retrospective Cohort Study Using Case Control Methods', *BMC Public Health* 8: 30.

Ritakallio, V.-M. and Bradshaw, J. (2006) 'Family Poverty in the European Union', in J. Bradshaw and A. Hatland, eds, *Social Policy, Employment and Family Change in Comparative Perspective* (Cheltenham: Edward Elgar).

Salm, M. and Schunk, D. (2008) 'Child Health Disparities, Socio-economic Status, and School Enrollment Decisions: Evidence from German Elementary School Entrance Exams', *Advances in Health Economics & Health Services Research* 20: 271–88.

Sassi, F. (2010) *Obesity and the Economics of Prevention: FIT NOT FAT* (Paris: Organisation for Economic Co-operation and Development).

Schneiders, J., Drukker, M., van der Ende, J., Verhulst, F. C., van Os, J. and Nicolson, N. A. (2003) 'Neighbourhood Socioeconomic Disadvantage and Behavioural Problems from Late Childhood into Early Adolescence', *Journal of Epidemiology & Community Health* 57: 699–703.

Scott, K. M., Von Korff, M., Alonso, J., Angermeyer, M. C., Bromet, E., Fayyad, J., de Girolamo, G., Demyttenaere, K., Gasquet, I., Gureje, O., Haro, J. M., He, Y., Kessler, R. C., Levinson, D., Medina Mora, M. E., Oakley Browne, M., Ormel, J., Posada-Villa, J., Watanabe, M. and Williams, D. (2009) 'Mental-physical Co-morbidity and its Relationship with Disability: Results from the World Mental Health Surveys', *Psychological Medicine* 39: 33–43.

Sen, A. (1992) *Inequality Re-examined* (Oxford: Oxford University Press).

Shakespeare, T. (2006) *Disability Rights and Wrongs* (London: Routledge).

Sheard, C., Clegg, J., Standen, P. and Cromby, J. (2001) 'Bullying and People with Severe Intellectual Disability', *Journal of Intellectual Disability Research* 45: 407–15.

Shima, I., Zólyomi, E. and Zaidi, A. (2008) *The Labour Market Situation of People with Disabilities in EU25* (Vienna: European Centre for Social Welfare Policy and Research).

Singer, G. H. (2006) 'Meta-analysis of Comparative Studies of Depression in Mothers of Children with and without Developmental Disabilities', *American Journal on Mental Retardation* 111(3): 155–69.

Spencer, N. J. (2000) *Poverty and Child Health* (Oxford: Radcliffe Medical Press).

Strømme, P. and Magnus, P. (2000) 'Correlations Between Socioeconomic Status, IQ and Aetiology in Mental Retardation: A Population-based Study of Norwegian Children', *Social Psychiatry & Psychiatric Epidemiology* 35: 12–18.

Sundrum, R., Logan, S., Wallace, A. and Spencer, N. (2005) 'Cerebral Palsy and Socioeconomic Status: A Retrospective Cohort Study', *Archive of Diseases of Childhood* 90: 2–3.

The Marmot Review (2010) *Fair Society, Healthy Lives: Strategic Review of Health Inequalities in England Post-2010* (London: The Marmot Review).

Thomas, C. (2007) *Sociologies of Disability and Illness. Contested Ideas in Disability Studies and Medical Sociology* (Basingstoke: Palgrave Macmillan).

Thornicroft, G., Brohan, E., Kassam, A. and Lewis-Holmes, E. (2008) 'Reducing Stigma and Discrimination: Candidate Interventions', *International Journal of Mental Health Systems* 2: 3.

Tropp, L. R. and Mallett, R. K. (2011) *Moving Beyond Prejudice Reduction: Pathways to Positive Intergroup Relations* (Washington, DC: American Psychological Association).

Tuffrey-Wijne, I., Hogg, J. and Curfs, L. (2007) 'End of Life and Palliative Care for People with Intellectual Disabilities Who Have Cancer or Other Life-limiting Illness: A Review of the Literature and Available Resources', *Journal of Applied Research in Intellectual Disabilities* 20: 331–44.

UNESCO (1994) *The Salamanca Statement and Framework for Action on Special Needs Education* (Paris: UNESCO).

UNICEF (2005) *Children and Disability in Transition in the CEE/CIS and Baltic States* (Florence: UNICEF Innocenti Research Centre).

United Nations (2006) *Convention on the Rights of Persons with Disabilities in the United Nations* (New York: United Nations).

Varela, M., Nohr, E., Llopis-Gonzalez, A., Andersen, A. N. and Olsen, J. (2009) 'Socio-occupational Status and Congenital Anomalies', *European Journal of Public Health* 19(2): 161–7.

White, C., Holland, E., Marsland, D. and Oakes, P. (2003) 'The Identification of Environments and Cultures that Promote the Abuse of People with Intellectual Disabilities: A Review of the Literature', *Journal of Applied Research in Intellectual Disabilities* 16: 1–13.

Whitfield, M. L., Langan, J. and Russell, O. (1996) 'Assessing General Practitioners' Care of Adult Patients with Learning Disability: Case Control Study', *Quality in Health Care* 5: 31–5.

WHO and The World Bank Group (2011) *World Report on Disability* (Geneva: World Health Organization).

Williams, B., Copestake, P., Eversley, J. and Stafford, B. (2008) *Experiences and Expectations of Disabled People* (London: Office for Disability Issues).

Williams, D. R. and Mohammed, S. A. (2009) 'Discrimination and Racial Disparities in Health: Evidence and Needed Research', *Journal of Behavioral Medicine* 32: 20–47.

Willis, D. S., Kennedy, C. M. and Kilbride, L. (2008) 'Breast Cancer Screening in Women with Learning Disabilities: Current Knowledge and Considerations', *British Journal of Learning Disabilities* 36(3): 171–84.

World Health Organization (2001) *International Classification of Functioning, Disability and Health* (Geneva: World Health Organization).

World Health Organization (2002) *World Health Report 2002: Reducing Risks, Promoting Healthy Life* (Geneva: World Health Organization).

World Health Organization (2007) *International Classification of Functioning, Disability and Health – Children and Youth Version. ICF-CY* (Geneva: World Health Organization).

World Health Organization (2008) *Closing the Gap in a Generation: Health Equity Through Action on the Social Determinants of Health. Final Report of the Commission on the Social Determinants of Health* (Geneva: World Health Organization).

World Health Organization Regional Office for Europe (2007) *The Challenge of Obesity in the WHO European Region and the Strategies for Response* (Copenhagen: World Health Organization Regional Office for Europe).

World Health Organization Regional Office for Europe (2010) *Interim First Report on Social Determinants of Health and the Health Divide in the WHO European Region* (Copenhagen: World Health Organization Regional Office for Europe).

Yang, J., Carmichael, S. L., Canfield, M., Song, J., Shaw, G. M. and National Birth Defects Prevention Study (2007) 'Socioeconomic Status in Relation to Selected Birth Defects in a Large Multicentered US Case-control Study', *American Journal of Epidemiology* 167(2): 145–54.

20

DISABILITY IN DEVELOPING COUNTRIES

Tom Shakespeare

Introduction

On 3 May 2008 the United Nations (UN) Convention on the Rights of Persons with Disabilities came into force, marking perhaps the end of the first phase of the global disability rights movement, which can be said to have begun in 1981 with the formation of Disabled Peoples' International. Principles and practices such as the social model of disability, independent living, inclusive education and community-based rehabilitation, and slogans such as 'nothing about us without us' are now commonly used across the world, despite the survival of charitable ways of thinking and the continued dominance of professional approaches in the disability field. While negative attitudes remain common, in many high-income countries there is a new generation of people with disabilities who have grown up expecting access to education, employment and community participation. Rather than needing to self-identify as disability activists and join a struggle for civil rights, young people with disabilities increasingly have the option of living in the mainstream and expressing their individuality without reference to their impairment. Access is expected as a right, not a privilege.

Yet many of these benefits have not reached the majority of the world's population, who live in conditions far removed from what pertains in North America, Europe or Australasia. The human rights discourse may have permeated the planet – with 151 states having signed the UN Convention (as of 1 October 2011) – but the everyday living situation is not just or equitable. This chapter explores some of the ways in which the majority of people with disabilities remain disadvantaged, and highlights several signs of hope that the situation might improve in future.

Preparation of the World Health Organization (WHO)/World Bank *World Report on Disability* (2011), on which this chapter is largely based, has identified considerable problems with the data and research on global disability. In many areas, we lack solid evidence about the lives of people with disabilities in developing countries and the problems they face. Frequently, and for the best of motives, numbers – on education, on poverty, on health – are used for advocacy purposes, but are not supported by good research, or sometimes any research at all. The *World Report on Disability* aimed to fill the gap by bringing together the best available scientific evidence. However, the majority of research and analysis of disability remains relevant to the minority of people with disability in the world (Grech 2009). It is for this reason, as well as for reasons of space, that the discussion in this chapter is necessarily incomplete.

Disability from the global to the local

Disability is a global phenomenon, although there are local differences in magnitude and characteristics. In low-income countries, infectious diseases, malnutrition, accidents and injuries may lead to a high incidence of disability, particularly among children, but poverty and lack of health care mean that people with disabilities may suffer premature mortality. By contrast, in high-income countries, congenital anomalies have become a highly significant cause of childhood disability, because communicable diseases have largely been eliminated (McCandless *et al.* 2003).

However, there are important areas of convergence between the epidemiology of disability in different settings. The non-communicable diseases – diabetes, hypertension, heart disease – which are major causes of disability in high-income countries are now becoming significant problems in regions such as south-east Asia (Dans *et al.* 2011). With increased longevity in all societies, disabilities associated with ageing are on the rise everywhere. A final commonality is the high burden of depression and other mental health conditions. According to the Global Burden of Disease study (World Health Organization 2004), unipolar depression is the fourth leading contributor to the global burden of disease, accounting for nearly 12 per cent of total years lived with disability worldwide, and by 2020 will be the second highest contributor to the global burden of disease (Üstün *et al.* 2004).

While disability is ubiquitous, the responses to it vary, depending on context, culture and resources. For example, Allotey *et al.* (2003) challenge assumptions surrounding the Disability Adjusted Life Year (DALY) by showing that paraplegia has very different implications in Australia and Cameroon. What they describe as the social determination of the severity of disease means that people with paraplegia in the high-income context, while disadvantaged, can nevertheless participate and live good lives. In Cameroon, 50 per cent of rural and 15 per cent of urban participants in the study did not own or have access to a wheelchair. Transport was almost impossible to access, roads and paths were impassable, sanitation was limited and toilets were inaccessible. As a result of these factors, it is common that in low-income settings, people with paraplegia only live for a few years after injury, due to the impact of avoidable complications such as pressure sores and urinary tract infections (UTIs). While Australian respondents reported stigma, pain and spasms, and UTIs, together with restricted employment options, the majority rated their health as very good; they had manual or motorized wheelchairs and could expect access to buildings and public spaces. As a result, Australians with paraplegia scored much better than their counterparts in Cameroon: 'the single-room experience of a person with paraplegia in Cameroon, who now smells so badly that she is socially isolated, has no corollary in the Australian experience' (Allotey *et al.* 2003: 957).

Impact of impairment/priority of prevention

Prevention of health conditions associated with disability is a controversial topic (Wang 1998; Lollar and Crews 2003). The social model approach has sometimes been interpreted as meaning that rather than preventing impairment, the emphasis should be only on preventing disabling barriers. The UN Convention on the Rights of Persons with Disabilities does not mention prevention, except insofar as persons with disabilities should receive health services that can prevent them developing secondary conditions or co-morbidities. Many disability rights activists would prefer to see policies addressing prevention of health conditions kept entirely separate from policies promoting the rights of persons with disabilities.

Nevertheless, the difficulties and realities of life with impairment in low-income countries suggest that interventions to prevent avoidable impairment should have high priority. Indeed, the efforts of international agencies such as the WHO, UNAIDS and the Global Partnership are largely dedicated towards reducing the incidence of avoidable conditions such as HIV, tuberculosis, malaria, polio, glaucoma and so on, as well as the impact of causes of illness and impairment, such as road traffic injury, childhood injury, violence, etc.

There need be no contradiction between preventing impairments and promoting rights and inclusion for people with disabilities. Emma Stone (1996) has pointed out that China, which has been criticized by activists and ethicists for the preventive stance of its Maternal and Infant Health Care Law, also has gone further than many developing countries in achieving provision and inclusion for its citizens with disabilities. It is also the case that organizations controlled by people with disabilities have sometimes taken a lead in prevention initiatives: for example, the QuadPara Association of South Africa campaigns for better road safety using the slogan 'Buckle up: we don't want new members'.

Cultural differences

Are concepts such as the social model of disability (Oliver 1990) or independent living applicable outside the developed countries in which they were first developed? Miles (2003) challenges the application of European or American models of autonomous individualism to disabled people's organizations in south Asia. Speaking broadly, while in all societies family members provide care, in non-Western societies it is more common, and more culturally normative, for people with disabilities to be supported within the family and community. An anthropological distinction is often drawn between 'ego-centric' Western societies and 'sociocentric' developing societies, where family and community are more important than individualism (Ingstad and Whyte 1995; Shakespeare 2000). This does not mean that international human rights standards such as the UN Convention on the Rights of Persons with Disabilities are not relevant in developing country settings. But it does mean that aspiring to live independently, in the Western individualist sense, may not be such an important goal in a culture where traditionally everyone is inter-dependent and most people live with their extended families. Moreover, many cultures (e.g., Maasai, indigenous Australian, etc.) may not share the unitary conception of 'disability' which underpins, for example, the International Classification of Functioning, Disability and Health (2001), or the social model of disability (Oliver 1990). People in traditional cultures may have different beliefs about the origins and nature of disability. Despite the problems of poverty and access to services that are elaborated in this chapter, in some ways, people with disabilities may be more included in the relational cultures of low-income countries than in Western, individualistic societies.

Barriers to participation

This section reviews some of the evidence about areas of life where people with disabilities may experience unmet need or face barriers to participation. It should be noted that disability is a heterogeneous experience (see, for example, Grech 2008). People with different impairments may experience different levels of disadvantage, with people with intellectual impairments and mental health conditions often facing most barriers (World Health Organization/World Bank 2011). Women can experience the double burden of gender inequality in addition to disability. People with disabilities who come from high-income families, in low-income settings, will do much better than the general population. Those in urban areas are generally better served than those living in rural or remote areas.

Environments

Disabled people are particularly disadvantaged due to environmental barriers in low-income countries (Allotey *et al.* 2003; Coulson *et al.* 2006). While there are barriers in all settings, generally, people in rural areas are additionally disadvantaged because services tend to be concentrated in urban areas, and because transport opportunities are limited.

To list some of the problems in the home: pit latrines are difficult to use for people with physical or visual impairments; dwellings may be cramped, lacking space for people who use wheelchairs; steps or other obstacles may render buildings inaccessible. To list some of the problems in the wider environment: paths or roads may be uneven, potholed and impassable in wet weather; high kerbs, or lack of kerbs and lack of safe crossings make it dangerous to cross roads; there may be concerns about security. Transport options may be limited to inaccessible buses or vans, with taxis being unaffordable or else taxi drivers being prejudiced against carrying disabled people because of extra time and hassle. All of these common problems in low-income settings are usually multiplied in informal settings, in refugee camps and after disasters (Tipple and Coulson 2009).

However, the need to rebuild and the inflow of development aid can create opportunities to build more accessible dwellings, as happened with one Sri Lankan housing project after the Boxing Day tsunami; the project achieved low-cost level access and accessible bathrooms (World Health Organization/World Bank 2011). Moreover, there are models for more accessible solutions in informal settings, for example a seated platform next to a communal hand pump, or a bench fitted over a pit latrine (Jones and Reed 2005). In transport, bus rapid transit schemes have been developed to ensure access for all, for example in Curtiba, Brazil, and metro schemes in cities such as Delhi have been constructed with accessibility in mind. Examples of efforts to develop training in universal design for architects and engineers can be found in countries including India and Malaysia (World Health Organization/World Bank 2011).

Health and rehabilitation

While disability should not be considered a health issue, people with disabilities clearly do have health care needs, and sometimes more complex and continuing needs than non-disabled people. These include needs for treatment, management and rehabilitation for primary conditions, and mainstream health care needs for health promotion, screening and treatment – for example, for conditions such as HIV/AIDS, to which people with disabilities might be disproportionately vulnerable.

However, people with disabilities often experience inequities in health. People with disabilities are often poorer, and thus suffer increased exposure to social determinants of ill health. Moreover, low-income countries are less likely to have universal health systems than high-income countries, which means that costs of health care, in the form of 'catastrophic health expenditure', can tip people with disabilities into poverty. The WHO *World Health Survey* found that catastrophic health expenditure was experienced by nearly a third of respondents with disabilities in low-income countries, but less than a fifth of people with disabilities in high-income countries (World Health Organization/World Bank 2011). A study in Sierra Leone, for example, found that persons with severe or very severe disabilities spent on average 1.3 times more on health care than non-disabled respondents (Trani *et al.* 2010).

People with disabilities, who may have higher needs for health care, face barriers in receiving the care they require. These may arise from inadequate provision, access or transport difficulties, discrimination or prejudice in health care. Analysis of the WHO *World Health Survey* found that people with disabilities in low-income countries were more than twice as likely to find provider skills or equipment inadequate; nearly three times as likely to be denied care; and up to four times as likely to be treated badly (World Health Organization/World Bank 2011). Problems with attitudes, information and communication are particularly important: a survey commissioned by the Zimbabwe Parents of Handicapped Children Association found that people with disabilities were excluded from general HIV/AIDS services because voluntary counselling and testing services were not offered in sign language for people with hearing impairments, and education and communication materials were not offered in Braille for people with visual impairments (Banda 2006). A study in rural areas of the Gambia reported that out of 380 people with epilepsy only 16 per cent knew that preventive treatment was possible. Of the 48 per cent of people with epilepsy who had never used biomedical treatment, 70 per cent did not know that clinics offered treatment for seizures (Coleman *et al.* 2002).

In a review of childhood hearing impairment, where proven neonatal interventions (e.g., vaccination, hygiene, education) can reduce the impact, the authors conclude: 'National health systems in most developing countries are too weak to bear the added burden of non-fatal but disabling disorders without external technical and financial support' (Olusanya and Newton 2007: 1316).

Mental health is a particular area of unmet need. In a large multi-country survey supported by the WHO, it was shown that 76.3 per cent and 85.4 per cent of people with serious mental health conditions in developing countries received no treatment in the year prior to the study, compared with high-income treatment gaps of 35.5 per cent to 50.3 per cent (World Mental Health Survey Consortium 2004). Access to psychiatric medicines has been found to be particularly problematic (Raja *et al.* 2009).

Rehabilitation is another neglected area of health care, despite its proven value in enabling people with impairments to improve functioning. Data from four southern African countries found only between about 17.3 per cent and 36.6 per cent of those who needed assistive devices actually received them. Between 26.3 per cent and 54.8 per cent of those in need of medical rehabilitation received this service, while between 8.4 per cent and 23.6 per cent of respondents received the welfare services they needed (Eide *et al.* 2003a, 2003b; Eide and Loeb 2006). A study of people identified as disabled from three districts in Beijing, China, found that 75 per cent of those interviewed expressed a need for rehabilitation services of different types, of which only 27 per cent had received such services (Zongjie *et al.* 2007).

Assistive devices such as wheelchairs, artificial limbs, hearing aids and splints are vital for achieving independence and participation in society. A national study in 2007 on rehabilitation needs in China found that the level of unmet need for rehabilitation services was particularly high in the areas of assistive devices and rehabilitation therapy (Qiu 2007). It is estimated that 30 million people in Africa, Asia and Latin America need prosthetic and orthotic services (Lindström 2008), requiring an estimated 180,000 rehabilitation professionals with varying levels of training. In 2005 there were 24 prosthetic and orthotic schools in developing countries, graduating a total of 400 trainees annually. Worldwide, existing training arrangements for prosthetic and orthotic professionals and other providers of essential rehabilitation services are completely inadequate in comparison to the need (World Health Organization/International Society for Prosthetics and Orthotics 2005).

Education

Most of the available cross-section data for education suggests that children with disabilities tend to have lower school attendance rates. For example, Deon Filmer (2008) reported on surveys from

14 countries that showed gaps in attendance between disabled and non-disabled children of up to 50 per cent. In India a survey estimated the share of disabled children not enrolled in school at more than five times the national rate, even in the more prosperous states. In Karnataka, the best performing major state, almost one quarter of children with disabilities were out of school, and in poorer states, such as Madhya Pradesh and Assam, more than half (World Bank 2009). SINTEF data from Malawi, Namibia, Zambia and Zimbabwe show that between 9 per cent and 18 per cent of children of age 5 years or older without a disability had never attended school, but between 24 per cent and 39 per cent of children with a disability had never attended (Loeb and Eide 2004; Eide *et al.* 2003a, 2003b). The exclusion of disabled children from school is particularly important because without education, people with disabilities are less likely to become employed, and are more likely to remain poor.

Clearly, global initiatives to promote Education For All have failed to include children with disabilities effectively. Barriers to participation in education include: lack of political commitment and leadership; inaccessible schools; distance of travel to school; negative attitudes and low expectations from teachers and families; rigid curricula and lack of appropriate teaching methods and materials. Lack of funding means that there are very few specialist schools in low-income countries, so expansion of this provision is neither cost effective nor desirable in terms of the UN Convention's emphasis on inclusive education systems.

A number of low-income countries have taken steps to improve access to education for children with disabilities. For example, after support and input from Finland, Ethiopia's Sebeta Teacher Training Institute now ensures that teachers are prepared to teach children with disabilities and meet diverse learning needs (Lasonen *et al.* 2005). Lao People's Democratic Republic (PDR) has promoted inclusive education in 539 schools (Grimes 2009), although this only reaches 3,000 children with disabilities (less than a tenth of the total population of children with disabilities in Lao PDR). Vietnam ran a campaign to identify excluded children and to train teachers and parents, reaching 4,000 children with disabilities. Again, the majority of Vietnamese disabled children remain excluded (Villa *et al.* 2003). Non-governmental organizations (NGOs) have developed small-scale projects in many low-income countries, such as the Oriang project in western Kenya, supported by Leonard Cheshire Disability (Ogot *et al.* 2008). While these bring benefits to the 2,568 children involved in five primary schools, of whom 282 are disabled, this has limited impact on a national scale.

Employment

While it is well known that there are major gaps in employment between disabled and non-disabled people in high-income countries (OECD 2003), the existing data reveals that the gaps in low-income countries are less pronounced. In Zambia, for example, SINTEF researchers (Eide and Loeb 2006) found that the employment rate of people with disabilities was 45.5 per cent, as compared to 56.5 per cent of the general population, giving an employment ratio of 0.81. In India, Mitra and Sambamoorthi (2006) found that 37.6 per cent of disabled people were employed, as compared to 62.5 per cent of the general population, giving a ratio of 0.61. In China, Buckup (2009) found that 48.9 per cent of disabled people and 73 per cent of non-disabled people were unemployed, giving a ratio of 0.67. Given that in Britain and many Organisation for Economic Co-operation and Development (OECD) countries disabled people are on average twice as likely to be unemployed as non-disabled people (i.e. a ratio of 0.5), this suggests that the differential is less acute in low-income countries. This is due to the lower overall employment rates in developing countries, for example South Africa, where people with mild to moderate disabilities have an employment rate of 46.96 per cent

(Statistics South Africa 2006) compared with the non-disabled rate of 48 per cent, or Sierra Leone, where 56.1 per cent of people with mild or moderate disabilities were working, compared with 60.4 per cent of non-disabled adults.

The implication is that as a country develops economically, the employment inequalities between disabled and non-disabled people are likely to increase. Many people in low-income countries, disabled or non-disabled, are engaged in household agricultural activity or the informal economy. However, people with more severe impairments are likely to be disadvantaged in any setting or sector: the evidence from Sierra Leone shows that only 29.6 per cent of adults with severe or very severe disabilities were working (Trani *et al.* 2010), and Grech (2008) paints a grim picture of the struggle for subsistence in rural Guatemala.

Poverty and social protection

Poverty is one of the areas where evidence is particularly weak in low-income settings. Data is scarce, and methodologies often inadequate (Braithwaite and Mont 2009).

It is commonly asserted that people with disabilities are disproportionately poor. In high-income settings there is strong evidence to substantiate this claim (Zaidi and Burchardt 2005; Braithwaite and Mont 2009, Cullinan *et al.* 2011). However, while it is always assumed that the problem is worse in low-income settings – intuitively, most people believe this must be the case – there is little hard evidence. Where the mass of the population are vulnerable to poverty, it may be that people with disabilities do not fare much worse than their neighbours. The SINTEF studies of southern African countries showed that the gap was very narrow for many indicators of household well-being (Loeb and Eide 2004; Eide *et al.* 2003a, 2003b; Eide and Loeb 2006). Research in Sierra Leone told a similar story (Trani *et al.* 2010).

In South Africa, adults who are unable to support themselves economically because of disability receive the disability grant, and families with children who require extra care and attention receive the care dependency grant (Swartz and Schneider 2006). Recipients of these grants rose from 732, 322 in April 1997 to 1,270,964 in April 2004. In most cases, the grant relieves poverty for an entire family. In the context of a society in which up to a quarter of people are living in chronic poverty, it may consequently be the case that families with disabled members could be better off than their non-disabled members. However, South Africa is unusual. Few low-income countries have social safety nets, particularly safety nets aimed at people with disabilities. However, countries including Bangladesh, Ghana and Zambia are beginning to experiment with social protection programmes (Marriott and Gooding 2007).

People with disabilities face material hardship in low-income countries. Yet because poverty is ubiquitous, the gap between households with disabled members and households without disabled members may often be less extreme than the gaps in high-income settings. A recent analysis of the WHO *World Health Survey* found that while disability was associated with higher multidimensional poverty in most of the developing countries in the study, households with disabilities were not worse off when measured by average non-health expenditure (Mitra *et al.* 2011). This is not to say that disabled people are not poor in low-income countries, only to say that so is everyone else. However, given that people with disabilities have additional costs – for health care and other support – they require a higher income to end up at the same level as others, which Amartya Sen has called 'conversion handicap'. When Braithwaite and Mont adjusted Vietnam data for the extra costs of disability, they found that the poverty rate for households with disabled members jumped from 16.4 per cent to 20.1 per cent in Vietnam, where the overall poverty rate is 13.5 per cent (Braithwaite and Mont 2009).

Ways forward

The disabled people's movement is not limited to high-income countries. As authors such as Diane Driedger (1989) and James Charlton (1998) have shown, the principle of 'nothing about us without us' has become ubiquitous in disability communities worldwide, and international networks such as Disabled Peoples' International, World Blind Union and the World Federation of the Deaf have a very broad global membership. At a local level, countries like South Africa and Uganda have strong guarantees on disability rights in their constitutions, and good provision for representation of people with disabilities within government and civil society (Matsebula *et al.* 2006). Where well-funded and effectively led, strong disabled people's organizations (DPOs) can campaign for change and develop information and independent living services for their members, and help individuals to empower themselves. However, DPOs themselves need to ensure that they are representative of all disabled people, that they are based on a human rights approach and that they are accountable to their members (Lang 2009).

Worldwide, the advocacy of the disability movement was a key factor in achieving the UN Convention on the Rights of Persons with Disabilities in 2006. Now ratified by more than 100 countries, this international treaty sets out clearly what states and other duty bearers need to do to implement the human rights and ensure the social development of people with disabilities. Having achieved this landmark, the next stage is to hold countries to account and to use the Convention as a tool for positive social change – removing barriers, challenging attitudes, improving services. International cooperation (Article 32) is an important way of achieving these goals. Better data and research is also explicitly mentioned in Article 31 as a means to improve policies and identify barriers. However, as Raymond Lang (2009) argues, the Convention is not a panacea: it is a necessary tool, but not sufficient to implement disability rights. In particular, the states responsible for its implementation need to prove capable of delivering on its promises.

Within the context of the human rights agenda epitomized by the Convention, it is important to mention international development assistance and community-based rehabilitation (CBR) as two relevant tools for helping overcome the problems previously described in this chapter.

Development assistance

While international NGOs have often created very progressive initiatives – around livelihood, education, rehabilitation and other needs – these welcome initiatives to foster development and disability inclusion need to be put into context. Roger Riddell points out that aid represents less than 10 per cent of the gross national income of the world's 50 poorest countries and estimates that less than 5 per cent of all overseas direct aid is used for disability projects and programmes (Riddell 2010: 44). Often, quick fixes like immunization programmes are preferred by funders to complex and long-term interventions such as building rehabilitation services or making education inclusive. For states, let alone DPOs, to access funding can be difficult and time consuming. For example, there are more than 200 official donor agencies, and fear of corruption and waste means that monitoring and reporting requirements can be onerous (Riddell 2010: 33).

One overarching framework for development is the Millennium Development Goals (MDGs) – agreed on by the international community in 2000 and endorsed by 189 countries. The MDGs are a unified set of development objectives addressing the needs of the world's poorest and most marginalized people, and are supposed to be achieved by 2015. The goals are as follows:

Goal 1: Eradicate extreme poverty and hunger.
Goal 2: Achieve universal primary education.

Goal 3: Promote gender equality and empower women.
Goal 4: Reduce child mortality.
Goal 5: Improve maternal health.
Goal 6: Combat HIV/AIDS, malaria, and other diseases.
Goal 7: Ensure environmental sustainability.
Goal 8: Develop a global partnership for development.

The MDGs are a compact between developing and developed nations. They recognize the efforts that must be taken by developing countries themselves, as well as the contribution that developed countries need to make through trade, development assistance, debt relief, access to essential medicines, and technology transfer.

While the background documents explicitly mention people with disabilities, they are not referred to in the MDGs, nor in the material generated as part of the process to achieve them. The MDGs will be impossible to achieve if people with disabilities are not included in policies and programmes, and in monitoring and evaluation of these programmes. This is particularly true for achievement of universal primary education and reduction in child mortality: the UNICEF Multiple Indicator Cluster Survey revealed that children at risk of disabilities are disproportionately likely to be not attending school, to be underweight and to be stunted (Gottlieb *et al.* 2009), and therefore addressing these inequities is part of achieving the goals.

The 2010 MDG report is the first to mention disabilities, noting the limited opportunities faced by children with disabilities, and the link between disability and marginalization in education. The Ministerial Declaration of July 2010 recognizes disability as a cross-cutting issue essential for the attainment of the MDGs, emphasizing the need to ensure that women and girls with disabilities are not subject to multiple or aggravated forms of discrimination, or excluded from participation in the implementation of the MDGs (E/2010/L.8, OP 9). The UN General Assembly concluded its high level meeting on the MDGs in September 2010 by adopting the resolution 'Keeping the promise: united to achieve the Millennium Development Goals' (64/299), which recognizes that 'policies and actions must also focus on persons with disabilities, so that they benefit from progress towards achieving the Millennium Development Goals' (A/RES/64/299, OP 28).

The existing framework and mechanisms of the MDGs can include disability. Data are available that could be used to encourage the inclusion of people with disabilities in the MDG process. The implications of General Assembly discussions are that data collection, targets and strategies around the MDGs should include disability, accessibility and inclusion. In addition, persons with disabilities need to be actively involved in planning, implementing and monitoring to make the MDGs achievable (in line with Article 32 of the UN Convention on the Rights of Persons with Disabilities, and the UN resolution 'Realizing the MDGs for Persons with Disabilities').

Donors do appear to be committed to the inclusion of disability in their programmes. Bilateral donors such as Norad (Norway) and SIDA (Sweden) have emphasized mainstreaming of disability in development assistance. AusAid (Australia) has also developed a progressive policy, *Development for All: Towards a Disability-Inclusive Australian Aid Program 2009–14*. However, it should be noted that previous attempts at mainstreaming disability by USAID, the World Bank, NORAD (Norway) and the Department for International Development (UK) had mixed success (Albert *et al.* 2005). Interestingly, some DPOs in developed countries – such as the Norwegian Council on Disability are themselves raising funds to support their counterparts in low-income settings. In Finland, the Finnish Disabled People's International Development Association brings together six DPOs to promote human rights and improvement of living conditions of disabled people in developing countries, in partnership with the Finnish Ministry of Foreign Affairs.

Community-based rehabilitation

CBR began as a way of ensuring that disabled people accessed rehabilitation in community settings, given the scarcity of tertiary facilities in low-income countries. However, the approach was taken up by other agencies such as the International Labour Organization (ILO) and UNESCO, and evolved into a broader strategy for social inclusion, poverty reduction and community development, particularly after the 2004 joint position paper of the WHO, the ILO and UNESCO. CBR services are delivered by professional workers, by trained volunteers, by other members of the community, including family members, and by people with disabilities themselves. CBR projects vary in the extent to which they remain focused around medical rehabilitation or take a broader approach, and in the extent to which people with disabilities are centrally involved, within a commitment to human rights and empowerment. CBR programmes are increasingly oriented not just at supporting individuals, but towards removing social barriers – for example, providing access to water and sanitation or transport (Rule *et al.* 2006), or challenging negative attitudes and promoting inclusion in education (Dalal 2006).

Although more than 90 countries now have CBR programmes, and while CBR networks now exist in the Asia-Pacific, African and South American regions, provision of CBR remains uneven and variable. In some countries (e.g., Mongolia) governments use CBR as a strategy, whereas in other countries it is left to international or national NGOs to develop projects, which often have limited coverage and reach. A typical example of implementation is Malawi, where CBR was first introduced in 1988 and which is now working towards establishing a national programme (Eggen *et al.* 2009). The Malawi Council for the Handicapped (MACOHA) – a subsidiary of the Ministry of Persons with Disabilities and the Elderly (MPWDE) – is the main implementing agency, working in partnership with other government ministries, the Federation of Disability Organisations in Malawi (FEDOMA), Christoffel Blindenmission (CBM), the Norwegian Association of the Disabled (NAD) and Sightsavers International. The MACOHA is using the *CBR Guidelines* as a framework to align the various CBR initiatives in Malawi into one comprehensive programme.

Evidence for the effectiveness of CBR varies (Mitchell 1999), but research and evaluation is increasingly being conducted (Mannan and Turnbull 2007; Kuipers *et al.* 2008; Finkenflügel *et al.* 2005), and information sharing is increasing through regional networks such as the CBR Africa Network (CAN), the CBR Asia-Pacific Network and the CBR American and Caribbean Network. Key principles for effective CBR include promoting inter-sectoral collaboration (e.g., between health, education and livelihood initiatives) and partnership (e.g, between professionals, families and disabled people). One future challenge is to better involve DPOs in the development of CBR, and another is to develop accredited training for CBR workers (Rule *et al.* 2006). The recently published *CBR Guidelines* (World Health Organization 2010) position CBR as a strategy for implementing the UN Convention on the Rights of Persons with Disabilities, and emphasize the need to promote the empowerment of people with disabilities.

Conclusion

Disability studies cannot be focused solely on Western experiences. It would be deeply regrettable if researchers spent their time exploring theoretical issues while neglecting practical and applied research to support social change. The diverse experiences of the millions of people with disabilities living across the world's countries and cultures are fascinating, while the poverty and social exclusion endured by the majority are far in excess of anything experienced in developed countries. Both curiosity and social commitment demands that Western researchers contribute to expanding the knowledge base on global disability.

This chapter has given a very brief overview of some of the issues, citing some of the available research and data from low- and middle-income countries. A much fuller analysis, providing extensive guidance on ways forward, can be found in the WHO/World Bank *World Report on Disability* (2011). It is important to reiterate the need for more and better research on the living conditions of people with disabilities and on what works to remove barriers and foster participation. There are many examples of good practice and low-cost solutions in developing countries, but evaluations need to be conducted and disseminated to share best practice and shape policy. This information will be vital to successful implementation of the UN Convention on the Rights of Persons with Disabilities.

The priority is therefore to foster research collaborations between developed and developing countries, and to contribute to training of researchers in low-income settings, particularly researchers with disabilities. In this endeavour, it is necessary not simply to export Western notions – for example, the social model of disability or independent living – but to respect and learn from different traditions and ways of including and empowering people with disabilities.

Acknowledgement and disclaimer

This chapter draws on evidence gathered for the *World Report on Disability* (World Health Organization/World Bank 2011), of which the author was an editor and lead author. 370 different individuals contributed to the *World Report*, and this chapter draws on their work. The author is a staff member of the World Health Organization. The author alone is responsible for the views expressed in this publication and they do not necessarily represent the decisions or policies of the World Health Organization.

References

Albert, B., Dube, A. K., Riis-Hansen, T. C. (2005) 'Has Disability Been Mainstreamed into Development Cooperation?' Disability Knowledge and Research Programme; available online at http://www.dfid.gov.uk/r4d/Search ResearchDatabase.asp?OutPutId=173465 (accessed 6 October 2011).

Allotey, P., Reidpath, D., Kouamé, A. and Cummins, R. (2003) 'The DALY, Context and the Determinants of the Severity of Disease: An Exploratory Comparison of Paraplegia in Australia and Cameroon', *Social Science and Medicine* 57(5): 949–58.

Banda, I. (2006) 'Disability, Poverty and HIV/AIDS. *Newsletter of Disabled Persons*, South Africa.

Braithwaite, J. and Mont, D. (2009) 'Disability and Poverty: A survey of the World Bank Poverty Assessments and Implications', *ALTER European Journal of Disability Research* 3: 219–32.

Buckup, S. (2009) *The Price of Exclusion: The Economic Consequences of Excluding People with Disabilities from the World of Work* (Geneva: ILO).

Charlton, J. (1998) *Nothing About Us Without Us: Disability, Oppression and Empowerment* (Berkeley, CA: University of California Press).

Coleman, R., Loppy, L. and Walraven, G. (2002) 'The Treatment Gap and Primary Health Care for People with Epilepsy in Rural Gambia', *Bulletin of the World Health Organization* 80: 378.

Coulson, J., Napier, M. and Matsebe, G. (2006) 'Disability and Universal Access: Observations on Housing from the Spatial and Social Periphery', in B. Watermeyer, L. Swartz, T. Lorenzo, M. Schneider and M. Priestley, eds, *Disability and Social Change: A South African Agenda* (Cape Town: Human Sciences Research Council Press): pp. 325–49.

Cullinan, J., Gannon, B. and Lyons, S. (2011) 'Estimating the Extra Cost of Living for People with Disabilities', *Health Economics* 20: 582–99.

Dalal, A. K. (2006) 'Social Interventions to Moderate Discrimination Attitudes: The Case of the Physically Challenged in India', *Psychology, Health and Medicine* 11(3): 374–82.

Dans, A., Nawi, N., Varghese, C., Tai, E. S., Firestone, R. and Bonita, R. (2011) 'The Rise of Chronic Non-communicable Diseases in Southeast Asia: Time for Action', *The Lancet* 9766: 680–89.

Driedger, D. (1989) *The Last Civil Rights Movement* (London: Hurst).

Eggen, O., Nganwa, A. B. and Suka, A. D. (2009) As Strong as the Weakest Link: An Evaluation of the Community Based Rehabilitation Programme (CBRP) in Malawi (Oslo: Norwegian Institute of International Affairs); available at http://english.nupi.no/Publications/Books-and-reports/2009/As-Strong-as-The-Weakest-Link (accessed 1 October 2011).

Eide, A. H. and Loeb, M. E., eds, (2006) *Living Conditions Among People with Activity Limitations in Zambia* (Oslo: SINTEF).

Eide, A. H., Nhiwatiwa, S., Muderedzi, J. and Loeb, M. E. (2003a) *Living Conditions Among People with Disabilities in Zimbabwe: A Representative, Regional Study* (Oslo: SINTEF).

Eide, A. H., van Rooy, G. and Loeb, M. E. (2003b) *Living Conditions Among People with Disabilities in Namibia: A National, Representative Study* (Oslo: SINTEF).

Filmer, D. (2008) 'Disability, Poverty, and Schooling in Developing Countries: Results from 14 Household Surveys', *The World Bank Economic Review* 22: 141–63.

Finkenflügel, H., Wolffers, I. and Huijsman, R. (2005) 'The Evidence Base for Community-based Rehabilitation: A Literature Review', *International Journal of Rehabilitation Research* 28: 187–201.

Gottlieb, C. A., Maenner, M. J., Cappa, C. and Durkin, M. S. (2009) 'Child Disability Screening, Nutrition and Early Learning in 18 Countries with Low and Middle Incomes: Data from the Third Round of UNICEF's Multiple Indicator Cluster Survey (2005–06)', *The Lancet* 374(970): 1831–9.

Grech, S. (2008) 'Living with Disability in Rural Guatemala: Exploring Connections and Impacts on Poverty', *International Journal of Disability, Community and Rehabilitation* 7(2); available online at http://www.ijdcr.ca/VOL07_02_CAN/articles/grech.shtml (accessed 1 October 2011).

Grech, S. (2009) 'Disability, Poverty and Development: Critical Reflections on the Majority World Debate', *Disability and Society* 24(6): 771–84.

Grimes, P. A. (2009) *Quality Education for All: A History of the Lao PDR Inclusive Education Project 1993–2009* (Vientiane: Save the Children Norway).

Ingstad, B. and Whyte, S. R. (1995) *Disability and Culture* (Berkeley: University of California Press).

Jones, H. and Reed, R. (2005) *Water and Sanitation for Disabled People and Other Vulnerable Groups: Designing Services to Improve Accessibility* (Loughborough: Loughborough University, Water and Development Centre).

Kuipers, P., Wirz, S. and Hartley, S. (2008) 'Systematic Synthesis of Community-based Rehabilitation (CBR) Project Evaluation for Evidence-based Policy: A Proof-of-Concept Study', *BMC International Health and Human Rights* 8: 3.

Lang, R. (2009) 'The United Nations Convention on the Right and Dignities for Persons with Disability: A Panacea for Ending Disability Discrimination?' *Alter* 3: 266–85.

Lasonen, J., Kemppainen, R. and Raheem, K. (2005) Education and Training in Ethiopia: An Evaluation of Approaching EFA Goals (Jyväskylä: Institute for Educational Research, University of Jyväskylä); available online at http://ktl.jyu.fi/arkisto/verkkojulkaisuja/TP_23_Lasonen.pdf (accessed 1 October 2011).

Lindström, A. (2008) 'Appropriate Technologies for Assistive Devices in Low-income Countries', in J. D. Hsu, J. W. Michael and J. R. Fisk, eds, *AAOS Atlas of Orthoses and Assistive Devices* (Philadelphia: Mosby/Elsevier).

Loeb, M. E. and Eide, A. H., eds, (2004) *Living Conditions Among People with Activity Limitations in Malawi: A National Representative Study* (Oslo: SINTEF).

Lollar, D. J. and Crews, J. E. (2003) 'Redefining the Role of Public Health in Disability', *Annual Review of Public Health* 24: 195–208.

McCandless, S. E., Brunger, J. W. and Cassidy, S. B. (2003) 'The Burden of Genetic Disease on Inpatient Care in a Children's Hospital', *American Journal of Human Genetics* 74: 121–7.

Mannan, H. and Turnbull, A. (2007) 'A Review of Community Based Rehabilitation Evaluations: Quality of Life as an Outcome Measure for Future Evaluations', *Asia Pacific Disability Rehabilitation Journal* 64: 1231–41.

Marriott, A. and Gooding, K. (2007) *Social Assistance and Disability in Developing Countries* (Haywards Heath: Sightsavers International).

Matsebula, S., Schneider, M. and Watermeyer, B. (2006) 'Integrating Disability within Government: The Office on the Status of Disabled Persons', in B. Watermeyer, L. Swartz, T. Lorenzo, M. Schneider and M. Priestley, eds, *Disability and Social Change: A South African Agenda* (Cape Town: Human Sciences Research Council Press): pp. 85–92.

Miles, M. (2003) 'Disability in South Asia: Millennium to Millennium', *Journal of Religion, Disability and Health* 6(2/3): 109–15.

Mitchell, R. (1999) 'The Research Base of Community-based Rehabilitation', *Disability and Rehabilitation* 121(10–11): 459–68.

Mitra, S. and Sambamoorthi, U. (2006) 'Employment of Persons with Disabilities: Evidence from the National Sample Survey', *Economic and Political Weekly* 41: 199–203.

Mitra, S., Posarac, A. and Vick, B. C. (2011) *Disability and Poverty in Developing Countries: A Snapshot from the World Health Survey, World Bank Social Protection Working Paper No. 1109* (Washington, DC: World Bank).

OECD (2003) *Transforming Disability into Ability: Policies to Promote Work and Income Security for Disabled People* (Paris: Organisation for Economic Co-operation and Development).

Ogot, O., McKenzie, J. and Dube, S. (2008) 'Inclusive Education (IE) and Community-based Rehabilitation', in S. Hartley and J. Okune *CBR: Inclusive Policy Development and Implementation* (Norwich: University of East Anglia).

Oliver, M. (1990) *The Politics of Disablement* (Basingstoke: Macmillan).

Olusanya, B. O. and Newton, V. E. (2007) 'Global Burden of Childhood Hearing Impairment and Disease Control Priorities for Developing Countries', *The Lancet* 369: 1314–1317.

Qiu, Z. (2007) *Rehabilitation Needs of People with Disability in China: Analysis and Strategies* (Beijing: Huaxia Press).

Raja, S., Kippen, S. and Reich, M. R. (2009) 'Access to Psychiatric Medicines in Africa, in E. Akyeampong, A. Hill and A. Kleinman, eds, *Culture, Mental Illness and Psychiatric Practice in Africa* (Bloomington: Indiana University Press).

Riddell, R. (2010) 'Poverty, Disability and Aid: International Development Cooperation', in T. Barron and J. M. Ncube, eds, *Poverty and Disability* (London: Leonard Cheshire Disability/UCL).

Rule, S., Lorenzo, T. and Wolmarans, M. (2006) 'Community-based Rehabilitation: New Challenges', in B. Watermeyer, L. Swartz, T. Lorenzo, M. Schneider M and M. Priestley, eds, *Disability and Social Change: A South African Agenda* (Cape Town: Human Sciences Research Council Press): pp. 273–90.

Shakespeare, T. (2000) *Help*. (Birmingham: Venture Press).

Stone, E. (1996) 'A Law to Protect, a Law to Prevent: Contextualising Disability Legislation in China', *Disability and Society* 11(4): 469–84.

Swartz, L. and Schneider, M. (2006) 'Tough Choices: Disability and Social Security in South Africa', in B. Watermeyer, L. Swartz, T. Lorenzo, M. Schneider and M. Priestley, eds, *Disability and Social Change: A South African Agenda* (Cape Town: Human Sciences Research Council Press): pp. 234–44.

Tipple, G. and Coulson, J. (2009) Enabling Environments: Reducing Barriers for Low-income Disabled People (Newcastle: Global Urban Research Unit, Newcastle University); available at http://www.ncl.ac.uk/guru/research/project/2965 (accessed 1 October 2011).

Trani, J.-F. with Bah, O., Bailey, N., Browne, J., Groce, N. and Kett, M. (2010) *Disability in and Around Urban Areas of Sierra Leone* (London: UCL/Leonard Cheshire Disability).

Ustün, T. B., Ayuso-Mateos, J. L., Chatterji, S., Mathers, C. and Murray, C. J. (2004) 'Global Burden of Depressive Disorders in the Year 2000', *British Journal of Psychiatry* 184: 386–92.

Villa, R. A., Tac, L. V., Muc, P. M., Ryan, S., Thuy, N. T. M., Weill, C. and Thousand, J. S. (2003) 'Inclusion in Viet Nam: More than a Decade of Implementation', *Research and Practice for Persons with Severe Disabilities* 28: 23–32.

Wang, C. C. (1998) 'Portraying Stigmatized Conditions: Disabling Images in Public Health', *Journal of Health Communication* 3: 149–59.

WHO World Mental Health Survey Consortium (2004) 'Prevalence, Severity, and Unmet Need for Treatment of Mental Disorders in the World Health Organization World Mental Health Surveys', *Journal of the American Medical Association* 291: 2581–90.

World Bank (2009) *People with Disabilities in India: From commitments to Outcomes* (Washington, DC: World Bank).

World Health Organization (2001) *International Classification of Functioning, Disability and Health* (Geneva: World Health Organization).

World Health Organization (2004) *Global Burden of Disease* (Geneva: World Health Organization).

World Health Organization (2010) *CBR Guidelines* (Geneva: World Health Organization).

World Health Organization/International Society for Prosthetics and Orthotics (2005) *Guidelines for Training Personnel in Developing Countries for Prosthetics and Orthotics Services* (Geneva: World Health Organization).

World Health Organization/World Bank (2011) *World Report on Disability* (Geneva: World Health Organization).

Zaidi, A. and Burchardt, T. (2005) 'Comparing Incomes When Needs Differ: Equivalization for the Extra Costs of Disability in the UK', *Review of Income and Wealth* 51: 89–114.

Zongjie, Y., Hong, D., Zhongxin, X. and Hui, X. (2007) 'A Research Study into the Requirements of Disabled Residents for Rehabilitation Services in Beijing', *Disability and Rehabilitation* 29: 825–33.

PART 4

Disability studies and interdisciplinarity

21

SOCIAL ENCOUNTERS, CULTURAL REPRESENTATION AND CRITICAL AVOIDANCE

David Bolt

Cultural disability studies is an explicitly interdisciplinary field, synthesizing, as it often does, scholarship in both disability and various forms of cultural production. Probing the very point of that interdisciplinarity, this chapter considers two interrelated questions. Does the study of culture deepen our understanding of disability? Does the study of disability enrich our understanding of culture? Specifically, the friction and avoidance that may result from encounters between those of us who have impairments and those of us who do not are analysed and theorized with reference to the influence of cultural representation. This discussion helps to explain why, increasingly, the established discipline of disability studies pertains to cultural factors. But also illustrated is the fact that a critical appreciation of disability can greatly inform the study of cultural representations, be they literary, filmic, artistic, musical, or whatever. The two interrelated questions raise a challenging issue on which I reflect here and elsewhere, for although the field of cultural disability studies is undoubtedly growing, it remains generally ignored within the humanities. In effect, the avoidance that results from some encounters between those of us who have impairments and those of us who do not have impairments is duplicated in the academy on a curricular level. It is to this scenario that I attach the label *critical avoidance*.

Before exploring some manifestations of critical avoidance, the chapter focuses on under-pinning notions about social encounters between those of us who have impairments and those of us who do not. The encounters might involve nothing more than passing someone in a corridor, standing next to someone in a queue, sharing a table with someone in a café, and so on. These and other such mundane meetings between virtual or complete strangers are considered with reference to mid-twentieth-century sociology and social psychology, classic studies that predicate my reading of a selection of first and second wave works of cultural disability studies. The sources resonate with my own experiential knowledge of disability and provide a basis for a metatheory of the problematics of social encounters. First, though, I contextualize my approach with a necessarily brief and thus wholly inadequate summary of the field.

The emergence of cultural disability studies

It has now been over a decade and a half since Lennard Davis's *Enforcing Normalcy: Disability, Deafness, and the Body* (1995) defined disability as a term that should have been added to the race, class, gender triad. One of the key points made in that seminal work of cultural disability studies was that while many 'progressive intellectuals' decried racism, sexism and class bias, it did not occur to most of them that the very foundations on which their information systems were built, their very practices of 'reading and writing, seeing, thinking, and moving' were 'laden with assumptions about hearing, deafness, blindness, normalcy, paraplegia, and ability and disability in general' (Davis 1995: 4–5). Indeed, when it came to informed critical theory, the humanities had been anything but inclusive of disability. Not surprisingly, then, Davis was considered a pioneer, bringing, as he did, poststructuralist cultural history to bear on the concept of disability, thereby giving 'disability studies greater historical and theoretical depth' and poststructuralism a 'much-needed specificity with regard to theories of the "normal" body' (Bérubé 2002: x). Several comparably significant monographs were published contemporaneously (e.g., Brueggemann 1999; Couser 1997; Garland-Thomson 1997; Kleege 1999), but Davis was singled out when his contribution came to be anthologized in a text set at numerous universities around the world, irrespective of whether or not they were particularly interested in disability studies. That is to say, one measure of his success in helping to move disability studies 'from sideshow to midway' was the *Norton Anthology of Theory and Criticism*, which juxtaposed excerpts from *Enforcing Normalcy* with the work of Homi Bhabha, Henry Louis Gates, Dick Hebdige and Judith Butler, among others (Bérubé 2002: x–xi). Albeit tentatively, then, disability was starting to be recognized as a theoretical basis for cultural criticism alongside gender, ethnicity, sexuality, class and so on.

Edited collections made an important contribution to the emerging field. Most obviously, the success of *Enforcing Normalcy* was followed by that of the *Disability Studies Reader* (Davis 1997). Currently celebrating its third edition, this book set out to place disability in a political, social and cultural context, bringing together, as it did, the work of eminent scholars such as Rosemarie Garland-Thomson and David Mitchell. I mention these two authors in particular because around the same time they too were involved in editing what have now become standard works of cultural disability studies – namely, *Freakery: Cultural Spectacles of the Extraordinary Body* (Garland-Thomson 1996) and *The Body and Physical Differences: Discourses of Disability* (Mitchell and Snyder 1997). Such anthologies continued to constitute a driving force at the start of the twenty-first century (e.g., Snyder *et al.* 2002; Wilson and Lewiecki-Wilson 2001). Indeed, the multidisciplinarity if not interdisciplinarity of the emerging field was exemplified in *Disability/Postmodernity: Embodying Disability Theory* (Corker and Shakespeare 2002). Juxtaposing the work of scholars based in the social sciences (e.g., Peter Beresford, Dan Goodley, Carol Thomas, Nick Watson) and the humanities (e.g., Johnson Cheu, Petra Kuppers, Shelley Tremain), the aim of this controversial volume was to address what in some circles was deemed a hindrance to disability studies – namely, a failure to engage with poststructuralism and postmodernism. That is to say, though edited by two eminent social scientists (Tom Shakespeare must have one of the highest profiles of current disability scholars in the United Kingdom (UK)), the much-read collection was of explicit relevance to those of us who work in the humanities.

There was something of a second wave when the first decade of the century also spawned a number of important monographs (e.g., Couser 2003; Kuppers 2003, 2007; McRuer 2006; Murray 2008; Nussbaum 2003; Quayson 2007; Serlin 2004; Snyder and Mitchell 2006). The second wave, like the first, benefited hugely from the exemplary work of David Mitchell and Sharon Snyder, most obviously *Corporealities: Discourses of Disability* (University of Michigan Press). This series endorsed, and continues to endorse, a broad range of work on representational meanings of disability (e.g., Couser 2009; Davidson 2008; Deutsch and Nussbaum 2000; Mitchell and Snyder 2000; Sandahl and Auslander 2005; Siebers 2008; Stoddard Holmes 2004; Tremain 2005). What is more, it led the way for comparable projects such as Stuart Murray and Robert McRuer's *Representations: Health, Disability, Culture and Society* (2008), which set out to make interdisciplinary research on cultural representations of health and disability more widely accessible.

It was amid this progress that the need for a specialized periodical was addressed by what is now known as the *Journal of Literary & Cultural Disability Studies (JLCDS)*. Launched at the inaugural conference of the Cultural Disability Studies Research Network, published by Liverpool University Press, promptly selected for Project MUSE, briefly affiliated with Lancaster University's Centre for Disability Research and now permanently based in Liverpool Hope University's Centre for Culture and Disability Studies, *JLCDS* furthered progress in the field with a number of special issues (e.g., Barker and Murray 2010; Burke 2008; Davidson 2007; Ferris 2007; Kleege 2009; Kuppers and Overboe 2009; Snyder and Mitchell 2010). Along with the general issues, these specials plugged a gap that was left by other journals, although it must be acknowledged that *Disability & Society*, for example, had already published some articles that came under the rubric of cultural disability studies (e.g., Hevey 1993; Shakespeare 1994; Waltz 2005). Indeed, I have generally found people working in disability studies very willing to accommodate those of us who focus on cultural representation – the invitation to write the present chapter being a case in point.

Does the study of culture deepen our understanding of disability?

Davis's *Disability Studies Reader* brought together a number of authors who in some ways grounded the field of cultural disability studies, including Mikhail Bakhtin, Judith Butler, Jacques Derrida, Michel Foucault, Sander Gilman, Kaja Silverman and Susan Sontag, as well as the sociologist to whom I now turn – namely, Erving Goffman. Most poignantly, Goffman's well-known book, *Stigma: Notes on the Management of Spoiled Identity* (1963), recognizes that 'all human differences are potentially stigmatizable' and that 'stigmas reflect the value judgments of a dominant group' (Coleman 1986: 217). Importantly, he also problematizes the very notion of the norm by asserting that there is just one unblushing male in America: 'a young, married, white, urban, northern, heterosexual Protestant father of college education, fully employed, of good complexion, weight and height and a recent record in sports' (Goffman 1963: 153). This profile may be understood as the subject position of the American male, a narrow ideal by which others would judge themselves and inevitably emerge wanting.

Goffman is particularly interested in what happens when so-called normals and stigmatized people are in one another's company, be it in an intimate or crowded setting. He goes so far as to assert that when we enter one another's immediate presence, especially if we attempt to engage in conversation, there occurs 'one of the primal scenes of sociology; for, in many cases, these moments will be the ones when the causes and effects of stigma must be directly confronted by both sides' (Goffman 1963: 24). It is in this primal scene of sociology that I detect the influence of cultural production.

So intense is the encounter between normals and the stigmatized that its very anticipation may lead to avoidance, the full significance of which is illustrated in Gordon Allport's *The Nature of Prejudice* (1954). This classic study, informed by the horrors of Nazi-Germany, proposes that the behavioural component of prejudice has five incremental stages: antilocution, avoidance, discrimination, physical attack and extermination (Allport 1954). While the vast majority of the human race has always been opposed to extermination, the same cannot be said of antilocution or avoidance. The problem is that the second stage of prejudice is predicated on the first, the third on the second, and so on, meaning that 'activity on one level makes transition to a more intense level easier' (Allport 1954: 15). Most obviously, Hitler's antilocution led many Germans to avoid their Jewish neighbours, making it easier to enact laws of discrimination that, in turn, made anti-Semitic attacks seem somehow acceptable, the final stage being the concentration camps in which millions died. Of course, avoidance does not necessarily lead to the more extreme forms of prejudicial behaviour but, like antilocution, it contributes to a divisive ethos of social exclusion that is often bolstered by cultural representations. I must therefore amend Allport's model by making explicit that pejorative cultural representations are, at the very least, on a par with antilocution.

Not only anthologized in the *Disability Studies Reader*, Goffman's *Stigma* is also revisited in Rosemarie Garland-Thomson's *Extraordinary Bodies: Figuring Physical Disability in American Culture and Literature* (1997). Though understandably critical of the assumption that femaleness has no part in the proposed normative subject position, Garland-Thomson expands on Goffman's conception of normals productively. She coins the term *normate*, thereby designating the 'veiled subject position of cultural self, the figure outlined by the array of deviant others whose marked bodies shore up the normate's boundaries' (Garland-Thomson 1997: 8). This neologism denotes the 'constructed identity of those who, by way of the bodily configurations and cultural capital they assume, can step into a position of authority and wield the power it grants them' (Garland-Thomson 1997: 8). The sense of an elevated status is so ubiquitous that people often aspire desperately to accord with the normate subject position, trying to fit what constitutes a prohibitively exclusive ideal. I say this because although, unlike Goffman, Garland-Thomson does not go so far as to invoke a single exemplary person, she does refer to a narrowly defined profile that describes only a minority of real people.

Goffman's primary scene of sociology becomes, for Garland-Thomson, more specifically an encounter between normate and disabled people. She acknowledges that in any initial meeting a large amount of information must be organized and interpreted, that each person 'probes the explicit for the implicit, determines what is significant for particular purposes, and prepares a response that is guided by many cues, both subtle and obvious' (Garland-Thomson 1997: 12). However, she asserts, if one person has an impairment the interaction tends to be particularly strained because the other may feel fear, pity, fascination, repulsion and/or surprise; feelings that cannot be expressed in a society that has aspirations of political correctness. As well as experiencing this cognitive dissonance it is extremely likely that the person who does not have an impairment will not know how to act toward the person who has an impairment, 'how or whether to offer assistance; whether to acknowledge the disability; what words, gestures, or expectations to use or avoid' (Garland-Thomson 1997: 12). It is acknowledged that the person who has an impairment may anticipate and perhaps fear subsequent avoidance, but the encounter is deemed especially stressful for the person who does not have an impairment, given that he or she is likely to be less skilled when dealing with such situations.

The concept of the normate is one of the main sources for Ato Quayson's *Aesthetic Nervousness: Disability and the Crisis of Representation* (2007). In this book the encounter between the normate and disabled people becomes a 'primary scene of extreme anxiety' (Quayson 2007: 17). Of particular interest are the various relational elements that disclose themselves not as power but as anxiety, dissonance and disorder. Following Garland-Thomson, Quayson recognizes corporeal difference as part of a structure of power that is based on the normate's unmarked regularities, but it is stressed that the impulse to categorize during interpersonal encounters is part of an assumed ideal of order. Because this chapter comes to focus on the metanarrative of disability it is especially important to note that, for Quayson, what Garland-Thomson calls the probing of the explicit for the implicit constitutes part of a quest for an order that is thought to lie elsewhere. That being so, the impaired body may be ascribed metaphysical or divine significance. But because impairment is often deemed a manifestation of disorder, the normate impulse for order must be revaluated and aesthetic nervousness results. Indeed, the normate position is necessarily insecure, given that everyone is subject to radical contingency, and people who have impairments tend to be perceived socially as reminders of that fact. Hence, those of us who have impairments will be very familiar with the phrase *there but for the grace of God go I.*

The other source for Quayson's notion of aesthetic nervousness is the reformulation of literary history from a perspective informed by disability studies (e.g., Davis 2002; Mitchell and Snyder 2000). Though not really departing from Quayson, here, I focus on issues of narrative in particular. This is largely because in my capacity as editor of *JLCDS* I have noticed that many (if not most) submissions explore and illustrate Mitchell and Snyder's concept of narrative prosthesis. That is to say, disability is often recognized as the 'crutch' on which narratives 'lean for their representational power, disruptive potentiality, and analytical insight' (Mitchell and Snyder 2000: 49). While the concept of narrative prosthesis is illustrated very fruitfully with reference to works of literature in both the eponymous monograph and the many derivative studies, it should be stressed for the purpose of this chapter that such examples are by no means exhaustive. After all, any discourse may be placed under the rubric of narrative, from which it follows that any discursive dependence on disability may be understood in terms of narrative prosthesis. I would certainly go as far as to say the term is applicable to any instance of a narrative in which impairment or disability is inserted for effect. Of course, we might bring to mind the work of William Faulkner, J. D. Salinger, Harper Lee, Ken Kesey, and so on, following the reliable lead of Mitchell and Snyder. But it might also be the case that a student unnecessarily invokes her tutor's impairment when querying a grade. It might be that political parties are described as autistic or retarded. It might be that a country is said to be crippled by war or natural disaster. It might be that someone is deemed blind to the facts, that her or his question has fallen on deaf ears. Indeed, when thinking of disability as a device on which authors depend for their 'disruptive punch' (Mitchell and Snyder 2000: 49), it might well be ableist or disablist jokes that spring to mind. The list of familiar examples could go on and on, the key commonality being that nothing informed is said about the lives of the people invoked.

Given this unawareness of (or disregard for) experiential knowledge and agency, it is perhaps not surprising that when normate thoughts do turn to impairment it is often associated with a story, placed in a narrative (Davis 1995). Thus, in an encounter between a person who has an impairment and a person who does not have an impairment, according to Davis's account of the ways in which normalcy is enforced, the impairment may be rendered part of a Bakhtinian chronotope – that is to say, it becomes embedded in a story, part of a time-sequenced narrative. Irrespective of the facts of the matter, a person is assumed to have been born quadriplegic, or to have been blinded in an accident, or to have become deaf as a result of some illness, and so on. He or she is thereby objectified, framed in a narrative that bolsters the normate subject position. I say this because, in effect, the person who has an impairment is written into the story of the person who does not have an impairment. The person who does not have an impairment assumes a kind of authorship, indeed authority, as the person who has an impairment is told rather than asked about her or his own life.

When thinking of discourse that bolsters the normate subject position we should not forget the way in which those of us who have impairments are often left out of our own conversation. Does he take sugar? The question is now a cliché, but the underpinning attitude is by no means a thing of the past. Just recently, for example, a colleague and I accompanied one of our disability studies classes on a visit to a resource centre for people who have visual impairments. It was our intention to facilitate a wider understanding of practical matters, but something far more profound was demonstrable within a few minutes of entering the centre. Once the brief introductions were over, having noticed my visual impairment, the person in charge turned to my colleague and asked if she would be taking me around. On this occasion I was not that bothered about the erroneous assumption that because I was using a guide dog I would necessarily be unable to browse unassisted. In fact, the assumption happens to be quite correct in my case (which is why my colleague had already indicated to me that she was more than happy to provide any necessary assistance). Nor did I give that much thought to the issues raised by the problematical application of the verb *taking*. Rather, the point of interest was my exclusion from the normate discourse, especially as it was initiated by someone we all expected to be fairly appreciative of disability. The resource centre, by definition, is meant to empower people who have visual impairments. However, the person in charge unwittingly subjected me to a discursive form of avoidance – something I must deem pertinent for a place in Allport's model of prejudicial behaviour.

The critical point about interpersonal encounters is that when one person has a visible impairment it tends to dominate the other's processing of perceptions, having a disruptive influence on her or his initial reactions: 'Perhaps most destructive to the potential for continuing relations is the normate's frequent assumption that a disability cancels out other qualities, reducing the complex person to a single attribute' (Garland-Thomson 1997: 12). This normate reductionism may explain my encounter in the resource centre, for example, where communication skills and indeed my very agency were both obscured by the apparent significance of visual impairment. Of course, like many of us who have impairments, I could list innumerable examples that are far more important and/or interesting. I refer to this particular instance largely because it was witnessed by several budding disability scholars (effectively during a lesson), but also because the context was overtly supportive of people with visual impairments.

What I want to stress about such interpersonal encounters is that as well as the normate assumption that impairment cancels out other qualities, reducing the complex person to a single attribute, there is a consequential but apparently immediate invocation of extraneous details. Not simply reduced to the facts of, say, visual impairment, the complex person is lumbered with what have been called the 'old vestments' of blindness (Kuusisto and Kuppers 2007: 74). In other words, people who have visual impairments are frequently keyed to a metanarrative of blindness that is shaped by cultural representations.

What I mean by a metanarrative, here, is the cloud of a story under which those of us who have impairments often find ourselves, an overriding narrative that seems to displace agency. With reference to one element of the metanarrative of blindness, for instance, it has been asserted that, 'Although the number of blind beggars is rather small, it is the image of the beggar that is most commonly called to mind by the words "blind man"' (Monbeck 1973: 8). This association is bolstered by two aspects of cultural production. First, there is the recurrent use of tropes such as the blind beggar in Robert Louis Stevenson's *Treasure Island* (1883) and J. M. Synge's *The Well of the Saints* (1905). Second, there is what I call critical avoidance, the general lack of informed tropological criticism in the humanities. That is to say, the absence of critical readings that are appreciative of disability effect a covert perpetuation of recurrent tropes. After all, while there is no denying that stereotypes 'in life become tropes in textual representation' (Garland-Thomson 1997: 11), it is the lack of profound if not general engagement with the tropes that ensures their return.

Having mentioned Stevenson, Synge and Monbeck, apparently dated sources from the nineteenth and twentieth centuries, I should perhaps emphasize that like the does-he-take-sugar cliché the image of the blind beggar cannot be dismissed as a thing of the past. Just a few days before my visit to the resource centre, I encountered another pertinent instance of normate reductionism. I had arranged to meet a friend for a few drinks at a bar in the city centre. I allowed half an hour for the journey but, owing to an unexpectedly low volume of traffic, arrived 20 minutes early. Because the bar was very noisy, making it difficult for me to order a drink and/or find somewhere to sit (relying in part, as I often do, on auditory cues), I decided to wait outside. After ten minutes or so someone walked past, paused and then turned back. I stepped forward slightly in case it was my friend, but it was a stranger who indicated in a non-aggressive tone that he was trying to hand me something. I imagined it must be a flier of some description (material not readily accessible to me) and so did not raise my hand. He seemed perplexed at my lack of engagement, pausing again before asking if I was not collecting for the blind. At that point a proverbial penny dropped for both of us. I explained that I was just waiting for someone and he apologized convincingly as he walked away. In the mind of the stranger, I was evidently reduced to the characteristic of visual impairment, but also keyed to the metanarrative in which the blind beggar is a stock character. My very presence was implicitly explained by a cultural construct.

As well as by others, those of us who have impairments may be keyed by ourselves to the metanarrative of disability. For instance, though well aware of the stereotypical possession of extraordinary senses, I cannot help feeling a little pleased when someone notices if I am first to hear the arrival of a taxi at the end of an evening with friends. Because in such situations I am accustomed to listening for the sounds of the engine and closing door, it is not really surprising if I am aware of the taxi's arrival before the driver rings the doorbell. That is the fact of the matter, but for a fleeting moment I may secretly embrace the so-called positive stereotype and all its cool mysteries. What is more, I am then likely to save myself from the internal displacement of identity by nervously cracking some joke about the extraordinary hearing of the blind. In other words, albeit through irony, I invoke the metanarrative of blindness overtly as well as covertly.

Before leaving these anecdotes aside, I should add a few details to expand a little on their context. For more than 20 years my visual impairment has been overt in so far as I have used guide dogs for mobility. In that time I have only experienced two of the blind-beggar encounters and, just for the record, in neither was I holding a can or a hat or anything that could have been mistaken for a begging bowl. The other situations, however, are far more common. I am certainly spoken about, rather than to, on a weekly if not daily basis and must admit to internalizing various stereotypes from time to time. Although in such instances I tend to be reduced not only to the characteristic of visual impairment but also to my own laughter, thereby demonstrating the point that 'real social relations are always dynamic' (Garland-Thomson 1997: 11), I do appreciate that cultural representations may have a profoundly disturbing and disabling influence on those of us who have impairments. After all, is it not the idea rather than the lived reality of acquiring an impairment that has the greater pejorative impact on the person? Are these ideas not frequently given currency in cultural representation?

It surely follows that the study of culture does indeed enrich our understanding of disability. Whichever models we invoke, be they tragic, charitable, religious, individual, medical, social or affirmative, cultural factors cannot be ignored. However we choose to approach disability, the fact remains that people who have impairments, or people with disabilities, or disabled people, or the disabled, are frequently keyed to a metanarrative by which all is supposedly explained. In relation to the radical social model, for instance, there cannot be a more ardent proponent than Colin Barnes, but it would be grossly erroneous to say that his work does not recognize cultural factors (e.g., Barnes 1997, 2008; Barnes and Mercer 2003). It has been argued that the social model reveals subliminal cultural assumptions about people who have impairments, raising the possibility that people who do not have impairments may 'ultimately be brought to recognize the sources of the constructedness of the normate and the prejudices that flow from it' (Quayson 2007: 17–18). This model is generally invoked to reveal discrimination, the third stage in Allport's model of prejudicial behaviour, and the more extreme stages, too, have cultural components. Insofar as it pertains to decisions about the type of person who inhabits the world, for example, selective abortion must be said to fall under the rubric of extermination. Women are 'expected to implement the society's eugenic prejudices by "choosing" to have the appropriate tests and "electing" not to initiate or to terminate pregnancies if it looks as though the outcome will offend' (Hubbard 1990: 199). The point, here, is that this offence, this expectation and these prejudices are all perpetuated by the recurrent tropes of cultural representation.

Does the study of disability enrich our understanding of culture?

Given the ways in which those of us who have impairments may key and be keyed to a metanarrative as we go about our day-to-day lives, the study of disability is bound to enrich the understanding of culture. If stereotypes become tropes in textual representation, does it not follow that studies of the one enhance those of the other? The hegemonic aspect of representations of disability is every bit as important and interesting as those of gender, ethnicity, class, sexuality, and so on. Indeed, without key concepts such as ableism, aesthetic nervousness, autistic presence, crip theory, enforcing normalcy, narrative prosthesis and the normate subject position, the study of cultural representation would be both dated and deficient. These and other such concepts, models and theories facilitate informed critical engagement with the numerous portrayals of disability that overtly and covertly influence society. The more we learn about disability, the more we discover about cultural representation.

This is where the problem of critical avoidance becomes evident. Generally, as I have said, those of us who work in disability studies do not deny the influence of cultural representations. Contrarily, though, while cultural disability studies is growing as an interdisciplinary field of enquiry, it still tends to be the case that scholars based in the humanities do not engage with disability studies. Disabled characters frequent most if not all of the primary texts that are being studied in the academy, but that level of representation is not reflected in the critical responses: it is often the case that the topic of disability is avoided, and generally so that any engagements are not informed by disability studies.

Critical avoidance is demonstrable in most prospectuses that pertain to courses in the humanities. This point may be illustrated with reference to various sample groups. Here in the UK, for instance, the Russell Group is said to represent the 20 universities that are most outstanding in their research, their teaching and learning, and their associations with business and the public sector. Visiting the online prospectus of each university in the group and selecting undergraduate English literature as a subject example, I find that several aspects of identity and ideology are posited as selling points for the courses. The University of Cambridge refers to 'Commonwealth and Post-Colonial Writing', much as the University of Southampton has a course called 'Post-Colonial Literature'. University College London offers 'Literary Representation and the History of Homosexuality'. King's College London mentions courses in both of these areas, referring, as it does, not only to 'Post-Colonial Australian Literature and Post-Colonial Perspectives', but also to 'Early Modern Sexualities and Critically Queer: Literature, Culture & Queer Theory'. Still more impressive is the University of Manchester, for as well as 'Contemporary Post-Colonial Fiction and Film', 'Post-Colonial Literature and Theory', and 'Politics, Sexuality and Identity in British Gothic Writing', the courses available include 'Power and Gender in Early Modern Literature' and 'Gender, Sexuality and Culture'. I am not inferring, here, that universities in the Russell Group necessarily avoid drawing on disability studies during their English literature courses. Indeed, I know for a fact that, at The University of Leeds, Stuart Murray runs an exemplary course in cultural disability studies. But all 20 universities certainly remain united insofar as they avoid referring or alluding to disability studies as a selling point for undergraduate courses in English literature. This is a tangible aspect of critical avoidance. Something similar can be said of the 1994 Group, too, for although madness, the body, and even health studies are all mentioned explicitly, disability studies is avoided.

Conclusion

What I draw from all this is a way forward for the field of cultural disability studies – namely, curricular reform. Focusing on issues of friction and avoidance, this chapter has illustrated that disability studies is supplemented by cultural studies and vice versa. The absence of one from the other, therefore, in an irresistibly Derridian turn, reveals deficiency. Accordingly, those of us who work in disability studies are generally open to research and scholarship on literary and other cultural factors. Those of us based in the humanities, however, are likely to tell a very different story, for critical avoidance is still the general rule. The chapter has considered how social encounters between people who have impairments and people who do not have impairments may be problematical, partly because the ever-present metanarrative of disability contains an independence–dependence, usefulness–uselessness, needed–needy, helper–helped binary logic. What this means in the first instance is that many assumptions may be made about the person who has an impairment, positing the person who does not have an impairment in the role of provider. The frequently overlooked point is that if and when these roles are realized they are also likely to be traded, a reversal that itself causes anxiety for some people who do not have impairments. Helping the proverbial blind man across the road is one thing, but recognizing the achievements, ideas, knowledge, influence, experience or authority of someone who has an impairment can prove profoundly difficult for some people who do not have impairments, as though a funda-mental order would thereby be disrupted. It is this very reluctance that becomes manifest in the humanities when the work of disability studies is dismissed as irrelevant. Much as those of us who have impairments deal with prejudicial behaviour, including avoidance, on a daily basis, those of us who work in disability studies must take the initiative in making and/or maintaining links with the humanities. In the academy, in the UK at least, the word on everyone's lips at the moment is *impact*. But with local, regional, national and international contexts in mind, we are in danger of forgetting that impact begins at home – that is, in our own institutions. As an explicitly interdisciplinary field, cultural disability studies informs and is informed by the humanities as well as the social sciences, yet this is far too rarely recognized in the work of our colleagues in literary studies, cultural studies, film studies, media studies, and so on. Indeed, many of our colleagues in the humanities are unaware of what is meant by disability studies, let alone the relevance to their own work. In this climate, critical avoidance is a matter of course.

References

Allport, Gordon W. (1954) *The Nature of Prejudice* (London: Addison-Wesley Publishing Company).

Barker, Clare and Stuart Murray, eds, (2010) 'Disabling Postcolonialism', special issue, *Journal of Literary & Cultural Disability Studies* 4(3).

Barnes, Colin (1997) 'A Legacy of Oppression: A History of Disability in Western Culture', in Len Barton and Mike Oliver, eds, *Disability Studies: Past, Present, and Future* (Leeds: The Disability Press): pp. 3–24.

Barnes, Colin (2008) 'Generating Change: Disability, Culture and Art', *Journal for Disability and International Development* 19(1): 4–13.

Barnes, Colin and Geoff Mercer (2003) *Disability* (Cambridge: Polity Press).

Bérubé, Michael (2002) 'Foreword', in Lennard J. Davis, *Bending Over Backwards: Disability, Dismodernism and Other Difficult Positions* (New York and London: New York University Press): pp. vii–xii.

Brueggemann, Brenda (1999) *Lend Me Your Ear: Rhetorical Constructions of Deafness* (Washington, DC: Gallaudet University Press).

Burke, Lucy, ed., (2008) 'Representations of Cognitive Impairment', special issue, *Journal of Literary & Cultural Disability Studies* 2(1).

Coleman, Lerita M. (1986) 'Stigma: An Enigma Demystified', in Lennard J. Davis, ed., (1997) *The Disability Studies Reader* (London: Routledge): pp. 216–31.

Corker, Mairian and Tom Shakespeare, eds, (2002) *Disability/Postmodernity: Embodying Disability Theory* (London: Continuum).

Couser, G. Thomas (1997) *Recovering Bodies: Illness, Disability, and Life Writing* (Madison: University of Wisconsin Press).

Couser, G. Thomas (2003) *Vulnerable Subjects: Ethics and Life Writing* (Ithaca: Cornell University Press).

Couser, G. Thomas (2009) *Signifying Bodies: Disability in Contemporary Life Writing* (Ann Arbor: University of Michigan Press).

Davidson, Michael, ed., (2007) 'Disability and the Dialectic of Dependency', special issue, *Journal of Literary & Cultural Disability Studies* 1(2).

Davidson, Michael (2008) *Concerto for the Left Hand: Disability and the Defamiliar Body* (Ann Arbor: University of Michigan Press).

Davis, Lennard J. (1995) *Enforcing Normalcy: Disability, Deafness, and the Body* (London: Verso).

Davis, Lennard J., ed., (1997) *The Disability Studies Reader* (London: Routledge).

Davis, Lennard J. (2002) *Bending Over Backwards: Disability, Dismodernism and Other Difficult Positions* (New York and London: New York University Press).

Deutsch, Helen and Felicity Nussbaum, eds, (2000) *'Defects': Engendering the Modern Body* (Ann Arbor: University of Michigan Press).

Ferris, Jim, ed., (2007) 'Disability and/as Poetry', special issue, *Journal of Literary & Cultural Disability Studies* 1(1).

Garland-Thomson, Rosemarie, ed., (1996) *Freakery: Cultural Spectacles of the Extraordinary Body* (London: New York University Press).

Garland-Thomson, Rosemarie, ed., (1997) *Extraordinary Bodies: Figuring Physical Disability in American Culture and Literature* (New York: Columbia University Press).

Goffman, Erving (1963) *Stigma: Notes on the Management of Spoiled Identity* (Middlesex: Penguin).

Hevey, David (1993) 'From Self-love to the Picket Line: Strategies for Change in Disability Representation', *Disability & Society* 8(4): 423–9.

Hubbard, Ruth (1990) 'Abortion and Disability: Who Should and Who Should Not Inhabit the World?', in Lennard J. Davis, ed., (1997) *The Disability Studies Reader* (London: Routledge): pp. 187–200.

Kleege, Georgina (1999) *Sight Unseen* (New Haven and London: Yale University Press).

Kleege, Georgina, ed., (2009) 'Blindness and Literature', special issue, *Journal of Literary & Cultural Disability Studies* 3(2).

Kuppers, Petra (2003) *Disability and Contemporary Performance: Bodies on Edge* (London: Routledge).

Kuppers, Petra (2007) *The Scar of Visibility: Medical Performances and Contemporary Art* (Minneapolis: University of Minnesota Press).

Kuppers, Petra and James Overboe, eds, (2009) 'Deleuze, Disability, and Difference', special issue, *Journal of Literary & Cultural Disability Studies* 3(3).

Kuusisto, Stephen and Petra Kuppers (2007) 'Auto-Graphein or "the Blind Man's Pencil": Notes on the Making of a Poem', in Jim Ferris, ed., 'Disability and/as Poetry', special issue,. *Journal of Literary & Cultural Disability Studies* 1(1): 74–80.

Leitch, Vincent B., William E. Cain, Laurie Finke, Barbara Johnson, John McGowan and Jeffrey Williams, eds, (2001) *The Norton Anthology of Theory and Criticism* (New York: W.W. Norton & Company).

McRuer, Robert (2006) *Crip Theory: Cultural Signs of Queerness and Disability* (New York: New York Press).

Mitchell, David T. and Sharon L. Snyder, eds, (1997) *The Body and Physical Differences: Discourses of Disability* (Ann Arbor: University of Michigan Press).

Mitchell, David T. and Sharon L. Snyder (2000) *Narrative Prosthesis: Disability and the Dependencies of Discourse* (Ann Arbor: University of Michigan Press).

Mitchell, David T. and Sharon L. Synder (2005) *Corporealities: Discourses of Disability* (Ann Arbor: University of Michigan Press).

Monbeck, Michael E. (1973) *The Meaning of Blindness: Attitudes Toward Blindness and Blind People* (London: Indiana University Press).

Murray, Stuart (2008) *Representing Autism: Culture, Narrative, Fascination* (Liverpool: Liverpool University Press).

Murray, Stuart and Robert McRuer (2008) *Representations: Health, Disability, Culture and Society* (Liverpool: Liverpool University Press).

Nussbaum, Felicity (2003) *The Limits of the Human: Fictions of Anomaly, Race, and Gender in the Long Eighteenth Century* (Cambridge: Cambridge University Press).

Quayson, Ato (2007) *Aesthetic Nervousness: Disability and the Crisis of Representation* (New York: Columbia University Press).

Sandahl, Carrie and Philip Auslander, eds, (2005) *Bodies in Commotion: Disability and Performance* (Ann Arbor: University of Michigan Press).

Serlin, David (2004) *Replaceable You: Engineering the Body in Postwar America* (Chicago: University of Chicago Press).

Shakespeare, Tom (1994) 'Cultural Representation of Disabled People: Dustbins for Disavowal?', *Disability & Society* 9(3): 283.

Siebers, Tobin (2008) *Disability Theory* (Ann Arbor: University of Michigan Press).

Snyder, Sharon and David Mitchell (2006) *Cultural Locations of Disability* (Chicago: University of Chicago Press).

Snyder, Sharon L. and David T. Mitchell, eds, (2010) 'The Geopolitics of Disability', special issue, *Journal of Literary & Cultural Disability Studies* 4(2).

Snyder, Sharon. L., Brenda J. Brueggemann and Rosemarie Garland-Thomson, eds, (2002) *Disability Studies: Enabling the Humanities* (New York: Modern Language Association of America).

Stevenson, Robert Louis (1962) [1883] *Treasure Island* (London: Longman).

Stoddard Holmes, Martha (2004) *Fictions of Affliction: Physical Disability in Victorian Culture* (Ann Arbor: University of Michigan Press).

Synge, John Millington (1905) *The Well of the Saints. Collected Plays and Poems and the Aran Islands* (London: Everyman): pp. 66–108.

Tremain, Shelley, ed., (2005) *Foucault and the Government of Disability* (Ann Arbor: University of Michigan Press).

Waltz, Mitzi (2005) 'Reading Case Studies of People with Autistic Spectrum Disorders: A Cultural Studies Approach to Issues of Disability Representation', *Disability & Society* 20(4): 421.

Wilson, James C. and Cynthia Lewiecki-Wilson, eds, (2001) *Embodied Rhetorics: Disability in Language and Culture* (Carbondale and Edwardsville, USA: Southern Illinois University Press).

22

WHAT CAN PHILOSOPHY TELL US ABOUT DISABILITY?

Simo Vehmas

Introduction: what can I tell you about philosophy and its uses in understanding disability?

It makes all the sense in the world to assume that philosophy can tell us something important about disability. After all, philosophers have since antiquity been considered lovers of wisdom who have a deeper understanding of the way things are than us regular mortals. The word 'philosophy', however, has various meanings nowadays, and it is often used to refer to the general scheme of things of virtually any human activity. People talk about the philosophy of tennis coaching, charity work, guitar solos, tasting wines, selling nail varnish, and so on. The word 'philosophy' implies profoundness related to the activity in question: guitar solos, for example, are not necessarily just a form of entertainment, they can also be pathways to deity. Thus, it seems that before I can go any further, I need to define 'philosophy'. And this, exactly, is when things get complicated.

Briefly, philosophy examines the conceptual boundaries of human thought by means of examples and counter-examples. This means that 'it is done just by asking questions, arguing, trying out ideas and thinking of possible arguments against them, and wondering how our concepts really work' (Nagel 1987: 4). Philosophy thus relies on thought, not on experiments or observation like science, nor does it have formal methods of proof, like mathematics. Philosophy can be described as a way of thinking whose distinctive features are its use of logical argumentation as well as the analysis and clarification of concepts. Philosophers are usually concerned about questioning and understanding common ideas that all of us use every day without thinking about them. For example, disability scholars and activists often talk about the oppression that people with disabilities experience. Philosophy, however, would typically respond to this by asking: by virtue of what should something count as 'oppression' or 'disability', and what makes a group of people an entity that can be meaningfully called 'people with disabilities'. Philosophy thus investigates ideas that are taken for granted most of the time with an aim to push our understanding of the world a bit deeper. Virtually any conceivable human thought can be questioned and scrutinized in philosophy, which makes it a dizzying and often tiring activity whose results usually don't go unchallenged for long (Nagel 1987: 5; Warburton 1992: 1–2).

Thus, the basic use of philosophy for disability studies is to question and examine carefully its essential concepts and conceptions, their rational credibility, logical tenability and normative soundness. Academic philosophy can be defined and divided in various ways but one traditional way is to divide it into ontology or metaphysics (studying the nature of being), epistemology (the study of knowledge), philosophy of science and logic (studying the nature of scientific knowledge and thinking) and, finally, ethics and political philosophy (studying practical and normative questions). My discussion in this chapter concentrates on the ontology of disability, ethics and the moral significance of disability and, finally, political philosophy and its implications for disabled people's social status.

Philosophical ontology and disability theory

Disability studies perspectives typically reject essentialist views of human beings. What is considered as characteristically 'human' or 'normal' for the physical or mental make-up of beings does not depend on human essence (whatever that might be), but on culturally produced norms. Humanity and normality are socially constructed. Accordingly, as much as bodies and impairments are biological entities, they are also cultural and social entities: 'the impaired body has a history and is as much a cultural phenomenon as it is a biological entity' (Paterson and Hughes 1999: 600). Social constructionism is one crucial ontological and epistemological basis of disability studies and, consequently, it has become the framework for understanding what disability is all about, as well as how one construes information about it (Albrecht 2002; Barnes *et al.* 1999: 93–5; Linton 1998: 37–45; Taylor 1996).

Social constructionism has been a politically liberating stance because it has provided a basis to question the dominance of medicine in explaining disability. The human world is an interpreted, construed world. Yet it would be intellectually and politically disastrous to conclude that impairments are not primarily or even secondarily physical facts and that nothing exists until it is spoken of or written about. Views of the ontology of disability are politically significant because the way phenomenon is understood inevitably directs institutional responses to it. This explains partly some of the heated theoretical debates in disability studies (Oliver 2007; Shakespeare 2006; Thomas 2008; Vehmas 2008): the one with the best story is supposedly seen to win the political battle as well. I will now briefly explain the ontological structure of disability, drawing heavily on John Searle's (1995) theory of social ontology, and clarify the conceptual difference between impairment and disability.

First, an important distinction between the senses of 'objective' and 'subjective' as for epistemology and ontology must be recognized. Epistemic sense of objective–subjective distinction refers simply to discussions about our judgments of how things are in the world and their credibility. A judgment is subjective if its correctness depends on the attitudes, feelings or points of view of the maker and the hearer of the judgment. A judgment is objective if its truth is settled by facts in the world that are independent of the maker and hearer of the judgment. In other words, if a statement is objective in the epistemic sense then there is an objective fact in the world which makes it true (Searle 1995: 8).

In the ontological sense, objective and subjective are predicates of the entities in the world, the types of entities and their mode of existence. Objective entities exist independently of any perceiver or mental state, whereas subjective entities are dependent on perceivers and mental states. So, in the ontological sense pains are subjective entities because their existence depends on a subject's experience. But mountains, for example, are ontologically objective because their mode of existence is independent of any perceiver; mountains would stay in the world even if all the humans and other subjects with senses disappeared from the Earth (and if the reader finds this implausible, he or she can test this statement by waiting for an oncoming train on the railway track instead of waiting for it on the platform, and see to what extent the existence of entities is dependent on people's views about them). Here, we need to distinguish between the senses of objective and subjective, that is, we can make epistemically subjective statements about entities that are ontologically objective, and similarly, we can make epistemically objective statements about entities that are ontologically subjective. For example, the statement 'Individuals with spina bifida are an oppressed group of people' is about an ontologically objective entity, but makes a subjective judgment about it. On the other hand, the statement 'The fact that my child has spina bifida causes me emotional distress' reports an epistemically objective fact in the sense that it is made true by the existence of an actual fact that is not dependent on any opinion of observers. Nevertheless, the phenomenon itself, the actual emotional distress, has a subjective mode of existence (Searle 1995: 9–11).

Various entities thus have different kinds of modes of existence, and they can exist independently from each other. Spina bifida is not inherently connected to oppression because the existence of a neural tube defect is an *intrinsic feature* which exists independently of our views about it. Spina bifida does, however, include *observer-relative* features as well; the kind of features that exist relative to observers. Oppression, for example, is fundamentally rooted in human experience and can only exist if subjects with experiences exist. The observer-relative features of the world do not add any material objects to reality, but they can add epistemically objective features to reality where the features in question exist relative to human beings (Searle 1995: 9–11).

If one is not willing to commit to completely nihilistic premises, we do know for a fact that certain statements are either true or false. For example, it is true that the Earth goes around the Sun. It is also true that spina bifida is caused by the failure of the fetus's spine to close completely during the first month of pregnancy. These are the kinds of facts, or truths, that as facts exist independently of human beings and their views. John Searle calls them *brute facts* as distinct from *institutional facts*, which can exist only within human institutions. But before we can name or agree on any facts, that is, to have institutional facts, we have to have brute facts. In order to have money, games, schools, medical diagnoses or any other human institution, for each there must be some physical realization, some brute fact on which we can impose its social function. All sorts of substances can be money. Whether it is bits of metal or pieces of paper or magnetic traces on plastic cards, it has to exist in some physical form. Institutional facts are hierarchically structured and they exist on top of brute facts, as it were (Searle 1995: 34–5; for some qualifications see Searle 2010: 19–24).

According to the British social model of disability, disability as a social phenomenon is about oppression and discrimination against people with impairments (e.g., Oliver 1990). By definition, then, disability as a social phenomenon does not include a mere institutional level of facts, but a brute level of facts as well, namely, impairments. Disability cannot thus be satisfactorily conceptualized purely in terms of institutional facts, such as oppression. The problem with some formulations in the social model tradition is that they downplay the significance of the inevitable physical foundation of social phenomena, with the result that these accounts are based on the upper stairs of the ontological ladder, as it were (see, for example, Shakespeare 2006: 38–43). Thus, ignoring the physical basis of disability results ontologically in an insufficient, or even a flawed, account. It should be noted that this flaw is more serious in the case of those impairments that include clearly verifiable brute facts like, for example, the causes of spina bifida and Trisomy 21. However, the situation is not that clear in the case of so-called social impairments such as attention deficit hyperactivity disorder (ADHD); it is far from clear whether these kinds of conditions are impairments in the proper sense or whether they are first and foremost institutional facts. After all, there is no certainty about the physiological causes of particular behaviour patterns, so the only brute fact that we know of at the moment for sure regarding ADHD is a certain kind of behaviour (Vehmas and Mäkelä 2009).

Attempts to understand the ontology and construction of the phenomena of impairment and disability can be primarily descriptive without any political or other normative commitments. Rather, metaphysical endeavours should involve first and foremost a methodological commitment to get our ontology right. After that, we have the necessary tools to build agendas to change the possibly oppressive status quo. An ontology that emphasizes both the physical origins of impairment and the relational nature of disability enables us to eradicate both organic and social factors that have resulted in people's distress. In other words, we can be more flexible and efficient in aiming to increase equality and well-being of all individuals in society when we recognize whether people need either physical responses (e.g., operations and therapies) or social responses (e.g., a more accessible built environment), or both.

As phenomena, disability and impairment consist of both natural and social factors. *Impairment* is a class name for natural properties that, depending on the context, in part cause or constitute functional limitations – although the limiting implications of the property in question can in part be explained in social terms. Impairment always involves a physical element, a condition of some sort which is seen as undesirable regarding people's organic or social functioning. Thus, impairment is a physical or organic phenomenon whose identification and definition is determined culturally and socially; it is inevitably about attaching some meaning to individual properties. *Disability*, however, is an ontologically subjective (mind-dependent) and institutional phenomenon that consists in the relation between the natural properties or features on the one hand, and the surrounding social and physical world on the other. Disability is inevitably, and self-evidently, a social construct. What distinguishes disability from impairment is that it can become dissociated from people's physical conditions. Disability often involves very general social structures and mechanisms that cannot be reduced to people's physical or mental characteristics. Disability has started to have a life of its own, as it were (Vehmas and Mäkelä 2009).

Thus, disability as a social phenomenon does not necessarily require impairment in the proper sense; some individual features and ways of acting can become labelled as impairments although they may have no verifiable organic basis. Sometimes the ontological formation of institutional facts may precede the recognition of brute facts, meaning impairments are ontologically objective physical phenomena which may epistemically come into existence after a disability has been classified. For instance, people with an extra chromosome 21 had existed long before the physiological cause of the characteristic features of these people was recognized. Similarly, various learning disabilities have come into existence due to the growing cognitive demands of contemporary societies. Some of these disabilities may very well have an organic basis, but the interest to recognize organic factors (i.e., brute facts) that may cause these disabilities is based on social demand.

To conclude, impairment and disability include both physical and social dimensions. Spina bifida, for example, is a medical matter, and the social participation of a person with spina bifida is both a medical and a political matter. In other words, impairment in general is often both a brute fact and an institutional fact, and disability is an institutional fact based on the hierarchy of facts which all ultimately rest on brute facts.

Philosophical ethics and the moral significance of disability

Ethical issues related to disability fall into applied normative ethics where normative moral theories and concepts are applied to ethical issues with practical significance. The main business of normative ethics is the general study of goodness and right action. The main questions of ethics are: 'What kinds of beings should we be like?' and 'How are we to live?' Philosophical ethics thus aims to describe the best features of human character and manner in a way that could be the basis for normative rules and even law-making and jurisdiction. The practical aim of normative ethics is to produce decision procedures or mental tools that can be used to guide correct moral reasoning about matters of moral concern. The theoretical aim of philosophical ethics, on the other hand, is coming to understand the underlying nature of right and wrong actions, good and bad persons (Timmons 2002: 3–4). Further questions concerning disability include the question in moral psychology, namely, whether disability can be significant regarding one's moral responsibility.

In addition to being an ontological concept, disability is also a normative concept that reflects the ideas concerning what kind of beings humans ought to be, both mentally and physically. It is also related to ideas about how society and social arrangements ought to be constructed in order to treat the members of society fairly. Despite our possibly differing views about the causal origins of disability, having a 'disability' implies an undesirable state of functioning or being of an individual – either to him or herself or to other people and society. Physical or mental abilities are essential constituents of humanity, not merely because these abilities differentiate us from most non-human animals, but because they make possible the social and relational aspects of human life. The concept of *dis*ability reflects the idea that persons considered as disabled lack certain abilities, or possibilities, that could contribute to their individual well-being or to their social adequacy. Abilities and possibilities are considered good and useful, whereas *dis*ability is seen as an impediment regarding human well-being. Thus, the essential core of the concept of disability is ethical. The tenets of the traditional individual approaches to disability imply that disability is a matter of an individual's insufficient abilities. This inevitably places persons with impairments in an unfortunate and even tragic position. Supporters of the social views of disability do not usually regard impairments as such as necessarily undesirable conditions. Disability, however, seems to be considered an undesirable state of functioning, or phenomenon, arising primarily or at least in part from unjust social arrangements. In other words, all individualistic and social approaches to disability contain a strong normative dimension that implies what is good or bad for an individual and what is right or wrong as regards social arrangements (Vehmas 2004).

The crucial point, then, is to examine the relevance and soundness of the norms that cause us to define certain phenomena, conditions and ways of functioning as disabilities. There are roughly two kinds of considerations to examine the issue: instrumental and intrinsic. Instrumental factors are those things that enhance human well-being, and are means to achieve things that are of intrinsic value. However, it is very difficult to judge whether impairments enhance, hinder or are in any way relevant regarding the achievement of intrinsically valuable things. Consider, for example, severe intellectual disabilities, which most people see as tragic or at least as undesirable conditions. From an instrumental viewpoint, this common notion seems obvious because severe intellectual disabilities, which often include multiple disabilities, seem to prevent people from pursuing various meaningful activities. Jeff McMahan, among many others, has argued that 'the more limited an individual's capacities are, the more restricted his or her range of well-being will be' (McMahan 1996: 7) and, therefore, whereas us normal human beings can pursue successfully the various dimensions of a good life 'the profoundly cognitively impaired are incapable, for example, of deep personal and social relations, creativity and achievement, the attainment of higher forms of knowledge, aesthetic pleasures, and so on' (McMahan 1996: 7–8).

McMahan's statement raises empirical and evaluative concerns. Empirically, some of McMahan's claims may be true; some of them are highly questionable or are without foundation. People with various forms of intellectual disability indeed are capable of forming deep personal and social relations, as well as having aesthetic pleasures. Eva Kittay, for example, describes her daughter Sesha, who was diagnosed as being severely to profoundly retarded, as an 'enormously responsive' person who, while listening to Beethoven's Emperor Concerto at home, 'gazes out the window enthralled, occasionally turning to us with a twinkle in her eye when she anticipates some really good parts' (Kittay 2005: 127). There is generally a difference in the narratives of philosophers who identify as having family members with severe intellectual disabilities compared with those who have had little or no contact. It is hardly surprising that people with intellectual disabilities, or people in general for that matter, tend to be more competent with people close to them than they are with people who they interact with only occasionally (Vehmas 1999). Many philosophers, such as McMahan, give hopelessly biased and flawed descriptions of the lives of people with intellectual disabilities and their families. Selectivity in the use of empirical data and factual statements of a non-ethical sort gives a framework to the arguments and directs the conclusions. On the basis of their simplified conception of disability, these philosophers can present questions of moral justification as less problematic. But wrong facts do not create merely false, but also potentially harmful, arguments that may reinforce prejudice and discrimination against people with impairments (Kittay 2009; Vehmas 1999).

In evaluative terms, and assuming that the things McMahan mentions should actually be seen as constitutive of human well-being, his position raises an epistemic concern about the conditions of our judgments regarding the quality of people's experiences. His claims seem to require some reliable standard that would help us to judge when, for instance, personal and social relations are deep, what kind of knowledge is of higher form, or when aesthetic pleasures are truly aesthetical. Now, I know personally academics who are keen to engage in abstract conversations but who are next to incompetent dealing with emotional issues with their friends, spouses or children. I have also met many persons with various levels of intellectual disability who are unable to analyse, say, Aristotle's virtue ethics, but who are very empathetic, kind and seem to thrive socially, as well as to have emotionally intimate relations with people close to them. In other words, ability for mutual communication of one's feelings does not require an ability to appreciate abstract thought, and it seems clear that the former is more crucial for the quality (or deepness) of one's personal and social relations than the latter. As for aesthetic pleasures, a friend of mine with a classical training in music is not convinced that my ecstatic responses to classic hard rock music qualify as genuine aesthetic pleasure. It is quite possible to maintain that the emotionally challenged but intellectually gifted academics, and people who are able to understand, say, the complexity of Bach fugue and see presumably correctly hard rock as pointless racket, can pursue more successfully the various dimensions of a good life. This kind of position would, however, exclude most people from higher levels of well-being. Even so-called non-disabled people achieve forms of well-being in degrees that vary greatly. Impairment is merely one factor among many other things that may affect one's chances to pursue different dimensions of well-being.

Instrumentally, it is difficult to prove the role of impairment in people's lives because one can always, and quite plausibly as well, argue that the significance of impairments regarding well-being depends mostly on social circumstances. Impairments are often a predicament, as Tom Shakespeare (2006: 63–4) has argued, but so are many other things in human lives. In most cases it is probably correct to pinpoint the significant sources of one's well-being at the intersection of various factors (personal, social, physical, cultural, etc.). For example, the significance of an inability to read and write due to intellectual disability, or an inability to form and maintain a relationship due to emotional issues, depends largely on social context and its values. Still, some impairments seem to cause distress and downright suffering regardless of the environmental and social conditions. I have in mind particularly some difficult forms of autism spectrum and psychiatric conditions that can, subjectively speaking, make the lives of people with these conditions, and people close to them, quite miserable.

It would be foolish to deny the significant impacts that impairments often have on people's lives and well-being. For example, persons with intellectual disabilities have limitations in intellectual functioning and in adaptive behaviour. This is due to their impairments and the requirements of competence in the particular society (although the most severe forms of intellectual disability would disable a person no matter what the social context) (Vehmas 2010). But intellectual disabilities do not necessarily prevent one from faring well; people with such disabilities indeed are capable of aesthetic pleasures, forming deep relationships, and so on. Yet it is true that some persons with milder forms of intellectual disability do realize their difference and various limitations, and suffer from it. But on the other hand, what else is new? It is the common fate of most of us humans to come to terms with our insecurities and feelings of inadequacy because there are always people that are more intelligent, attractive, virtuous, or what have you, than we see ourselves to be.

Most people who have had any contact with persons with intellectual disabilities would probably admit that intellectual disabilities as such do not make one's life miserable. Often it seems to be quite the opposite. And indeed, well-being is essentially a subjective concept by its very nature; it unavoidably concerns 'what is good or bad *for the subject in question*' (Sumner 1995: 767) regardless of whether one evaluates an individual's good in the light of her experiences, desires or some objective standards (e.g., Crisp 2008). Even many philosophers would probably accept the empirical observation that environment and relationship with others often count a great deal more than intellectual competence when assessing one's subjective well-being (Vehmas 1999). But surely, we think, there must be something wrong with impairments and particularly cognitive impairments as such, especially if they compromise one's subjective welfare? It seems highly counter-intuitive to view impairments as neutral, and not as harmful qualities.

If this instrumental starting-point seems insufficient we need to ask whether it is possible to stipulate intrinsic factors that would form an objective and a substantial foundation for the normative examination of disability. However, the problem with intrinsic values is that, ultimately, they require either an essentialist account of humanity or an objective account that undeniably explains why certain things are good and valuable in their own right. If we are to say that some quality is of intrinsic value to human beings, in the essentialist framework we need to point out how it is necessary in the fulfilment of the human ideal. Aristotle's theory is an example of an openly species-specific account: all creatures have a nature and their existence has an end that is based on their nature (Griffin 1986: 56–72). So all we need to do in an Aristotelian framework is to deduce from human nature our natural telos.

Another possibility in explaining the value of certain things in people's lives is to see how they correspond with things that are intrinsically valuable, that is, valuable in a way that needs no further explanation or justification. What could such things be? The most common answer is happiness. Traditionally philosophers are not content with a purely subjectivist understanding of happiness. This is apparent and undeniable in cases where someone takes pleasure from harming others. One could also argue that some ways of fulfilling one's happiness are not actually in line with a good life. John Rawls (1972: 432) has presented an example of a mathematically gifted man whose only pleasure is to count blades of grass in various geometrically shaped areas such as park squares and well-trimmed lawns. To many of us, this man's happiness would seem peculiar – not the kind of happiness that would be of intrinsic value. This is because subjective well-being and sense of happiness are often seen as relevant only when they have resulted from living according to the ideals that form the idea of a good life; meaning, you have to be happy for the right reasons. This view naturally raises questions about the contents of the good and its justification. There are various objective accounts of morality and the good life but there is no consensus as to why we should adopt a particular theory as the ultimate criterion for a good human life. Also, it would be curious to detach goodness or badness altogether from a subjective perspective. Knowledge, rational activity, love and many other things may be valuable in their own right, but they would also be pointless if they were entirely devoid of pleasure. Moral ideals that do not benefit beings under moral realm are, at the end of the day, useless. For instance, the badness of a pain consists in its being disliked; it is not disliked because it is bad. What is of value, or is good for someone, requires an individual's desire for it (Parfit 1986: 499–502).

Another factor that can possibly be seen as having intrinsic value is opportunity. According to John Harris, disabilities are the kind of harmed conditions that someone has a strong rational preference not to be in (Harris 2000, 2001). A harmed condition is relative both to one's rational preferences and to possible alternatives. In other words, some condition is a disability if it implies the deprivation of worthwhile experiences and the possibility of exploring them: 'The intellectually disabled do miss out on some dimensions of experience which are closed to them in the way that music is closed to the deaf. And this is a disability' (Harris 2001: 384). Thus, Harris conceptualizes disability in terms of missed possibilities and opportunities. Disability is something to do with individuals' abilities for pursuing various enriching experiences and possibilities in life.

Harris's formulation gives the impression that opportunities as such are valuable and that the more opportunities one has to pursue worthwhile experiences, the better. But this clearly is not true. Being spoilt for choice does not guarantee one's happiness, rather, sometimes it may cause stress and constant feelings of inadequacy. For example, I personally have little talent in academic scholarship, music and sports, and I enjoy all these activities. But at the same time, I often feel that I am very poor doing these things partly because I do not have enough time to improve my talents in all those three areas. Hence, I might be better off if I could concentrate on improving my performance in only one of these areas. Harris's account also raises the question of what kinds of possibilities are *relevant* in the sense that the lack of them amounts to a disability and harm. Harris (2000: 97) thinks that hearing is an invaluable faculty and people are disabled if they cannot enjoy 'Mozart, and Beethoven, and dance music, and the sound of the wind in the trees, and the waves on the shore'. This seems intuitively clear to hearing people but it does not provide a satisfactory argument for the notion that loss of hearing inevitably amounts to a disability – especially since many deaf people do not consider themselves disabled or unfortunate (depending, of course, on whether they were born deaf or impaired later in their lives). Harris does not seem to take into account the fact that certain functions are regarded vital for human well-being because they are 'sources of shared experience and social interaction' and also because 'our social life and culture are built around some of those functions' (Wasserman 1996: 133). This is why people usually do not feel impaired in lacking a sixth sense or the acoustic range or olfactory sensitivity of a typical dog. Thus, functions and faculties are regarded as good for people on the basis of actual cultural and social accommodation and requirements, regardless of how much these, or some other functions and faculties, could enrich our lives in some other circumstances (Vehmas 2004).

To conclude, despite its intuitive appeal to most people, it is very difficult to argue either on instrumental or intrinsic grounds that impairments are necessarily harmful regarding human well-being. But it would also be unconvincing to claim that impairments sometimes wouldn't cause some kind of predicament or downright suffering to people. It is important to distinguish something being a *disadvantage* and something being *disadvantageous* on balance (Steinbock 2000: 112–3). Deafness, for example, is a disadvantage in the sense that it precludes the possibility for many activities and careers but also leaves many other opportunities available. So, on balance, deafness may not amount to a disadvantage although the impairment in itself may be considered a disadvantage; something one might prefer not to have. All people face undesirable limitations in their lives as embodied beings that are not disadvantageous on balance. Ultimately, the significance of any characteristic to one's well-being depends largely on social values and arrangements.

305

Political philosophy and disability policy

Philosophical ethics aims to produce well-argued norms that could, first of all, contribute to people's pursuit of a good life and, second, regulate social life. Ethics is thus closely linked to political philosophy, which involves reflections on how best to arrange our collective lives. Political philosophy aims to answer the question: what would institutionally be the best way to arrange our social life, and how can and should these arrangements be justified? Typically, political philosophers discuss the meaning and significance of, for instance, liberty, justice and equality. Western political thought has evolved from contractarian tradition, where people voluntarily commit to follow norms and laws they have established in order to ensure a peaceful social life. The normative force of the contractarian political theory is seen to be based on a mutually advantageous contract between different parties. The point is not *what* individuals and communities choose to pursue in this contract but, rather, *how* they choose it. The contractarian model thus emphasizes the procedure over the contents of the contract. The correct procedure in making the agreement is based on autonomous and rational decision-making. Also, the parties acting as representatives of citizens should be endowed with mental and physical abilities that lie within the 'normal' range. The most well-known representative of the contractarian model, John Rawls (1972), assumes that in an imaginary negotiation between parties with sufficiently similar mental and physical abilities the interests of all are interconnected, which implies that it is only rational for the negotiators to consider the interests of all parties. Yet, this logic does not work in situations where people's interests and needs do not overlap. Contractarianism does not tell us how to treat beings whose lives do not concern us directly (e.g., Mulhall and Swift 1992: 1–33; Nussbaum 2006: 17).

Contractarianism has been criticized for excluding people who do not conform to the demands of normality from the negotiating table and thus from the spheres of justice. Contractarianism conflates the negotiators of justice with the benefactors of justice, with the result that the negotiators agree on arrangements that concern first and foremost themselves. People with impairments have virtually been ignored in contractarian tradition. This concerns especially people with cognitive impairments because they have been regarded as lacking the essential cognitive capacities required for autonomous and rational moral agency. Contractarianism has been based on a one-sided view of humanity and has failed to recognize sufficiently the human diversity, and to 'attend to the fact of human dependency and the consequences of this dependency on social organization' (Kittay 1999: 76). Thus, those highly dependent on other people's care have been pushed to the fringes of humanity and the political system.

One influential political theory that addresses these concerns is the capabilities approach developed by Amartya Sen (1992) and Martha Nussbaum (2006). In this theory ethically significant equality means what people are actually able to do and to be; the actual freedom to pursue and exercise things and activities that are significant regarding human well-being. Thus, the capabilities approach is 'an account of core human entitlements that should be respected and implemented by the governments of all nations, as a bare minimum of what respect for human dignity requires' (Nussbaum 2006: 70). Satisfactory political theory must, according to Nussbaum, be *pluralist* in the sense that it takes into account cultural variation. At the same time, and to a degree, it should also be normatively *objective* due to the fact that people often submit to the status quo against their own interest. In other words, in some cultures the upbringing of certain people (e.g., women and people with impairments) has been hedged around discrimination and inequality, with the result that the people who are actually discriminated against do not acknowledge this negative experience, have submitted to the prevailing circumstances and have the subjective experience of doing well. According to Nussbaum, political theory should be based on an objective (albeit an open-ended and subject to ongoing revision and rethinking) list of components of well-being and relevant capabilities. Such capabilities include, for example, health, adequate nourishment, bodily integrity, social bases of self-respect and non-humiliation, and right of political participation (Nussbaum 2006: 69–81).

Conceptions of what kinds of beings humans are and especially what kinds of beings we ought to be are politically crucial because these ideas, in their part, form the basis for social arrangements. Western philosophical tradition has emphasized the importance of mental capacities regarding humanity and human dignity. The rationality of human beings has been seen to distinguish us from other animals. The capabilities approach withdraws from this tradition by pointing out that corporality and animality is the foundation of human life, and that rationality and animality should be seen as thoroughly unified. Since we are fundamentally corporeal beings, our existence is characterized by various physical needs and dependencies throughout our lives. Dependency is not characteristic merely to infants, old people and people with impairments but, rather, it is something that unites all human beings. Therefore, it is only expedient to consider dependency and the need for care as inseparable features of human condition and, consequently, of social order as well. This means that we should not include effectively into our social organization merely those who are dependent upon others, but also those who attend to their needs. Eva Kittay, for example, has argued that work within the family, conducted mostly by women, should be recognized as proper work and that family members performing care work should be eligible for a salary (Kittay 1999: chapters 1, 2 and 5; Nussbaum 2006: 159–60, 211–16).

In the capabilities approach people's lives are seen to consist of both social and individual features. This has inevitable implications regarding social arrangements. First of all, capabilities crucial for well-being and a good life are determined largely on the grounds of environmental factors. For example, the level of free education that the state should provide its citizens with or what is the proper school-leaving age depends, to an extent, upon the type of economy and employment in the state. Second, capabilities and their realization relate to an individual's features. Freedom of religion may have very little importance to an individual with a severe intellectual disability, whereas the recognition of his or her needs for individualized support and care may be vital. All institutional arrangements of care and social participation must acknowledge human diversity in order to be efficient and of use. However, Nussbaum (2006: 186–95) emphasizes the political, strategic and normative significance of insisting that capabilities are important to *all* individuals despite their characteristics. This is important because 'it reminds us of the respect we owe to people with mental impairments as fully equal citizens' and because it 'also reminds us of the continuity between so-called normal people and people with impairments' (Nussbaum 2006: 190–1).

The practical implications of the capabilities approach are not always easily discerned. Consider, for example, educational arrangements for pupils with impairments (or with 'special needs'). It is largely taken for granted in disability studies that all segregated special education is oppressive and that inclusive education is the only ethically and politically justifiable arrangement (e.g., Oliver 2004). But the issue is not, perhaps, all that simple. Let me explain. A genuine inclusion in social life manifests in three ways. First, there is the technical inclusion in social life, which means the provision of the material facilities that enable persons to take part in social life (e.g., an accessible built environment). Second, there is the institutional inclusion in social life, which refers to an institutionally enforced position as a person and a citizen (typically manifested in rights). Finally, there is the interpersonal inclusion in social life, which means being included in concrete events and contexts of interaction through the attitudes of or attention given by relevant others who are also partakers in them – that is, to be respected, valued and loved by other people (Ikäheimo 2009).

Now, the three dimensions of social inclusion mentioned above seem to contradict segregated teaching, and support the notion of inclusive education. This kind of conclusion may, however, be a bit hasty in the light of the experiences of students in various educational settings. Many students have experienced segregated teaching as demeaning and humiliating, whereas many other students have reported mainly positive experiences and outcomes regarding their personal life course (e.g., Beltempo and Achille 1990; Jahnukainen and Järvinen 2005). Also, an educational policy that does not tolerate any exceptions might be highly inappropriate and harmful to some students. For example, deaf students need their own institutions in order to strengthen their language, identity and culture, and some students with difficult psychiatric conditions could find it impossible to appreciate group dynamics and simply not feel comfortable in groups no matter how respectful those groups would be towards them. Thus, social (including educational) arrangements should probably be, to an extent, flexible; one method or arrangement does not suit all. Whether it is possible to improve everyone's capabilities in the best possible manner in the same setting is, fundamentally, an empirical matter that should be judged in relation to different values such as justice, human well-being and common good. What matters from a disability perspective is a commitment to politics that, first, rests on the assumption that taking care of those that are dependent on others benefits us all in the end, and second, that putting into practice this assumption is seen primarily as society's moral obligation that does not need any further justification.

References

Albrecht, G. L. (2002) 'American Pragmatism, Sociology and the Development of Disability Studies', in C. Barnes, M. Oliver and L. Barton, eds, *Disability Studies Today* (Cambridge: Polity Press): pp. 18–37.

Barnes, C., Mercer, G. and Shakespeare, T. (1999) *Exploring Disability: A Sociological Introduction* (Cambridge: Polity).

Beltempo, J. and Achille, P. A. (1990) 'The Effect of Special Class Placement on the Self-concept of Children with Learning Disabilities', *Child Study Journal* 20: 81–103.

Crisp, R. (2008) 'Well-Being', in E. N. Zalta, ed., *Stanford Encyclopedia of Philosophy*; available online at http://plato.stanford.edu/entries/well-being/ (accessed 6 October 2011).

Griffin, J. (1986) *Well-Being: It's Meaning, Measurement and Moral Importance* (Oxford: Clarendon Press).

Harris, J. (2000) 'Is There a Coherent Social Conception of Disability?', *Journal of Medical Ethics* 26: 95–100.

Harris, J. (2001) 'One Principle and Three Fallacies of Disability Studies', *Journal of Medical Ethics* 27: 383–7.

Ikäheimo, H. (2009) 'Personhood and the Social Inclusion of People with Disabilities: A Recognition-Theoretical Approach', in K. Kristiansen, S. Vehmas and T. Shakespeare, eds, *Arguing About Disability: Philosophical Perspectives* (London and New York: Routledge): pp. 77–92.

Jahnukainen, M. and Järvinen, T. (2005) 'Risk Factors and Survival Routes: Social Exclusion as a Life-Historical Phenomenon', *Disability & Society* 20: 669–82.

Kittay, E. F. (1999) *Love's Labor: Essays on Women, Equality, and Dependency* (New York and London: Routledge).

Kittay, E. F. (2005) 'At the Margins of Moral Personhood', *Ethics* 116: 100–31.

Kittay, E. F. (2009) 'The Personal is Philosophical is Political: A Philosopher and Mother of a Cognitively Disabled Person Sends Notes From the Battlefield', *Metaphilosophy* 40: 606–27.

Linton, S. (1998) *Claiming Disability: Knowledge and Identity* (New York: New York University Press).

McMahan, J. (1996) 'Cognitive Disability, Misfortune, and Justice', *Philosophy and Public Affairs* 25: 3–35.

Mulhall, S. and Swift, A. (1992) *Liberals and Communitarians* (Oxford: Blackwell).

Nagel, T. (1987) *What Does It All Mean? A Very Short Introduction to Philosophy* (New York and Oxford: Oxford University Press).

Nussbaum, M. (2006) *Frontiers of Justice: Disability, Nationality, Species Membership* (Cambridge: Harvard University Press).

Oliver, M. (1990) *The Politics of Disablement* (Basingstoke: Macmillan).

Oliver, M. (2004) 'Does Special Education Have a Role to Play in the 21st Century?', in G. Thomas and M. Vaughan, eds, *Inclusive Education: Readings and Reflections* (Maidenhead: Open University Press): pp. 111–115.

Oliver, M. (2007) 'Disability Rights and Wrongs?', *Disability & Society* 22(2): 230–4.

Parfit, D. (1986) *Reasons and Persons* (Oxford: Clarendon Press).

Paterson, K. and Hughes, B. (1999) 'Disability Studies and Phenomenology: The Carnal Politics of Everyday Life', *Disability & Society* 14: 597–610.

Rawls, J. (1972) *A Theory of Justice* (Oxford: Oxford University Press).

Searle, J. R. (1995) *The Construction of Social Reality* (London: Penguin).

Searle, J. R. (2010) *Making the Social World: The Structure of Human Civilization* (New York: Oxford University Press).

Sen, A. (1992) *Inequality Reexamined* (Oxford: Clarendon Press).

Shakespeare, T. (2006) *Disability Rights and Wrongs* (London and New York: Routledge).

Steinbock, B. (2000) 'Disability, Prenatal Testing, and Selective Abortion', in E. Parens and A. Asch, eds, *Prenatal Testing and Disability Rights* (Washington, DC: Georgetown University Press): pp. 108–23.

Sumner, L. W. (1995) 'The Subjectivity of Welfare', *Ethics* 105: 764–90.

Taylor, S. (1996) 'Disability Studies and Mental Retardation', *Disability Studies Quarterly* 16: 4–13.

Thomas, C. (2008) 'Disability: Getting it "Right"', *Journal of Medical Ethics* 34(1): 15–17.

Timmons, M. (2002) *Moral Theory: An Introduction* (Lanham: Rowman and Littlefield).

Vehmas, S. (1999) 'Newborn Infants and the Moral Significance of Intellectual Disabilities', *Journal of the Association for Persons with Severe Handicaps* 24: 111–21.

Vehmas, S. (2004) 'Ethical Analysis of the Concept of Disability', *Mental Retardation* 42: 209–22.

Vehmas, S. (2008) 'Philosophy and Science: The Axes of Evil in Disability Studies?', *Journal of Medical Ethics* 34: 21–3.

Vehmas, S. (2010) 'The Who or What of Steve: Severe Cognitive Impairment and its Implications', in M. Häyry, T. Takala, P. Herissone-Kelly and G. Árnason, eds, *Arguments and Analysis in Bioethics* (Amsterdam and New York: Rodopi): pp. 263–80.

Vehmas, S. and Mäkelä, P. (2009) 'The Ontology of Disability and Impairment: A Discussion of the Natural and Social Features', in K. Kristiansen, S. Vehmas and T. Shakespeare, eds, *Arguing about Disability: Philosophical Perspectives* (London and New York: Routledge): pp. 42–56.

Warburton, N. (1992) *Philosophy: The basics* (London and New York: Routledge).

Wasserman, D. (1996) 'Some Moral Issues in the Correction of Impairments', *Journal of Social Philosophy* 27: 128–45.

23

THE PSYCHOLOGY OF DISABILITY

Dan Goodley

Introduction

Disability studies theory and research have emerged in response to the politicization of disabled people. Disability studies attends to the social, cultural, material, economic and material conditions of exclusion. Often missing from these analyses is the psychology of disability. This exemption is understandable. Psychology has a troubling and troubled status in disability studies. When disability and psychology cross they tend to in terms of rehabilitation, treatment, therapy and cure. While there have been recent attempts to colonize psychology with disability studies (Goodley and Lawthom 2005a, 2005b, 2005c), psychology has the potential to individualize the material, political and cultural foci of disability studies. Disabled people remain un(der)represented on psychology courses (Olkin 2003), and, as indicated in the accounts of Levinson and Parritt (2005) and Stannett (2005), disabled psychologists remain excluded from the profession. Despite these problems, following (Goodley 2011a), merging disability studies and psychology might allow us to address a number of issues, including: theorizing the psychological impact of living with an impairment in a disabling society; exploring the ways in which disabled people psychologically deal with demanding publics and exposing non-disabled people's unresolved, unconscious conflicts around disability. While addressing these issues might well contribute to the development of disability studies, the idea of developing a psychology of disability raises two significant questions. Does a turn to psychology risk individualizing the phenomenon of disability? What psychological orientations already exist that may enhance our understandings of disability? This chapter will address these questions by making a case against 'a functionalist psychology of disability' and developing, as an alternative, an argument for 'a phenomenological psychology of disability'. I will argue that a psychology of disability, which positions psychology as a functionalist science, that develops as *the* discipline of the individual, treats individuals in ways that maintain the disablist status quo. In contrast, a critical psychology of disability that recasts psychology as phenomenological inquiry, develops psychology as a discipline of and for the community and seeks to treat the community in ways that challenge disabling conditions of everyday life.

A functionalist psychology of disability: mainstream psychological disability studies

That disabled researcher who came to speak at your disability seminar – what's wrong with him?

(A question asked of me by a professor of psychology, somewhere in the United Kingdom)

I was reading through my lecturer's new textbook the other day – the 'Abnormal psychology' text – and I thought, 'do you know, I think I am depressed, schizophrenic, autistic and many other things!'

(Anonymized comments of a third-year psychology undergraduate student)

A university lecturer was teaching a second-year undergraduate class on research methods in psychology. During the first session she asked the class, 'How would you find out how your friend was feeling?' After at least three minutes of silence, a student cautiously raised her hand to answer, 'I would send her a questionnaire.' The lecturer acknowledged that as a valid psychological measure. A short time later another member of the class raised her hand to suggest, 'Could you just … eh, ring and ask how she was feeling?'

(An anecdote shared by an academic colleague, Goodley 2011a: 75)

This being a chapter on psychology, I will start with a confession; I am a psychology graduate. I feel an acute sense of trepidation in admitting this. Perhaps I should feel less concerned when disability studies luminaries such as Vic Finkelstein are themselves psychologists by background and training (Finkelstein and French 1993). The uncomfortable truth, that I do not want to avoid in this chapter, is that psychology has led a troubled existence in the disability studies world. The anecdotes presented above – picked out of the academic context of psychology – hint at some of the problems inherent in psychological science, theory and research. Implicit within these anecdotes are assumptions of lack, deficit and pathology associated with disability: a phenomenon that encompasses physical and sensory impairments as well as 'impairments of mind' such as intellectual disabilities and mental health issues. We can also detect a mode of research production and level of analysis that dominates psychology: the *scientific* study of an *individual's* mind and behaviour. In this section, then, I want to worry away at my own feelings of negativity to address the first question posed at the outset of the chapter: does a turn to psychology risk individualizing the phenomenon of disability? I will argue that there are real problems inherent with an approach to psychology that threatens to understand disability as a product of a deficient, flawed, lacking individual.

Psychology is a broad discipline that encompasses many different theoretical positions including humanism, cognitivism, behaviourism, psychoanalysis, existentialism and biogenic. There are a number of professional psychological roles including educational, clinical, counselling, health, psychotherapeutic, educational, forensic and occupational. In recent years psychology has been territorialized by a number of politicized and transformative positions including feminist, queer, class and disability theories. Nonetheless, a positivist and experimentalist approach to the study of psychology continues to dominate the field, especially in those arenas where psychology seeks scientific status and authority. A consequence of this dominance is a tacit and sometimes unthinking reliance on scientific method. While I am not suggesting that science is inherently problematic for disabled people, a scientific approach to the study of psychology has the potential to lead to, at the very least, a limited conception of disability as a cultural, social and economic phenomenon. This is particularly so when we consider that for many psychologists the unit of analysis is the individual. Scientific analyses of the individual will, inevitably, lead to individualistic understandings of psychological and social phenomena. To develop this observation further, let us turn to a study.

Study 1

As a consequence of a severe reduction in their autonomy, the social life of people with quadriplegia becomes highly routine. In addition, the social environment becomes very limited because people without disabilities may feel awkward around, or have an aversion to, people with quadriplegia. A pet animal often facilitates social interactions between humans, and in this study we investigated the influence of a capuchin monkey companion on the social environment of a person with quadriplegia. In three different public areas, we compared the behaviors of passers-by confronted with a person with quadriplegia or a person who had no disabilities, either alone or with a capuchin companion. In both situations the capuchin companion greatly modified the behaviors of the passers-by, inducing more positive social behaviors such as smiles, and higher frequencies of visual contact. In addition, passers-by tended to avoid the person with quadriplegia less often when the capuchin was present. The presence of a capuchin companion potentially improves the social environment of people with quadriplegia.

(Hien and Deputte 1997: 101)

By citing this study I am in no way suggesting that it is representative of psychological studies of disability. I would accept that it is a mischievous choice and an easy target. What I do think this study captures, though, are some of the ways in which a positivistic and individualistic approach to the study of psychological processes – such as social isolation, autonomy and the response of (non-disabled) others – may reinforce particular conceptions of disability and impairment. Using the case study as a point of reflection, we will consider some of the ways in which a 'psychology of disability' draws on a distinct psychological orientation which is at odds with the aims and ambitions of disability studies.

Our first consideration is *psychology as a functionalist science*. Too often what counts as 'good psychology' is framed in terms of a scientific approach to research, which C. Wright Mills (1970: 61–5) defined as 'abstracted empiricism'; a pronounced tendency to study phenomena only within the curiously self-imposed limitations of an arbitrary epistemology. The epistemology Wright Mills was describing relates to a form of positivistic empirical psychology in which the individual subject is manipulated, controlled and measured in order to understand something objectively valid and reliable within that individual. This is the mode of research associated with experimentation and one strongly advocated by psychologists who view their discipline as a science akin to the natural sciences. Hien and Deputte's (1997) study elegantly captures this approach to abstracted empiricism, where the disabled subject is reduced to a passive object of experimental investigation. A number of conditions of the experiment are manipulated (a person with quadriplegia or a person who had no disabilities, either alone or with a capuchin companion), replicable measures are taken (positive social behaviours such as smiles, and higher frequencies of visual contact on the part of passers-by) in order to address hypotheses (whether or not the presence of a capuchin companion potentially improves the social environment of people with quadriplegia). Disabled individuals emerge as variables of the experiment and objects of inquiry. Leaving aside, for now, the problems disabled people might have with being objectified by this research, the study does at least take seriously their social location and seeks to address the problem of isolation. However, inherent within this study is a view not simply of disabled people but, more generally, of the individual.

This leads neatly to our second consideration: *psychology as the discipline of the individual*. Psychology is an academic discipline that is interested in the thoughts (cognitions), emotions (affect) and behaviours (responses) of individuals. A psychology of disability would, therefore, translate into a psychology of disabled individuals. When individualism and functionalist science fold into one another then there is always the potential for developing scientific theories about the relative functionality of disabled individuals. Hien and Deputte's (1997) study is predicated on the assumption that individuals with quadriplegia lack autonomy which directly impinges on their functionality in community settings. As Prilleltensky (2001: 750) observes, a commonly held view around social justice within psychology is the concept that psychologists can improve societies by helping one individual at a time. Hence, the Hien and Deputte (1997) study is clearly under-pinned by a human aim – to improve the social environments of wheelchair users – but is ultimately focused on the individual. The danger inherent in this perspective is that the problem of disability is seen as lying with the disabled person rather than a social world that responds negatively to disability. The notion of discipline extends beyond university walls. As Michel Foucault (1973a, 1973b, 1977, 1978) recognized, the 'individual' has a long socio-political history and etymology. It is tied to the enlightenment rise of the *reasoned* individual and *his* democracy, over the sovereignty of church and monarchy. The 'individual' is also the creation of capitalism, a convenient signifier of an alienating symbolic order, which masks the inequities of social and political life. And individuals populate consumerist and marketized forms of education, work and leisure. Those able to benefit from this meritocracy flourish while the less able tend to flounder. In dominant ideas of everyday life, the 'individual' remains the key site of understanding for the aetiology of disablism. As Spivak (1985: 344) coins it, 'individualism in an age of imperialism relates to the making of human beings – the constitution and interpellation of the subject not only as an individual but as individualist'. Psychology's individualistic functionalism has contributed markedly to the development of social policies, legislative and educational systems that seek to discipline the individual:

> The individual becomes the hub around which is organised the maintenance of discipline, citizenship, rights and responsibilities demanded of democratic governments and its institu-tions of school, prison, welfare institution and workplace. Discourses of these institutions and their professionals served the disciplining of the individual. Human and social sciences informed their knowledge about the individual. But these sciences did not simply provide understandings of the individual: they made the individual in their own image.
>
> *(Goodley 2011a: 69)*

Questions are raised about the type of (disabled) individual that emerges through the discipline and *disciplining* of psychology. This individual is incommensurate with disability studies that aim to promote understandings of the disabled world whilst recognizing the resistance of disabled people.

Our third consideration, *psychology's treatment of the individual*, addresses the problems of disability at the level of human being. This approach dominates the professional and service experiences of disabled people who are subjected to a number of interventions from professionals allied to medicine (PAMs) (Finkelstein 1999a, 1999b). Psychology tends to defer reference to material and social structural influences on personhood by subordinating these influences to cognitive processes, following the dictum that 'problems follow from people's perceptions and evaluations of the events in their lives rather than from the events themselves' (Cromby and Harper 2009: 342). Hence, Hien and Deputte's (1997) study makes some tentative conclusions around the responses of non-disabled passers-by to a disabled person (with or without a capuchin monkey present). While these findings might be helpful in describing response sets, the actual material and social origins of these responses remain unchallenged. Indeed, Hien and Deputte's (1997) reason-ing around the origins of isolation implicates only disabled people; their isolation is the consequence of their 'severe reduction of autonomy' (Hien and Deputte 1997: 101). Unsurprisingly, then, their preferred intervention is a therapeutic one: focused on improving the life of the individual through the introduction of a monkey. This approach leaves the social world intact. While a few passers-by are encouraged to engage with the monkey (and perhaps the disabled person), the community remains relatively untroubled. Following C. Wright Mills (1970: 14–16), social isolation is tackled only as a 'private trouble' of individuals that occur in their relationships with others (often when their own values are threatened) and does not become understood or engaged with as a 'public issue' of organizations and institutions (that often arise as a crisis of institutional arrangements). There are real dilemmas in keeping disability a private matter because this will influence more general societal responses to disability:

> What shall we do now you are disabled?
>
> We shall cure you.
>
> How shall you live when our cure fails and you are now permanently disabled?
>
> You shall adjust.
>
> (Michalko 2002: 30)

For social change to occur, Wright Mills advocates that research must concern itself with private troubles *and* public issues.

Our fourth consideration, *psychology as handmaiden of society*, follows the suggestion made by a number of critical commentators that psychology has historically helped to maintain the status quo (Kitzinger 1993). Venn (1984) argues that psychology contributes, in no small part, to a particular view of the individual of contemporary society: namely the unitary rational subject or the sovereign self of modern individualism. Psychology is not just the science of the individual but, crucially, a discourse that participates positively in the construction of the social world and the instrumental rationality of the individual (Venn 1984: 122). Psychology is a science that speaks of the person. Psychology has long held implicit assumptions (that are then made explicit) *about* people, and conversely, what is *required* to be a person. Following Goodley (2011a: 72), the accepted individual of contemporary society, whom many of us are expected to mirror, is adult, male, middle class, heterosexual, rule abiding, sane, non-disabled and European. The converse – the Other – is the unacceptable; child, female, working class, homosexual, criminal, insane, disabled and resolutely non-European. Venn suggests that in order to promote the desired individual what is required is an obsessional focus on the abject Other; normalizing and disciplining this section of the population as part of the quest for the model citizen and rational self. The individual of post/industrial societies is a 'normal' one who will contribute to the making of society as a body-of-functions (Michalko 2002: 156). A key site of the oppression of disabled people pertains to those moments when they are judged to fail to match up to the ideal individual; when they are categorized as embodying the failing individual. Mintz (2002: 162) suggests that social discourses about disability are not about disability at all. Rather, they relate to the need to guarantee the privileged status of the non-disabled citizen; 'a need that, in turn, emerges from fears about the fragility and unpredictability of embodied identities'. Similarly, Marks (1999a) observes that disabled people constitute a huge problem for non-disabled society precisely because they disrupt cherished views of the normative individual:

> The person that dribbles, she comments, disrupts a culture that emphasises bodily control and associated cultural norms around manners, convention and bodily comport-ment. An individual whose speech is difficult to understand is assumed to have a problem because they challenge a colonising stance of certainty about how people should speak. People who do not walk are understood as tragic because they do not embody the

idealised mobility of the autonomous walker (Oliver, 1993). People with learning difficulties, who fail to meet developmentalist stages, are discarded from mainstream educational systems because of their lack of fit with educational prerogatives. Individuals who depend on – or require connections with – others to live are not individuals at all.

(Goodley 2011: 79)

Disabled people are their impairment. *They* are broken individuals. *They* lack development. *They* cannot do. *They* are burdens. *They* do not have the abilities to lead an independent life. In assigning the problems of disability to the bodies and personhood of disabled people then psychology leaves the social world untouched; under-theorizing and unchallenged.

A phenomenological psychology of disability: critical psychological disability studies

We now turn to our second question: What psychological orientations already exist that may enhance our understandings of disability? In answering this question I want to consider the contribution of phenomenology – a perspective that has gathered force in a movement defined as 'critical psychology'. In a recent book I offer the following overview:

Critical psychologists contest the modernist view that psychology is a progressive science. For Fox and Prilleltensky (1997), psychology has hindered social justice, to the detriment of all communities and to oppressed groups in particular. Critical psychologists confront psychological practices that sustain oppression and seek, instead, to promote an ethical and politicised psychology that works alongside activists, users and survivors of psychology. The 1970s 'crisis in social psychology' saw a paradigm shift in thinking about how psychology should go about its business. For Parker (1989) a key site of contestation appeared through interpretivists, phenomenologists, feminists and Marxist writers challenging the dominating forces of positivism. The 'crisis' marked a sustained rejection of psychological functionalism: a mistaken view of isolated beings in socio-political vacuums: the roots of psychologisation. Overall, the crisis pushed psychologists towards meaning-oriented persuasions often with political affiliations. …Critical psychology shares much with disability studies. Each are reactions to hegemonic constructions of elitist subjectivities, the medicalisation of distress and the segregation of some from the mainstream. Each oppose the diagnosis, assessment and treatment of isolated individuals and seek to change cultural and environmental forms of alienation and marginalisation. Similarly, each has produced epistemologies that invite criticality on the part of activists, theorists and practitioners. They share a commitment to forming communities of practice that are engaged with social change. Critical psychologists have deconstructed and reconstructed, revised and rejected psychology.

(Goodley 2011a: 87–8)

There have been a number of recent disability studies writings that have unambiguously drawn on what have been termed 'critical psychology' resources, for example in education and childhood (Billington 2000, 2002), in relation to reappraising the psychologist's role (Olkin 2001, 2002, 2003, 2008, 2009; Olkin and Pledger 2003; Levinson and Parritt 2005) and in ontological accounts of disablism (Chinn 2006; Reeve 2008). Analyses of critical disability studies have been made in reference to psychoanalysis (Marks 1999a, 1999b; Goodley 2011b), humanistic (Swain and French 2000; Swain *et al.* 2003), post-structuralist (Todd 2005) and discursive psychology (Rapley 2004). All of these contributions contest the individualization of disability but aim to expose some of the psychological elements of living with an impairment in a disabling world. For this chapter I want to turn to the contribution of phenomenology to a critical psychology of disability.

Study 2

When Rod Michalko's sight finally became so limited that he no longer felt safe on busy city streets or traveling alone, he began a search for a guide. The Two-in-One is his account of how his search ended with Smokie, a guide dog, and a dramatically different sense of blindness. Few people who regularly encountered Michalko in his neighborhood shops and cafes realized that he was technically blind; like many people with physical disabilities, he had found ways of compensating for his impairment. Those who knew about his condition thought of him as a fully realized person who just happened to be blind. He thought so himself. Until Smokie changed all that. In this often moving, always compelling meditation on his relationship with Smokie, Michalko probes into what it means to be at home with blindness. Smokie makes no judgment about Michalko's lack of sight; it simply is the condition within which they work together. Their partnership thus allows Michalko to step outside of the conventional – and even 'enlightened' – understanding of blindness; he becomes not simply resigned to it but able to embrace it as an essential part of his being in the world. Drawing on his training as a sociologist and his experience as a disabled person, Michalko joins a still small circle of scholars who examine disability from the inside. More rare still – and what will resonate with most readers – is Michalko's remarkable portrayal of Smokie; avoiding sentimentality and pathos, it is a deeply affectionate yet restrained and nuanced appreciation of his behavior and personality. From their first meeting at the dog guide training school, Smokie springs to life in these pages as a highly competent, sure-footed, take-charge, full-speed-ahead, indispensable partner. 'Sighties' are always in awe watching them work; Michalko has even persuaded some of them that the Smokester can locate street addresses – but has a little difficulty with odd numbers! Readers of The Two-in-One can easily imagine Rod and Smokie sharing the joke as they continue on their way.

(Book cover of Michalko 1999)

As with the first case study of this chapter, we should not view this study as a perfect example of a critical psychological approach to the study of disability. Indeed, Michalko (1999) describes his work as a sociological critique. However, Michalko's work directly extends into a psychological terrain through his use of phenomenology. This approach to the study of psychology places the dilemmas and possibilities of disability at the level of embodiment (Hughes and Paterson 1997, 2000; Hughes 2002; Michalko 2002; Titchkosky 2003; Overboe 2007). Following Goodley (2011a: 56), phenomenologists attend to the capacities of the body to be a source of self and society. This has been termed a carnal sociology, drawing on the work of such people as Merleau-Ponty (1962), to theorize the body as *the* place where self and society interact. Embodiment refers to how the body operates in the world at the intersections of the corporeal and institutional (Sherry 2006). Comportment, for example, reflects conventions. Ability is a response to environmental demands. Illness is a narrative written onto and lived with through recourse to a whole host of powerful narratives such as medicine and self-help. The phenomenology of the everyday (Turner 2008: 12) engages with the 'lieb': the living, feeling and sensing facets of bodily experience (Crossley 1995). Bodies are sites for subjectivity and consciousness, our active vehicles for being in the world. Practical engagements with our surroundings inform the intentionality of the body. Senses provide thickness of meaning that then constitute the world around us. We open ourselves and bodies onto, and by doing so create, environments (Merleau-Ponty 1962). Overboe (2007), for example, argues that the disabled self can be embraced as a unique embodied entity through which to revise how bodies should and could be lived in. While there is this potential, critics accuse phenomenology of being nothing more than an individualistic account of embodiment, from the point of individual bodies, lacking a sociological and historical context (Turner 2008: 52).

Michalko's (1999) book, like the work of Hien and Deputte (1997), considers the relational interface between humans and animals. The similarities stop there, though, as Michalko approaches the study of disability from a very different angle.

First, let us consider *psychology as phenomenological inquiry*. Michalko's work is the antithesis of scientific, objective, quantifiable, experimental study. His work is an interpretivist inquiry that makes use of the creation, elaboration and celebration of stories that people bring to research (Haydon 2008). Michalko (1999) reflects upon the intimate, sustained and in-depth experience of walking through blindness with a guide dog. Unlike Hien and Deputte's work (1997), which isolates human and animal as distinct variables requiring analysis, Michalko's (1999) work provides deeply personal, qualitative reflections on the blurring of embodied realities between himself and his guide, Smokie. This account stands in stark contradistinction to functionalist science. Michalko (1999) is not simply a variable of a study: he is the active researcher of his relationship between human and animal and their shared encounters with the social world. For example, he argues that:

> Being 'at home with blindness' is to be an anomaly in the sighted world, and thinking of oneself as an anomaly does little for a blind person's quest for integrity and dignity. ... Anomalies, to this way of thinking, are accidental: things should have been otherwise. But for disease or accident, blind persons should and would be able to see. When we see blindness in this way we see it as a home unworthy of habitation. This leaves the blind person with only one choice – to be at home with blindness and not in blindness. ... This was how I understood my blindness before I had Smokie – as a condition that I had to overcome – and I believed that Smokie would help me do so. But my understanding soon began to change.
>
> *(Michalko 1999: 101–2)*

Michalko's inquiry draws on emergent reflections of everyday life in order to expose his own values around disability whilst illuminating societal and cultural values that already exist around disability. This being-in-the-world is a phenomenological position that may well give very different understandings of disability to those that already exist in the community. At the very least this approach foregrounds the perspectives of disabled researchers as they grapple with the complexities of meanings, relationships and interactions of the everyday. Phenomenological inquiry assumes that one has a life to recount, presents (disabled) informants as moral agents and situates the locus of culture in the interactions of self and others (McRuer and Wilkerson 2003: 11). This is a form of inquiry intrigued with what many of us would understand psychologists to be interested in: a sense of self; the distinction of self from another; reflections on the body and explorations of cognition, affect and action. However, unlike the functionalist science described above, phenomenology interrogates an individual's being-in-the-community.

Second, we can resituate *psychology as a discipline of and for the community*. Edwards (2002) argues that for communities to change this has to be accompanied by phenomenological change. Michalko supports this argument when he writes:

> Smokie and I move through our world *alone together,* focusing on one another in the midst of the plurality of our world and its many blindnesses. Smokie keeps me company in this estranged familiarity of opinion. I experience my blindness *together* with Smokie in this plurality. My focus is on Smokie and on myself. The world we generate springs from our communication in the midst of the world and from our movements through it. (italics in the original)
>
> *(Michalko 1999: 186)*

One way in which Michalko's (1999) study throws the spotlight onto the community is evidenced in his representation and explanation of many awkward (and at times exclusionary) comments and reactions that he (and Smokie) receive during their everyday encounters. These include: a stranger placing a one-dollar coin in Michalko's hand while he waits for a friend with Smokie outside a coffee bar; strangers asking if Smokie is a 'blind dog' ('Jeez: I hope not' is Michalko's retort) and the difficulties in negotiating the terrain of sidewalks when Saturday shoppers have pulled up onto the kerbs to park their cars. These mundane experiences draw attention to the ways in which the embodied and physical nature of the community can be likened to the 'demanding public' described by Hochschild (1983). Following Williams (2003) and Goodley (2011a: 92), disabled people are expected to emotionally *labour* in response to demanding publics. Emotions are corporeal thoughts, embodied processes, imbricated with social values and frequently involved in preserving social bonds, social rules and displays of behaviour (Williams 2003: 519–20). Our analysis of disability moves away from an analysis of individual deficit to problems inherent within demanding communities that expect particular responses from disabled people. This approach resonates with Finkelstein's (1999a, 1999b) vision of the professional allied to the community: a concept we will return to in the conclusion.

Third, *we may revise psychology's treatment of the community*. A critical psychology of disability has much to say about the constitution and functioning of society. Community psychologists pitch their analysis of psychology in the community as *the* place in which to address issues of social change and well-being. This is an orientation that fits neatly with the focus of disability studies on societal exclusion and disabling public discourses that are to be found in communities. Hence, following Oliver (1996), while people have impairments (cognitively, sensorially or physically) they also experience disability (marginalization in a society that is not designed to meet the needs with impairments). While bodies may function in different ways – some lacking, others apparently more productive – we live in a culture of disablism: 'a form of social oppression involving the social imposition of restrictions of activity on people with impairments and the socially engendered undermining of their psycho-emotional well being' (Thomas 2007: 73).

For Michalko (1999: 174) while he lives *with* blindness (that which is normally understood as the biological reality of visual impairment) he also lives *in* blindness (public discourses and societal responses to blindness). Our task, then, is to address and challenge many taken-for-granted assumptions that exist in the sighted world. Such a change of tack fits with Dorwick and Keys's (2001: 5) orientation of community psychology, which moves inquiry from an emphasis on an individual's deficits to an emphasis on their rights (concerned with access and barriers to access) and ultimately to an emphasis on empowerment (concerned with both needs and rights and with individuals' choice and control of their own lives). Community psychologists face issues similar to those faced by disability studies researchers regarding involvement by participants, the importance of context, the tension between scientific scepticism and social action, and the impact of the researcher on the research process.

> In the future, we hope that there will be more collaboration between the field of disability studies and community psychology. Such collaboration will expose disability studies scholars to valuable theory and research concerning community phenomena and give community psychologists a deeper understanding of the experience of disability.
>
> *(Dorwick and Keys 2001: 12)*

While these hopes seem very laudable, perhaps we can claim that disability studies – such as that adopted by Michalko (1999) – is already sensitizing us to the community and phenomenological experiences of disability. Disability studies preempts many of the paradigmatic changes demanded by community psychologists:

> While clinical psychology defined problems in terms of individuals, community psychology adopted ecological metaphors that encompassed various levels of analyses. While traditional applied psychology concentrated on professional help, community psychology fostered self-help and mutual help organizations taking place in natural settings. While clinicians operated very much as experts, community psychologists saw themselves as collaborators. The latter wanted to build on the strengths of individuals and groups, and not just concern themselves with diagnosis of pathologies.
>
> *(Prilleltensky 2001: 749)*

A community psychological engagement therefore engages with disability at both levels of private troubles and public issues (Wright Mills 1970). Disability studies and community psychology merge together through the private/public; self/community and intimate/formal engagement of phenomenological inquiry:

> Compassion at the interpersonal level is both wonderful and insufficient. There is a definite need to expand the implementation of values from the group and neighborhood contexts to the political context. …Efforts should always be directed toward the long-term goal of making society more humane for everyone.
>
> *(Prilleltensky 2001: 758)*

Fourth, we can promote *psychology as a critic of society*. When disability studies scholars only recognize functionalist scientific approaches to psychology, then they forget some of psychology's more radical histories. For example, *the Frankfurt school* of the early to mid-twentieth century included scholars such as Adorno, Marcuse, Horkheimer, Habermas, Fromm and Reich who shared critical and revolutionary ambitions (see Frosh 1987).

> these scholars aspired to question the 'nature' of human essence; unpick ideology as a form of false consciousness; challenge practices of excessive repression that served the aims of capitalism (for example, in relation to the arts, creativity or sexuality); explored the contradictory maxims of Marx ('life determines consciousness') and Freud ('anatomy is destiny'); struggled with the conflict between individual desire/ creativity and social prohibition/management; recovered bodily pleasures (inc: original sensuous child-like polymorphous perversity of our bodies) from the normalising pressures of labour; celebrated alternative forms of institutional and relational

arrangement (matriarchal rather than patriarchal society). All writers shared the aim of synthesising the sociology of Marx and the psychology of Freud in the name of radical social theory (Giroux 2009).

(Goodley 2011a: 58)

Parker (2007: 116–117) describes the critical theory of the Frankfurt school, and other radical humanists, as opposing positivist neutrality; a shift from crude economics to consciousness; a view of individualism as destructive and a shared ambition to recover human potential from the oppressive and dialectical markings of capitalist life. Giroux's (2009) account of the Frankfurt school captures the shared ambitions of this group of writers to rescue reason from technocratic rationality and positivism. Naïve positivism informs capitalist ideologies through the fetishization of facts and the sidelining of subjectivity. In contrast, the radical humanism of the Frankfurt school views theory as ever-present, and dialectical, with the potential to inform emancipatory practice: to subvert ideology. Dialectical theory reveals incompleteness where completeness is claimed and views culture as colonized by ruling ideas and hegemonic practices. A critical community psychology of disability seeks to recognize and build further on these revolutionary psychological tendencies. Michalko's (1999) book has many revolutionary lessons for disability studies and psychologists. One of these relates to his demand to think again about pathological concepts of

Table 23.1 Professional allied to professionals – or – the community

Professional allied to professionals	Professional allied to the community
Psychology of disability	Critical psychology of disability
Individual, moral and medical models of disability	Social, minority, cultural and relational models of disability
Functionalist science	Phenomenological inquiry
Individual rehabilitation	Community regeneration
Disabled people are service users	Disabled people are expert citizens
Individual adjustment and repair	Systemic change and community cohesion
Attitudinal change	Ideological and structural change
Care and cure	Support and hope
Individual	Relational
Participation	Emancipation
Health	Well-being
Advocacy	Politicization
Expertise	Collective empowerment
Deficit model	Capacity thinking
Service centred	Community centred
Alliances with other professionals and services	Alliance with organizations of disabled people
Services culture	Community culture
Segregation	Inclusion
Rights, in/dependence and mastery	Rights, interdependence and vulnerability
Diagnosis	Recognition
Marketization	Democratization
Paid employment	Cultural and community contribution

Source: Adapted from Goodley (2011a: 174). Drawing on Dunst (2008), Rioux (1994), Finkelstein and Stuart (1996), Finkelstein (1999a, 1999b), Oliver (1996), Kagan (2002), Kagan and Burton (2002).

blindness and, instead, conceive it as a space of productive reflection and insight of one's own psychology and its place in the world:

> Smokie has reminded me, too, of the value of intimacy. … Without intimacy, relations between nature and society become a mere matter of dominance and submission in which 'society' dominates and 'nature' submits. Intimacy allows the relationship between dominance and submission to be reciprocal, fluid and dialectical. This is what life with Smokie has taught me. With his guidance, I have become intimate with him, with my world, and with my blindness.
>
> *(Michalko 1999: 188)*

Conclusions

In this chapter we have explored two distinct psychologies of disability. We have considered the ways in which a functionalist psychology maintains an individualistic conception of disability, while a phenomenological psychology opens up possibilities for addressing disablism in the social relationships and interactions of the community. These are not just debates about theory. Psychology produces practitioners. We might ask how these two psychologies could play out in practice. Finkelstein's (1999a, 1999b) concept of the professional allied to medicine and the professional allied to the community provides a useful framework for pitching our two psychologies (see Table 23.1).

Psychology continues to occupy a strong position in service provision and professional practice in the lives of disabled people. It is therefore crucial that disability studies engages with psychology in ways that enhance the community's recognition of disabled people and their allies.

References

Billington, T. (2000) *Separating, Losing and Excluding Children: Narratives of Difference* (London: Routledge Falmer).

Billington, T. (2002) 'Children, Psychologists and Knowledge: A Discourse Analytic Narrative', *Educational and Child Psychology* 19(3): 32–41.

Chinn, D. (2006) 'All Parents Together: Professionals Talk about Parents with Developmental Disabilities'. Paper presented at the British Disability Studies Association 3rd Annual Conference, Lancaster, 18–21 September.

Cromby, J. and Harper, D. (2009) 'Paranoia: A Social Account', *Theory and Psychology* 19(3): 335–61.

Crossley, N. (1995) 'Merleau-Ponty, the Elusive Body and Carnal Knowledge'. *Body and Society* 1(1): 43–63.

Dorwick, P. W. and Keys, C. B. (2001) 'Community Psychology and Disability Studies', *Journal of Prevention & Intervention in the Community* 21(2): 1–14.

Dunst, C. (2008) 'Participatory Opportunities, Capacity Building Processes and Empowerment Actions'. Keynote presentation to Intellectual Disability Conference: Empowering People with Intellectual Disabilities, their Families and Supporters: Reflections on Research and Practice, Park Building, University of Portsmouth, 12–13 September.

Edwards, S. (2002) 'Evaluating Models of Community Psychology: Social Transformation in South Africa', *International Journal of Behavioral Medicine* 9(4): 301–8.

Finkelstein, V. (1999a) 'A Profession Allied to the Community: The Disabled People's Trade Union', in E. Stone, ed., *Disability and Development: Learning from Action and Research on Disability in the Majority World* (Leeds: The Disability Press): pp. 21–4.

Finkelstein, V. (1999b) *Professions Allied to the Community* (PACS II); available online at www.leeds.ac.uk/disability-studies/archive (accessed 5 October 2011).

Finkelstein, V. and French, S. (1993) 'Towards a Psychology of Disability', in J. Swain, V. Finkelstein, S. French and M. Oliver, eds, *Disabling Barriers – Enabling Environments* (London: Sage): pp. 26–33.

Finkelstein, V. and Stuart, O. (1996) 'Developing New Services', in G. Hales, ed., *Beyond Disability: Towards an Enabling Society* (London: Sage): pp. 165–72.

Foucault, M. (1973a) *The Birth of the Clinic: An Archaeology of Medical Perception*, trans. A. M. Sheridan (New York: Pantheon Books).

Foucault, M. (1973b) *Madness and Civilisation: A History of Insanity in the Age of Reason*, trans. R. Howard (New York: Vintage/Random House).

Foucault, M. (1977) *Discipline and Punish: The Birth of the Prison*, trans. R. Howard (New York: Pantheon Books).

Foucault, M. (1978) *The History of Sexuality*, Volume I (New York: Vintage Books).

Fox, D. and Prilleltensky, I., eds, (1997) *Critical Psychology: An Introduction* (London: Sage).

Frosh, S. (1987) *The Politics of Psychoanalysis: An Introduction* (London: Macmillan).

Giroux, H. (2009) 'Critical Theory and Educational Practice', in A. Darder, M. P. Baltodano, R. D. Torres, eds, *The Critical Pedagogy Reader* (2nd edn) (New York: Routledge): pp. 27–56.

Goodley, D. (2011a) *Disability Studies: An Interdisciplinary Introduction* (London: Sage).

Goodley, D. (2011b) 'Social Psychoanalytic Studies', *Disability & Society*.

Goodley, D. and Lawthom, R. (2005a) 'Journeys in Emancipatory Disability Research: Alliances between Community Psychology and Disability Studies', *Disability & Society* 20(2): 135–52.

Goodley, D. and Lawthom, R., eds, (2005b) *Disability and Psychology: Critical Introductions and Reflections* (London: Palgrave).

Goodley, D. and Lawthom, R. (2005c) 'Disability Studies and Psychology: New Allies', in D. Goodley and R. Lawthom, eds, *Psychology and Disability: Critical Introductions and Reflections* (London: Palgrave): pp. 1–16.

Haydon, M. (2008) '"Ooh, Where Did that Come from?": Celebrating Systemic Practice in Services for Adults with Intellectual Disability', *Context: The Magazine for Family Therapy and Systemic Practice* 100: 16–17.

Hien, E. and Deputte, B. L. (1997) 'Influence of a Capuchin Monkey Companion on the Social Life of a Person with Quadriplegia: An Experimental Study', *Anthrozoos: A Multidisciplinary Journal of The Interactions of People & Animals* 10(2–3): 101–7.

Hochschild, A. R. (1983) *The Managed Heart: Commercialisation of Human Feeling* (Berkeley: University of California Press).

Hughes, B. (2002) 'Disability and the Body', in C. Barnes, L. Barton and M. Oliver, eds, *Disability Studies Today* (Cambridge: Polity Press): pp. 58–76.

Hughes, B. and Paterson, K. (1997) 'The Social Model of Disability and the Disappearing Body: Towards a Sociology of "Impairment"', *Disability & Society* 12(3): 325–40.

Hughes, B. and Paterson, K. (2000) 'Disabled Bodies', in P. Hancock, B. Hughes, E. Jagger, K. Paterson, R. Russell, E. Tulle-Winton and M. Tyler, eds, *The Body, Culture and Society: An Introduction* (Buckingham: Open University Press): pp. 29–44.

Kagan, C. (2002) 'Making the Road by Walking It'. Inaugural professorial lecture, Manchester Metropolitan University, 30 January.

Kagan, C. and Burton, M. (2002) 'Community Psychology: Why this Gap in Britain?' *History and Philosophy of Psychology* 4(2): 10–23.

Kitzinger, C. (1993) 'Depoliticizing the Personal: A Feminist Slogan in Feminist Therapy', *Women's Studies International Forum* 16: 487–96.

Levinson, F. and Parritt, S. (2005) 'Against Stereotypes: Experiences of Disabled Psychologists', in D. Goodley and R. Lawthom, eds, *Disability and Psychology: Critical Introductions and Reflections* (Basingstoke: Palgrave Macmillan): pp. 111–22.

McRuer, R. and Wilkerson, A. (2003) 'Cripping the (Queer) Nation', *GLQ: A Journal of Lesbian and Gay Studies* 9(1–2): 1–23.

Marks, D. (1999a) *Disability: Controversial Debates and Psychosocial Perspectives* (London: Routledge).

Marks, D. (1999b) 'Dimensions of Oppression: Theorizing the Embodied Subject', *Disability & Society* 14(5): 611–26.

Merleau-Ponty, M. (1962) *The Phenomenology of Perception* (London: Routledge).

Michalko, R. (1999) *The Two-in-One: Walking with Smokie, Walking with Blindness* (Philadelphia: Temple University Press).

Michalko, R. (2002) *The Difference that Disability Makes* (Philadelphia: Temple University Press).

Mintz, S. B. (2002) 'Invisible Disability: Georgina Kleege's *Sight Unseen*', in K. Q. Hall, ed., Feminist Disability Studies [Special issue], *NWSA Journal* 14(3): 155–77.

Oliver, M. (1993) *'What's So Wonderful About Walking?'*, inaugural professorial lecture, University of Greenwich, London.

Oliver, M. (1996) *Understanding Disability: From Theory to Practice* (London: Macmillan).

Olkin, R. (2001) 'Disability-affirmative Therapy', *Spinal Cord Injury Psychosocial Process* 14(1): 12–23.

Olkin, R. (2002) 'Could You Hold the Door for Me? Including Disability in Diversity', *Cultural Diversity & Ethnic Minority Psychology* 8(2): 130–7.

Olkin, R. (2003) 'Women with Physical Disabilities Who Want to Leave Their Partners: A Feminist and Disability-affirmative Perspective', *Women and Therapy* 26(3/4): 237–46.

Olkin, R. (2008) 'Physical or Systemic Disabilities', in J. Worell and C. Goodheart, eds, *Handbook of Girls' and Women's Psychological Health* (New York: Oxford University Press): pp. 94–102.

Olkin, R. (2009) *Women with Physical Disabilities Who Want to Leave Their Partners: A Feminist and Disability-affirmative Perspective* (California: California School of Professional Psychology and Through the Looking Glass, Co).

Olkin, R. and Pledger, C. (2003) 'Can Disability Studies and Psychology Join Hands?', *American Psychologist* 58(4): 296–304.

Overboe, J. (2007) 'Disability and Genetics: Affirming the Bare Life (the State of Exception), in Genes and Society: Looking Back on the Future, special issue of *Canadian Review of Sociology* 44(2): 219–35.

Parker, I. (1989) '*Discourse and Power*', in J. Shotter and K. J. Gergen, eds, *Texts of Identity* (London: Sage).

Parker, I. (2007) *Revolution in Psychology: Alienation to Emancipation* (London: Pluto Press).

Prilleltensky, I. (2001) 'Value-based Praxis in Community Psychology: Moving Toward Social Justice and Social Action', *American Journal of Community Psychology* 29(5): 747–77.

Rapley, M. (2004) *The Social Construction of Intellectual Disability* (Cambridge: Cambridge University Press).

Reeve, D. (2008) *Negotiating Disability in Everyday Life: The Experience of Psycho-emotional Disablism*. Lancaster: Unpublished PhD thesis.

Rioux, M. (1994) 'Towards a Concept of Equality of Well Being: Overcoming the Social and Legal Construction of Inequality', in M. Rioux and M. Bach, eds, *Disability is Not Measles: New Directions in Disability* (Ontario: L'Institut Roeher): pp. 67–108.

Sherry, M. (2006) *If I Only Had a Brain. Deconstructing Brain Injury* (London: Routledge).

Spivak, G. C. (1985) 'Three Women's Texts and a Critique of Imperialism', *Critical Inquiry* 12(1): 243–61.

Stannett, P. (2005) 'Disabled and Graduated: Barriers and Dilemmas for the Disabled Psychology Graduate', in D. Goodley and R. Lawthom, eds, *Disability and Psychology: Critical Introductions and Reflections* (Basingstoke: Palgrave Macmillan): pp. 77–83.

Swain, J. and French, S. (2000) 'Towards an Affirmation Model of Disability', *Disability & Society* 15(4): 569–82.

Swain, J., Griffiths, C. and Heyman, B. (2003) 'Towards a Social Model Approach to Counselling Disabled Clients', *British Journal of Guidance and Counselling* 31(1): 137–52.

Thomas, C. (2007) *Sociologies of Disability, 'Impairment', and Chronic Illness: Ideas in Disability Studies and Medical Sociology* (London: Palgrave).

Titchkosky, T. (2003) *Disability, Self and Society* (Toronto: University of Toronto Press).

Todd, L. (2005) 'Enabling Practice for Professionals: The need for Practical Post-Structuralist Theory', in D. Goodley and R. Lawthom, eds, *Disability and Psychology: Critical Introductions and Reflections* (Basingstoke: Palgrave Macmillan).

Turner, B. (2008) *The Body and Society* (3rd edn) (London: Sage).

Venn, C. (1984) 'The Subject of Psychology', in J. Henriques, W. Hollway, C. Urwin, C. Venn and V. Walkerdine, *Changing the Subject: Psychology, Social Regulation and Subjectivity* (London: Methuen): pp. 115–47.

Williams, C. (2003) 'Sky Service: The Demands on Emotional Labor in the Airline Industry' *Gender, Work and Organisation* 10(5): 513–51.

Wright Mills, C. (1970) *The Sociological Imagination* (Oxford: Oxford University Press).

24

HISTORY AND DISABILITY STUDIES

Evolving perspectives

Anne Borsay

Introduction

Despite physical and mental impairment being central to the human condition, disability history has only recently emerged as a vibrant field of intellectual enquiry. As the late Paul Longmore and Laura Umansky argued in their seminal edited collection, the reasons for this late development are bound up with the low status that societies have imposed upon disabled people. Historians have assumed that disabled people are too marginal to generate significant primary sources. Medicalization has construed them as the passive victims of biological deficit. And this persona-lization has promoted 'individual case histories' at the expense of social, cultural and political analysis. But most pervasive is the 'existential anxiety' that comes from challenging the norms of independence, autonomy and control (Longmore and Umansky 2001: 6–9). These obstacles have been most effectively overcome in the United States (US). From the late 1970s – following a trajectory similar to women's history (Purvis 1995) – disability activists engaged in 'heritage hunting', celebrating the achievements of those who had triumphed over impairment. During the 1980s, these 'compensatory' histories, which 'unwittingly' confirmed mainstream stereotypes, were joined by studies of 'abuse, discrimination, and oppression'. More recently, attention has turned to 'the cultures, values, and activism of disabled people themselves' and to the implications of factors such as gender, class and race for their experiences (Longmore and Umansky 2001: 18). Furthermore, disability is now being promoted as a primary category of historical analysis that is foundational to both cultural life and material living (Kudlick 2003).

In Britain, where the services of the welfare state undercut the emphasis on individual rights that fuelled the American movement, this 'new' disability history has been slower to develop. The purpose of this chapter is to trace its evolution, looking at how histories of disabled people have been told and at what disability studies has contributed to their telling. The discussion will be organized around the three key approaches to British disability history identified by Jan Walmsley and Dorothy Atkinson (2000): biography; service evaluation; and the contextualization of impairment through a 'turn' first to the social and then to the cultural.

Biography

Although the concept of biography dates back to the classical period, studies based on historical scholarship only began to gather momentum after 1850. By the turn of the century, the 'life and times' methodology had become well-established, not only making 'the … actions of the subject more comprehensible' but also enabling an assessment of their impact (Davies 2003: 48). Yet whilst some historians praise biography as a holistic approach that 'cut[s] across arbitrary divisions' (Jordanova 2000: 41), others criticize its preoccupation with individual agency at the expense of structural constraints. A rich cache of primary sources is also fundamental. For disabled people who rose to fame, this is not a problem (Davies 2003). Helen Keller – the blind and deaf American icon – has thus inspired a string of biographies. Not until recently, however, has Keller's image as 'the wild child transformed … by the civilizing influence of female devotion' (Chinn 2006: 241) been complemented by any serious consideration of her adult life and the ways in which disability more than gender compromised her citizenship and frustrated her radical political ambitions (Nielsen 2001).

Outside the small circle of renowned disabled people, the raw materials for biography are generally lacking. Occasionally, autobiographical pieces survive – allegedly, just one for the pre-modern period: the narrative of Teresa de Cartagena, a Castilian nun, living in the second half of the fifteenth century, who was deaf (Juárez 2002). Legal documents are another potential source. In 1747, for instance, an Edinburgh court was called upon to determine 'the mental capacity of Hugh Blair … and thus to confirm or dissolve a marriage' that he had contracted in the previous year. Testimonies from the 29 witnesses, who eventually concluded that he was a 'natural fool' and 'void of common sense', offer a fascinating insight into how 'local society' in south-west Scotland 'understood what it meant to be mentally capable'. But in their historical-clinical analysis of this case, Rab Houston and Uta Frith do not interpret the evidence from the perspective of Hugh Blair himself. Instead, he is an absent presence, used to test the reductionist hypothesis that he was autistic and to 'expose the unchanging core' of the condition without regard to the influence of cultural relativity in medical diagnosis (Houston and Frith 2000: 1, 4, 53).

The advent of oral history created new opportunities to capture the biographical voices of disabled people. Originating in ancient songs, legends and stories passed on by word of mouth, oral sources were rejected as unreliable during the nineteenth century as humanities disciplines aspired to the methods of the natural sciences. The arrival of *social* history in the 1960s put oral history back on the map, its potential for more democratic, socially conscious research resonating with the egalitarian ethos of the times. Of course, there are drawbacks. Only recent history is accessible; chronologies may be uncertain; meanings may be reconstituted over time; and stereotyped social roles may be reproduced. But the capacity of oral history to rescue groups missing from the written record and to correct distorted images makes it a vital tool for disability history (Thompson 1978). Its exploitation has been slow. Nonetheless, we now have striking testimonies of what it was like to be a disabled person in the early twentieth century. David Swift, for instance, was interviewed for the Channel 4 programme *Out of Mind* during 1992. Born in Nottingham in 1936, he had a hereditary muscular disease, which among other things caused him to limp. His father, a miner, was intolerant of his deteriorating impairment:

> When my legs were getting worse my dad said I was walking like a drunken man. And I said I couldn't do anything to change that. So he made me sit on the sofa and he says, 'Right, straighten your feet.' And I'm sitting there trying to straighten them. I told him that I couldn't and he got really angry, kept shouting, 'Straighten them, put your legs together!' And hitting my legs, beating them. I think he was trying to shock me into doing it 'cos he thought my disability was something in my mind.
>
> *(Humphries and Gordon 1992: 28)*

Service evaluation

Whereas oral history is open to practitioners as well as disabled people, histories of service delivery are spoken exclusively from the viewpoint of the expert – primarily in medicine – whose job was 'the management, repair, and maintenance of physical and cognitive incapacity' (Mitchell and Snyder 1997: 1). The development of charitable and statutory provision was thus assumed to be beneficial for recipients; this progressive mentality resonating with the Whiggish optimism that characterized social policy history as a whole (Thane 1998). The assumption that impairment was a personal deficiency did not inevitably ensue, for the American philanthropist Douglas C. McMurtrie was insisting in 1919 that 'the greatest handicap is not a loss of limb or other disability but the weight of public opinion': an impediment which included not just pejorative social attitudes but also poor education, restricted employment, poverty, inadequate housing and social care, and an inaccessible environment (Kudlick 2003: 772). In the main, however, these structural problems were ignored. Furthermore, the requirements of disabled people were seen not as the legitimate entitlements of citizenship but as needs that compromised their status. Therefore, when the relative effectiveness of different care strategies was evaluated, their performance was assessed against a professionally defined yardstick that sidelined the views of recipients (Walmsley and Atkinson 2000).

Although the First World War overshadowed precedents in the management of 'difference' that followed the American Civil War (Yuan 1997), it did seemingly trigger a novel interest in the history of disability – at least in Britain (Metzler 2006). The subjects were not war-damaged veterans but the children who were swelling the lists of orthopaedic surgeons. The authors of these histories were drawn from medicine and its philanthropic penumbra. In 1924, G. R. Girdlestone published *The Care and Cure of Crippled Children*. The preface claimed that 'the past and present ... [would be] reviewed from the point of view of the cripple'. However, Girdlestone – an orthopaedic surgeon at the Wingfield Hospital in Oxford – prepared the book to promote a national scheme of charitable orthopaedic hospitals and after-care clinics that were being coordinated by the Central Council for the Care of Cripples. To buttress his professional credibility, he recruited Sir Robert Jones – director of orthopaedics for the army during the war – to write the foreword. Jones supplied the historical backdrop, painting a picture of enduring misery until the dawn of the twentieth century. 'The cripple has always presented a problem awaiting solution', he declared:

> and his story is unequalled in its tragic sequence of obloquy and neglect. In ancient days he was the embodiment of magic, and in medieval times had fallen to the estate of public mockery. ... Again, in a later period, when Puritanism sought the hand of God in all things, normal and abnormal, the cripple was frowned upon as an outcast, and crawled through his miserable distorted life as an example of divine punishment and humiliation. So for long centuries deformity remained little more than a text for theological discussion, and even in the light of more modern times his destiny has been seriously disputed upon the pseudo-scientific doctrine of the survival of the fittest.
>
> *(Girdlestone 1924)*

From the late nineteenth century, however – thanks to changes in 'public consciousness' – Jones saw help at hand in the shape of a more healthy lifestyle, the development of orthopaedic surgery, and the establishment of the first charitable hospitals for disabled children and then military hospitals for disabled soldiers. Accordingly, it was the First World War that finally transformed attitudes to the 'cripple', who 'by his fine courage and endurance can become a source of spiritual pride and envy to the strong' (Girdlestone 1924: 3, 7–9).

History emanating from the voluntary sector – as opposed to medicine – was equally replete with stereotyped images of pity and punishment, tragedy and heroism. In 1930, Frederick Watson published *Civilization and the Cripple*. Married to Robert Jones's daughter, Watson was not only the moving force behind the Voluntary Orthopaedic Association in Montgomeryshire but also editor of *The Cripples' Journal* (Hunt 1938). Despite its title, this periodical – first produced in 1924 by the Shropshire Orthopaedic Hospital in Oswestry – was primarily intended for 'institutions, medical men, nursing staffs and helpers' (*The Cripples' Journal* 1924, editorial). The book, which aimed to 'outline … some past and future problems of disablement in domestic life and industry', was similarly positioned, arguing that advances in orthopaedic surgery had encouraged a sense of journey's end. For Watson, that journey was not an escape from the relentless suffering that Girdlestone portrayed because, 'There were periods – like those sudden endearing serenities of April sunshine – when even the cripple was not an outcast.' Nevertheless, during centuries of neglect, orthopaedics had resorted at best to 'rudimentary knowledge' and at worst to 'gross superstition and quackery'. Indeed, even in the nineteenth century, 'there was … no light in the darkness' since germ theory had caused the 'cripple' to be 'deserted by modern surgery'. Not until John Little – 'the first great apostle of orthopaedic surgery in England'– and those who took up his baton did orthopaedics become established as a special branch of surgery (Watson 1930: vii, 2–3, 8–9, 12–13, 15).

Despite praising medical professionals and voluntary workers, Watson recognized that they were incapable of overcoming the economic and social conditions from which patients arrived. Industrialization was not the sole culprit because pre-modern domestic industries such as lace-making also 'contributed … [their] fair share of lives crippled in mind and limb'. 'The delicate beauty of the lace', wrote Watson, meant 'almost universal distortion of children's spines, premature blindness, chronic ill-health and maternal fatalities through malformation.' Yet acknowledging these factors neither diminished the power of professional expertise nor increased the autonomy of disabled people (Watson 1930: vii, 4–5, 6–7, 8, 10). In line with the social corporatism that informed inter-war debates about the future welfare state (Baxendale and Pawling 1996; Parker 1998), orthopaedists managed to reconcile structural inequalities with personal culpability. Poverty begat 'laxity', asserted Watson, and so 'to provide a new house … [did] not bestow a new sense of the responsibilities of … civic life' (Watson 1930: 82). With this mentality in place, the expansion of medical treatment, far from liberating disabled people, reinforced their stigmatized position.

In the aftermath of the Second World War, the welfare state was slow to take on board disability services. Outside education and compensation for industrial injury, there were thus few statutory obligations; and where local authorities had permissive powers, they often continued to use charitable bodies. Histories of the voluntary sector rejoiced in this ongoing reliance and hailed the role of disabled pioneers in disability organizations. In 1957, for instance, Mary Thomas published a study of the Royal National Institute for the Blind, founded in 1868 initially to produce embossed literature. In the author's note, she claimed that, as a former member of staff, it would be inappropriate for her 'either to extol or criticise policy'. But in the allegedly 'much more modest task merely to record facts', she had no reservations about showing 'how, from a small beginning and the devotion of one blind man to his fellows, one of the largest and most democratically controlled voluntary organizations in this country has developed'. That one blind man was the founder, Thomas Rhodes Armitage. And he was not the only leading figure to be lauded. Indeed, even the anonymous staff of the Sunshine Homes for young blind children received 'tribute' for their efforts (Thomas 1957: author's note, 22, 32, 80).

The institutional study remained an enduring feature of the history of disability (see, for example, Grant 1990). Furthermore, the prominence of charity meant that disability was almost invisible in general histories of public intervention (see, for example, Bruce 1961; Fraser 1973). And although past services were discussed in contemporary texts (see, for example, Parker 1965; Forder 1969), specific accounts – such as D. G. Pritchard's (1963) *Education and the Handicapped from 1760 to 1960* – were rare. Coverage of the state sector – like that of the voluntary – was far from abrasive, concentrating attention on the 'nuts and bolts' of service operation. This approach resonated with the broadly held consensus that the welfare state was meeting its objectives; only fine-tuning was necessary to resolve a few residual problems. By the mid-1960s, however, the rediscovery of poverty was prompting more fundamental questions about the relationship between social welfare and social structure (Coates and Silburn 1970); whilst social history – the new sub-discipline nurturing oral testimony – was also stressing the influence of social class (Tosh 1991). But these trends were slow to establish themselves. Therefore, studies such as Kathleen Jones's *A History of the Mental Health Services* (1972) are aptly described as 'practitioner-pragmatist' views, in which it is assumed that 'the authorities were essentially benign, if under-resourced' and that 'more services meant a better life for the people who needed care' (Walmsley and Atkinson 2000: 191). Only in 1984 with *The Disabled State* did the American political scientist Deborah Stone begin the process of moving beyond the mechanics to the underlying social context in her comparative study of social security policies in Britain, Germany and the US.

The social turn

For Stone, the 'social turn' (Dolan 2010: 398) was a material one marked out by a 'distributive dilemma' about reconciling the demands of employment and social need 'without undermining the productive side of the economy'. Her principal concern was the role of the state in defining and redefining the boundaries of dependency by establishing categories which expressed 'a culturally legitimate rationale for nonparticipation in the labor system'. Those categories that were chronologically based on childhood or old age were easily validated exemptions, but disability was not. Diverse, unstable and prone to abuse by impostors who feigned illness or impairment in order to obtain assistance, it was ripe for the picking by eighteenth- and nineteenth-century medical professionals as their power and status climbed. Therefore, clinical judgement overtook the old ways of detecting trickery (Stone 1984: 15, 22, 51).

Although Stone incorporated an economic driver for the social construction of impairment, her polarization of work and welfare assumed that 'the distributive dilemma' was universal. Furthermore, the fixation with official categories led to a narrow convergence on government activity. From the early 1970s, however, economic crisis had been undermining the pale pink political consensus typical of British society since 1945; and with the shift to the political right at the end of the decade came a thriving historiographical interest in the mixed economy of welfare, which looked beyond the state to champion the commercial sector, the voluntary sector of charitable and mutual aid organizations, and the informal sector of relatives, friends and neighbours (Kavanagh and Morris 1989; Finlayson 1994). The outcome was a string of historical studies of disability that not only challenged the ascendancy of medicine and the public services but also situated disabled people in their families and local communities, outside the institution that had dominated previous research (see, for example, Bartlett and Wright 1999; Borsay 1999; Jackson 2000).

The intellectual home of these studies was the social history of medicine, but none peddled a crude medical mission. Instead, they strove to tease out the economic, social and political connotations of the services under scrutiny in a way that reflected their commitment to contextualization (Jordanova 1995). Thus, in his meticulous empirical study of British orthopaedic medicine between 1880 and 1948, Roger Cooter unpicked 'the socio-economic interests, political relations, conceptual formulations and ideologies that underlay ... the divisions of labour that came to be embedded in the structure of the NHS' (1993: 4). Similarly, Mathew Thomson's fine account of *The Problem of Mental Deficiency* between *c.*1870 and 1959 interpreted policy development as a response to democracy that sought to harness the resources of the modern state to exclude those judged unfit to vote from the newly extended franchise. Dismissive of dualistic theories of social control, he plotted an intricate 'process of negotiation between providers and recipients' reflective of their shared values. Nevertheless, families like this one – living in London in 1919 – lacked the knowledge, confidence and financial resources to secure the release of relatives: 'I suppose you are longing to come home as we are longing for you. ... Father is going up and make them understand that you were in fit state when you went to that place' (Thomson 1998: 240, 268). But though Thomson conceded that power was heavily skewed towards the authorities, neither he nor Cooter engaged explicitly with disability studies.

The disability studies perspective flourished with the disability movement: one of a series of social movements that emerged in the 1980s as – like the welfare state – the political structures of the consensual era lost credibility. The disability studies' attack on individual models or explanations discredited both their sharp distinction between different types of impairment and the search for causes exclusively within the 'defective' disabled person, who was expected to adapt to society by resorting to professional expertise. In sharp contrast, the social model's emphasis on the common ground between different types of impairment and their joint causes in economic, social and political organization outlawed dogmatic notions of 'normality' and unlocked disabled people from the burden of trimming themselves to fit the dimensions of 'ordinary' society (Oliver 1983). The implications for terminology are well-known. In 1976, the Union of the Physically Impaired Against Segregation defined impairment as 'lacking all or part of a limb, or having a defective limb, organ or mechanism of the body'. Disability, on the other hand, was 'the disadvantage or restriction caused by a contemporary social organization which takes no or little account of people who have physical impairments and thus excludes them from the mainstream of social activities' (Union of the Physically Impaired Against Segregation 1976: 3–4).

The historical application of the social model was heavily indebted to Marxism, focusing especially on the transition from feudalism to modern industrial capitalism. Vic Finkelstein began the debate in 1980 with his provocative but imprecise distillation of three 'phases'. In Phase 1, physically impaired people were congregated at the bottom of the economic pile in the company of poorly paid workers, the unemployed and the mentally ill. Attempts were made to differentiate the poverty of unfortunate 'cripples' from the poverty of sturdy beggars, but impairment was typically regarded as a consequence of sin or wanton behaviour that required no special social provision. Phase 2 saw the arrival of segregated disability institutions in response to 'a new productive technology'; 'large scale industry with production-lines geared to able-bodied norms' excluded impaired people who had previously been integrated and socially active members of their class and community. Furthermore, the growth of hospital-based medicine encouraged the expansion of professionals whose expert knowledge was disabling. Yet, paradoxically, public services also helped disabled people to acquire social independence and dispute the professional control of their lives. It was this critique that triggered the birth of the social model and the onset of Phase 3 (Finkelstein 1980: 11).

Finkelstein's schema was a useful ice-breaker. On his own admission, however, it sought 'to say something about the context in which attitudes ... [were] formed' and was not 'a historical analysis' (Finkelstein 1980: 8). Therefore, neither the dynamics of the industrial process nor its social and political outcomes were made plain. Mike Oliver tackled both shortcomings in 1990 with *The Politics of Disablement*. First, he complicated the influence of the economic base by arguing that whereas fully fledged capitalism was exclusive, 'agriculture or small-scale industry ... did not preclude the great majority of disabled people from participating in the production process'. To the impact of the economy was added the 'mode of thought' and the problem of order. The evolution of intellectual concepts 'from a religious interpretation of reality' to a metaphysical and then a scientific one interacted with the disruption thrown up by the rise of capitalism to alter 'historical perceptions of deviance' and to propagate new medical and institutional methods for subduing it (Oliver 1990: 27, 29–30).

This tripartite model of economy, ideology and politics presented a more intricate analysis of economic development than Finkelstein, and the dissection of service delivery was situated within a political matrix that reached beyond the administrative state to include beliefs and values, and the policing of disorder. In 1999 the historical geographer, Brendan Gleeson, added a socio-cultural dimension, envisaging disability 'as part of a broader process of social embodiment' in which 'roles and representations' were ascribed 'to body types that varie[d] in time and space'. Like Oliver, however, he shared Finkelstein's assumption that the Industrial Revolution was a watershed, preventing economic integration by turning impairments – previously unproblematic – into disabilities. In short, he used a historical, economic and political framework akin to the social model (Gleeson 1999: 34).

Undoubtedly, this materialist interpretation exaggerated the impact of industrialization. Negative attitudes to disability were evident both in the religions and cultures of ancient Greece and Rome, and in the art and literature of Renaissance Europe. The struggle of the Tudor poor law to distinguish 'deserving' from the 'undeserving' applicants also suggests that the work ethic was a preoccupation in pre-modern Britain (Barnes 1991). And although the factory system with its heavy machinery did ultimately entrench a geographical separation of home and work that became a defining feature of industrial societies, this change was slow in coming. In fact, as late as 1851 only 6 per cent of the total labour force was working in textile factories – the sole employment sector where this mode of production had made major inroads (Evans 1983: 103). But the social model is not only historically inaccurate. For more than a decade, social scientists and disabled people themselves have alleged that it omits the structural factors that interact with impairment: social class, gender, age and ethnicity. Likewise condemned is the neglect of personal pain, fatigue, depression and the internalized oppression that arises from the psychology of exclusion (Barnes and Mercer 1996). Above all, there is the accusation of being too deterministic, of selling short the ability of disabled people to undermine institutional constraints, and of denying them the agency to give their lives meaning (Patterson and Hughes 1999).

The cultural turn

A cultural turn in the social approach to disability was the response to these criticisms. As Tom Shakespeare has pointed out, there are affinities between the social model and a 'family' of more nuanced 'social-contextual approaches', which date back to the 1960s (Shakespeare 2006: 2). But the assault on materialism was more than a call for greater sophistication in the analysis of social interaction. It reflected the penetration of postmodernist ideas, which were gathering momentum from the 1980s with the collapse of the post-war consensus. Postmodernism was dismissive of the grand narratives that Western societies had used to make sense of reality since the Enlightenment – rationality, science, Christianity and the Marxism that underpinned the social model (Kumar 1995). The rejection of these totalizing explanations not only created space for the marginal and subordinate whose story did not fit the big picture but also acknowledged diversity within such groups (Shakespeare 2006). However, this fragmentation was additionally driven by a new intellectual ethos. Monolithic accounts were untenable because knowledge was a product of power, and power was 'local and unstable' – not the 'consolidated and homogenous domination' by a particular individual or group or class (Foucault 1980: 98, 142). The resulting multiplicity of narratives was compounded by a challenge to the previously fixed relationship between words and objects (Hollinger 1994). The combined effect of such diffused power and fluid language was a deep scepticism towards the prospects for universal truth, a collapse of the boundary between fact and fiction, and hence a loss of confidence in the old narratives of modernity.

Architects of the social model, such as Mike Oliver and Colin Barnes, were scathing of this postmodern world 'somehow constructed through discourse alone'; social change, they averred, could only be delivered by addressing concrete deprivation (Oliver and Barnes 1998: xv). The fear that cultural difference was easily used as a defence for structural injustice is understandable (Riddell and Watson 2003). However, its effect was that disability studies and disability history in Britain were slow to respond to the cultural turn. In France, conversely, the path-breaking *Corps Infirmes et Sociétés* (*A History of Disability*) by Henri-Jacques Stiker was published way back in 1982, venturing into physical impairment: that 'whole continent', which Foucault – one of the high priests of postmodernism – had left 'unexplored' (1999: 92). Stiker ranged over a broad chronological canvass, beginning with the biblical era and moving on to Western antiquity, the Middle Ages and the era from *c*.1500 to 1900. Unlike Foucault, he did not envisage 'history as a series of ruptures or breaks', arguing 'for a continuum of effects in which one epoch's beliefs continue to inform the practices of succeeding generations' (Mitchell 1999: viii). Nevertheless, his most strident criticism was directed at a final phase: the birth of rehabilitation during the period of the First World War, when a 'collection of medical, therapeutic, social, and professional actions' were aimed 'at those … grouped under the generic term of disabled' in order to 'efface their difference' and make them 'identical' to an 'empirical norm' (Stiker 1999: 121, 134, 150–1). As he wrote in elaboration:

> prosthesis is not only the pieces of wood, iron, now plastic that replace the missing hand or foot. It is also the very idea that you can *replace*. The image of the maimed person and of the society around him becomes prosthetic. Replacement, re-establishment of the prior situation, substitution, compensation – all this now becomes possible language.
>
> *(Stiker 1999: 123–4)*

In adopting this interpretation, Stiker concurred with the perception of the social model that disabled people were expected to adjust to society, but on unequal terms that did not integrate them 'on the same level economically and socially' (Stiker 1999: 151). However, his approach was set apart by two distinctive features. First, his methodology involved the close reading of a variety of sources from 'literary texts as exemplary of dominant myths to discussions of the etymology of disability terminology to medical taxonomies of specific conditions and test cases to an examination of current legislative initiatives' (Mitchell 1999: vii). Second, his theoretical framework embraced the transient meanings of disability as a category of analysis. 'There is no history of thought', he maintained, 'outside the history of *systems* of thought. There is no speech outside systems of language. … There is no disability, no disabled, outside precise social and cultural constructions; there is no attitude to disability outside a series of societal references and constructs' (Stiker 1999: 14).

Stiker's *A History of Disability*, not translated into English until 1999, was differential in its effect. In the US, for instance, the literary scholars David Mitchell and Sharon Snyder picked up the notion of 'prosthesis' and applied it to narrative (Mitchell and Snyder 2000); far from being absent in cultural imagery, they insisted, disability had functioned 'throughout history as a crutch on which literary narratives lean for their representational power, disruptive potentiality, and social critique' (Mitchell 2002: 17). In Britain, whilst disability historians acknowledged Stiker's cultural ideas, they continued to see a role for 'material factors as setting the agenda, the problems to which individuals, groups and, metaphorically speaking, cultures try to adapt or respond' (Burke 1991: 18). Therefore, in charting the social exclusion imposed by institutional and community services post-1750, Anne Borsay (2005) challenged the postmodernist contention that power and the capacity to resist were significantly dispersed to groups such as disabled people.

Technology and war have been the themes most commonly used to unpick the relationship between the material and the cultural. The meanings attached to total hip replacement, for example, have been examined via 'the interactions between patients, professionals, companies and governments' – although, in this case, patients did not regard themselves as disabled, instead welcoming surgery because it brought 'the prospect of a near normal life' (Anderson *et al.* 2007: 5, 143).

Wheelchairs have also been interrogated. Again, close attention was paid to the politics of policy, teasing out the links between professionals and the state. In the case of adaptive wheelchair seating – which 'controls contractures, prevents skeletal deformities, and allows occupants to breathe, swallow, and communicate' – Watson and Woods concluded that 'it was innovative technologists who created a new cohort of users' (2005: 460, 473). With the earlier tubular steel, folding and powered wheelchairs that emerged from the 1950s, however, the political influence of disabled people was identified as they campaigned for the mobility and independence that was impossible in chairs designed for the housebound or institutionalized (Woods and Watson 2004). But complementing this analysis was the recognition that wheelchairs were not only aids to mobility but also cultural artefacts onto which the values associated with disability – 'loss, tragedy, passivity and dependency' – were inscribed. Using a wheelchair 'symbolised either the failure of medicine to find a cure, and/or that the wheelchair user had given up on rehabilitation'. Therefore, the battle for better technologies confronted the reconfiguration of cultural values as well as improved physical and social access (Parr *et al.* 2006: 162–3).

The disability history of war similarly confronted this material/cultural axis. In *The War Come Home*, Deborah Cohen (2001) examined the integration of disabled veterans after the First World War. She maintained that 'social peace' was more effectively achieved in Britain because, although public intervention was minimal relative to the services provided in Germany, 'civil society' – 'defined … as the dense network of voluntary … organizations' – 'mediated between the individual and the state' (Cohen 2001: 4). In other words, the political response of veterans was not alone determined by material standards of living, guaranteed by government. Cultural perceptions of social value, generated from involvement by the community, also played an important part, despite their philanthropic origins.

In Ana Carden-Coyne's *Reconstructing the Body* (2009), the cultural emphasis was uppermost as she unravelled how the classical tradition of ancient Greece and Rome merged with early twentieth-century modernism to influence exercise enthusiasts, beauticians, dancers and sexual reformers as well as the doctors and rehabilitation therapists who mended disabled veterans. The adoption of this classical imagery was not a 'retreat to the safe past'. Rather, the modern science of prosthetics was applied to reconstituting the disabled ex-serviceman in accordance with heroic, 'classical visions of wholeness', which ensured a body empowered to work. In reality, some prosthetic devices were impractical to use, painful or out of reach to the majority of disabled veterans whom the government abandoned to charity. But these material contradictions were overridden by the cultural appeal of wholeness which, in a world broken by violent conflict, extended beyond the body to embrace the political order and harmony that was also a feature of classicalism (Carden-Coyne 2009: 2, 190).

Conclusion

In this chapter we have mapped the changing relationship between disability, history and disability studies. Three key approaches to the history of disabled people in Britain have been pursued: biography; service evaluation; and the situation of impairment within first its social and then its cultural context. In disability studies, a historical dimension was slow to develop and there was a reluctance to acknowledge a cultural dimension to both the past and the present. Disability is indeed strongly – if not irrevocably – correlated with economic, social and political disadvantage, and so we neglect the material underpinnings of culture at our peril. Nevertheless, as Iris Young has pointed out, cultural imperialism is also a form of social oppression (1990). Disability history has recognized this by integrating economic, social and political causation with cultural construction. The challenge now is to ensure that the experiences of disabled people – accessible through a critical reading of traditional documentary sources as well as through the direct personal testimony of autobiographies, diaries and oral history – are central not only to disability history but also to the discipline as a whole.

References

Anderson, J., Neary, F. and Pickstone, J. (2007) *Surgeons, Manufacturers and Patients: A Transatlantic History of Total Hip Replacement* (Basingstoke: Palgrave Macmillan).

Barnes, C. (1991) *Disabled People in Britain and Discrimination: A Case for Anti-Discrimination Legislation* (London: Hurst).

Barnes, C. and Mercer, G., eds, (1996) *Exploring the Divide: Illness and Disability* (Leeds: Disability Press).

Bartlett, P. and Wright, D., eds, (1999) *Outside the Walls of the Asylum: The History of Care in the Community, 1750–2000* (London: Athlone Press).

Baxendale, J. and Pawling, C. (1996) *Narrating the Thirties: A Decade in the Making – 1930 to the Present* (Basingstoke: Macmillan).

Borsay, A. (1999) *Medicine and Charity in Georgian Bath: A Social History of the General Infirmary, c.1739–1830* (Aldershot: Ashgate).

Borsay, A. (2005) *Disability and Social Policy in Britain since 1750: A History of Exclusion* (Basingstoke: Palgrave Macmillan).

Bruce, M. (1961) *The Coming of the Welfare State* (London: Batsford).

Burke, P. (1991) 'Overture: The New History', in P. Burke, ed., *New Perspectives on Historical Writing* (Cambridge: Polity): pp. 1–23.

Carden-Coyne, A. (2009) *Reconstructing the Body: Classicism, Modernism, and the First World War* (Oxford: Oxford University Press).

Chinn, S. E. (2006). 'Gender, Sex and Disability from Helen Keller to Tiny Tim' *Radical History Review* (Special Issue: *Disability and History*) 94: 240–8.

Coates, K. and R. Silburn (1970) *Poverty: The Forgotten Englishmen*, 1970 (Harmondsworth: Penguin).

Cohen, D. (2001) *The War Come Home: Disabled Veterans in Britain and Germany, 1914–1939* (Berkeley: University of California Press).

Cooter, R. (1993) *Surgery and Society in Peace and War: Orthopaedics and the Organization of Modern Medicine, 1880–1948* (Basingstoke: Macmillan).

Cripples' Journal (1924) Editorial: 'The Gist of the Matter': p. 1.

Davies, S. (2003) *Empiricism and History* (Basingstoke: Palgrave).

Dolan, B. (2010) 'History, Medical Humanities and Medical Education', *Social History of Medicine* 23: 393–405.

Evans, E. J. (1983) *The Forging of the Modern State: Early Industrial Britain, 1783–1870* (London: Longman).

Finkelstein, V. (1980) *Attitudes and Disabled People: Issues for Discussion* (New York: World Rehabilitation Fund).

Finlayson, G. (1994) *Citizen, State, and Social Welfare in Britain, 1830–1990* (Oxford: Clarendon Press).

Forder, A., ed., (1969) *Penelope Hall's Social Services of England and Wales* (London: Routledge and Kegan Paul).

Foucault, M. (1980) 'Two Lectures', in C Gordon, ed., *Michel Foucault Power/Knowledge: Selected Interviews and Other Writings 1972–1977* (Brighton: Harvester Press).

Fraser, D. (1973) *The Evolution of the British Welfare State* (London: Macmillan).

Girdlestone, G. R. (1924) *The Care and Cure of Crippled Children* (Bristol: John Wright).

Gleeson, B. (1999) *Geographies of Disability* (London: Routledge).

Grant, B. (1990) *The Deaf Advance: A History of the British Deaf Association* (Edinburgh: Pentland Press).

Hollinger, R. (1994) *Postmodernism and the Social Sciences: A Thematic Approach* (Thousand Oaks, California: Sage).

Houston, R. and Frith, U. (2000) *Autism in History: The Case of Hugh Blair of Borgue* (Oxford: Blackwell).

Humphries, S. and Gordon, P. (1992) *Out of Sight: The Experience of Disability, 1900–1950* (Plymouth: Northcote House).

Hunt, A. (1938) *This is My Life* (London: Blackie).

Jackson, M. (2000) *The Borderland of Imbecility: Medicine, Society and the Fabrication of the Feeble Mind in Late Victorian and Edwardian England* (Manchester: Manchester University Press).

Jones, K. (1972) *A History of the Mental Health Services* (London: Routledge and Kegan Paul).

Jordanova, L. (1995) 'The Social Construction of Medical Knowledge', *Social History of Medicine* 8: 361–78.

Jordanova, L. (2000) *History in Practice* (London: Arnold).

Juárez, E. (2002) 'The Autobiography of the Aching Body in Teresa Cartegena's *Arboleda de los Enfermmos*', in S. L. Snyder, B. J. Brueggemann and R. Garland-Thomson, eds, *Disability Studies: Enabling the Humanities* (New York: Modern Language Association of America): pp. 131–43.

Kavanagh, D. and Morris, P. (1989) *Consensus Politics from Attlee to Thatcher* (Oxford: Basil Blackwell).

Kudlick, C. J. (2003) 'Disability History: Why We Need Another "Other"', *American Historical Review* 108: 763–93.

Kumar, K. (1995) *From Post-industrial to Post-modern Society: New Theories in the Contemporary World* (Oxford: Blackwell).

Longmore, P. K. and Umansky, L. (2001) 'Disability History: From the Margins to the Mainstream', in P. K. Longmore and L. Umansky, eds, *The New Disability History: American Perspectives* (New York: New York University Press): pp. 1–29.

Metzler, I. (2006) *Disability in Medieval Europe: Thinking about Physical Impairment During the High Middle Ages, c.1100–1400* (Abingdon: Routledge).

Mitchell, D. T. (1999) 'Foreword', in H.-J. Stiker, *A History of Disability* (Ann Arbor: University of Michigan Press): pp. vii–xiv.

Mitchell, D. T. (2002) 'Narrative Prosthesis and the Materiality of Metaphor', in S. L. Snyder, B. J. Brueggemann and R. Garland-Thomson, eds, *Disability Studies: Enabling the Humanities* (New York: Modern Language Association of America): pp. 15–30.

Mitchell, D. T. and Snyder, S. L. (1997) 'Disability Studies and the Double Bind of Representation', in D. T. Mitchell and S. L. Snyder, eds, *The Body and Physical Difference: Discourses of Disability* (Ann Arbor: University of Michigan Press): pp. 1–31.

Mitchell, D. T. and Snyder, S. L. (2000) *Narrative Prosthesis: Disability and the Dependencies of Discourse* (Ann Arbor: University of Michigan Press).

Nielsen, K. (2001) 'Helen Keller and the Politics of Civic Fitness', in P. K. Longmore and L. Umansky, eds, *The New Disability History: American Perspectives* (New York: New York University Press): pp. 268–90.

Oliver, M. (1983) *Social Work with Disabled People* (Basingstoke: Macmillan).

Oliver, M. (1990) *The Politics of Disablement* (Basingstoke: Macmillan).

Oliver, M. and Barnes, C. (1998) *Disabled People and Social Policy: From Exclusion to Inclusion* (London: Longman).

Parker, J. (1965) *Local Health and Welfare Services* (London: George Allen and Unwin).

Parker, J. (1998) *Citizenship, Work and Welfare: Searching for the Good Society* (Basingstoke: Macmillan).

Parr, S., Watson, N. and Woods, B. (2006) 'Access, Agency, and Normality: The Wheelchair and the Internet as Mediators of Disability', in A. Webster, ed., *New Technologies in Health Care: Challenge, Change and Innovation* (Basingstoke: Palgrave Macmillan).

Patterson, K. and Hughes, B. (1999) 'Disability Studies and Phenomenology: The Carnal Politics of Everyday Life', *Disability & Society* 14: 597–610.

Pritchard, D. G. (1963) *Education and the Handicapped* (London: Routledge and Kegan Paul).

Purvis, J. (1995) 'From "Women Worthies" to Poststructuralism? Debate and Controversy in Women's History in Britain', in J. Purvis, ed., *Women's History: Britain, 1850–1945* (London: UCL Press): pp. 1–22.

Riddell, S. and Watson, N. (2003) *Disability, Culture and Identity* (London: Pearson Education).

Shakespeare, T. (2006) *Disability Rights and Wrongs* (London: Routledge).

Stiker, H.-J. (1982) *Corps Infirmes et Sociétés* (Paris: Aubier-Montaigne).

Stiker, H.-J. (1999) *A History of Disability*, trans. William Sayers (Ann Arbor: University of Michigan Press).

Stone, D. (1984) *The Disabled State* (Basingstoke: Macmillan).

Thane, P. (1998) 'Histories of the Welfare State', in W. Lamont, ed., *Historical Controversies and Historians* (London: UCL Press): pp. 49–64.

Thomas, M. G. (1957) *The Royal National Institute for the Blind, 1868–1956* (London: Royal National Institute for the Blind).

Thompson, P. (1978) *The Voice of the Past: Oral History* (Oxford: Oxford University Press).

Thomson, M. (1998) *The Problem of Mental Deficiency: Eugenics, Democracy and Social Policy in Britain, c.1870–1959* (Oxford: Clarendon Press).

Tosh, J. (1991) *The Pursuit of History: Aims, Methods and New Directions in the Study of Modern History* (Harlow: Longman).

Union of the Physically Impaired Against Segregation (1976) *Fundamental Principles of Disability* (London: UPIAS).

Walmsley, J. and Atkinson, D. (2000) 'Oral History and the History of Learning Disability', in J. Bornat, R. Perks, P. Thompson and J. Walmsley, eds, *Oral History, Health and Welfare* (London: Routledge).

Watson, F. (1930) *Civilization and the Cripple* (London: John Bale).

Watson, N. and Woods, B. (2005) 'The Origins and Early Development of Special/Adaptive Wheelchair Seating', *Social History of Medicine* 18: 459–74.

Woods, B. and Watson, N. (2004) 'In Pursuit of Standardization: The Ministry of Health's 8F Model Wheelchair, 1948–1962', *Technology and Culture* 45: 540–68.

Young, I. (1990) *Justice and the Politics of Difference* (Princeton: Princeton University Press).

Yuan, D. D. (1997) 'Disfigurement and Reconstruction in Oliver Wendell Holmes's "The Human Wheel, Its Spokes and Felloes"', in D. T. Mitchell and S. L. Snyder, eds, *The Body and Physical Difference: Discourses of Disability* (Ann Arbor: University of Michigan Press): pp. 71–88.

25

DISABILITY, SPORT AND PHYSICAL ACTIVITY

A critical review

Brett Smith and Andrew C. Sparkes

Scholarly activity on disability, sport and physical activity has burgeoned in recent years. We now have numerous books (e.g., Berger 2009; Brittain 2009; DePauw and Gavron 1995; Fitzgerald 2009; Goosey-Tolfrey 2010; Howe, 2008; Thomas and Smith 2009), several journal special editions (e.g., *Leisure Studies* 2009, vol. 28; *Sociology of Sport Journal* 2001, vol. 18; *Sport, Ethics and Philosophy* 2009, vol. 2; *Qualitative Research in Sport, Exercise and Health*, forthcoming 2012), a number of specialist journals (e.g., *Adapted Physical Activity Quarterly*; *European Journal of Adapted Physical Activity*) and a throng of journal papers devoted to disability, sport and physical activity. Scholarship also spans a range of disciplines, including sport sociology, physical education, sport and exercise physiology, sport biomechanics, and exercise and sport psychology. Given this situation, in this chapter our aspirations are modest. Many stones are left unturned and, given our background, we limit ourselves to work done in the social sciences.[1] The main aim is to give a flavour of some of the scholarly social scientific activity and offer some research directions scholars might take in the future. The first section focuses on elite disabled sport. In the second section, we examine leisure time physical activity. Finally, we reflect on some challenging issues in the area of disability, sport and physical activity, and consider directions of travel for each issue.

Elite disability sport

Although disability sport is a relatively recent phenomenon, there is a history of organized disabled sport and a noticeable growth in participation in elite sporting competitions. For example, in Germany in 1888 sports for deaf people were organized by deaf communities, and by the 1920s sports federations for the deaf had emerged in several countries. In England, Sir Ludwig Guttmann and colleagues in 1948 founded competitive sport for people with spinal cord injuries (SCIs). In 1960 in Italy persons with SCIs participated in the first Paralympic Games. In 1964 in France the International Organization for the Disabled was created with the intention of giving athletes with amputations, visual impairments and cerebral palsy an opportunity to participate in competitive sport. The Paralympics in 1972 for the first time gave disabled people other than those with an SCI an opportunity to compete. Moving forward, in 1989 the International Paralympic Committee (IPC) – the global governing body of the Paralympic Movement – was founded to organize multi-disability competitions for a range of disabled people through the Summer and Winter Paralympic Games. Nearly 4,000 athletes from 146 countries competed at the Beijing 2008

Paralympics. The IPC currently also serves as the International Federation for nine sports, for which it supervises and coordinates the World Championships and other competitions.

Against this brief historical background and growth in the participation of sport, scholars within the social sciences have increasingly turned their attention to elite disabled sport. For example, sport psychologists have explored the following: how athletes with disabilities[2] can effectively use psychological skills and benefit from psychological skills training to enhance their performance (Hanrahan 2007; Martin 2010); the physical self-perceptions and self-esteem of elite Portuguese wheelchair basketball players (Ferreira and Fox 2008); the challenges wheelchair athletes face when leaving sport (Martin 2000); the role of self-efficacy and the effect on the training and performance of wheelchair road racers (Martin 2002); and stress, emotion and coping strategies in elite Paralympian athletes (Campbell 2002; Martin 2011). Another popular issue that sport psychologists have examined is motivation (Hanrahan 2007). For instance, in their qualitative study, Page *et al.* (2001) examined the factors underlying the motivation for coming to sport and staying in it among elite disabled powerlifters and track and field athletes. They found that one key motivating factor was fitness. Sport further allowed participants to feel competent and to prove competence to oneself and others. In so doing, sport was perceived to help them feel empowered and challenge the negative perceptions of incompetence held by others. Participants also said that what motivated them to engage in sport was the common social outlet it provided them as disabled people. As one participant put it when asked why he plays sport:

> I would say the camaraderie of teammates. It's always fun to go someplace where everybody has the same common goals. It's an understanding [of your sport], because ... people out in the community have no idea – some people have no knowledge. And it's always nice to sit down and say, 'Hey, what did you do last night?' And you can have the lingo chat of sport and you can relate to each other.
>
> *(Page et al. 2001: 48)*

In addition to sport psychologists, sport sociologists have studied elite disabled sport. However, compared with sport psychologists, sociologists of sport have engaged in more intense debate about elite disabled sport and turned a more critical eye towards it. For instance, the various systems of classification used to organize competitive sport for disabled people have been subjected to critical debate (Howe and Jones 2006; Thomas and Smith 2009). The use of technological aids by Paralympians, such as Oscar Pistorius, has come under critical scrutiny too (Edwards 2008; Hilvoorde and Landeweerd 2008; Thomas and Smith 2009). Elite disabled sport has been critiqued for being grounded firmly in the medical model and not engaging enough with other models of disability, such as the social model, that have individual and societal emancipatory potential (Brittain 2004). Further, Hargreaves (2000) has drawn attention to the fact that the Paralympic Games is a heavily male-dominated competition in terms of participation. For her, part of the explanation for the differential participation rates between men and women can be related to the view that 'in the main, disability sports organisations are organisations *for* the disabled and not *of* the disabled (p. 207). More recently Berger (2009) and Thomas and Smith (2009) have noted the gendered divisions in participation in elite sport between men and women as well as the social fissures that can develop between disabled athletes and non-disabled athletes, and between disabled athletes and non-athletes within the disability community. They have also suggested that disability sport has rarely been the focus of any sustained or clearly defined policy and political commitment.

Another popular issue that sport sociologists have turned their attention to is the representation of elite level disability sport in the media. Among the various key concerns raised has been that whilst media coverage of *some* major disability sport-specific competitions such as the Summer Paralympic Games is growing, particularly in Great Britain, it is, as Brittain (in press) points out, still very small. Coverage is also fleeting, limited to a few weeks surrounding the Paralympic Games. Moreover, what is presented in the media has raised questions. For example, as Thomas and Smith (2009) have noted, in many countries the media coverage of 'disabled sport has tended to focus on *particular athletes, with particular impairments, competing in particular sports*' (p. 151). In this limited focus, the researchers add, athletes have tended to be described in highly medicalized terms. Likewise, the athletes with disabilities focused on have often been depicted in the media as victims or courageous individuals who battle against the odds and overcome their tragic disabled fate (Brittain 2009, in press; Hardin and Hardin 2004; Kleiber and Hutchinson 1999; Peers 2009). Thus, the media has been critiqued for not only reinforcing negative perceptions of disability and perpetuating stereotypes, but also for turning athletes with disabilities into what has been described as a 'supercrip'; that is an athlete who with courage, hard work and dedication proves that one can accomplish the impossible and heroically triumph over the 'tragedy' of disability (Berger 2009).

One concern with supercrip athletes and the stories told about them in the media, as Berger (2009) has noted, is that they foster unrealistic expectations about what disabled people can achieve, or what they *should* achieve, if only they tried hard enough. This, so it is said, can lead to blaming disabled people who are not willing, or not able for bodily, structural or economic reasons, to engage in disabled sport. It is also suggested that when the media depicts elite sporting athletes as supercrips, as well as when athletes with disabilities themselves operate as or seek to be a supercrip, they support the low societal expectations of disabled people, reproduce a tragic image of disability, perpetuate heroic and hegemonic notions of masculinity and 'reinforce social systems of domination, equating individuals' self-worth with coming out on top in the competitive struggle for achievement' (Berger 2009: 131). The supercrip athlete in the media, in the flesh or in community talk may likewise be disempowering because what is generated, it is might be argued, is a de-politicized, pre-social and false impression that all is needed when one is impaired is heroic individual effort and inner drive to overcome societal barriers (Berger 2009; Hardin and Hardin 2004; Kleiber and Hutchinson 1999). In other words, the types of reform advocated by proponents of the social model are unnecessary because individuals by themselves can, and should, heroically rise to the challenge of overcoming barriers. Thus, it might be said, there are problems with supercrip athletes and how they are depicted not just in the media, but in everyday life too.

According to Berger (2009) and Hardin and Hardin (2004), a much more nuanced view of competitive disabled sport and the so-called supercrip athlete is needed. In their research with athletes with disabilities, they proposed that competitive sports can be *both* a potentially disempowering and empowering experience for disabled people. For example, the disabled people in Hardin and Hardin's (2004) study said that they found supercrip athletes to be inspiring and believed that such athletes can be an affirmative model for disabled people as well as the general public. The disabled sport stars Berger (2009) interviewed echoed these sentiments. They also cited numerous other benefits with competitive sport that, for Berger, need to be taken into account when critiquing supercrip athletes. These benefits, similar to those identified by Page *et al.* (2001) as well as Goodwin *et al.* (2009) and Huang and Brittain (2006), included: the camaraderie and affirmation they get from teammates and peers; improved physical conditioning and a sense of bodily mastery; a heightened sense of self-esteem and confidence; the mental strength to deal with stress in everyday life; intrinsic enjoyment of playing sport; and increased opportunities for travel.

That said, as Berger (2009) argued, whilst there are benefits to sport, there are also problems associated with the supercrip athlete. The problems highlighted in Berger's study included the unintended consequence of creating a subcultural milieu that alienates the broader disabled community and impedes the development of a collective identity or shared political vision for improving the lives of disabled people. Thus, in Berger's research it was not that he did not discover some disempowering elements of the supercrip phenomenon. Rather, as he stated:

> It's that a cavalier dismissal of these athletes fails to appreciate that they did not 'make it' on their own. While they mostly certainly deserve credit for their hard work, persever-ance, and accomplishments in the face of adversity, their lives must be understood in a social context – the actions they took were enabled by significant others and institutional resources that were available to them during their lives.
>
> *(Berger 2009: 43)*

Similarly, Peers (2009) offered a more nuanced view of competitive disabled sport than has traditionally been offered. Reflecting autoethnographically on her experiences as a Paralympian, she highlighted that, in similar ways identified by Berger (2009), she benefited from sport. At the same time, there were costs for her. She felt that the pedestal she was put on as a Paralympic athlete turned the social inequality of disability into something to overcome, rather than something to challenge and change. She revealed how, for her, the heroic Paralympian relied on narratives of the 'pitiful cripple' who can't overcome and the burdensome 'gimp' who won't. Peers also commented that these narratives served to set disabled people apart, 'whether up on the pedestal or down in the gutter: they enable others not to look us in the eye, they induce us not to look into each other's and they encourage us not to look inside of ourselves (Peers 2009: 654). Further problematizing overly simplistic critiques of the supercrip, she wrote:

> I know that many athletes thrive through sport. I know that they build communities and resistances. I know that they actively organise, disorganise, invent and pervert the sports that they play. I know that these athletes have names and that they have stories that neither originate in disability nor terminate with their sporting careers. I know this because of the stories that athletes tell each other. We tell each other stories that help us remember the historically irrelevant. We tell stories that help us resist the institutiona-lised silences. We also tell stories, however, that help us raise ourselves above others: stories that reproduce the pedestals from which we speak and the gutters on which these pedestals are built.
>
> *(Peers 2009: 662)*

Taking into account all of the above, it would seem there are problems with elite sport that cannot be glossed over and debates that cannot be ignored. At the same time, as we have seen, elite sport for many disabled people has physical, psychological and social benefits. But, of course, not all disabled people can be, or wish to be, an elite athlete.

Leisure time physical activity

Although still comparatively rare, researchers in sport and exercise have in recent years widened their focus from elite sports to include what is broadly termed leisure time physical activity. This, as described by Martin Ginis and colleagues (2010a, b), is physical activity that people choose to do during their free time, such as exercising at a fitness centre, playing amateur sport and going for a wheel or walk. One popular issue focused on by social scientists, like in elite sport, relates to motivation and the benefits of leisure time physical activity. Research has revealed that for many disabled people, the corporeal benefits that can come with being physically active are motivating in themselves. For example, Kehn and Kroll (2009) noted that people with SCIs exercise because it has been shown to decrease the risk of secondary physical bodily conditions associated with spinal injury, including pressure sores, urinary tract infections, diabetes and arthritis. In addition, the psychological benefits that might come with being physically active can motivate disabled people to engage in leisure time physical activity. For instance, it has been suggested in quantitative and qualitative studies that participation in activities such as amateur sport and exercise in a gym has the potential to enhance self-esteem, improve body satisfaction, boost confidence, help escape worries associated with disability and impairment, reduce stress and open opportunities to socialize with others (e.g., Guthrie and Castelnuovo 2001; Goodwin and Thurmeier 2004; Kerstin *et al.* 2006; Martin Ginis *et al.* 2010a, b; Semerjian 2009; Shapiro and Martin 2010; Swanson *et al.* 2008).

Complementing this research, researchers have focused on the barriers to leisure time physical activity. One barrier identified is the socio-environment. Linked to this, the outdoor climate, lack of transport, lack of accessible facilities, unsafe neighbourhoods, cost, lack of peer support and negative attitudes towards disabled people, for example, are barriers that can prevent them from engaging in physical activities in their leisure time. Likewise, a lack of information is a barrier (Martin Ginis *et al.* 2010a, b; Semerjian 2009). For instance, disabled people have reported that they do not know how to be physically active or have the information to know where to be active. This is compounded by the fact that disabled people are rarely targeted for health promotion (Kehn and Kroll 2009). Further limiting or impeding a disabled person's potential to engage in physical activity are such corporeal matters as pain and fatigue. Other reasons reported by disabled people for not being physically active are a lack of motivation and confidence as well as a belief that disability equates to inability (Brittain 2004). In relation to the latter point, Seymour (1998) and Sparkes and Smith (2002), in their work on SCIs and amateur sport pointed out that for many of the participants in their study, reversing the damage done to their bodies and regaining their former able body was vital. This, however, operated as a barrier to participating in disability sport because engaging in it was seen as both futile (why do disabled sport when I'll be walking again?) and harmful to their sense of self (sport reminds me that I'm impaired, not who I was, nor who I want to be).

Another theme to emerge out of an interest in disability and leisure time physical activity relates to people's experiences of suffering an SCI through playing amateur sport. For example, over the years we have examined the experiences of amateur sportsmen who have suffered an SCI and become disabled as a result of playing rugby union football (see, for example, Smith and Sparkes 2008, 2011; Sparkes and Smith 2002, 2009). Our analysis of the men's stories has revealed that most of their experiences were shaped and framed by the restitution narrative, as defined by Frank (1995), with its notions of concrete hope tied to a medical cure, attendant metaphors that include fighting to make a comeback and walk again, and time tenses that conceptualize the future as located in the past and associated with the able body. We argued that the restitution narrative can be problematic. There is little talk of commitment when living restitution stories to challenging disabling barriers or ableist attitudes. The plot of this story is also concerning because it might not come to fruition, and, even if it does and a medical cure does arrive, it will be a narrative that some can purchase and others cannot. That said, we also argued that the restitution narrative has various benefits, including offering a coherent storyline. Other people's responses to this narrative added further nuance and complexity to our understandings of what it might mean to live by restitution. When we have presented restitution stories to audiences, individuals have responded to them with concern and worry. In many cases, though, people have responded with understanding and approval because the stories fit with how they themselves would react if they became impaired and disabled. Moreover, this narrative fits with dominant notions of heroic masculinity that call for stoicism and courage in the face of challenges and high levels of motivation to overcome adversity (see Smith and Sparkes 2011).

Some of the men in our study, however, primarily told stories framed by what Frank (1995) termed the quest narrative. This narrative calls on metaphors associated with a journey of self-discovery, notions of being changed for the better, transcendent hope and time tenses that link the person to living fully in the immediate present. The person telling quest narratives communes with other bodies. The stories can also challenge disabling barriers or ableist attitudes. As with the restitution narratives, we have relayed quest stories to audiences who receive and react to them with approval, as a 'positive' way to live with disability and 'grow' as a person.

In contrast to the quest and restitution narratives, one person embodied a story framed by what Frank (1995) calls the chaos narrative (see Smith and Sparkes 2008). This narrative imagines life never getting better. The person is sucked under the undertow of impairment and disability and the disasters that may occur as a result of them. Further, when in chaos, there is seemingly no end in sight to living this way. The present is empty and the future appears desolate. Consequently, self and identities fragment, and some dissolve. Life is deemed to be meaningless and devoid of purpose. When we have presented the chaos story to various audiences, we have sensed the anxiety, discomfort and fear it instils in them and their need, at times, to respond to the story. When people do respond, they offer a story in which the chaotic person needs to move out of chaos.

Whilst most people agree that people in chaos need to get out of this story, what counts as 'to move out of' is contested among them. Some call for the person in chaos to seek psychological therapy (depression-therapy restitution response). Some, though, believe a biotechnological breakthrough, such as stem cell surgery, is what is needed to release the person from chaos (breakthrough restitution response). Others think the man in chaos needs to witness his story (solace response) whilst others consider that what is needed to get out of chaos is the removal of barriers 'out there' in society that act to oppress disabled people and create conditions in which chaos is produced (social model response). Our own responses to the chaos narrative have further complicated matters. Rather than giving one single response to this story, we have in our heads and hearts oscillated between each of these different responses just noted, changing across and shifting among them. Our uncertainties and dilemmas remain as we continue the process of travelling with stories of chaos. We also continue to wonder, if none of these responses is wholly adequate (though each has its rationale and strengths), what can be said? Or are we left in a scenario like in Conrad's Kurtz book *Heart of Darkness* (1999): 'the horror'? Maybe, for some amateur athletes who suffer an SCI, dark as that is, that's how it is? (see Smith and Sparkes 2011).

Challenging issues and potential directions of travel

Earlier in this chapter we offered a partial review of the burgeoning literature on disability, elite sport and physical activity in a modest attempt to make sense of the field. We now reflect on *some* challenging issues in the field and offer some possible indications of the direction of travel for the future. Of the many challenges and directions that may be taken, we will consider four.

First, there is the challenge of developing knowledge on elite disability sport. One direction of travel researchers might take to help meet this challenge is to examine the legacy of the Paralympics on both athletes with disabilities and disabled people in general. Likewise, research is needed that examines the impact that sports such as wheelchair rugby or tennis have on players' health, personal growth and inter-generational relationships in the run-up to, during, and after a Paralympic Games. Another direction of travel is concerned with the media.

As we noted earlier, there has been much work analysing the content of the media in relation to disability and sport. However, the audience remains, in large part, an absent presence in disability sport media research. For example, there is a scarcity of research on audience interpretations of what is said and shown, that is, media reception. Equally, the relationship between disability sport in the media and the audiences' everyday social experiences and uses of it has escaped empirical enquiry. Thus, it is very difficult to know empirically the precise impact that disability sport media coverage has on disabled and able-bodied people. Do people interpret media depictions of athletes with disabilities as, for instance, courageous individuals who battle against the odds and overcome their tragic disabled fate? Are media depictions of athletes with disabilities interpreted in negative and/or positive terms? Outside the typical research setting of audience reception focus groups, do people 'use' media depictions of sport and disability? If so, how and with what effects on them and other people? Do people in their everyday lives subvert and/or reinforce tragic, overly medicalized media depictions of disability? Can portraying self-worth as aligning one's actions with those of the athletes with disabilities not only create an unrealistic ideal that most individuals cannot live up to, but also direct the course of recovery in personally limiting ways? Does a lack of exposure of athletes with disabilities lessen the possibility of non-participating disabled people becoming aware of disabled sport or inspired to take part themselves? Do disabled people who simply engage in leisure time physical activity feel inferior to those at the elite sport level? Accordingly, without denying the need for substantial time and resources to examine such questions, researchers might consider engaging also with audiences in both traditional research settings (e.g., research interviews) and in their everyday lives (e.g., ethnographic work) rather than them being a ghostly presence, hovering over and around research on disability sport media work. Such an engagement, for us, might benefit disability sport media research by developing a more nuanced understanding of it.

Second, there is the challenge of extending our understanding on disability leisure time physical activity. One important direction to take is concerned with positive psychology and the role of disability leisure time physical activity in facilitating or hindering resilience and post-traumatic growth. An associated direction to take is concerned with barriers. As we noted earlier, whilst there are numerous health benefits from engaging in leisure time physical activity, the path towards a physically active lifestyle is fraught with various obstacles for many disabled people. Given this, we urgently need work that seeks to facilitate ways for disabled people to engage in leisure time physical activity if they so wish. This could include identifying preferred messengers (e.g., disabled peers, family, or physical therapists), preferred methods (e.g., face-to-face contact, internet, or written stories), and ideal times (e.g., acute rehabilitation) for effectively conveying physical activity information in such a manner that addresses different impairments, gender, age, ethnicity, marital status and socio-economic status (Martin Ginis *et al.* 2010a, b). Future work on barriers may also involve developing interventions that focus on psychological factors, such as resilience and implementation intentions (Latimer *et al.* 2006). Moreover, to create or enhance access to spaces and places for participating in leisure time physical activity there is a need to take action at the socio-environmental level and policy level. This is especially so since there is a growing amount of research on physical activity and disability that, explicitly or implicitly, promotes the health role.

According to Shilling (2008), the health role places on people the responsibility to be productive and maintain their bodies at the fittest and most adaptable, by being physically active, not smoking, and so on, in order to be responsible citizens and personally prevent disability or illness. However, the health role assumes each person has the desire to be physically active, that all individuals can prevent their body from being ill or impaired and that everybody can be physically active. As Shilling commented, the health role, like its antecedent sick role, can be seen as implicating individuals within a new and more demanding mechanism of social control which banishes disability, impairment and illness from everyday life, and associates ill-health or an impaired body with a lack of inner individual strength and motivation.

In these circumstances, it is easy for the chronically ill or impaired to 'feel that they are culturally illegitimate, unaccepted in the wider society'. … This is not only because the health role ignores individual or group differences, but because it ignores the significance that the *physical environment* has on people's capacities to approximate to the health role.

(Shilling 2008: 108)

Another important direction to take to meet the challenge of extending our understanding of leisure time physical activity is to examine the potential for disabled people of what has been termed 'the blue gym' (Depledge and Bird 2009). The blue gym is about engaging in activities within our water environment, such as wheeling or walking along the coast, playing in rivers or fishing in the sea. This moves traditional notions of the gym as an indoor, machine-filled contained physical place and space to conceptualizing it as part of our multi-sensory natural environment, city surroundings or maritime culture. The blue gym has exploded in interest in the United Kingdom, and is spreading globally. However, to date there is no research on this social space and place in relation to disability. This gap in knowledge needs to be rectified because the blue gym could be a leisure time physical activity environment that is liberating, empowering, positive for health and well-being, disabling and/or oppressive. This is not to deny that some people with certain bodily impairments will always struggle to engage in some activities within the blue gym. For example, a person with a high level spinal injury would struggle to surf unaided in the sea or travel long distances alone in their wheelchair along a sandy beach. That said, failure to consider disabled people in the blue gym risks this place and space being simply associated with able-bodied leisure time physical activity. There is the danger that if disabled people are ignored the blue gym becomes an environment where ableist attitudes and the ableist structures of society are perpetuated, the needs and rights of people with impairments are not acknowledged, and disabled people cannot benefit from it if they so wish.

Third, with respect to both elite disabled sport and leisure time physical activity, there is the theoretical and empirical challenge of understanding the *body*. There has been an increasing amount of work in the field of elite disabled sport and disabled leisure time physical activity on the body. However, with rare exceptions, much of the work on the body, sport and physical activity has failed to engage with the body as *simultaneously* biological, lived and social. As a consequence, one, but frequently more, of the following occurs: the body is depicted as independent from society; the materiality of lived experience is a shadowy presence; very little is said about oppression and disabling barriers; impairment is reduced to a discursive production (i.e. a product of discourse); experiences of embodiment are overlooked; the emotional expressive body is obfuscated; and/or people's bodies disappear behind the social and cultural constructions that produce them, obscuring the human agent. Of course, understanding the body as simultaneously biological, a place where we experience the world, and a social construction is no easy matter. That said, we share the view of Thomas (2007), who argued, 'it should be possible to understand the "impaired body" as simultaneously biological, material and social – in short, as bio-social in character' (p. 135).

Given this, what direction of travel might researchers take to understand the body as biological, lived and social? One exciting possibility is to operate as a theoretical bricoleur via the 'body made flesh' perspective described by Evans *et al.* (2009). For them, this perspective directly addresses body/mind/biology/culture relationships while attempting to avoid the limitations of perspectives that either exclude or underplay the possibility that social life also has a material as well as a discursive and subjective component. Complementing this perspective, and building on a feminist non-reductionist materialist ontology of the body as described by Thomas (2007), we might talk also of embodied narratives. There are a number of reasons for this, the most important of these being the bio-social nature of narratives.

In relation to the biological character of bodies, as we have suggested in our work on SCI and becoming disabled through playing sport (Smith and Sparkes 2008; Sparkes and Smith 2009), narratives have a material component. For example, the kind of body that one *has* and *is* becomes crucial to the kind of narrative told. Narratives also play a key role in constituting and expressing our emotions either through verbal stories the body tells or through the body's gestures, sweat and blood. Further, the nature of narrative is to endow biological happenings, like SCI, with meaning. SCI often disrupts the body's capacity to map its sensory experiences and to translate this mapping into what neurophysiologist Damasio (2000) calls the *movie-in-the-brain*, which is the beginning of human storytelling. The movie-in-the-brain *is* what we take to be the world we perceive: the world of continuous, flowing, meaningful movements, in which each instant of perception is understood as following sequentially from the moment before and leading to the moment after. SCI itself, and the pain, pressure sores and other bodily matters that can follow from this injury, can disrupt the body's capacity to map itself and to produce a coherent and meaningful movie-in-the-brain. Narrative works to repair those moments of disruption of the movie-in-the-brain by restoring flow to a life's story, and with that flow, the coherence of things happening in consequence of recognized antecedent events and having predictable consequences, thereby giving meaning to the 'stuffness' of life that includes bodily sensations and experiences.

This said, and making the connection with the social and cultural nature of embodied lives, the body is not free to restore flow to its life's story, make meaning or construct just any story it wishes about itself. In commenting on the dialectic between the individual body and the societies and cultures it inhabits, Frank (1995) emphasized that although the corporeal experiences and the reported biographical events may be unique to the individual, the manner in which they are given meaning via narration is structured according to socially shared conventions of reportage and, just as importantly, conventions regarding the hearing and reception of stories. Hence, the story somebody tells is shaped, but not determined, by the stories 'out there' in society. Given this, examining people's stories helps us not only illuminate the social quality of our bodies, but also the body's agency. Bodies are shaped and inscribed by stories that society and culture supply us. These stories help make meaning and restore flow to lives following impairment. Yet within the constraint of power, narrative resources and the realness of fleshy bodies, disabled people can and do edit, weave and strategically construct the stories they tell, organizing experience in the process and resisting any idea that a person as some*body* is determined by biology, culture and society.

Fourth, there is the challenge of expanding the *qualitative methods* used in research on elite disability sport and disability leisure time physical activity. Much qualitative work done with people has tended to rely on a one-shot interview as the main data collection technique. This is not to say that such interviews should be abandoned or that we should elevate one kind of source of data over another. Our point is that for certain purposes and under certain circumstances we might consider harnessing the potential of not just multiple interviews over time but also other forms of data collection. For example, researchers might utilize vignettes or naturalistic data. Another untapped direction in the field of disability and sport that researchers might travel is concerned with visual methods. These include drawing, film and researcher directed photography.[3] Researchers may also consider using the visual method of auto-photography. This, as Phoenix (2010) explained, involves turning the camera over to participants to document the images/ footage they choose, and in some instances to story their meanings collaboratively with investigators. Such a method can provide an additional layer of insight into individual lives by enabling researchers to view the participant's world through their eyes. It can, suggested Phoenix, provide participants with a sense of 'agency and opportunity to speak for themselves, and subsequently help to erase the traditional power imbalance between researcher and participant. ... Moreover, participants are able to use their bodies and the space around them to *"show"* rather than just *"tell"* about their lives (p. 99).

Furthermore, researchers for certain purposes might consider using what has been termed mobile methods (Ross *et al.* 2009). Departing from sedentarist methods that treat people as static, and drawing on the 'spatial turn', mobilities research embraces people's social experiences of moving in and between spaces. It foregrounds the corporeal body as an effective and multi-sensory vehicle through which we move and construct emotional, sensorial geographies. To examine the experiences of bodies in motion – whether that is strolling along the coast, wheeling in a rugby game, driving to the beach, running for fun, playing in a park, travelling on a bus to go swimming, or negotiating the machines in a gym – and the flows of bodies that move inside gyms, researchers use methods 'in motion'. For example, visual methods such as auto-photography might be used. Researchers might use 'time and space diaries', in which participants record what they were doing and where, how they moved during those periods, and how they felt during them. The power of 'walking or wheeling interviews' might also be harnessed (Ross *et al.* 2009). Here, rather than simply interviewing people sitting down in their home or in a university office as is traditionally the case, researchers might interview people on the move (e.g., while walking along the coast in the blue gym or travelling to an international sporting competition), asking questions about matters such as previous social interactions, one's relationship with space, environmental barriers faced and sensory experiences of noise and smell.

Conclusion

In this chapter we have presented a limited selection of some key issues that have swirled through the growing social scientific study of disability, sport and physical activity. In a modest attempt to expand our understandings of disabled people's lives, cultural landscapes and the psycho-social worlds in which they live, we have offered some critical reflections on the many challenges faced and suggested directions in which we could go. Of course, none of these challenges are straightforward. Nor are the proposed directions of travel easy to make. However, for us, ultimately social scientific research on disability, sport and physical activity will not flourish without taking some risks. We look forward, then, to travelling into a future that is bursting with possibilities.

Notes

1 See, for example, Goosey-Tolfrey (2010) for accounts of disability and sport physiological research.
2 The term 'athletes with disabilities' is used when referring to elite athletes as in the literature. Elite disabled athletes often state they prefer to be known as athletes first (e.g., Berger 2009; Huang and Brittain 2006).
3 For sport and physical activity examples, see the 2010 special edition of *Qualitative Research in Sport and Exercise* 2(2).

References

Berger, R. (2009) *Hoop Dreams on Wheels* (London: Routledge).
Brittain, I. (2004) 'Perceptions of Disability and Their Impact upon Involvement in Sport for People with Disabilities at all Levels', *Journal of Sport and Social Issues* 28(4): 429–52.
Brittain, I. (2009) *The Paralympic Games Explained* (London: Routledge).
Brittain, I. (in press) 'British Media Perceptions of the Paralympics', in O. J. Schantz and K. Gilbert, eds, *Heroes or Zero's: The Media Portrayal of Paralympic Sport* (Champaign: Commonground Publishing).
Campbell, E. (2002) 'Cognitive Appraisal of Sources of Stress Experienced by Elite Male Wheelchair Basketball Players', *Adapted Physical Activity Quarterly* 19: 100–8.

Conrad, J. (1999) *Heart of Darkness and Selections from the Congo Diary* (New York: The Modern Library).

Damasio, A. (2000) *The Feeling of what Happens: Body, Emotion and the Making of Consciousness* (London: Vintage Press).

DePauw, K. and Gavron, S. (1995) *Disability and Sport* (Champaign: Human Kinetics).

Depledge, M. and Bird, W. (2009) 'Editorial', *Marine Pollution Bulletin* 58: 947–8.

Edwards, S. (2008) 'Should Oscar Pistorius be Excluded from the 2008 Olympic Games?', *Sports, Ethics & Philosophy* 2(2): 112–25.

Evans, J., Davies, B. and Rich, E. (2009) 'The Body Made Flesh: Embodied Learning and the Corporeal Device', *British Journal of Sociology of Education* 30: 391–406.

Ferreira, P. and Fox, K. (2008) 'Physical Self-perceptions and Self-esteem in Male Basketball Players with and without Disability: A Preliminary Analysis Using the Physical Self-perception Profile', *European Journal of Adapted Physical Activity* 1(1): 35–49.

Fitzgerald, H., ed., (2009) *Disability and Youth Sport* (London: Routledge).

Frank, A. W. (1995) *The Wounded Storyteller: Body, Illness and Ethics* (Chicago: The University of Chicago Press).

Goodwin, D. L. and Thurmeier, R. (2004) 'Inadequate Bodies or Inadequate Contexts?: Reactions to the Metaphors of Disability', *Adapted Physical Activity Quarterly* 21: 379–98.

Goodwin, D. L., Johnson, K., Gustafson, P., Elliott, M., Thurmeier, R. and Kuttai, H. (2009) 'It's Okay to be a Quad: Wheelchair Rugby Players' Sense of Community', *Adapted Physical Activity Quarterly* 26(2): 102–17.

Goosey-Tolfrey, V., ed., (2010) *Wheelchair Sport* (Champaign: Human Kinetics).

Guthrie, S. R. and Castelnuovo, S. (2001) 'Disability Management Among Women with Physical Impairments: The Contribution of Physical Activity', *Sociology of Sport Journal* 18(1): 5–20.

Hanrahan, S. J. (2007) 'Athletes with Disabilities', in G. Tenenbaum and R. Eklund, eds, *Handbook of Sport Psychology* (3rd edn) (Hoboken, NJ: Wiley): pp. 845–58.

Hardin, M. and Hardin, B. (2004) 'The "Supercrip" in Sport Media: Wheelchair Athletes Discuss Hegemony's Disabled Hero', *Sociology of Sport Online* 7(1); available online at http://physed.otago.ac.nz/sosol/v7i1/v7i1_1.html (accessed 6 October 2011).

Hargreaves, J. (2000) *Heroines of Sport* (London: Routledge).

Hilvoorde, I. and Landeweerd, L. (2008) 'Disability or Extraordinary Talent – Francesco Lentini (Three Legs) Versus Oscar Pistorius (No Legs)', *Sports, Ethics & Philosophy* 2(2): 97–111.

Howe, P. D. (2008) *The Cultural Politics of the Paralympic Movement: Through the Anthropological Lens* (London: Routledge).

Howe, P. D. and Jones, C. (2006) 'Classification of Disabled Athletes: (Dis)empowering the Paralympic Practice Community', *Sociology of Sport Journal* 23(1): 29–46.

Huang, C. J. and Brittain, I. (2006) 'Negotiating Identities through Disability Sport: From Negative Label to Positive Self-identification', *Sociology of Sport Journal* 23(4): 352–75.

Kehn, M. and Kroll, T. (2009) 'Staying Physically Active After Spinal Cord Injury: A Qualitative Exploration of Barriers and Facilitators to Exercise Participation', *BMC Public Health* 9: 168.

Kerstin, W., Gabriele. B. and Richard, L. (2006) 'What Promotes Physical Activity After Spinal Cord Injury? An Interview Study from a Patient Perspective', *Disability & Rehabilitation* 28(8): 481–8.

Kleiber, D. and Hutchinson, S. (1999) 'Heroic Masculinity in the Recovery from Spinal Cord Injury', in A. C. Sparkes and M. Silvennoinen, eds, *Talking Bodies: Men's Narratives of the Body and Sport* (Finland: University of Jyväskylä): pp. 135–55.

Latimer, A. E., Martin Ginis, K. A. and Arbour, K. P. (2006) 'The Efficacy of an Implementation Intention Intervention for Promoting Physical Activity Among Individuals with Spinal Cord Injury: A Randomized Controlled Trial', *Rehabilitation Psychology* 51: 273–80.

Martin, J. (2000) 'Sport Transitions Among Athletes with Disabilities', in D. Lavellee and P. Wylleman, eds, *Career Transitions in Sport: International Perspectives* (West Virginia: Fitness Information Technology): pp. 161–8.

Martin, J. (2002) 'Training and Performance Self-efficacy, Affect, and Performance in Wheelchair Road Racers', *The Sport Psychologist* 16: 384–95.

Martin, J. (2010) 'Psychological Skills for Athletes with Physical Disabilities', in S. Hanrahan and M. Andersen, eds, *Handbook of Applied Sport Psychology* (London: Routledge).

Martin, J. (2011) 'Coping and Emotion in Disability Sport', in J. Thatcher, M. Jones and D. Lavellee, eds, *Coping and Emotion in Sport* (2nd edn) (London: Routledge): pp. 194–212.

Martin Ginis, K. A., Jetha, A., Mack, D. and Hetz, S. (2010) 'Physical Activity and Subjective Well-being Among People with Spinal Cord Injury: A Meta-analysis', *Spinal Cord* 48(1): 65–72.

Martin Ginis, K. A., Latimer, A. E., Arbour-Nicitopoulos, K. P., Buchholz, A., Bray, S. R., Craven, B., Hayes, K. C., Hicks, A. L., McColl, M., Potter, P. J., Smith K. and Wolfe, D. L. (2010a) 'Leisure-time Physical Activity in a Population-based Sample of People with Spinal Cord Injury Part I: Demographic and Injury-related Correlates', *Archives of Physical Medicine and Rehabilitation* 91: 722–8.

Martin Ginis, K. A., Latimer, A. E., Arbour-Nicitopoulos, K. P., Buchholz, A., Bray, S. R., Craven, B., Hayes, K. C., Hicks, A. L., McColl, M., Potter, P. J., Smith K. and Wolfe, D. L. (2010b) 'Leisure-time Physical Activity in a Population-based Sample of People with Spinal Cord Injury Part II: Activity Types, Intensities and Durations', *Archives of Physical Medicine and Rehabilitation* 91: 729–33.

Page, S., O'Connor, S. and Peterson, K. (2001) 'Leaving the Disability Ghetto: A Qualitative Study of Factors Underlying Achievement Motivation Among Athletes with Disabilities', *Journal of Sport and Social Issues* 25(1): 40–55.

Peers, D. (2009) '(Dis)empowering Paralympic Histories: Absent Athletes and Disabling Discourses', *Disability & Society* 24(5): 653–65.

Phoenix, C. (2010) 'Seeing the World of Physical Culture: The Potential of Visual Methods for Qualitative Research in Sport and Exercise', *Qualitative Research in Sport and Exercise* 2(2): 93–108.

Ross, N., Renold, E., Holland., S. and Hillman, A. (2009) 'Moving Stories: Using Mobile Methods to Explore the Everyday Lives of Young People in Public Care', *Qualitative Research* 9: 605–23.

Semerjian, T. (2009) 'Disability in Sport and Exercise Psychology', in T. Ryba, R. Schinke and G. Tenenbaum, eds, *The Cultural Turn in Sport and Exercise Psychology* (West Virginia: Fitness Information Technology): pp. 259–85.

Seymour, W. (1998) *Remaking the Body* (London: Routledge).

Shapiro, D. and Martin, J. (2010) 'Athletic Identity, Affect, and Peer Relations in Youth Athletes with Physical Disabilities', *Disability and Health Journal* 3: 79–85.

Shilling, C. (2008) *Changing Bodies. Habit, Crisis and Creativity* (London: Sage).

Smith, B. and Sparkes, A. C. (2008) 'Changing Bodies, Changing Narratives and the Consequences of Tellability: A Case Study of Becoming Disabled Through Sport', *Sociology of Health and Illness* 30(2): 217–36.

Smith, B. and Sparkes, A. (2011) 'Multiple Responses to a Chaos Narrative', *Health: An Interdisciplinary Journal for the Social Study of Health, Illness and Medicine* 15(1): 38–53.

Sparkes, A. and Smith, B. (2002) 'Sport, Spinal Cord Injury, Embodied Masculinities, and Narrative Identity Dilemmas', *Men & Masculinities* 4(3): 258–85.

Sparkes, A. and Smith, B. (2009) 'Men, Spinal Cord Injury, Memories, and the Narrative Performance of Pain', *Disability & Society* 23(7): 679–90.

Swanson, S. R., Colwell, T. and Zhao, Y. (2008) 'Motives for Participation and Importance of Social Support for Athletes with Physical Disabilities', *Journal of Clinical Sports Psychology* 2: 317–36.

Thomas, C. (2007) *Sociologies of Disability and Illness* (London: Palgrave).

Thomas, N. and Smith, A. (2009) *Disability, Sport, and Society* (London: Routledge).

26

WHAT CAN THE STUDY OF SCIENCE AND TECHNOLOGY TELL US ABOUT DISABILITY?

Stuart Blume

The neglect of technology

For all but its poorest inhabitants, life in a wealthy industrial society depends on a host of sophisticated technologies: for travel, communication, learning, carrying out household tasks, entertainment and leisure, and, of course, work. Engaging in these activities without recourse to airplanes, telephones, computers, microwave ovens, DVD players, and so on, requires imagination and effort. People who choose to live their lives with only minimal use of modern technology, such as the Amish, are generally regarded as quaint or eccentric. For many more people a vacation provides an opportunity for returning to 'the simple life': a precisely delimited period of time in which walking replaces driving, conversation replaces television, and the thermostatically controlled central heating gives way to the log fire. The rest of the time we strive for increased convenience or efficiency – enhanced functionality. But the effects of how we use all this technology go beyond this. Social life is experienced as structured by and around technologies. Widespread use of communications technologies (e-mail, MSN, social network-ing, texting, and so on) in particular seems to be leading to forms of sociality very different from those of the past.

In thinking about this multitude of devices, we normally group them in terms of what they enable us to do: to carry out household chores, to gather information, to entertain ourselves and our friends, and so on. But there is at least one class of technologies that is distinguished differently. The United States Assistive Technology Act of 1998 [105–394, S.2432] defines an 'assistive technology device' as 'any item, piece of equipment, or product system, whether acquired commercially, modified, or customized, that is used to increase, maintain, or improve functional capabilities of individuals with disabilities'. There are a number of difficulties with this definition. One is a degree of ambiguity. Who are 'people with disabilities'? Is it a matter of functional limitation, as a rehabilitation professional might assess it, or is it a matter of sense of self, of identity? What of people whose orthopaedic problems make them candidates for a hip replacement? Numbers of people with artificial hips have grown rapidly in recent decades, and although most of them are elderly, numbers of young people have been rising (Anderson *et al.* 2007: 111). Despite the fact that hip replacement provides greatly increased mobility, few regard themselves as disabled. Their aim is 'not to live life skilfully with a disability … it is to be cured' (loc. cit. 143). Another difficulty with the definition is more fundamental. Since 'all useful technology is assistive', why do we 'stipulate that some devices are assistive while others need no qualification' (Ott *et al.* 2002: 21)? Since we all depend on technological aids for getting about (bicycles, trains, cars), what is involved in designating users of particular mobility aids, such as wheelchairs, as different?

Leaving these difficulties aside for the moment, any number of indicators (sales, hospital procedures, research publications, patents) show that there are more and more such technologies, that their sophistication and performance are being constantly extended and that their users are increasingly numerous. Underlying this growth is a variety of factors, including ageing populations, a growing unwillingness to accept restrictions on lifestyle, and legislative changes. In the United States (US) the 1990 Americans with Disabilities Act (ADA) required employers, municipalities, 'places of public accommodation' and telephone service providers to remove barriers to access faced by people with disabilities. Because compliance with the requirements of the ADA meant that large institutions were obliged to provide a variety of aids and accommodations, the market for such devices was enhanced, with the result that development and design work in the field became more economically attractive (Berven and Blanck 1999).

Despite this growth there have been relatively few studies of how these technologies are developed, made available or used. Sandra Tanenbaum's early study of the 'Boston elbow' (a sophisticated above-the-arm prosthesis) has had few successors (Tanenbaum 1986).[1] Few studies have 'sought to ask people with disabilities about their use of and attitude towards technologies' (Lupton and Seymour 2000). In disability studies, even though pioneers such as Finkelstein and Oliver pointed early on to the importance of technology, the significance of technology for life with a disability has received little attention. The reasons for this neglect are not hard to discern. The social movement of people with disabilities had more urgent priorities. Inspired by the social model of disability, it set out to identify and confront the structural and legal barriers that stood in the way of disabled people's full participation and citizenship. From the perspective of the social model, 'assistive technologies', typically having their origins in rehabilitation medicine, represented precisely those attempts at compensating for individual impairments that were to be rejected and opposed. This is not to say that little has been written about technology and disability. The opposite is the case. But that literature is dominated by 'perspectives from outside the disability movement – designers and retailers of new technologies, funders of pilot projects, and the providers of social and health care services. This means that important issues about choice, control and access to the wider environment are at serious risk of being overlooked as the technological bandwagon picks up pace' (Johnson and Moxon 1998: 243). Reviewing the scant treatment of technology from within the disability movement, Johnson and Moxon find a wide range of opinions, ranging from those who see technology as most commonly subverting the goals of disabled people to those who emphasize the emancipatory potential of technology.

Underlying this chapter is the claim that studying the use (and non-use) of technologies can provide valuable insights into the meaning of disability. But how? What concepts and research tools do we need, and where precisely should we look? Science and technology studies (or STS) has a lot to offer in this regard.

Science and technology studies

It is not possible in the compass of this chapter to provide an overview of the origins, scope or theoretical orientations that mark the field of STS.[2] Both theoretically and methodologically the field today shares much common ground with a number of social sciences (anthropology, sociology, political science), and with history and cultural studies. Suffice it to say that STS has always been concerned with the processes through which the products of science and technology (concepts, classifications, theories – even facts – as well as technological devices and systems) are conceived, tested, legitimated, enter into and transform social life. Often these concepts, classifications, theories or devices become taken for granted, unquestioned and unquestionable, ubiquitous, the basis for further progress. How is this achieved?

To study any technology from such a starting point is to uncover its emergence from a complex configuration of actors with distinctive interests, values and knowledge. It is to uncover a process through which an initial concept, sketch or vision of what might be possible is given shape, turned into one or more prototypes, then tested in practice according to some or other criteria of performance, and finally prepared for regulatory approval and commercialization. The details of the process depend on the differing authority, influence and expert resources that each participant can bring to bear, but they are also influenced by prior technological developments, or 'innovation trajectories'. Over time, particular configurations of actors accumulate authority and influence. Through much of the twentieth century, this was true of the 'medical industrial complex' (Blume 1992). Medical specialists and the industrial corporations supplying them with the tools they sought, aligned their interests and came to enjoy considerable influence over the formulation of health policy. At the same time popular conceptions of health, and of the sources of better health, became increasingly identified with advanced medical technology. It is this accretion of authority, influence and discursive power that has given *medical* technology a dynamic that few other areas of technology could until recently match (though information and communications technology (ICT) may now be comparable). We have been led to see technological progress as inevitable (referred to by Daniel Sarewitz as 'the myth of infinite benefit') and as a legitimate source of hope (Sarewitz 1996). It is as a result of this dynamic, or momentum, that the preferences of users lacking either professional authority or market power have had relatively little influence. Thus, patients and their organizations have had to struggle hard to obtain any influence: much of the influence they now appear to enjoy (in parts of the world at least) may represent no more than token accommodations. Though STS scholars have long emphasized the important roles that users play in successful innovation (Oudshoorn and Pinch 2003), matters here seem to be different. It is because of the absence of this dynamic that *non-medical* technologies representing the search for participation rather than functional betterment are realized with so much more difficulty.

The lack of user influence and the difference in dynamic between medical and non-medical technologies can be illustrated by comparing the origins of two technologies both intended specifically to benefit deaf people.

In many cases of total deafness the problem lies in the inner ear, or cochlea. It is in this small snail-shaped organ that sound waves are converted into electrical stimuli that are carried to the brain. Until a few decades ago, medicine could do little or nothing for totally deaf people, who have little benefit from conventional hearing aids. In the middle decades of the twentieth century physicians and technologists, working together, developed the cochlear implant. This surgically implanted device was to provide totally deaf people with a form of hearing. From the 1980s, when the first cochlear implants reached the market, manufacturers and physicians around the globe lobbied extensively and effectively for its reimbursement by medical insurance schemes. Though professional discourse focused on the restoration of some, variable, degree of function, popular accounts in the mass media presented the implant as turning a deaf person into a hearing one: as signalling 'the end of deafness' (Blume 2010). The first cochlear implants were developed for people who had lost their hearing in adult life, and could therefore assess for themselves what they had lost and what they had regained. Soon, however, both biomedical assumptions and market considerations led to the development of paediatric devices. In the early 1990s implantation programmes specifically for deaf children were established. Today something like 200,000 people worldwide have had a cochlear implant, about half of them children. The Cochlear Corporation, the leading manufacturer of cochlear implants, has become one of Australia's most successful and profitable companies. All this took place despite the profound objections expressed by organizations of deaf people in many countries and (through the World Federation of the Deaf) globally.

Compare this with a very different technological advance, and one that deaf communities strongly supported. The closed captioning of television programmes, offering deaf viewers the possibility of reading what they cannot hear, provides an example of a technological advance addressing participation. In the early 1980s closed captioning was being used on a growing scale (Gregg 2006). In the US, the deaf community lobbied major television networks, demanding the captioning of programmes. The special decoders that had to be attached to TV sets in order to read the closed captions were, however, expensive, and relatively few deaf and hard of hearing people had them. Moreover, it was argued that because of the stigma attached to hearing problems, many people might be discouraged from buying the special decoder, or might not know how to obtain it. In 1990 the Television Decoder Circuitry Act (TDCA) was signed into law as a supplement to the ADA and became effective in 1993. The new law required *all* TV sets 13 inches and larger to have a built-in chip, enabling them to decode closed captions without the need of an external decoder.

From the perspective of the deaf community the implantation of deaf children was seen as yet another attempt at 'repathologizing' deafness: a challenge to the progress that had been made in gaining acceptance for sign language (Lane 1992). Closed captioning technology was perceived very differently by deaf communities. It involved the deployment of technology in support of the inclusion of all deaf people in a widely shared social practice (viewing television). Deaf communities thus lobbied against the implant and in favour of closed captioning.

In the field of technologies for people with disabilities, policy analysts have pointed out that users (people with disabilities themselves) should be involved in development and design work. As early as 1982 the Office of Technology Assessment (OTA) of the US Congress found that the system of funding, coordinating and providing 'appropriate technologies' to 'handicapped people' was in many respects inadequate. One of many problems it identified was the inadequate involvement of people with disabilities in the development and delivery of technologies. 'Consumer involvement is frequently discussed, however, and everyone seems to believe in the concept – yet few satisfactory schemes or actual actions to improve the situation exist' (Office of Technology Assessment 1982).

Responding to concerns like these, new structures aimed at better coordination and dissemination of information relating to assistive technologies were created, some of them explicitly seeking to establish new partnerships with potential users.[3] Yet the problem remains. Kim Anderson, a scientist with a spinal cord injury (SCI), surveyed people with SCI regarding how they felt the use of neurostimulation[4] could best contribute to a better quality of life (Anderson 2004). Nearly 700 people responded, half of them paraplegic and half quadriplegic. The study showed that for quadriplegics the return of hand and arm function was most important, whereas for paraplegics a much-desired improvement was in sexual functioning: an area receiving little attention. Regaining bladder and bowel control was a concern of both groups, since bowel accidents are not only physically uncomfortable but also socially humiliating. Neurostimulation is noted as a potentially very promising approach. However, noting that the 'mismatch of desired outcomes with outcomes usually targeted by researchers is a concern to the SCI population', Anderson argues that scientists must learn to draw on 'the intimate knowledge of the people living with the disease'. The 'experiential knowledge' of people with disabilities and chronic illnesses still plays little role in the development of technologies intended to benefit them. The problem has not gone away. But because thinking about public policy has changed in the quarter century since the OTA wrote its report, solutions proposed today are different. Thus, in the US a

National Task Force on Technology and Disability, established in 2001, reporting three years later, wrote:

> In the accessible nation envisioned by the Task force, people with disabilities will purchase technology in an expanded, reorganized and consumer-driven process that takes advantage of scale. Some of the challenges inherent in this vision include increasing coordination of services at the federal and state levels, facilitating consumer informed choice, reducing the cost of AT [assistive technologies], and ensuring affordable access to emerging technologies. The overriding challenge is to make AT more affordable and available to those who need it, and reduce costs to consumers, government and private insurers.
>
> *(National Task Force on Technology and Disability 2004: 14)*

The free market-based thinking that came to dominate public policy debates from the 1980s stressed consumer choice. Instead of people with disabilities obtaining the devices needed under the aegis of the state, generally on the basis of medical advice, they would decide for themselves which devices (and which services) they required. An ideal system, from this perspective, is one in which people with disabilities function as 'informed consumers', choosing and purchasing from among a range of technological options. The notion that to be able to choose, (as) in a consumer market, is to be 'empowered' has wide currency today.

And indeed, this is how it seems to be experienced. People value the possibility of choosing between a variety of available forms, or designs, of a device, and they have different preferences. Users both of wheelchairs and of hearing aids were found to differ in what exactly they wanted (Ravneberg 2009). One of Bodil Ravneberg's interviewees, Julie, wanted her wheelchair to be as neutral in colour as possible. For her, the important thing was that people pay attention to her, not the wheelchair. And though a powered wheelchair would appear to offer greater convenience, Julie preferred a manual chair, 'as it signalled less dependency'. It was this 'signalling' rather than ease of use that appeared to matter to Julie. Brian, a hearing aid user in his twenties, had recently decided he no longer wanted a flesh-coloured aid. He wanted a silver-coloured one, since many people today use silver-coloured Bluetooth headsets. Eva, by contrast, wanted as discrete as possible a hearing aid, since she regarded them as stigmatizing, focusing other people's attention on her hearing loss.

An STS approach requires that we probe more deeply into the origins and consequences of new technologies. Rather than taking them as givens, we need to look at the decisions, the trade-offs, the evidence and its interpretations, the political strategies, involved in constructing a device and in rendering it 'natural', and at how it is used and understood by those for whom it is intended. What sorts of studies might these be?

Studying technologies

Writing about the study of medical technologies Stefan Timmermanns and Mark Berg argued for studies of 'technologies-in-practice': of what technologies do in particular situations (that is, configurations of other technologies, practices and interests). Fine-grained descriptions are needed of the ways in which technologies are used in particular settings: affecting and affected by the identities, (inter) subjectivities, categorizations and practices constitutive of that setting (Timmermans and Berg 2003). The seductive power of controversial or 'hyped' technologies (genomics, stem-cells, nanotechnology) has to be resisted. It's the ubiquitous technologies, such as clinical guidelines, home-care technologies and patient records, from which we can best learn. But *what* might we learn from studying technologies in practice?

Studies along these lines draw attention to the complex processes of adjustment involved in beginning to make use of a new technology. Where one device is exchanged for another, a common experience for people with impairments of all kinds, these processes become visible. Over the course of time the device used is changed, whether because of bodily change, technological development, or some other reason. Such moments involve a foregrounding of the body, evoking powerful emotions. Kay Toombs, who suffers from multiple sclerosis, has written about this. She speaks of shame, for example, as the declining strength of her muscles obliges her to change one form of mobility aid for another.

> [My] feelings of shame have been most intense whenever I have had to adopt a new kind of mechanical aid to assist me in getting around (first the cane, then the crutches, then the walker, then the wheelchair and scooter).
>
> *(Toombs 1995: 18)*

Changes in technology can also work very differently, as they did for Dag, whose story Ingunn Moser has recounted (Moser 2005). At the age of 22 Dag had suffered severe brain injury as the result of a car accident. It left him unable to speak and able to move only his head and eyes. At the time of the interview he was living in a nursing home. He'd been provided with a device called a Digivox: a speech machine that included 24 pre-programmed messages, each of which could be activated by a specific pad. All the messages were to do with physical needs: for food, drink, changing position in the wheelchair, and so on. Later he got a new device called a Lightwriter. With this he could compose his own messages. In the course of the interview, Dag had his Lightwriter produce a wolf whistle. Then he had it ask whether there were any nice girls around. He was using the new device to express something that had not been possible with the old device: that he was a young male, a sexual being, as well as a person with a disability.

If the exchange of one aid (or technology more generally) for another is an occasion at which new possibilities or impossibilities are created, emotions evoked and social relationships potentially brought into question, then the process of experimentation – trying out – a new device becomes a valuable site for research. Myriam Winance has pursued this line of investigation (Winance 2006). Drawing on fieldwork conducted in France, Winance presents the case of David, a 20 year old and paraplegic as a result of a car accident, though with important mobility of the trunk and arms. Accompanied by his occupational therapist and a physiotherapist, he is choosing a new manual wheelchair. Four wheelchairs seem to fit David's criteria, though in the course of trying out the wheelchairs these criteria prove open to reconsideration. One design will enable him to enter very small rooms, but not mount kerbs. Another will allow him to mount kerbs, but not enter small rooms. There is an ambivalence, and David 'is smiling and hesitating'. Winance wants us to see ambivalence as inherent to the process of adjustment, as the rigidity of various links (relationships) is tested. André's muscular dystrophy is progressing to the stage at which he cannot easily operate his electric wheelchair. Feeling insecure, he prefers to have his mother accompany him when he goes out. She helps him drive the wheelchair and corrects his position when necessary. André and his parents are now looking for a new wheelchair that he can drive himself. After two hours of trial, and however positioned, André does not like the new wheelchair. The advice of the physiotherapist is that André keep his old chair, just changing the joystick. André and his chair have become so adjusted, one to the other, 'that it has become impossible to detach them'. Winance's emphasis on 'adjustment' shows us how choice of a technical aid involves a renegotiation of social relationships as well as sensate experimentation with the device (see also Kurzman 2002).

As noted above, Anderson asked people with SCIs what they would particularly like a neural stimulator to do for them. A few years later, when such devices were already being used to treat a number of conditions, including SCI and Parkinson's disease, a subsequent study addressed a very different question. How do people with Parkinson's disease, who have received a neural implant, feel about its effects on their lives (Gisquet 2008)? When interviewed, many said that compared with the medications they'd used before, they had less control over managing their illness. They had been able to adjust the amount of medication they took, but had now lost this element of control. Other aspects of their lives had also been affected: 'problems such as mood changes, irritability or apathy appear in a way which is strange or destabilizing for patients, because they have the feeling that their identity has been affected' (Gisquet 2008: 1849). The study found that most recipients were little aware of the profound adaptations that use of the device entailed, because they hoped that the implant would 'magically wipe away all problems'. A consequence was that their strategies for coping with their illness had been disrupted.

How do studies such as these contribute to our understanding of the meaning of disability?

Today some social scientists, both within disability studies and working adjacent to it, question the adequacy of the social model and of the clear distinction it draws. Carol Thomas has provided a valuable analysis of their (varied but partly overlapping) objections (Thomas 2004). In contesting the barriers imposed by social structures and by inadequate public policies, the social model has failed to acknowledge the extent to which our life experiences are constituted by and through our individual bodies, with their varying perfections and imperfections. The difficulties that people with disabilities confront are not only a matter of access to resources and physical spaces. They are cultural and aesthetic too, but most importantly they are also embodied. Chronic pain; fatigue; the gradual loss of muscular functioning in the case of a degenerative condition; loss of memory, sight or hearing: these are central to the experience of many people with disabilities. To exclude them from consideration by insisting on a clear separation between disability and impairment is to ignore something vital. For critics, this is, in effect, to accept medicine's claim to jurisdiction over the body. The distinction should be abandoned and the corporeal quality of disabled experience reclaimed. If the social model of disability neglects the 'lived body' of daily experience, with all its pains and its joys, then the question is 'how can this omission be rectified?' Hughes and Paterson (1997) argue for a phenomenological approach to what they term a 'sociology of impairments'. Phenomenology rejects the Cartesian separation between mind and body. We simultaneously experience our bodies and experience through our bodies.[5] Drawing on earlier discussions of the body-in-pain, Hughes and Paterson start by emphasizing that the 'normal' body, neither sick nor in pain, is normally backgrounded: it disappears from our conscious awareness. By contrast the body reappears, though problematically, as it experiences pain. Though pain is internally experienced, it also rearranges our daily living: the ways in which we deal with space, with time, with others. Reflecting on her own experience of life with multiple sclerosis Toombs, who is a professional philosopher, has made a powerful case for a phenomenological account of life with a disability (Toombs 1995). It is through the lived body, she explains, that one orients oneself to the world (through the senses, through the placing and actions of the body) and that one actively engages with the world. In both these respects disability (in her case the loss of mobility) engenders 'a profound disruption of the lived body' (p. 11). Her subjective experience of space must be continually renegotiated as the progressive nature of her conditions gradually reduces her mobility. More is involved than a loss of function. There is a loss of intentionality too, as tasks can no longer be accomplished, and a sense of diminishment, of shame.

Studies of technologies can help bridge the conceptual gap that has been created between the social impediments to integration and the embodied experience of disability. Studying what is involved in adjusting to a new technology, whether an implant, a wheelchair, or an artificial hip, represents the move from embodiment. But such studies need to be complemented by studies of another kind. What determines the choices available to David and André (in Winance's study)? Why *these* particular models and not others? Is a design conceivable, but not available, that would have better met their needs? So we return to the other side of the coin: to approach the ways in which technologies are developed and made available, to the assumptions about their intended users on which design and prescription are based, to the influence that intended users have on processes and assumptions, and to the factors restricting this influence. This move can be seen as an extension of the concerns to which the social model of disability directs attention: an extension from civil rights to also include research, development and design.

An important focus here should be the kinds of evidence on the basis of which, as a technology is constructed, professionals try to establish its value. At least in theory, professional consensus is 'evidence based'. But what counts as evidence?

In 1995, soon after the first cochlear implantation programmes for deaf children were established, the National Institutes of Health (NIH) convened a Consensus Development Conference to review the state of the technology (Blume 2010: 55–6). It was acknowledged that cochlear implant outcomes were more variable in children than in adults. 'Nonetheless,' the Conference concluded, 'gradual, steady improvement in speech perception, speech production, and language does occur.' There were still major gaps in knowledge. There was a troubling 'unexplained variability' in the performance of implant users. Little or nothing was known of the effects of implantation on children's language development. Despite these important gaps in knowledge the consensus panel was convinced that the benefits of implantation in both adults and children had been established.

There was a large body of evidence for the effectiveness of the implant, but that evidence was limited in scope. Consensus had been reached on the basis of evidence relating almost exclusively to speech perception and production. Only minimal attention had been paid to the possible consequences of implantation for children's linguistic, cognitive and psycho-social development. Though these many areas of ignorance were acknowledged, they did not impede the consensus process. The point was that the implant did seem to give deaf children better understanding of speech, and this single variable is what everyone focused on. The gaps in knowledge could be addressed later (as they have been in studies focusing on educational attainment, on quality of life and so on), but *after* the technology had become firmly established in medical practice.

Deaf communities argued that being brought up as a member of the signing deaf community had far more to offer the deaf child in terms of cognitive, linguistic and social competences, and a positive sense of self. Hearing parents typically knew nothing of the lives that deaf people led, and were said to be misled by over-enthusiastic media reporting of this 'wonder technology' and by the hope that their child could be made 'normal'. Why did none of this appear in the assessments of the implant on the basis of which professional consensus was established? Because to have done otherwise, to have made professional consensus dependent on the results of psycho-social and linguistic studies (let alone on the experiences of deaf people) would have been to compromise professional status and jurisdictional authority. Deaf advocates were posing a challenge to medicine. They were questioning the competence, the authority and the right of the profession to assess an intervention that it defined as medical in its own restricted terms. The proper test was not 'improved hearing', as in practice measured with audiological scales and instruments, but a far more complex metric rooted in psychology, linguistics and the reflexive understanding of deaf people. However, hearing and its measurement, and these alone, lay within the undisputed jurisdiction of the medical and audiological professions.

The study of technologies entering practice illuminates the gap between the forms of knowing on which their evaluation and acceptance in professional circles, and among their users, are based. Struhkamp, Mol and Swierstra focus on what is meant by 'independence': a major goal of rehabilitation medicine (Struhkamp *et al.* 2009). They start by presenting an instrument, an evaluative scale known as the FIM™, by means of which professionals can assess the improvement in a particular person's life, or the benefits of a particular treatment or procedure. What is measured is the degree of functional independence, aggregated across a number of dimensions (self-care, communication, mobility, cognition, etc). Despite their acknowledged limitations, 'measurement scales of functional independence, such as the FIM™ instrument are ubiquitous in rehabilitation assessment' (p. 60). In the real world, and in the rehabilitation clinic, independence cannot be aggregated to a single dimension. Being independent or dependent (and on whom), and for what, matter differently in different circumstances. In Struhkamp *et al.*'s study, Petra Brand compares her electric and her manual wheelchairs.

> Her electric chair allows Petra to negotiate doorsills, rough terrain, and long distances without too much pain and exhaustion. But it is awkward in social interaction and makes her feel more disabled. It may get her far into town, but it limits her in her living room. In the living room, then, a manual chair is the better tool. It allows one to sit as close to the dinner table as the rest of the family. ... So the question is not which chair helps Petra Brand most. Each chair has its own drawbacks and advantages, and the added value of these differs from one situation to another.
>
> *(Struhkamp et al. 2009: 63)*

People will differ in the importance they attach to independence in one or other situation.

> In the clinic, then, the aim of professionals and patients is not that the latter accumulates the ability to engage in as many predefined activities as possible. Rather, disabled people and professionals experimentally seek to fine-tune and balance various in/dependencies in such a way that daily life becomes as good as it can be.
>
> *(Struhkamp et al. 2009: 66)*

The standard assessment instruments with which the utility of a new device is determined, whether in establishing professional consensus or for an individual client or patient, allow neither for such contingencies nor for those elements of experience that lie beyond the compass of medical practice.

In studying how technologies emerge and are made available the focus cannot be on assistive technologies such as implants and wheelchairs alone. In a consumer culture, consumer goods and services are far more deeply implicated in 'projects of self-identity' than is captured by the notion of 'enhanced functioning' of which these devices speak (Hughes *et al.* 2005). Trying to embrace 'mainstream cultures of consumption', young disabled people face numerous forms of exclusion which include, but go beyond, lack of financial resources. Designers of coveted consumer goods are little aware of disabled people's projects of self-identity, and change here has to be fought for, as the closed captioning example illustrates.

There is something else. The significance of technologies within our society is not wholly captured by what they enable us to do. Some kinds of devices (but not others) have acquired an important symbolic function. The choice of a consumer technology – a car, a mobile phone – may be an important opportunity to 'make a statement' about who I am, or how I would like to be seen. This is what the participants in Ravneberg's study were expressing. But there is more to it than this. For one thing, we can't control the statements we are seen as making. Choosing a 'neutral' or a 'screaming neon' wheelchair enables the user to distinguish him/herself from those who made the other choice, but whether it is this choice or the fact of being a wheelchair user that dominates the perceptions of others is a contingent matter. The symbolic meanings of technologies vary with time and place. A century ago, to walk with a cane was a sign of wealth and power. Now it is a symbol of dependency (Anderson *et al.* 2007: 136). Toombs speaks of patients learning to accept mobility aids as 'extensions of bodily space, rather than as symbols of disability' (1995: 20). Yet how far can, and how far should, the culturally determined symbolic significance of a technology be set aside?

What made the cochlear implant problematic for deaf community leaders? Not the daily experiences of its users. Most users are probably satisfied with the device. The sources of the objections were different. First, they were in response to the vastly exaggerated (and sometimes erroneous) claims for the device that circulated in the mass media. Second, they were based on a historical and structural analysis of deaf experience, emphasizing the many ways in which, throughout history, deaf people had been oppressed, often denied basic human rights, and in which their sign languages had been suppressed. It was not individual experiences in using the device, but this historical consciousness that underlay their protests.

Beverley Biderman, a university-educated Canadian woman with a progressive hearing loss, describes how, at age 46, she decided to obtain a cochlear implant. Biderman tells her story not so much in terms of what learning to hear again entailed but rather as the painful remaking of her autobiography. She found herself having to confront the anger and the frustration her deafness had caused her as a teenager. This remaking of autobiography brought grief with it. Grieving for the teenage girl she had been was 'a belated but necessary step for me finally to accept my deafness'. Her defective hearing, which had previously just been there, a frustration and an inconvenience, was brought sharply into focus. 'Am I becoming a hearing person?' she asks herself. The effort of interrogating her status as a deaf person was wrenching. She describes it as an 'unravelling' of the fabric of her life. She is still a deaf person, she explains, but one who, thanks to the implant, can communicate quite effectively via spoken language. She is confident that her deafness will become less and less of an inconvenience, with time and experience. Nevertheless, her knowledge of what it is to grow up deaf leaves her with considerable sympathy for the deaf community's opposition to cochlear implants.

> I understand this opposition with regard to the Deaf asserting that their lives are not so terrible as hearing people looking at their world from the outside may think. Strangely, I even find myself, almost against my will, extending my sympathy and understanding to their opposition to cochlear implants. I find myself comprehending it on a level where my own pain about deafness resides.
>
> *(Biderman 1998: 119)*

Biderman's understanding of the implant draws on, and moves between, two different registers: one of daily experience, the other of collective memory. As collective memory becomes codified through the work of historians of disability, the resources for reflexion are rendered richer and more complex.

How can studying technology provide insights into the nature of disability?

In this chapter I have tried to argue that studies of technology that draw on the conceptual and methodological tools that STS provides can add significantly to understanding of disability, and can provide disability studies with a new research agenda.

Studying the use of technology-in-practice can help bridge the gap between the social impediments to integration on which the social model of disability has focused and the embodied experience of disability emphasized by its critics. We have to look both at the technologies called 'assistive' and those with no such predicate. Such studies need to be complemented by other studies that explore how the technologies were designed and the knowledge and the assumptions that went into the design process. How did professional and/or commercial interests constrain the significance attached to lived experience of disability? How can this experience – contingent and variable though it may be – be made relevant for the work of design and evaluation? 'Experience', however, is neither simple nor standardizable. Reflecting on, and articulating their experience, people with disabilities draw on much more than their daily conveniences and inconveniences. Their stories, as Biderman's shows so well, and as disability studies pioneers so well recognized, are imbued also by a historical and cultural consciousness.

In the aftermath of war, to walk with an artificial leg may be, and has been, a source of pride. It marks its wearer as one who has made a sacrifice in the service of his country. As years pass, as memories of war fade and attention focuses on economic reconstruction, the symbolic meaning of the artificial leg changes. Even if the prosthesis is more sophisticated, its use points to dependency rather than sacrifice, shame rather than pride. To understand what technology means for life with a disability requires that we study not only its use in daily practice, and not only how the experiences, concerns and values of its intended users were (or were not) brought to bear on its development. Universal design – the design of products, environments, programmes and services to be usable by all people, to the greatest possible extent, without the need for adaptation or specialized design – certainly has a great deal to offer. The example of the closed caption decoder is illustrative. But until such a time as all products are designed according to these principles, a time that may never come, there is something else that has to be understood and, perhaps, contested. That is the cultural dynamics through which the symbolic significance of a technological device evolves, thereby helping shape how it is used, and how its users interpret their experience of its use.

Notes

1 Though in addition to the studies cited in this chapter, see Woods and Watson 2003.
2 For such an overview, see Hackett *et al.* 2007.
3 These include academic centres such as the University of Washington Center for Technology and Disability Studies, and the T. K. Martin Center for Technology and Disability at Mississippi State University. In the United Kingdom they include the Foundation for Assistive Technology (FAST), established as a charity in 1998 (http://www.fastuk.org).
4 Neurostimulation involves the implantation of an electrode to electrically stimulate paralyzed muscles, and thereby provide functional enhancement (Bhadra and Chae 2009). The cochlear implant can be seen as an early example.
5 For a more detailed, and ambitious, exposition of the empirical possibilities of phenomenology, see Csordas 1990. Following Merleau-Ponty, Csordas sees an approach based on embodiment as 'not restricted to micro-analytic application' but as offering a new 'foundation for analysis of culture and history' (p. 39).

References

Anderson, Julie, Francis Neary and John Pickstone (2007) *Surgeons, Manufacturers and Patients. A Transatlantic History of Total Hip Replacement* (London: Palgrave Macmillan).
Anderson, Kim D. (2004) 'Targeting Recovery: Priorities of the Spinal Cord-Injured Population', *Journal of Neurotrauma* 21(10): 1371–83.
Berven, Heidi M. and Peter D. Blanck (1999) 'Assistive Technology Patenting Trends and the Americans with Disabilities Act', *Behavioral Sciences and the Law* 17: 47–71.

Bhadra, Niloy and John Chae (2009) 'Implantable Neuroprosthetic Technology', *Neurorehabilitation* 25: 69–83.

Biderman, Beverly (1998) *Wired for Sound. A Journey into Hearing* (Toronto: Trifolium Books).

Blume, Stuart (1992) *Insight and Industry. The Dynamics of Technological Change in Medicine* (Cambridge, MA: MIT Press).

Blume, Stuart (2010) *The Artificial Ear: Cochlear Implants and the Culture of Deafness* (New Brunswick: Rutgers University Press).

Csordas, Thomas J. (1990) 'Embodiment as a Paradigm for Anthropology', *Ethos* 18: 5–47.

Gisquet, Elsa (2008) 'Cerebral Implants and Parkinson's Disease: A Unique Form of Biographical Disruption?', *Social Science & Medicine* 67: 1847–51.

Gregg, Jennifer L. (2006). Policy-making in the Public Interest: A Contextual Analysis of the Passage of Closed-captioning Policy', *Disability & Society* 21(5): 537–50.

Hackett, Edward J., Olga Amsterdamska, Michael Lynch and Judy Wajcman, eds, (2007) *Handbook of Science and Technology Studies* (London and Cambridge, MA: MIT Press).

Hughes, Bill and Kevin Paterson (1997) 'The Social Model of Disability and the Disappearing Body: Toward a Sociology of Impairment', *Disability & Society* 12(3): 325–40.

Hughes, Bill, Rachel Russell and Kevin Paterson (2005) 'Nothing to be had "Off the Peg": Consumption, Identity and the Immobilization of Young Disabled People', *Disability & Society* 20(1): 3–17.

Johnson, Liz and Eileen Moxon (1998) 'In Whose Service? Technology, Care and Disabled People: The Case for a Disability Politics Perspective', *Disability & Society* 13(2): 241–58.

Kurzman, Steven (2002) '"There's No Language for This". Communication and Alignment in Contemporary Prosthetics', in Katherine Ott, David Serlin and Stephen Mihm, eds, *Artificial Parts, Practical Lives. Modern Histories of Prosthetics* (New York and London: New York University Press): pp. 227–46.

Lane, Harlan (1992) *The Mask of Benevolence* (New York: Knopf).

Lupton, Deborah and Wendy Seymour (2000) 'Technology, Selfhood and Physical Disability', *Social Science & Medicine* 50: 1851–62.

Moser, Ingunn (2005) 'On Becoming Disabled and Articulating Alternatives. The Multiple Modes of Ordering Disability and their Interferences', *Cultural Studies* 19(6): 667–700.

National Task Force on Technology and Disability (2004) *Within Our Reach: Findings and Recommendations of the National Task Force on Technology and Disability*.

Office of Technology Assessment (1982) *Technology and Handicapped People* (Washington, DC: Congress of the United States).

Ott, Katherine, David Serlin and Stephen Mihm, eds, (2002) *Artificial Parts, Practical Lives. Modern Histories of Prosthetics* (New York and London: New York University Press).

Oudshoorn, Nelly and Trevor Pinch, eds, (2003) *How Users Matter: The Co-construction of Users and Technology* (London and Cambridge, MA: MIT Press).

Ravneberg, Bodil (2009) 'Identity Politics by Design: Users, Markets and the Public Service Provision for Assistive Technology in Norway', *Scandinavian Journal of Disability Research* 11(2): 101–15.

Sarewitz, Daniel (1996) *Frontiers of Illusion. Science, Technology and the Politics of Progress* (Philadelphia: Temple University Press).

Struhkamp, Rita, Annemarie Mol and Tsjalling Swierstra (2009) 'Dealing with In/dependence: Doctoring in Physical Rehabilitation Practice', *Science, Technology & Human Values* 34(1): 55–76.

Tanenbaum, Sandra J. (1986) *Engineering Disability. Public Policy and Compensatory Technology* (Philadelphia: Temple University Press).

Thomas, Carol (2004) 'How is Disability Understood? An Examination of Sociological Approaches', *Disability & Society* 19(6): 569–83.

Timmermans, Stefan and Marc Berg (2003) 'The Practice of Medical Technology', *Sociology of Health & Illness* 25: 97–114.

Toombs, S. Kay (1995) 'The Lived Experience of Disability', *Human Studies* 18: 9–23.

Winance, Myriam (2006) 'Trying Out the Wheelchair. The Mutual Shaping of People and Devices Through Adjustment', *Science Technology & Human Values* 31(1): 52–72.

Woods, Brian and Nick Watson (2003) 'A Short History of Powered Wheelchairs', *Assistive Technology* 15: 164–80.

PART 5

Contextualizing the disability experience

27

FEMINISM AND DISABILITY

A cartography of multiplicity

Ana Bê

Introduction

This chapter aims to map the main debates in the growing interdisciplinary field of feminist scholarship and disability studies or, as Rosemarie Garland-Thomson termed it, *feminist disability studies* (2005, 2006). The chapter will also briefly explore some possible paths for the future. Feminists within disability studies have brought forth a number of vital theoretical debates, insights and contributions that remain crucial in both domains. However, more often than not, such contributions remain underplayed or even unacknowledged by mainstream debates in both disciplines. Despite this slow process of acknowledgement, contributions in this area have continued to grow and there is by now a solid and diversified body of work available. This chapter cannot, therefore, refer to every single publication or author in this area, but rather offer an overview of selected debates and contributions.

Early contributions and debates

As the disabled people's movement grew in importance throughout the later decades of the twentieth century, contributions from activists and scholars interested in both feminism and disability also began to take shape. The 1980s saw a number of important publications that focused on disabled women's lived experiences (Deegan and Brooks 1985; Fine and Asch 1988; Driedger 1989; Morris 1989). Most of these earlier publications focused on bringing to light some of the issues that most affected disabled women by presenting case studies and statistics showing that disabled women were often at a relative disadvantage to both disabled men and non-disabled women, and that their specific issues and experiences remained invisible. Likewise, they called our attention to the fact that disabled women had difficulty having their points of view acknowledged – both in the women's movement and the disabled people's movement (Deegan and Brooks 1985; Fine and Asch 1988).

Furthermore, disabled women of this era also contended that disabled people could not be considered as a whole since the issues faced by disabled women were often different from those faced by disabled men. Therefore, identifying and recognizing the gender differences was seen as absolutely essential (Fine and Asch 1985: 9; Begum 1992: 72).

In addition, feminists within disability studies thoroughly challenged and deconstructed ableist[1] ideas within feminism. This was a crucial step. They argued that the inability to include disabled women's concerns was not due to some unexplainable lack of awareness about the existence of disability among women but was mostly due to common misconceptions, stereotypes and what would later be termed ableist ideas about disabled people in general (Asch and Fine 1988; Begum 1992; Morris 1989, 1991, 1996; Thomas 1999; Wendell 1996). This can perhaps best be illustrated by Asch and Fine:

> The popular view of women with disabilities has been one mixed with repugnance. Perceiving disabled women as childlike, helpless, and victimized, non-disabled feminists have severed them from the sisterhood in an effort to advance more powerful, competent, and appealing female icons. As one feminist academic said to the non-disabled co-author of this essay: 'Why study women with disabilities? They reinforce traditional stereotypes of women being dependent, passive and needy.'
>
> *(Asch and Fine 1988: 3–4)*

These early writings were also important in demonstrating that new emancipatory models about disability had been developed by disabled men and women themselves, and these really challenged traditional individual and medical models of disability. An example of this is notably the social model of disability (Morris 1989, 1991, 1996; Thomas 1999; Wendell 1996). This new thinking exposed the ableist ideas and (mis)conceptions about 'being disabled' that are deeply engraved in our culture and ways of being, as well as the difficulty in changing them. Feminists would take their time to truly listen and, in some ways, mainstream feminisms[2] have not yet quite heard the voices of disabled feminists.

Building new horizons: constructing a body of work

The last decade of the twentieth century was crucial for the disability movement, with a series of equal rights conquests achieved in some countries, and also the appearance of a number of influential works in disability studies. It was also the decade that saw a sudden growth in the number of publications by feminists within disability studies and, consequently, the amplification of debates and contributions in this area.

These feminist writers found it important to continue to focus on the lives of disabled women by bringing their experiential stories to light (Thomas 1999) and organizing anthologies of first-person narratives (Driedger and Gray 1992). Consequently, as more studies appeared in the era of new ideas and models about disability, disabled feminists were better equipped to theorize dimensions of social life in novel and sophisticated emancipatory ways.

In a groundbreaking and essential book, *Pride Against Prejudice* (1991), Jenny Morris explored in detail how disabled people experienced prejudice and, indeed, how ideas and perceptions of disability are to a great extent defined by the non-disabled world (Morris 1991: 37). The devaluing of disabled people's lives and existence by the non-disabled world can also affect the value disabled people ascribe to their own lives. This is exactly why, as Morris states: 'We need to value our lives, and we also must value the lives of other disabled people and refuse to make assumptions about the quality of life based on the nature of a particular disability' (Morris 1991: 59). Moreover, Morris argues, this devaluing of disabled people's lives often leads to the widespread perception that these are 'lives not worth living' and that, therefore, they should be extinguished, for instance, by preventing disabled people from being born in the first place, by defending the use of euthanasia for disabled people, or by systematically persecuting, erasing and policing their lives and experiences. In its extreme, as Morris points out, it can lead to a policy of mass murder for disabled people, similar to what happened in Germany in the 1930s and early 1940s (Morris 1991: 51–8).

In the same book, Morris also analysed other aspects of the problematic relationship that mainstream feminists had with disability. While Morris continuously pointed out the ways in which feminisms had excluded disabled women and their issues from research and theoretical agendas, she was also clear to state that she had 'brought the perspective of feminism to an analysis of the experience of disability, using the principle of making the personal political as [her] primary analytical tool' (Morris 1991: 9). This remains an important political point for feminists within disability studies. The reason they felt it was important to point out both feminism's ableism and disability studies' often gendered character was exactly because, being situated in two different social locations as women and disabled people, they wanted and felt the need to draw from both feminist and disability studies' frameworks in original conceptual moves.

For example, in Britain – where the social model of disability played a key role from the 1970s – deconstructing traditional ideas about 'care' became both possible and essential. The activities of the disabled people's movement and the Independent Living Movement laid the groundwork for feminist thinkers in disability studies to redefine notions of dependency and care (Morris 1993; Thomas 2007). It was argued that Western culture constructed disabled people as 'passive', 'dependent' and 'in need of care' – a position that immediately placed them under the control of others. The point was that disabled women and men needed to have control over their own lives, including choices and self-determination related to accessing support and personal assistance, otherwise they would always be under the control of other people (for instance institutional carers or informal carers) and not have the power to determine their own lives (Morris 1993). Disabled feminists contributed to this debate by critiquing how some mainstream feminists *accepted* the normative constructions that 'disability equals dependency' and, thus, had unthinkingly made disabled and older women invisible and/or 'needy' when they discussed the important role of (non-disabled) women as carers in society (Thomas 2007). Disabled feminists such as Jenny Morris (1993, 1996) led this critique by referring to research she had conducted that demolished notions that disabled women were simply 'burdens of care' or mere 'passive recipients of care'. She concluded that: 'people who are commonly considered to be passive recipients of others' help can also be "care-givers" themselves' (Morris 1993: 89). Indeed, disabled women often had caring responsibilities of their own, and relationships that involved reciprocity were common (Morris 1993; Thomas 2007: 110). In Britain the care debate remains a heated one, and disabled feminists continue to bring forth essential contributions.

Rethinking impairment

The use of the old feminist maxim 'the personal is political' would profoundly influence the debate in Britain during the 1990s over the role of impairment in the social model of disability – a discussion that would deeply engage disabled feminists (French 1993; Crow 1996; Morris 1996; Meekosha 1998; Corker 1999; Thomas 1999). As the social model slowly began to establish itself in Britain, it also began to be under some scrutiny from disabled people themselves. One of the major sites of contention was the debate around the experience of impairment and the role of the body in the social model of disability. Proponents of the social model made a strong distinction between 'impairment' and 'disability' in order to dissociate disability from the personal tragedy rhetoric of the individual model, and to place the focus more unambiguously on the disabling barriers that exclude and oppress in the social sphere. For example, Michael Oliver clearly mentions that the social model does not deny the proximity of impairment to the body, adding that 'impairment is, in fact, nothing less than a description of the physical body' (Oliver 1996: 35). To the social model disability is therefore about: 'all the things that impose restrictions on disabled people; ranging from individual prejudice to institutional discrimination, from inaccessible public buildings to unusable transport systems, from segregated education to excluding work arrangements, and so on' (Oliver 1996: 33).

Some disabled feminists began to insist that this strong impairment/disability distinction dismissed the *experience* of impairment and the 'body-felt' altogether. They argued that this division actually mirrored the classic patriarchal split that mainstream feminists had challenged – the split between the public and private, where the 'private' becomes a personal arena of no collective significance (Morris 1996; Crow 1996). It is not entirely a surprise, therefore, that disabled feminists felt the need to question this split as replicated in disability studies: disability as public and impairment as private. While they understood that talking about the experience of impairment held the danger of reinforcing negative stereotypes about disabled people as 'victims' and 'hostages' of their bodies, they also realized that if disabled people do not reconceptualize their knowledges of the body and impairment *in their own terms*, then that would always constitute a gap that the individual or medical model would eagerly claim and occupy. As Liz Crow eloquently puts it:

> External disabling barriers may create social and economic disadvantages but our sub-jective experience of our bodies is also an integral part of our everyday reality. [...] Recognizing the importance of impairment for us does not mean that we have to take on the non-disabled world's ways of interpreting our experiences of our bodies.
>
> *(Crow 1996: 210, 211)*

Coming at it from a postmodern perspective, Mairian Corker and Sally French also contended that in the social model framework: 'disability and impairment is presented as a dualism or dichotomy – one part of which (disability) tends to be valorised and the other part (impairment) marginalized or silenced'. As such, in the authors' view, this framework fails 'to conceptualize a mutually constitutive relationship between impairment and disability which is both materially and discursively (socially) produced' (Corker and French 1999: 2, 6).

Social model proponents responded by remaining firm in their belief that impairment had no role to play in a model that had always intended to focus on the social barriers that cause disability rather than on the personal restrictions of impairment (Oliver 1996: 38). The debate continues.

New concepts

On the basis of the earlier work of disabled feminists, newcomers were encouraged to actively construct ideas and proposals that could bridge conceptual gaps. It was in this context that British feminist sociologist Carol Thomas formulated two important proposals that were to move thinking along. These were first developed in the context of Thomas's study about the lived experiences of disabled women in Britain (Thomas 1999). Her book, *Female Forms: Experiencing and Understanding Disability* (1999), remains an essential book for its innovative methodology and for its enduring theoretical contributions to disability studies. For example, Thomas argued that socially imposed restrictions that shape disabled people's identity and subjectivity by working along psychological and emotional pathways – what she termed the psycho-emotional dimensions of disablism – should be taken much more seriously by disability studies (Thomas 1999: 46). She went on to conclude that the impact of disablism in both how disabled people act in the face of disabling barriers (doing) and who they are in the face of psycho-emotional disablism (being) is interactive and compounding in individuals' lives (Thomas 1999: 46). This is a vital contribution towards a deeper understanding of the ways the non-disabled world contributes to shaping the inner existence of disabled people and has rightly gained a key role in disability studies.

In the course of her oeuvre, Thomas has continued to develop this concept and in her book, *Sociologies of Disability and Illness* (2007), she states that:

> [P]sycho-emotional disablism involves the intended or unintended 'hurtful' words and social actions of non-disabled people (parents, professionals, complete strangers, others) in inter-personal engagements with people with impairments. It also involves the creation, placement and use of denigrating images of 'people with impairments' in public spaces by the non-disabled. [...] The effects of psycho-emotional disablism are often profound: the damage inflicted works along psychological and emotional path-ways, impacting negatively on self-esteem, personal confidence and ontological security.
>
> *(Thomas 2007: 72)*

Another central and helpful concept coined by Thomas in this context has been that of 'impair-ment effects' (1999, 2007, 2010). In a recent publication, Thomas defines impairment effects as 'the *direct and unavoidable* impacts that impairments (physical, sensory, intellectual) have on individuals' embodied functioning in the social world. Impairments and impairment effects are always bio-social in character, and may occur at any stage in the life course' (Thomas 2010: 37 – author's emphasis). For Thomas, then, the bio-social nature of impairment effects is crucial since neither impairments nor their effects can be reduced to mere biology. They are both corporeal *and* social in nature. For instance, someone's particular morphology – Thomas gives the example of someone who is born missing a hand – has particular consequences for how that person does certain things in the world, or what one might call certain restrictions of activity. However, if other people see a person who is missing a hand as being unfit to work or carry out any other activity, or indeed if biomedicine labels this person as 'abnormal' because having two hands is what is deemed 'normal' in contemporary societies, then this experience is always already immersed in the social and is thus never *only* biological.

Additionally, I would add, if we as a society come to embrace the multiverse-of-bodies that constitute human presence, stop being rigid about what parts of our bodies 'should do', and come to accept that people might be creative in the ways they use their bodies (e.g., drinking a glass of water can be done in very different ways by different people – maybe by using just lips, elbows or feet instead of hands), then the experience of not having a hand might be conceptualized in another way altogether. As Thomas mentions, it then becomes very evident that 'the bio-material always intersects with the socio-cultural' (Thomas 2007: 137). Given this, Thomas is clear to conclude that: 'The distinctions made between impairment and disability (disablism) cannot [...] be mapped onto familiar biological/social or natural/cultural dualisms, nor should impairment be sidelined as an irrelevant category' (Thomas 2007: 137).

In other words, by using an inter-relational approach, Thomas does not really conceive of 'impairment' and 'disability' as completely separate entities that have nothing to do with each other, or that refer to completely different realms. Rather, she sees them both as inherently related and interconnected. Furthermore, she is clear to state that they both have bio-social processes and factors involved and are not *only* biological or *only* social.

Once again inspired by the feminist maxim 'the personal is political', many disabled feminists' personal experiences were also often featured in their own work, therefore refusing the pseudo-neutrality of positivist and male traditions of thought. Susan Wendell (1996), for example, talked openly about her own experiences with chronic illness in her book *The Rejected Body: Feminist Philosophical Reflections on Disability*. This is an essential and enduring book in disability studies and feminism wherein Wendell interweaves her own personal story with an interdisciplinary theore-tical framework to construct a powerful critique of biomedical power and the cultural and social forces that construct disabled people as 'other'. Wendell is clear to place the book theoretically as a 'feminist philosophical discussion of disability' (1996: 1) and one can clearly find a well-crafted analysis and discussion of fundamental issues around disability. The book therefore remains an essential introduction to the novice and a constant place of return for those already working in the area. Like Morris, Wendell is interested in calling our attention to the links between disability and ageing, reminding us that we construct our environments 'to fit a *young* adult, non-disabled, male paradigm of humanity' (1996: 19 – author's emphasis). Furthermore, when we think about ageing as inherently disabling we realize that non-disabled people are only temporarily non-disabled and, consequently, it is in everyone's interest to structure society in a way that enables people of all abilities to participate fully.

Wendell's careful discussion of what may count as disability, the complexities of who identifies as disabled and who counts as disabled, remains fundamental. She reminds us that disability is often viewed from the outside as a taken-for-granted and stable category that is clearly recognizable. However, many people who may be perceived as disabled by others may not in fact identify as disabled (e.g., members of the Deaf community), whereas some people who do consider themselves disabled are not identified as such by everyone else (e.g., people with 'invisible' or what I prefer to call undistinguishable impairments such as chronic illnesses). It therefore remains essential to problematize notions of perceived dis/ability.

Wendell's work (1996, 2001), along with that of Thomas (1999, 2007), has also been instrumental in opening up the field by arguing for the inclusion of chronic illnesses and other disabling conditions in the disabled people's movement and in disability studies. This particular theme has continued to be of interest for many feminists engaged with disability, as can be seen for instance in the edited collection *Dissonant Disabilities: Women with Chronic Illnesses Explore Their Lives* (Driedger and Owen 2008). While understanding the initial desire to dissociate illness from disability because this might fuel ableist stereotypes of the 'totally incapacitated' disabled person, Wendell calls for a more nuanced analysis that recognizes that while some disabled people may be either well or very healthy, others may experience illness and may therefore be exposed to particular forms of disablism. Further, as she mentions: 'like healthy people with disabilities, most people who have disabilities due to chronic or even life-threatening illnesses are not "globally incapacitated". [...] Thus there are issues of access for people with chronic and life-threatening illnesses that need to be addressed' (Wendell 1996: 20).

Following from this important point, I would argue that it is now important to begin to realize that disability studies has itself tended to uncritically accept dualistic and opposing notions of health and illness, conceptualized in very similar ways to those of the biomedical model. Thus, as the experience of chronic illness demonstrates, it is now important to rethink dualistic and exclusionary models of health and illness by presenting more fluid, interlacing and interdependent models that focus on the importance of fostering a standard of well-being in the experience of illness and on questioning standard assumptions about what health is and how it is conceptualized (Zola 1983).

Bodies of knowledge

Susan Wendell also reminds us of the complex ways in which disabled people have been constructed as 'the other' in society, and the disabling consequences that has had in disabled people's lives. However, influenced by the feminist notion of *standpoint*, she argues that this particular location may invite a specific standpoint for disabled people stemming from disabled people's unique and specific knowledges and accumulated experiences (Wendell 1996: 73). In fact, I would add that along the lines of the project of modernity, where only some knowledges are valued (most notably scientific knowledge) in detriment of others, disabled people's specific knowledges have been deemed unimportant or indeed nonexistent and therefore do need to be recovered and cast in a new light. Adopting standpoint theory can greatly aid this project.

Contributing to the importance of uncovering how normalcy is constructed, Wendell draws on feminist theory to conclude that the: 'disciplinary practices of physical normality [...] are in many ways analogous to the disciplinary practices of femininity. [...] Like the disciplines of femininity, they require us to meet physical standards, to objectify our bodies and to control them' (1996: 88). Yet, as Wendell so eloquently mentions, while criticizing constructions of femininity, mainstream feminisms have often constructed their own bodily ideals around the importance of ablebodiness and strength, often refusing to confront the frailty of the body. Thus: 'Until feminists criticize our own body ideals and confront the weak, suffering, and uncontrollable body in our theorizing and practice, women with disabilities are likely to feel that we are embarrassments to feminism' (1996: 93).

One of the major obstacles Wendell identifies as crucial to coming to terms with 'the full reality of the bodily life is the widespread myth that the body can be controlled' (1996: 93). As she mentions, both biomedicine and alternative therapies are proficient in the notion that the mind can fully control the body and, consequently, that people are responsible for their illnesses. Such influences have grave consequences for those involved, including the stigma and guilt experienced by those whose bodies seem 'out of control'. Additionally, as Wendell postulates: 'by creating a culture of individual responsibility for illness and accident, the myths of individual control and medical control through cure, discourage any search for possible social and environmental causes of diseases and disabilities, thus inhibiting efforts to prevent them' (1996: 106).

Wendell's carefully constructed critique of the power of biomedicine remains one of the most authoritative in the disability studies context and an essential point of departure for anyone interested in this issue. Her concept of 'epistemic invalidation' (1996: 122) highlights the ways in which personal knowledges and experiences of our bodies are simply disregarded or even denied by biomedicine while scientifically produced discourses are the only ones considered authoritative. Her analysis is a fundamental contribution to understanding the many ways biomedical power operates in disabled people's lives.

Diversification

As debates from a framework of feminism and disability became more and more sophisticated, the field welcomed an increasingly bigger amount of theoretical and geographical diversity. Influenced by postmodernism, the work of Janet Price and Margrit Shildrick is important in feminist disability studies, often challenging concepts that are taken for granted, inviting us to move beyond modernist standards as well as to look at the importance of reclaiming the 'uncontrollable body' (Price and Shildrick 1998, 2002; Shildrick 2009).

As disability scholarship and communication spreads throughout the world, several important contributions have appeared that draw from both feminism and disability studies. Helping to introduce readers to research in the Nordic countries, *Gender and Disability Research in the Nordic Countries* is an exciting collection edited by Kristjana Kristiansen and Rannveig Traustadóttir (2004) that applies a joint framework of gender and disability to Nordic perspectives. Writing from an Indian perspective, the work of Anita Ghai (2002, 2003) weaves together disability studies, feminist theory and postcolonial theory to produce a crucial view of the struggles faced by disabled people in the South as well as a fundamental theoretical contribution that is relevant for anyone interested in disability studies.

Inviting the humanities

In the United States, where disability studies has always been much more connected with the humanities (especially literary and cultural studies), feminists engaging with disability have shown how feminist disability studies can both draw from and enrich these areas. The work of Rosemarie Garland-Thomson truly stands out in this context, providing numerous and important insights for those wanting to engage with the humanities and cultural studies. From the start, Garland-Thomson's project has been a bold but fundamental one. In her riveting book *Extraordinary Bodies: Figuring Physical Disability in American Culture and Literature* (1997), she explores the intricacies that allow for the construction of the disabled body in culture, and the role of medical, political, cultural and literary narratives in shaping an exclusionary discourse that constructs certain bodies as inferior. Her purpose, then, soon becomes explicit: 'to alter the terms and expand our understanding of the cultural construction of bodies and identity by reframing "disability" as another culture-bound, physically justified difference to consider along with race, gender, class, ethnicity, and sexuality' (1997: 5).

By clearly placing disability alongside race, gender and sexuality in culture, Garland-Thomson is drawing our attention to the similar processes they may share when constructed as categories of 'otherness'. She is equally addressing the fact that the disabled figure, or what she eloquently terms the *extraordinary body*, had been missing from the broad critical enquiry that had allowed other cultural categories such as gender, race and sexuality to be destabilized to the point of implosion. Analysing the role of bodies in culture, and exactly how and why some are constructed as 'inferior' and 'lacking', the author reminds us that this is not due to some inherent physical characteristics but, rather, to the imposition of powerful social norms that value and legitimize certain physical characteristics over others. In this particular work, as would happen in her subsequent works, Garland-Thomson calls on the role of several cultural discourses in the construction of disability, and examines the exclusionary position of liberal individualism as well as the role of representation in specific literary and cultural sites. As such, her work has effectively reached the goal she first formulated in *Extraordinary Bodies*: to foster and create a true place of presence for disability studies as a subfield of literary criticism and cultural studies.

In *Extraordinary Bodies* Garland-Thomson joins voices with other feminists within disability studies by wishing to bring their discussions to the attention of mainstream feminisms and vice versa. She also reminds us that *both* female and disabled bodies have been historically constructed as inferior and lacking, and that these are associations that must be acknowledged:

> Many parallels exist between the social meanings attributed to female bodies and those assigned to disabled bodies. Both the female and the disabled body are cast as deviant and inferior; both are excluded from full participation in public as well as economic life; both are defined in opposition to a norm that is assumed to possess natural physical superiority.
>
> *(Garland-Thomson 1997: 19)*

In this context, the author reminds us that such association began as far back as Aristotle's *Generation of Animals*, where the female is described as a deviation from the normate male and as a 'deformed male' (Garland-Thomson 1997: 19–20). This form of taxonomy, then, as the author points out:

> [I]nitiates the discursive practice of marking what is deemed aberrant while concealing what is privileged behind an assertion of normalcy. This is perhaps the original operation of the logic that has become so familiar in discussions of gender, race, or disability: male,

white, or able-bodies superiority appears natural, undisputed, and unremarked, seemingly eclipsed by female, black, or disabled difference.

(Garland-Thomson 1997: 20)

One is thus, once again, reminded of the intricate ways in which the unmarked body (be it male or white or able) is constructed only in regards to its fictional opposite – a process that requires contrast, hierarchy and exclusion.

Although Garland-Thomson finds a constructionist perspective helpful in understanding the body as culturally constructed within social relations and in destigmatizing the differences we have come to know as gender, race or disability, she also recognizes that constructionism may contribute to erasing the material and bodily effects of those differences and the social categories we claim to be important. In the case of disability this can still be problematic because, as she wisely points out:

> [A] disability politics cannot at this moment, however, afford to banish the category of disability according to the poststructuralist critique of identity [.] [...] [W]hile in the movement toward equality, race and gender are generally accepted as differences rather than deviances, disability is still most often seen as a bodily inadequacy or a catastrophe to be compensated for with pity or good will, rather than accommodated by systemic changes based on civil rights.
>
> *(Garland-Thomson 1997: 23)*

As a result, while the constructionist argument is helpful in addressing the fact that disability is *not* a state of bodily insufficiency but rather comes into existence via the interaction of physical difference with the surrounding environment, it is also important to recognize that the material existence of the disabled body demands *accommodation* as well as *recognition*. This is a very powerful observation that still rings true today.

As an interdisciplinary area with much to contribute, Garland-Thomson also calls for disability studies to become a discourse that is recognized as 'structuring a wide range of thought, language, and perception that might not be explicitly articulated as "disability"' (Garland-Thomson 1997: 22). As disability studies establishes itself in ever greater increments, it is hopefully almost inevitable that this will be so.

Possible futures: intersectionality

There are many possible bright futures for feminist disability studies. There is no doubt that this interdisciplinary area will continue to expand. As an example, I want to suggest that engaging with theories of intersectionality can provide another interesting way forward, and I would like to briefly focus on some of its possible contributions.

Disability studies has always struggled when it comes to the integration and theorizing of multiple location subjects. Some authors have used additive approaches and the notion that, for instance, disabled women have a double disadvantage. Terms such as double oppression or multiple oppression have also been used but from the early years, authors such as Morris have warned that such an analysis can shift attention away from the socio-structural problems and risk subjects being looked at as mere passive victims of oppression (Morris 1993: 57; Morris 1996: 89). Both Thomas (2007: 73) and Garland-Thomson (2005) agree that additive analysis can be overly simplistic and that more complex approaches are necessary. Feminisms have had to face the same kind of issues, and intersectionality arose as a paradigm of research precisely from the need to tackle 'internal diversity' in a more sophisticated manner. Even though many internal debates have risen over the concept of intersectionality in mainstream feminisms, it remains helpful. Leslie McCall even argues that 'intersectionality is the most important theoretical contribution that women's studies, in conjunction with related fields, has made so far' (McCall 2005: 1771). As such, it can prove a helpful tool to disability studies too and a way forward for future explorations. It is beyond the scope of this article to define and summarize debates in this area, but for more on inter-sectionality see, for instance, Crenshaw [1989] 2003; Collins 1990; Brah and Phoenix 2004; McCall 2005; Hancock 2007.

Exploring intersectionality from a joint framework of race and gender, Evelyn Nakano Glenn recognizes the importance of identifying: 'a framework in which race and gender are defined as mutually constituted systems of relationships [...] organized around perceived differences. This definition focuses attention on the processes by which racialization and engendering occur, rather than on characteristics of fixed race or gender categories' (Nakano Glenn 2002: 12).

Perhaps one of the most interesting articulations Nakano Glenn makes resides in her take on the importance of relationality. In her view, this concept is important because it helps problema-tize how the dominant categories always establish themselves by way of contrast. It also helps to highlight how the lives of different groups are inexorably interconnected. Lastly, the author points out that relationality helps to address the critique that abandoning fixed categories means race and gender can mean anything one wants them to mean: 'Viewing race and gender categories and meanings as relational partly addresses this critique by providing "anchor" points – though these points are not static' (Nakano Glenn 2002: 14).

I want to expand on Nakano Glenn's notion of anchor point by suggesting that this notion may be helpful to theories of intersectionality in disability studies in two ways. First, it may be useful when addressing our own internal diversity as disabled people, or the internal diversity of the other categories attached to disabled people. It is crucial to address the needs of internal diversity in a nuanced way that is non-exclusionary. In the case of disabled people, this is even more paramount since disabled people experience a wide range of impairments and experiences that are, at times, very variable – yet, not devaluing any of our experiences remains fundamental. Furthermore, as many authors mention, disability studies has at times struggled to embrace its own internal diversity either in addressing who can be counted as disabled (Goodley 2004; Wendell 1996; Driedger and Owen 2008) or what sort of issues can be deemed relevant (Morris 1991; Crow 1996; Hughes 2004). Accepting everyone's experience as equally valid, while still being able to find a political commonality and a common articulation as an anchor point, is crucial. An anchor point can thus be perceived as a location from which to be temporarily rooted, in which to set a temporary anchor. This does not mean it is static but, indeed, that it invites fluidity and, above all, constant awareness of what is being excluded. The anchor point can certainly be easily adjusted and relocated. If we are to be able to keep fighting oppression and question ableism, it is therefore crucial that we are able to continually articulate the commonality of what unites us while acknowledging our own internal diversity.

Second, the notion of anchor point is helpful when one wishes to draw from intersectionality theories to conceptualize the role of different categories. For instance, if one wants to be aware of the place of class, race, gender and disability in a certain context, or in the life or a certain subject, one can think of all of these as temporary satellite anchor points that constantly travel and change their point of approximation. They may not all have the same weight or presence in different contexts – because in some contexts disability may be more present and in need of highlighting, while in others this might be true of gender or race or sexuality. But it remains important that one anchor point is not obliterated by another, such as what happened in the past with disabled women. Indeed, as recently as 2006, both Susan Wendell (2006) and Rosemarie Garland-Thomson (2006) were still calling our attention to the fact that mainstream feminisms do not recognize disability as one dimension of reality that is part of many women's lives. On the other hand, disability studies has only recently began to engage more fully with other social categories (race, sexuality, age, etc) that may interlace with disability. Yet the articulation of other categories with disability is also fundamental to address the complexities of all disabled people's lives.

Final words

In summary, I hope to have shown that a joint framework of feminism and disability has significantly enriched debates in disability studies and often helped to accommodate, even celebrate, internal diversity. The contributions of authors drawing from this joint framework, and the value of debates brought forth, should therefore be recognized and indeed be fully incorporated in disability studies and feminisms instead of being viewed as a localized perspective pertaining only to disabled women. Furthermore, I hope to have been able to illustrate the luscious heterogeneity that stems from authors inspired by both feminism and disability. As the field develops, one can clearly perceive an increasing diversity of locations and debates offered, as well as a growing number of publications. A good example of this is a collection edited by Diane Driedger focusing on the Canadian experience: *Living the Edges: A Disabled Women's Reader* (2010). Therefore, even though it remains sadly true that mainstream feminisms have not yet incorporated disability as a fundamental axis of presence in their writings, it is certain that it is their analysis that remains the poorer. Additionally, newcomers to the area, as well as newly curious, will not find a desert of absence. On the contrary, they will easily find a strong place of presence and belonging in the wide variety of writings that this interdisciplinary area has to offer.

Notes

1 I define ableism as a system of beliefs that privileges normate notions of the body/mind and ability that are culturally constructed and views disabled people as inferior and lacking. It focuses on how society artificially constructs notions of normalcy.
2 By 'mainstream feminisms' I mean those parts of feminist theory that are generally better known, widely taught, discussed, quoted and circulated. For example, while feminist disability studies is clearly *part of* feminisms, its contributions are not yet widely taught or known.

References

Asch, Adrienne and Fine, Michelle (1988) 'Introduction: Beyond Pedestals', in Michelle Fine and Adrienne Asch, eds, *Women with Disabilities: Essays in Psychology, Culture and Politics* (Philadelphia: Temple University Press): pp. 1–39.

Begum, Nasa (1992) 'Disabled Women and the Feminist Agenda', *Feminist Review*, 40 (spring): 70–84.

Brah, Avtar and Phoenix, Ann (2004) 'Ain't I a Woman? Revisiting Intersectionality', *Journal of International Women's Studies* 5(3): 75–86.

Collins, Patricia Hill (1990) *Black Feminist Thought: Knowledge, Consciousness, and the Politics of Empowerment* (Boston: Unwin Hyman).

Corker, Mairian (1999) 'New Disability Discourse, The Principle of Optimization and Social Change', in Mairian Corker and Sally French, *Disability Discourse* (Buckingham: Open University Pres): pp. 192–209.

Corker, Mairian and French, Sally (1999) 'Reclaiming Discourse in Disability Studies', in Mairian Corker and Sally French, *Disability Discourse* (Buckingham: Open University Press): pp. 1–11.

Crenshaw, Kimberlé Williams ([1989] 2003) 'Demarginalizing the Intersection of Race and Sex: A Black Feminist Critique of Antidiscrimination Doctrine, Feminist Theory, and Antiracist Politics', in Adrien Wing, ed., *Critical Race Feminism: A Reader* (New York: New York University Press): pp. 23–33.

Crow, Liz (1996) 'Including All of Our Lives: Renewing the Social Model of Disability', in Jenny Morris, ed., *Encounters with Strangers: Feminism and Disability* (London: The Women's Press).

Deegan, Mary Jo and Brooks, Nancy A., eds, (1985) *Women and Disability: The Double Handicap* (New Brunswick: Transaction Books).

Driedger, Diane (1989) *The Last Civil Rights Movement – Disabled People's International* (London: C. Hurst & Co).

Driedger, Diane, ed., (2010) *Living the Edges: A Disabled Women's Reader* (Toronto: Inanna Publications and Education, Inc).

Driedger, Diane and Gray, Susan, eds, (1992) *Imprinting Our Image, An International Anthology by Women with Disabilities* (Charlottetown: Gynergy Books).

Driedger, Diane and Owen, Michelle, eds, (2008) *Dissonant Disabilities: Women with Chronic Illnesses Explore Their Lives* (Toronto: Canadian Scholars' Press Inc./Women's Press).

Fine, Michelle and Asch, Adrienne (1985) 'Disabled Women: Sexism without the Pedestal', in Mary Jo Deegan and Nancy A. Brooks, eds, *Women and Disability: The Double Handicap* (New Brunswick: Transaction Books): pp. 6–23.

Fine, Michelle and Asch, Adrienne, eds, (1988) *Women with Disabilities: Essays in Psychology, Culture and Politics* (Philadelphia: Temple University Press).

French, Sally (1993) 'Disability, Impairment or Something in Between?', in John Swain, Vic Finkelstein, Sally French and Mike Oliver, eds, *Disabling Barriers – Enabling Environments* (London: Sage/Open University Press): pp. 17–25.

Garland-Thomson, Rosemarie (1997) *Extraordinary Bodies: Figuring Physical Disability in American Culture and Literature* (New York: Columbia University Press).

Garland-Thomson, Rosemarie (2005) 'Feminist Disability Studies', *Signs: Journal of Women in Culture and Society* 30(2): 1577–87.

Garland-Thomson, Rosemarie (2006) 'Integrating Disability, Transforming Feminist Theory', in Lennard J. Davis, ed., *The Disability Studies Reader*, 2nd edn (New York: Routledge): pp. 257–75.

Ghai, Anita (2002) 'Disability in the Indian Context: Post-colonial Perspectives', in Mairian Corker and Tom Shakespeare, eds, *Disability/Postmodernity: Embodying Disability Theory* (London: Continuum).

Ghai, Anita (2003) *(Dis)embodied Form: Issues of Disabled Women* (New Delhi: Har-Anand Publications).

Glenn, Evelyn Nakano (2002) *Unequal Freedom: How Race and Gender Shaped American Citizenship and Labor* (Harvard: Harvard University Press).

Goodley, Dan (2004) 'Who is Disabled? Exploring the Scope of the Social Model of Disability', in John Swain, Sally French, Colin Barnes and Carol Thomas, eds, *Disabling Barriers – Enabling Environments*, 2nd edn (London: Sage): pp. 118–25.

Hancock, Ange-Marie (2007) 'When Multiplication Doesn't Equal Quick Addition: Examining Intersectionality as a Research Paradigm', *Perspectives on Politics* 5(1): 63–79.

Hughes, Bill (2004) 'Disability and the Body', in John Swain, Sally French, Colin Barnes and Carol Thomas, eds, *Disabling Barriers – Enabling Environments*, 2nd edn (London: Sage): 63–9.

Kristiansen, Kristjana and Traustadóttir, Rannveig (2004) *Gender and Disability Research in the Nordic Countries* (Lund: Studentlitteratur).

McCall, Leslie (2005) 'The Complexity of Intersectionality', *Signs: Journal of Women in Culture and Society* 30(3): 1771–800.

Meekosha, Helen (1998) 'Body Battles: Bodies, Gender and Disability', in Tom Shakespeare, ed., *The Disability Reader: Social Science Perspectives* (London: Continuum): pp. 163–80.

Morris, Jenny (1989) *Able Lives, Women's Experiences of Paralysis* (London: The Women's Press).

Morris, Jenny (1991) *Pride Against Prejudice* (London: The Women's Press).

Morris, Jenny (1993) *Independent Lives, Community Care and Disabled People* (Basingstoke: Macmillan).

Morris, Jenny (1996) 'Introduction', in Jenny Morris, ed., *Encounters with Strangers: Feminism and Disability* (London: The Women's Press).

Oliver, Michael (1996) *Understanding Disability: From Theory to Practice* (Basingstoke: Palgrave).

Price, Janet and Shildrick, Margrit (1998) 'Uncertain Thoughts on the Dis/abled Body', in Margrit Shildrick and Janet Price, eds, *Vital Signs, Feminist Reconfigurations of the Bio/logical Body* (Edinburgh: Edinburgh University Press): pp. 224–50.

Price, Janet and Shildrick, Margrit (2002) 'Bodies Together: Touch, Ethics and Disability', in Mairian Corker and Tom Shakespeare, eds, *Disability/Postmodernity: Embodying Disability Theory* (London: Continuum): pp. 62–76.

Shildrick, Margrit (2009) *Dangerous Discourses of Disability, Subjectivity and Sexuality* (Basingstoke: Palgrave Macmillan).

Thomas, Carol (1999) *Female Forms: Experiencing and Understanding Disability* (Buckingham: Open University Press).

Thomas, Carol (2007) *Sociologies of Disability and Illness: Contested Ideas in Disability Studies and Medical Sociology* (Hampshire: Palgrave Macmillan).

Thomas, Carol (2010) 'Medical Sociology and Disability Theory', in Graham Scambler and Sasha Scambler, eds, *New Directions in the Sociology of Chronic and Disabling Conditions* (Hampshire: Palgrave Macmillan): pp. 37–57.

Wendell, Susan (1996) *The Rejected Body: Feminist Philosophical Reflections on Disability* (New York: Routledge).

Wendell, Susan (2001) 'Unhealthy Disabled: Treating Chronic Illnesses as Disabilities', *Hypatia* 16(4): 17–33.

Wendell, Susan (2006) 'Toward a Feminist Theory of Disability', in Leonard J. Davis, ed., *The Disability Studies Reader* (New York: Routledge): pp. 243–57.

Zola, Irving Kenneth (1983) *Socio-Medical Inquiries, Recollections, Reflections and Reconsiderations* (Philadelphia: Temple University Press).

28

RACE/ETHNICITY AND DISABILITY STUDIES

Towards an explicitly intersectional approach[1]

Deborah Stienstra

The late Chris Bell, disability studies scholar, challenged disability studies to be more consciously reflective (and reflexive) about race and ethnicity, and specifically its whiteness (Bell 2010). In this chapter, I take up his challenge and identify themes in the existing literature as well as the tools, including both storytelling and intersectional analysis, which may help this process of reflection.

Chris and I shared a space at the 2009 Canadian Disability Studies Association meetings. I spoke on the theme of 'Canadian multiculturalism and the space for disability culture'. He was the respondent. We were a mixed bag, each reflecting our lived and intellectual experiences. I am racialized white, perceived by many to be non-immigrant Canadian (although I am a first generation Dutch immigrant), a political scientist by training – with a strong feminist analysis – and someone who has come to thinking about race and ethnicity because of my commitments to intersectional analysis. I framed stories about inherent racism and ableism in Canadian immigration policies as a way of uncovering and disrupting the myths and narratives of Canadian multi-culturalism and inclusion. Chris was racialized black, an American, and well versed in narrative analysis. His response was eloquent and replete with probing questions and demanding insights. I was challenged to think and respond. In this chapter, I continue that conversation with Chris, despite his absence, and respond to his challenge to uncover and go beyond the whiteness of disability studies.

Where have we been on race/ethnicity and disability?

In 2002, for a Canadian government-sponsored seminar on intersections of diversity I developed a literature review on the intersection of certain identity markers, specifically race/ethnicity, heritage language and religion, with disability. At that time I argued:

> It could be appropriate to do an analysis of disability and these identity markers, including those within dominant racial/ethnic groups such as white, Anglo-Saxon Canadians with disabilities. Yet most of the literature on disability fails to be that self-conscious about race and ethnicity. For the most part, when we consider race and ethnicity we find research about those in subordinated or minority groups within society.
>
> *(Stienstra 2002: 5)*

Much of the literature that addresses both race/ethnicity and disability comes from the United States (US) and addresses the situations of African Americans with disabilities.

As well, I noted that the literature about race/ethnicity and disability mirrors the fault lines of disability research identified by Simi Linton (1998). 'The research is found almost exclusively in applied fields, especially rehabilitation, special education and social work. Much of the research isolates and seeks to treat the individual with impairments rather than addressing the broad context that creates disability' (Stienstra 2002: 3).

In terms of service provision to people with disabilities in minority cultural groups, the studies in my review are:

> primarily by professionals, including some organizations, who recognize the cultural diversity among their clients and want to address cultural differences appropriately. They suggest that there is an underutilization of services related to disability by those from racial/ethnic minority backgrounds as a result of communication barriers, (negative) perceptions about the causes of disability and the inaccessibility and incompatibility of the mainstream service system for these people.
>
> *(Stienstra 2002: 8–9)*

Two studies, one Canadian and one British, which adopted participatory research and the social model of disability, have also illustrated this fault line around service provision.

> [T]hey [the researchers] all seek to provide better services and better recognition of the particular concerns of ethno-racial people with disabilities ... by building links with the families in the context of their own communities, it is likely the services that are provided will be seen more as 'insider' services (or community-based services), rather than those provided by 'outsiders' to the community.
>
> *(Stienstra 2002: 10)*

From these findings, the literature review suggested several gaps and areas for future work.

> [R]esearch related to disability should focus on the social, political and economic contexts of how impairment changes into disability. Less attention should be paid to how to provide better 'culturally competent' services, and more paid to what causes the inequities that result in the need for differing services, or services at all.

> We also need to develop research that originates from the communities of those who experience the intersections between race/ethnicity/heritage languages/religion and disability. We need to use methods that allow their voices to be heard authentically, and develop research programs together with these communities in ways that will benefit them.

> For those who are studying majority communities, or are making broad statements about the lives of people with disabilities, we need to be more self-conscious about the generalizations we make about affected communities. Our research needs to reflect the limitations within which we gathered our data, and needs to be clear about the extent of commentary we can make with those limitations.

> Much more research is needed to develop our understanding of the different perspectives and inequalities people of colour with disabilities face, immigrants with disabilities face

and Aboriginal people with disabilities face. We know little about their experiences of racism as it intersects with their experiences of ableism. The intersections of race/ethnicity and disability, however, are not only found among ethno-racial people with disabilities, they also intersect for people who provide support or services.

So much research is needed that it is impossible to prioritize, except to return to the need for research to recognize the full participation of ethno-racial people with disabilities and their communities in the research process, from their vantage point, recognizing and valuing their expertise and addressing their benefit. This will create rich, credible and reliable research that speaks to the inequalities that shape the lives of ethno-racial people with disabilities.

(Stienstra 2002: 20–2)

While many of the fault lines still exist almost ten years later, there has been a growth in the number of qualitative and narrative accounts of the experiences of people with disabilities from minority ethno-racial backgrounds. Despite that increasing wealth, the reflexivity around whiteness that Chris Bell invited has yet to emerge. In the subsequent sections, I will briefly illustrate the fault lines and what they demonstrate. From there I will discuss how intersectional and narrative analyses provide tools to bring forward the stories and experiences of those rendered invisible. In doing so, as Parin Dossa suggests:

Persons from marginalized social locations bring into relief the fault lines of the system and suggest avenues for change. What they have to say both in the way of experiential knowledge and subsequent reflection – embedded in storytelling – is of value to the larger society … margins engage with the centre and in the process shift its pivotal points.

(Dossa 2009: 5)

Culture, disability and service provision

One of the continuing fault lines in the literature around race/ethnicity and disability is related to how culture and race/ethnicity are addressed in service delivery to people with disabilities. There continues to be significant literature in this area primarily found in special education, learning disabilities, mental health services and rehabilitation. Recent literature on racial/ethnic minority people with disabilities and service provision echoes earlier work calling for 'culturally competent service delivery'. While there is some modest recognition of the effect of the race/ethnicity of service providers as well as service recipients, most of the literature continues to address minority culture or race/ethnicity without reflecting on majority culture. As well, in this literature, disability is often presented as uncontested and embedded exclusively in people's bodies. In the quantitative data analysis, disability and impairment are presented as identical. Disability is rarely understood as an interaction between an individual's impairments and barriers in the environment, or included as a culture to be addressed through culturally competent services.

How does this theme emerge?

Attention to culture and disability in the context of service provision has come about largely because of identified gaps in the presence and effects of impairment and access to services between white and non-white people with disabilities, predominantly in the US.[2]

This significant literature identifies several themes, largely drawing from US quantitative data. There are racial disparities in disability framed in comparison to the situations of white or

Caucasian Americans,[3] including: more disability in the activities of daily living among African Americans and Spanish-speaking Hispanic Americans (Dunlop *et al.* 2007); earlier onset of disability among African Americans (Taylor 2008; Resnick and Allen 2006); a quicker decline in functioning (Thorpe *et al.* 2009); poorer adaptation to impairments in African American elders (McKinzie *et al.* 2007); and later or no diagnosis among African American and Hispanic children (Mandell *et al.* 2009). Some racial gaps in disability are attributed to access to health care in the US as well as socio-economic status (Taylor 2008; Fuller-Thomson *et al.* 2009) and as such begin to shift the focus from race/ethnicity as physical or biological characteristics to the social and economic inequalities that can create disadvantage.

Racial disparities also exist among those people with disabilities accessing services, including vocational rehabilitation (Arang-Lasprilla *et al.* 2009; Cavenaugh *et al.* 2006) and mental health services (Omar *et al.* 2009), with some evidence that these differences are also linked to socio-economic status (Fulda *et al.* 2009; Dunlop *et al.* 2007). In research related to American Indian (Aboriginal or indigenous) populations, Mays *et al.* suggest: 'Racial/ethnic minority disparities in mental health can emerge from a lack of culture-specific and in-depth understanding of the issues involved in the constellation of precipitating causes, appropriate diagnostics, and culturally appropriate treatment and intervention' (2009: 77). In the United Kingdom people from some black and minority ethnic groups are three times more likely than average to be admitted as mental health patients (Allen 2008) and there are significantly lower rates of service utilization among South Asian children with intellectual disability compared with white British children with intellectual disabilities (Dura-Vila and Hodes 2009). Racial disparities are evident in the rates of employment for people with disabilities, with lower rates among racial minorities in the US (Krause *et al.* 2009; Hasnain and Balcazar 2009).

In the US, there are disproportionately more people with disabilities from minority cultures than majority cultures in special education (Powell 2010; Blanchett 2009; Beratan 2008; Harry and Klingner 2006). Artiles *et al.* (2010: 279–80) suggest 'students from historically underserved groups are and have been disproportionately placed in special education. We use the terms historically underserved groups to describe "students from diverse racial, cultural, linguistic and economically disadvantaged backgrounds who have experienced sustained school failure over time".' Oesterreich and Knight (2008) argue that this over-representation in special education has implications for the possibility and success of these students in college education. Blanchett *et al.* (2009) indicate that African-American students who have been identified as having a developmental disability face a complex set of barriers to equitable education, including:

> institutionalized racism, White privilege, and an increased risk for being identified as having developmental disabilities not because being African American or of color results in a disability but instead due to being more likely to live in poverty, receive inadequate prenatal care, and have limited access to early intervention services.
>
> *(2009: 392)*

Much of the research on racial disparities and disability also suggests that programmes specific to language or cultural groups may lower racial/ethnic disparities (Arang-Lasprilla *et al.* 2009; Krause *et al.* 2009; Allen 2008; Dunlop *et al.* 2007; Cavenaugh *et al.* 2006). It is not surprising from this analysis of the gaps that the solution is to provide more culturally relevant and sensitive services, rather than to address the reasons for the inequalities.

Culturally sensitive or competent service provision

To address the gap in services for people with disabilities from minority racial/ethnic backgrounds, as well as service provision for minority populations without disabilities, many service providers refer to culturally sensitive or culturally competent services.

> Cultural sensitivity is knowing that cultural differences and similarities exist, without value judgment. Cultural competence refers to the ability to work effectively with individuals from different cultural and ethnic backgrounds, or in settings where several cultures co-exist. It includes the ability to understand the language, culture and behaviours of other individuals and groups, and to make appropriate recommendations.
>
> *(Raghavan 2009: 17)*

Others echo the importance of culturally competent services that can address many of the barriers faced by people with disabilities from minority backgrounds.

> [C]ulturally and linguistically responsive services are those services that recognize, value, and infuse individuals of color with developmental disabilities' ethnic, cultural, and linguistic knowledge to inform pedagogical and service delivery practices and to employ that knowledge to design instructional strategies, communication strategies, assessment tools, and service delivery models. Service providers who provide culturally and linguistically relevant services acknowledge that the American special education system is grounded in American macrocultural values concerning communication and language, and as such, it disproportionately favors parents for whom English is their first language and those who speak and comprehend the 'official' language.
>
> *(Blanchett et al. 2009: 403)*

Some suggest that without a cultural immersion, providing culturally competent services is impossible. Reflexivity and cultural awareness can lead people to engage in cultural humility, that is, 'having a lifelong commitment to self-evaluation and self-critique in the service of redressing power imbalances' (Mays *et al.* 2009: 79).

Others critique culturally competent service approaches for their lack of attention to the cultural or identity elements of disability in addition to race/ethnicity. For example, Lightfoot and Williams (2009a) suggest that in domestic violence programmes cultural competence was required in terms of race and ethnicity, but 'that the notion of cultural competency rarely was expanded to include disability. ... Another strong theme was that cultural competence in domestic violence service providers rarely extended to include disability or Deaf culture' (2009a: 147–8). Mpofu and Harley (2006) suggest people of colour with disabilities have unique career counselling needs because they have identities both as people of colour and people with disabilities.

Finally, a small part of the literature in this area is beginning to recognize that the significance of race/ethnicity and culture is not simply for service recipients and those in minority populations, but that it shapes everyone, including majority culture service providers and their organizations. Raghavan eloquently makes the case that all humans have ethnic identities:

> our ethnic identity plays an important role in terms of our beliefs, attitudes and behaviours. All human beings have an ethnic identity, but often when we talk about ethnicity or cultural diversity we do not think of our own ethnicity but tend to think about people with different skin colours, cultures or religions to our own.
>
> *(2009: 14)*

The implications of this insight for majority culture service providers are identified by Whitfield *et al.* who suggest that: 'Rehabilitation professionals should be aware of the ethnicities of the communities that they serve and how the ethnicities of the office in which they work may interact with the ethnicities in the community' (2010: 102–3).

Much of the current literature reflects the fault lines that identify racial disparities among disabled people largely in terms of minority cultures and calls for creating culturally sensitive and competent services that value these differences and provide services for different groups. A small portion of the literature reflects upon the inequalities that exist outside of race/ethnicity including poverty, access to health care and socio-economic status.

Multiple and intersecting identities result in multiple and intersecting oppressions

Over the past decade, there has been an increasing number of articles and books published drawing from the experiences of people with disabilities from minority racial/ethnic groups. Most use qualitative research methods, some draw on narrative analysis and storytelling. In general what they suggest is that the multiple and intersecting identities of minority race/ethnicity and disability (among others) create situations of disadvantage, marginalization and oppression that differ from the experiences of those who are disabled, or who are racial minorities. For many, these are experiences of being rendered invisible, being made – or made to feel – an outsider, and being constrained or restrained as a result of their multiple identities. The words used to describe these experiences are powerful and tell the stories of people with disabilities from minority racial/ethnic groups in ways that illustrate the multiple and intersecting oppressions they experience.

Intersectionality

One of the common features of this literature is an increasing commitment to the practice of intersectionality, that is, identifying, understanding and explaining the ways in which multiple identities or experiences combine to create unique barriers. 'Intersectional discrimination means people are discriminated against in qualitatively different ways as a consequence of the combination of their individual characteristics' (Cramer and Plummer 2009: 164).

This means, for example, that the explanations provided by considering disability are not sufficient for understanding the situations of women immigrants with disabilities. We also need to consider immigration status, gender, culture and religion, and the ways in which they may reinforce experiences of marginalization or exclusion, as well as challenges to the status quo. Parin Dossa provided rich stories of intersections in some women's lives. 'My work aims to show that race and gender matter and that these social markers of difference cannot be dismissed under the seemingly neutral category of disability, the reference point for which is young white males' (Dossa 2009: 5).

Multiple possible intersections emerge when we begin to use this approach, including the unique barriers for older persons with disabilities (including older immigrants with disabilities), the increased presence of poverty of women with disabilities, the higher unemployment and underemployment rate for persons of colour with disabilities, the benefits of culturally specific services for parents of children with disabilities, the lack of services for Aboriginal children with disabilities in First Nations communities and the jurisdictional barriers for Aboriginal people with disabilities living in urban areas (Lo 2010; Cramer and Plummer 2009; Hirji-Khalfan 2009; Shackel 2008).

Krissy's stories as an African American woman labelled as having learning disabilities illustrate the challenges that multiple and, at times conflicting, identities can present.

> Many of us are fragmented selves, individuals who chose at one time or another to assume a different role or identity. In Krissy's case her choices were limited. Many multiple identities had been imposed upon her, notably not one of which most people would choose for themselves. In coming to know and understand Krissy it occurred to me that she had little choice but to negotiate these conflicting identities. Like a chameleon, she accentuated one identity while downplaying or denying another. It was how she survived. In doing so she was unable to fully express herself as an embodied human being.
>
> *(Petersen 2006: 730)*

The barriers that Krissy encountered, as well as those identified when we use intersectional analysis, illustrate some common and significant barriers faced when people live with both disability and as part of a minority race/ethnic group. These include being invisible or an outsider as well as being restrained and constrained.

Outsider and invisible

The intersections of race/ethnicity and disability often lead people to feel like they are outsiders to the mainstream society. For some, this includes a perception that they do not measure up to a standard.

> One of the first stories she [Krissy] told me was that of being a transplant. 'A what?' I asked, immediately needing clarification. 'You know a transplant,' Krissy said, 'I would have gone to East High School, but my mom open enrolled me to the [university] lab school instead. She thought I could get a better education there. You know, she wanted me to have a better life than she had'. … Later on she told me 'You know, we were below middle class, like almost there, but not quite'. I wondered if the words middle class might be substituted with 'white', 'men' or 'able bodied'. I began to understand what Krissy meant by transplant. In so many words, Krissy expressed feeling like an outsider, someone who was not quite good enough or was perceived as not measuring up.
>
> *(Petersen 2006: 724)*

For others, that experience of outsider renders them invisible or rejected. Parin Dossa suggests that:

> The immigrant racialized woman is constructed as an outsider; add disability to this construct, and she is rendered socially invisible. If she is identified, she is 'designated by the term "problem"; and she lives beneath the shadow of that problem which envelops and obscures her'. It must be noted that able-bodied racialized women are desirable for their labour, whereas women who have disabilities – deemed to be neither waged workers nor homemakers (unpaid workers) – are constructed as a social burden. They are construed as recipients, rather than givers, of care.
>
> *(Dossa 2009: 24)*

For people with disabilities who want to immigrate to Canada and other places, their status as disabled renders them ineligible to do so (Capurri 2010), and refugee women with disabilities are not wanted.

Able-bodied refugee women may be granted asylum with the expectation that they will take up dead-end and poorly paid jobs. A disabled body, erroneously assumed to be unfit for waged work, is not wanted. Constructing racialized people who have disabilities as the Other of the Other, Canadian immigration policy bars the entry of applicants with disabilities, the significance of which cannot be overstated. Racialized women who have disabilities are not part of the multicultural and gendered landscape of Canadian society. Finding themselves isolated and unwanted, they are left to their own devices to negotiate the realities of their lives in their new homeland.

(Dossa 2009: 34)

The experiences of feeling like an outsider may also turn into experiences of being disenfranchised and discarded. Stories of 13 lawful residents or citizens of Australia who had been wrongly detained as a result of the intersections of race and disability illustrate how being made an outsider happened. 'Racism (in the initial formation of suspicion) and disability discrimination (in the maintenance of suspicion and silencing of disabled voices) were critical aspects of all these cases, aspects so far not adequately investigated' (Soldatic and Fiske 2009: 293). The authors tell stories including that of Vivian Alvarez.

Vivian Alvarez was an Australian citizen who had a mental illness and additionally sustained a head injury and memory loss, probably in an accident shortly before being found in a park at midnight. She was taken to Lismore Hospital, New South Wales on 30 March 2001 and was later transferred to a psychiatric clinic, where a social worker called the Immigration Department and said she suspected Vivian was an 'illegal immigrant'. Immigration officers interviewed her on 3 May 2001 and assumed she had been trafficked into Australia as a sex worker. They did not complete comprehensive database searches for her name and instead began deportation pro-ceedings. Vivian stated on a number of occasions that she was an Australian citizen, that she held an Australian passport and gave her correct name and date of birth, however, immigration officers persisted in their opinion that she was an unlawful non-citizen without conducting adequate searches based on information she gave and on 20 July 2001 Vivian was deported to the Philippines … Vivian had a mental illness and was from a non-English speaking background. Additionally, Vivian was Filipina, an ethnic group stereotypically associated in Australia with mail order brides and sex workers.

(Soldatic and Fiske 2009: 291)

In the stories of the 13 lawful residents or citizens of Australia and Vivian, it is the intersection of disability and minority race/ethnicity that can create experiences of being an outsider, invisibility, or being set outside the protections and rights that non-disabled, majority culture citizens access and expect.

Contained and restrained

An intersectional analysis of disability and race/ethnicity also illustrates the ways in which social restraint and containment are used as vehicles to manage the people who experience these intersections. In an innovative project with participant researchers narrating their experiences of the intersections of disability, race and class in special education, Connor (2009) suggests that the intersection of these identities led to experiences of restraint or containment.

Comments from participant researchers reveal experiences and understandings of having their movements literally inhibited in terms of disability (segregated classes, IEP diplomas), race (workplaces, public places, school locations), and class (opportunities for further education, job expectations, neighbourhoods to live in). Thus, the feeling of limitations imposed upon these individuals is exacerbated by negotiating all three discourses that indicate very real forms of social restraint. Furthermore, these restraints are often not seen, felt, or understood by those without the same marker(s) of identity.

(2009: 465)

For Michael, restraint was the extension or outcome of being labelled an outsider.

As a student labeled LD [learning disabled], he is stigmatized and ostracized by peers. Unlike race and class, LD does not trigger 'pride,' but rather shame. Stereotypic mainstream expectations of Michael position him as lazy and/or 'unable' because of misperceptions of LD and long held assumptions of racial inferiority. His fate is 'sealed' in special education because his working-class mother, while to some extent a class-straddler is still unable to 'take on' the intricacies of special education bureaucracy. Unlike middle-class students, Michael does not have a sense of entitlement to attend college; he knows he has to work extra hard to transcend the expectations placed upon him. At the less valued side of three binaries, Michael understands the sense of restraint placed upon him as a black, 'disabled' learner, from a working-class background.

(Connor 2006: 163)

Dossa tells the story of how the complexities of race, gender, disability and immigration status intertwined in Mehrun's life to force her to live, constrained, in two different ways – first being constrained not to eat or drink as required and, as a 'solution', removal to a hospital for more than a year even though she wasn't ill.

While her mother went to work her father took care of her but there was one problem: Mehrun could not go to the bathroom.

'My father would have taken me to the bathroom but I felt uncomfortable. Before my Mum went to work she took me to the bathroom and again when she came home in the evening. I had to be careful with what I ate or drank in the day. I could hardly eat or drink.'

Social marginalization translates into deprivation of basic human needs which in this case amounted to coerced starvation for close to a year because there was no female available to assist Mehrun with personal hygiene.

The social worker placed Mehrun in a hospital so that her father could undertake waged work. In Mehrun's words: 'The social worker said: "he cannot stay at home for ever. He needs to work." Taking care of his daughter was not considered work. ... In the hospital Mehrun was compelled to live with a disability identity, reinforced by the fact that she was among people with different kinds of disabilities. She was looked upon as a woman with polio. Her gender and race were relegated to the background because her disabled body became the focus of attention. Her one- and-a-half-year stay at the hospital was humiliating as Mehrun was not sick.

(Dossa 2005: 2530)

These are very sharp examples of the daily, lived experiences of the intersections of race/ethnicity and disability, experiences in which solutions to the 'problems' these people posed were to contain and restrain them in ways that are often considered appropriate by broader society. But the insights from this research also illustrate how people with these multiple and intersecting identities recreate their worlds by claiming their citizenship rights and access to programmes and services and by using their stories to give meaning to these experiences and share them with a wider audience.

Responding to multiple, intersecting oppressions

Despite assumptions of many, those who experience the intersections of disability and minority race/culture are not simply victims of injustice and oppressions, even though these experiences shape their lives. Using their stories and experiences, they also have challenged the structural, cultural and individual perceptions and actions that render them invisible, outsiders, restrained and constrained.

Claiming citizenship rights

As the mother of two children with disabilities and a racialized Muslim immigrant woman, Tamiza challenged the discourses that might render her and her children invisible, outsiders or constrained. She recognized that 'as a citizen and as a taxpayer' she was entitled to services like everyone else.

> She recognizes that some good programs are in place but that people do not know of their existence. She stated that she was able to secure services in bits and pieces of information gathered from the people she interacted with on a daily basis or through chance encounters, such as a conversation with another mother while waiting to see a doctor. Once she learnt about the services, she noted that it was not easy to secure them. 'There were papers to be filled and you had to prove that you were entitled to the services. They asked for medical reports.' Tamiza felt that as a minority it was more difficult for her 'as you do not know the system as well as they [mainstream people] do.' Yet, she noted that because she had family support she had the time to inquire 'what is out there.' Her fluency in English helped her to secure services though she emphasized that it was an uphill battle. ... Her experiences of raising two children convinced her that she was entitled to services. She believed that 'as a citizen and as a taxpayer,' it was her right to access and use the social provision that her children needed to live like everyone else. Tamiza then advocated for their/her rights as well as those of the others.
>
> *(Dossa 2008: 94)*

The discourse of claiming the rights of citizenship and the responsibilities as taxpayers is also used by the Council of Canadians with Disabilities (CCD), the national Canadian advocacy organization of people with disabilities. Marie White, former chair of CCD, argued that people with disabilities in Canada want to be taxpayers, which is one of the recognized ways of contributing to Canada as nation-builders, and thus have greater legitimacy in contributing to discussions on how those tax funds are spent.

> People with disabilities don't want to be sitting on the sidelines of life due to barriers in our community. The National Action Plan on Disability shares some steps on how Canada's federal, provincial and territorial governments can assist Canadians with disabilities to exercise their rights and responsibilities.
>
> *(Council of Canadians with Disabilities 2008)*

People who experience the intersections of minority race/ethnicity and disability also recognize they are citizens with rights. Their experiences of exclusion and barriers make it difficult to claim those rights, and they receive little support through advocacy organizations of people with disabilities since issues about minority race/ethnicity remain at the edges of the overall priorities of these organizations. Not only do they have to advocate for their own situations and rights as individual citizens, but frequently disability advocacy organizations remain firmly entrenched in the disability discourse and an unstated majority culture view.[4]

Some have recognized this lack of responsiveness by disability advocacy organizations to issues of minority race/ethnicity by creating organizations that explicitly work on issues that emerge for those experiencing these intersections. In Canada, the Ethno Racial People with Disabilities Coalition of Ontario (ERDCO)[5] is an unusual and very active example of those who bring attention, support and resources about both culture and disability.

People with disabilities from minority race/ethnicity groups in collaboration with researchers are also using storytelling and narrative as a way to share experiences of these intersections and recreate the world in ways that include them.

Remaking the centre through storytelling and narrative

Throughout this chapter, stories from Krissy, Vivian, Michael, Tamiza and Mehrun have told us about how they experienced these intersections. In foregrounding their experiences, names and narratives we learn several lessons. First, stories alert us to what those who experience the intersections identify as important in these experiences (although clearly mediated through the researcher/author). By bringing the stories forward, we set them out as valuable, important and worthy of attention (Connor 2006: 155). Stories also give those who tell the story a chance to make meaning from their experiences, even if they are painful, and to share them with others and receive a response (Dossa 2006: 353).

Part of the act of storytelling is also the making of social change, of recreating the world, with the stories of individuals who have been excluded, marginalized and constrained included.

> [S]tories/narratives have the potential to effect social change, provided they form part of the larger political, social, historical, cultural and literary landscapes of societies. Racialized women with disabilities are not part of the Canadian landscape. Their structural and social exclusion are intense. Yet their stories must be heard if we want to write a different kind of Canadian history: a history where women with different abilities and from different cultural backgrounds have an active presence.
>
> *(Dossa 2008: 91)*

Researchers have a responsibility to ensure that these stories are valued and gathered and told in ways that are culturally respectful, recognizing the potential the stories have to bring about social change. This requires research methods that are culturally appropriate, including reflecting upon majority cultural values that find their way into dominant research practices and values. In Canada, the academic funding agencies have recognized some of the 'whiteness' of research ethics in their inclusion of particular ethics practices required for working in and with Aboriginal communities.[6]

While telling the stories of people who have been excluded and marginalized as a result of disability and minority race/ethnicity is a critical step forward in a more inclusive and authentic account of the world, it is not enough. As Chris Bell reminded us, part of reflecting on race/ethnicity and disability is also recognizing the often-unstated experiences, privileges and perspectives that arise from majority race/ethnicity and disability experiences. It is talking about how white privilege and use of English has shaped the culture and practices of schools, income security, and health and social services; how racial disparities in the presence of impairments and the use of services also tell us about the situations of those from majority cultures; and that when we speak of the barriers faced by people with disabilities we are really speaking of those from minority and majority race/ethnicity backgrounds and should provide those experiences in common and those that vary as a result of intersections.

Notes

1 My deep thanks go to Natalie Brewer for her assistance with this work.
2 This comment must be qualified as evident in the English literature that primarily reflects upon US, Canadian, British and Australian data. I did not review literature in languages other than English.
3 Disability in this section is being used as it is used in the literature, as impairment.
4 The exclusionary Canadian immigration policy has come under attack regularly from the Council of Canadians with Disabilities for its exclusion of people with disabilities, but the Council provides little analysis of the racialized intersections of these exclusions.
5 For more information, see http://www.erdco.ca (accessed 10 September 2011).
6 These are included in the second edition of the *Tri-Council Policy Statement: Ethical Conduct for Research Involving Humans*, Chapter 9; available online at http://www.pre.ethics.gc.ca/eng/policy-politique/initiatives/tcps 2-eptc2/Default/ (accessed 10 September 2011).

Bibliography

Allen, Daniel (2008) 'Count Me In or Count Me Out?', *Mental Health Practice* 11(5): 6.

Arang-Lasprilla, Juan Carlos, Ketchum, Jessica M., Stevens, Lillians Flores, Balcazar, Fabricio, Wehman, Paul, Forster, Lauren and Hsu, Nancy (2009) 'Ethnicity/Racial Differences in Employment Outcomes Following Spinal Cord Injury', *NeuroRehabilitation* 24: 37–46.

Artiles, Alfredo J., Kozleski, Elizabeth B., Trent, Stanley C., Osher, David and Ortiz, Alba (2010) 'Justifying and Explaining Disproportionality, 1968–2008: A Critique of Underlying Views of Culture', *Exceptional Children* 76(3): 279–99.

Bell, Chris (2010) 'Is Disability Studies Actually White Disability Studies?', in Lennard J. Davis, ed., *The Disability Studies Reader*, 3rd edn (Routledge).

Beratan, Gregg D. (2008) 'The Song Remains the Same: Transposition and the Disproportionate Representation of Minority Students in Special Education', *Race Ethnicity and Education* 11(4): 337–54.

Blanchett, Wanda J. (2009) 'A Retrospective Examination of Urban Education from *Brown* to the Resegregation of African Americans in Special Education – It is Time to "Go for Broke"', *Urban Education* 44(4): pp. 370–88.

Blanchett, Wanda J., Klingner, Janette K. and Harry, Beth (2009) 'The Intersection of Race, Culture, Language, and Disability: Implications for Urban Education', *Urban Education* 44(4): 389–409.

Capurri, Valentina (2010) '*Canadian Public Discourse around Issues of Inadmissibility for Potential Immigrants with Diseases and Disabilities, 1902–2002*'. *PhD dissertation* (York: York University, Department of History).

Cavenaugh, Brenda S., Giesen, Martin and Steinman, Bernard A. (2006) 'Contextual Effects of Race or Ethnicity on Acceptance for Vocational Rehabilitation of Consumers Who are Legally Blind', *Journal of Visual Impairment & Blindness*, July: 425–36.

Connor, David J. (2006) 'Michael's Story: "I Get into so Much Trouble Just by Walking": Narrative Knowing and Life at the Intersections of Learning Disability, Race, and Class', *Equity & Excellence in Education* 39(2): 154–65.

Connor, David J. (2009) 'Breaking Containment – The Power of Narrative Knowing: Countering Silences within Traditional Special Education Research', *International Journal of Inclusive Education* 13(5): 449–70.

Council of Canadians with Disabilities (CCD) (2008) 'Waiting to Be Tax Payers', 18 September; available online at http://www.ccdonline.ca/en/socialpolicy/elections/2008/091808 (accessed 6 October 2011).

Cramer, Elizabeth P. and Plummer, Sara-Beth (2009) 'People of Color with Disabilities: Intersectionality as a Framework for Analyzing Intimate Partner Violence in Social, Historical, and Political Contexts', *Journal of Aggression, Maltreatment & Trauma* 18(2): 162–81.

Dossa, Parin (2005) 'Racialized Bodies, Disabling Worlds: "They [Service Providers] Always Saw Me as a Client, Not as a Worker"', *Social Science and Medicine* 60: 2527–36.

Dossa, Parin (2006) 'Disability, Marginality and the Nation-State – Negotiating Social Markers of Difference: Fahimeh's Story', *Disability & Society* 21(4): 354–58.

Dossa, Parin (2008) 'Creating Alternative and Demedicalized Spaces: Testimonial Narrative on Disability, Culture, and Racialization', *Journal of International Women's Studies* 9(3):79–98.

Dossa, Parin (2009) *Racialized Bodies, Disabling Worlds: Storied Lives of Immigrant Muslim Women* (Toronto: University of Toronto Press).

Dunlop, Dorothy D., Song, Jing, Manheim, Larry M., Daviglus, Martha L. and Chang, Rowland W. (2007) 'Racial/Ethnic Differences in the Development of Disability Among Older Adults', *American Journal of Public Health* 97(12): 2209–15.

Dura-Vila, G. and Hodes, M. (2009) 'Ethnic Variation in Service Utilisation Among Children with Intellectual Disability', *Journal of Intellectual Disability Research* 53(II): 939–48.

Fulda, Kimberly G., Lykens, Kristine, Bae, Sejong and Singh, Karan (2009) 'Factors for Accessing a Medical Home Vary Among CSHCN from Different Levels of Socioeconomic Status', *Maternal and Child Health Journal* 13: 445–56.

Fuller-Thomson, Esme, Nuru-Jeter, A., Minkler, Meredith and Guralnik, Jack M. (2009) 'Black White Disparities in Disability Among Older Americans: Further Untangling the Role of Race and Socioeconomic Status', *Journal of Aging and Health* 21(5): 677–98.

Harry, B. and Klingner, J. (2006) *Why are So Many Minority Students in Special Education? Understanding Race and Disability in Schools* (New York: Teachers College Press).

Hasnain, Rooshey and Balcazar, Fabricio (2009) 'Predicting Community- Versus Facility-based Employment for Transition-aged Young Adults with Disabilities: The Role of Race, Ethnicity, and Support Systems', *Journal of Vocational Rehabilitation* 31: 175–88.

Hirji-Khalfan, Raihanna (2009) 'Federal Supports for Aboriginal People with Disabilities', *Critical Disability Discourse/Discours Critique dans le Champ du Handicap* vol. 1; available online at http://pi.library.yorku.ca/ojs/index.php/cdd/issue/view/1440 (accessed 6 October 2011).

Islam, Zoebia (2008) 'Negotiating Identities: The Lives of Pakistani and Bangladeshi Young Disabled People', *Disability & Society* 23(1): 41–52.

Krause, James S., Saunders, Lee and Staten, David (2009) 'Race-Ethnicity, Education, and Employment After Spinal Cord Injury', *Rehabilitation Counselling Bulletin* 53: 78–86.

Lightfoot, Elizabeth and Williams, Oliver (2009a) 'The Intersection of Disability, Diversity, and Domestic Violence: Results of National Focus Groups', *Journal of Aggression, Maltreatment & Trauma* 18(2): 133–52.

Lightfoot, Elizabeth and Williams, Oliver (2009b) 'Domestic Violence and People of Color with Disabilities: An Overview', *Journal of Aggression, Maltreatment & Trauma* 18(2): 129–32.

Linton, Simi (1998) *Claiming Disability: Knowledge and Identity* (New York: New York University Press).

Lo, Lusa (2010) 'Perceived Benefits Experienced in Support Groups for Chinese Families of Children with Disabilities', *Early Child Development and Care* 180(3): 405–15.

McKinzie, Charla A., Reinhardt, Joann P. and Benn, Dolores (2007) 'Adaptation to Chronic Vision Impairment: Does African American or Caucasian Race Make a Difference?', *Research on Aging* 29(2): 144–62.

Mandell, David S., Wiggins, L. D., Carpenter, L. A., Daniels, J., DiGuiseppi, C., Durkin, M. S., Giarellia, E., Morrier, M. J., Nicholas, J. S., Pinto-Martin, J. A., Shattuck, P. T., Thomas, K. C., Yeargin-Allsopp, M. and Kirby, R. S. (2009) 'Racial/Ethnic Disparities in the Identification of Children with Autism Spectrum Disorders', *American Journal of Public Health* 99(3): 493–8.

Mays, Vickie M., Gallardo, Miguel, Shorter-Gooden, Kumea, Robinson-Zanartu, Carol, Smith, Monique, McClure, Faith, Ruri, Siddarth, Methot, Laural and Ahhaity, Glenda (2009) 'Expanding the Circle: Decreasing American Indian Mental Health Disparities Through Culturally Competent Teaching About American Indian Mental Health', *American Indian Culture and Research Journal* 33(3): 61–83.

Mpofu, Elias and Harley, Debra A. (2006) 'Racial and Disability Identity: Implications for the Career Counseling of African Americans with Disabilities', *Rehabilitation Counseling Bulletin* 50(1): 14–23.

Oesterreich, Heather A. and Knight, Michelle G. (2008) 'Facilitating Transitions to College for Students with Disabilities from Culturally and Linguistically Diverse Backgrounds', *Intervention in School and Clinic* 43(5): 300–4.

Omar, Gudino G., Lau, Anna S., Yeh, May, McCabe, Kristen M. and Hough, Richard L. (2009) 'Understanding Racial/Ethnic Disparities in Youth Mental Health Services: Do Disparities Vary by Problem Type?', *Journal of Emotional and Behavioral Disorders* 17(1): 3–16.

Ostrander, R. Noam (2008) When Identities Collide: Masculinity, Disability and Race, *Disability & Society* 23(6): 585–97.

Petersen, Amy (2006) 'An African-American Woman with Disabilities: The Intersection of Gender, Race and Disability', *Disability & Society* 21(7): 721–34.

Powell, Justin J. W. (2010) 'Change in Disability Classification: Redrawing Categorical Boundaries in Special Education in the United States and Germany, 1920–2005', *Comparative Sociology* 9(2): 241–67.

Raghavan, Raghu (2009) 'Improving Access to Services for Minority Ethnic Communities', *Learning Disability Practice* 12(7): 14–18.

Resnik, Linda and Allen, Susan (2006) 'Racial and Ethnic Differences in Use of Assistive Devices for Mobility: Effect Modification by Age', *Journal of Aging and Health* 18(1): 106–24.

Shackel, D. W. (2008) 'The Experiences of First Nations People with Disabilities and Their Families in Receiving Services and Supports in First Nations Communities in Manitoba'. MA thesis, University of Manitoba.

Soldatic, K. and Fiske, L. (2009) 'Bodies "Locked Up": Intersections of Disability and Race in Australian Immigration', *Disability & Society* 24(3): 289–301.

Stienstra, Deborah (2002) 'The Intersection of Disability and Race/Ethnicity/Heritage Languages/ Religion'. Presented to the Intersections of Diversity seminar, Ottawa, 8 March 8; available online at http://canada.metropolis.net/events/Diversity/litreview_Index_e.htm (accessed 6 October 2011).

Taylor, Miles G. (2008) 'Timing, Accumulation, and the Black/White Disability Gap in Later Life: A Test of Weathering', *Research on Aging* 30(2): 226–50.

Thorpe Jr., Roland J., Weiss, Carlos, Xue, Quan-Li and Fried, Linda (2009) 'Transitions Among Disability Levels or Death in African American and White Older Women', *Journal of Gerontology: Medical Sciences* 64(6): 670–4.

Whitfield, Harold W., Venable, R. and Broussard, S. (2010) 'Are Client Counselor Ethnic/Racial Matches Associated with Successful Rehabilitation Outcomes?', *Rehabilitation Counseling Bulletin* 53(2): 96–105.

29

MOTHERING AND DISABILITY

Implications for theory and practice

Claudia Malacrida

Mothers with disabilities are inadequately researched; they are also notoriously underserved by policies relating to families and parenthood. Further, this lack of information about and accommodation for the experiences and needs of mothers with disabilities is often at the root of the challenges faced by disabled women in having, raising and maintaining custody of their children. The dearth of information, policy and services relating to disabled mothering is firmly embedded in historical and enduring ideas about disability and the right to reproduce and rear children. Indeed, it is not unreasonable to speculate that this elision operates as a covert yet consistent extension of the history of disability in general and eugenics in particular. In this chapter, I begin with a brief discussion concerning disability and attitudes regarding the 'appropriateness' of parenting with a disability. This is followed by a consideration of gender specificity in mothering a child with disabilities. I then move on to give an overview of some intersections between current policies and services and the experiences of mothers with disabilities in the West. I conclude with some suggestions for researching and theorizing mothering and disability, arguing specifically for a feminist and poststructural approach to understanding the barriers and possibilities in policies and practices relating to mothering with a disability.

The underlying issues – eugenics, disability and mothering

In Western Europe and North America up until the late nineteenth and early twentieth century, it was common for people with disabilities to live at home and remain in their communities. Nevertheless, they were rarely encouraged to marry and have families. Instead, people with mental, physical, sensory and intellectual disabilities were often hidden from the public eye and kept in social isolation, fostering and reflecting a common understanding of people with disabilities as dependent and incapable of filling adult roles of intimacy, sexuality and parenthood (Rafter 1997; James W. Trent 1994). In the early years of the twentieth century, a progressivist belief in the power of education and medicine to cure social ills led to the rise of small schools and residential centres for people with intellectual, physical, mental health and sensory disabilities. Originally, at least some of these institutions were premised on an expectation of 'improvement' of the residents and the hope of community reintegration and full citizenship. However, when it became apparent that not all institutionalized people would be easily rehabilitated, and when the helping professionals involved began to build their own empires based on constructing disabled people as requiring continuing care, these small, short-stay training centres soon burgeoned into a system of large, long-term institutions (Albrecht 1993; Johnson 2003; James W. Trent 1994). The institutional system operated as a form of passive eugenics, often sequestering people for their entire lives as a way of ensuring that they would not 'pollute' their societies with 'tainted' offspring. The institutions also operated in more active eugenic ways. In Canada and the United States, some were the sites of regulatory bodies that either funnelled their residents into the eugenic system or in some cases even performed sterilizations in-house on inmates, in the hope of improving the stock of the general population; others offered 'voluntary' sterilization as a condition of discharge or as a means of avoiding internment (Radford 1994; Ramsay 2000; Schoen 2001; James W. Trent 1993). Eugenics, of course, targeted people with disabilities outside of the institutional system as well, and in their communities, women with disabilities were disproportionately victims of involuntary or coerced sterilizations (Grekul *et al.* 2004). In the United Kingdom (UK), although there were no official involuntary sterilizations, the 1913 Mental Deficiency Act illustrated widespread support for 'voluntary' eugenics, and it is speculated that many disabled people – and women in particular – were sterilized unwittingly or without their fully informed consent (Walmsley 2000). Eugenic programmes involving varying passive and active eugenic methods, and varying approaches to voluntarism and degrees of 'success' were effected in Japan, Germany, Scandinavia and Northern Europe, and again, these disproportionately regulated the sexuality of women rather than men with disabilities (Burleigh 1997; Drouard 1996; Kevles 1995; Morita 2001). Further, such eugenic efforts did not necessarily die off with changed political and social sensibilities. Despite the reality that most disabilities are not heritable, there is still evidence that women with disabilities in particular continue to be pressured by family members and helping professionals to consider sterilization as a way to avoid the purported impossibility of mothering a child while living with a physical, mental or intellectual disability (Aunos and Feldman 2002; Brady 2001).

It should also be noted that eugenic beliefs continue to be expressed in indirect ways through a persistent ambivalence concerning all aspects of sexuality for women with disabilities. There is a strong need for information, on the one hand, about achieving a full adult sexual life and in obtaining support – both physical and cultural – for people with disabilities to develop and enjoy a healthy and satisfying sexuality (Dotson *et al.* 2003; Earle 1999; Mona 2003; Wilkerson 2002). On the other hand, there is little information available specific to disability concerning inappropriate sexual contact, harassment, sexual exploitation and sexual violence, to which women with disabilities are particularly vulnerable not only from friends and lovers, but also from helping professionals and care providers (Asch *et al.* 2001). Finally, there is woefully little information available about giving birth or obtaining post-partum care that is specific to mothers with disabilities (Disability, Pregnancy and Parenthood International 2002). Taken as a whole, the dearth of information for and about disabled women on these important axes of sexuality and reproduction indicates a remarkably robust scepticism about the appropriateness of disabled women to making, birthing or raising children in modern Western societies.

The underlying issues – gender, structure and disablism

Inevitably, there will be readers who question a focus on 'mothering' rather than 'parenting' and disability, but reproductive control and parenting support are both highly gendered arenas in which women bear an unequal burden. As noted above, potential motherhood for disabled women has been highly regulated in Western societies, as is evidenced through the inordinate targeting of women during the eugenics programmes of the twentieth century, by the routinization of hidden eugenics in the form of pressures on women with disabilities to use both temporary and permanent forms of birth control, and by the lack of information about and support for disabled women's sexuality (Gerodetti 2003; O'Toole 2002). In part, this heightened control of women's sexuality is an offshoot of a general tendency to police all women's sexuality; women are seen to be both vulnerable and dangerous as sexual actors and are held responsible for men's sexual behaviour as well as their own (Abramowitz 1996). Further, this victim-blaming has been most virulently levelled against women who are marginalized due to poverty, poor health or single motherhood, all of which are heightened possibilities for women with disabilities. Given the unequal sexual policing of women's reproduction in general, coupled with heightened cultural anxieties about disabled women's reproduction in particular, it is clear that disabled mothers' sexual and reproductive bodies act as dense transfer points of power relations (Foucault 1990), and are heavily burdened by moral, social, legal and economic regulation.

In addition to reproductive and sexual control, women with disabilities, because of gendered norms and structures, are more vulnerable to perceived and actual parenting challenges than are disabled men. While all people with disabilities face educational and occupational barriers and a higher than average likelihood of living in poverty, women with disabilities are even less likely than disabled men to be encouraged to achieve educationally, and they thus find fewer work opportunities at lower pay than men with disabilities or than women who are not disabled (Malacrida 2010). If women with disabilities are mothers, and particularly – as is quite likely – if they are single mothers, these lowered educational, employment and income opportunities will have significant impacts on their and their family's quality of life, and can pose challenges to mothers in providing a 'good enough' home situation for their children (Asch *et al.* 2001). As a result of educational and employment barriers and a heightened likelihood of parenting alone, women with disabilities are also more likely to face dependency on state funding than most citizens (Asch *et al.* 2001). In turn, this can make disabled women vulnerable to state interventions that while ostensibly offered as 'help' may in fact be profoundly disruptive; there is ample evidence that intervention into family life also increases a likelihood of surveillance, particularly in homes where there is poverty or social marginalization (Strega *et al.* 2002; Swift 1995).

Mothers with disabilities often find themselves at heightened risk for scrutiny, and while this is in part because of the poverty and marginalization that can accompany disability, this can also occur because the embodied qualities of disability can mean that workers and state employees, in providing care and support to disabled women, also breach the bounds of privacy that other citizens are likely to enjoy. This dual relationship of service provider and public employee can create difficulties; it has been argued that helping professionals, social workers and the family court system operate from a *deficit model of disability*, frequently characterizing women with disabilities as inappropriate for the role of mothering and as incompetent regardless of their actual mothering practices (Breeden *et al.* 2008; Malacrida 2009a, 2009b; McConnell and Llewellyn 1998). As with many aspects of disability oppression, these negative ascriptions and their effects are worsened if a mother has an intellectual disability, a profound physical disability or mental health problems (Booth *et al.* 2005; Mosoff 1997).

A final reason to concentrate on mothers rather than all parents with disabilities is because of the gendered qualities of parenting itself. Despite feminist attempts to denaturalize ideals of maternal responsibility for childcare, mothers are normatively expected to provide nurturance to the men in their lives through emotional support, and to the children in their lives through active, involved and expert mothering – indeed, being a mother/care-giver is a master status for adult women in modernity (Hays 1996; McMahon 1995). The ideal mother in Western culture is positioned as a woman who mothers naturally, is always and immediately present to care for her baby or child, and who does this mothering selflessly and seamlessly (Choi *et al.* 2005). In short, in the current ideology of intensive mothering, modern mothers are ideally expected to be all things at all times to their children: strong role models, endlessly nurturant, child-focused and without limits to their capacity for care (Hays 1996). Women with disabilities who experience limited economic and social resources, who may have their own requirements for care, and who often do not receive adequate support from disability and family services providers, undoubtedly face challenges in living up to this ideal.

The ideology of intensive mothering is often expressed in formal institutional practices: social services, medical and educational institutions and government agencies continue to consider mothers as the primary moral guardian in the modern family (Swift 1995; Abramowitz 1996). Further, mothers with disabilities are particularly likely to be judged by helping professionals as offering an inadequate or *not* 'good enough' sort of mothering, coloured by the myth of the upside-down family. This myth, and a broad professional literature that draws upon it, presumes that disabled mothers not only fall short of ideal mothering, but that they also depend on their *children* for care and services, exploiting these 'young carers' and robbing them of their childhoods (Booth and Booth 1998b).

Not only are mothers seen by policy-makers, social workers, teachers and medical personnel as naturally and completely responsible for the care and safety of their children, they are also conceived of as being responsible for choosing safe partners and for regulating their partners' behaviour: ultimately, mothers are held culpable when *any* type of family violence or breakdown occurs, even when they are themselves victims (Knowles 1996; Roberts 1999). This responsibility is particularly onerous when we consider that women with disabilities are far more likely than other groups of women to be victims of sexual, psychological, economic and physical violence both from their intimate partners (Brownridge 2006; Olkin 2003) and – ironically – from the helping professionals and institutions that are charged with providing mothers with support and services (McCarthy and Thompson 1996; Nicki 2001; Saxton *et al.* 2001).

Women with disabilities face enhanced challenges in achieving idealized mothering on the one hand, and they are particularly vulnerable to mother-blame and heightened scrutiny on the other. This is in part because women with disabilities often engage in mothering with fewer resources and more barriers in the public and private spheres than do women without disabilities. In the public sphere, disabled women's mothering is often constrained by poverty, inadequate housing and the inaccessibility of public spaces (Blackford 1993; Grue and Laerum 2002; Thomas 1997). In the private sphere, in addition to heightened probabilities of lone parenting, poverty and vulnerability to abuse, disabled women's embodied differences are not accommodated through policies and service programmes (Blackford 1993, 1999), a topic which will be explored further below.

In sum, mothers with disabilities face economic, social and environmental barriers to their mothering in the public sphere while at the same time bearing particular burdens in the private sphere. These barriers – poverty, heightened vulnerability to abuse, the stigmatization of disability and normative notions that women with disabilities are 'naturally' unsuited to motherhood – comprise a disablist culture for mothers with disabilities, and this disablist culture is in many ways the most challenging aspect of engaging in motherhood for women with disabilities. Thus, the balance of this chapter examines policy and service delivery issues relating to women with disabilities and their families. This is a critical aspect of disabled mothering, since it is clear that policies and programmes relating to housing, income, employment, personal and child care services, family support and community inclusion are themselves disabling to women and their children (Asch *et al.* 2001; Chouinard 2006; Chouinard and Crooks 2005; Hyde 2000).

Challenges – policies and programming for disabled mothers

The cultural ambivalence concerning motherhood for women with disabilities is clearly evidenced by the dearth of information available for and about such women in mainstream family policy; indeed, if one were to explore research or policy on families, one could be forgiven for assuming that all mothers are people who do not have any physical, intellectual, sensory or mental health issues. In terms of government research, for example, recent Canadian census data includes information about disabilities, and information about family and marital status, but there is no indication of the numbers of parents (or mothers) with disabilities, or the type and severity of the disabilities parents experience. These data are available for *children* with disabilities, but embedded in the census is a presumption that people with disabilities will *not* have children. Similarly, in the UK, while there has been a late recognition that people with disabilities will be parents, and while English policy for disabled people compares favourably with some other Western countries, disability-specific parenting policy is maintained and presented as separate from 'regular' family policy. In turn, this means that many family-related policies do not include disability-specific information, while disability-specific family policies do not include general information about family benefits, schooling or children's programmes. In short, in the UK, family policy and policy concerning parents with disabilities remain distinct from and marginal to each other. A telling example can be found in the Sure Start programme, which provides families with a system of 'affordable, quality childcare … children's centres and health and family support, particularly in disadvantaged areas where they are most needed'(Government of the United Kingdom 2007a). Despite the reality that parents with disabilities are highly likely to face financial, housing and social disadvantages and so be amongst the programme's target group, the policy does not mention disabled parents or make the programme accountable to them, and as with other policies, the information is written and presented inaccessibly and is not linked to information for parents with disabilities (Government of the United Kingdom 2007a, 2007b).

Disabled parenting is not only marginalized or absent in government policy, but it is also underrepresented in family and disability-specific research. Traditional helping professional and academic research on families and disability has tended (in a way similar to government research) to focus on children with disabilities in families, indicating an unspoken assumption that disabilities and parenting are incompatible. When traditional helping professional and academic literature *has* focused on parents, the perspective has been from a deficit model, where parents with disabilities are seen as operating from a position of inadequacy, rather than acknowledging that it is the *systems* relating to disabled parenting that are inadequate (Family Rights Group 2009; Malacrida 2009c). The little supportive research we do have has come primarily from the field of disability studies, and this literature is relatively sparse. Perhaps this is because in so many Western countries (although this is arguably particularly the case in the UK), the social model of disability is ascendant. The social model has concentrated its analyses along materialist lines, with a focus on access to labour force inclusion, access to education and accessibility in the built environment (Thomas 2007). In turn, this has meant a lack of attention to 'non-productive' labour and the private sphere (Thomas 2007) and a neglect of feminist concerns, including motherhood (Thomas 1997; Wendell 1996); as feminists have argued more broadly, materialist approaches have failed to account for reproduction, child-rearing and labour in the private sphere (Hartsock 1998). Not surprisingly, the social model of disability's focus on workplace and education has been particularly detrimental to mothers with disabilities, whose challenges are perhaps more likely to be in the private than in the public sphere.

Given the above, what are some of the challenges specific to disabled mothering, and how do these intersect with policy gaps and erasures? In the following section, I offer a brief overview of some of these issues.

Erasing and undermining motherhood in disability research and policy

Policy is, of course, much more than words, comprising a template that guides practices across the board for mothers with disabilities. Policies concerning financial support, home care and personal support services, education, employment, daycare, housing, transportation, child custody and child welfare programmes affect virtually every aspect of disabled women's lives. Despite this, most of these policies are not written accessibly and – more central to this argument – they typically fail to take the possibility of motherhood and disability into account. It is thus crucial to speak with mothers themselves about how these policies and practices impinge on their parenting.

In my own research, I have spoken with disabled mothers whose narratives often point out inconsistencies in policy and programme delivery, and whose situations also indirectly highlight gaps in current research approaches to understanding disability. These mothers describe barriers in the public sphere that are not generally considered in mainstream disability policy and social model research relating to accessibility, with its focus on public buildings and the paid workplace. In addition to their concerns about public spaces such as shops and worksites, mothers describe how inaccessible playgrounds and parks mean that mothers either cannot accompany their children while they play or must watch from a distance, potentially compromising their children's safety. Parent-child groups, often held in church basements, private homes or inaccessible community centres, preclude mothers' community involvement and increase their and their children's social isolation. Children's schools, pre-schools and daycare are often inaccessible unless designed specifically to be inclusive for *children* with disabilities, and these accessible schools are rare, so that mothers must choose (where such choice is possible) between allowing their children to attend school in their local community or driving them (where such an action is possible) to an accessible school far from their neighbourhood (Malacrida 2007, 2009b). In all of these public sphere issues, listening to the voices of mothers about how they live their lives exposes gaps in both policy and research that erase disabled mothering. These stories also illustrate how such gaps can potentially contribute to negative perceptions about disabled women's 'failed' mothering; mothers whose children cannot go to school with their friends, who cannot attend developmental educational programmes with their mothers or who cannot enjoy simple child-hood play in a public space can be seen by outsiders (including helping professionals) as children who are being poorly mothered. In this context, the real culprits such as poor policy and research, and inadequate planning and programme implementation, can remain unexamined and hence blame-free.

In a similar vein, the issues confronting mothers in the field of employment can be different from those described in much disability research, and disabled mothers' workplace issues are often directly related to policy gaps and programme designs that fail to accommodate mothers' family-related needs. In mainstream disability research, there is a strong focus on accommodation for disability in the paid workplace, and although there has recently been somewhat more attention paid to gendered problems, particularly in terms of analysing lowered income and educational opportunities for women, there is little direct consideration of the special challenges that mothers with disabilities face. Only rarely does the literature consider that unpaid labour comprises a significant portion of women's working lives, and that the lack of compensation and/or support for accomplishing that work amounts to workplace discrimination (McDonough 1996); even more rare is an acknowledgement that mothering can be and often is a job for disabled women that should be supported through both family and disability-related policies and programmes. Not surprisingly, in terms of policy and programme delivery, there is virtually no state compensation to disabled women for their challenges in homemaking or caregiving, and receiving such services that will facilitate disabled women's mothering roles as part of disability compensation is rare indeed. Instead, disability-related services typically offer support to the individual with the disability alone, which can mean that mothers receive in-home care but their young children, who are not themselves entitled to care services, are left to fend for themselves, an issue that will be discussed more fully below (Malacrida 2007, 2009a).

While there is virtually no research that takes on the question of financial compensation for disabled mothers' child-related labour, there is also little consideration in research or policy of the temporal and career trajectory issues faced by disabled mothers. Mothers, particularly mothers of young children, often take time off from paid work during the intensive early childcare years, and once those years have passed, such women are often challenged to find their place again on the career ladder (Hartsock 1998; Leth-Sorenesen and Rohwer 2001). For women with disabilities, who are amongst the most discriminated-against workers (Government of Canada 2008), a decision to step out of the paid workface to accommodate childbirth, recovery from childbirth and early infant and childcare can mean the death knell to career aspirations; these women face tremendous challenges in finding work in the first place, let alone after a hiatus that poses challenges to any female returning to the paid workforce. In turn, this can heighten mothers' dependency on either a partner or the state for income support. In the first instance, this can mean that women can become trapped in relationships that are abusive or unhappy; in the latter 'option', it can mean impoverishment and vulnerability to surveillance. In Canada, the question of forced dependency on a male partner is further compounded by policies that provide income support only for the disabled person, without any provision for dependent children who also require financial support (Malacrida 2009d).

Finally, it is important to add that part-time work is often a solution for many mothers with younger children or who are returning to the workplace after taking time from birthing and raising children. However, for mothers with disabilities, the option of part-time work can often mean rescinding one's rights to income or disability benefits; many programme benefits cease with *any* paid employment. Again, the result can be that disabled mothers find themselves either declining their due benefits or staying out of the workplace, resulting in impoverishment, social isolation, dependency on the state or a partner, and in a diminished lifestyle for themselves and their children. In short, the failure of income support and workplace-related policies and programmes to accommodate the particular situations and needs of mothers with disabilities actually contributes to negative aspects of living with a disability.

One last issue that deserves consideration in terms of eliding and/or erasing disabled mothers' experiences is that of disability service delivery. I will use two examples to illustrate a need for research that moves beyond traditional disability studies' approaches and for policy that recognizes the possibility that disabled women are frequently mothers. Mainstream research on disability service delivery focuses on the challenges that persons with disabilities face in obtaining adequate, affordable services. In this literature, services for persons with disabilities are typically characterized as *under-serviced*, meaning that programmes and benefits for disabled people are inadequate, difficult to access, fragmented and not designed to meet the needs of persons with disabilities. In this vein, researchers have pointed out that many of the policies and programmes offering support for individuals with disabilities are inaccessible to people with disabilities because they are couched in dense language or available only in print form rather than Braille, plain language, signing or spoken language (McVilly 1995). Others have noted that not only the form, but also the intention and content of disability-related policies can impose barriers to access. Thus, many individuals who require these services are deemed to be ineligible for them, or they are only provided with services that only partially meet their needs, or they must deal with hostile or untrained workers who can also act as gatekeepers to services (Gill *et al.* 1994). Further research on disability-related agencies as *under-serviced* indicates that service providers are plagued by lengthy waiting lists and they face difficulties in filling their mandate due to difficulties in maintaining a dedicated workforce (Roeher Institute 2001).

While these barriers to services also exist for mothers with disabilities, the extant research does not acknowledge how disability service delivery can pose additional burdens for mothers with disabilities in two distinct ways. First, in addition to the traditional concerns raised by disability research on under-serviced programme delivery, mothers with disabilities can also experience disability service delivery as *over-serviced*. By this, and drawing on both feminist conceptions of power as written on women's bodies in the private sphere and on poststructural conceptions of power as deployed through the uses of knowledge and seemingly benign practice, I mean to say that service delivery can act as a point of penetration and surveillance for state workers into the lives of mothers with disabilities. Because many of the services disabled mothers require involve the home front and intimate personal care, inviting workers into the home can operate as a way of controlling women, of knowing and judging their intimate practices and of finding them wanting. Mothers are themselves very aware of the threat of surveillance that is attached to intervention; for example, many women interviewed in the UK and in Canada describe declining to seek help for fears of being judged as inadequate, preferring to rely on their own resources to compensate for policy shortfalls rather than run that risk (Malacrida 2009c). It is important to note that these mothers' perceptions about being seen as inadequate are not without grounds; mothers' disability status has been used successfully to disqualify their claims to custody, particularly if the mothers have intellectual disabilities, mental health problems or profound mobility limitations (Booth and Booth 1998a; Mosoff 1995).

The second way that programme delivery problems are compounded for women with disabilities is that much service delivery does not include an understanding that mothers' lives are lived in relationship with their children. This seems a fairly obvious thing to state, however; most programmes (like much of the research) relating to disability are designed for individuals, without consideration of the individual's embodied and embedded responsibilities in the private sphere. In Canada, home care services that include personal hygiene, feeding and house-keeping are specifically designed for the recipient alone. Thus, it is not uncommon for women to receive home care services wherein the worker is permitted to feed, dress and clothe the mother, but cannot provide the same services to a baby or toddler unless that child is also labelled as disabled. Likewise, in the UK, where at least technically there is policy acknowledgement that disabled people can also be parents, services for adults and services for children are administered and delivered separately. Thus, in a similar vein to Canada, while a mother may indeed be eligible for personal care services, unless her child is eligible in its own right to such care, the service for the child will not be forthcoming. As with the issue of fragmentation and under-serviced programme delivery, the net result of separating children's and mothers' needs means that, for many mothers with disabilities, the choice is to either privatize their care via family and friends, or to 'make do' to the best of their capacity and hope that this will result in – and be seen as – 'good enough' mothering (Malacrida 2009a, 2009b). Either way, service delivery is yet another example of ways that policy, research and programmes, because they elide and erase disabled motherhood as a possibility, add to the burdens carried by disabled mothers and their families.

Thus, in addition to the usual problems of inadequacy and inappropriateness associated with disability service delivery, surveillance issues and a lack of consideration of mothers' roles can create a dilemma for mothers with disabilities. Ironically, the presence of disability support workers in the home can mean that, on the one hand, the children in the home are not entitled to any services and, on the other, it can open up the private home to scrutiny from those workers who are there to support the parent (Malacrida 2009a, 2009c).

Future considerations – bringing mothers in

Historically, disability and motherhood have been both understood and managed as though antithetical. From formal active eugenic policies, through passive eugenics in the form of institutionalization, to a persistent lack of research, education, accommodation and support for disabled women's sexuality and mothering roles, continuities persist in terms of cultural ambivalence over disabled motherhood. Thus, while in the current context such ambivalence is no longer sustained and expressed through active and official eugenics programmes, a wide range of research, policy and service delivery both erases and undermines the realities of disabled mothers.

Mainstream disability studies has offered a trenchant critique of medical models of disability and provided important insights into the experiences of disabled people in general, but that critique can only provide partial insight into and policy recommendations for the issues faced by disabled mothers. As we have seen, disability research that takes a materialist analysis often overlooks the intersections between disabled women's multiple sources of oppression and their embodied relationships of interdependency. Research on workplace accommodation and inclusion, while valuable, cannot offer the kinds of insights and subsequent policy recommendations needed by women whose labour is embedded in caregiving in the private sphere. For example, traditional research relating to disabililty accommodation in the built environment, with its focus on the accessibility of the workplace and educational institutions, has not accounted for the barriers women encounter in accessing playgrounds, daycare, schools and social spaces that are crucial to their children's development and to perceptions of the mothers' parenting as 'good enough'. Likewise, while research relating to services for people with disabilities can make important contributions to our understanding of service shortfalls, when that same research fails to include the reality that disabled mothers are not only receivers of care but also must be providers of it and that women's families are made vulnerable by service shortfalls, the critique offered by this research falls short for disabled women and their children. Resulting policies and programmes are not only doomed to fail mothers, but they leave them open to heightened scrutiny and negative family intervention.

Thus, it is important to expand our theoretical framings of disability to include gendered inequalities and to accommodate a research approach that takes women's specifically situated perspectives into account. Narrative methodologies, taken from the perspectives and experiences of people with disabilities, can offer an important counterpoint to traditional formulations of disabled people as operating from deficit or lack (Jongbloed 2007; Morgan 2001; Reinelt and Fried 1993). Drawing on arguments concerning narrative work in the feminist tradition, narrative studies with mothers with disabilities can offer insights into the embodied, interactional aspects of disability, and can be highly political, by connecting personal narratives with broader social structures (Linton 2006; Mairs 1996). Here, moving from individual narratives to the structures that constrain women, narrative work is able to include traditional materialist concerns as well as 'non-productive' aspects of living with a disability, such as sexuality, mothering, intimacy and embodiment. If we wish to make the connections between women's lived experiences and the institutions and practices that constrain them, it is important to – as feminist philosopher Dorothy Smith argues – begin where women live, and build upward (Smith 1990). Playing feminist narrative methods against critical discourse analysis illuminates how a lack of acknowledgement for disabled mothering disciplines mothers into an individualist, forced self-sufficiency in the current model of family and disability, leaving women to fend for themselves, sometimes at the cost of their own health, and increasing their risks of surveillance and intervention. Blending these theoretical and methodological approaches can expose the casual brutality that policy and research omissions impose on disabled women and their children in deeply critical and crucial ways.

References

Abramowitz, M. (1996) *Regulating the Lives of Women: Social Welfare Policy from Colonial Times to the Present (Revised Edition)* (Boston, MA: South End Press).

Albrecht, G. L. (1993) *The Disability Business: Rehabilitation in America (SAGE Library of Social Research)* (Thousand Oaks, CA: Sage).

Asch, A., Rousso, H. and Jefferies, T. (2001) 'Beyond Pedestals: The Lives of Girls and Women with Disabilities', in H. Rousso and M. L. Wehmeyer, eds, *Double Jeopardy: Addressing Gender Equity in Special Education* (Albany: State University of New York Press): pp. 13–48.

Aunos, M. and Feldman, M. A. (2002) 'Attitudes Towards Sexuality, Sterilization and Parenting Rights of Persons with Intellectual Disabilities', *Journal of Applied Research in Intellectual Disabilities* 15: 285–96.

Blackford, K. A. (1993) 'Erasing Mothers with Disabilities through Canadian Family-related Policy', *Disability, Handicap & Society* 8(3): 281–94.

Blackford, K. A. (1999) 'Caring to Overcome Differences, Inequities, and Lifestyle Pressures: When a Parent Has a Disability', in K. A. Blackford, M.-L. Garceau and S. Kirby, eds, *Feminist Success Stories* (Ottawa: University of Ottawa Press): pp. 279–87.

Booth, T. and Booth, W. (1998a) 'Introduction', in T. Booth and W. Booth, eds, *Growing Up With Parents Who Have Learning Difficulties* (London: Routledge): pp. 1–7.

Booth, T. and Booth, W. (1998b) 'The Myth of the Upside Down Family', in T. Booth and W. Booth, eds, *Growing Up With Parents Who Have Learning Difficulties* (London: Routledge): pp. 146–68.

Booth, T., Booth, W. and McConnell, D. (2005) 'The Prevalence and Outcomes of Care Proceedings Involving Parents with Learning Difficulties in the Family Courts', *Journal of Applied Research in Intellectual Disabilities* 18: 7–17.

Brady, S. M. (2001) 'Sterilization of Girls and Women with Intellectual Disabilities: Past and Present Justifications', *Violence Against Women* 7(4): 432–61.

Breeden, C., Olkin, R. and Taube, D. J. (2008) 'Child Custody Evaluations When One Divorcing Parent Has a Physical Disability', *Rehabilitation Psychology* 53(4): 445–55.

Brownridge, D. A. (2006) 'Partner Violence Against Women with Disabilities: Prevalence, Risk, and Explanations', *Violence Against Women* 12(9): 805–22.

Burleigh, M. (1997) *Ethics and Extermination: Reflections on Nazi Genocide* (Cambridge: Cambridge University Press).

Choi, P., Henshaw, C., Baker, S. and Tree, J. (2005) 'Supermum, Superwife, Supereveything: Performing Femininity in the Transition to Motherhood', *Journal of Reproductive and Infant Psychology* 23(2): 167–80.

Chouinard, V. (2006) 'On the Dialectics of Differencing: Disabled Women, the State and Housing Issues', *Gender, Place and Culture* 13(4): 401–17.

Chouinard, V. and Crooks, V. A. (2005) '"Because They Have All the Power and I Have None": State Restructuring of Income and Employment Supports and Disabled Women's Lives in Ontario, Canada', *Disability & Society* 20(1): 19–32.

Disability Pregnancy and Parenthood International (2002) 'Sharing Good Practice in Supporting Disabled Adults in Their Parenting Role'; available online at http://www.dppi.org.uk/journal/journal-articles.php (accessed 6 October 2011).

Dotson, L. A., Stinson, J. and Christian, L. (2003) '"People Tell Me I Can't Have Sex": Women with Disabilities Share their Personal Perspectives on Health Care, Sexuality, and Reproductive Rights', *Women and Therapy* 26(3/4): 195–209.

Drouard, A. (1996) 'A Case of Democratic Eugenics: Forty-Five Years of Genetics Hygiene in Denmark', *La Recherche* 287: 78–81.

Earle, S. (1999) 'Facilitated Sex and the Concept of Sexual Need: Disabled Students and their Personal Assistants', *Disability & Society* 14(3): 309–23.

Family Rights Group (2009) 'Supporting Disabled Parents: Social Care Services for Parents and Adults in a Parenting Role'; available online at http://www.frg.org.uk/pdfs/6.%20ssfor%20disabled%20parents.pdf (accessed 6 October 2011).

Foucault, M. (1990) *The History of Sexuality. Volume I: An Introduction* (New York: Vintage Books).

Gerodetti, N. (2003) *'Disabling' Femininities and Eugenics: Sexuality, Disability and Citizenship in Modern Switzerland* (Lausanne: University of Lausanne).

Gill, C. J., Kirschner, K. L. and Reis, J. P. (1994) 'Health Services for Women with Disabilities: Barriers and Portals', in A. Dan, ed, *Reframing Women's Health: Multidisciplinary Research and Practice* (Thousand Oaks, CA: Sage Publications): pp. 357–66.

Government of Canada (2008) *Participation and Activity Limitation Survey 2006: Labour Force Experience of People with Disabilities in Canada*; available online at http://www.statcan.ca/english/freepub/89-628-XIE/89-628-XIE2008007.pdf (accessed 6 October 2011).

Government of the United Kingdom (2007a) *Sure Start Maternity Grant Factsheet*; available online at http://www.direct.gov.uk/en/MoneyTaxAndBenefits/BenefitsTaxCreditsAndOtherSupport/Expecting orbringingupchildren/DG_10018854 (accessed 6 October 2011).

Government of the United Kingdom (2007b) *Sure Start Maternity Grant from the Social Fund*.

Grekul, J., Krahn, H. and Odynak, D. (2004) 'Sterilizing the "Feeble-minded": Eugenics in Alberta, Canada, 1929–1972', *Journal of Historical Sociology* 17(4): 358–84.

Grue, L. and Laerum, K. T. (2002) '"Doing Motherhood": Some Experiences of Mothers with Physical Disabilities', *Disability & Society* 17(6): 671–83.

Hartsock, N. (1998) 'The Feminist Standpoint: Developing the Ground for a Specifically Feminist Historical Materialism', in N. Hartsock, ed, *The Feminist Standpoint Revisited and Other Essays* (Boulder: Westview): pp. 105–32.

Hays, S. (1996) *The Cultural Contradictions of Motherhood* (New Haven: Yale University Press).

Hyde, M. (2000) 'From Welfare to Work? Social Policy for Disabled People of Working Age in the United Kingdom in the 1990s', *Disability & Society* 15(2): 327–41.

Johnson, H. M. (2003) 'The Disability Gulag', *New York Times Magazine*: pp. 1–15.

Jongbloed, L. (2007) 'Disability Income: Narratives of Women with Multiple Sclerosis', in V. Raoul, C. Canam, A. Henderson and C. Paterson, eds, *Unfitting Stories: Narrative Approaches to Disease, Disability, and Trauma* (Waterloo, ON: Wilfred Laurier University Press): pp. 209–16.

Kevles, D. J. (1995) *In the Name of Eugenics: Genetics and the Uses of Human Heredity* (edn) (Cambridge, MA: Harvard University Press).

Knowles, C. (1996) *Family Boundaries: The Invention of Normality and Dangerousness* (Peterborough, Ontario: Broadview Press).

Leth-Sorenesen, S. and Rohwer, G. (2001) 'Work Careers of Married Women in Denmark', in H. P. Blossfeld and S. Drobnic, eds, *Careers of Couples in Contemporary Societies: From Male Breadwinner to Dual Earner Families* (New York: Oxford University Press): pp. 261–80.

Linton, S. (2006) *My Body Politic: A Memoir* (Ann Arbor: University of Michigan Press).

McCarthy, M. and Thompson, D. (1996) 'Sexual Abuse by Design: An Examination of the Issues in Learning Disability Services', *Disability & Society* 11(2): 205–17.

McConnell, D. and Llewellyn, G. (1998) 'Parental Disability and the Threat of Child Removal', *Family Matters* 51(Spring/Summer): 33–6.

McDonough, P. A. (1996) 'The Social Production of Housework Disability', *Women & Health* 24(4): 1–25.

McMahon, M. (1995) *Engendering Motherhood: Identity and Self-transformation in Women's Lives* (New York: The Guilford Press).

McVilly, K. R. (1995) 'Interviewing People with a Learning Disability About their Residential Service', *British Journal of Learning Disability* 23: 138–42.

Mairs, N. (1996) *Waist-High in the World: Life Among the Nondisabled* (Boston: Beacon Press).

Malacrida, C. (2007) 'Negotiating the Dependency/Nurturance Tightrope: Dilemmas of Disabled Motherhood', *Canadian Review of Sociology* 144(4): 469–93.

Malacrida, C. (2009a) 'Gendered Ironies in Home Care: Surveillance, Gender Struggles and Infantilization', *International Journal of Inclusive Education* 13(7): 741–52.

Malacrida, C. (2009b) 'Performing Motherhood in a Disablist World: Dilemmas of Motherhood, Femininity and Disability', *International Journal of Qualitative Studies in Education* 23(1): 99–117.

Malacrida, C. (2009c) 'Services for Mothers with Disabilities: Surveillance, Gender Struggles and Infantilization', in G. Katsas, ed., *Sociology in a Changing World* (Athens: Athens Institute for Education and Research): pp. 271–82.

Malacrida, C. (2009d) '"The AISH Review is a Big Joke": Contradictions of Policy Participation and Consultation in a Neoliberal Context', *Disability & Society* 24(1): 5–18.

Malacrida, C. (2010) 'Parents with Disabilities', in D. Cheal, ed., *Canadian Families Today: New Perspectives* (Toronto: Oxford University Press): pp. 213–33.

Mona, L. R. (2003) 'Sexual Options for People with Disabilities: Using Personal Assistance Services for Sexual Expression', *Women and Therapy* 26(3/4): 211–20.

Morgan, R. (2001) 'Using Life Story Narratives to Understand and Identify in South Africa', in M. Priestley, ed., *Disability and the Life Course: Global Perspectives* (Cambridge: Cambridge University Press): pp. 89–100.

Morita, K. (2001) 'The Eugenic Transition of 1996 in Japan: From Law to Personal Choice', *Disability & Society* 16(5): 765–71.

Mosoff, J. (1995) 'Motherhood, Madness and Law', *University of Toronto Law Journal* 45(2): 107–42.

Mosoff, J. (1997) '"A Jury Dressed in Medical White and Judicial Black": Mothers with Mental Health Histories in Child Welfare and Custody', in S. B. Boyd, ed., *Challenging the Public/Private Divide: Feminism, Law and Public Policy* (Toronto: University of Toronto Press): pp. 227–52.

Nicki, A. (2001) 'The Abused Mind: Feminist Theory, Psychiatric Disability, and Trauma', *Hypatia. Special Issue: Disability and Feminism I* 16(4): 80–223.

Olkin, R. (2003) 'Women with Physical Disabilities Who Want to Leave their Partners: A Feminist and Disability-Affirmative Perspective', in M. E. Banks and E. Kaschak, eds, *Women with Visible and Invisible Disabilities: Multiple Intersections, Multiple Issues, Multiple Therapies* (Haworth Press): pp. 237–46.

O'Toole, C. J. (2002) 'Sex, Disability and Motherhood: Access to Sexuality for Disabled Mothers', *Disability Studies Quarterly* 22(4): 81–101.

Radford, J. P. (1994) 'Eugenics and the Asylum', *Journal of Historical Sociology* 7(4): 462–73.

Rafter, N. (1997) *Creating Born Criminals* (Urbana and Chicago: Illinois University Press).

Ramsay, S. (2000) 'Enforced Sterilization in Sweden Confirmed', *Lancet* 355 (8 April): 1252.

Reinelt, C. and Fried, M. (1993) '"I Am This Child's Mother": A Feminist Perspective on Mothering with a Disability', in M. Nagler, ed., *Perspectives on Disability: Text and Readings* (Health Markets Research): pp. 195–202.

Roberts, D. E. (1999) 'Mothers Who Fail to Protect their Children: Accounting for Private and Public Responsibility', in J. E. Hanigsberg and S. Ruddick, eds, *Mother Troubles* (Boston, MA: Beacon): pp. 31–49.

Roeher Institute (2001) *Disability-related Support Arrangements, Policy Options and Implications for Women's Equality* (Ottawa: Status of Women Canada).

Saxton, M., Curry, M. A., Powers, L. E., Maley, S., Eckels, K. and Gross, J. (2001) '"Bring My Scooter So I Can Leave You": A Study of Disabled Women Handling Abuse by Personal Assistance Providers', *Violence Against Women* 7(4): 393–417.

Schoen, J. (2001) 'Between Choice and Coercion: Women and the Politics of Sterilization in North Carolina, 1929–1975', *Journal of Women's History* 13(1): 132–56.

Smith, D. E. (1990) *The Conceptual Practices of Power: A Feminist Sociology of Knowledge* (Toronto: University of Toronto Press).

Strega, S., Callahan, M., Rutman, D. and Dominelle, L. (2002) 'Undeserving Mothers: Social Policy and Disadvantaged Mothers', *Canadian Review of Social Policy* (49–50): 175–97.

Swift, K. (1995) *Manufacturing 'Bad Mothers': A Critical Perspective on Child Neglect* (Toronto: University of Toronto Press).

Thomas, C. (1997) 'The Baby and the Bathwater: Disabled Women and Motherhood in Social Context', *Sociology of Health and Illness* 19(5): 622–43.

Thomas, C. (2007) *Sociologies of Disability and Illness: Contested Ideas in Disability Studies and Medical Sociology* (Basingstoke: Palgrave Macmillan).

Trent, J. W. (1993) 'To Cut and Control: Institutional Preservation and the Sterilization of Mentally Retarded People in the United States', *Journal of Historical Sociology* 6(1): 56–73.

Trent, J. W. (1994) *Inventing the Feeble Mind: A History of Mental Retardation in the United States* (Berkeley: University of California Press).

Walmsley, J. (2000) 'Women and the Mental Deficiency Act of 1913: Citizenship, Sexuality and Regulation', *British Journal of Learning Disabilities* 28: 65–70.

Wendell, S. (1996) *The Rejected Body: Feminist Philosophical Reflections on Disability* (New York and London: Routledge).

Wilkerson, A. (2002) 'Disability, Sex Radicalism, and Political Agency', *NWSA Journal* 14: 33–57.

30

UNDERSTANDING DISABLED FAMILIES

Replacing tales of burden with ties of interdependency

Janice McLaughlin

Introduction

Family life in the context of disability has been the focus of a significant amount of research across a range of disciplines. Health care studies, medicine, social policy and psychology all have a long-term interest in disability and family life; collectively they have produced a particular image of the lives of families with disabled members that documents their burden of care and celebrates the ability of those non-disabled family members able to cope with that burden. This narrow approach has been criticized by the disability movement as yet another version of disability as tragedy. To counter this, new research within disability studies, sociology and anthropology is seeking to represent alternative and positive understandings. The aim of this chapter is to discuss this new work.

Before mapping out the new perspectives emerging from contemporary work on family and disability it will be useful to clarify a few points. First, what is family? Family is one of those commonplace terms whose regular, everyday use makes it easy to miss the complex social processes that lie behind framing it in certain ways. Without going too far into the sociology of family, or the anthropology of kinship, it is important to stress that while our most immediate image of family is that of the nuclear family – of mum, dad, children, sharing both biology and a household – we know that this is a social construct, however dominant (Carsten 2004; Edwards *et al.* 1999; Finch 2007; Franklin and McKinnon 2001; Morgan 1996). There is much debate about whether we live – in the West – in an era where there is greater recognition of varied forms of family life, which means that many no longer live in the nuclear family model presented above (ONS 2010). Therefore, it is important that research exploring 'family' does not begin with too many presumptions of what it is that is being studied, and provides a space for people to define what family means to them. This is particularly important in the context of disability, where the caring networks around disability are rarely contained by household or by family as equating to biological relations. Instead, neighbours and friends can be equally, if not more, important in mutual caring activities. Second, the research on families and disability has significantly focused on families where the child or children are disabled (my own research has had much of this focus). This is an important area to look at, but it is also important not to exclude other ways in which disability and family come into contact, in particular the experiences and perspectives of disabled parents, and the specific issues created by the forms of disability that come with ageing. In this chapter I will use the phrase 'disabled families' to equate to family formations, however constituted, where at least one member is disabled. In such contexts it is the family as a whole who live and experience disability, although the specifics of those experiences amongst the members will vary, as well as the response to being a disabled family. The phrasing symbolizes the ways in which others, formal services, the community and neighbourhood respond to the family differently in light of disability. The chapter will highlight some of these dynamics. Much of the discussion will concentrate on issues related to childhood disability, but I will also bring in issues relating to disabled parents and disability across the life course.

Third, a core theme of this chapter is to challenge dominant narratives around family and disability that emphasize the burden disability produces and the qualities of families who are able to cope. Below I will discuss why this framing is problematic. Nevertheless, while advocating different ways in which family and disability can be understood, I do not want to suggest that disabled families do not face difficulties. We should not be aiming to replace one problematic nightmare scenario with an equally problematic fairytale. Statistical data, with all the caveats around reliability, point to the economic difficulties families face through: (a) the extra costs of looking after someone who is disabled (Beresford 1994; Preston 2006); (b) the removal of family members from the labour force to provide care (Carmichael *et al.* 2008); (c) the consequences of those in a family who would usually be in the labour market being unable to work due to the problems disabled people face gaining and remaining in employment (Magadi 2010); and (d) the lack of sufficient benefits for those unable to work due to disability (Barnes and Mercer 2005). Families also talk of the difficulties and battles they encounter in getting appropriate support from formal services, while also being concerned about the level of scrutiny their lives fall under from those services – an issue felt particularly strongly by disabled parents (Swain and Cameron 2003). In addition, work with people who are disabled, whether children or adults, has identified forms of abuse and neglect that they have suffered at the hands of family members and the inadequacy of social services in response. Finally, existing social hierarchies, for example located in terms of class or capital (Gillies 2005; Sharma 2002) and ethnicity (Chamba *et al.* 1999; Shah 1995), have inevitable consequences for access to resources and support for families.

As mentioned above, my own research is particularly focused on childhood disability. Throughout the discussion in this chapter I will draw from a completed research project that I was a member of which explored the perspectives of parents with disabled infants and babies. The details of the project and its methodology are published elsewhere (McLaughlin *et al.* 2008). I want to acknowledge here the work of the other members of the research project, in particular Dan Goodley, Emma Clavering, Pamela Fisher and Claire Tregaskis. This chapter is split into three sections. The first outlines the problems with the burden fixation and the alternatives that are emerging. The second section explores the significance of medical therapies and treatments in the lives of disabled families. The final section explores the meanings associated with care and the value of recognizing the interdependencies that lie at the heart of all family life.

Disability as a burden and families who cope

Read (2000) and Runswick-Cole (2007) highlight ways in which disabled families are often assumed to be problem families, both in how the state responds in the provision of support and how others around them withdraw from contact. When not faced with hostility or suspicion, instead what many report is the language of pity. This focus on pity is not just found in social responses, but is also visible in the expansive research literature found amongst health care studies, medicine and social policy. A search for articles on disability and family will come up with an array of work focused and framed around burden (just a few examples include Brinchmann 1999; Canam 1993; Dyer 1996; Hannam 1988; Kim *et al.* 2010; Partington 2002; Snell and Rosen 1997).

To some degree there has been a move away from the burden fixation in contemporary health care and social policy literature. We now have tales of families who overcome difficulties, who learn to cope, followed by psychological profiles of which families adapt or accommodate to disability and the strategies they develop in order to do so. The media and charity spotlight is often on such families too, particularly if it is a non-disabled sibling or child who cares for their disabled sibling or parent. The problems with such media stories and family models are manifold. First, for those families judged not to cope blame is easily placed. If some can manage, why can't others? Second, such explanations easily fall into stereotypes and assumptions. For example, the wonders of the British Asian extended family and the way in which it simply absorbs caring responsibilities (Katbamna *et al.* 2004). Or, in contrast, assumptions that disabled parents or a single parent household will be unable to cope. Such assumptions are problematic because they do not reflect the social realities of any of these groups' lives. It is not necessarily the case that within an Asian context there is an extended family ready and waiting to take on such responsibilities (Ali *et al.* 2001). Neither should it be assumed that a disabled parent or single parent household cannot cope, nor that they do not live within an extended care network that is ready and willing to help share caring activities (Traustadóttir and Sigurjonsdottir 2008). Third, the focus is on the non-disabled person and their trials and tribulations; this focus places the disabled person as 'other' to the family. Fourth, the analysis presents disability as both a pathology and something which comes from outside a family; a family whose life was previously good and who must now accommodate an alien presence. Finally, the focus remains with the individual and their innate abilities to cope, or how they can learn to cope, via the right adoption of techniques and strategies.

What becomes invisible in such accounts are the social contexts that produce burden and the significance of multiple forms of capital and resources in enabling some to 'cope' better than others (McKeever and Miller 2004). What families talk of as burdensome in their lives is not the disability they or a family member has, it is the battles with social services and health care providers to receive adequate and appropriate care provision. The current difficulty is that the long-term trend in welfare provision across Europe is a move away from universal entitlement towards conditionality (Dwyer 2000, 2004); that is the requirement to prove need – either financial or support – before services are allocated. This is seen in a range of support services related to disability in the United Kingdom (UK), for example Disability Living Allowance and statements of need in education. Every indication suggests that conditionality in welfare will only increase for the foreseeable future; the implication is that having to pursue services will continue to grow as an element of the caring activities of disabled families. If this is where burden is found, then it is important that research agendas remain concerned with what is occurring within welfare regimes and challenge this direction of travel in provision.

As discussed above the burden literature produces a sense that the disabled child is an intrusion in to what otherwise would be a productive and happy family life. Such an approach is exemplified in literature on siblings of disabled children or children of disabled parents. Here, again the dominant voice and concern has been one revolving around the non-disabled children whose lives are disrupted by having a sibling or parent who is disabled. In both scenarios the common themes include: such children have to grow up too quickly as they must care for themselves; their lives are centred around caring for others, whether parent or sibling; they grow up resentful of the way in which having a disabled parent or sibling means that they are not provided with enough attention and instead lead lives of isolation where things such as holidays or having friends over is made impossible by the presence of disability within their childhood (Bischoff and Tingstrom 1991; Cuskelly and Gunn 2006; Giallo and Gavidia-Payne 2006). It would be wrong, as before, to suggest that such problems do not occur or that it is untrue that non-disabled children who grow up around disability may feel a sense of loss when they compare their childhood with that of others (Heaton *et al.* 2005; Hodapp and Urbano 2005). But this is not the only element of the story and the only people to be concerned about. Research with children themselves, disabled and non-disabled, paints a different picture of what growing up in a context of disability within one's family also provides. For non-disabled siblings or children of disabled parents, their experiences can also be positive as they grow up with different priorities, interests and world views on disability and the value of being in caring relationships with people who are 'different' (Canary 2008; Stalker and Connors 2004).

Highlighting the perspectives of disabled siblings, also highlights that earlier work leaves the impression that only non-disabled children can be siblings. Instead disabled children are siblings too, siblings who can provide something positive to the lives of others in the families they are part of. Anthropological literature exploring relationships between disabled and non-disabled siblings has done a better job than other social science disciplines of considering how the siblings become part of each other's lives, supporting each other, changing each other, and carrying those relationships (positive and negative) into adult life (Davis and Salkin 2005). Crucially what this research also points to is the importance of doing research with the children themselves (Balen *et al.* 2006; Clavering and McLaughlin 2010; Marchant 2004; Save the Children 1999) in order to find out what they define as significant to them, what influences their world view and what they see as the key areas that affect their lives negatively and positively. There is now a growing body of research doing this, often using innovative and participatory methodology to examine disabled children's views and experiences of the barriers to social participation (Susinos 2007); the importance of play (Goodley and Runswick-Cole 2010), their quality of life (Dickinson *et al.* 2007; Young *et al.* 2007), their developing sexuality (Addlakha 2007); their disability in the context of other aspects of who they are (Islam 2008; Singh and Ghai 2009); and transitions within health care, education and into adulthood (Galambos *et al.* 2007).

The search for cure or therapy

There is substantial research literature that highlights how parents with a child who is developing or behaving differently will seek medical explanations and treatment. This is particularly marked in areas such as attention deficit hyperactivity disorder (ADHD) and autism spectrum disorder (ASD) (Bull and Whelen 2006; Singh 2004), where both the diagnosis and some of the relevant treatment options (in particular the use of medications to subdue behaviour and mood) are highly contentious within disability groups. Other writers have explored why parents may seek 'normalizing' surgery for their children, for example leg lengthening in the case of restricted growth, or facial cosmetic surgery in the case of Down's syndrome (Hansen and Hansen 2006; McGrath 2001; Thiruchelvam *et al.* 2001; Woodgate and Degner 2004). Parents often frame such strategies in the quest for some kind of normality. However, there is a wide debate in disability studies and medical sociology as to whether medical diagnosis and therapy, while obtained in an effort to help the child, also contribute to emphasizing the child's difference and medicalizing their identity (Blum 2007; Conrad and Potter 2000; Gillman *et al.* 2000; Hedgecoe 2003; Rapp *et al.* 2001). The research I participated in with parents of disabled children indicated that parents seek from medicine abdication from blame and a promise that through a cure the child could one day be normal (McLaughlin and Goodley 2008). Medicine can also be understood as a response to parents' own discomfort with disability. At times the research did highlight how parents contributed to positioning their disabled child as not a full member of the family through expressions of failure to bond, comparisons to other 'normal children' and through parental desires to 'normalize' their child's behaviour so they – the child and the parent – experienced less social discomfort. However, it is important to explore why parents may struggle, at least initially, with raising a disabled child (Allen 2004; Ferguson 2001; Green 2004).

This understanding requires an appreciation of contemporary contexts of parenting. All parents in the West are under a heightened gaze through increased levels of medical advice and guidance on how to raise perfect children: the more this is emphasized and wished for, the more parents of disabled children and the children themselves are constructed as failures (Landsman 1999; Larson 1998; Rigazio-DiGilio 2000). Parents are failures both via the assumption that they must have done something wrong to produce this disabled child and also to have produced a child, which it is assumed, will not be able to grow to be the socially useful citizen expected by the state and others (McKeever and Miller 2004). As such, disabled families can find themselves falling into the same 'problem' categories of other 'troublesome' families, such as single parent households or 'workless/workshy' families. Disabled children do not fit contemporary narratives of family life, contributing to the difficulties parents may face finding a space within their own family narratives for their child (Dowling and Dolan 2001; Jenks 2005). Such contexts encourage a sense amongst families that a disabled child is a different child, and that the solution, for everyone's interests, is to minimize that difference, through whatever routes.

However, while such contexts can be important and are a motivation to involving medicine in a child's life, this is not the only dynamic at play in the involvement of parents with medicine. First, the quest for normality is not shared by all parents, or a quest that all stay rooted to. In the research my colleagues and I carried out with parents, some talked of recognizing the costs of too much time spent trying to find the medical explanation for their child's differences, or trying to get them closer to the developmental markers they had fallen behind on. Instead they began to explore new ways of thinking of their child, their family and their futures together that incorporated difference and impairment. Crucially, parents talked of the importance of the child's own identity and character in reshaping family life. In a counterpoint to the notion of burden, here the disabled child brings something of value in to the family which changes the family and signals the child's centrality and importance to the lives they are a part of. Second, researchers need to be careful to avoid seeing all inclusion of medical therapies and treatments – including drugs in the context of behavioural problems – as necessarily problematic. In the cases of some long-term and degenerative conditions these treatments can be absolutely necessary in keeping the child alive, in providing improved quality of life and in enabling the child to grow up to adulthood. This is most clearly seen in conditions such as cystic fibrosis and Duchenne muscular dystrophy, where improved medical intervention and better social care are clearly significant in the improved quality of life and increased life span of people with these degenerative conditions. The reality for many disabilities is that medicine is part of life. The social and political implication of this for disabled families is to ensure that this involvement with medicine does not become the key factor in shaping the person's life and identity, or that of those around them, and that medical actors do not become too powerful in dictating the choices and experiences of that person and family (Larson 1998).

Understanding how medicine affects disabled families' lives is best done by studying the interactions between families and medical actors and organizations, rather than presuming what will occur. In our own research, after diagnosis, parents can become focused on acquiring and participating in therapies and treatments to aid their child. They may willingly take on such activities; however, it also may be something which they – particularly mothers – are assumed to want to get involved in. This assumption can lead to question marks being raised about parents who appear unwilling to play their role in such treatments and therapies. Mothers can feel little choice but to participate in such interventions. However, they can also question both the validity of the intervention and their participation in it. In particular, they can become aware of the risk that therapies may change the dynamics of the intimate space of family life. This can lead parents to become choosier about medical interventions and appointments they feel it necessary to attend; in so doing they seek to reclaim their child and provide space for a range of the child's development to occur more freely. Rejection of certain medical practices can be understood as elements in ongoing processes of redefining family life in the context of disability (Frank 1995; Jenks 2005; Taylor 2000).

Some of the technologies that families have to learn to use to enable a disabled person to be at home, particularly technologies that aid breathing or eating, are both intensive and intrusive (Place 2000). However, work influenced by social studies of technology is also highlighting how over time, families, both the disabled and non-disabled members, work together to minimize the disruption and dominance of medical interventions or therapies into their lives and spaces of intimacy. In such processes they can also seek to positively incorporate such interventions and technologies, which do not deny their presence or benefit, into their lives. This way of under-standing the social aspects of medical equipment and technology highlights the agency of disabled users who are not dictated to by the technology, but instead make it something that responds to their needs and life. One example of this is the creative use of assistive communicative technologies by disabled young people to experiment with new ways of representing themselves and producing forms of identity and subjectivity which break free of notions of them as 'technologically dependent'.

Care and interdependency

Care is a problematic category in disability debates. Feminists have rightly been criticized for being solely bothered by the 'burden' of care within the gendered division of labour within families. While fundamentally important to feminism in the 1970s and 1980s (Finch and Groves 1983; Land 1978; Ungerson 1987, 1990), and an important challenge to state approaches to depositing care responsibility on to the family (for the most part women, particularly with respect to the care of children and older relatives), this work was problematic for how it approached disability. In addition, via the significance of charitable organizations in 'caring' for disabled people, care is sometimes framed as an act of charity. Disability writers have pointed out that the language of charity is inappropriate; in particular how it acts to disallow the sense that the disabled person has a right to query the care they receive (Hughes 1999; Lindemann 2003). Charitable caring for Hughes 'mobilised the emotions invested in the tragic and the pitiful' (Hughes 2002: 577), while Kittay suggests that care is understood not as a right but instead is provided 'out of a gratuitous kindness, a kindness they have no right to demand' (2002: 271).

While acknowledging these concerns, I would argue that in the contexts of understanding the lives of disabled families, care is both something to be interrogated and also reclaimed from its problematic associations (McLaughlin 2006; Traustadóttir 1991, 1999). This can be done by understanding the relationship between care and subjectivity, politics and interdependency. Without denying the problems found in feminist work, there is much in contemporary feminist explorations of care within and outside the family that is of value here. Still pivotal in such work are the arguments of Finch and Mason (1991, 1993). They propose that the processes through which women become the predominant carers involve 'negotiations' within families; negotiations which often leave women with the least socially acceptable excuses to leave care to others outside or inside the family. For many women, the role of carer gives them value and appreciation, providing them with a socially acceptable identity, which is not available elsewhere:

> People's identities are being constructed, confirmed and reconstructed – identities as a reliable son, a generous mother, a caring sister or whatever it might be. … If the image of a 'caring sister' is valued as part of someone's identity then it eventually becomes too expensive to withdraw from those commitments through which that identity is expressed and confirmed.
>
> *(Finch and Mason 1993: 170)*

Skeggs (1997) also explores the gendered subjectivity of the carer, and the social conditions that support and legitimate particular identities. Being a carer becomes something that is not just incorporated into things women do. It is also translated into aspects of the self, providing respectability and recognition; a process that Campbell and Carroll (2007) argue is not as possible for men due to the influence of hegemonic masculinity (Connell 1987). Therefore, exploring the social, cultural and political contexts within which care occurs is important to understanding its significance (Kittay 1999).

Such contexts that lead to women being seen as the natural carers and women adopting such identities appear particularly marked in the care of disabled children. When mothers are asked to provide key roles in the day-to-day treatments and therapies for their child, this is based on their presumed inherent ability to care. Over time this becomes part of the processes that consolidate the gendered division of care. The expertise mothers develop in treatment and supporting the child leads them to continue to be seen as the obvious carers for their child, which excludes others from participating in those activities. In our research with families, fathers' identities as carers were often unrecognized by others, while mothers were readily identified and identified themselves as carers.

However, such assumptions and identity dynamics are not the same when the mother is disabled. Instead, whether the child is disabled or not, the first response by formal services and often others around the woman is to assume that she will lack core skills which others must provide, justifying significant scrutiny of her and her relationship with her child (Berman and Wilson 2009; Booth and Booth 1994, 1997, 1998; Booth *et al.* 2006). This is not to say, like all mothers, disabled women would not benefit from support and advice; the problem is the way assumptions tied to their disability impose readings of their mothering as inevitably lacking (Coren *et al.* 2010; Llewellyn 1995, 1997; Llewellyn and McConnell 2002). In such contexts it is difficult for disabled mothers to define for themselves what type of support they would benefit from and to set the boundaries to when it is legitimate for others to question their parenting skills. Increasingly, however, research is including an appreciation of the ways in which disabled parents 'can be assisted to live successful family lives in the community' (Traustadóttir and Sigurjonsdottir 2008: 331).

The assumptions made about non-disabled women as carers and disabled women as inadequate carers take us towards a consideration of the politics of care. There are a variety of ways through which to bring politics into the discussion of care. One is the significance of the variety of social discourses embedded in gender, class, disability, age, and race and ethnicity in framings of who can and cannot care. Another I wish to discuss here is in considerations of what the content and boundaries to care are (McLaughlin 2006). In my research with colleagues, mothers found new meaning and senses of self in their caring role; in particular, fighting injustice experienced by their children and others became an important part of what they defined as the caring role and was embedded in their identity. In defining their caring role, mothers included their battles with statutory services on behalf of their child. Therefore, their caring identity was not perceived as a private role, it spread out into the public realm of challenges to resources and against inequality. This allows for a broader understanding of the relations, experiences, engagement, interdependences and politics involved in caring activities (Watson *et al.* 2004). It also creates a space to recognize the agency and identity of disabled people within caring roles, pushing towards a position that blurs the notion that there are those who care and those who are cared for (Fine and Glendinning 2005; Lloyd 2000, 2003).

Care can be rescued from associations with charity if it is remembered that all those participating in care are nested in sets of reciprocal relations and obligations (Kittay 1999). These relations emerge from the significance of vulnerability to the human condition (Shildrick 1997). Recognizing the inevitability of vulnerability brings with it recognition of interdependency, in contrast to charitable notions of dependency and burden. The value of interdependency is also the way in which it asks questions of society and the state and pushes care out of the privacy of the family into the public sphere and debates about citizenship (Sevenhuijsen 1998). It points to the broader social responsibility to participate in care practices with all kinds of people. It broadens the responsibilities of good citizens to include participation in ties of caring interdependence (Held 1995).

From this perspective, evaluating the contexts around disabled families includes questioning to what degree professional, institutional and community settings provide spaces for the development of affirmative and productive relationships with them. A turn to the complexities of interdependency provides us with more productive ways of conceptualizing the lives of disabled families. Without a debate about the responsibilities of the state and society to care, rather than just the family, the privatization of care goes on unquestioned and the marginalization of such families continues. Where care provision is presented as individualistic, as focused only on the 'condition' rather than the person, as a form of charity and private responsibility rather than public right and entitlement, families remain locked in marginalized positions that construct them as 'troubling' to society and enforce the caring role on the mother.

Conclusion

This chapter has sought to present aspects of the lives of disabled families that become invisible when the focus is on burden. Instead of a disabled family member being thought of as someone or something a family has to manage, cope with or adapt to, here I have explored disabled family members as full and valued participants in family life. While the language of burden is problematic we do need to remember the routes through which disabled families are marginalized in society, in particular via the ways in which caring responsibilities are naturalized as private and gendered. Instead we need an understanding of disability and family that integrates disabled people into the families they are a part of (rather than seeing them as an unwelcome intrusion) and integrates family into its social, political and cultural contexts. This can occur via recognizing ties of interdependency that refute clear boundaries between the carer and the cared for, the private and the public and the disabled and the non-disabled.

References

Addlakha, R. (2007) 'How Young People with Disabilities Conceptualize the Body, Sex and Marriage in Urban India: Four Case Studies', *Sexuality and Disability* 25(3): 111–23.

Ali, Z., Fazil, Q., Bywaters, P., Wallace, L. and Singh, G. (2001) 'Disability, Ethnicity and Childhood: A Critical Review of Research', *Disability & Society* 16(7): 949–67.

Allen, C. (2004) 'Bourdieu's Habitus, Social Class and the Spatial Worlds of Visually Impaired Children', *Urban Studies* 41(3): 487–506.

Balen, R., Blyth, E., Calabretto, H., Fraser, C., Horrocks, C. and Manby, M. (2006) 'Involving Children in Health and Social Research: "Human Becomings" or "Active Beings"?', *Childhood* 13(1): 29–48.

Barnes, C. and Mercer, G. (2005) 'Disability, Work, and Welfare: Challenging the Social Exclusion of Disabled People', *Work, Employment and Society* 19(3): 527–45.

Beresford, B. (1994) *Positively Parents: Caring for a Severely Disabled Child* (London: HMSO).

Berman, R. C. and Wilson, L. (2009) 'Pathologizing or Validating: Intake Workers' Discursive Constructions of Mothers', *Qualitative Health Research* 19(4): 444–53.

Bischoff, L. G. and Tingstrom, D. H. (1991) 'Siblings of Children with Disabilities: Psychological and Behavioural Characteristics', *Counselling Psychology Quarterly* 4: 311–41.

Blum, L. M. (2007) 'Mother-blame in the Prozac Nation – Raising Kids with Invisible Disabilities', *Gender & Society* 21(2): 202–26.

Booth, T. and Booth, W. (1994) *Parenting Under Pressure: Mothers and Fathers with Learning Difficulties* (Buckingham: Open University Press).

Booth, T. and Booth, W. (1997) 'Making Connections: A Narrative Study of Adult Children of Parents with Learning Difficulties', in C. Barnes and G. Mercer, eds, *Doing Disability Research* (Leeds: The Disability Press).

Booth, T. and Booth, W. (1998) *Growing up with Parents who have Learning Difficulties* (London: Routledge).

Booth, T., McConnell, D. and Booth, W. (2006) 'Temporal Discrimination and Parents with Learning Difficulties in the Child Protection System', *British Journal of Social Work* 36(6): 997–1015.

Brinchmann, B. S. (1999) 'When the Home Becomes a Prison: Living with a Severely Disabled Child', *Nursing Ethics* 6(2): 137–43.

Bull, C. and Whelen, T. (2006) 'Parental Schemata in the Management of Children with Attention Deficit-Hyperactivity Disorder', *Qualitative Health Research* 16(5): 664–78.

Campbell, L. D. and Carroll, M. P. (2007) 'The Incomplete Revolution – Theorizing Gender when Studying Men who Provide Care to Aging Parents', *Men and Masculinities* 9(4): 491–508.

Canam, C. (1993) 'Common Adaptive Tasks Facing Parents of Children with Chronic Conditions', *Journal of Advanced Nursing* 18(1): 46–53.

Canary, H. E. (2008) 'Negotiating Dis/ability in Families: Constructions and Contradictions', *Journal of Applied Communication Research* 36(4): 437–58.

Carmichael, F., Hulme, C., Sheppard, S. and Connell, G. (2008) 'Work–life Imbalance: Informal Care and Paid Employment in the UK', *Feminist Economics* 14(2): 3–35.

Carsten, J. (2004) *After Kinship* (Cambridge: Cambridge University Press).

Chamba, R., Ahmad, W., Hirst, M., Lawson, D. and Beresford, B. (1999) *On the Edge: Minority Families Caring for a Severely Disabled Child* (York: The Policy Press).

Clavering, E. K. and McLaughlin, J. (2010) 'Children's Participation in Health Research: From Objects to Agents?', *Child: Care, Health and Development* 36(5): 603–11.

Connell, R. W. (1987) *Gender and Power* (Cambridge: Polity Press).

Conrad, P. and Potter, D. (2000) 'From Hyperactive Children to ADHD Adults: Observations on the Expansion of Medical Categories', *Social Problems* 47(4): 559–82.

Coren, E., Hutchfield, J., Thomae, M. and Gustafsson, C. (2010) 'Parent Training Support for Intellectually Disabled Parents', *Cochrane Database of Systematic Reviews*: p. 6.

Cuskelly, M. and Gunn, P. (2006) 'Adjustment of Children who have a Sibling with Down Syndrome: Perspectives of Mothers, Fathers and Children', *Journal of Intellectual Disability Research* 50: 917–25.

Davis, C. S. and Salkin, K. A. (2005) 'Sisters and Friends – Dialogue and Multivocality in a Relational Model of Sibling Disability', *Journal of Contemporary Ethnography* 34(2): 206–34.

Dickinson, H. O., Parkinson, K. N., Ravens-Sieberer, U., Schirripa, G., Thyen, U., Arnaud, C., Beckung, E., Fauconnier, J., McManus, V., Michelsen, S. I., Parkes, J., Colver, A. (2007) 'Self-reported Quality of Life of 8–12-year-old Children with Cerebral Palsy: A Cross-sectional European Study', *Lancet* 369: 2171–8.

Dowling, M. and Dolan, L. (2001) 'Families with Children with Disabilities – Inequalities and the Social Model', *Disability & Society* 16(1): 21–35.

Dwyer, P. (2000) *Welfare Rights and Responsibilities: Contesting Social Citizenship* (Bristol: The Policy Press).

Dwyer, P. (2004) 'Creeping Conditionality in the UK: From Welfare Rights to Conditional Entitlements?', *Canadian Journal of Sociology* 29(2): 265–87.

Dyer, B. (1996) *Seeming Parted* (Middlesex: New Millennium).

Edwards, J., Franklin, S., Hirsch, E., Price, F. and Strathern, M. (1999) *Technologies of Procreation: Kinship in the Age of Assisted Conception* (2nd edn) (London and New York: Routledge).

Ferguson, P. M. (2001) 'Mapping the Family: Disability Studies and the Exploration of Parental Response to Disability', in G. L. Albrecht, K. D. Seelman and M. Bury, eds, *Handbook of Disability Studies* (Thousands Oaks: Sage).

Finch, J. (2007) 'Displaying Families', *Sociology* 41(1): 65–81.

Finch, J. and Groves, D., eds, (1983) *A Labour of Love: Women, Work, and Caring* (London: Routledge and Kegan Paul).

Finch, J. and Mason, J. (1991) 'Obligations of Kinship in Contemporary Britain – Is there Normative Agreement?', *British Journal of Sociology* 42(3): 345–67.

Finch, J. and Mason, J. (1993) *Negotiating Family Responsibilities* (London: Routledge).

Fine, M. and Glendinning, C. (2005) 'Dependence, Independence or Inter-dependence? Revisiting the Concepts of "Care" and "Dependency"', *Ageing & Society* 25: 601–21.

Frank, A. W. (1995) *The Wounded Storyteller: Body, Illness and Ethics* (Chicago: University of Chicago Press).

Franklin, S. and McKinnon, S. (2001) 'Relative Values: Reconfiguring Kinship Studies', in S. Franklin and S. McKinnon, eds, *Relative Values: Reconfiguring Kinship Studies* (Durham: NC: Duke University Press).

Galambos, N. L., Darrah, J. and Magill-Evans, J. (2007) 'Subjective Age in the Transition to Adulthood for Persons with and without Motor Disabilities', *Journal of Youth and Adolescence* 36(6): 825–34.

Giallo, R. and Gavidia-Payne, S. (2006) 'Child, Parent and Family Factors as Predicators of Adjustment for Siblings of Children with a Disability', *Journal of Intellectual Disability Research* 50(12): 937–48.

Gillies, V. (2005) 'Meeting Parents' Needs? Discourses of "Support" and "Inclusion" in Family Policy', *Critical Social Policy* 25(1): 70–90.

Gillman, M., Heyman, B. and Swain, J. (2000) 'What's in a Name? The Implications of Diagnosis for People with Learning Difficulties and their Family Carers', *Disability & Society* 15(3): 389–409.

Goodley, D. and Runswick-Cole, K. (2010) 'Emancipating Play: Dis/abled Children, Development and Deconstruction', *Disability & Society* 25(4): 499.

Green, S. E. (2004) 'The Impact of Stigma on Maternal Attitudes Toward Placement of Children with Disabilities in Residential Care Facilities', *Social Science & Medicine* 59(4): 799–812.

Hannam, C. (1988) *Parents and Mentally Handicapped Children* (Bristol: Bristol Classical Press).

Hansen, D. L. and Hansen, E. H. (2006) 'Caught in a Balancing Act: Parents' Dilemmas Regarding their ADHD Child's Treatment with Stimulant Medication', *Qualitative Health Research* 16(9): 1267–85.

Heaton, J., Noyes, J. and Sloper, P. (2005) 'Families' Experiences of Caring for Technology-dependent Children – A Temporal Perspective', *Health and Social Care in the Community* 13(5): 441–50.

Hedgecoe, A. M. (2003) 'Expansion and Uncertainty: Cystic Fibrosis, Classification and Genetics', *Sociology of Health & Illness* 25(1): 50–70.

Held, V. (1995) 'The Meshing of Care and Justice', *Hypatia* 10(2): 128–34.

Hodapp, R. M. and Urbano, R. C. (2005) 'Siblings of Persons with Disabilities: Towards a Research Agenda', *Mental Retardation* 43: 334–8.

Hughes, B. (1999) 'The Constitution of Impairment: Modernity and the Aesthetic of Oppression', *Disability & Society* 14(2): 155–72.

Hughes, B. (2002) 'Bauman's Strangers: Impairment and the Invalidation of Disabled People in Modern and Post-modern Cultures', *Disability & Society* 17(5): 571–84.

Islam, Z. (2008) 'Negotiating Identities: The Lives of Pakistani and Bangladeshi Young Disabled People', *Disability & Society* 23(1): 41–52.

Jenks, E. B. (2005) 'Explaining Disability – Parents' Stories of Raising Children with Visual Impairments in a Sighted World', *Journal of Contemporary Ethnography* 34(2): 143–69.

Katbamna, S., Ahmad, W., Bhakta, P., Baker, R. and Parker, G. (2004) 'Do They Look After Their Own? Informal Support for South Asian Carers', *Health & Social Care in the Community* 12(5): 398–406.

Kim, K. R., Lee, E., Namkoong, K., Lee, Y. M., Lee, J. S. (2010) 'Caregiver's Burden and Quality of Life in Mitochondrial Disease', *Pediatric Neurology* 42(4): 271–6.

Kittay, E. F. (1999) *Love's Labour: Essays on Women, Equality and Dependency* (New York: Routledge).

Kittay, E. F. (2002) 'When Caring is Just and Justice is Caring: Justice and Mental Retardation', in E. F. Kittay and E. K. Feder, eds, *The Subject of Care: Feminist Perspectives on Dependency* (Oxford: Rowan and Littlefield Publishers).

Land, H. (1978) 'Who Cares for the Family?', *Journal of Social Policy* 3(7): 357–84.

Landsman, G. (1999) 'Does God Give Special Kids to Special Parents: Personhood and the Child with Disabilities as Gift and as Giver', in L. L. Layne, ed., *Transformative Motherhood: On Giving and Getting in a Consumer Culture* (New York and London: New York University Press).

Larson, E. (1998) 'Reframing the Meaning of Disability to Families: The Embrace of Paradox', *Social Science & Medicine* 47(7): 865–75.

Lindemann, K. (2003) 'The Ethics of Receiving', *Theoretical Medicine* 24: 501–9.

Llewellyn, G. (1995) 'Relationships and Social Support: Views of Parents with Mental Retardation/ Intellectual Disability', *Mental Retardation* 33: 349–63.

Llewellyn, G. (1997) 'Parents with Intellectual Disability Learning to Parent: The Role of Informal Learning and Experience', *International Journal of Disability, Development and Education* 44(3): 243–61.

Llewellyn, G. and McConnell, D. (2002) 'Mothers with Learning Difficulties and their Support Networks', *Journal of Intellectual Disability Research* 46: 17–34.

Lloyd, L. (2000) 'Caring About Carers: Only Half the Picture?', *Critical Social Policy* 20(1): 136–50.

Lloyd, L. (2003) 'Caring Relationships: Beyond "Carers" and "Service Users"', in K. Stalker, ed., *Reconceptualising Work and Carers: New Directions for Policy and Practice. Research Highlights 43* (London: Jessica Kingsley).

McGrath, P. (2001) 'Findings on the Impact of Treatment for Childhood Acute Lymphoblastic Leukemia on Family Relationships', *Child and Family Social Work* 6: 229–37.

McKeever, P. and Miller, K. L. (2004) 'Mothering Children Who Have Disabilities: A Bourdieusian Interpretation of Maternal Practices', *Social Science & Medicine* 59(6): 1177–91.

McLaughlin, J. (2006) 'Conceptualising Intensive Caring Activities: The Changing Lives of Families with Young Disabled Children', *Sociological Research Online* 11(1); available online at http://www.socresonline.org.uk/11/1/mclaughlin.html (accessed 6 October 2011).

McLaughlin, J. and Goodley, D. (2008) 'Seeking and Rejecting Certainty: Exposing the Sophisticated Lifeworlds of Parents of Disabled Babies', *Sociology* 42(2): 317–35.

McLaughlin, J., Goodley, D., Clavering, E. K., Fisher, P. (2008) *Families Raising Disabled Children: Enabling Care and Social Justice* (Basingstoke: Palgrave Macmillan).

Magadi, M. (2010) 'Risk Factors for Severe Child Poverty in the UK', *Journal of Social Policy* 39(2): 297–316.

Marchant, R. (2004) 'Adopting a More Inclusive Approach to Listening', *Early Years Education* 6(3): 54–6.

Morgan, D. H. J. (1996) *Family Connections* (Cambridge: Polity Press).

ONS (2010) *Social Trends 40: How UK Life has Changed Since the 1970s* (London: Stationery Office).

Partington, K. (2002) 'Maternal Responses to the Diagnosis of Learning Disabilities in Children: A Qualitative Study Using a Focus Group Approach', *Journal of Learning Disabilities* 6(2): 163–73.

Place, B. (2000) 'Constructing the Bodies of Critically Ill Children: An Ethnography of Intensive Care', in A. Prout, ed., *The Body, Childhood and Society* (Basingstoke: Palgrave).

Preston, G. (2006) 'Families with Disabled Children, Benefits and Poverty', *Benefits: Journal of Poverty and Social Justice* 14(1): 39–43.

Rapp, R., Heath, D. and Taussig, K.-S. (2001) 'Genealogical Dis-ease: Where Hereditary Abnormality, Biomedical Explanation and Family Responsibility Meet', in S. Franklin and S. McKinnon, eds, *Relative Values: Reconfiguring Kinship Studies* (Durham, NC: Duke University Press).

Read, J. (2000) *Disability, the Family and Society: Listening to Mothers* (Buckingham: Open University Press).

Rigazio-DiGilio, S. A. (2000) 'Relational Diagnosis: A Co-constructive-developmental Perspective on Assessment and Treatment', *Journal of Clinical Psychology* 56(8): 1017–36.

Runswick-Cole, K. (2007) '"The Tribunal was the Most Stressful Thing: More stressful than My Son's Diagnosis or Behaviour": The Experiences of Families who go to the Special Educational Needs and Disability Tribunal', *Disability & Society* 22(3): 315–28.

Save the Children (1999) 'Involving Young Researchers', available online at http://www.savethechildren.org.uk/en/54_2334.htm (accessed 6 October 2011).

Sevenhuijsen, S. (1998) *Citizenship and the Ethics of Care* (London: Routledge).

Shah, R. (1995) *The Silent Minority: Children with Disabilities in Asian Families* (London: National Children's Bureau).

Sharma, N. (2002) *Still Missing Out? Ending Poverty and Social Exclusion: Messages to Government from Families with Disabled Children* (Basildon: Barnardo's Publications).

Shildrick, M. (1997) *Leaky Bodies and Boundaries* (London: Routledge).

Singh, I. (2004) 'Doing their Jobs: Mothering with Ritalin in a Culture of Mother-blame', *Social Science and Medicine* 59: 1193–1205.

Singh, V. and Ghai, A. (2009) 'Notions of Self: Lived Realities of Children with Disabilities', *Disability & Society* 24(2): 129–45.

Skeggs, B. (1997) *Formations of Class and Gender* (London: Sage).

Snell, S. A. and Rosen, K. H. (1997) 'Parents of Special Needs Children Mastering the Job of Parenting', *Contemporary Family Therapy* 19(3): 425–42.

Stalker, K. and Connors, C. (2004) 'Children's Perceptions of their Disabled Siblings: "She's Different but it's Normal for Us"', *Children & Society* 18: 218–30.

Susinos, T. (2007) '"Tell Me in Your Own Words": Disabling Barriers and Social Exclusion in Young Persons', *Disability & Society* 22(2): 117–27.

Swain, P. A. and Cameron, N. (2003) '"Good Enough Parenting": Parental Disability and Child Protection', *Disability & Society* 18(2): 165–77.

Taylor, S. J. (2000) '"You're not a Retard, You're Just Wise": Disability, Social Identity, and Family Networks', *Journal of Contemporary Ethnography* 29(1): 58–92.

Thiruchelvam, D., Charach, A. and Schachar, R. (2001) 'Moderators and Mediators in Long-term Adherence to Stimulant Treatment in Children with ADHD', *Journal of the American Academy of Child and Adolescent Psychiatry* 40(8): 922–28.

Traustadóttir, R. (1991) 'Mothers Who Care: Gender, Disability and Family Life', *Journal of Family Issues* 12(2): 221–8.

Traustadóttir, R. (1999) 'Gender, Disability and Community Life, Toward a Feminist Analysis', in H. Bersani, ed., *Responding to the Challenge: Current Trends and International Issues in Developmental Disabilities* (Cambridge, MA: Brookline Books).

Traustadóttir, R. and Sigurjonsdottir, H. B. (2008) 'The "Mother" Behind the Mother: Three Generations of Mothers with Intellectual Disabilities and Their Family Support Networks', *Journal of Applied Research in Intellectual Disabilities* 21(4): 331–40.

Ungerson, C. (1987) *Policy is Personal: Sex, Gender, and Informal Care* (London: Tavistock).

Ungerson, C., ed., (1990) *Gender and Caring: Work and Welfare in Britain and Scandinavia* (Hemel Hempstead: Harvester Wheatsheaf).

Watson, N., McKie, L., Hughes, B., Hopkins, D., Gregory, S. (2004) '(Inter)dependence, Needs and Care: The Potential for Disability and Feminist Theorists to Develop an Emancipatory Model', *Sociology* 38(2): 331–50.

Woodgate, R. L. and Degner, L. F. (2004) 'Cancer Symptom Transition Periods of Children and Families', *Journal of Advanced Nursing* 46(4): 358–68.

Young, B., Rice, H., Dixon-Woods, M., Colver, A., Parkinson, K. N. (2007) 'A Qualitative Study of the Health-related Quality of Life of Disabled Children', *Developmental Medicine and Child Neurology* 49: 660–65.

31

CONCEPTUAL ISSUES IN CHILDHOOD AND DISABILITY

Integrating theories from childhood and disability studies

John Davis

Introduction and context

This chapter considers a range of different theoretical positions concerning disabled childhoods (e.g., deficit, social model, holistic and postmodern/structuralist). It charts a shift from medical model writing that judged disabled children as being passive victims in need of being fixed (e.g., in respect to the 'norm' for their age) (Watson and Shakespeare 1998; Priestley 1998; Davis *et al.* 2003), through social model approaches that pointed to the social-structural, materialist and attitudinal aspects of disablement, to complex postmodern/structural notions of disability and childhood that consider issues of agency, politics and social justice. It concludes by promoting a more complex and politically nuanced approach to childhood and disability that recognizes the diverse identities of disabled children and balances notions of agency, fluidity and social oppression.

Medical models of disability

Disabled children have been described as being unable to make choices (requiring their lives to be structured or controlled by adults), as posing a danger to others and as socially or educationally inept (Davis and Watson 2001, 2002). A number of writers have connected the reification of disabled children's inabilities with Piagetian notions of age or stage and the medicalization of childhood (Alderson 2000; Davis and Watson 2002). Piaget connected different age stages to how individual children interpret, organize and use information from their environment to construct concepts (mental structures) about their physical and social world. In the 1970s, researchers in child development aimed to solve children's life problems by identifying and explaining developmental milestones and identifying factors that led to deviations from the norm (Woodhead 2009). Attempts to solve children's life problems by child development were critiqued on several grounds. Developmentalists were critiqued for over-emphasizing their ability to provide solutions and for failing to recognize their inability to influence issues outside the individual child. In particular they were critiqued for ignoring the power relations of their work roles and for failing to value diversity (Davis 2011).

'Medical model' ideas pathologized children who failed to meet standardized developmental targets, viewed disability as the natural consequence of impairment rather than being caused by society, ignored the structural and cultural barriers that blocked disabled children's inclusion, and resulted in professionals becoming over-preoccupied with measuring children's bodies and minds rather than facilitating their inclusion into society (Priestley 1998; Alderson and Goodey 1998).

Traditional approaches in social work, health and education tended to concentrate on disabled children's 'need' for care, highlight their status as a dependent, emphasize their vulnerability and assume they should be kept separate from society (Watson and Shakespeare 1998; Priestley 1998). However, it was not simply ideas from psychology that downplayed disabled children's ability. For example, some sociologists represented children in general as passive, arguing that society should appropriate the child, take it over and mould it (Parsons and Bales 1955). These writers traditionally viewed children who deviated from the norm as a threat to society (Parsons and Bales 1955). Such approaches were criticized in sociology for over-emphasizing the individual child pathology, for promoting cultural/behavioural universality and for defining children's lives too prescriptively (Alderson 2000). For example, very often professionals used such concepts to justify behaviourist approaches that attempted to control children through processes of punishment, reward and repetition (Alderson 2000). Similarly, they led to the expectation that children who did not fit with development and social norms should not be included in mainstream schools (Alderson and Goodey 1998).

Corsaro (1997) critiqued such approaches in psychology and sociology because they reduced children to the state of passive objects who received socialization but could not think for themselves, viewed children as a worry and pushed them to the margins of society. He suggested children were rarely viewed in a way that appreciated what they were in the present. Other critiques emerged, including the view that children's peer groups were not being taken seriously or were rarely viewed as a potentially positive influence, that children were treated as a homogeneous group when they in fact had very complex, diverse, fluid identities, and that children's abilities to make reflective choices in contrasting social contexts were being underplayed (James *et al.* 1998; Davis 2011). Contemporary psychologists echoed this critique suggesting that traditional writing on child development downplayed children's abilities, views, rights and feelings (Stanton-Rogers 2001; Woodhead and Faulkner 2000; Burman 1994, 1996). In particular, rigid approaches in sociology and psychology were criticized for lacking an understanding of cultural diversity, for not fully assessing the social context of children's behaviour and for imposing adult ideas of what children should be (Alderson 2000; Davis 2006). Contrasting writing highlighted the creative and innovative nature of childhood (Corsaro 1997; James and Prout 1990; James *et al.* 1998). This general critique of traditional approaches to childhood had major implications for writers in childhood and disability studies, particularly when connected with critiques that emerged from the disability movement.

Social and holistic approaches to disability and childhood

In the 1970s disabled people challenged medical and psychological definitions of disability and argued that disability was/is socially constructed (e.g., Finkelstein 1975; UPIAS 1976). This 'social model' of disability suggested that disability was/is caused by social barriers in society (Abberley 1987; Oliver 1990; Morris 1991; Barnes 1991; Zarb 1995). The social model of disability led to studies on disabled childhood that emphasized the structural context of childhood disability (e.g., links to poverty) (Humphries and Gordon 1992; Lewis 1995; Middleton 1996; Norwich 1997; Priestley 1998) and promoted the idea of inclusive schooling as not simply being integrated into buildings but having an equitable level of experience (e.g., access to both social and academic interaction) (Booth and Ainscow 2000).

There are strong connections between social model approaches to disability studies and the work of materialist writers about childhood (e.g., Thompson 1994; Qvortrup 1994). Such writers suggested that childhood was a social phenomenon that included young people not being able to participate fully in social life (e.g., they don't vote, work, drink alcohol, go out on their own, etc.). Such writers related childhood experiences to economic, social and structural issues (e.g., national policies, poverty and parental employment).

In childhood sociology Corsaro (1997) contrasted the psychological constructivist *'linear' view of development* (that children develop in a straight line from child to adult) with a more sociocultural complex *'orb-web' or 'spider's-web' model* that illustrated that children gain experiences across a range of sites, institutions and locations (e.g., religion, politics, school, family experiences and community encounters). Similarly, in psychology, holistic models emerged (e.g., Bronfenbrenner's 1989 ecological model) that defined the child as the centre of a series of rings that included friends, school, neighbours, local services, cultures and the media. Ecological models in psychology emerged in response to critiques of child development. They moved beyond individualized approaches to recognize the systems around the child and family (Dolan 2008). Such ideas were utilized in social policy that sought to take a multifaceted approach to assessment, planning and delivery in children's services and that encouraged service providers to include children, families and communities in discussions concerning service development (Davis 2011).

However, there is a tendency for holistic models in children's services to ignore the power and politics of children's lives (e.g., issues of change, power and conceptual hierarchy in children's services) (Fitzgerald and Kay 2008; Anning *et al.* 2006; Dillon *et al.* 2001; Smith and Davis 2010; Smith 2007). For example, Davis (2011) demonstrated a tendency for different professional approaches to assessment, planning and delivery of child and adolescent mental health services to fail to take account of children's own views, for practitioners to fail to question medical model presumptions and for professionals to vary in their conceptual approach. He found children and young people critiqued professionals who claimed to take neutral approaches to their work and judged professionals in inter-relation ways (e.g., whether they cared, were trustworthy, enabled choice and took time to explain processes). This work contrasted four different conceptual approaches to assessment/treatment:

- *individualized* approaches that highlighted the individual child's pathology and judged children against normative criteria related to developmental age and stage;
- *ecological* approaches that considered the social context outside of the individual child (e.g., friends, school, neighbours, local services, national culture, government and the media) but rarely questioned the politics of the professional role;
- *multi-agency* approaches that aimed to ensure that no one professional solely defined children's problems/solutions; and
- *politically nuanced holistic models* that challenged hierarchies (e.g., the assumption that the medical professional knows best) and recognized that service users are the experts on their own lives.

Such writing highlighted the social as well as the organizational aspects of disabled children's lives. It has been argued that disabled young people want to be more proactive in their communities (e.g., to be involved in disability equality events; projects to improve public transport; and policy development that provides better transition to work and greater inclusion in education, leisure, play and sport). Yet, service providers don't always recognize the ways that their own perspectives and prejudices can create barriers to such involvement and change (Davis 2000, 2011; Davis *et al.* 2006; Davis and Hogan 2004). Indeed, disabled children and young people have been found to be frustrated by the limitations of participatory processes and to wish to see a change in the power relations between service providers and themselves (Davis 2011).

It is important when outlining the socio-political marginalization of disabled children's 'voice' and highlighting discriminatory practices in health, education and social services that we do not at the same time solely define disabled children as social victims (Davis and Watson 2002). Many writers in disability studies have painted a picture of a 'disabled child' who has been denied the same rights/choices as other children and been cut off from non-disabled children (Morris 1997; Alan 1996; Tomlinson and Colquhoun 1995; Middleton 1996; Norwich 1997; Alderson and Goodey 1998). Disabled children were believed to be prevented from developing social skills and self-confidence because their lives were controlled by other people (Morris 1997; Norwich 1997; Alderson and Goodey 1998). This suggestion can be connected to Mayall's (1996) view that children are rarely given choices about how they govern their own bodily practice and Ennew's (1994) idea that children's lives are structured by time. Ennew (1994) defines a number of types of time: biological (children eating, drinking, sleeping and toileting); social (controlled interaction at school or in sports clubs); parents' (where a judgement is made as to whether a child's time/ activities is/are profitable); danger (unsupervised risky time); free (children choose what to do); and play (children interact with others or artefacts). Such writers critique the social control of childhood but occasionally there is a tendency for the powerless nature of childhood to be overplayed.

As Swain and French (2000) state, one of the central assumptions of the medical/tragedy model is that disabled people want to be other than themselves. So we have to ensure that whilst highlighting the structural issues that disabled children experience (considering the social model) we also recognize disabled people's abilities, diverse experiences and positive identities (collective and individual) (Swain and French 2000). Swain and French (2000) encourage us to build on the social model (that sites the problem with society) to promote an affirmative model that:

- challenges perspectives which identify problems with impairments by asserting value and validity to impairment;
- celebrates difference; and
- recognizes disabled people's right to have control of what is done to their bodies.

The affirmative model can be connected to writers in family and community studies who are concerned with the concept of social justice. For example, Dolan (2008) drew from Honneth (2000) to define social justice as the person's right to be treated with regard/care, to be entitled to legal rights, and to be recognized as having attributes and strengths.

An example of more affirmative approaches to disabled children can be found in the work of Norwich (1997), who argued that disabled children used diverse strategies to both ignore the negative influences on their lives and to challenge negative stereotypes of themselves. Similarly, Connors and Stalker (2003) critiqued the tendency for medical professionals to attempt to remove difference, to demonstrate that childhood and disability are not unifying concepts (e.g., children are not homogeneous) and to highlight how the ways that children, parents and teachers manage concepts of difference can have a strong influence on children's abilities to promote positive identities in schools. The concept of difference has been analysed heavily in disability studies; the final section of this chapter reviews some of the key arguments in relation to disabled children.

Culture, difference and postmodernism

The previous section raised questions concerning the management of difference. Writers such as Thomas (1978), Lewis (1995), Middleton (1996), Morris (1997), Norwich (1997) and Alderson and Goodey (1998) have attempted to differentiate between disabled children's childhoods in terms of race, class and gender. This is similar to writing in childhood studies where authors have defined children's groupings by adult rather than children's ideas of difference and tended to fail to recognize the fluidity of children's cultures (e.g., Mauthner 1997; Mayall 1994; Hallden 1994; Hendry *et al.* 1993). In contrast, a number of authors have recognized children's abilities to develop their own cultures. They have suggested that children are innovative and creative, that they not only internalize culture but also actively contribute to shaping and changing culture, and that they are not simply restrained by the structures they encounter, but also shape them (Corsaro 1997; James and Prout 1990). Many authors have promoted the concept of child agency, which argues that children are not empty vessels, they can interact with more than one social group at a time and are capable of making choices and of influencing adult culture (James and Prout 1990; Waksler 1991).

A number of authors highlighted the complexity of inter-generational relations and argued that power relations could be two-way between children and adults (Mayall 2000). A more complex approach to childhood emerged that argued that childhood was a social construction that could not be separated from issues of class, gender or ethnicity but also that children's social relationships and cultures were worthy of study in their own right (James and Prout 1990; Waksler 1991). This perspective argued that children should be viewed as actively involved in the construction of their own social lives (and the lives of those around them) and that different children used or gave different meaning to the same cultural artefacts (James and Prout 1990; Hardman 2001). This work suggested that children's cultural lives were complex and it led to calls within disability studies for more nuanced approaches that would investigate disabled children's capacities to develop complex and multiple identities and to take action to confront stereotypes about themselves (Davis and Watson 2002; Priestley 1998). It should be noted that such shifts (related to shifts in the sociology and anthropology of childhood) also occurred in child development. In an attempt to move to more complex notions of childhood agency, developmental psychology as a discipline has become more self-critical (see Woodhead and Faulkner 2000 and Hogan 2005 for further discussion of these issues). Similarly, post-Vygotskian writers in psychology have examined the complexity of systems (see social cultural activity theory: Leadbetter *et al.* 2007). They have argued that we need to understand better the relationships, contradictions and tensions that exist in systems. This approach sees systems as complex and dynamic (Leadbetter *et al.* 2007). These perspectives have led to the conclusion that children are not simply restrained by the structures they encounter but also shape them.

The recognition of children's analytical abilities and their ability to develop contrasting social relations in different contexts has led a number of writers to challenge single representations of childhood (Mills 2000; Valentine 1999; Dyck 1999). The development of more complex characterizations of childhood that take into account children's own beliefs, practices and fluid identities has taken many forms of writing including:

- the challenging of the idea that young carers have a universal victim status (Stables and Smith 1999);
- the description of the multifaceted nature of power relationships and control in out-of-school clubs (Smith and Barker 2000);
- the examination of the fluid and diverse identities of men working in childcare (Robb 2001);
- the recognition of diverse life experiences of 'refugee children' (Candappa and Egharevba 2002);

- the illustration of the complex construction of illness among young people in Ecuadorian Andes (e.g., perceptions of self, economic migration by fathers, emotional and physical exhaustion, parenting styles and changes in community relationships) (Pribilsky 2001);
- the explanation of the complex fusion of issues relating to technology and health in everyday school life (Robinson and Delahooke 2001);
- the connecting of new forms of technology with new forms of independence (Lee 2001).

In disability studies, the traditional social model has been adapted in an attempt to overcome simplistic characterization of 'disability culture' (Davis 2000; Corker and Davis 2001; Davis and Corker 2001). Disability studies in the United Kingdom (UK) has tried to better understand notions of difference and the relationships between disability and inequality that relate to 'gender', 'race' and 'sexuality' (Morris 1992; Vernon 1997). A number of writers have argued that there are many 'social models' of disability, including materialist and postmodern (Corker and Shakespeare 2001; Corker 1999a, 1999b). Corker and Shakespeare (2001) were particularly concerned with understanding the connections between disability studies and postmodernism. They separated out three types of postmodernism:

- *Radical postmodernism* (considers truth to be contested, there to be various perspectives on a social event and social life to be ambiguous);
- *Psychoanalytical approaches* (highlight the diverse and fragmented nature of identity, conflict concerning legitimate behaviour and the contradictory nature of people's lives and thoughts);
- *Performativity* (stresses the expressive nature of identity, the ability of people to adopt or 'perform' different roles in various contexts and the opportunity for people to interpret reality and construct identities through social practice rather than genetics).

Postmodern perspectives encourage listeners, readers and observers to consider the complex nature of disability, culture and identity (Corker and Davis 2000, 2001). They can be connected to writing in other fields which suggest young people 'do' identities rather than are or have one identity (e.g., the different ways in which young people 'do ethnicity') (Nayak 2009). Such writing suggests that adults and children's identities are constructed in a range of complex ways publically and privately (Corker and Davis 2000, 2001).

The political nature of childhood relationships was highlighted by a number of writers. For example, Davis and Watson (2001) found that some adults in mainstream and special schools unreflexively employed markers of difference when ignoring the wishes and aspirations of disabled children.

> Our data suggest that very few adults in schools question the processes and social contexts in which they construct notions of difference. Much emphasis on inclusion is placed on the removal of structural barriers. Whilst this is important, our findings suggest that personal and institutional cultural values also need to be addressed. Policies which aim to create positive outcomes for disabled children within the education system should not be based simply on structural issues but should be based on a more nuanced multi-level approach which challenges the structural, cultural and individual conditions which create disability. Schools have to address the issues which lead to unreflexive adult practices. These include: poor resources and training, the unquestioning use of discourses of difference and the privileging of teachers own cultural beliefs and hierarchical notions of ability.
>
> *(Davis and Watson 2001: 19–20)*

419

This shift in childhood and disability studies recognized the complex nature of children's identities and questioned the taken-for-granted practices of professionals. This shift mirrored changes in counselling studies that led writers to suggest that identity was complex and involved power relations (Miller and De Shazer 2000; Berg and De Jong 1996; De Shazer and Molnar 1987). In particular, this enabled the notion of collaborative practice to emerge that aimed to celebrate the expertise of all people involved in a counselling process and questioned the power relations between relatives, clients and counsellors (Corker and Shakespeare 2001).

However, the postmodern shift has had its problems. For example, a number of texts have been criticized for overplaying the social construction of childhood, the crisis of adult power and legitimacy, the emergence of discourses of control/child powerlessness, the notion of a troubled global youth, the pressure from various forms of media and the need for professionals and parents to collaborate to keep control of children (e.g., social constructionists such as Jenks 1996; Finn 2001; Postman 1982). Such approaches have been critiqued for over-emphasizing the social aspects of childhood, creating social victims (in a similar way to the social model discussed earlier), ignoring the role of the body being acted upon and replicating the very dogma they aimed to replace (Prout 2000; Griffin 2001).

The body, childhood and disability

The principal objection to social constructionism has been that it has failed to investigate the interconnectedness of 'the body' to social places and overlooked writers that have highlighted the need to understand the role of social relations in different social locations (e.g., Dyck 1999; Stables and Smith 1999; Valentine 1999). A number of writers in disability and childhood studies now see the social world as a fusion of biological, cultural, individual and social issues (Corker and Shakespeare 2001; Davis and Watson 2002; Prout 2005; Davis 2007).

In childhood studies, Prout (2005) promoted a notion of nature-culture that suggested that biology is influenced by the social, that the social is influenced by biology and that the variables of social life are in constant interplay not (as is the case with the ecological model) rings that are distant. This can be connected to writing by Davis and Watson (2002) that highlighted the connectedness of the biological and social when illustrating the embodied resistance of disabled children, e.g., the interplay of impairment (visual impairment), disability experiencing peer (bullying) and agency (also being the bully) was related to a specific young man who in a vigorous way did not accept any victim status. Similarly, Corker and Davis (2000) illustrated the way that professionals connected notions of body, impairment and normality when attempting to ascribe identities on disabled children and the consequences of resistance in health settings (e.g., including an example where young peoples' liberty was withdrawn because they did not conform to health professionals' notions of normality). In particular these texts attempted to understand the social construction of impairment (Abberley 1987; Hughes and Paterson 1997; Paterson and Hughes 1999) and the relationship between impairment, disability and illness (Corker 1999b). Prout (2005) suggested that we needed to understand better the connections between biology, the social and processes of change. He considered the different contexts of systems, suggesting that systems with similar starting points can end up in quite different places due to the fluidity of the nature-culture relationship and the complexity of systems.

It is important to consider the fluid nature of change in disability and childhood studies, particularly when we are encouraging professionals to engage more effectively with disabled children. There are strong connections between fluid ideas of disability culture and the social model of disability, particularly in relation to challenging stereotypes concerning disabled children. However, we need to recognize the tension between individual and collective rights and the difficulties faced by professionals who work with groups of children. The postmodern shift recognizes the complexity of political systems (e.g., vested interests, claims on scarce resources and in-fighting between professionals) (Smith and Davis 2010) and requires those that study and work with disabled children to investigate their views and collaborate with disabled children to make their wishes come to fruition. Yet, we know that this process is very difficult because of the dynamic nature of children's everyday lives and the pressures placed on service providers (Davis 2007, 2006).

Many writers have called for children to be put at the centre of solving their own life problems (Dolan 2006; Davis 2006). However, this requires us to confront hierarchical ideas about disability and childhood and develop approaches to working with children where professionals become experts at facilitating processes of change (Dolan 2008; Davis 2007). Moss and Petrie (2002) argued against thinking in terms of adult rules, norms and principles. They believed that we should approach childhood in an ambiguous way, develop processes that enable dialogue and adopt practices that enable us to be surprised by the outcomes that children are prepared to negotiate. Prout (2005) suggested that processes of change were dependent on the nature of systems, whether they were balanced, chaotic, rhythmically repetitive or oscillating between two poles. Such perspectives have encouraged us to understand that disabled children's lives will be different depending on the systems they live in, the way that their identities are constructed by and for them, the relationship between impairment and disability, the availability of opportunities to have their opinions heard and the likelihood that they have the chance to live the lives that they wish for. But they will also be different because they themselves can construct diverse identities, influence the people they encounter and support the learning of others. At the heart of this analysis is the idea that disabled children's identities can be fluid; they and their impairments will have different meanings in different social contexts and there will be times when they do not wish to be defined as disabled in the social model sense because (disability being a social construct) they are not encountering barriers at that specific moment.

In disability studies, it has been argued that postmodern approaches can provide a focus to encourage professionals to include service users in service development (Beresford 1999). However, it has also been argued that this requires service providers to consider issues of equality and respect, recognize disabled people as capable, value/validate disabled people's contributions and shift ownership/control to disabled people. This requires a shift in power relations that recognize the connection between policy, theory and practice, that encourage service providers to be clear about the concepts of disability and childhood that underpin their practice, and to embrace complexity. In particular, postmodern ideas of ambiguity, dialogue and contested truth need to be unpacked with professionals (Parton 2000).

Professionals are just as complex human beings as children and the development of flexible approaches is not easy in situations where bureaucratic processes reduce professionals' abilities to respond quickly to disabled children's ideas (Davis 2011). We can conclude from postmodern accounts in both childhood and disability studies that we need to examine further the oppressive barriers that both children and adults encounter in social spaces and that we cannot understand disabled children's lives in isolation from the adults that they interact with. We can also conclude that we should not assume (as academics) that any approach to disabled children's lives is superior to another. It is for disabled children themselves (in partnership with others) to identify the individual, social, economic, biological and political issues that they wish change in their lives and it is for researchers in this field to support such processes of analysis, dialogue and discovery.

Conclusion

The chapter has briefly charted recent shifts in thinking in relation to disability and childhood studies. It concludes that disabled children and young people have complex identities, their lives involve agency and can be dynamic (influence the present as well as the future). Disabled children should not be characterized as homogeneous groups, or as perpetual victims. They have the potential to act in powerful ways (both integrative and divisive) (Davis 2007). The shift documented here in social theory has enabled us to move away from patronizing and rigid approaches to disability and childhood. Very often writers characterize the medical/social model division as a division between psychological and sociological accounts of disability. Such writers overlook the shift in both disciplines that is concerned with the tension between control and self-realization in childhood (Prout 2000). They also ignore the fact that contemporary sociological theories that create social victims and overplay the notion of oppression can be equally as limiting as outdated psychological deficit model approaches. This leads this chapter to conclude that we need to be much more precise when critiquing writing related to disability and childhood and not simply assume that any single discipline has all the answers.

References

Abberley, P. (1987) 'The Concept of Oppression and the Development of a Social Theory of Disability', *Disability, Handicap and Society* 2(1): 5–19.

Alan, J. (1996) 'Foucault and Special Educational Needs: A "Box of Tools" for Analysing Children's Experience of Mainstreaming', *Disability & Society* 11(2): 219–33.

Alderson, P. (2000) *Young Children's Rights: Exploring Beliefs, Principles and Practice* (London: Jessica Kingsley).

Alderson, P. and Goodey, C. (1998) *Enabling Education: Experiences in Special and Ordinary Schools* (London: Tufnell Press).

Anning, A., Cottrell, D., Frost, N., Green, J. and Robinson, M. (2006) *Developing Multiprofessional Teamwork for Integrated Children's Services* (Maidenhead: Open University Press).

Barnes, C. (1991) *Disabled People in Britain and Discrimination: A Case for Anti-discrimination Legislation* (London: Hurst & Co).

Beresford, P. (1999) Theorising Social Work Research, 'Social Work: What Kinds of Knowledge?' seminar, Brunel University, May.

Berg, I. K. and De Jong, P. (1996) 'Solution-building Conversations: Co-constructing a Sense of Competence with Clients', *Families in Society* 77(6): 376–91.

Booth, T. and Ainscow, M. (2000) *Index on Inclusion* (Bristol: Centre for Studies on Inclusive Education).

Bronfenbrenner, U. (1989) 'Ecological Systems Theory', in R. Vasta, ed., *Annals of Child Development 6* (Greenwich, CT: JAI Press): pp. 187–249.

Burman, E. (1994) *Deconstructing Developmental Psychology* (London: Routledge).

Burman, E. (1996) 'Local, Global or Globalized? Child Development and International Children's Rights Legislation', *Childhood* 3(1): 45–66.

Candappa, M. and Egharevba, I. (2002) 'Negotiating Boundaries: Tensions Within Home and School Life for Refugee Children', in R. Edwards, ed., *Children, Home and School: Autonomy, Connection or Regulation?* (London: Falmer Press).

Connors, C. and Stalker, K. (2003) *The Views and Experiences of Disabled Children and their Siblings* (London: Jessica Kingsley).

Corker, M. (1999a) 'New Disability Discourse: The Principle of Optimisation, and Social Change', in M. Corker and S. French, eds, *Disability Discourse* (Buckingham: Open University Press).

Corker, M. (1999b) 'Differences, Conflations and Foundations: The Limits to the Accurate Theoretical Representation of Disabled People's Experience', *Disability & Society* 14(5): 627–42.

Corker, M. and Davis, J. M. (2001) 'Portrait of Callum: The Disabling of a Childhood', in R. Edwards, ed., *Children, Home and School: Autonomy, Connection or Regulation?* (London: Falmer Press).

Corker, M. and Davis, J. M. (2000) 'Disabled Children – Invisible Under the Law', in J. Cooper and S. Vernon, eds, *Disability and the Law* (London: Jessica Kingsley).

Corker, M. and Shakespeare, T. (2001) 'Mapping the Terrain', in M. Corker and T. Shakespeare, eds, *Disability and Postmodernity* (London: Continuum).

Corsaro, W. A. (1997) *The Sociology of Childhood* (London: Pine Forge Press).

Davis, J. M. (2000) 'Disability Studies as Ethnographic Research and Text: Can We Represent Cultural Diversity Whilst Promoting Social Change?', *Disability & Society* 15(2): 191–206.

Davis, J. M. (2006) 'Disability, Childhood Studies and the Construction of Medical Discourses: Questioning Attention Deficit Hyperactivity Disorder; a Theoretical Perspective', in G. Lloyd, J. Stead and D. Cohen, eds, *Critical New Perspectives on ADHD* (London: Taylor and Francis).

Davis, J. M. (2007) 'Analysing Participation and Social Exclusion with Children and Young People: Lessons from Practice', *International Journal of Children's Rights* 15(1): 121–46.

Davis, J. M. (2011) *Integrated Working in Children's Services* (London: Sage).

Davis, J. M. and Corker, M. (2001) 'Disability Studies and Anthropology: Difference Troubles in Academic Paradigms', *Anthropology in Action* 8(2): 18–27.

Davis, J. M. and Watson, N. (2001) 'Where are the Children's Experiences? Analysing Social and Cultural Exclusion in "Special" and "Mainstream" Schools', *Disability & Society* 16(5): 671–87.

Davis, J. M. and Watson, N. (2002) 'Countering Stereotypes of Disability: Disabled Children and Resistance', in M. Corker and T. Shakespeare, eds, *Disability and Postmodernity* (London: Continuum).

Davis, J. M. and Hogan, J. (2004) Research with Children: Ethnography, Participation, Disability, Self Empowerment', in C. Barnes and G. Mercer, eds, *Implementing the Social Model of Disability: Theory and Research* (Leeds: The Disability Press).

Davis, J. M., Watson, N., Corker, M. and Shakespeare, T. (2003) 'Reconstructing Disabled Childhoods and Social Policy in the UK', in A. Prout and C. Hallet, *Hearing the Voices Of Children* (London: Falmer Press).

Davis, J. M., Tisdall, K., Hill, M. and Prout, A., eds, (2006) *Children, Young People and Social Inclusion: Participation for What?* (Cambridge: Policy Press).

De Shazer, S. and Molnar, A. (1987) 'Solution-focused Therapy: Toward the Identification of Therapeutic Tasks', *Journal of Marital and Family Therapy* 13(4): 349–58.

Dillon, J., Statham, J. and Moss, P. (2001) 'The Role of the Private Market in Day Care Provision for Children in Need', *Social Policy and Administration* 35(2): 127–44.

Dolan. P. (2006) 'Family Support: From Description to Reflection', in P. Dolan, J. Canavan and J. Pinkerton, eds, (2006) *Family Support as Reflective Practice* (London: Jessica Kingsley).

Dolan. P. (2008) 'Social Support, Social Justice and Social Capital: A Tentative Theoretical Triad for Community Development', *Community Development* 39(1): 112–119

Dyck, I. (1999) 'Body Troubles: Women, the Workplace and Negotiations of a Disabled Identity', in R. Butler and H. Parr, eds, *Mind and Body Spaces: Geographies of Illness, Impairment and Disability* (London: Routledge).

Ennew, J. (1994) 'Time for Children or Time for Adults?' in J. Qvortrup, M. Bardy, G. Sgritta and H. Wintersberger, eds, *Childhood Matters: Social Theory, Practices and Politics* (Aldershot: Avebury).

Finkelstein, V. (1975) 'To Deny or Not to Deny Disability', *Magic Carpet* 28(1): 31–8.

Finn, J. (2001) 'Text and Turbulence: Representing Adolescence as Pathology in the Human Services', *Childhood* 8(2): 167–92.

Fitzgerald, D. and Kay, J. (2008) *Working Together in Children's Services* (London: Routledge/David Fulton).

Griffin, C. (2001) 'Imagining New Narratives of Youth', *Childhood* 8(2): 147–66.

Hallden, G. (1994) 'The Family – A Refuge from Demands or an Arena for the Exercise of Power and Control – Children's Fictions on their Future Families', in B. Mayall, ed., *Children's Childhoods Observed and Experienced* (London: Falmer).

Hardman, C. (2001) Can there be an Anthropology of Children?', *Childhood* 8(4): 501–17. First published in (1973) *Journal of the Anthropology Society of Oxford* iv(11): 85.

Hendry, L. B., Glendenning, A., Love, J. and Shucksmith, J. (1993) *Young People's Leisure and Lifestyles* (London: Routledge).

Hogan, D. (2005) 'Researching the Child in Developmental Psychology', in S. Green and D. Hogan, eds, *Researching Children's Experience* (London: Sage).

Honneth, A. (2000) 'Suffering from Indeterminacy: An Attempt at a Reactualisation of Hegel's Philosophy of Right', *Two Lectures*. Assen: Van Gorcum.

Hughes, B. and Paterson, K. (1997) 'The Social Model of Disability and the Disappearing Body: Towards a Sociology of Impairment', *Disability & Society* 12(3).

Humphries, S. and Gordon, P. (1992) *Out of Sight: The Experience of Disability 1900–1950* (Plymouth: Northcote House).

James, A. and Prout, A. (1990) 'Contemporary Issues in the Sociological Study of Childhood', in A. James and A. Prout, eds, *Constructing and Reconstructing Childhood* (London: Falmer).

James, A., Jenks, C. and Prout, A. (1998) *Theorising Childhood* (Cambridge: Polity Press).

Jenks, C. (1996) 'The Postmodern Child', in J. Brannen and M. O'Brien, eds, *Children in Families* (London: Falmer).

Leadbetter, J., Daniels, H. R. J., Edwards, A., Martin, D. M., Middleton, D., Popova, A., Warmington, P. C., Apostol, A. and Brown, S. (2007) 'Professional Learning within Multi-agency Children's Services: Researching into Practice', *Educational Research* 49(1): 83–98.

Lee, N. (2001) 'The Extensions of Childhood: Technologies, Children and Independence', in I. Hutchby and J. Moran-Ellis, eds, *Children, Technology and Culture: The Impact of Technologies in Children's Everyday Lives* (London: Falmer).

Lewis, A. (1995) *Children's Understandings of Disability* (London: Routledge).

Mauthner, M. (1997) 'Methodological Aspects of Collecting Data from Children', *Children & Society* 11: 16–28.

Mayall, B. (1994) 'Children in Action at Home and School', in B. Mayall, ed., *Children's Childhoods Observed and Experienced* (London: Falmer).

Mayall, B. (1996) *Children, Health and the Social Order* (Buckingham: Open University Press).

Mayall, B. (2000) 'Conversations with Children: Working with Generational Issues', in P. Christensen and A. James, eds, *Research with Children* (London: Falmer).

Middleton, L. (1996) *Making a Difference: Social Work with Disabled Children* (Birmingham: Venture Press).

Miller, G. and De Shazer, S. (2000) 'Emotions in Solution-focused Therapy: A Re-examination', *Family Process* 39: 5–23.

Mills, R. (2000) 'Perspectives of Childhood', in J. Mills and R. Mills, eds, *Childhood Studies: A Reader in Perspectives of Childhood* (London: Routledge).

Morris, J. (1991) *Pride Against Prejudice: Transforming Attitudes to Disability* (London: Women's Press).

Morris, J. (1992) 'Personal and Political: A Feminist Perspective in Researching Physical Disability', *Disability, Handicap and Society* 7(2): 157–66.

Morris, J. (1997) 'Gone Missing? Disabled Children Living Away from their Families', *Disability & Society* 12(2): 241–58.

Moss, P. and Petrie, P. (2002) *From Children's Services to Children's Spaces* (London: Taylor and Francis).

Nayak, A. (2009) 'Race, Ethnicity and Young People', in H. Montgomery and M. Kellet, eds, *Children and Young People's Worlds: Developing Frameworks for Integrated Practice* (Bristol: Policy Press).

Norwich, B. (1997) 'Exploring the Perspectives of Adolescents with Moderate Learning Difficulties on their Special Schooling and Themselves: Stigma and Self-perceptions', *European Journal of Special Needs Education* 12(1): 38–53.

Oliver, M. (1990) *The Politics of Disablement* (Basingstoke: Macmillan).

Parsons, T. and Bales, R. F. (1955) *Family Socialisation and the Interactive Process* (New York: The Free Press).

Parton, N. (2000) 'Some Thoughts on the Relationship between Theory and Practice in and for Social Work', *British Journal of Social Work* (2000) 30: 449–63.

Paterson, K. and Hughes, B. (1999) 'Disability Studies and Phenomenology: The Carnal Politics of Everyday Life', *Disability & Society* 14(5).

Postman, N. (1982) *The Disappearance of Childhood* (New York: Random House).

Pribilsky, J. (2001) 'Nervios and "Modern Childhood"', *Childhood* 8(2): 251–73.

Priestley, M. (1998) 'Childhood Disability and Disabled Childhoods: Agendas for Research', *Childhood* 5(2): 207–23.

Prout, A. (2000) 'Children's Participation: Control and Self-realisation in British Late Modernity', *Children and Society* 14: 304–16.

Prout, A. (2005) *The Future of Childhood. Towards the Interdisciplinary Study of Children* (London: Flamer Routledge).

Qvortrup, J. (1994) 'Childhood Matters: An Introduction', in J. Qvortrup, M. Bardy, G. Sgritta and H. Wintersberger, eds, *Childhood Matters: Social Theory, Practices and Politics* (Aldershot: Avebury).

Robb, M. (2001) 'Men Working in Childcare', in P. Foley, J. Roche and S. Tucker, eds, *Children in Society: Contemporary Theory, Policy and Practice* (Basingstoke: Open University Press/Palgrave).

Robinson, I. and Delahooke, A. (2001) 'Fabricating Friendships', in I. Hutchby and J. Moran-Ellis, eds, *Children, Technology and Culture: The Impact of Technologies in Children's Everyday Lives* (London: Falmer).

Smith, F. and Barker, J. (2000) 'Contested Spaces: Children's Experiences of Out-of school Care in England and Wales', *Childhood* 7(3): 315–33.

Smith, M. (2007) 'What is Family Support Work? A Case Study within the Context of One Local Authority in Scotland', University of Edinburgh.

Smith, M. and Davis, J. M. (2010) 'Constructions of Family Support: Lessons from the Field', *Administration* 58(2): 69–83.

Stables, J. and Smith, F. (1999) '"Caught in the Cinderella Trap": Narratives of Disabled Parents and Young Carers', in R. Butler and H. Parr, eds, *Mind and Body Spaces: Geographies of Illness, Impairment and Disability* (London: Routledge).

Stanton-Rogers, W. (2001) 'Constructing Childhood – Contrasting Child Concern', in P. Foley, J. Roche and S. Tucker, eds, *Children in Society* (Basingstoke: Open University Press).

Swain, J. and French, S. (2000) 'Towards an Affirmation Model of Disability', *Disability & Society* 15(4): 569–82.

Thomas, D. (1978) *The Social Psychology of Childhood Disability* (London: Methuen).

Thompson, P. (1994) 'Transmission Between Generations', in J. Brannen and M. O'Brien, eds, *Childhood and Parenthood* (London: Institute of Education).

Tomlinson, S. and Colquhoun, R. (1995) 'The Political Economy of Special Educational Needs in Britain', *Disability & Society* 10(2): 191–202.

UPIAS (1976) *Fundamental Principles of Disability* (London: Union of the Physically Impaired Against Segregation).

Valentine, G. (1999) 'What it Means to Be a Man: The Body, Masculinities, Disability', in R. Butler and H. Parr, eds, *Mind and Body Spaces: Geographies of Illness, Impairment and Disability* (London: Routledge).

Vernon, A. (1997) 'Reflexivity: The Dilemmas of Researching from the Inside', in C. Barnes and G. Mercer, eds, *Doing Disability Research* (Leeds University: The Disability Press).

Waksler, F. C. (1991) 'Beyond Socialisation', in F. C. Waksler, ed., *Studying the Social Worlds of Children: Sociological Readings* (London: Falmer).

Watson, N. and Shakespeare, T. (1998) 'Theoretical Perspectives on Disabled Childhood', in C. Robinson and K. Stalker K, eds, *Growing Up with Disability* (London: Jessica Kingsley).

Woodhead, M. (2009) 'Child Development and the Development of Childhood', in J. Qvortrup, W. A. Corsaro and M.-S. Honig, eds, *The Palgrave Handbook of Childhood Studies* (London: Palgrave).

Woodhead, M. and Faulkner, D. (2000) 'Subjects, Objects or Participants? Dilemmas of Psychological Research with Children', in P. Christiensen and A. James, eds, *Research with Children* (London: Falmer).

Zarb, G., ed., (1995) *Removing Disabling Barriers* (London: Policy Studies Institute).

32

'I HOPE HE DIES BEFORE ME'

Unravelling the debates about ageing and people with intellectual disability

Christine Bigby

Improvements to health care and the impact of deinstitutionalization have significantly increased the life expectancy of people with intellectual disability, few of whom survived past their early twenties in the first part of the twentieth century. Most people with mild intellectual impairment now have a life expectancy comparable with that of the general population and, while differences still exist for people with more severe impairments or specific genetic syndromes, the gap between their lifespan and population norms has reduced significantly (Patja *et al.* 2000). For example, between 1960 and 1995 the lifespan of people with Down's syndrome more than tripled from an average of 15 to 50 years (Haveman 2004). In Australia, people with mild, moderate and severe levels of impairment can expect to live for 74.0, 67.6 and 58.6 years respectively compared with a population median of 78.6 years (Bittles *et al.* 2002). Increased longevity means that adults with intellectual disability are much more likely to outlive their parents than in previous decades. As the quote in the title, taken from an Australian report, suggests, however, parental attitudes towards the extended life course of their adult children are often associated with anxiety and fear rather than celebration and recognition of potential for new opportunities (Bigby 2000; Keyzer *et al.* 1997a, b).

The broad goals found in national and international social and disability policies recognize people with intellectual disability as citizens with equal rights and seek to further choice, autonomy, independence and social participation. For example, ratification of the United Nations Convention on the Rights of Persons with Disabilities carries the expectation that governments will take effective and appropriate measures to facilitate participation and inclusion in the community (United Nations 2006: 13). Strategies adopted have been deinstitutionalization, self-directed funding, services that aim to support individualized lifestyles, community development to foster inclusive communities and improved access to mainstream services. The advent of middle and old age for people with intellectual disability is a new phenomenon, requiring disability advocates, policy makers and practitioners, for the first time, to apply these key concepts to the mid and latter part of the life course. This chapter highlights some of the debates that arise in doing so.

Primary challenges are balancing a focus on the centrality of family in the lives of middle-aged people with intellectual disability whilst not overshadowing individual needs, replicating the roles played by family and friends for those who lack these primary relationships, reconciling tensions between the 'disability' and 'ageing' worlds, navigating the interface of quite distinct service systems, and adapting mainstream and disability-specific services to accommodate people ageing with intellectual disability. Whilst many of the issues raised are similar for people ageing with other types of impairments, the focus of this chapter is people with intellectual disability. The institutionalization during their younger years of some of the current cohort who are ageing and the lifelong co-residence with parents of others distinguishes them from many other disabled people. The very nature of intellectual impairment adds a complex layer of issues associated with supporting independence, choice, autonomy and decision making that are also fairly unique to this group. The perspectives of people with intellectual disability have not been influential in the wider disability movement due to a lack of effective support and adaptation of participatory processes, and issues associated with intellectual impairment have not been widely considered by disability scholars (Chappell 1998; Frawley and Bigby 2011). Significantly, however, there is a well-established body of policy and practice research about ageing people with intellectual disability, although here too their own perspectives are largely missing (Bigby 2004). In comparison, issues of ageing with lifelong physical impairments have been taken up more by bio-psycho-medical researchers than those interested in social or policy spheres (Kemp and Mosqueda 2004).

This chapter adopts a life course perspective that draws attention to the influence of earlier parts of the life course on ageing, by examining 'how problems, needs and patterns of adaptations of older people are shaped by their earlier life experiences and historical conditions' (Hareven 2001: 142). For example, in the case of people with intellectual disability, the influence of earlier opportunities for personal development, quality of health care and lifestyle, formation of social networks and employment are significant to the issues likely to arise as people age. They lead to questions such as – what experiences might typify middle age in the absence of career, spouse or children? What relevance do retirement or superannuation policies have for ageing people with intellectual disability who have never worked? What type of support is necessary to ensure participation in social activities and community organizations when an older person has few friends or lacks resources such as transport, or the knowledge and skills to choose, locate and negotiate access to meaningful activities?

The starting point too is the dynamic interaction between the nature of impairment and social structures and processes, which leads to questions such as – should age care services targeted at the 'old old', people who are in their eighties, be accessible to people with Down's syndrome in their fifties who are ageing prematurely? Allied to this, is the fundamental influence of service systems in determining the types of adaptations to ageing that need to be contemplated and lead to questions such as – would adaptations to ageing be needed if individualized flexible supports were already a feature of disability service systems? Or should allied health and social programmes that aim to support ageing and which are in place for the general population of people who live in private homes in the community be equally available to older residents with intellectual disability in small group homes in the community or is this 'double dipping'? Such questions are tackled in later sections, but first I focus on a slightly earlier part of the life course, highlighting the almost total neglect of middle age in the intellectual disability literature which skips from an undifferentiated period of adulthood to old age (see, for example, Brown and Percy 2007; Grant *et al.* 2010).

Middle aged – or prematurely old?

Too often middle-aged people with intellectual disability are regarded as being old. Premature ageing that affects some subgroups such as people with Down's syndrome is wrongly assumed to apply to all people with intellectual disability, or those who are middle aged are thought to be 'old' because they are simply the oldest participants in a service. Perceptions of premature ageing have been compounded by researchers who often adopt an earlier chronological age for 'older people' with intellectual disability, at times as young as 40 years, to ensure sufficient participants, and avoid exclusion of subgroups who do age prematurely from studies (Bigby and Balandin 2004). Such practices have meant that the negative connotations associated with ageing have prematurely enveloped people with intellectual disability and masked middle age as a stage in the life course that holds significant possibilities and is worthy of attention in its own right.

In middle age the majority of people with intellectual disability live with their parents. It has been the 'off cycle' family life course of older parents that has been associated with the middle age of people with intellectual disability. The continued parental caring role has been problematized in light of parents' reduced physical stamina, juxtaposed with their desire to 'retire'. Identification of the new phenomenon of 'older parental carers' has coincided with the growth of the Carers Movement, drawing attention to the stress and burden of informal caring more generally and generating programmes to support carers, which some suggest has been both disempowering and diverted attention from pursuit of services that support the rights and citizenship of people with disabilities (Fyffe *et al.* 2011; Shakespeare 2006).

Parental concerns about future safety and security, and who will 'care' for their middle-aged son and daughter with intellectual disability have framed people as 'dependants', or 'care recipients', whose future must be planned. Parents and service systems alike have been exhorted to plan for future care, to ensure replacement of parents as lifelong primary carers. The emphasis on future planning has overshadowed a focus on the present, as plans focus on a fixed, static future characterized by security rather than the continuing developmental potential of adults to learn new skills or acquire new interests and relationships in middle age and beyond. Studies about the nature of planning suggest that in many instances middle-aged adults with intellectual disability are not included in discussions about their own future, and plans are made around rather than with them (Bigby 2000; Knox and Bigby 2007). Seldom have questions been raised about the viability or desirability of encouraging parents to plan for the rest of their middle-aged child's life, which may be another 40 or 50 years (Bigby 2000). A few programmes, such as that developed by Heller and colleagues at the University of Chicago, recognize that planning for the future is not the sole preserve of parents but must occur in tandem with middle-aged adults (Heller *et al.* 2000). An evaluation of training curricula designed to educate and provoke discussion about ageing issues among adults with intellectual disability demonstrated the importance of their involvement. It also illustrated participants' dissatisfaction with their current lives, when they were exposed to the range of potential choices and opportunities about their own futures. Significant personal development does occur when middle-aged people leave the parental home, and one study suggested the most effective type of planning was for a key person able to advocate, respond flexibly to change and support the person with intellectual disability to negotiate support as issues arose, rather than the formulation of more rigid residential plans that might lock a person into particular long-term arrangements (Bigby 1996).

Possibilities of middle age

Various theoretical perspectives divide the life course into stages; psychological theorists take a developmental or psychodynamic approach to define characteristics, whilst sociologists use gender experiences, family formation, intergenerational commitments, or relationships to work or wider communities (Erikson 1959; Brody 2004). Most schemas identify specific challenges associated with 'middle age', and the media and pop psychology abound with comments about the mid-life crisis, when individuals take life-changing decisions about work, relationships and lifestyle. Middle age is the seventh age in Erikson's eight-stage theory of psycho-social development, a time when the individual may feel their life has become stuck, and tensions between generativity and stagnation arise. Generativity extends beyond the personal spheres of family and career to include the wider social world where the investment of the skills and wisdom gained from life experiences can lead to the creation of ideas and contributions to culture, arts and society (Erikson 1959). Sociological approaches suggest middle age is a time of change in career direction, family roles and relationships, particularly in respect of parenting and caring. The chronological age span encompassed by middle age is perceived as 45–65 years although culture and socio-demographic trends influence the timing and nature of the events or transitions that occur during this period. Until the 1980s in Western societies for example, middle age was associated with the 'empty nest', a time when adult children had departed and couples remained in the family home, left alone to renegotiate their relationship (Neugarten 1968). Higher divorce rates have changed for some the need to renegotiate relationships in mid life, and later marriage, greater access to higher education and housing inflation have extended the period adult children remain at home. In twenty-first century Australia, rather than being a norm for middle-aged couples, the empty nest has become an aspiration to joke about, with adult children being portrayed as nesting in the attic.

Brody (2004) identified the 'parent care years' as a period in women's lives when they are 'in the middle', with caring responsibilities for both children and parents. The absence of spouse, children or career in the lives of most people with intellectual disability means that in middle age they may not confront many of the issues faced by people who have acquired these attributes of modern life. Many do, however, occupy key family roles and face challenges in negotiating these relationships. Walmsley (1996) and others have identified the reciprocal relationships and interdependence that frequently exist between an older parent and their middle-aged son or daughter with intellectual disability who lives at home; each dependent on the other for the continued capacity to remain in the community (Knox and Bigby 2007). It is notable in this context that some research suggests that older parental carers of middle-aged people with intellectual disability experience less care giving stress and have greater well-being compared with other caring groups (Seltzer and Krauss 1994). Interdependent relationships with parents have more recently been termed 'mutual caring' by the Foundation for People with Learning Disabilities (2010) and, though still narrowly conceptualizing the potential of people with intellectual disability, this extends their identity beyond that of care recipient. This idea of mutual caring highlights the costs to lifestyle and autonomy of interdependent relationships with elderly parents and the challenge of reconciling conflicting needs. For example, in Bigby's (2000) study, many of the older adults with intellectual disability who had lived at home with parents until middle age seemed to live lifestyles more typical of an older person. They described accompanying their parents to activities and clubs geared towards senior citizens and shared relationships with parental friends rather than people from their own generation. They spoke too about the restrictions that living with parents placed on their own lives. One man said, for example:

> I couldn't have been able to come to functions here or at the church. If I went to the cricket all day Saturday I'd come home and find mum on the floor and she wouldn't be able to get any help, she wouldn't be able to ring up. I just couldn't get away and leave her on her own. I'd have to stay with my mum. I couldn't do the things which I would like to do.
>
> *(Bigby 2000: 76)*

In a similar vein, Walmsley (1996) suggests that whilst middle-aged adults provide significant support to elderly parents, parents retain control over the life of their adult son or daughter. In Bigby's study for example, siblings talked about the protective stance taken by parents and their own difficulty in challenging this. For example, one said about the way her mother had regarded her then middle-aged brother, 'Phillip's her little boy … mother was too dominant' (Bigby 2000: 116).

Little thought has been given to the self-identity of middle-aged people with intellectual disability or to the potential contribution they could make to their communities. In Australia where the employment rates of adults with intellectual disability are decreasing (Australian Institute of Health and Welfare (AIHW) 2008) their primary form of occupation is likely to be supported employment, or a segregated day programme. The anecdotal accounts of middle-aged people dropping out by refusing to attend day programmes hint of the stagnation that attendance at such programmes over many years may bring to people's lives. Work, the self-advocacy movement, peer education and mentoring programmes, volunteering in community organizations and participation in inclusive research groups, though seldom including more than a small minority, all provide examples of opportunities for people with intellectual disability to use their life experiences in creative, meaningful ways to make a wider contribution. Drama groups such as that described by Hall (2010) or arts programmes similarly provide opportunities for creative contributions and inclusion as part of a wider arts community. In families, for example, potentially new roles exist for single middle-aged members, such as that of the family maiden aunt (made famous by Australian folk singer Judy Small) whose relationship with nephews and nieces can be unencumbered by parental authority or responsibility.

The grey literature from the United States (US), Canada and the United Kingdom (UK) holds many examples of the success of person-centred planning and middle-aged people with intellectual disability being valued members of community groups, or with a network of acquaintances and friends with whom they have reciprocal relationships (O'Brien and Lyle O'Brien 2002; Wightman 2009). Such examples, however, are usually the exception that flourish with well-resourced family support, but which for many, especially those who have lived in institutions, is absent. Evidence is beginning to indicate that more formal person-centred planning alone has little impact on the formation of social networks (Robertson *et al.* 2006). Recent statistics about the social isolation and the continuing 'distinct social space' occupied by middle-aged adults with intellectual disability raise the importance of exploring strategies by which network building or construction of circles of support might be replicated for those without resourceful families (Clement and Bigby 2009; Todd *et al.* 1990). For example, Australian studies of middle-aged people with intellectual disability have found that 62 per cent of residents in group homes had no one outside the service system who knew them well (Bigby 2008a) and only 28 per cent of residents had weekly contact with a family member, friend or acquaintance without intellectual disability outside their home in contrast to 96 per cent of the general Australian population (Bigby *et al.* 2011b). The absence of robust informal relationships for many middle-aged people with intellectual disability through which self-identify and self-esteem can be gained or that act as a vehicle for social participation, poses a significant challenge to the disability system to make the ideal of generativity, social inclusion and contribution a reality for more than a small minority of middle-aged people. Such attributes are also fundamentally important as the foundations for a good old age.

Old age – double jeopardy

Aspects of old age, like other parts of the life course, are socially constructed. Expectations about retirement and the participation of older people in family, work and social roles differ between culture and historic time, mediated by prevailing economic conditions and demographic trends. For example, mandated and different retirement ages for men and women in countries such as

Australia disappeared as anti-discriminatory legislation strengthened; early retirement as a solution to unemployment and technological change in the mid-1980s has given way to expectations of an extended working life and a rise in the age criteria for state pensions; efforts to reduce the welfare state have led to self- rather than state-funded retirement and the growth of private superannuation. Theorizing about the sociological nature of ageing has changed dramatically since Henry and Cumming, writing in the 1960s, considered disengagement to be a core element and Butler (1975) identified ageism and the poverty, isolation and illness that characterized experiences of ageing in the US.

The earliest writing about the ageing of people with intellectual disability, dating back to the mid-1980s, reflected the contemporary social attitudes of that time towards ageing and warned of the double jeopardy they faced, as negative and devaluing attitudes towards people with disabilities were compounded by similar attitudes towards older people. MacDonald and Tyson (1988) referred to the 'deca-jeopardy' faced by older people with intellectual disability as members of multiply disadvantaged groups, the 'aged', 'disabled', 'poor', 'women' and 'socially isolated'. Wolfensberger (1985) discussed the challenges of applying the theory of social role valorization and the risks of replicating for older people with intellectual disability the devalued status of older people in the general community. His writing questioned the application of norms such as retirement, which he saw as stripping people of key identities and roles. He proposed the lifestyle of the rich and famous should provide the valued role model for people with intellectual disability rather than the lives of ordinary older people. He and others drew attention to the philosophies and approach of aged care services that were diametrically opposed to those of disability services, by providing 'care' rather than 'support', fostering 'dependence' rather than 'independence' and continuing 'segregation' rather than 'integration'. Such factors together with the relatively poor quality of aged care services compared with disability services and the already devalued status of people with intellectual disability were seen to heighten their risk of using such services. It was suggested too, that people with intellectual disability would be alienated by other older service users, who with their own self-image already under threat, would regard proximity to people with a lifelong disability as a further assault on their status.

Empirical evidence for the relative merits of the aged care and disability systems was provided by several early UK studies that illustrated the diminished opportunities for participation and engagement that age care services offered to older people with intellectual disability (Moss *et al.* 1992; Walker and Walker 1998). Whilst the jeopardy of using aged care services was uncovered, research also identified the inherent ageism of disability services, illustrating the dangers of being prematurely labelled as older. Walker *et al.* (1995) found that in disability services, older participants were given fewer opportunities, despite in some instances having lower support needs than their younger more severely disabled counterparts, and concluded:

> if older people with intellectual disability are to have positive futures, then as an essential starting point, the implicit age discrimination that regards older people with intellectual disability as having lesser needs than younger ones should be tackled root and branch within all service provision agencies.
>
> *(Walker et al. 1995: 241)*

Strong messages from this early writing were the need to change and adapt the intellectual disability system to take account of ageing people, the potential advantages of remaining in the disability service system and the dangers of using aged care services. Since then, debate has continued about how needs should be met and by which system but in a context of changing aged care policies and services.

Reformulating old age

In the last 20 years the proportion of older people has increased in Western societies and their numbers continue to be swelled by the baby boom generation. This growth has been accompanied by reformulation of theories about old age and policy reform, resulting in greater alignment between the philosophies of aged care and disability sectors. More recent theories about ageing have a much more positive spin, framing it as having the possibility of being 'successful' or 'active' (Rowe and Kahn 1998; World Health Organization 2002). The concept of 'Active Ageing', founded on the United Nations' principles of the rights of older people (independence, participation, care, self-fulfilment and dignity), exemplifies this shift (World Health Organization 2002). It promotes Active Ageing as 'the process of optimizing opportunities for health, participation and security in order to enhance quality of life as people age'. This is very similar to the emphasis in disability policy of rights, participation, choice and inclusion. Both sectors have adopted new service models based on person-centred care and planning and individual self-directed services (Nay and Garratt 2009). Differences remain, however, in the extent to which aims are realized in front line service delivery, and residential aged care services are significantly larger than supported accommodation services in the disability sector (AIHW 2009). Despite facing similar structural issues, such as discrimination, differences continue in the way these are framed, which in turn affects where advocacy efforts are directed. Issues are perceived at a more personal and individual level by the ageing sector whilst the disability sector has a stronger focus on social structural factors (Priestley and Rabiee 2002; Gibson and Grew 2002).

There are different perceptions of what constitute ageing and who is an older person between the two sectors, which has implications for access to services. In Western countries, it is the over-80 year-old group who have experienced the most rapid expansion in recent years, and the greatest age-associated changes to biological and health status occur after the age of 75 years, when the prevalence of chronic disease and other disabling health conditions increases quite dramatically. Reflecting this standard trajectory of chronological ageing, in Australia and elsewhere, the bulk of the aged care system is focused on the frail aged, and eligibility criteria are normally set at 70 years (AIHW 2009).

In contrast, as suggested earlier, disability service providers tend to prematurely label people with intellectual disability in their forties and fifties as old, often associated with reduced expectations of capacity and development and assumptions that health problems are simply related to ageing. Chronological demarcation of old age for people with intellectual disability is complicated by their diversity. Most older people with intellectual disability do not age prematurely although some subgroups have a unique pattern of ageing. Some experience age-related disorders relatively early, or acquire additional health needs associated with the progression of secondary impairments, chronic health conditions or the consequences of a lifetime of poor-quality health care. People with Down's syndrome, for instance, have higher prevalence and earlier onset of age-related sensory and musculoskeletal disorders resulting in additional disability as well as having the exceptional risk of developing dementia in the sixth decade (Holland 2000; Torr *et al.* 2010). Higher age-specific mortality rates mean that most people with more severe and multiple impairments do not live to old age and, as a result, older people with intellectual disability are predominantly the 'younger old' in their sixties and seventies, rather than the 'old old' in their eighties. They are the 'healthy survivors', who as a group have milder impairment levels than their younger peers.

The life experiences of people with an intellectual disability mean that ageing occurs from a particularly disadvantageous position. After the transition from parental care in mid life, and perhaps a period of co-residence with siblings or a more independent option, a high proportion of older people with an intellectual disability live in disability-supported accommodation, where it is more complex to adapt to age-associated changed support needs than in a private home. As a result of lifelong unemployment, most older people have no superannuation, are reliant on a state-funded pension for income, and have limited wealth to enable the exercise of choice or access to private health systems. As well as the possibility of health-related complications that arise from genetic conditions or secondary impairments, the health of older people with intellectual disability may be compromised by an unhealthy lifestyle during their adult years. They have much higher rates of obesity, nutritional problems and cholesterol and lower rates of physical activity and exercise than the general population. Potentially these all increase the chances of later-life diseases such as diabetes, hypertension, heart disease and arthritis (Bigby 2004). When parents die, siblings are likely to be the closest relatives of people with intellectual disability and the limited informal support networks they carry over from middle age will have consequences for well-being in terms of social relationships, inclusion and availability of advocates. All of these factors exemplify the significance of access to quality health care and other support services to enable people to age well.

Adapting services to age-associated change

As people with intellectual disability age they continue to need many of the services they have used previously, such as aids and equipment, accommodation, advocacy and support with participation in purposeful activities. Age-related changes may mean that the nature and intensity of the support required changes; for example, physical modifications to reflect reduced mobility, more intensive health monitoring or night-time support. Issues arise about the source of resources necessary to intensify support, whether adapting to age-related changes will alter too radically the original intent of a disability service, such as a group home, and the potential impact on other service users. Some types of service, such as vocational, may no longer be required. The need for new types may arise, such as geriatric health care, dementia assessment, allied health and leisure or volunteering programmes. This type of service will already be available in the mainstream health, aged or community care systems. Issues arise, however, about access, quality and responsiveness of mainstream services to people with intellectual disability who may need access at an earlier age, and may fall outside eligibility criteria on the grounds of age or already be receiving disability services.

Despite many of these issues being flagged by researchers and advocacy groups for the past 20 years they have not been resolved at a policy level (Moss 1993; Bigby 2010). Governments have been reluctant to formulate policy that would, for example, articulate reasonable expectations of support to enable ageing in place, provide funding for partnership initiatives between sectors, or agreement about which sector is responsible for additional resourcing. The lack of policy means inconsistency and uncertainty that impacts on their quality of life, places stress on family members, advocates and staff, and means older people with intellectual disability are often unable to access support appropriate to their needs (see, for example, Bigby *et al.* 2011a; Bigby and Knox 2009; Webber *et al.* 2010a). The lack of policy formulation may be explained by the complexity of designing and implementing policy that requires a multiplicity of stakeholders from different sectors – health, disability and aged care – and the existence of strong drivers in some jurisdictions towards cost shifting between sectors caused by separate administration of service systems.

Ageing place in group homes – an exemplar issue

In the last decade, in Australia as elsewhere, policies of community care and ageing in place have aimed to avoid the institutionalization of older people and provide more supportive environments in their own homes (Howe 2001). Services to support older people to remain in the community have expanded and now replicate in some instances the level of care available in residential aged care facilities. Such services, together with tighter entry criteria and the establishment of assessment gate-keeping services have meant that the average age of admission to residential care has increased significantly (now 84 years) along with the level and complexity of care required by new residents (AIHW 2009).

Mainstream approaches

An application of the principles embedded in disability policy suggests that ageing in place should be as applicable to residents in group homes as it is to other older people who live in the community. A 'mainstreaming' model assumes the inclusion of people with intellectual disability is an integral part of the design of policy and services, and expects that the types of services available to others in the community are also accessible to group home residents, complemented by disability services where necessary (United Nations Economic and Social Council 2007). Thus, an older resident of a group home, diagnosed with a chronic health condition or dementia, would expect to access geriatric health care or dementia-specific services for diagnosis, treatment and ongoing management of the condition, as well as aspects such as modifications to make their home more dementia capable. In addition, continuing support would be expected from the disability system in the form of, for example, a group home, which would adapt its programme to take account of things such as: increased medical appointments and interface with hospitals and other health care professionals; retirement from full-time attendance at a day programme; changed resident dynamics and compatibility; extra resources such as active night staff and the necessity for front line and supervisory staff to have additional knowledge or access to advice on management of age-related conditions (Fyffe *et al.* 2007). Attention too would be given to the accessibility and responsiveness of mainstream health and aged care services to people with intellectual disability and removal of any restrictive discriminatory criteria based on age. A small pilot programme in Australia based on this approach provided 'top up' funding to purchase aged care expertise and health planning for residents in group homes assessed as eligible for residential aged care and supported aged care professionals with knowledge specific to working with people with intellectual disability. The validity of this approach was demonstrated by the delayed admission and extended period residents aged in place, as well as the lesser cost to the aged care system than would occur if the resident had moved into residential aged care (AIHW 2006). The logic of this approach suggests that if the health and functional capacity of an older group home resident is declining and reaches the stage where they need 24-hour nursing care, they should access the care option available to other older people with similarly high health needs which reflects community norms – a residential aged care facility in their local area. If they do so, however, they may still require access to disability services for support with disability-related needs that are not available within the aged care system. For example, support with decision making, advocacy or to participate in meaningful activities. The aged care facility may also need some advice and training to enable staff to respond appropriately to a resident with intellectual disability, which could be provided either from the disability sector or a specialist resource embedded in the aged care system.

Avoidance of double dipping

The application of a mainstream model described above is obstructed by concern about 'double dipping', which means an older person with intellectual disability is regarded as either a person with a disability or an older person rather than both simultaneously or as a citizen (Bigby 2008b,

2010). In the resulting model, the disability system becomes responsible for adapting the nature of its support to older service users, for whom, because they are already in receipt of substantial government resources, it would be inequitable to provide additional resources from either the disability or aged care sectors. The strength of this position is evident when the indicative per capita figure of 43 pounds sterling for supported accommodation in the disability sector is compared with 14–20 pounds sterling in residential aged care (Thompson *et al.* 2004). The assumption of this model, which is common in the UK and Australia, is that disability service organizations should adapt group home programmes from within their existing resources or move residents out. Multiple adaptation strategies have included: changes to the profile of staff skills; partnerships with day programme providers; house modifications; and variation to service design such as regrouping residents (Fyffe *et al.* 2007; Wilkinson *et al.* 2004). The strategic plan developed by the Daughters of Charity in Ireland to adapt its services to the projected increase of residents with dementia used strategies such as the establishment of a dedicated mobile memory clinic to provide regular screening, early diagnosis and clinical support to staff; provision of education programmes for staff, family and peers; and endorsement of organizational standards for dementia care (McCarron 2010). Adaptations occur in a context of little available expertise or responsiveness of mainstream aged care or geriatric health services to people with intellectual disability, and often restricted access for the 'younger old', in their fifties and sixties, or simply because a person is already in receipt of a disability service.

The frail aged – in place progression or transfer out

It is clear that ageing in place in a group home will not always be the most appropriate option especially if insufficient additional resources and expertise are available, or if a person requires continuous nursing, medical care or monitoring. One strategy has been 'in place progression' where older residents age in place in the wider disability service but move from their home to a dedicated programme for older people as their needs change. Advantages are suggested to be the capacity to concentrate skilled staff and provide specialist support. Disadvantages are the disloca- tion from one's home, familiar locale and co-residents, and the segregation of older people often in larger facilities within disability services. Potentially such strategies result in the development of large-scale specialist aged care facilities in the disability system which do not reflect the principles in broader disability policy and lead to premature (re) institutionalization. In New South Wales, Australia, for example, a 100-bed aged care facility built as part of an institutional closure programme is now part of the disability service infrastructure (NSW Government 2006). For facilities such as this to remain fully occupied and economically viable, given the relatively small number of frail aged people with intellectual disability, they have to draw potential residents from a large geographic area and have less stringent entry criteria than mainstream aged care facilities.

There are some indications that 'transferring out' of a group home and the disability service system is a common option for older residents in the UK and Australia (Bigby *et al.* 2011a; Thompson 2003; Wilkinson *et al.* 2004). A move to residential aged care can be precipitated by a combination of factors: the degree of change in the residents' health needs; the impact of their changed needs on staff and other residents; the coexistence of other issues that affect the operation of the home; and the flexibility of resources or success in garnering additional ones (Bigby *et al.* 2011a). There seems to be no identifiable objective indictor of the level of 'care' that triggers a move, rather it is relative to each person's context and the degree of change experienced. Group home residents with relatively low support needs seem to be at higher risk, as the degree of change in their support needs and extra resources required may well be greater than residents with pre-existing high support needs, for whom supports such as mobility modifications or active night staff are already in place. A major issue of concern is the processes of decision making about an older person's move, which has been found to be hurried, made at times of acute health crisis and have little involvement of the person themselves, their family or external advocates (Bigby *et al.* 2011a). These findings suggest that, in the case of older people, little attention is paid to the principles embedded in disability policy, which reinforces the importance of every person having access to an advocate external to the service system and family members having an awareness of the person's rights.

Some evidence from both the UK and Australia suggests that people with intellectual disability move prematurely and are often misplaced in mainstream aged care facilities (Bigby *et al.* 2008; Thompson 2003). As a group they are significantly younger, with lower rates of dementia but stay much longer than other residents (Bigby *et al.* 2008). Their entry is associated with the inability of other forms of accommodation to continue to provide support, often due to a lack of resources, the death or ill health of a family carer or a lack of other options, rather than severity of health or support needs. The quality of mainstream aged care facilities differs within and across jurisdictions. Whilst a recent Australian study suggests they might provide better quality health care than is available in a group home, this and other studies suggest residents with intellectual disability fare less well on social aspects such as community access, participation in meaningful activity and relationships with friends and family compared either with co-resident peers or age peers in disability-supported accommodation (Thompson *et al.* 2004; Higgins and Mansell 2009; Bigby *et al.* 2008; Webber *et al.* 2010b).

Concluding comments

There is no simple formula to apply to questions about aging in place, given the diverse quality of aged care and disability service systems. Establishment of large-scale facilities in the disability service system that congregate and segregate people with intellectual disability on the basis not only of their disability but also their age is well out of step with the current principles of disability policy. It is not clear whether the risk of premature institutionalization and dislocation from place by building large disability-specific aged care facilities is outweighed by the advantages of retaining older people within the disability service system and the disadvantages of reliance on mainstream residential aged care facilities if a resident can no longer be accommodated in a group home. How these issues are weighed up depends on the comparative quality of facilities in each sector. It can be argued, as Wolfensberger (1985) did in the past, that in some countries mainstream aged care facilities should be avoided at all costs as the quality remains so significantly below that in the disability system and they represent larger scale institutionalization than would be found in the disability sector. A 'mainstream' position that seeks the adaptation of disability support services and accessible, responsive mainstream aged care services, both community based and residential, and which takes account of the particular needs of people ageing with an intellectual disability, most closely aligns with aims of social inclusion and continued community living as the best means to ensure an optimal quality of life.

Although the numbers are growing, older people constitute a small proportion of people with intellectual disability and an even smaller fraction of the general ageing population. They may benefit most from being identified as a middle-aged or older person rather than just a person with a disability, and thus benefit from active ageing initiatives for the younger old and the greater scrutiny and reform of aged care services likely to stem from the growth in the number of older people. The focus on the need for 'care' when parents die, which characterizes concerns about middle age, and the increased life expectancy of people with intellectual disability have dangers that stem from the 'plasticity of care' (Baldock 1997). To governments and those disconnected from the lives of people with intellectual disability, the paramount issue is likely to that 'care' is provided, and as different types of care are thought of as easily substituted for one another, little attention will be paid to its quality, and the extent to which it reflects the principles embedded in disability policies may remain largely invisible and of little concern. A continuing case must be made that despite age-associated changes, the principles and visionary aims of disability policy are as applicable to middle-aged and older people with intellectual disability as they are to their younger peers – the need is much more than care. These new parts of the life course provide opportunities for people with intellectual disability to continue the development of their own self-identity and contributions to family and the wider community. Realization of these aims requires individualized support, adaptation of service systems, social and attitudinal change. The overriding aim of advocates and practitioners alike must be to ensure mid and later adulthood is a bonus for people with intellectual disability, by creating a social context and service infrastructure that supports an optimal quality of life, rather than it being a perilous period as imagined by parents, characterized by the threat of institutionalization and multiple losses.

References

AIHW (2006) *National Evaluation of the Aged Care Innovative Pool Disability Aged Care Interface Pilot: Final Report* (Canberra: Australian Institute of Health and Welfare).

AIHW (2008) *Disability in Australia, Intellectual Disability* (Canberra: Australian Institute of Health and Welfare).

AIHW (2009) *Australia's Welfare 2009*. Series no. 9. Cat. no. AUS 117 (Canberra: Australian Institute of Health and Welfare).

Baldock, J. (1997) 'Social Care in Old Age: More than a Funding Problem', *Social Policy and Administration* 31(1): 73–89.

Bigby, C. (1996) 'Transferring Responsibility: The Nature and Effectiveness of Parental Planning for the Future of Adults with Intellectual Disability Who Remain at Home Until Mid-life', *Journal of Intellectual and Developmental Disabilities* 21(4): 295–312.

Bigby, C. (2000) *Moving on without Parents: Planning, Transitions and Sources of Support for Middle-aged and Older Adults with Intellectual Disability* (Baltimore: P. H. Brookes).

Bigby, C. (2004) *Aging with a Lifelong Disability: Policy, Program and Practice Issues for Professionals* (London: Jessica Kingsley).

Bigby, C. (2008a) 'Known Well by No-one: Trends in the Informal Social Networks of Middle-aged and Older People with Intellectual Disability Five Years after Moving to the Community', *Journal of Intellectual and Developmental Disability* 33(2): 148–57.

Bigby, C. (2008b) 'Beset by Obstacles: A Review of Australian Policy Development to Support Aging in Place for People with Intellectual Disability', *Journal of Intellectual and Developmental Disabilities* 33(1): 1–11.

Bigby, C. (2010) 'A Five Country Comparative Review of Accommodation Support Policies for Older People with Intellectual Disability', *Journal of Policy and Practice in Intellectual Disability* 7: 3–15.

Bigby, C. and Balandin, S. (2004) 'Issues in Researching the Aging of People with Intellectual Disability', in E. Emerson, T. Thompson, T. Parmenter and C. Hatton, eds, *International Handbook of Methods for Research and Evaluation in Intellectual Disabilities* (London: Wiley): pp. 221–36.

Bigby, C. and Knox, M. (2009) '"I Want to See the Queen": The Service Experiences of Older Adults with Intellectual Disability', *Australian Social Work* 62(2): 216–31.

Bigby, C., Bowers, B. and Webber, R. (2011a) 'Planning and Decision Making about the Future Care of Older Group Home Residents and Transition to Residential Aged Care, *Journal of Intellectual Disability Research* 55(8): 777–89.

Bigby, C., Cooper, B. and Reid, K. (2011b) *Making Life Good in the Community: Measures of Resident Outcomes and Staff Perceptions of the Move from an Institution* (Melbourne: Department of Human Services).

Bigby, C., Webber, R., McKenzie-Green, B. and Bowers, B. (2008) 'A Survey of People with Intellectual Disabilities Living in Residential Aged Care Facilities in Victoria', *Journal of Intellectual Disability Research* 52: 404–14.

Bittles, A., Petterson, B., Sullivan, S., Hussain, R., Glasson, E. and Montgomery, P. (2002) 'The Influence of Intellectual Disability on Life Expectancy', *Journal of Gerontology: Medical Sciences* 57A(7): M470–M472.

Brody, E. (2004) *Women in the Middle: Their Parent Care Years* (2nd edn) (New York: Springer).

Brown, I. and Percy, M., eds, (2007) *A Comprehensive Guide to Intellectual and Developmental Disabilities* (Baltimore: Paul H. Brookes).

Butler, R. (1975) *Why Survive? Being Old in America* (New York: Harper and Row).

Chappell, A. (1998) 'Still Out in the Cold: People with Learning Difficulties and the Social Model of Disability', in T. Shakespeare, ed., *The Disability Reader: Social Science Perspectives* (London: Cassell).

Clement, T. and Bigby, C. (2009) 'Breaking Out of a Distinct Social Space: Reflections on Supporting Community Participation for People with Severe and Profound Intellectual Disability', *Journal of Applied Research in Intellectual Disabilities* 22(3): 264–75.

Erikson, E. (1959) *Identity and the Life Cycle* (New York: International Universities Press).

Foundation for People with Learning Disabilities (2010) *Mutual Caring: Supporting Older Families who are Looking after Each Other*, available online at http://www.learningdisabilities.org.uk/our-work/family-friends-community/mutual-caring/ (accessed 6 October 2011).

Frawley, P. and Bigby, C. (2011) 'Inclusion in Political and Public Life: The Experiences of People with Intellectual Disability on Government Disability Advisory Bodies in Australia', *Journal of Intellectual and Developmental Disability* 36(1): 27–38.

Fyffe, C., Bigby, C. and McCubbery, J. (2007) *Exploration of the Population of People with Disabilities who are Ageing, Their Changing Needs and the Capacity of the Disability and Age Care Sector to Support Them to Age Positively* (Canberra: National Disability Administrators Group).

Fyffe, C., Pierce, G., Ilsley, B. and Paul, P. (2011) 'The Next Steps: Adults with a Disability and Caring Families', in C. Bigby and C. Fyffe, eds, *State Disability Policy for the Next Ten Years – What Should it Look Like? Proceedings of the Fifth Roundtable on Intellectual Disability Policy* (Melbourne: La Trobe University School of Social Work): pp. 69–73.

Gibson, D. and Grew, R. (2002) 'New Models and Approaches to Care' (from a series of eight commissioned papers prepared for *2020: A Vision for Aged Care in Australia*) (Melbourne: The Myer Foundation).

Grant, G., Ramcharan, P., Flynn, M. and Richardson, M., eds, (2010) *Learning Disability: A Life Cycle Approach*, 2nd edn (Maidenhead: Open University Press).

Hall, E. (2010) 'Spaces of Social Inclusion and Belonging for People with Intellectual Disabilities', *Journal of Intellectual Disability Research* 54: 48–57.

Hareven, T. (2001) 'Historical Perspectives on Aging and Family Relations', in R. Binstock and L. George, eds, *Handbook of Aging and the Social Sciences* (San Francisco: Academic Press): pp. 141–59.

Haveman, M. (2004) 'Disease Epidemiology and Aging People with Intellectual Disabilities', *Journal of Policy and Practice in Intellectual Disabilities* 1(1): 16–23.

Heller, T., Miller, A., Hsieh, K. and Sterns, H. (2000) 'Later-life Planning: Promoting Knowledge of Options and Choice-making', *Mental Retardation* 38(5): 395–406.

Higgins, L. and Mansell, J. (2009) 'Quality of Life in Group Homes and Older Persons' Homes', *British Journal of Learning Disabilities* 37(3): 207–212.

Holland, A. (2000) 'Incidence and Course of Dementia in People with Down's Syndrome: Findings from a Population Based Study', *Journal of Intellectual Disability Research* 44(2): 138–46.

Howe, A. (2001) 'Recent Developments in Aged Care Policy in Australia', *Journal of Aging and Social Policy* 13: 101–16.

Kemp, B. and Mosqueda, L. (2004) *Aging with a Disability. What the Clinician Needs to Know* (Baltimore: John Hopkins University Press).

Keyzer, P., Carney, T. and Tait, D. (1997a) '"Against the Odds": Parents with Intellectual Disability'. Report to the Disability Services Sub-Committee, Canberra.

Keyzer, P., Carney, T. and Tait, D. (1997b) '"I hope he dies before me": Caring for Ageing Children with Intellectual Disabilities'. Report to the Disability Services Sub-Committee, Canberra

Knox, M. and Bigby, C. (2007) 'Moving Towards Midlife Care as Negotiated Family Business: Accounts of People with Intellectual Disabilities and their Families', *Journal of Disability, Development and Education* 54(3): 287–304.

McCarron, M. (2010) 'Models of Good Practice in Health and Social Support for Ageing People with ID: Strategic Planning for Ageing and Dementia at the Daughters of Charity'. Presentation at the nineteenth roundtable of the IASSID special interest research group on aging and intellectual disability; available online at https://www.iassid.org/sirgs/aging/activities (accessed 6 October 2011).

MacDonald, M. and Tyson, P. (1988) 'Deca-jeopardy – The Aging and Aged Developmentally Disabled', in J. Matson and A. Marchetti, eds, *Developmental Disabilities: A Lifespan Perspective* (San Diego: Grune and Stratton): pp. 256–91.

Moss, S. (1993) *Aging and Developmental Disabilities: Perspectives from Nine Countries* (Durham, NH: IEEIR).

Moss, S., Hogg, J. and Horne, M. (1992) 'Individual Characteristics and Service Support of Older People with Moderate, Severe and Profound Learning Disability with and without Community Mental Handicap Team Support', *Mental Handicap Research* 6: 3–17.

Nay, R. and Garratt, S. (2009) *Older People: Issues and Innovations in Care* (Sydney: Elsevier).

Neugarten, B., ed., (1968) *Middle Age and Aging: A Reader in Social Psychology* (Chicago: University of Chicago Press).

New South Wales Government (2006) *Stronger Together: A New Direction for Disability Services in NSW 2006–2016* (Sydney: New South Wales Government).

O'Brien, J. and Lyle O'Brien, C., eds, (2002) *Implementing Person-centered Planning: Voices of Experience* (Toronto: Ontario Inclusion Press).

Patja, K., Iivanainen, M., Vesala, H., Oksanen, H. and Ruoppila, I. (2000) 'Life Expectancy of People with Intellectual Disability: A 35 Year Follow Up Study', *Journal of Intellectual and Disability Research* 44(5): 591–9.

Priestley, M. and Rabiee, P. (2002) 'Same Difference? Older People's Organisations and Disability Issues', *Disability & Society* 17(6): 597–612.

Robertson, J., Emerson, E., Hatton, C., Elliott, J., McIntosh, B., Swift, P., Krinjen-Kemp, E., Towers, C., Romeo, R., Knapp, M., Sanderson, H., Routledge, M., Oakes, P. and Joyce, T. (2006) 'Longitudinal Analysis of the Impact and Cost of Person-centered Planning for People with Intellectual Disabilities in England', *American Journal on Mental Retardation* 111(6): 400–16.

Rowe, J. and Kahn, R. (1998) *Successful Aging* (New York: Random House).

Seltzer, M. and Krauss, M. (1994) 'Aging Parents with Co Resident Adult Children: The Impact of Lifelong Caring', in M. Seltzer, M. Krauss and M. Janicki, eds, *Life Course Perspectives on Adulthood and Old Age* (Washington: AAMR): pp. 3–18.

Shakespeare, T. (2006) *Disability Rights and Wrongs* (Abingdon: Routledge).

Thompson, D. (2003) 'Policy into Practice. Growing Older with a Learning Disability', *Research Policy and Planning* 21(3): 71–8.

Thompson, D., Ryrie, I. and Wright, S. (2004) 'People with Intellectual Disabilities Living in Generic Residential Services for Older People in the UK', *Journal of Applied Research in Intellectual Disabilities* 17: 101–8.

Todd, S., Evans, G. and Beyer, S. (1990) 'More Recognised than Known: The Social Visibility and Attachment of People with Developmental Disabilities', *Australia and New Zealand Journal of Developmental Disabilities* 16(3): 207–18.

Torr, J., Strydom, A., Patti, P. and Jokinen, N. (2010) 'Ageing in Down Syndrome: Morbidity and Mortality', *Journal of Policy and Practice in Intellectual Disabilities* 7(1): 70–81.

United Nations (2006) *Convention on the Rights of Persons with a Disability*; available online at www.un.org/disabilities (accessed 6 October 2011).

United Nations Economic and Social Council (2007) 'Mainstreaming Disability in the Development Agenda': note by secretariat, 23 November.

Walker, A. and Walker, C. (1998) 'Age or Disability? Age Based Disparities in Service Provision for Older People with Intellectual Disabilities in Great Britain', *Journal of Intellectual and Developmental Disability* 23(1): 25–40.

Walker, C., Walker, A. and Ryan, T. (1995) 'What Kind of Future: Opportunities for Older People with a Learning Difficulty', in T. Philpott and L. Ward, eds, *Values and Visions. Changing Ideas in Services for People with Learning Difficulties* (Oxford: Butterworth Heinemann): pp. 232–43.

Walmsley, J. (1996) 'Doing What Mum Wants Me to Do: Looking at Family Relationships from the Point of View of Adults with Learning Disabilities', *Journal of Applied Research in Intellectual Disabilities* 9(4): 324–41.

Webber, R., Bowers, B. and Bigby, C. (2010a) 'Hospital Experiences of Older People with Intellectual Disability', *Journal of Intellectual and Developmental Disability* 35(3): 155–64.

Webber, R., Bowers, B. and Bigby, C. (2010b) 'Residential Aged Care: A Good Place to Be for People with ID?', *Journal of Applied Research on Intellectual Disability* 23(5): 417.

Wightman, C. (2009) *Connecting People: Steps to Making it Happen* (London: Foundation for People with Learning Disabilities).

Wilkinson, H., Kerr, D., Cunningham, C. and Rae, C. (2004) *Home for Good? Preparing to Support People with a Learning Disability in a Residential Setting When They Develop Dementia* (Brighton: Joseph Rowntree Trust/Pavilion).

Wolfensberger, W. (1985) 'An Overview of Social Role Valorisation and Some Reflections on Elderly Mentally Retarded Persons', in M. Janicki and H. Wisniewski, eds, *Aging and Developmental Disabilities: Issues and Approaches* (Baltimore: Brookes): pp. 61–76.

World Health Organization (2002) *Active Ageing: A Policy Framework* (Geneva: World Health Organization).

INDEX

Note: Page numbers in italics represent tables and figures.